Business Information Systems

Business Information Systems

Technology, Development and Management
for the E-Business

Fifth edition

PAUL BOCIJ, ANDREW GREASLEY AND SIMON HICKIE

PEARSON

Harlow, England • London • New York • Boston • San Francisco • Toronto • Sydney • Auckland • Singapore • Hong Kong
Tokyo • Seoul • Taipei • New Delhi • Cape Town • São Paulo • Mexico City • Madrid • Amsterdam • Munich • Paris • Milan

PEARSON EDUCATION LIMITED

Edinburgh Gate
Harlow CM20 2JE
United Kingdom
Tel: +44 (0)1279 623623
Web: www.pearson.com/uk

First published 1999 (print)
Second edition published 2003 (print)
Third edition published 2006 (print)
Fourth edition published 2008 (print)
Fifth edition published 2015 (print and electronic)

© Pearson Education Limited 2015 (print and electronic)

The screenshots in this book are reprinted by permission of Microsoft Corporation.
Pearson Education is not responsible for the content of third-party internet sites.

The Financial Times. With a worldwide network of highly respected journalists, *The Financial Times* provides global business news, insightful opinion and expert analysis of business, finance and politics. With over 500 journalists reporting from 50 countries worldwide, our in-depth coverage of international news is objectively reported and analysed from an independent, global perspective. To find out more, visit www.ft.com/pearsonoffer.

ISBN: 978-0-273-73645-5 (print)
     978-0-273-73646-2 (PDF)
     978-0-273-78045-8 (eText)

British Library Cataloguing-in-Publication Data
A catalogue record for the print edition is available from the British Library

Library of Congress Cataloging-in-Publication Data
Bocij, Paul.
  Business information systems : technology, development and management for the e-business / Paul Bocij, Andrew Greasley and Simon Hickie. – Fifth edition.
      pages cm
  Includes bibliographical references and index.
  ISBN 978-0-273-73645-5 (print) – ISBN 978-0-273-73646-2 (PDF) – ISBN 978-0-273-78045-8 (eText)
  1. Business – Computer network resources. 2. Business information services. 3. Electronic commerce.
I. Greasley, Andrew. II. Hickie, Simon. III. Title.
  HF54.56.B63 2015
  658.4'038011–dc23
                                2014030404

10 9 8 7 6 5 4 3 2 1
18 17 16 15 14

Cover image: © vs 148/Shutterstock

Print edition typeset in 10/12pt Minion Pro Regular by 73

Print edition printed and bound in Slovakia by Neografia

NOTE THAT ANY PAGE CROSS REFERENCES REFER TO THE PRINT EDITION

The authors would like to dedicate this book to Lin Mellor, teacher, mentor and colleague. A consummate professional and example to educators everywhere.

To Clare, without whom my contribution would never have happened.
From Simon

To my wife, Mik.
From Paul

Brief contents

Preface xv
Guided tour xxii
Plan of the book xxiv
About the authors xxv
Authors' acknowledgements xxvi
Publisher's acknowledgements xxvii

Contents in detail

Part 2
BUSINESS INFORMATION SYSTEMS DEVELOPMENT

17 Ethical, legal and moral constraints on information systems 599

Supporting resources

Visit **www.pearsoned.co.uk/bis** to find online resources for instructors

Preface

Introduction

With the prominence of the concept of e-business and the increased use of business information systems (BIS) within organisations, the need for all working professionals to have a good knowledge of ICT and IS has also increased. With the vast, rapidly changing choice of IS available, important business skills are understanding and assessing the range of options available, and then choosing the solution best suited to the business problem or opportunity. This is, essentially, our aim in writing this book: to provide a source of knowledge that will explain how the right systems can be chosen by a business, then developed appropriately and managed effectively.

Despite the rising expenditure on IS, surveys also show that the potential of IS is often not delivered, often due to problems in the management, analysis, design or implementation of the system. The intention in this book is to acknowledge that there are great difficulties with developing and using IS and to explain the measures that can be taken to try to minimise these difficulties in order to make the systems successful.

Why study business information systems?

Information systems form an integral part of modern organisations and businesses. Computer-based IS are now used to support all aspects of an organisation's normal functions and activities.

New technology creates new opportunities for forward-thinking companies. Higher levels of automation, high-speed communications and improved access to information can all provide significant benefits to a modern business organisation. However, the benefits of new and emerging technologies can only be realised once they have been harnessed and directed towards an organisation's goals.

The hybrid manager

The traditional view of managers is as functional specialists having specialised knowledge and expertise in a particular area, such as finance. The modern business environment requires a new kind of manager, often called a *hybrid manager*. The hybrid manager combines management and business skills with expertise in the areas of ICT and IS. This type of manager is able to undertake a wide variety of roles and can operate across functional areas. The study of IS plays an important part in the development of an individual so that they may become a competent and effective manager as well as providing prospective managers with important problem-solving skills that can be applied to a range of situations and problems. Specifically, the hybrid manager will need to:

- define the IS strategy for their workgroup, department or company;
- identify potential uses of IS to improve company performance;
- select and then acquire new IS from appropriate suppliers;
- oversee the development and implementation of these new systems;
- manage the IS to ensure they are effective in delivering information of the appropriate quality to users.

Aims

This book is intended to provide a comprehensive, yet accessible, guide to choosing the right systems for an organisation, developing them appropriately and managing them effectively. The book was conceived as a single source book that undergraduate business students would refer to throughout their course, without the need to purchase a separate book for different topics such as ICT; information management; systems analysis and design; and strategy development. It covers, in detail, the software and hardware technologies which form IS, the activities involved in acquiring and building new IS, and the elements of strategy required to manage IS effectively.

Key skills necessary to participate in the implementation of ICT in businesses are developed, and these skills, which form the main themes of the book, are:

- understanding of the terms used to describe the components of BIS to assist in selection of systems and suppliers;
- assessing how BIS applications can support different areas of an organisation;
- managing IS development projects;
- systems analysis and design;
- developing an IS or e-business strategy and managing its implementation.

The book assumes no prior knowledge of IS or ICT. New concepts and terms are defined as simply as possible, with clear definitions given in the margins of the book. It explains the importance of information in developing a company business strategy and assisting decision making. The use of relevant hardware and software components of computer systems are defined and explained in the context of a range of business applications. The book also explains the benefit of specialised innovative applications such as data warehouses and geographical information systems. The application of IS to business process re-engineering and initiatives is also described.

After using the book as part of IS modules on their course, students will be able to:

- evaluate and select ICT solutions for deployment within different functional parts of a business to achieve benefits for the business;
- actively participate in ICT projects, applying skills such as selection of suppliers, procurement of hardware and software, systems analysis and design, and project management;
- communicate effectively with ICT specialists when collaborating on a task or project;
- use ICT to access a wide range of information sources for research and acquisition of knowledge.

Changes for the fifth edition

The logical structure of the fourth edition has been retained, but many changes have been incorporated based on lecturer and student feedback. The main changes are as follows:

- Chapter 3 and Chapter 4 from the fourth edition have been combined to make a new chapter 3.
- A new chapter 4 titled Databases and Business Intelligence has been incorporated.
- Numerous new case studies with questions have been included in the fifth edition.

The structure of this book

The book is divided into three parts, each covering a different aspect of how BIS are used within organisations to help achieve competitive advantage:

- *Part 1* focuses on the hardware and software technologies, known collectively as ICT, which make up IS. It is intended for introductory courses in ICT and BIS.

- *Part 2* explains how IS are acquired and developed by considering the activities involved with each of the stages of developing an IS. This part is intended for more advanced courses in systems analysis and design.

- *Part 3* describes how IS need to be managed, and a strategy developed, to ensure they effectively support the mission of the business. This part is appropriate for courses which consider the strategic management of IS.

Each part is self-contained and is the equivalent of what might be covered in a single module, or course, in a programme of study.

Part 1: Introduction to business information systems

Part 1 introduces the basic concepts of BIS. Its main focus is the technology that forms BIS, but it starts by reviewing the importance of information and what makes good-quality information. Many people who work in the ICT industry tend to believe it is the technology part of ICT that is important, whereas most business people will tell you it is the information part of ICT that is crucial to business performance. To enable a business user to communicate effectively with their suppliers of ICT, a knowledge of the often bewildering terminology used to describe the components of IS, and a basic idea of how these components interact is important. To aid understanding, basic concepts and characteristics of IS are reviewed in Chapter 2. Hardware, software, communications and networking technologies are then described in subsequent chapters.

The different aspects of ICT are introduced as follows:

- *Chapter 1: Basic concepts – understanding information* provides an introduction to how information is used within a business.

- *Chapter 2: Basic concepts – an introduction to business information systems* introduces the different types of BIS, including the concept of e-business, and how they can be used to gain strategic advantage.

- *Chapter 3: Hardware and software* describes the issues in the selection of different hardware components of IS which are used to capture, process, store and output information. It also reviews the selection and use of general-purpose applications software such as word processors, spreadsheets and databases, which are often referred to as 'productivity software'. Internet software is also covered.

- *Chapter 4: Databases and business intelligence* explains the role of databases in storage and sharing of information and the use of Business Intelligence systems to provide information for decision making.

- *Chapter 5: Networks, telecommunications and the Internet* explains how BIS are linked using telecommunications links which form networks within and between businesses.

- *Chapter 6: Enterprise and functional BIS* considers how BIS can be implemented as enterprise or functional business systems. The chapter also covers departmental applications of BIS.

Part 2: Business information systems development

Part 2 focuses on how BIS are acquired and built. A basic understanding of this is necessary to every business user of BIS so that they can appreciate the context of their use of the system and this can be of particular importance when they are involved in testing or using a new system since they will need to understand the reason for introducing new systems as well as their limitations. A more detailed understanding of building BIS is important to users and managers who are responsible for, or are involved in a systems development project. In this case they will need to know the different stages of systems development to help plan the project or work with the developers of the system. They will also need to be aware of the different alternatives for sourcing IS, such as buying pre-written 'off-the-shelf' systems or specially written 'bespoke' systems, to decide which is best for their company or department.

This book provides a reference framework known as the 'systems development lifecycle' which puts all the activities involved with building a system into a business context. Chapters give guidelines on how best to approach system development, giving examples of activities that need to occur in order to avoid any pitfalls and enabling a quality system to be produced which meets the needs of the users and the business. The chapters in Part 2 are sequenced in the order in which activities occur in the systems development lifecycle:

■ *Chapter 7: An introduction to acquiring and developing BIS* gives an introduction to alternatives for acquiring new systems. It also introduces the software development lifecycle which acts as a framework for the next chapters.

■ *Chapter 8: Initiating systems development* covers the initiation phase of system development when the need for the new system and the feasibility of different development methods are assessed.

■ *Chapter 9: BIS project management* describes how project management can be used to ensure the new system is built within the time and budget constraints, while also providing the features and quality required by the business and end-users.

■ *Chapter 10: Systems analysis* details system analysis techniques including methods of capturing the requirements for the system and summarising them. Different diagramming techniques are also covered.

■ *Chapter 11: Systems design* reviews different aspects of the design of IS from overall architectural or system design to aspects of detailed design, such as data-base and user interface design.

■ *Chapter 12: System build, implementation and maintenance: change management* describes the final stages of a systems development project when the system is released to end-users, following programming, testing and installation, and is then maintained. The area of change management at the levels of software, IS and the organisation is also considered.

Part 3: Business information systems management

Part 3 considers issues involved with the management of IS within an organisation. Of these, probably the most important is ensuring that the strategy defined is consistent with the mission and objectives of the business. Techniques for achieving this are reviewed, together with trends in IS strategy, such as location of IS within a large company and outsourcing IS management to third-party companies. Key issues in implementing the strategy are detailed in the areas of ensuring IS are secure; managing end-user facilities such as desktop PCs, development tools and the help desk; and ensuring the company is acting within moral, ethical and legal guidelines.

The chapters are structured as follows:

■ *Chapter 13: Information systems strategy* considers tools for developing IS strategy, including the integration of the IS and business strategy.

■ *Chapter 14: Information systems management* explores the management of IS investments and the location of IS resources.

■ *Chapter 15: Managing information security* describes how information and systems can be protected through controls from threats such as destruction, failure or loss as part of business continuity planning.

■ *Chapter 16: End-user computing – providing end-user services* explains why managing use of systems and, in particular, development by end-users is a significant trend in IS.

■ *Chapter 17: Ethical, legal and moral constraints on information systems* discusses the importance of protecting personal data and other ethical, moral and legal requirements which must be met by the IS manager.

Who should use this book?

The book discusses key aspects of BIS development and management for students who need to understand the application of ICT to assist businesses. It is designed for college students, undergraduate degree and postgraduate students taking courses with modules giving a grounding in the practical

ICT skills of selection, implementation, management and use of business information systems (BIS). The main types of reader will be:

- *Undergraduates taking general business courses* such as Business Administration and Business Studies or *specialised business courses* such as Accounting, Marketing, Tourism and Human Resources Management.

- *Undergraduates on computer science courses* in Business Information Systems or e-commerce which involve the study of business applications of information technology and the management of the development of IS.

- *Students at college aiming for vocational qualifications* such as the HNC/HND in Business Management or Computer Studies.

- *Postgraduate students on MBA, Certificate in Management, Diploma in Management Studies or specialist masters degrees* which involve courses on information management or IS strategy or electives in e-business and e-commerce.

Managers in industry involved in the development and use of IS who will also find the practical sections in this book of use are:

- *Business analysts* working with customers to identify business problems and propose solutions.

- *Systems analysts and software designers* specifying how the solution will be implemented.

- *'Hands-on' managers* responsible for implementing ICT solutions as either a supplier or a client.

What does it offer to lecturers teaching these courses?

The book is intended to be a comprehensive guide to the business applications, development and management of BIS. As such, it can be used across several modules to help integrate different modules. Lecturers will find the book has a good range of excellent case studies to support their teaching. These include industry case studies of the applications of BIS together with problems encountered and simplified practical exercises for systems analysis and design. Web references are given in the text to important information sources for particular topics.

Student learning features

A range of features have been incorporated into this book to help the reader get the most out of it. They have been designed to assist understanding, reinforce learning and help readers find information easily. The features are described in the order you will encounter them.

At the start of each chapter:

- *Chapter introductions*: succinct summaries of why the topic is relevant to the management of IS and its content and structure.

- *Learning outcomes*: lists describing what readers should learn through reading the chapters and completing the exercises.

- *Links to other chapters*: a summary of related information in other chapters.

In each chapter:

- *Definitions*: when significant terms are first introduced the main text contains explanations and succinct definitions in the margin for easy reference.

- *Web links*: where appropriate, web addresses are given as reference sources to provide further information on a particular topic. They are provided in the main text where they are directly relevant as well as at the end of the chapter.

- *Case studies*: real-world examples of how technologies are used to support businesses. Case studies are taken from around the world but there is a particular emphasis on the UK and Europe. They are referred to from related material within the text they support. Questions at the end of the case study are intended to highlight the main learning points from each case study.

- *Mini case studies*: short examples which give a more detailed example, or explanation, than is practical in the main text. They do not contain supplementary questions.

- *Activities*: exercises in the main text which give the opportunity to practise and apply the concepts and techniques described in the text.

- *'Focus on' sections*: used to consider topical issues of IS in more detail. Such sections may be used to support the essay or discussion-style questions, or may provide areas for further student research, perhaps giving ideas for student dissertations and projects.

- *Chapter summaries*: intended as revision aids which summarise the main learning points from chapters.

At the end of each chapter:

- *Self-assessment exercises*: short questions which will test understanding of terms and concepts described in the chapters.

- *Discussion questions*: require longer essay-style answers discussing themes from the chapters, and can be used for essays or as debate questions in seminars.

- *Essay questions*: conventional essay questions.

- *Examination questions*: typical short-answer questions which would be encountered in an exam and can also be used for revision.

- *References*: these give details of books, articles or papers referred to within the chapter.

- *Further reading*: supplementary text or papers on the main themes of the chapter. Where appropriate a brief commentary is provided on recommended supplementary reading on the main themes of the chapters.

- *Web links*: extensive lists of relevant web sites and particular articles together with a brief description of what information is available.

At the end of the book:

- *Glossary*: a list of all definitions of key terms and phrases used within the main text.

- *Index*: all key words, abbreviations and authors referred to in the main text.

Support material

An Instructor Manual for this book is available for download from **www.pearsoned.co.uk/bis**

Guided tour

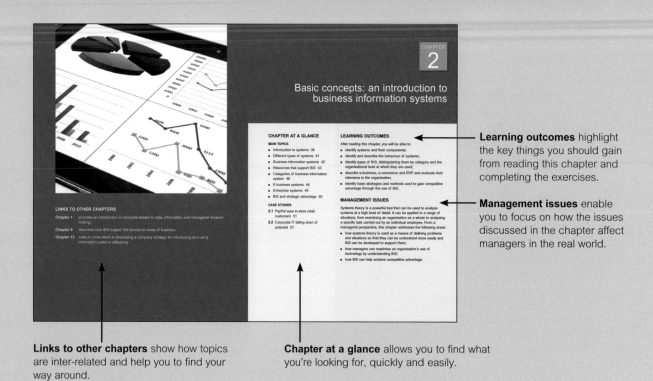

Learning outcomes highlight the key things you should gain from reading this chapter and completing the exercises.

Management issues enable you to focus on how the issues discussed in the chapter affect managers in the real world.

Links to other chapters show how topics are inter-related and help you to find your way around.

Chapter at a glance allows you to find what you're looking for, quickly and easily.

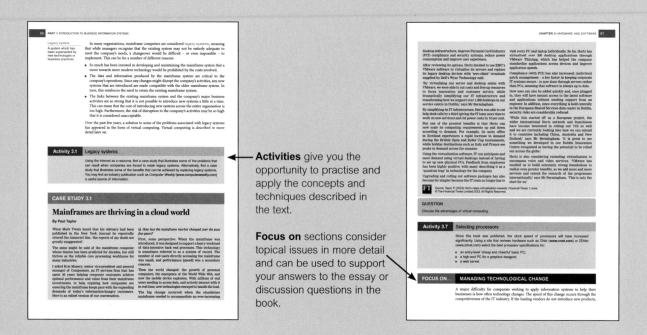

Activities give you the opportunity to practise and apply the concepts and techniques described in the text.

Focus on sections consider topical issues in more detail and can be used to support your answers to the essay or discussion questions in the book.

Case studies and **mini case studies** show real-world examples of how technologies are used to support businesses.

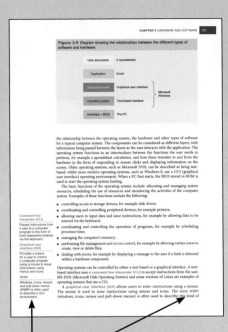

Definitions – key terms are highlighted in the text and explained in the margin for easy reference.

These are also available in the glossary.

Questions at the end of each case study highlight the main learning points.

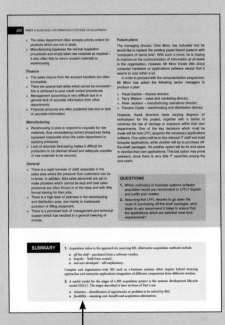

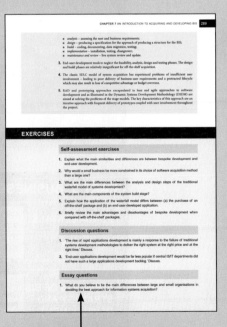

Chapter summaries appear at the end of every chapter summarising the main learning points.

A variety of **Exercises** and **Questions** test your understanding of the key concepts described in each chapter. Exercises require short answers, discussion and essay questions require longer answers and exam questions can be used for revision.

Plan of the book

PART 1 INTRODUCTION TO BUSINESS INFORMATION SYSTEMS

FUNDAMENTALS OF BUSINESS INFORMATION SYSTEMS	CHAPTER 1 INFORMATION	CHAPTER 2 SYSTEMS	
BUSINESS INFORMATION SYSTEMS TECHNOLOGIES	CHAPTER 3 HARDWARE AND SOFTWARE	CHAPTER 4 DATABASES AND BUSINESS INTELLIGENCE	CHAPTER 5 NETWORKS
BUSINESS APPLICATIONS	CHAPTER 6 ENTERPRISE AND FUNCTIONAL BIS	EXAMPLES THROUGHOUT CHAPTERS 1 TO 5	

PART 2 BUSINESS INFORMATION SYSTEMS DEVELOPMENT

FUNDAMENTALS OF BIS DEVELOPMENT	CHAPTER 7 ACQUIRING AND DEVELOPING	CHAPTER 9 PROJECT MANAGEMENT		
BIS DEVELOPMENT LIFECYCLE	CHAPTER 8 INITIATION	CHAPTER 10 SYSTEMS ANALYSIS	CHAPTER 11 SYSTEMS DESIGN	CHAPTER 12 SYSTEM BUILD, IMPLEMENTATION AND MAINTENANCE

PART 3 BUSINESS INFORMATION SYSTEMS MANAGEMENT

FUNDAMENTALS OF BIS STRATEGY	CHAPTER 13 INFORMATION SYSTEMS STRATEGY	CHAPTER 14 INFORMATION SYSTEMS MANAGEMENT	
ELEMENTS OF BIS STRATEGY AND DEVELOPMENT	CHAPTER 15 PROTECTING BIS	CHAPTER 16 END-USER SERVICES	CHAPTER 17 LEGAL AND ETHICAL ISSUES

About the authors

Paul Bocij is a Senior Teaching Fellow at Aston Business School. An experienced educator, he has worked for a wide variety of institutions, including universities, colleges and numerous commercial organisations. His commercial experience includes time spent in the fields of programming, management, training and consultancy. Previous clients for consultancy services include Cashco, British Red Cross, Barclaycard, Ministry of Defence, WROX Press, Bank of Ireland, JCB, Cardiff NHS Trust, Youth Hostels Association. Paul is a Member of the British Computer Society and is a Chartered IT Practitioner. He is also a Senior Fellow of the Higher Education Academy, a Fellow of the Institute for Learning, a member of the Society of Authors and a member of the British Association of Journalists. As a professional writer, he has produced or contributed to more than 20 books, including several best-selling titles and a number of academic texts. In addition, he is also the author of numerous articles, magazine columns, academic papers, training guides and other materials related to information systems and information technology. He is an active researcher and his research interests are largely concerned with the impact of technology on society, with a particular emphasis on deviant forms of behaviour, such as harassment. He is also interested in the use of educational technology in higher education, especially in areas such as the use of computer-based assessment systems.

Andrew Greasley MBA, PhD, FHEA is a lecturer in the Operations and Information Management Group at Aston Business School, Aston University. He has over 80 publications and has published in journals such as the *International Journal of Operations and Production Management, Journal of the Operational Research Society, Technovation and SIMULATION*. He is the sole author of the texts *Operations Management* published by John Wiley & Sons, *Operations Management: Short Cuts* published by Sage Publications Ltd, *Enabling a Simulation Capability in the Organisation* published by Springer Verlag and *Simulation Modelling for Business* published by Ashgate Publishing Ltd.

Simon Hickie has worked for some 20 years as a senior lecturer in business information systems, having previously worked for 10 years in the management information systems field in a variety of roles including programmer, project manager and trainer. His particular interests lie in the areas of information systems in SMEs, change management and strategic information systems management. He retired recently from the University of Derby to pursue his interests in photography which include lecturing, training and competition judging. He is married with three adult children.

Authors' acknowledgements

The authors would like to thank the assistance of the team at Pearson Education in the compilation of this book. Thanks also go to the team of reviewers for their constructive comments which have helped develop the book. Valuable feedback has also been obtained from students completing exercises and case studies. We thank everyone who has contributed in this way.

Reviewers and contributors

The following people contributed to the first edition of this book by commenting on the initial plan, or by providing detailed feedback on the entire manuscript:

Linda Charnley, Robert Gordon University; Neil Doherty, Loughborough University; Glenn Hardaker, University of Huddersfield; Alan Hunt, Robert Gordon University; Chris Percy, Oxford Brookes University; David Rowe, Kingston University; Daune West, University of Paisley.

For the second edition, in addition to the invaluable feedback provided by a full review panel, the publishers and authors would particularly like to thank the following people for their insightful and constructive feedback on the new manuscript as it was written:

Professor Mogens Kuehn Pedersen, Copenhagen Business School; Rebecca Chandler-Wilde, Lead Tutor, Henley Management College; Lisa Jackson, Lecturer at the Department of Informatics, Halmstad University; Roger Hammond, Senior Lecturer, University of Gloucester Business School.

For the third edition, the publishers and authors would particularly like to thank the following people for their insightful and constructive feedback:

Zahid Hussain, Bradford University; Milena Bobeva, Bournemouth University; Donna Champion, Loughborough University; Bruce Bluff, Bournemouth University; Andreas Panayiotidis, Kingston University; Michael Martin, Buckinghamshire University College; John McKeown, Canterbury Christchurch University College; Brian Telford, Glamorgan University; Ann Mulhaney, Liverpool John Moores University; Roel Ronken, Maastricht University; David Targett, Imperial College; Sunil Choenni, Nyenrode University; Feng Li, Newcastle University; Des McLaughlin, Dublin City University.

For the fourth edition, the publishers would like to thank:

Eric van Hoek, RSM Erasmus University; Alan Hunt, Robert Gordon University; Owen Johnson, University of Leeds; Andy Jones, Staffordshire University; Abdullah Khaled, Essex University; Catherine Maria Toase, University of Central Lancashire; Tom McMaster, University of Salford.

Finally, the publishers and authors would like to recognise the co-authorship of Dave Chaffey (www.davechaffey.com) during the first three editions of this book. Dave is a freelance consultant and lecturer, and author of a number of other books on e-business and information systems.

Publisher's acknowledgements

We are grateful to the following for permission to reproduce copyright material:

Figures

Figure 4.5 from IBM Cognos Enterprise screenshot, courtesy of International Business Machines Corporation, © 2014 International Business Machines Corporation; Figures 4.7, 4.8 from A Closer Look at Scorecards and Dashboards *Dashboard Insight* (Wise, L. 2010), http://www.dashboardinsight. com/articles/digital-dashboards/fundamentals/a-closer-look-at-scorecards-and-dashboards. aspx, Image courtesy of Dundas Data Visualization, Inc. - www.dundas.com; Figure 4.9 from A BAM dashboard displaying realtime data in a browser, http://www.oracle.com/technetwork/ middleware/bam/loanflow-098007.html; Figure 4.10 from http://www.esri.com/news/arcuser/0611/ graphics/newbizgis_3_lg.jpg, used with permission, © 2011 Esri, ArcUser, all rights reserved; Figure 6.1 from www.sap.com, © SAP SE, all rights reserved; Figure 11.3 from Information system integration, *Communications of the ACM*, vol. 43(6), pp. 33–8 (Hasselbring, W., 2000), © 2000 Association for Computing Machinery, Inc. Reprinted by permission. http://dl.acm.org/citation. cfm?doid=336460.336472; Figure 12.4 from Oracle; Figure 13.3 adapted from How information gives you the competitive advantage, *Harvard Business Review*, July/August, pp. 149–60 (M.E. Porter and V.E Millar, 1985), © 1985 by the Harvard Business School Publishing Corporation; all rights reserved; Figure 13.6 from *Competitive Advantage: Creating and Sustaining Superior Performance*, Free Press (Porter, M.E.) Fig. 2.2, p. 37, © 1985, 1998 by Michael E. Porter, all rights reserved; Figure 14.1 from Beyond strategic information systems: towards an IS capability, *Journal of Strategic Information Systems*, vol.13(2), pp. 167–94 (Peppard, J. and Ward, J., 2004), copyright 2004, with permission from Elsevier; Figure 16.3 from Information success: The quest for the dependent variable', *Information Systems Research*, vol.3(1) (DeLone, W. and McLean, E., 1992), copyright 1992, the Institute for Operations Research and the Management Sciences (INFORMS), 7240 Parkway Drive, Suite 310, Hanover, MD 21076, USA Reproduced with permission. http://www.informs.org.

Tables

Table 5.4 after Road map to the e-revolution, *Information Systems Management Journal*, vol.17(2), pp. 8–22 (Kampas, P.J., 2000), Reprinted by permission of the publisher (Taylor & Francis Ltd, http:// www.tandfonline.com); Table 12.6 from *The Essence of Business Process Re-engineering*, Prentice Hall (Peppard, J. and Rowland, P., 1995) p. 181.

Text

Case Study 1.1 from The new model sharing economy: technology sponsors a complementary form of capitalism, *Financial Times*, 11/08/2013, © The Financial Times Limited, All Rights Reserved; Case Study 1.2 from Dealing with the data deluge, *Financial Times*, 01/02/2013 (Cookson, C.), © The Financial Times Limited, All Rights Reserved; Case Study 2.1 from PayPal eyes in-store retail customers, *Financial Times*, 28/03/2013 (Dembosky, A.), © The Financial Times Limited, All Rights Reserved; Case Study 2.2 from Corporate IT falling short of potential, *Financial Times*, 18/01/2013 (Taylor, P.), © The Financial Times Limited, All Rights Reserved; Case Study 3.1 from Mainframes are thriving in a cloud world, *Financial Times*, 22/04/2013 (Taylor, P.), © The Financial Times Limited, All

Rights Reserved; Case Study 3.2 from Hertz reaps virtualisation rewards, *Financial Times*, 01/06/2013 (Tayor, P.), © The Financial Times Limited, All Rights Reserved; Case Study 3.3 from Rise of the paperless meeting, *Financial Times*, 09/04/2012 (Stevenson, A.), © The Financial Times Limited, All Rights Reserved; Case Study 3.4 from Cloud is silver lining for German online bank Fidor, *Financial Times*, 28/01/2014 (Bird, J.), © The Financial Times Limited, All Rights Reserved, Case Study on page 171 adapted from A redesign of a road traffic accident reporting system using business process simulation', *Business Process Management Journal*, Vol.10(6), pp. 636–644 (Greasley, A. 2004), © Emerald Group Publishing Limited all rights reserved; Case Study on pages 154–155 from How to get rid of 'devil customers', *Financial Times* (Rubens, P.), © The Financial Times Limited. All Rights Reserved; Case Study on pages 162–163 from Traders' tools turn tables on dodgy deals, *Financial Times*, 10/07/2013 (Masters, B.), © The Financial Times Limited. All Rights Reserved; Case Study 4.1 from Big data put under the spotlight as never before, *Financial Times*, 26/06/2013 (Taylor, P.), © The Financial Times Limited, All Rights Reserved; Case Study 4.2 from Making business intelligence work, *Financial Times*, 06/10/2010 (Cruickshank, B.), © The Financial Times Limited, All Rights Reserved; Case Study 4.3 from After 160 years, the value of maps is starting to be appreciated, *Financial Times*, 20/07/2009 (Waite, R.), © The Financial Times Limited, All Rights Reserved; Case Study 5.2 from Death of a matchmaker, *Financial Times*, 22/02/2013 (Kaminska, I.), © The Financial Times Limited, All Rights Reserved; Case Study 5.2 from Tipping point for media viewing as couch potatoes go digital, *Financial Times*, 01/08/2013 (Steel, E.), © The Financial Times Limited, All Rights Reserved; Case Study 5.3 from Asian mobile chat apps challenge Western dominance, *Financial Times*, 01/08/2013 (Bland, B. et al.), © The Financial Times Limited, All Rights Reserved, Case Study on page 231 from The supply chains that could bind unsuspecting managers (abridged version)., *Financial Times*, 28/11/2006 (Stern, S.), © The Financial Times Limited. All Rights Reserved; Case Study 6.1 from A convincing case must be made before investment, *Financial Times*, 20/03/2012 (Twentyman, J.), © The Financial Times Limited, All Rights Reserved; Case Study 6.2 from Managing the supply chain, *Financial Times*, 08/02/2011 (Teijken, R.), © The Financial Times Limited. All Rights Reserved; Case Study 8.1 from Recession reveals the dark side of advanced IT, *Financial Times*, 24/07/2013 (Moschella, D.), © The Financial Times Limited, All Rights Reserved; Case Study 8.2 from Case study: Sedgemoor District Council, *Computing* (Kelly, L.), www.computing.co.uk/computing/analysis/2200923/case-study-sedgemoor-district; Case Study on page 322 from The key to . . project planning, The Times, 26/05/2005 (Plummer, J.); Case Study 9.1 from Putting an all-inclusive price tag on successful IT, *Financial Times*, 30/05/2007 (Barker, R.), © The Financial Times Limited, All Rights Reserved; Case Study 9.2 from Project management: lessons can be learned from successful delivery, *Financial Times*, 19/08/2012 (Kortekaas, V.), © The *Financial Times* Limited, All Rights Reserved; Case Study 11.1 from Case study: Beaverbrooks the Jewellers, *Computing* (Linda More), http://www.computing.co.uk/ctg/analysis/1821325/case-study-beaverbrooks-jewellers; Case Study 11.2 from Systems management: driving innovation should be the main objective, *Financial Times*, 06/11/2012 (Bird, J.), © The Financial Times Limited, All Rights Reserved; Case Study on page 444 from Jim Goodnight: crunching the numbers, *Financial Times*, 28/03/2005 (Dempsey, M.), © The Financial Times Limited. All Rights Reserved; Case Study 13.1 from Which cloud model will prevail?, *Financial Times*, 22/05/2012 (Taylor, P.), © The Financial Times Limited. All Rights Reserved; Case Study 13.2 from Next generation of clients forces pace of IT change, *Financial Times*, 07/05/2013 (Thompson, J.), © The Financial Times Limited, All Rights Reserved; Case Study on pages 516–57 from *Computing*, www.computing.co.uk/itweek/news/2185966/customers-admit-blame; Case Study 14.1 from Outsourcing: beware false economies, *Financial Times*, 06/12/2011 (Bird, J.), © The Financial Times Limited, All Rights Reserved; Case Study 14.2 from IT trends shape future corporate strategies, *Financial Times*, 23/05/2013 (Taylor, P.), © The Financial Times Limited, All Rights Reserved; Case Study on page 543 from Complacent staff weak link in combating cyber criminals, *Financial Times*, 30/06/2013 (Burgess, K.), © The Financial Times Limited. All Rights Reserved; Case Study 15.1 from Online cybercrime rings forced to home in on smaller prey, *Financial Times*, 19/07/2013 (Kortekaas, V.), © The Financial Times Limited, All Rights Reserved; Case Study 15.2 from Cybercrime costs US $100bn a year, report says, *Financial Times*, 23/07/2013 (Taylor, P.), © The Financial Times Limited, All Rights Reserved; Case Study on pages 577–578 from Cyberslacking: employees surf non-work-related web sites, *Financial Times*, 17/05/2006 (Allison, K.),

© The Financial Times Limited. All Rights Reserved; Case Study 16.1 from It's not just an IT issue any more, *Financial Times*, 21/07/2004 (Baxter, A.), © The Financial Times Limited, All Rights Reserved; Case Study 16.2 from Time to call the helpdesk?, *Financial Times*, 13/06/2007 (Twentyman, J.), © The Financial Times Limited, All Rights Reserved; Case Study on pages 625–626 from Pirate Bay hacker jailed for two years, *Financial Times*, 20/06/2013 (Milne, R.), © The Financial Times Limited. All Rights Reserved; Case Study 17.1 from Small mistakes attract the biggest trouble, *Financial Times*, 13/05/2012 (Kellaway, L.), © The Financial Times Limited, All Rights Reserved; Case Study 17.2 from Sony fined after lapses at games network, *Financial Times*, 24/01/2013 (McCarthy, B.), © The Financial Times Limited, All Rights Reserved.

Photographs

123rf: 123; **Corbis:** Smithsonian Institution/Corbis 393; **Getty Images:** Atomic Imagery 573, Mike Kiev 293, Miguel Navarro 263; **Shutterstock.com:** asharkyu 177, Brian A. Jackson 439, Maksim Kabakou 539, Val Lawless 5, David Mail 217, Leigh Prather 507, Bruce Rolff 599, Semisatch. 391, Sergey Nivens 145, sheelamohanachandran2010 477, vichie81 349, vovan 35, White78. Shutterstock 65, Zadorozhnyi Viktor 319.

All other images © Pearson Education

In some instances we have been unable to trace the owners of copyright material, and we would appreciate any information that would enable us to do so.

Introduction to business information systems

PART 1 INTRODUCTION TO BUSINESS INFORMATION SYSTEMS

FUNDAMENTALS OF BUSINESS INFORMATION SYSTEMS	CHAPTER 1 INFORMATION	CHAPTER 2 SYSTEMS	
BUSINESS INFORMATION SYSTEMS TECHNOLOGIES	CHAPTER 3 HARDWARE AND SOFTWARE	CHAPTER 4 DATABASES AND BUSINESS INTELLIGENCE	CHAPTER 5 NETWORKS
BUSINESS APPLICATIONS	CHAPTER 6 ENTERPRISE AND FUNCTIONAL BIS	EXAMPLES THROUGHOUT CHAPTERS 1 TO 5	

PART 2 BUSINESS INFORMATION SYSTEMS DEVELOPMENT

FUNDAMENTALS OF BIS DEVELOPMENT	CHAPTER 7 ACQUIRING AND DEVELOPING	CHAPTER 9 PROJECT MANAGEMENT		
BIS DEVELOPMENT LIFECYCLE	CHAPTER 8 INITIATION	CHAPTER 10 SYSTEMS ANALYSIS	CHAPTER 11 SYSTEMS DESIGN	CHAPTER 12 SYSTEM BUILD, IMPLEMENTATION AND MAINTENANCE

PART 3 BUSINESS INFORMATION SYSTEMS MANAGEMENT

FUNDAMENTALS OR BIS STRATEGY	CHAPTER 13 INFORMATION SYSTEMS STRATEGY	CHAPTER 14 INFORMATION SYSTEMS MANAGEMENT	
ELEMENTS OF BIS STRATEGY AND DEVELOPMENT	CHAPTER 15 PROTECTING BIS	CHAPTER 16 END-USER SERVICES	CHAPTER 17 LEGAL AND ETHICAL ISSUES

Introduction to Part 1

When beginning the study of the use of information systems (IS) in business, it is important to understand a number of concepts drawn from a variety of different fields. In order to create, improve and manage business information systems (BIS), one must combine an understanding of information, systems concepts, business organisations and information technology (IT). Part 1 is intended as an introductory section to IS which provides a background supporting further study in Parts 2 and 3. In addition to explaining basic terms and concepts, Part 1 shows, through examples in each chapter, why IS are vital to business today. The role of BIS in transforming organisations through the application of electronic commerce and electronic business is also introduced in Part 1.

Understanding the terms and components that define IS is necessary in order that business users can communicate with the IT suppliers building and maintaining their systems. All systems involve transforming inputs such as data into outputs such as information by a transformation process. The UK Academy for Information Systems defines information systems as follows:

> Information systems are the means by which organisations and people, using information technologies, gather, process, store, use and disseminate information.

In simpler terms, a business information system can be described as a system that provides the information needed by managers to support their activities in achieving the objectives of a business. A computer-based information system can be described as an IS which uses information technology in the form of hardware, software and communications links. The term 'information and communications technology' (ICT) is often used to emphasise the growing importance of communications technology such as local area networks and the Internet. Throughout this book, the terms 'information technology' and 'information and communications technology' are used interchangeably. Note that an IS can be paper-based or computer-based. For simplicity, computer-based information systems and business information systems are referred to as BIS throughout this book.

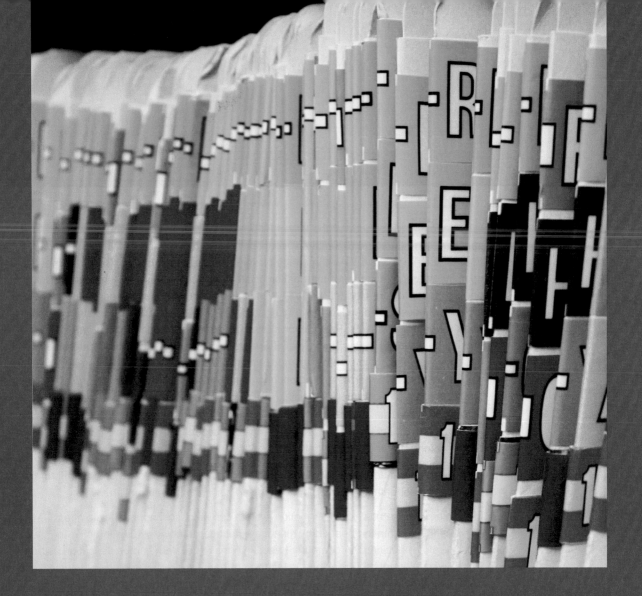

LINKS TO OTHER CHAPTERS

Chapter 2   builds upon the concepts described within this chapter and introduces new ideas, such as BIS.

Chapter 6   gives examples of how decision support systems assist decision making.

Chapter 10   describes the techniques used in analysing information flows within an organisation.

Chapter 13   reviews the ways in which information systems can support an organisation's business strategy.

Chapter 15   considers techniques for increasing the security of information.

Basic concepts – understanding information

CHAPTER AT A GLANCE

MAIN TOPICS

FOCUS ON . . .

CASE STUDIES

LEARNING OUTCOMES

After reading this chapter, you will be able to:

- distinguish between data, information and knowledge;
- describe and evaluate information quality in terms of its characteristics;
- classify decisions by type and organisational level;
- identify the information needed to support decisions made at different organisational levels;
- identify some of the tools and techniques used to help make decisions.

MANAGEMENT ISSUES

The purpose of business information systems (BIS) is to produce high-quality information that can be used to support the activities of an organisation. In order to gain a good understanding of BIS, managers must first understand the nature of information and how effective decisions are made. From a managerial perspective, this chapter addresses the following areas:

- the importance of managing information and knowledge as a key organisational asset;
- the transformation process from data to information of high quality;
- the process and constraints of decision making;
- the different kinds of decisions that managers make and how these affect the organisation.

INTRODUCTION

The general aim of this chapter is to introduce readers to the basic concepts needed to gain a thorough understanding of business information systems (BIS). However, before looking at BIS themselves, it is important to understand something of the nature of information. For BIS to be effective, the quality of information provided is vital. In this chapter, we look at how we can assess and improve the quality of data and information. The topics covered are intended to give readers an understanding of:

- the nature of data, information and knowledge;
- the value of information;
- the characteristics that can be used to describe information quality;
- information in the context of the e-business environment;
- managerial decision making, including the characteristics of decisions at different organisational levels;
- the information needed to support decision making.

DATA AND INFORMATION

As will be shown a little later, much of a manager's work involves using information to make decisions and ensuring that information flows through the organisation as efficiently as possible. Increasingly, technology is used to capture, store and share information throughout the organisation and with business partners. Many organisations are keenly aware that using information – and information technology – effectively can have an impact on every aspect of their operations, from reducing running costs to dealing with competition in the marketplace. In his best-selling book, *Business at the Speed of Thought*, Bill Gates (2001) says 'Information technology and business are becoming inextricably interwoven. I don't think anybody can talk meaningfully about one without talking about the other.' In this chapter we present an insight into the natures of data, information and knowledge to provide a foundation for learning about BIS.

Russell Ackoff's 'DIKW' model (Rowley, 2007: 176) provides a good framework for helping to understand the relationships between data, information, knowledge and wisdom. As can be seen in Figure 1.1, these concepts can be shown as a hierarchy. The hierarchy suggests three important ideas. The first is that data becomes information, information becomes knowledge and knowledge ultimately becomes wisdom. In other words, there is a progression from one level to the next. The second idea is that knowledge and wisdom are somehow more valuable, desirable or important than data and information. This is because wisdom and knowledge sit at the top of the triangle. In turn, this leads to the third idea, that data are relatively common while knowledge and wisdom are less so.

We will look at each of the levels in the hierarchy in detail throughout the rest of this chapter, starting with data in the next section.

What is meant by data?

Data

A collection of non-random facts recorded by observation or research.

Data are raw facts or observations that are considered to have little or no value until they have been processed and transformed into information. A single piece of data is called a datum. Unrelated items of data are considered to be essentially without meaning and are often described as 'noise'. It is only when data have been placed in some form of context that they become meaningful to a manager.

Figure 1.1 The 'DIKW' model

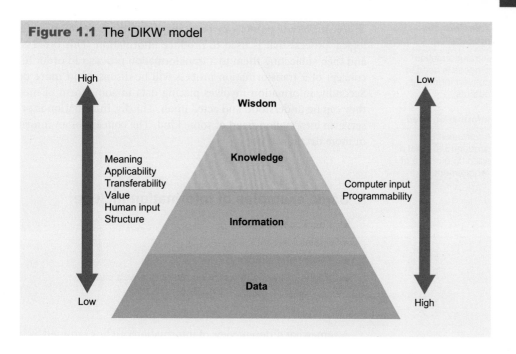

There are several definitions for data that are in common use:

- a series of non-random symbols, numbers, values or words;
- a series of facts obtained by observation or research and recorded;
- a collection of non-random facts.

Examples of data include:

- today's date;
- measurements taken on a production line;
- records of a business transaction, such as a single visit to a web site.

Data can exist naturally or can be created artificially. Naturally occurring data need only to be recorded. In business, organisations often establish procedures to make sure data are recorded properly. When a customer makes a telephone enquiry, for example, staff may be instructed to ask for up-to-date contact details and make sure they are recorded in the company's database.

Artificial data are often produced as a by-product of a business process. Processing an organisation's accounts, for example, might produce the number of sales made in a particular month.

What is information?

Information

Data that have been processed so that they are meaningful.

As with the concept of data, there are several definitions of information that are in common use:

- data that have been processed so that they are meaningful;
- data that have been processed for a purpose;
- data that have been interpreted and understood by the recipient.

Transformation process

A transformation process is used to convert inputs into outputs.

Information need

Information is produced to meet a specific purpose or requirement.

Three important points can be drawn from these definitions. First, there is a clear and logical process that is used to produce information. This process involves collecting data and then subjecting them to a transformation process in order to create information. The concept of a transformation process will be discussed in more detail in the next section. Secondly, information involves placing data in some form of meaningful context, so that they can be understood and acted upon. Thirdly, information is produced for a purpose, to serve an information need of some kind. The concept of an information need is described in more detail later on.

Some examples of information include:

- a bank statement;
- a sales forecast;
- a telephone directory;
- graphs of trends in visitor numbers to a web site.

A somewhat different view of information can be examined by introducing an additional definition:

> Information acts to reduce uncertainty about a situation or event.

Although uncertainty can never be eliminated entirely, it can be *reduced* significantly. Information can help to eliminate some possibilities or make others seem more likely. Managerial decision making can be improved by using information to reduce uncertainty. Information is said to influence *decision behaviour*, the way in which people make decisions. Managerial decision making is dealt with in more detail in a later section.

To summarise the key points made in the preceding section. Information:

- involves transforming data using a defined process;
- involves placing data in some form of meaningful context;
- is produced in response to an information need and therefore serves a specific purpose;
- helps to reduce uncertainty, thereby improving decision behaviour.

CREATING INFORMATION

Data process

A process used to convert data into information. Examples include summarising, classifying and sorting.

Processing data is necessary to place them into a meaningful context so that they can be easily understood by the recipient. Figure 1.2 illustrates the conversion of data into information.

A number of different data processes can be used to transform data into information. Data processes are sometimes also known as 'transformation processes'. The next section describes a range of common data processes.

Figure 1.2 Transforming data into information using a data process

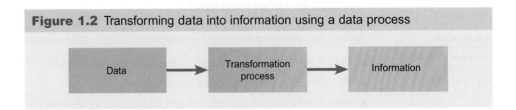

Data processes

Some examples of data processes include the following:

- *Classification*. This involves placing data into categories, for example categorising an expense as either a fixed or a variable cost.

- *Rearranging/sorting*. This involves organising data so that items are grouped together or placed into a particular order. Employee data, for example, might be sorted according to surname or payroll number.

- *Aggregating*. This involves summarising data, for example by calculating averages, totals or subtotals.

- *Performing calculations*. An example might be calculating an employee's gross pay by multiplying the number of hours worked by the hourly rate of pay.

- *Selection*. This involves choosing or discarding items of data based on a set of selection criteria. A sales organisation, for example, might create a list of potential customers by selecting those with incomes above a certain level.

It is worth noting that any action that serves to place data into a meaningful context can be considered a valid data process. In addition, several processes may be used in combination to produce information.

Activity 1.1	Data v. information

From the point of view of a student at university, which of the following might be examples of information? Which might be examples of data?

(a) the date;

(b) a bank statement;

(c) the number 1355.76;

(d) a National Insurance number;

(e) a balance sheet;

(f) a bus timetable;

(g) a car registration plate.

Value of information

Tangible value

A value or benefit that can be measured directly, usually in monetary terms.

It is often possible to measure the value of information directly. The **tangible value** of information is often measured in terms of financial value. An example might be the use of inventory information to improve stock control procedures. A simple calculation can be used to determine the value of a given item or collection of information:

$$\text{Value of information} - \text{Cost of gathering information}$$

However, in many cases, it is not possible to calculate the value of information directly. Although it is certain that the information is of benefit to the owner, it is difficult – or even impossible – to quantify its value. In such cases, the information is said to have **intangible value**. A good example might involve attempting to measure the extent to which information can improve decision behaviour. Such a calculation might appear as shown below:

Intangible value

A value or benefit that is difficult or impossible to quantify.

$$\text{Improvements in decision behaviour} - \text{Cost of gathering information}$$

There can be little doubt that the ability to make better decisions can be of great value to any organisation. However, one cannot readily quantify any improvements in decision making since a large number of other factors must also be taken in account. We will see in later chapters that this makes performing a cost–benefit analysis for BIS difficult (Chapters 8 and 14).

Activity 1.2	Tangible and intangible information

When information is used effectively, it can bring about many of the improvements listed below. State and explain why each of the items listed illustrates a tangible or intangible value of information:

(a) improved inventory control;

(b) enhanced customer service;

(c) increased production;

(d) reduced administration costs;

(e) greater customer loyalty;

(f) enhanced public image.

Activity 1.3	Information value

Using the Internet as a resource, find three case studies that show the value of information in the context of a business organisation. As an example, you might locate a news story in *Computer Weekly* (**www.computerweekly.com**) describing the savings made as a result of implementing a new stock control system.

Sources of information

Formal communication

Formal communication involves presenting information in a structured and consistent manner.

Informal communication

This describes less well-structured information that is transmitted by informal means, such as casual conversations between members of staff.

Information can be gathered through both formal and informal communication. **Formal communications** can include reports and accounting statements. **Informal communications** can include conversations and notes.

Formal communication

Information transmitted by formal communication tends to be presented in a consistent manner. Company reports, for example, will often use the same basic format. This allows the recipient to locate items of interest quickly and easily. Since formal communications tend to be presented in a more structured manner, they are also more likely to present a more comprehensive view of the situations or circumstances they describe. In addition, the information transmitted in this way is likely to be accurate and relevant, since it is normally created for a specific purpose.

BIS can be used to help apply a 'house style' for standard documents. Memos, reports and other documents are produced by making use of the templates that are found in most modern word processing packages. These templates contain the basic structure of a given document and can be compared to completing a standard form. Templates can also contain detailed instructions that specify what information should be included in the document and, more importantly, what information should be excluded.

However, formal communication also has several disadvantages. The structure imposed on information is often inflexible, sometimes limiting its type, form and content. In addition, formal communications often overlook information obtained by informal means. This can affect the decision-making process, reducing the quality and accuracy of any decisions made. Finally, formal communications often ignore group and social mechanisms. A formal report, for example, might marginalise or ignore staff opinions, causing offence and leading to reduced morale.

Informal communication

Informal communication is always present in an organisation, regardless of its size or nature. Information of this kind can be considered a valuable resource and one of the aims of knowledge management (described later in this chapter) is to harness it to work for the benefit of the organisation. Perhaps the most common means by which informal communication takes place is by word of mouth. This kind of communication is sometimes known as *water-cooler conversation*. In a sales organisation, for example, a casual conversation between a salesperson and a client might yield information that can be used to enhance a product or find new ways of making it more attractive to customers. If this information is not recorded the feedback will not be available to the new product development group.

Informal communication tends to offer a high degree of flexibility since there is more freedom to choose how information is structured and presented. Information obtained in this way also tends to be highly detailed, although it may often contain inaccuracies and may not be entirely relevant.

Activity 1.4	Informal communication

Consider the role of informal communication within an organisation such as a local government department or hospital.

The scope of information obtained in this way is often very narrow, relevant only to localised problems and situations. However, even at a local level, this can improve problem solving and decision making since it allows managers to gain a more detailed and in-depth understanding of a given situation.

One of the major disadvantages of informal communication is that it cannot deal with large volumes of information. Furthermore, as a means of communication, it is relatively slow and inefficient. Informal communication can also be highly selective, for example a person taking part in a conversation may be able to restrict what information is transmitted and who is able to receive it. Perhaps a more serious disadvantage is that informal communication is often ignored in favour of formal communication.

QUALITIES OF INFORMATION

Attributes of information quality

A group of characteristics by which the quality of information can be assessed, normally grouped into categories of time, content and form.

Information can be said to have a number of different characteristics that can be used to describe its quality. The differences between 'good' and 'bad' information can be identified by considering whether or not it has some or all of the attributes of information quality.

Lucey (2005) provides a list of characteristics likely to be present in information considered to be of good quality. However, others, such as O'Brien and Marakas (2006), take a more structured approach and describe the attributes of information quality as being divided into three basic categories: time, content and form. Table 1.1 summarises information characteristics that can be used to assess quality. Note that each column is independent; reading down each column lists the attributes associated with a particular factor.

Table 1.1 Summary of attributes of information quality

Time	Content	Form	Additional characteristics
Timeliness	Accuracy	Clarity	Confidence in source
Currency	Relevance	Detail	Reliability
Frequency	Completeness	Order	Formatted correctly
Time period	Conciseness	Presentation	Appropriateness
	Scope	Media	Received by correct person
			Sent by correct channels

Time dimension

Time dimension

Characteristics of information quality such as timeliness, currency and frequency which are related to the time of collection and review.

The **time dimension** describes the time period that the information deals with and the frequency at which the information is received.

- *Timeliness*. The information should be available when needed. If information is provided too early, it may no longer be current when used. If the information is supplied too late, it will be of no use.

- *Currency*. The information should reflect current circumstances when provided. One can go further and suggest that as well as being up-to-date the information should also indicate those areas or circumstances liable to change by the time the information is used.

- *Frequency*. In addition to being available when needed, information should also be available as often as needed. This normally means that information should be supplied at regular intervals, for example some organisations may require weekly sales reports whilst others need only monthly reports.

- *Time period*. The information should cover the correct time period. A sales forecast, for example, might include information concerning past performance, current performance and predicted performance so that the recipient has a view of past, present and future circumstances.

Content dimension

Content dimension

Characteristics of information quality such as accuracy, relevance and conciseness which are related to the scope and contents of the information.

The **content dimension** describes the scope and contents of the information.

- *Accuracy*. Information that contains errors has only limited value to an organisation.

- *Relevance*. The information supplied should be relevant to a particular situation and should meet the information needs of the recipient. Extraneous detail can compromise other attributes of information quality, such as conciseness.

- *Completeness*. All of the information required to meet the information needs of the recipient should be provided. Incomplete information can compromise other attributes of information quality, such as scope and accuracy.

- *Conciseness*. Only information relevant to the information needs of the recipient should be supplied. In addition, the information should be provided in the most compact form possible. As an example, sales figures are normally provided in the form of a graph or table – it would be unusual for them to be supplied as a descriptive passage of text.

- *Scope*. The scope of the information supplied should be appropriate to the information needs of the recipient. The recipient's information needs will determine whether the information should concern organisational or external situations and whether it should focus on a specific area or provide a more general overview.

Form dimension

Form dimension

Characteristics of information quality related to how the information is presented to the recipient.

The **form dimension** describes how the information is presented to the recipient.

- *Clarity*. The information should be presented in a form that is appropriate to the intended recipient. The recipient should be able to locate specific items quickly and should be able to understand the information easily.
- *Detail*. The information should contain the correct level of detail in order to meet the recipient's information needs. For example, in some cases highly detailed information will be required whilst in others only a summary will be necessary.
- *Order*. Information should be provided in the correct order. As an example, management reports normally contain a brief summary at the beginning. This allows a manager to locate and understand the most important aspects of the report before examining it at a higher level of detail.
- *Presentation*. The information should be presented in a form that is appropriate to the intended recipient. Different methods can be used to make information clearer and more accessible to the recipient, for example it is common to present numerical information in the form of a graph or table.
- *Media*. Information should be presented using the correct medium. Formal information, for example, is often presented in the form of a printed report, whereas a presentation might make use of a video projector.

Additional characteristics

In addition to the attributes described above, one might also add several others. Of particular importance is *confidence* in the source of the information received. Recipients are more likely to accept and trust the information they obtain if it is received from a source that has been accurate and reliable in the past.

A further attribute of information quality is that of *reliability*. It can be argued that recipients should be confident that they can rely upon information being available when required and that the information will be of a consistent quality in terms of other attributes of information quality, such as accuracy and conciseness.

The widespread use of computer-based information systems raises a number of issues related to the sheer quantity of information that is freely available via sources such as the Internet. In addition, the use of computer-based information systems also raises concerns in relation to security. In view of this, one might suggest that a further attribute of information quality is that the information provided should be *appropriate* to the recipient's activities. This might restrict information from being supplied if it is of a confidential nature or beyond the duties or responsibilities of a person's role.

The past decade has also seen an increased emphasis on finding new ways to exploit the huge quantities of information available to organisations. Many of the tools and techniques developed use technology to analyse information automatically. In order to do this effectively, it is necessary to store the information in a form that makes it easy to process by machine. In this way, we can say that information often needs to be *formatted correctly*, according to its intended use. Data to be processed by computer often needs to be placed in a specific format – usually following one or more standards – before it can be used. We see many of these standards in use every day. On the Internet, for instance, web pages are formatted using the HTML specification. The formats and standards used

proprietary

related to an owner or ownership

by an organisation can be its own internal ones, or can follow national or international standards. Internal data formats are often described as being **proprietary** while national and international standards are usually defined by official agencies. In the UK, for instance, official standards are usually set by the British Standards Institute (BSI). International standards are often set by the International Organisation for Standardistation (ISO).

The semantic web is often used to describe information accessible via the Internet that is meaningful to computers. This allows computers to deal with information more like human beings by understanding the meaning of the information and its associations with other pieces of information. One of the ways in which information can be made more accessible to machines is by including metadata. We can think of metadata as 'data about data' meaning that it is used to provide information about the content of a given item. A word processing document, for instance, will contain more than just text; it will contain additional information such as the name of the author, the date and time the document was created, comments and more.

According to the World Wide Web Consortium (W3C, 2001):

> The Semantic Web is about two things. It is about common formats for integration and combination of data drawn from diverse sources, where on the original Web mainly concentrated on the interchange of documents. It is also about language for recording how the data relates to real world objects. That allows a person, or a machine, to start off in one database, and then move through an unending set of databases which are connected not by wires but by being about the same thing.

It also seems natural to suggest that some confirmation that the information has been *received by the correct person* is required. Unless the information has been received and acted upon, then it is of no value. Thus, it can be suggested that an additional attribute of information quality is that it can be verified that the information has been received and understood.

Finally, it can be argued that another attribute of information quality is that that information should be capable of being transmitted via the *correct channels*. Most organisations have formal policies and procedures for dealing with particular situations. For example, a complaint against a member of staff is normally presented in a written form and travels upwards through the management hierarchy until it is received by the correct person. If the information were to be sent in any other way, for example by word of mouth, it might not reach its destination or might become garbled during the journey.

Semantic web

Refers to information accessible via the Internet that is understandable by machines. Such information has been placed in a form that allows machines to understand the meaning of the information and its associations with other pieces of information.

Metadata

Additional information used to describe the content of a given item. Metadata is often described as 'data about data'.

Activity 1.5   Information quality

Visit the web sites of two different online booksellers. For each example, assess whether the information provided about a particular book is of 'good' or 'poor' quality. Explain your reasoning with reference to the characteristics of information described in this chapter, and in particular Table 1.1. Can you differentiate between the offerings of the companies using the information provided?

CASE STUDY 1.1

Technology sponsors a complementary form of capitalism

The foundation of modern economics is Adam Smith's observation that an individual who aims only for his gain may still be led 'by an invisible hand' to make choices that bring economic benefits to others.

Last week, the Financial Times reported that a complementary view is emerging in the form of a 'sharing economy'. Most productivity growth may still be powered by self-interest. But modern information technology is helping the invisible hand become a whole lot more collaborative.

There has been too much breathless talk of how IT would revolutionise the economy, so it is useful to distinguish changes that are truly transformational from those that merely make it easier to do what one was already doing. Three broad trends assert themselves.

First, the internet makes it much cheaper for individuals to offer traditional goods and services to a larger market. Take short-term accommodation: there have always been homeowners wanting to rent out a spare room, and the hotel industry is of course of old vintage. IT does not bring fundamental innovation in this case. But – as websites such as Airbnb show – making it possible, for free, to connect with customers anywhere in the world cuts transaction costs and shrinks the advantage of scale that hotel chains hold over homey bed and breakfast operations.

A lower cost structure is not itself a shift from the pursuit of one's self-interest to a passion for sharing. It it nonetheless significant. When it becomes profitable to occupy rooms that would previously have stayed empty, it is a boost to the efficient use of society's resources. The same can be said for how the internet has made more personal services affordable for those outside the ranks of the super-rich. Those with more cash than time can outsource small chores to those in the opposite situation. The vehicles are sites that match tasks – from picking up the laundry to settling the utility bills – to those with time to spare.

Second, the information revolution facilitates genuine sharing in consumption. Barter – long seen as the height of inefficiency – is enjoying a revival through house swaps, where the internet can deepen the pool of swappers, making compatible pairings more likely. Many city residents are ditching car ownership in favour of web-facilitated car sharing. Car clubs that allow down to half-hour car rentals exist in cities around the globe. Car pooling websites allow for a virtual form of hitchhiking that does away with the inefficient waiting at the roadside. In France, **buzzcar.com** allows 'peer-to-peer rental': private car owners rent out their vehicles when they do not need them.

Sharing can be a lifestyle as well as an economy. Demand is growing for consumption that offers a personal experience beyond the standardised good or service. It also reflects a change in attitude to exclusive ownership, traditionally the measure of material success.

This underpins the third, most innovative and exciting trend: sharing in production. The open-source movement in software coding, Wikipedia, and some artists' renunciation of standard copyright show how work that is carried out voluntarily and co-ordinated spontaneously can result in economically valuable products. It is the antithesis of Taylorism.

None of these trends represents alternatives to capitalism; rather they are complements to standard practice and should be celebrated as such. Like traditional capitalism, they rely on trust and on supporting institutions for their success. These can be provided by the market itself – from the informal, such as user reviews, to the formal, such as Creative Commons licensing standards. At times state quality regulation is needed. In all cases the goal should be neither to force sharing nor to ban it, but to give those who want to share the confidence to do so.

 Source: Comment section (2013) Technology sponsors a complementary form of capitalism. *Financial Times*. 11 August. © The Financial Times Limited 2013. All Rights Reserved.

QUESTIONS

1. Using the case study, explain how IT enables a sharing economy.
2. How does a sharing economy improve overall productivity?

KNOWLEDGE AND WISDOM

Knowledge

Knowledge can be thought of as the combined result of a person's experiences and the information they possess.

Although there are numerous definitions of knowledge, many tend to agree that it involves harnessing a person's unique abilities, such as his or her perceptions, experiences, intuition and analytical skills. When these abilities are combined with the information the person holds, this represents knowledge. In other words, knowledge can be thought of as the combined result of a person's experiences and the information he or she possesses. This idea can be seen clearly in common definitions, such as this one proposed by Wang, Hjelmervik and Bremdal (2001):

> Knowledge is the full utilisation of information and data, coupled with the potential of people's skills, competencies, ideas, intuitions, commitments and motivations

We can also see this idea in more recent definitions, such as Rainer and Cegielski's (2011):

> Knowledge consists of data and/or information that have been organised and processed to convey understanding, experience, accumulated learning, and expertise as they apply to a current business problem.

In general, knowledge can be described as explicit or tacit. It may help to think of explicit knowledge as 'know-what' and tacit knowledge as 'know-how'.

Explicit knowledge is easily captured and stored within documents and other media. This type of knowledge tends to be highly detailed, formal and systematic. It is often stored in the form of manuals, documents, procedures and database files. Examples of explicit knowledge include minutes of meetings, employee handbooks and user manuals. Since explicit knowledge tends to be structured, it is easy to transmit to others.

Tacit knowledge is 'the intangible, internal, experiential, and intuitive knowledge that is undocumented and maintained in the human mind. It is a personal knowledge contained in human experience' (Waltz, 2003). Tacit knowledge is characterised by factors such as perceptions, beliefs, values, intuition and experience. Since a great deal of tacit knowledge may be held unconsciously, it is difficult to elicit, describe or record. Examples of tacit knowledge include skills (e.g. riding a bike), knowing how to respond in social situations and knowing how to respond to management reports.

Knowledge management (described in more detail later on) is involved with collecting (*eliciting*) knowledge and converting (*codifying*) it into a form that allows it to be shared across the organisation. A key part of this process involves gathering tacit knowledge and converting it into explicit knowledge.

For completeness, it is also worth taking a brief look at the concept of wisdom. *Wisdom* combines the characteristics of knowledge with the ability to apply such knowledge to new situations and problems. Wang, Hjelmervik and Bremdal (2001: 43), for instance, define wisdom as 'sufficiently generalised approaches and values that can be applied in numerous and varied situations'. Spitzer (2007: 106) offers a fairly similar definition: 'Wisdom is deep, rich understanding and insight that usually develops through a combination of extensive knowledge (knowing) and personal experience (doing) over time.'

A good way of thinking about wisdom involves the journey many people take as they move from being beginners to experts in many different areas. In engineering, for instance, an apprentice spends several years learning a wide range of skills before becoming a craftsman. We might argue that the difference between an apprentice and a craftsman is that the latter has greater knowledge, experience and understanding.

Activity 1.6	What is knowledge?

Using the Internet, locate at least five definitions or descriptions of knowledge. What do these definitions have in common and how do they differ from each other?

THE BUSINESS ENVIRONMENT

Environment

All businesses operate within an environment that includes social, political and business influences.

All business organisations operate within an **environment** that influences the way in which the organisation operates. Legislation, for example, will act to control some of the organisation's activities. However, the actions of an organisation may also influence parts of the environment. For example, companies may launch an advertising campaign designed to draw customers away from a competitor.

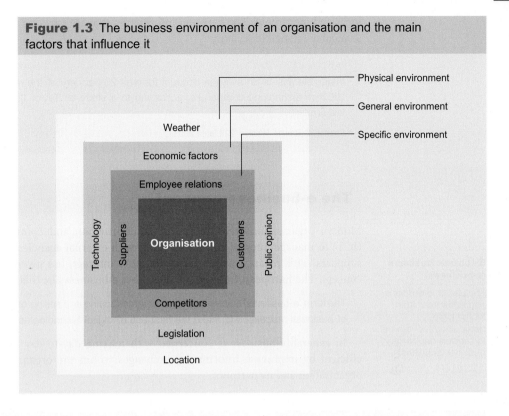

Figure 1.3 The business environment of an organisation and the main factors that influence it

Figure 1.3 illustrates some of the elements that may influence the way in which an organisation operates. For managers, gathering and using information about the external environment is an essential part of decision making. Increasingly, information systems are needed to help collect and make sense of information about the environment.

Internal business resources

Business resource base

The resources that a company has available to it which are made up of physical and conceptual resources known as tangible and intangible assets.

To operate within the business environment, organisations use a **business resource base** which supports their activities. The resource base consists of tangible resources (sometimes called 'physical resources') and intangible resources (sometimes called 'conceptual resources').

BIS can be applied to make best use of physical and conceptual resources to help an organisation to reduce costs, improve productivity and enhance overall efficiency.

Tangible assets (physical resource base)

Physical resources

Tangible assets or resources owned by a company such as land, buildings and plant.

Physical resources are often known as *tangible assets* and are normally directed towards the production of a product or service. Examples of physical resources include money, land, plant and labour power. The hardware and software making up BIS are also physical resources.

Intangible assets (conceptual resource base)

Conceptual resources

Non-physical resources or intangible assets owned by a company, such as organisational knowledge.

Conceptual resources are often known as intangible assets and are normally used to support an organisation's activities, for example by helping managers to make better decisions. Examples of intangible resources include experience, motivation, knowledge, ideas and judgement. The data and information that are part of a BIS can be thought of as a valuable intangible resource.

> Intangible assets on average account for over 20 per cent of the market capitalisation of UK high-technology companies, according to a study by Taylor Johnson Garrett, a City law firm.
>
> Source: *Computer Weekly*, 22 March 2001

The e-business concept

Electronic business (e-business)

The use of information and communication technologies, particularly the Internet, to support day-to-day business activities.

Modern organisations rely heavily upon information and communications technology (ICT) to manage internal communications with external agencies, such as customers and suppliers. This reliance upon, particularly the Internet, has given rise to the **e-business** concept. The European Commission describes e-business like this:

> The term 'e-business' covers both e-commerce (buying and selling online) and the restructuring of business processes to make the best use of digital technologies.

In general, e-business is concerned with making day-to-day business activities more efficient by improving information exchanges within the organisation and between the organisation and its partners.

MANAGERIAL DECISION MAKING

In order for an organisation to function effectively, all activities must be planned and monitored by managers according to well-informed decisions. In this part of the chapter we review the role of BIS in supporting different aspects of managerial decision making as follows:

1. An introduction to how managers use information, including their decision behaviour.
2. The three key levels of managerial decision making – operational, tactical and strategic.
3. A description of the decision-making process, assessing how BIS can assist at different stages of this process.
4. A section on decision-making theory, showing how structured decisions can be formally described in order to incorporate them into BIS.
5. The final section on knowledge management, illustrating how businesses are looking to manage information that can be used to assist less clearly structured decision making.

The information requirements of managers

Henri Fayol (1841–1925) devised a classic definition of management that is still widely used in both industry and academia. Of course, it is considered somewhat inappropriate nowadays to talk about commanding people:

> To manage is to forecast and plan, to organise, to command, to coordinate and to control.

Fayol's definition should make it clear that much of a manager's work involves making decisions about the best way to achieve the organisation's objectives and that there is a direct link between a manager's decision-making and planning activities. A forecast, for example, is created to help managers decide what actions are necessary to prepare the organisation for the future. The success of *all* of the activities described in Fayol's definition depends upon access to high-quality information. It is here that BIS have a role, as a means of supporting the manager's work by providing the information he or she needs. The next sections discuss managerial decision making in more detail.

Max Weber's (1864–1920) view of a *bureaucratic form* of organisation suggests that as an organisation grows in size and complexity, it becomes more difficult to control. For Weber, an ideal organisation displayed a number of characteristics, such as well-defined hierarchy or legitimate authority, the division of labour based on functional specialism and the existence of rules and procedures to deal with all situations and decisions. Large organisations, such as public utilities, often adopt some or all of the characteristics of a bureaucracy.

As organisations grow in size or complexity, the importance of effective and efficient management increases. In turn, greater reliance is placed upon the BIS used by the organisation. Put simply, as an organisation becomes larger, effective information systems become critical to continued survival.

Decision behaviour

Decision behaviour

The way in which managers make decisions.

The way in which managers make decisions, and the factors that influence those decisions, are often described as decision behaviour.

Decisions can be classed as structured or unstructured (sometimes referred to as 'programmable' and 'non-programmable' decisions). In reality, however, many decisions fall somewhere in between the two extremes and are known as *semi-structured decisions*.

Structured decisions

Situations where the rules and constraints governing the decision are known.

Structured decisions tend to involve situations where the rules and constraints governing the decision are known. They tend to involve routine or repetitive situations where the number of possible courses of action is relatively small. A good example involves stock control. The decision to reorder a given item will be governed by a fairly simple set of rules and constraints. When the amount of stock held falls below a certain point, a fixed quantity of new stock will be ordered. Structured decisions are often described as programmable, meaning that they are easily automated.

Unstructured decisions

Complex situations, where the rules governing the decision are complicated or unknown.

Unstructured decisions tend to involve more complex situations, where the rules governing the decision are complicated or unknown. Such decisions tend to be made infrequently and rely heavily on the experience, judgement and knowledge of the decision maker. A good example of an unstructured decision might be whether or not an organisation should open a new branch in a particular area.

Cognitive style

This describes the way in which a manager absorbs information and reaches decisions. A manager's cognitive style will fall between analytical and intuitive styles.

The behaviour of a manager will influence the way in which he or she absorbs information and reaches a decision. This is often referred to as a person's cognitive style. A manager's cognitive style will fall between analytical and intuitive styles.

The *analytical* manager typically displays a high level of analytical thought and is able to provide detailed justifications for any decisions made. He or she tends to prefer quantitative information as the basis for a decision and will often overlook any qualitative information received. This type of manager examines situations in fine detail and often overlooks the wider issues that might influence a decision.

Quantitative data

Includes use of figures, such as statistics. Also known as *hard data*, often collected in order to measure or quantify an object or situation.

Data are often described as 'hard data' or 'soft data'.

Hard data, also known as quantitative data, tend to make use of figures, such as statistics. Hard data are often collected in order to measure or *quantify* an object or situation.

Qualitative data

Describe without the use of figures, the qualities or characteristics of an object or situation. Also known as *soft data*.

Soft data, often known as qualitative data, tend to focus on describing the *qualities* or characteristics of an object or situation. Interviews, for example, are often used to collect qualitative data related to a person's opinions or beliefs.

The *intuitive* manager relies heavily on prior experience, judgement and intuition. He or she tends to examine situations as a whole, adopting a holistic view that takes into account the wide range of factors that might influence a decision. This kind of manager will also be more willing to accept qualitative information when making a decision.

It should be evident that a manager with an analytical cognitive style is likely to be most effective when making structured decisions. Intuitive managers are likely to be most effective when making unstructured decisions. Systems to assist in decision making are described in Chapter 6.

Levels of managerial decision making

The characteristics of the decisions taken in an organisation vary according to the level at which they are taken. Figure 1.4 shows the distribution of managerial responsibility within a typical organisation. As can be seen, the largest proportion of managers tends to be located at the operational level of the organisation. The smallest proportion of managers, typically less than 10 per cent, is located at the strategic level.

- At the *strategic* level, managers are largely concerned with long-term organisational planning. Decisions tend to be unstructured and are made infrequently. However, the decisions made at this level are likely to have a large impact on the organisation as a whole and cannot be reversed easily. An example of a decision taken at the strategic level might be a choice of new markets to move into.

- At the *tactical* level managers are largely concerned with medium-term planning. Managers monitor the performance of the organisation, control budgets, allocate resources and set policies. Decisions taken at this level are used to set medium-term goals that form stages leading to the accomplishment of the organisation's strategic objectives. An example of a decision taken at the tactical level might be setting a departmental budget.

- At the *operational* level managers deal with short-term planning and the day-to-day control of the organisation's activities. The decisions taken at this level direct the organisation's efforts towards meeting the medium-term goals, abiding by the budgets, policies and procedures set at the tactical level. Operational decisions tend to be highly structured and have little impact on the organisation as a whole. An example of a decision taken at the *operational* level might be setting a daily or weekly production schedule.

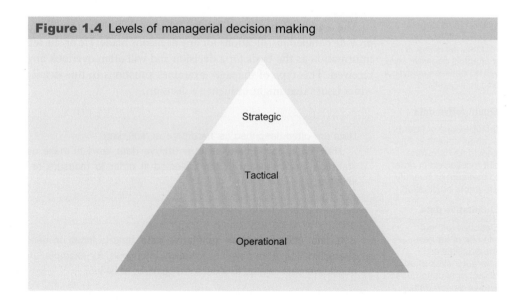

Figure 1.4 Levels of managerial decision making

Strategic

Tactical

Operational

Table 1.2 Decision characteristics and management level

Management level	Decision			
	Type of decision	Timescale	Impact on organisation	Frequency of decisions
Strategic	Unstructured	Long	Large	Infrequent
Tactical	↔	Medium	Medium	↔
Operational	Structured	Short	Small	Frequent

Example of decision types

Structured decisions: operational planning
- How should we process a sales order?
- What level of discount shall we give our customer on this order?

Semi-structured decision: tactical planning
- How do we target our most profitable customers and what are their characteristics?
- Which foreign markets should we target?
- What is the best pricing structure for this product?

Unstructured decision: strategic planning
- Which business area should the organisation be in?
- How should the organisation be structured?
- What should our distribution channels be?

A direct relationship exists between the management level at which a decision is taken and the characteristics of the information required to support decision making. Tables 1.2 and 1.3 illustrate how the characteristics of the information needed by managers change according to the type of decision being made.

Activity 1.7 Organisation-level decisions

Classify the following decisions by type (structured, semi-structured, unstructured) and organisational level (strategic, tactical, operational). In addition, determine whether or not the decision-making process could be automated, and if possible describe the name or type of BIS used.

(a) At what level should we set the budget for next year?

(b) Does this customer qualify for a discount on a large order?

(c) How should we deal with a takeover bid?

(d) Should we employ more staff to cope with an urgent order?

(e) Should we expand abroad?

(f) Should we launch an advertising campaign?

(g) Should we take a short-term loan to help our current cash flow position?

(h) What new markets should we move into?

(i) What should we do about a faulty machine?

Table 1.3 Information characteristics for decisions by management levels

Management level	Information					
	Time period	Frequency	Source	Certainty	Scope	Detail
Strategic	Wide	Infrequent	External	Less certain	Wide	Summarised
Tactical	↔	↔	↔	↔	↔	↔
Operational	Narrow	Frequent	Internal	More certain	Narrow	Detailed

Later (in Chapter 2, Figure 2.7 and in Chapter 6) we consider how particular types of BIS are used to support activities at the three different levels of operational, tactical and strategic.

The decision-making process

The work of H. Simon (1977) provides a framework from which to examine the way in which managerial decisions are made. Although presented in a modified form, this framework can be used to show how the act of making a decision involves moving through five stages. Each stage must be completed before it is possible to move on to the next. As you read about each stage, consider how BIS might be used to support it. Table 1.4 provides an overview of the decision-making process.

The *intelligence* stage involves gathering information concerning the decision to be made. It recognises that managers must be made aware that a problem exists before any action can be taken. Once a problem has been identified, information is collected in order to achieve a thorough understanding of the problem and the circumstances in which it arose. Unless this understanding is achieved, managers may take an inappropriate approach to the problem, resulting in a less efficient or even ineffective solution.

In the *design* stage, as many as possible of the potential solutions to the problem are identified and evaluated. At this point, the decision maker will begin to discard unsatisfactory solutions in order to reduce the number of alternatives as far as possible. The solution that will be implemented is then chosen during the *choice* stage.

Having made a decision, the action required to achieve a resolution to the problem is taken in the *implementation* stage. Following implementation, the *evaluation* stage considers how successful the solution has been. If further action is required, the decision maker returns to the intelligence stage and examines the problem again.

Table 1.4 A model of decision making

Stage	Activities
Intelligence	■ Awareness that a problem exists
	■ Awareness that a decision must be made
Design	■ Identify all possible solutions
	■ Examine possible solutions
	■ Examine implications of all possible solutions
Choice	■ Select best solution
Implementation	■ Implement solution
Evaluation	■ Evaluate effectiveness or success of decision

This model can be used to highlight two important points. First, it is important to recognise that information plays a critical part in arriving at an effective and successful decision. In the design stage, for example, it is essential to examine the implications of each possible solution. Unless the decision maker has access to adequate information, he or she may reject or accept possible solutions for the wrong reasons.

Secondly, the information required to support the decision-making process is determined by the decision itself. In other words, *decision needs determine information needs*.

Information need

The object of producing information is to meet a specific purpose or requirement.

> An information need can be thought of as a specific requirement for information. As an example, when a student sits an examination, he or she is asked to meet an information need by providing answers (information) to a series of specific questions.

CASE STUDY 1.2

Dealing with the data deluge

By Clive Cookson

At the turn of the millennium, many pundits described the 20th century as one of physics-based innovation and anticipated the 21st as the century of biology. Now, 13 years in, it looks increasingly as though we are living in the century of data.

Though research in biology and medicine continues to make exciting progress in the lab, it has yet to make much difference to the lives of most people. By far the biggest changes so far this century are due to the processing and communication of data (in the broad sense) from mass participation in the internet and associated social media to the digital takeover of writing, music and photography.

The issue of 'big data' – how to make the most of the truly gigantic deluge of data to emerge – is exercising the minds of many scientists and engineers. Trillions of bits of information are pouring out from billions of sources. Besides conventional websites, we have social networks leaving behind 'digital crumbs' for us to study, and the sensors embedded in everything from cars to cameras, creating the 'internet of things'. This data is largely unstructured.

Shirley Ann Jackson, president of Rensselaer Polytechnic Institute, New York, and a prominent figure in US science policy for two decades, is one of those considering this issue. I caught up with her on a visit to London to deliver a speech at the Royal Academy of Engineering.

'One could say that, concerning big data, we are still pre-web,' Jackson says. 'The world wide web is one huge 'library' but it has not yet provided uniform access to data. In a word, there is no Google for all data.'

Recovering information is difficult because there is no consistent system for tagging data to identify its origins, history, context, rights and so on. 'We need better means to take what may be implicit in the data,

and obvious in context, and make that explicit in its description,' Jackson says. 'We also need to improve the credibility of information by automating processes that cross-reference and cross-check.'

One remedy is the 'semantic web', a collaborative movement led by the World Wide Web Consortium to promote common data formats. The goal is to have a global mesh of information linked in a way that is easily processed by computers. The approach is based on semantic technology that encodes meanings separately from data in content files. This will allow intelligent software agents to search for connections among different data, by 'semantic inference'. 'One only can imagine what the impact will be, once this work is completed,' Jackson observes.

Jackson boasts several firsts as an African-American woman, including being the first elected to the US National Academy of Engineering and the first to lead a top research-orientated university. She is a passionate advocate of interdisciplinary working as the way to draw more power from the data deluge.

It is fashionable now to talk about the need to knock down academic silos and collaborate across all disciplines. But Jackson has been putting that approach into practice at Rensselaer since becoming president in 1999.

In Britain the term polytechnic has somewhat unfortunate associations of two-tier academic institutions, but Jackson has a much more positive view – and indeed advocates the 'new polytechnic' as an umbrella term to encompass multidisciplinary working to tackle the problems and opportunities of big data. 'I define the new polytechnic as an entirely fresh collaborative endeavour merging across a multiplicity of disciplines, sectors and global regions,' she says. 'It is animated by new technologies and tools – high-performance computing is an example – applied in new ways, with input from big data, amplified by new platforms such as the semantic web, probed by advanced analytics, and guided by societal concerns and ethics.'

We can look forward to many benefits from tackling big data in this way, in fields from climate change to genomic medicine. It will also be important to understand the effects of pervasive computing and communications technology itself on human behaviour.

How is the age of big data and pervasive information affecting us as people? Are we becoming more or less moral? If we can look anything up immediately on a mobile device, what will happen to our memories and our ability to learn? How will cognition respond to frequent and lengthy immersion in virtual reality? No one knows – and, as Jackson says, only by engaging the arts, humanities and social sciences are we likely to find out.

 Source: Cookson, C. (2013) Dealing with the data deluge. *Financial Times*. 1 February.
© The Financial Times Limited 2013. All Rights Reserved.

QUESTION

Explain the social and technical issues involved in extracting personal information from the web.

Decision-making theory

As mentioned earlier, structured decisions involve situations where the rules and constraints are known and where information needs can be clearly defined. These characteristics allow structured decisions to be automated by incorporating them within a business information system. Decision-making theory provides a framework for presenting structured decisions in a formal and systematic way.

A key concept associated with decision-making theory is that of the business rule. A **business rule** describes the actions that will be taken when a particular situation arises. Business rules are made up of three parts: an event that triggers the rule, a condition to test and the action(s) to be taken according to the outcome of the test. As an example, a bank might use a business rule that specifies only customers who have held an account for three or more years can be considered for a loan.

Since the business rules governing a particular situation can be complicated, various tools are used to make sure they applied in a logical and consistent way. Diagrams and tables, for instance, provide a standardised way of presenting rules that makes them easier to understand and follow. These tools also make it easier to implement business rules within computer programs. Although there are a number of different ways to present business rules, the example given earlier might be represented like this:

1	Name of event	Loan enquiry
2	Condition	Held account for 3+ years?
3	Possible results	Yes or no
4	Possible actions	Yes: allow application
		No: refuse application

As this example shows, the need to make a decision is usually triggered when an event occurs. In this case, the decision is triggered when the customer makes an enquiry about a loan. The condition governing the outcome of the business rule is usually expressed as a question. In this example the question is this: has the customer held an account for three or more years? If the result is 'no', the customer is not allowed to make a loan application, otherwise he or she is invited to apply.

This example has only a single condition with only two possible actions. However, more complex business rules may involve several questions and numerous actions. In these cases, it is common to use **decision trees** and **decision tables** to analyse a given situation. In general, a decision tree is drawn first, a decision table is then constructed using the decision tree as a basis.

Business rule

A rule describing what action the organisation should take when a particular situation arises. As an example, a bank might have a rule specifying that customers applying for a loan will only be considered if they have held an account for three years or more.

Decision tree

A diagram showing the events, conditions and outcomes associated with making a business decision. The decision tree is a graphical representation of the decision-making process.

Decision table

A means of representing the logic of a decision. A matrix is used to show all contingencies and the actions to be taken for each.

A decision tree is a diagram showing the events, conditions and outcomes associated with making a business decision. Diagrams are produced using flowchart notation. Figure 1.5 shows a simple decision tree for the loan application example.

A decision table breaks down a business process into a table that shows all the possible outcomes of the process. A matrix is used to show the different components of the decision and what outcomes will occur depending on the conditions governing the decision. Typically, the decision table uses the format shown in Figure 1.6.

A more detailed example may help to make the use of decision trees and decision tables clearer. Imagine the case of a customer applying for credit from a bank. The bank only offers loans to customers who have held an account for three or more years and who are in full-time employment or can offer some form of security. A simple decision tree is shown in Figure 1.7.

The process begins when the customer makes an enquiry at the bank. The first question asked is: has the customer held an account for three or more years? If so, the next question is whether or not the customer is in full-time employment. If they are, they can be offered credit. If they are not in full-time employment, they can still be offered credit if they are able to offer some other form of security. Otherwise, their application will be rejected.

Figure 1.8 shows the decision table for this example. The four rules correspond to the outcomes shown at the end of each branch in the decision tree in Figure 1.7. The upper part of the table shows the test conditions and all of the possible outcomes. The lower part of the table shows the possible actions to be taken according to the results of the test conditions. A dash signifies that the result of the test is unimportant. In the case of the first rule, for example, if the customer has not held an account for three or more years, their

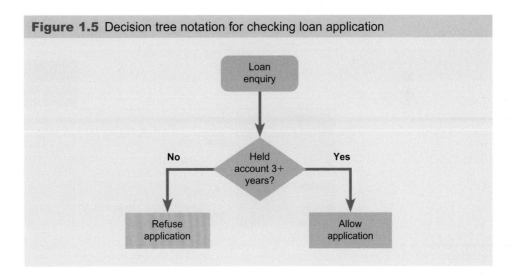

Figure 1.5 Decision tree notation for checking loan application

Figure 1.6 Framework for a decision table

Conditions	Condition alternatives
Actions	Action entries

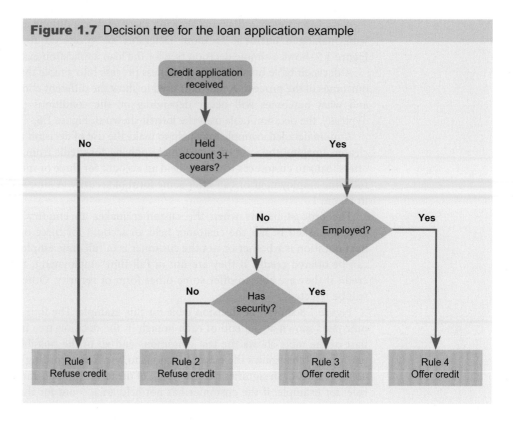

Figure 1.7 Decision tree for the loan application example

Figure 1.8 Decision table for Figure 1.7

		Rules			
		1	2	3	4
Conditions	Account 3+years	N	Y	Y	Y
	Employed	–	N	N	Y
	Security	–	N	Y	–
Actions	Offer credit			X	X
	Refuse credit	X	X		

application will be rejected regardless of their employment status or whether they are able to offer security.

As the example shows, decision tables provide clear and concise summaries of even the most complex business rules. A decision table can also help software developers incorporate the underlying logic of a business rule within an information system. For instance, it is fairly simple to translate a decision table into Structured English (also known as pseudocode) and from pseudocode into program code. Pseudocode is a simple but effective way of designing computer programs. Figure 1.9 shows the Structured English for the decision table in Figure 1.8.

Figure 1.9 Structured English program code for implementing the decision table shown in Figure 1.7

```
IF Held Account 3+ Years THEN
  IF Employed THEN
    Accept Application                    (Rule 4)
  ELSE
    IF Can Offer Security THEN
      Accept Application                  (Rule 3)
    ELSE
      Decline Application                 (Rule 2)
        ENDIF
    ENDIF
ELSE
  Decline Application                     (Rule 1)
ENDIF
```

FOCUS ON...　KNOWLEDGE MANAGEMENT

In this chapter we have shown that much of a manager's work involves making decisions about the best way to achieve the organisation's objectives. In addition, the quality of a manager's decisions depends upon the quality of the information he or she has access to. Since information influences almost every activity within an organisation, it is an important asset and must be treated accordingly.

Knowledge management is a fairly new term that describes a range of activities intended to make sure an organisation uses its information resources as effectively as possible. Bergeron (2003), defines knowledge management like this:

> Knowledge Management (KM) is a deliberate, systematic business optimisation strategy that selects, distils, stores, organises, packages, and communicates information essential to the business of a company in a manner that improves employee performance and corporate competitiveness.

In many countries there has been a general shift away from traditional industries, such as manufacturing, towards what has been termed the 'knowledge economy'. In the knowledge economy, companies exploit their knowledge and skills in order to generate profits. Many organisations have adapted to the knowledge economy by adopting new structures and by creating new roles for managers. The term *knowledge worker* describes a person whose role is based around creating, using, sharing and applying knowledge. Similarly, the work of a *knowledge engineer* focuses on eliciting knowledge from experts so that it can be recorded and shared with others within the organisation.

Although knowledge management is important within any organisation, it is of particular value in situations where organisations rely upon the knowledge and skills of individual staff. In such cases, the loss of a key person can cause significant disruption until an appropriate replacement can be found. Knowledge management aims to capture the knowledge and experience of key personnel, placing it in a form where it will remain accessible to the organisation at all times.

Many organisations have been enthusiastic about adopting knowledge management because of the potential benefits it brings. For example, CIO's online magazine suggests that an effective knowledge management programme will bring about one or more of the following benefits (Levinson, 2007):

- foster innovation by encouraging the free flow of ideas;
- improve customer service by streamlining response time;

- boost revenues by getting products and services to market faster;
- enhance employee retention rates by recognising the value of employees' knowledge and rewarding them for it;
- streamline operations and reduce costs by eliminating redundant or unnecessary processes.

Other writers, such as Bixler (2005) and Bergeron (2003) supply long lists of additional tangible and intangible benefits associated with effective KM programmes. We can summarise some of these benefits like this:

- an improved ability to sustain competitive advantage, leading to increased market share and market leadership;
- increased profit margins leading to increased shareholder satisfaction;
- the ability to identify best practices and better approaches towards problem solving;
- formalised system for transferring knowledge, allowing knowledge to be transferred between employees more easily and more efficiently;
- increased collaboration with customers;
- increased customer satisfaction, loyalty and retention;
- reduced costs through streamlining of internal processes and improved efficiency;
- higher staff morale and satisfaction, leading to lower staff turnover, increased innovation and greater productivity;
- increased organisational stability.

Applications of knowledge management are described in more detail later (in Chapters 4 and 6). They include:

- *Business intelligence (BI)*. BI is a general term that describes a range of techniques and technologies used to gather, store and analyse information from a variety of sources in order to improve decision making within an organisation. More information on business intelligence is covered later (in Chapter 4).
- *Document image processing (DIP)*. DIP involves converting printed documents into an electronic format that is more easily stored, searched and managed. The *Portable Document Format (PDF)* used by products such as Adobe Acrobat is an example of a common electronic format used to store documents. Documents stored as PDF files require very little storage space, can be searched quickly and are easy to manage.
- *Data mining*. This involves searching organisational databases in order to uncover hidden patterns or relationships in groups of data. Data mining software attempts to represent information in new ways so that previously unseen patterns or trends can be identified. An important feature of data mining is that it maximises the use of data the organisation already holds, making it relatively simple and inexpensive to perform. Uncovering patterns or trends in data can result in a number of important benefits, such as suggesting ideas for new products and services.

As these examples suggest, many of the activities associated with knowledge management are dependent upon the use of technology. DIP, for instance, would be impossible without the ability to digitise documents and convert them into their electronic equivalents. However, using technology effectively requires a firm grasp of elementary business concepts. As an example, before we can improve the way decisions are made within an organisation, we must first develop an understanding of decision theory. (Chapter 2 builds upon some of the concepts discussed here by introducing the topics of systems theory and competitive advantage.)

Competitive intelligence

Competitive intelligence (CI) is a typical example of knowledge management. As mentioned earlier, CI involves gathering information from a range of sources with the aim of maintaining or increasing competitive advantage. Although there are a number of definitions of competitive intelligence, most share some common elements. As an example, consider the definition given by the Institute for Competitive Intelligence (**www.institute-for-competitive-intelligence.com**).

> 'Competitive Intelligence' (CI) can be described as a systematic process of information retrieval and analysis, in which fragmented (raw) information on markets, competitors and technologies can be transformed into a vivid understanding of the corporate environment for the decision maker.

Compare this with the definition given in the *Competitive Intelligence Handbook* (**www .combsinc.com/handbook.htm**):

> Competitor intelligence is the analytical process that transforms disaggregated competitor intelligence into relevant, accurate and usable strategic knowledge about competitors, position, performance, capabilities and intentions.

As both definitions show, CI involves collecting data from a number of disparate sources and converting it into useful information about an organisation's competitors. The information gathered is used to support decision making within the organisation, allowing it to respond more effectively to competition.

CI is sometimes confused with activities such as industrial espionage. However, it is worth pointing out that CI is both legal and ethical; information is gathered lawfully, often openly, and usually from sources that are publicly accessible. This is echoed within the *Competitive Intelligence Handbook*:

> The objective of competitor intelligence is not to steal a competitor's trade secrets or other proprietary property, but rather to gather in a systematic, overt (i.e., legal) manner a wide range of information that when collated and analysed provides a fuller understanding of a competitor firm's structure, culture, behaviour, capabilities and weaknesses.

To read more about competitive intelligence visit the web sites listed at the end of the chapter.

SUMMARY

1. Data can be described as a collection of non-random facts obtained by observation or research.

2. Information can be described as data that have been processed so that they are meaningful. An alternative view of information suggests that it acts to reduce uncertainty about a situation or event.

3. Information can have tangible or intangible value. One view suggests that the value of information can be measured in terms of the improvements it brings to managerial decision making.

EXERCISES

Self-assessment exercises

1. What are the three dimensions of information quality?

2. How can the value of information be measured?

3. What are the functions of management?

4. What are the stages involved in making a decision?

5. How will a manager's cognitive style affect the decisions he or she makes?

6. Explain how the concept of knowledge management relates to data and information.

7. What differences in perspective about managerial decision making are introduced by the e-business concept?

8. In brief, what is knowledge?

Discussion questions

1. Some people argue that employees should be restricted in terms of the information they have access to in the course of their duties. Others argue that they are able to work more efficiently if they have access to *all* of an organisation's information resources. Using relevant examples, make a case for one side of this argument.

2. It has been said that decision needs should determine information needs. Is this always true or is there a case for an organisation gathering *all* available data and information?

3. Select an article of your choice from a newspaper, journal or magazine. Analyse the information contained within the article using concepts related to the attributes of information quality. Use the web links provided at the end of this chapter to locate suitable articles.

4. 'Knowledge management is nothing new, it is merely a repackaging of existing information management techniques.' Discuss.

Essay questions

1. Select an organisation you are familiar with. Identify at least one major decision that the organisation has taken recently. Describe the decision-making process that took place, paying particular attention to the following points:

   (a) describe how managers became aware that a problem existed and that a decision was required;
   (b) describe what information was gathered so that managers could achieve a good understanding of the problem;
   (c) provide examples of any alternative solutions that were considered and explain why these were eventually rejected;
   (d) explain why the final solution was selected and describe how it was implemented;
   (e) discuss how the solution was evaluated and whether or not it was successful.

2. The survival of a large organisation depends upon access to high-quality information. Discuss this statement, providing relevant examples where necessary.

3. The Microsoft Corporation is arguably one the most successful company's in the world. Conduct any research necessary to complete the following tasks:

   (a) Provide an overview of the company and its activities.
   (b) Selecting appropriate examples, describe the company's physical and conceptual resource bases.
   (c) Identify and describe some of the factors in the company's business environment. Provide examples of factors that act either to support or obstruct the company's activities.

4. Write a report on how knowledge management could enhance an organisation of your choice.

Examination questions

1. It is generally agreed that one of the key functions of management is decision making. Using specific examples, you are required to:

   (a) describe the types of decisions that managers are required to take;
   (b) explain the stages involved in making a decision;
   (c) describe the characteristics of decisions taken at different levels in an organisation.

2. An understanding of the nature of information is fundamental to the study of information systems. Using specific examples, you are required to:

   (a) define information;
   (b) describe the characteristics that will be present in information of high quality;
   (c) describe how the value of information can be determined.

3. Information can be transmitted via formal and informal means. Using specific examples, you are required to:

   (a) describe the advantages and disadvantages of each method;
   (b) discuss each method in terms of the attributes of information quality that are likely to be present.

4. In relation to the concept of knowledge management:

   (a) explain how knowledge differs from information;
   (b) describe two ways of classifying knowledge;
   (c) give an example of a business application for each of your answers in (b).

References

Bergeron, B. (2003) *Essentials of Knowledge Management*, John Wiley, Hoboken, NJ

Bixler, C. (2005) Developing a foundation for a successful knowledge management system in M. Stankosky (ed.) *Creating the Discipline of Knowledge Management*, Elsevier Butterworth–Heinemann, Oxford, pp. 51–65

Gates, B. (2001) *Business at the Speed of Thought: Succeeding in the Digital Economy*, Penguin, London

Levinson, M. (2007) *ABC: An Introduction to Knowledge Management (KM)* [online], CIO.com, Framingham, MA. Available at: www.cio.com/article/40343/40343/2#4

Lucey, T. (2005) *Management Information Systems*, 9th edition, Thomson Learning, London

O'Brien, J.A. and Marakas, G. (2010) *Introduction to Information Systems*, 15th edition, McGraw-Hill, New York

Rainer, K. and Cegielski, C. (2011) *Introduction to Information Systems: Enabling and Transforming Business*, 3rd edition, John Wiley & Sons, Hoboken, NJ

Rowley, J. (2007) 'The wisdom hierarchy: representations of the DIKW hierarchy', *Journal of Information Science*, 33, 2, 163–80

Simon, H. (1977) *The New Science of Management Decision*, Prentice-Hall, Englewood Cliffs, NJ

W3C (2001). *W3C Semantic Web Activity*. Available at: http://www.w3.org/2001/sw/

Waltz, E. (2003) *Knowledge Management in the Intelligence Enterprise*, Artech House, Boston, MA

Wang, K., Hjelmervik, O. and Bremdal, B. (2001) *Introduction to Knowledge Management: Principles and Practice*, Tapir Academic Press, Trondheim, Norway

Further reading

Laudon, K. and Laudon, J. (2013) *Management Information Systems: Managing the Digital Firm*, 13th edition, Prentice-Hall, Upper Saddle River, NJ. Chapters 11 and 12 deal with topics such as knowledge management and managerial decision making.

Turban, E., Rainer, R. and Potter, R. (2004) *Introduction to Information Technology*, 3rd edition, John Wiley, New York. Although lacking depth in some areas, this text is colourful and easy to read. Chapters 1 and 2 discuss basic concepts.

Web links

News sources for finding case studies about organisations

www.findarticles.com FindArticles provides searching through many newspapers, business magazines and some journals.

www.moreover.com Moreover provides searching through the world's newspapers. Particularly good for recent stories.

www.ft.com The *Financial Times* web site provides access to news stories from some 3000 publications. The searchable archive of news stories is a wonderful resource for a wide range of research activities.

www.guardian.co.uk The *Guardian* web site provides excellent news coverage and a wide variety of additional services.

www.reuters.com The official site for Reuters. Provides coverage of international news and financial information.

www.worldnews.com News stories from around the world. Major stories are categorised by city, e.g. New York, London. Some stories are accompanied by multi-media, such as Real Audio sound files. The site can be searched for items of interest.

http://news.bbc.co.uk The highly respected news service of the BBC. Coverage includes multi-media elements, such as sound and video.

www.infobeat.com Allows the creation of a personalised newspaper. Although the content received cannot be customised to a great extent, it nevertheless demonstrates the concept of delivering up-to-date, personalised information via the Internet.

www.mindtools.com/page2.html The Mind Tools site provides a series of brief articles that describe common approaches to problem solving in plain language.

www.eb.co.uk The *Encyclopaedia Britannica* web site.

Knowledge management and competitive intelligence

www.sveiby.com Karl-Erik Sveiby operates a web site containing a selection of well-written articles on knowledge management, including a regularly updated definition of different views of knowledge management. At the site, use the 'library' tag to locate articles of interest.

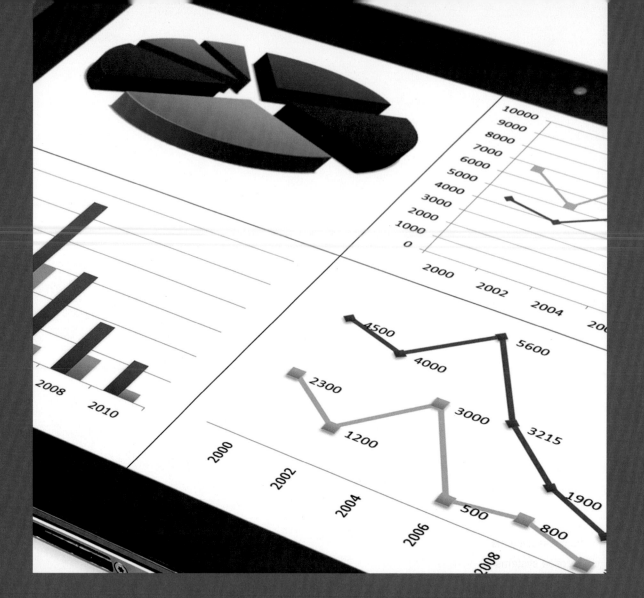

LINKS TO OTHER CHAPTERS

Basic concepts: an introduction to business information systems

CHAPTER AT A GLANCE

MAIN TOPICS

CASE STUDIES

LEARNING OUTCOMES

After reading this chapter, you will be able to:

- identify systems and their components;
- identify and describe the behaviour of systems;
- identify types of BIS, distinguishing them by category and the organisational level at which they are used;
- describe e-business, e-commerce and ERP and evaluate their relevance to the organisation;
- identify basic strategies and methods used to gain competitive advantage through the use of BIS.

MANAGEMENT ISSUES

Systems theory is a powerful tool that can be used to analyse systems at a high level of detail. It can be applied to a range of situations, from examining an organisation as a whole to analysing a specific task carried out by an individual employee. From a managerial perspective, this chapter addresses the following areas:

- how systems theory is used as a means of defining problems and situations so that they can be understood more easily and BIS can be developed to support them;
- how managers can maximise an organisation's use of technology by understanding BIS;
- how BIS can help achieve competitive advantage.

INTRODUCTION

This chapter builds upon the concepts introduced earlier (see Chapter 1) and introduces concepts related to the features of systems and competitive advantage. The topics covered are intended to give readers an understanding of:

- the basic characteristics of systems;
- the behaviour of systems;
- types of information systems;
- applications for information systems;
- the use of e-business and e-commerce;
- applying information systems for competitive advantage.

INTRODUCTION TO SYSTEMS

Systems theory

The study of the behaviour and interactions within and between systems.

Systems theory provides a powerful means of analysing and improving business processes. It can be applied to a wide variety of different areas and is fundamental to gaining a good understanding of the managerial application of BIS.

What is a system?

System

A collection of interrelated components that work together towards a collective goal.

Mission statement

A statement intended to encapsulate the overall goal(s) of an organisation.

A **system** can be defined as a collection of interrelated components that work together towards a collective goal. The function of a system is to receive inputs and transform these into outputs. Figure 2.1 illustrates the organisation of the input–process–output model. Note that though natural systems such as the solar system may not have an obvious goal, business systems often have multiple goals such as profit or improving the quality of a product. The overall goal of a business is often described within a **mission statement**.

An example will help to illustrate this concept and aid understanding. Earlier (in Chapter 1), the concept of a transformation process was used to explain how data can be converted into information. Using the model shown in the diagram, it can be said that data are used as the input for a process that creates information as an output.

However, this model illustrates a system that is essentially static. The performance of the system cannot be adjusted and there are no checks to ensure that it works correctly. In order to monitor the performance of the system, some kind of feedback mechanism is required. In addition, control must be exerted to correct any problems that occur and ensure that the system is fulfilling its purpose.

Adaptive system

A system with the ability to monitor and regulate its own performance.

If these additional components are added to the basic model of the system, it can be illustrated as shown in Figure 2.2. The model shown in the diagram is sometimes referred to as an **adaptive system**, in order to signify that it has the ability to monitor and regulate its own performance.

Figure 2.1 A basic model of a transformation process

Input → Process → Output

Figure 2.2 A generic model of a system

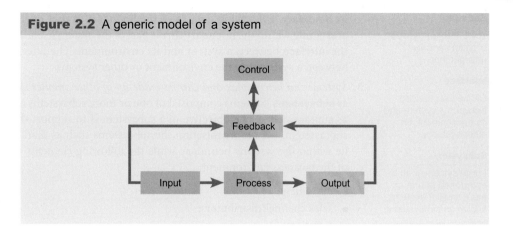

System components

At this point, it can now be argued that a generic system includes five components: input, process, output, feedback and control. Each of these components can now be described in more detail.

Input

The raw materials for a *process* that will produce a particular *output*.

Process

Inputs are turned into outputs by a transformation process.

Output

A product that is created by a system.

Feedback mechanism

Provides information on the performance of a system which can be used to adjust its behaviour.

Control mechanism

If alterations are needed to the system, adjustments are made by a control mechanism.

System objective

All components of a system should be related to one another by a common objective.

Environment

The surroundings of a system, beyond its boundary.

- The **input** to a system can be thought of as the raw materials for a process that will produce a particular output. Inputs can take many forms and are not necessarily purely physical in nature. Examples of inputs might include data, knowledge, raw materials, machinery and premises.

- Inputs are turned into outputs by subjecting them to a **transformation process**. The concept of a transformation process was described earlier (in Chapter 1).

- The **output** is the finished product created by the system. Again, the outputs produced by a system can take many forms. Examples might include information, products and services.

- Information on the performance of the system is gathered by a **feedback mechanism** (sometimes known as a 'feedback loop'). Measurements taken on a production line, or customer feedback on a web site are examples of feedback mechanisms.

- If alterations are needed to the system, adjustments are made by some form of **control mechanism**. In general, control is exerted as the result of feedback information regarding the performance of the system. The function of the control component is to ensure that the system is working to fulfil its objective (which is normally the creation of a specific output). Control tends to be exerted by adjusting the process and input components of the system until the correct output is achieved.

Other system characteristics

All systems share these characteristics:

1. *The components of a system work towards a collective goal.* This is known as the **system's objective**. The objective of a system is normally very specific and can often be expressed in a single sentence. As an example, the objective of a car might be expressed simply as: to transport people and goods to a specified location.

2. *Systems do not operate in complete isolation.* They are contained within an **environment** that contains other systems and external agencies. The scope of a system is defined by

Boundary

The interface between a system and its environment.

Interface

Defines exchanges between a system and its environment, or other systems.

Subsystem

Large systems can be composed of one or more smaller systems known as subsystems.

Suprasystem

A larger system made up of one or more smaller systems (subsystems).

Open system

Interaction occurs with elements beyond the system boundary.

Closed system

No or limited interaction occurs with the environment.

Coupling

Defines how closely linked different subsystems are. Loose coupling means that subsystems are not closely linked. Close-coupled systems are highly dependent on each other.

its **boundary**. Everything outside of the boundary is part of the system's environment, everything within the boundary forms part of the system itself. The boundary also marks the **interface** between a system and its environment. The interface describes exchanges between a system and the environment or other systems.

3. *Systems can be complex and can be made up of other smaller systems.* These are known as **subsystems**. Systems composed of one or more subsystems are sometimes referred to as **suprasystems**. The objective of a subsystem is to support the larger objective of the suprasystem. For an organisation the subsystems such as marketing and finance would lie within the system's boundary while the following elements would lie outside as part of the business environment:

- customers;
- sales channel/distributors;
- suppliers;
- competitors;
- partners;
- government and legislation;
- the economy.

An organisation will interact with all these elements which are beyond the system boundary in the environment. Systems that have a high degree of interaction with the environment are called **open systems**. Open systems are influenced by changes in the environment and can also influence the environment itself. Most information systems are open systems because they accept inputs and react to them. Totally **closed systems** which do not interact with their environment are unusual.

4. *Subsystems in an information system interact by exchanging information.* This is known as the *interface* between systems. For information systems and business systems, having clearly defined interfaces is important to an efficient organisation. For example, sales orders must be passed from the sales subsystem to the finance subsystem and the distribution subsystem in a clear, repeatable way. If this does not happen orders may be lost or delayed and customer service will be affected.

5. *The linkage or coupling between subsystems varies.* The degree of **coupling** defines how closely linked different subsystems are. It is a fundamental principle of systems theory and BIS design that subsystems should be loosely coupled.

Systems or subsystems that are highly dependent on one another are known as *close-coupled* systems. In such cases, the outputs of one system are the direct inputs of another. As an example, consider the way in which an examination system might operate. The letter that confirms a student's grade could be said to be the result of two subsystems working together very closely. One subsystem ensures that all examination scripts are marked and that a list of final results is produced. The second subsystem produces the letter of confirmation as its output. However, the letter of confirmation can only be produced once all marks have been confirmed and recorded. Thus, the output of the marking subsystem becomes the input to the subsystem that creates the confirmation letter.

The 'just-in-time' method used by a number of manufacturing organisations also illustrates a close-coupled system well. This method involves holding as few parts or raw materials as possible. In order to ensure that production is not halted, parts must be supplied 'just in time' to be used in the manufacturing process. Unless the manufacturing organisation has very close links with its suppliers, this approach cannot work effectively.

Decoupled systems (or subsystems) are less dependent on one another than coupled systems and so are more able to deal with unexpected situations or events. Such systems tend to have higher levels of autonomy, being allowed more freedom to plan and control their activities. Although decoupled systems are more flexible and adaptive than close-coupled systems, this very flexibility increases the possibility that inefficiencies might occur. The traditional method of production where material is held 'in-hand' as inventory is decoupled. In this arrangement it is not necessary for production to match sales so closely, but this results in higher costs of holding inventory.

6. *Systems are hierarchical.* Systems are made up of subsystems that may themselves be made up of other subsystems. From this, one should realise that the parts of a system are dependent on one another in some way. This **interdependence** means that a change to one part of a system leads to or results from changes to one or more other parts.

Interdependence

Interdependence means that a change to one part of a system leads to or results from changes to one or more other parts.

Control in organisational systems

Figure 2.3 shows the relationship between different parts of an organisation and how they are related according to systems theory. The control mechanism is indicated by the arrowed line from the output back to the input.

The role of an information system is to support managers in making decisions that will help the organisation to function properly and achieve its objectives. Control is being exercised correctly if the organisation – including all subsystems – is moving towards its objectives as efficiently as possible.

Open-loop control systems in business

Open-loop control system

An open-loop control system is one in which there is an attempt to reach the system objective, but no control action to modify the inputs or process is taken once the process has begun.

Figure 2.4 shows a generic **open-loop system**. An open-loop control system is one in which there is an attempt to reach the system objective, but no action is taken to modify the process or its input to achieve the targets once the process has begun. Open-loop systems have no mechanism for ensuring goals are met once the process is under way. As an example, an electronics manufacturer might predict a huge demand for its new product and decide to produce a large quantity of items. Once production begins, no changes will be made to the production plan even in response to, say, the launch of a similar product from a competitor.

Open-loop systems are inadequate in an organisational context because of the complexity of organisational systems and their environments. In other words, open-loop systems would only be successful in attaining the system objectives in cases where we could plan with certainty the events that would take place during the system's process.

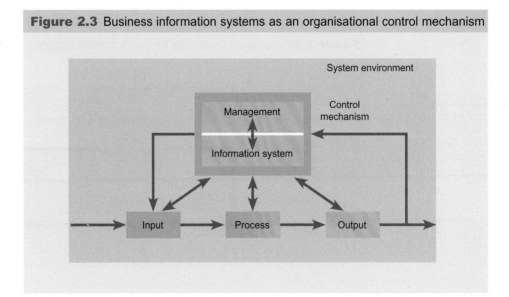

Figure 2.3 Business information systems as an organisational control mechanism

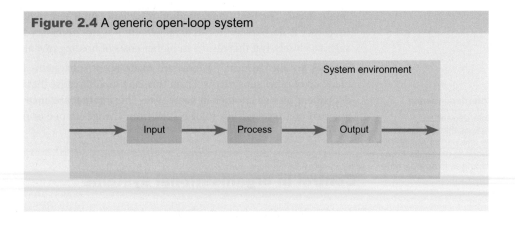

Figure 2.4 A generic open-loop system

Closed-loop control systems in business

Feedback control

The output achieved is monitored and compared to the desired output and corrective action is taken if a deviation exists.

Feedforward control

The environment and system process are both monitored in order to provide corrective action if it is likely that the system goal will not be met.

Two types of control mechanism that can be employed in this situation are **feedback control** and **feedforward control**. Feedback control responds to changes in the system or its environment *after* they have taken place, while feedforward control attempts to *predict* likely changes so that any delays before taking action are minimised.

Feedback control systems generally provide a relatively cheap method of reactive control and provide an effective method of bringing a system back under control. In a manufacturing company, for example, measurements taken on the production line can help to indicate when equipment needs to be adjusted. Figure 2.5 shows a generic closed-loop system.

Feedforward systems (Figure 2.6) provide a pro-active way of overcoming the timing delays associated with feedback systems but depend upon the accuracy of the plans on which they are based. Feedforward control systems attempt to overcome the overcorrection and time-delay disadvantages of feedback systems by incorporating a prediction element in the control feedback loop. Feedforward systems are not as common as feedback systems in business settings. Examples include inventory control systems which work to a planned sales level or material usage rate. Elements of project management can also be seen as feedforward control where plans are made for resource requirements over time.

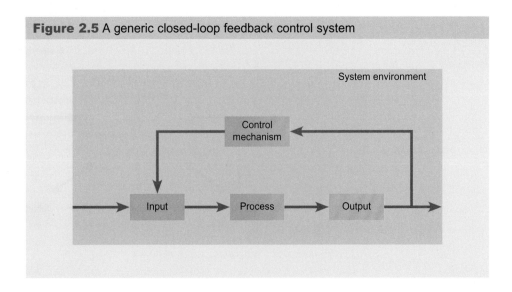

Figure 2.5 A generic closed-loop feedback control system

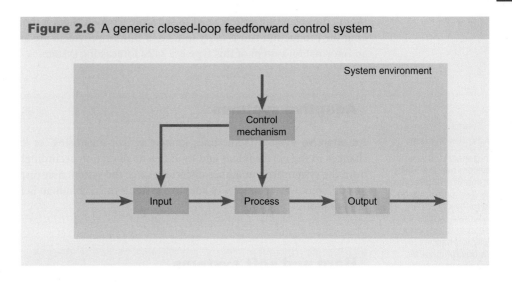

Figure 2.6 A generic closed-loop feedforward control system

Positive and negative feedback

Negative feedback is used to describe the act of reversing any discrepancy between desired and actual output. In a business setting, for example, a budget overspend in one area might be corrected by cutting spending in others.

An example of **positive feedback** might involve a company experiencing rapid sales growth, leading to increased production and higher sales levels. In general, a situation of positive feedback is unsustainable and some corrective action arising either from within the system or from the environment will occur. For example, if sales and production are increased, the company may experience cashflow problems caused by expanding too quickly.

The major difficulty with negative feedback systems is the potential for delays in the feedback control loop. In other words, the effect of a change in inputs to bring about a change in output may not be seen until after a period of time. This can lead to an output level that oscillates around the desired output because of overcorrection of input values during the feedback delay period. For example, the delay between the setting of interest rates and their effect on the output goal of a level of inflation can lead to a situation of overcompensation in either direction.

DIFFERENT TYPES OF SYSTEMS

In this final section on systems theory, we introduce some common terms for describing types of systems which you may encounter in business.

Deterministic and probabilistic systems

In a *deterministic* system (sometimes known as *mechanistic*), all of the system's outputs can be predicted by examining its inputs. An example of a deterministic system is an electronic calculator, where the results of carrying out a calculation can be predicted with complete accuracy.

In a *probabilistic* system (sometimes known as *stochastic*), the outputs of the system cannot be predicted with complete accuracy. An example of a probabilistic system is a production planning system used to schedule work. Although the system can predict how long the production run is *likely* to take, it cannot provide a precise figure. An example of an information system of this type is a sales forecasting system.

Adaptive systems

Adaptive system

In general, an adaptive system has the ability to monitor and regulate its own performance. In many cases, an adaptive system will be able to respond fully to changes in its environment by modifying its behaviour.

An adaptive system (sometimes known as 'self-organising' or 'cybernetic') responds to changes in the environment and modifies its operation accordingly. The outputs obtained from the system are sometimes uncertain since the system may respond to the same stimuli in a different way. Examples of adaptive systems include human beings, plants and business organisations.

Hard and soft systems

A *hard system* has an explicit objective and is governed by fixed rules and procedures such as those encountered for structured decision making (Chapter 1). The conditions in the system's environment tend to be stable and therefore more predictable. In turn, the system's outputs can be predicted more easily and its performance can be measured objectively. An example of a hard system is a production line.

A *soft system* operates in a relatively unpredictable environment where conditions may be uncertain or liable to rapid change. Soft systems usually involve people or socio-technical situations.

BUSINESS INFORMATION SYSTEMS

In this section, we introduce the concept of a business information system and consider the characteristics of computer-based information systems.

What is a business information system?

Business information systems

This describes information systems used to support the functional areas of business. For example, an organisation might use specialised information systems to support sales, marketing and human resource management activities.

Having examined concepts related to information, systems theory and decision making, it is possible to combine these to suggest a basic definition of a business information system:

A business information system is a group of interrelated components that work collectively to carry out input, processing, output, storage and control actions in order to convert data into information products that can be used to support forecasting, planning, control, coordination, decision making and operational activities in an organisation.

It should be noted that alternative definitions exist and it is worth taking a brief look at some aspects of these definitions.

Many definitions refer to 'data resources' that are converted into 'information products'. This underlines the notion that data form part of an organisation's intangible resource base and that the information derived from them is provided in a finished, useful form. The importance of information as a business resource is highlighted by John Talburt from the University of Arkansas at Little Rock, who says 'As modern society becomes increasingly information driven, the capability and maturity of an organization to manage the quality of its information can mean the difference between success and failure' (Al Hakim, 2007).

- Many definitions also specify that information systems involve the use of *information technology*. However, this can be disputed since it is possible to provide many examples of information systems that do not involve information technology at all. A simple example of such a 'manual' information system is a set of accounting ledgers.

- Some definitions specify that information systems are used only to support decision making. Again, this can be disputed since it is apparent that managers make use of information in a number of other ways, for example as feedback on various aspects of a company's performance.

- Although some definitions refer to organisations in general, others specify that they are concerned only with business organisations. However, it can be argued that it is sometimes very difficult to distinguish between profit-making and non-profit-making organisations.

RESOURCES THAT SUPPORT BIS

BIS typically rely on five basic resources: people, hardware, software, communications and data.

1. *People resources.* People resources include the users of an information system and those who develop, maintain and operate the system. Examples of people resources might include managers, data entry clerks and technical support staff.

2. *Hardware resources.* The term 'hardware resources' refers to all types of machines, not just computer hardware. Telephones, fax machines, switchboards are all valid examples of hardware. The term also covers any media used by these machines, such as compact discs or paper. (These resources are described in Chapter 3.)

3. *Software resources.* In the same way, the term 'software resources' does not only refer to computer programs and the media on which they are stored. The term can also be used to describe the procedures used by people. Within this context, examples of software include instruction manuals and company policies. (These resources are described in Chapter 4.)

4. *Communications resources.* Resources are also required to enable different systems to transfer data. These include networks and the hardware and software needed to support them. (These resources are described in Chapter 5.)

5. *Data resources.* 'Data resources' describes all of the data that an organisation has access to, regardless of its form. Computer databases, paper files and measurements taken by sensors on a production line are all examples of data resources.

Activity 2.1   Example of information systems

What information systems might be found in your newsagent's? For each system identified, list the people, hardware, communications, software and data resources involved.

Information technology

The terms 'information systems' (IS) and 'information technology' (IT) are often used interchangeably. This is an error, because the scope of the terms is different. The stress in IT is on the technology while IS not only refers to the technology, but also incorporates how it is applied and managed to contribute to the business. For this reason, we refer to

BIS throughout this book. Approaches to management of IS and IT as part of BIS strategy development are discussed in more detail later (see Chapter 13).

Computer-based information systems

Computer-based information system

An information system that makes use of information technology in order to create management information.

In modern organisations, most BIS make extensive use of information technology, such as personal computers. The reasons why computerised BIS have become widespread are evident in their advantages.

Some advantages of processing by computer

- *Speed*. Computers can process millions of instructions each second, allowing them to complete a given task in a very short time.
- *Accuracy*. The result of a calculation carried out by a computer is likely to be completely accurate. In addition, errors that a human might make, such as a typing error, can be reduced or eliminated entirely.
- *Reliability*. In many organisations, computer-based information systems operate for 24 hours a day and are only ever halted for repairs or routine maintenance.
- *Programmability*. Although most computer-based information systems are created to fulfil a particular function, the ability to modify the software that controls them provides a high degree of flexibility. Even the simplest personal computer, for example, can be used to create letters, produce cash flow forecasts or manipulate databases.
- *Repetitive tasks*. Computer-based information systems are suited to highly repetitive tasks that might result in boredom or fatigue in people. The use of technology can help to reduce errors and free employees to carry out other tasks.

These advantages combine to give major benefits to a business, as described in the section on *using information systems for strategic advantage* later in this chapter. There are, however, some disadvantages to computer-based BIS:

- *Judgement/experience*. Despite advances in artificial intelligence techniques and expert systems, computer-based information systems are considered incapable of solving problems using their own judgement and experience.
- *Improvisation/flexibility*. In general, computer-based information systems are unable to react to unexpected situations and events. Additionally, since most systems are created to fulfil a particular function, it can be difficult to modify them to meet new or changed requirements.
- *Innovation*. Computers lack the creativity of a human being. They are unable to think in the abstract and are therefore restricted in their ability to discover new ways of improving processes or solving problems.
- *Intuition*. Human intuition can play an important part in certain social situations. For example, one might use intuition to gauge the emotional state of a person before deciding whether or not to give them bad news. BIS cannot use intuition in this way and are therefore unsuitable for certain kinds of situations.
- *Qualitative information*. Managers often make unstructured decisions based on the recommendations of others. Their confidence in the person they are dealing with often has a major influence on the decision itself. Once again, BIS cannot act upon qualitative information of this kind.

Business applications of BIS

Earlier (in Chapter 1), it was shown how the characteristics of the decisions taken by managers vary according to organisational level from operational to strategic. The problems and decisions dealt with at the operational level of an organisation tend to have a high degree of structure. Frequent access to highly detailed information is often required to support the decision-making process. Since BIS are well suited to such situations, they are more common at this organisational level than at the strategic level where unstructured decision making based on qualitative data is more common.

Figure 2.7 illustrates areas of applications for BIS in a typical organisation. Note that there will be fewer applications and therefore lower levels of usage at the strategic level. A need for higher levels of automation and the structure of the tasks carried out mean that highest levels of usage will be at the operational level.

The key operational activities referred to in Figure 2.7 include **data processing** or handling the large volumes of data that arise from an organisation's daily activities. Although 'data processing' describes a wide range of activities, the most common are transaction processing and process control.

Transaction processing involves dealing with the sales and purchase transactions that an organisation carries out in the course of its normal activities. Banks, for example, handle millions of deposits and withdrawals each day. **Process control systems** deal with the large volume of data generated by production processes. As an example, a machine producing a precision component might take hundreds of measurements and use these to adjust the manufacturing process. (These types of system are described in more detail in Chapter 6.)

The speed, accuracy and reliability of computer-based information systems mean that they are able to handle repetitive tasks involving large volumes of data. Furthermore, they are best used in situations governed by clear, logical rules. This makes them ideally suited to transaction processing or process control applications. From this, it is reasonable to suggest that the widest use of computer-based information systems will be at the operational level of an organisation.

Data processing

Handling the large volumes of data that arise from an organisation's daily activities is described as data processing.

Transaction processing

Processing the sales and purchase transactions that an organisation carries out in the course of its normal activities.

Process control systems

Systems which manage manufacturing and other production processes.

Figure 2.7 Usage and applications of computer-based information systems by organisational level (shading denotes usage of BIS)

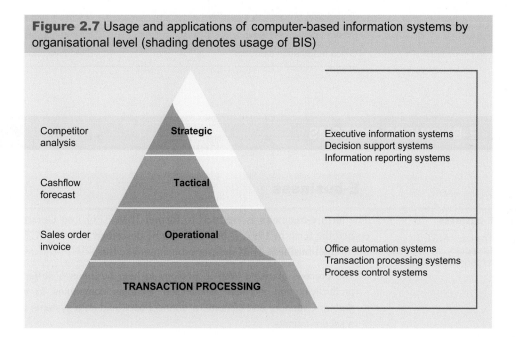

Competitor analysis — Strategic — Executive information systems / Decision support systems / Information reporting systems

Cashflow forecast — Tactical

Sales order invoice — Operational — Office automation systems / Transaction processing systems / Process control systems

TRANSACTION PROCESSING

CATEGORIES OF BUSINESS INFORMATION SYSTEM

Operations information systems

Systems required for the day-to-day activities of a business such as process control, transaction processing, communications (internal and external) and productivity.

Information systems are commonly divided into two broad categories: systems that support an organisation's business activities and systems that support managerial decision making.

- **Operations information systems** are generally concerned with process control, transaction processing, communications (internal and external) and productivity.
- **Management information systems** provide feedback on organisational activities and help to support managerial decision making. Managerial decision making can occur at the operational, tactical and strategic levels of an organisation.

Activity 2.2 — Online processing systems

Using the Internet as a resource, locate at least two examples of the use of online processing systems in business. As an example, both Sainsbury's and Boots use incentive programmes based around loyalty cards, where customers can redeem points against purchases using interactive kiosks.

Management information systems

Systems providing feedback on organisational activities and supporting managerial decision making.

As shown in Table 2.1, both of these broader categories can be subdivided into a number of additional categories. The following sections introduce these types of system. They are described in more detail later (in Chapter 6). Figure 2.7 also illustrates the typical use of each category of computer-based information system by management level.

Note that the categories given here represent a traditional view of computer-based information systems and tend to downplay the growing importance of new and emerging types of information systems, many of which might not fit neatly into the table. As an example, some people feel that systems based around the use of the Internet should be given their own category. The next section considers the concepts of e-business and e-commerce.

Table 2.1 Categories of computer-based information systems

Operations information systems	Management information systems
Transaction processing systems	Decision support systems
Process control systems	Information reporting systems
Office automation systems	Executive information systems

E-BUSINESS SYSTEMS

E-business

E-business

The use of ICT, especially the Internet, to conduct business.

The term **e-business** is credited to former IBM CEO Lou Gerstner, who is said to have coined the term in 1997. E-business can be described as using ICT, especially the Internet, to conduct business. IBM defines e-business like this:

> The process of using Web technology to help businesses streamline processes, improve productivity and increase efficiencies. Enables companies to easily communicate with partners, vendors and customers, connect back-end data systems and transact commerce in a secure manner.

As this definition shows, e-business involves several key activities: improving business processes, enhancing communications and providing the means to carry out business transactions securely. Three areas of business are enhanced by adopting an e-business approach. These are:

- *Production processes* – including procurement, ordering stock, payment processing, links with suppliers and production control.
- *Customer-focused processes* – including marketing, selling via the Internet, customer support and processing of customer orders and payments.
- *Internal management processes* – including training, recruitment, internal information sharing and other employee services.

Internet economy

This encompasses all of the activities involved in using the Internet for commerce.

E-business is part of a broader Internet economy which encompasses all of the activities involved in using the Internet for commerce. The CREC (Center for Research and Electronic Commerce) at the University of Texas has developed a conceptual framework for how the Internet economy works (**http://cism.mccombs.utexas.edu**). The Internet economy is made up of four layers:

1. *Internet infrastructure.* Companies that provide the hardware, software and other equipment for the Internet. Examples: ISPs, networking companies and manufacturers of PCs and servers.
2. *Internet applications infrastructure.* Companies that provide software facilitating Internet transactions. Also, companies that provide web development, design and consulting services. Examples: producers of web development software, web-enabled databases and search engines.
3. *Internet intermediaries.* Companies that link buyers and sellers, for example by providing content or by creating marketplaces where business can be transacted. Examples: travel agents, content providers and online brokerages.
4. *Internet commerce.* Companies that sell products and services to consumers or other companies. Examples: online retailers, subscription or fee-based services and manufacturers selling directly to the public.

Activity 2.3 | **The Internet economy**

Consider the framework of the Internet economy developed by the CREC (Center for Research and Electronic Commerce) at the University of Texas. Give at least three examples of companies for each layer in the framework.

E-commerce

E-commerce

Using technology to conduct business transactions, such as buying and selling goods and services.

A common activity associated with e-business is electronic commerce (e-commerce), which can be described as using technology to conduct business transactions, such as buying and selling goods and services. However, e-commerce involves more than merely conducting electronic transactions; it also encompasses a wide range of associated activities, such as after-sales support and even logistics.

The importance of e-commerce can be illustrated by looking at the rapid growth of online sales. In 2010 Forrester Research (**www.forrester.com**), for instance, predicted that online sales in the UK will grow at the rate of 10 per cent each year for the next five years. Online retail will reach 40 billion by 2014 and the number of online shoppers will grow from 31 million to 40 million over the same period. The UK has the largest proportion of consumers who make monthly online purchases: around 48 per cent, compared with a European average of 32 per cent.

In Western Europe, online retailing will grow at a rate of approximately 11 per cent each year, reaching 114 million by 2014. The number of Europeans who shop online will grow from 141 million to 190 million over the same period.

In the United States, online retail sales will grow to $249 billion by 2014, accounting for 8 per cent of all retail sales.

E-commerce activities can be broken down into five basic types:

1. *Business-to-business (B2B)*. Transactions take place between companies. Approximately 80 per cent of all e-commerce is of this type.

2. *Business-to-consumer (B2C)*. Companies sell products directly to consumers. B2C can involve activities such as product research (where consumers gather information and compare prices) and electronic delivery (where information products are delivered to consumers via e-mail or other means).

3. *Business-to-government (B2G)*. Transactions take place between companies and public-sector organisations.

4. *Consumer-to-consumer (C2C)*. Transactions take place between private individuals. Perhaps the best examples of C2C commerce are online auction sites and peer-to-peer systems.

5. *Mobile commerce (m-commerce)*. **M-commerce** is a relatively new development and involves selling goods or services via wireless technology, especially mobile phones and PDAs. A report from Juniper Research has found that annual retail payments on mobile handsets and tablets are expected to reach $707 billion by 2018, representing 30 per cent of all eRetail by that time. This compares with mobile retail spend of $182 billion in 2013, when mobile accounted for around 15 per cent of eRetail (**www.juniperresearch.com**).

M-commerce

Describes selling goods or services via wireless technology, especially mobile phones and PDAs.

There are many new types of e-commerce activity starting to appear or growing in popularity. As an example, exchanges between governments and citizens, employees and businesses are often described using the term *e-government*. These exchanges are also described using abbreviations like G2C (government-to-citizen), C2G (citizen-to-government), G2E (government-to-employee) or G2B (government-to-business).

Activity 2.4　E-commerce types

How many new or emerging types of e-commerce can you locate using the Internet? Which of these do you think will become most significant in the future?

Benefits of e-business

In general, the benefits of e-business include reduced costs, improved efficiency and access to larger markets.

By automating many of the administrative tasks associated with ordering, supplying and delivering goods or services, the cost of a typical business transaction can be reduced significantly. As an example, the NHS is the largest single healthcare delivery organisation in the world, with net planned expenditure for 2013–14 of £109.956 billion. E-procurement is used to reduce administrative costs and purchase goods at lower prices. Using e-procurement, it is possible to reduce the cost of making a purchase from £30 to just £4.

It was mentioned earlier that adopting an e-business approach could help to enhance three main areas of business: production processes, customer-focused processes and internal management processes. In terms of customer-focused processes, for example, the efficiency of customer services can be improved through the introduction of a help desk on the company's web site. Such a facility can be used to provide customers with help, information and advice on a 24-hour, 365-day basis. As well as helping customers, such a facility can also act to reduce costs by reducing pressure on other support services, such as telephone helplines.

Finally, the adoption of an e-business approach can help companies to reach a larger, global market. This is often one of the benefits of restructuring the relationship between manufacturer, retailers and customers. In a conventional business relationship, consumers buy products and services from a retailer and have little or no contact with the producer. However, the Internet provides access to a global marketplace, allowing manufacturers to sell to customers directly (called e-tailing) or form business relationships with retailers located anywhere in the world. Customers also benefit by being given a greater choice of products at more competitive prices.

E-tailing

The use of the Internet by manufacturers to sell goods directly to customers.

Activity 2.5   Benefits of e-business

The approaches used by companies such as Argos, Dell and eBay restructure the relationship between manufacturer, retailer and customer to the benefit of all involved. Discuss this statement with reference to the e-business and e-commerce concepts described in this section.

ENTERPRISE SYSTEMS

Enterprise systems

Enterprise systems aim to support the business processes of an organisation across any functional boundaries that exist within that organisation.

Enterprise systems aim to support the business processes of an organisation across any functional boundaries that exist within that organisation. They use Internet technology to integrate information within the business and with external stakeholders such as customers, suppliers and partners. The main elements of an enterprise system are enterprise resource planning (ERP) which is concerned with internal production, distribution and financial processes, customer relationship management (CRM) which is concerned with marketing and sales processes, supply chain management (SCM) which is concerned with the flow of materials, information and customers through the supply chain and supplier relationship management (SRM) which is concerned with sourcing, purchasing and the warehousing of goods and services. Other elements may include product lifecycle management (PLM), financial management and human capital management. Enterprise systems provide a single solution from a single supplier with integrated functions for major business functions from across the value chain such as production, distribution, sales, finance and human resources management. They are normally purchased as an off-the-shelf package which is then tailored. The main reason for implementing an enterprise system is explained by Figure 2.8. It compares an enterprise application with the previous company arrangement of separate data silos and applications (sometimes known as 'information islands') in different parts of the company. The problem of information silos arose as decentralisation of BIS selection became devolved, with the end-users in individual departments making their own purchasing decisions. This often led to separate applications from different vendors in different departments, often with poor data transfer between applications. (Enterprise systems are covered in detail in Chapter 6.)

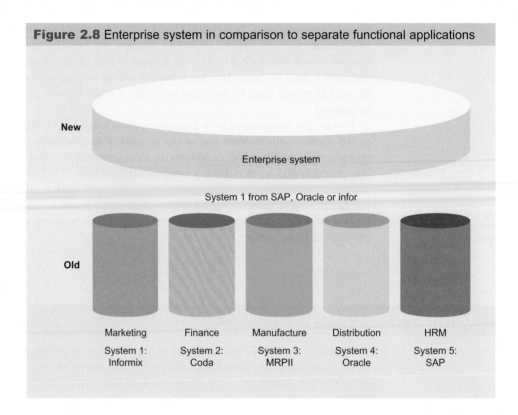

Figure 2.8 Enterprise system in comparison to separate functional applications

BIS AND STRATEGIC ADVANTAGE

Strategic advantage

Organisations gain
benefits through
developing distinctive
competencies.

In order to survive and grow in a competitive environment, organisations must seek to gain **strategic advantage** (or competitive advantage) over their competitors. BIS play a crucial part in gaining and sustaining a competitive edge over other organisations operating in the same industry.

This section introduces the concept of strategic advantage. Later (in Chapter 13) we describe how IS strategy can be developed in more detail. We also look at how a company reviews the benefits of a specific new system when assessing its feasibility (in Chapter 8).

Competitive strategies

In order to gain or maintain competitive advantage, organisations can adopt three basic strategies: cost leadership, differentiation or innovation.

Cost leadership

Cost leadership means simply providing goods or services at the lowest possible cost. In most cases this is achieved by reducing the organisation's costs in producing goods or providing services, for example by automating parts of the production process. However, cost leadership can also be achieved by helping suppliers and customers to reduce costs, usually by forming alliances and linkages that benefit all of the parties involved. In some cases, cost leadership is achieved by causing a competitor's costs to increase, for example by introducing new product features that will be expensive for a competitor to duplicate. Using Internet technologies for e-business can assist in achieving cost leadership by helping to reduce **transaction costs**. All business transactions have a variety of expenses associated

Transaction costs

The costs associated
with a business
transaction, such as
selling a product, or
ordering stock.

with them, such as the cost of advertising products, processing orders and so on. For many organisations, the largest transaction costs arise from the sale of goods or services. In recent years, companies have sought to reduce operating expenses by moving towards increased automation and by passing on transaction costs to customers. Sometimes this has been done directly, perhaps by imposing a small booking or order fee. In other cases, it has been done by encouraging customers to select, order and pay for goods themselves via the Internet. Such a move tends to result in significant savings since the company no longer needs to maintain expensive premises, such as showrooms, and can start to reduce staffing levels. easyJet is a good example of a company that has been able to reduce operating costs using this approach. By transferring over 90 per cent of its ticketing online, the company has been able to reduce staff costs dramatically.

Product differentiation

Differentiation involves creating a distinction between the organisation's products and those of its competitors. In many cases, differentiation is used to concentrate on a specific niche in the market so that the company can focus on particular goods and services. A car manufacturer, such as Rolls-Royce, provides a good example of product differentiation. The cars produced by Rolls-Royce are perceived as luxury items that indicate status and importance in society. They are considered far superior to standard production models in terms of quality, reliability and comfort. By creating this image, Rolls-Royce has succeeded in differentiating its products from those of its competitors.

Innovation

Innovation is concerned with finding new ways to approach an organisation's activities. Examples of innovation include improving existing products or creating new ones, forging strategic linkages, improving production processes and entering new markets. It is possible for companies operating in the same market to use entirely different competitive strategies. Large companies may also need to select different strategies for customers located in different regions.

CASE STUDY 2.1

PayPal eyes in-store retail customers

By April Dembosky in San Jose and California

Between the various charts and bar graphs projected on the screen at eBay's analyst day on Thursday was a cartoon of a woman in a shoe store.

Surrounded by dozens of pairs of pumps and dishevelled shoeboxes, a weary store clerk kneels before her, cradling her foot. 'This pair is so perfect,' she says. 'I can't wait to buy them cheaper online somewhere. What's your WiFi password?'

Don Kingsborough, vice president of retail for eBay-owned PayPal, said the scenario plays out every day in retail stores. The hundreds of retail executives he had spoken with in the last two years were all trying to figure out how to get the shoppers like the one in the cartoon to buy from them and not from online

behemoths like Amazon. Mr Kingsborough said PayPal wants to win those customers.

'Commerce is no longer about location, location, location,' he said. 'New commerce is about engagement, engagement, engagement.'

His team described various applications PayPal was developing to keep smartphone-obsessed shoppers buying at bricks and mortar stores, from loyalty programmes that offer discounts when people enter stores to ordering apps that allow people to place and pay for food orders over their phones then pick them up in the store without waiting in line.

The financial benefits would come not just to the retailers, but to PayPal, too, executives said. After

➡

doubling revenues in the last three years, the online and mobile payment company is expecting to double revenues again by 2015, up to $10.5bn.

Overall revenues for the company are projected to grow 50 per cent to $21.5bn in 2015, up from $14.1bn in 2012. Profits will grow between 15 and 19 per cent, according to Bob Swan, chief financial officer.

The focus of eBay's analyst day was how the company planned to work 'with retailers, not against them' in a world where people's shopping habits increasingly blend the online and offline worlds.

'It's an anti-Amazon play,' said one analyst, who believed retailers would find the various eBay technology offerings compelling in their quest to defend themselves against the e-commerce giant.

Shares in eBay rose more than 4 per cent on Thursday, closing at $54.22, then rose further in after-hours trading.

Analyst saw the most potential for growth in PayPal. They said its strong foundation in digital payments and its global reach position it well for taking advantage of the 'new commerce'.

'Building a payments business globally is really, really, really hard,' said David Marcus, president of PayPal. He took a slight dig at competitors in the financial services industry or technology industry who are competing with PayPal in building a digital wallet, including Visa and Google.

'They don't have the reach, scale, or innovation,' he said. 'It's easy to create buzz, but only a handful have been able to scale and build a large payments business globally.'

PayPal now has 125m digital wallets, he said.

Several analysts raised questions, however, about whether the company's investment in new technology and its move into the retail world would ultimately lower margins. Concerns have been growing that credit card companies will eventually follow the lead set by MasterCard in February and begin charging PayPal fees for using their networks in digital wallet transactions.

Mr Swan said no. He said analysts have been asking the broader question about margins for seven years, but the details have evolved – from PayPal's move toward working with larger retailers several years ago, through the regulations of the Dodd-Frank Act in 2011, to potential network fees today. But he predicted core transaction margins would in fact go up, from 60 per cent or more to 62 per cent or more.

John Donahoe, chief executive of eBay, concluded the day by calling the technological changes in consumer shopping and merchant offerings a 'commerce revolution' for large and small businesses alike.

'Retailers are beginning to fight back,' he said. 'Retail is not dead.'

 Source: Dembosky, A. (2013) PayPal eyes in-store retail customers. *Financial Times*. 28 March.

QUESTION

How are Paypal assisting bricks and mortar stores to compete against online-based retailers such as Amazon?

Value chain analysis

Michael Porter's work (Porter, 1980) includes the concept of a value chain: a series of connected activities that add value to an organisation's products or services. An analysis of an organisation's value chain can indicate which areas might provide the organisation with a competitive advantage.

Supply chain management (SCM)

The coordination of all supply activities of an organisation from its suppliers and partners to its customers.

Value chain

A model for analysis of how supply chain activities can add value to products and services delivered to the customer.

To understand value chain analysis we need also to consider an organisation's supply chain. **Supply chain management (SCM)** is the coordination of all supply activities of an organisation from its suppliers through to production of goods and services and their delivery to its customers. The **value chain** is a related concept that describes the different value-adding activities that connect a company's supply side with its demand side. We can identify both an internal value chain within the boundaries of an organisation and an external value chain where these activities are performed by partners. Traditional value chain analysis (Figure 2.9) distinguishes between primary activities that contribute directly to getting goods and services to the customer (such as inbound logistics, including procurement, manufacturing, marketing and delivery to buyers, support and servicing after sale) and support activities which provide the inputs and infrastructure that allow the primary activities to take place. Support activities include finance, human resources and information systems.

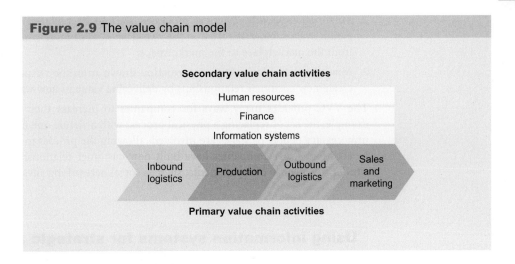

Figure 2.9 The value chain model

The virtual value chain

The preceding material should make it clear that Porter's value chain is largely concerned with business activities surrounding the production and supply of physical products. However, today's modern marketplace sees many companies concerned with producing and marketing non-physical products, such as subscription-based services. In these new industries, primary and secondary activities may be so transformed as to be virtually unrecognisable. As an example, delivering a digital product – such as a music track, movie or ring tone – to buyers may involve little more than sending an automated e-mail or text message.

Porter's work also overlooks the fact that as technology has developed, the information it can supply to managers has become essential to the operation of most businesses. This is understandable given that much of Porter's work was carried out in the 1970s and 1980s, well before personal computers became popular and affordable. The information supplied by modern BIS affects both primary and secondary activities by changing the activities themselves or by allowing the value chain to be configured differently. The Internet, for example, has transformed the way in which some products are marketed and delivered.

All of this raises two important questions. First, what is the role of information within the value chain? Second, can Porter's value chain be applied to a modern businesses that operates across the Internet or that markets virtual products and services?

For some people, information supports processes that add value, but is not a source of value itself. For others, information is a source of value because it can create competitive advantage when viewed from the right perspective and if applied correctly. As an example, Rayport and Sviokla (1995) state:

> The value chain model model treats information as a supporting element in the value-adding process, not as a source of value in itself. Managers often use information they capture on inventory, production, or logistics to help monitor or control those processes, for instance, but they rarely use information itself to create new value for the customer.

Virtual value chain (VVC)

The virtual value chain allows value chain analysis to be extended to modern businesses that operate across the Internet or market virtual products and services. In the VVC, physical processes are replaced by virtual ones and the marketplace is replaced by a virtual marketspace.

Rayport and Sviokla have suggested the concept of the **virtual value chain (VVC)** to explain how information can help to create competitive advantage. In doing this, they refer to the physical *marketplace* and its virtual counterpart, the *marketspace*. They suggest that companies adopting a virtual value chain tend to go through three phases. In each phase, companies have the opportunity to reduce costs, improve efficiency or find new ways of doing things:

1. *Visibility.* Companies use information to examine the physical value chain more closely. Technology is used to manage activities in the physical value chain more efficiently.

2. *Mirroring capability.* Physical processes start to be replaced by virtual processes. A parallel value chain is created in the marketspace. Put more simply, activities are moved from the marketplace to the marketspace.

3. *New customer relationships.* Information drawn from the virtual value chain is used to create new customer relationships by delivering value in new ways.

The VVC provides many ways for companies to increase their competitiveness. As an example, the act of replacing a physical process with a virtual one may reveal that too many unnecessary people or stages are involved, allowing the process to be made more efficient. In addition, many companies have built new customer relationships by establishing web sites or making use of social media, such as social networking sites.

Using information systems for strategic advantage

BIS can be also used to counter the five competitive forces of their environment described by Porter (1980). Examples of how this can be achieved are given later (in Chapter 13). The five forces are:

1. the threat of new entrants;
2. the bargaining power of suppliers;
3. the bargaining power of customers;
4. the threat of substitute products or services;
5. rivalry among existing competitors.

Porter's work can also be used to identify a number of ways in which BIS can be used to achieve competitive advantage. These include:

- improving operational efficiency;
- raising barriers to entry;
- locking in customers and suppliers;
- promoting business innovation;
- increasing switching costs;
- leverage.

Figure 2.10 summarises the main ways in which computer-based information systems can be used to achieve competitive advantage.

Improving operational efficiency

One of the most common ways of using computer-based information systems to achieve competitive advantage is by using them to improve *operational efficiency*. As an example, consider a typical manufacturing company wishing to adopt a cost leadership strategy. In a primary activity, such as production, an inventory control system might be used to manage stock levels, reducing storage and transportation costs. In addition, support activities, such as management and administration, might achieve higher levels of productivity through the introduction of office automation systems. The organisation might also realise additional benefits from this kind of approach, such as improved customer service.

Barriers to entry

In many industries, organisations have improved operational efficiency by investing heavily in BIS. Often, the systems employed are extremely complex and require ongoing

Figure 2.10 Applying computer-based information systems for competitive advantage

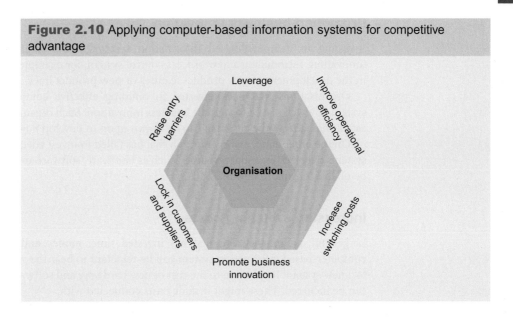

maintenance and development. This means that newcomers to the industry must be prepared to make a large initial expenditure so that they can acquire the computer-based information systems they need to be able to compete effectively. The level of expenditure needed may be so high that an *entry barrier* is created that deters or prevents the new competitor from entering the industry. Investing heavily in computer-based information systems may also deter existing competitors, since they too must invest in their information systems in order to maintain or improve their position in the industry. New technologies can decrease barriers to entry. For example, electronic banking removed the requirement for a branch network, leading to the establishment of Internet-only banks, such as Smile. However, entry barriers were so high that most required the backing of a major high-street bank or building society.

Locking in customers and suppliers

Linking an organisation's computer-based information systems to those of its customers and suppliers can help to strengthen business relationships. As an example, computer-based information systems can be used to provide higher levels of customer service, thereby encouraging clients to remain loyal to the company.

Close integration with a supplier's information systems can result in a number of business benefits, which include:

- the availability of raw materials or parts is more certain;
- cost savings can be realised through reduced administration overheads;
- suppliers are less likely to abandon the business relationship;
- the organisation can negotiate favourable terms and prices;
- competitors are excluded from the business relationship.

However, it should be noted that achieving high levels of integration can also have some significant disadvantages. Perhaps the single largest disadvantage is that the organisation may come to rely upon a relatively small number of suppliers. This reliance might lead to some suppliers' taking advantage of the relationship, for example by raising prices. The organisation may also find it difficult to maintain normal operations if the supplier goes out of business or experiences other problems.

Promoting business innovation

Investing in computer-based information systems often helps to stimulate business innovation. Introducing a new process control system, for example, might ultimately result in the development of new product features or new product lines.

Organisations that have invested in building effective computer-based information systems are well placed to support business innovation. Such organisations are likely to have established a resource base that can be drawn upon to develop new ideas.

On the other hand, an organisation that has failed to invest adequately in its information systems may lack essential resources, such as hardware, software and trained personnel, and be unable to explore new methods.

Increasing switching costs

In general, an organisation that has invested time, money and effort in developing a computer-based information system will be reluctant to bear the *switching costs* of moving to a new system. In addition to the cost of new hardware and software, a range of other costs can be incurred. These might include costs connected with:

- converting data for use with the new system;
- training staff;
- interruptions to the company's operations;
- lost opportunities to gain new business.

When an organisation links its information systems to those of its suppliers or customers, it will often ensure that switching costs are as high as possible. In this way, the supplier or customer is discouraged from switching to a competitor's system and competitors are excluded from the business relationship.

Leverage

Leverage

A way of increasing returns without increasing investment, usually by maximising the use of existing resources.

Information leadership

Enhancing a product or service using an organisation's specialised information or expertise.

Access to a resource base of this kind can provide a number of other benefits to an organisation as well as innovation. First, the organisation is equipped so that it can take advantage of any opportunities that arise in the business environment. Second, the organisation can begin to develop new products and services by maximising its use of existing resources. An example of leverage is when a travel agent creates a mailing list from its customer database so that it can offer customers new products or services, such as travel insurance or car rental.

Finally, the organisation may use its resources to gain competitive advantage through information leadership. Information leadership involves enhancing a product or service with an organisation's specialised information or expertise.

In some cases, organisations achieve information leadership by selling information or expertise in the form of a separate product. A good example might be selling a mailing list created from an organisation's customer database.

Mini case study	Capital One develops information leadership

As products become commoditised, it is often said that how companies use information is the key to competing successfully in the marketplace. Dave Buch, director at Capital One, has said: 'Back in 1987 we figured that our business is nothing to do about credit cards, it's about information. *Capital One is now a $14 billion company with 12 million customers.*'

CASE STUDY 2.2

Corporate IT falling short of potential

By Paul Taylor

A global survey of more than 2,000 company IT leaders published this week by Gartner, the IT market research firm, shows that, on average, enterprises are realising only 43 per cent of technology's business potential.

I asked Mark McDonald, group vice-president and Gartner Fellow, what chief information officers can do to address this issue and make better use of IT in 2013.

Q. The CIO Agenda 2013 survey reveals that chief information officers believe that their enterprises have realised less than half of technology's potential. How has this come about?

There are two reasons behind this: the past and the future.

For the past 10 years, IT has endured a decade of CIO IT budget devaluation because tending to current concerns and costs have limited IT's strategic relevance, resources and skills. This led many CIOs to believe that surviving meant keeping IT focused on muddling through with current operations and responsibilities. That approach in turn reduces the good business reasons for investing in technology.

This approach worked so long because there were no really new technologies to invest in. During these same 10 years there was something of a desert of technology and business innovation on the horizon, providing another reason why technology has been underused in the enterprise. But all of that has changed now.

The economic, competitive and customer context have all reduced the potential of existing technologies, particularly when a context change is not accompanied by a technology change. The digital future further accelerates these changes, as CIOs see mobile, information and cloud as reversing this trend. So now we have a new context, new technologies that reduce the potential of current technology operations and investment.

If executives, including the CIO, want to raise this number, then they will need to change the strategic relevance, resources and skills assigned to technology. This number cannot increase by repeating a past of 'doing more with less' if they expect to create value in the future.

Q. Can IT realise its full potential and support the enterprise going forward?

The answer is yes, but to fill such a big gap, CIOs cannot merely work harder, especially when they consider the factors that have changed the enterprise. Over the last 18 months, digital technologies have reached a tipping point with business executives. CIOs have little choice but to increase technology's potential in the enterprise,

and this means evolving IT's strategies, priorities and plans beyond tending to the usual concerns.

This means finding answers to a new central question: 'how will technology support growth?' This question replaces the prior one of 'how to control IT cost?'

Q. Will IT budgets be boosted in 2013 to allow CIOs to do this?

Without a change in context, this is unlikely. The survey showed that CIO IT budgets have been flat to negative ever since the dotcom bust of 2002. For 2013, IT budgets are projected to be slightly down, with a weighted global average decline of 0.5 per cent.

However, it is not appropriate to think that CIO's have to re-slice the IT budget pie to make room for digital technology investments. That is a 'more with less' view that is ultimately self-defeating.

The bottom line is that the CIO cannot expect to secure additional funding without assuming new responsibilities or producing new results. CIOs can get money to do new things; they just can't get more money to do the same old things.

Q. What are the top CIO priorities in 2013?

Digital technologies dominate CIO technology priorities for 2013. The top 10 global technology priorities revealed by the survey reflect a greater emphasis on externally oriented digital technologies, as opposed to traditional IT/operationally oriented systems.

Data and analytics were ranked as the key priority for CIOs in 2013, followed by mobile computing, cloud computing and collaboration technologies. CIOs see these technologies as disrupting business fundamentally over the next 10 years.

When asked which digital technologies would be most disruptive, 70 per cent of CIOs cited mobile technologies, followed by big data/analytics at 55 per cent, social media at 54 per cent and public cloud at 51 per cent. The disruptiveness of each of these technologies is real, but CIOs see their greatest disruptive power coming in combination, rather than in isolation.

Q. So what will corporate IT leaders be doing differently in 2013?

Digital technologies will certainly provide a platform to achieve results, but only if CIOs adopt new roles and behaviours to find digital value. CIOs require a new agenda that incorporates hunting for new digital innovations and opportunities, and harvesting value from products, services and operations.

However, IT needs new tools in order to find technology-intensive innovation and harvest raised business performance from transformed IT infrastructure, operations and applications. Without change, CIOs and IT will consign themselves to tending a garden of legacy assets and responsibilities.

Q. Will the CIO's role change as a result?

It should and for many it has. Sixty seven per cent of CIOs today have significant leadership responsibilities outside of traditional IT, ranging from chief process officer to business strategy to customer care.

Almost a fifth of CIOs now act as their enterprise's chief digital officer, leading digital commerce and channels. Though this nascent role varies in scope and style, it normally includes championing the digital vision for the business – that is ensuring that the business is evolving optimally in the new digital context.

The 2013 CIO Agenda focused on recognising these challenges and developing plans to win in a digital world. CIOs who merely stick to their current job in this quiet crisis are setting themselves up to lose that job in the future.

IT is not going away; it just needs to change – not because it is wrong, but because the world has changed and enterprises are realising only a fraction of technology's potential. That is why we have titled the 2013 CIO agenda 'Hunting and Harvesting in a Digital World.'

Mark McDonald is a group vice-president and Gartner Fellow. He is head of research in Gartner Executive Programs.

QUESTION

Explain why organisations are only realising less than half of information technology's potential.

SUMMARY

1. A system is composed of a group of interrelated components that work towards a common goal. These components include inputs, processes, outputs, feedback and control. A system also has a boundary that separates it from the environment. Systems can be made up of one or more smaller subsystems.

2. An information system converts data into information products. This information is used to support the activities of managers. Information systems make use of people resources, hardware resources, software resources and data resources.

3. Computer-based information systems take advantage of the benefits of information technology and are often grouped into two broad categories. Operations information systems are concerned with process control, transaction processing and productivity. Management information systems provide feedback on organisational activities and support managerial decision making. Computer-based information systems are referred to as 'information systems' in the remainder of the book for simplicity.

4. Operations information systems include transaction processing systems, process control systems and office automation systems.

5. Management information systems include information reporting systems, decision support systems and executive information systems.

6. Other categories of computer-based information systems include expert systems, business information systems, end-user computing systems and strategic information systems.

7. 'Electronic business' is a broader term referring to how technology can benefit all internal business processes and interactions with third parties. This includes buy-side and sell-side e-commerce.

8. Electronic commerce traditionally refers to electronically mediated buying and selling.

9. Sell-side e-commerce involves all electronic business transactions between an organisation and its customers, while buy-side e-commerce involves transactions between an organisation and its suppliers.

10. In large companies, applications functional areas are gradually being replaced by enterprise resource planning applications that provide functionality applicable across the organisation. In

smaller companies, accounting systems are being extended to use in other areas such as payroll, purchase ordering and inventory management.

11. In order to gain strategic advantage, companies will often adopt one of three basic competitive strategies: cost leadership, product differentiation or business innovation. BIS and e-business systems can be used to support attempts to gain competitive advantage through a number of different approaches. These include improving operational efficiency, raising entry barriers, creating high switching costs and gaining information leadership.

EXERCISES

Self-assessment exercises

1. Answer the following questions in relation to your college or university:

   (a) What are the institution's objectives?
   (b) Identify a range of typical inputs, processes and outputs.
   (c) What feedback mechanisms are in place and what kinds of information do they produce?
   (d) What control mechanisms exist?

2. In what ways can information systems support a manager's activities?

3. How can computer-based information systems help an organisation to achieve a strategic advantage over its competitors?

4. Match each term to the correct statement.

(a) input	1. provides information concerning the performance of a system
(b) process	2. describes exchanges between the system and its environment
(c) output	3. converts raw materials into a finished product
(d) feedback	4. contains everything outside of the system
(e) control	5. defines the scope of the system
(f) boundary	6. examples include raw materials, energy and labour power
(g) environment	7. examples include information, a product and service
(h) interface	8. adjusts the performance of the system

5. What is the virtual value chain?

6. What are transaction costs?

7. Explain the reasons for the adoption of enterprise resource planning systems by organisations.

Discussion questions

1. Can each of the following be described as a system? For each item, try to identify at least two inputs, processes and outputs. In addition, what feedback and control mechanisms exist?

   - a human being;
   - a plant;
   - a house;
   - a country;
   - a computer.

2. A small company is considering the purchase of a computer and accounting software to help it keep track of its finances. In general, what are the benefits of processing by computer? What other benefits might the company gain by taking this step?

3. Locate an annual report or article that describes a large organisation, such as a supermarket chain. From the information contained in the annual report, identify and describe the information systems that the company might use.

4. Discuss the following statement with reference to how an organisation should react to the Internet. 'Is the Internet a typhoon force, a ten times force, or is it a bit of wind? Or is it a force that fundamentally alters our business?' (Andy Grove, Chairman of Intel).

5. 'Enterprise resource planning software is likely to replace packages used in a single area of the organisation, such as accounting, logistics, production and marketing.' Discuss.

Essay questions

1. Use the Internet to research the SABRE system produced by American Airlines. This system demonstrates how BIS can be used to gain strategic advantage. Provide an analysis of this system. Your response should include discussion of the following areas:

   (a) Describe how the overall approach adopted by American Airlines incorporated the basic competitive strategies of cost leadership, innovation and product differentiation.
   (b) In what ways did SABRE provide American Airlines with a competitive advantage? Your analysis should refer to concepts related to the strategic use of information systems, for example entry barriers.
   (c) Although SABRE was undoubtedly successful, American Airlines was not able to maintain its competitive advantage beyond the late 1980s. What factors played a part in the erosion of the company's lead over its competitors and how did the company react?

2. Select an organisation you are familiar with. You may choose a department within a large organisation, if you wish. Analyse the structure and behaviour of the organisation using systems concepts. Your response should include the following elements:

   (a) Identify and describe at least two examples of the following: inputs, processes, outputs, feedback and control.
   (b) Identify and describe two decisions that will be taken at the strategic, tactical and operational levels of the organisation.
   (c) For each of the decisions described, identify at least two items of information that may be required. Describe some of the characteristics that each item of information will have.

3. Draw a diagram illustrating the subsystems occurring in a hospital. Label the inputs and outputs of each subsystem. Which subsystems are most closely coupled?

4. Do you believe that the advantages of enterprise resource planning applications outweigh their disadvantages? Illustrate your answer with reference to company examples.

Examination questions

1. Information systems play a critical part in supporting a company's activities. Using specific examples, you are required to:

   (a) define an information system;
   (b) describe the categories of computer-based information systems, providing relevant business examples for each category identified;

   (c) explain how computer-based information systems can support managers at each level
       of an organisation.

2. Computer-based information systems are critical to an organisation's survival in the modern
   competitive environment. Discuss this statement with reference to the following:

   (a) Porter's competitive forces model and the basic competitive strategies that can be used
       to gain advantage;
   (b) how computer-based information systems can support these strategies;
   (c) how an organisation's information resources can be used to create information
       leadership.

3. Large retail organisations employ a wide variety of computer-based information systems in
   order to support their activities. Considering a large supermarket chain, such as Sainsbury's,
   you are required to:

   (a) define the term 'computer-based information system';
   (b) identify the types of computer-based information systems that are likely to be found
       within a typical branch. Your response should describe the function of each system
       identified and the category to which it belongs.
   (c) selecting one of the systems identified in (a), describe the system in more detail,
       identifying the hardware, software, data and people resources it employs.

4. Draw a diagram illustrating the main components of a generic system.

5. Explain why feedback and control are important in business information systems.

6. Define an enterprise resource planning application. Name two main disadvantages of this
   type of approach.

References

Al Hakim, L. (2007) *Information Quality Management: Theory and Applications*, Idea Group
    Publishing, London

Porter, M. (1980) *Competitive Strategy*, Free Press, New York

Rayport, J. and Sviokla, J. (1995) Exploiting the virtual value chain, *Harvard Business Review*,
    73, 6, November/December, 75–85

Further reading

Laudon, K.C. and Laudon, J.P. (2013) *Management Information Systems: Managing the
    Digital Firm*, 13th edition, Prentice-Hall, Upper Saddle River, NJ. Although some might
    find this book a little dense and difficult to read, it is detailed and comprehensive in its
    coverage. Chapters 1 and 2 cover some basic concepts related to information systems,
    whilst Chapter 3 looks at areas such as decision making, competitive advantage, and
    so on.

O'Brien, J. and Marakas, G. (2011) *Management Information Systems*, 10th edition, McGraw-
    Hill, Boston. Chapter 1 deals with basic concepts such as systems theory and types of
    systems, whilst Chapter 2 deals with topics such as competitive advantage.

Turban, E., Rainer, R. and Potter, R. (2004) *Introduction to Information Technology*, 3rd edition,
    John Wiley, New York. Although lacking depth in some areas, this text is colourful and easy
    to read. Chapters 1, 2 and 11 deal with basic topics, such as the concept of an information
    system, data, knowledge, decision making and decision support.

Web links

E-business

www.e-consultancy.com E-consultancy.com is an excellent online digest of consultant and analyst reports.

www.revolutionmagazine.com Revolution magazine has a web site for monthly UK magazine on new media – mainly sell-side e-commerce.

Competitive advantage

http://encyclopedia.thefreedictionary.com The Free Dictionary provides access to a series of brief, easy-to-read articles that summarise key ideas and concepts. A search for 'competitive advantage', for example, brings up a concise summary with links to additional, related articles.

www.optimizemag.com *Optimize* is a free magazine dedicated to business strategy. A search for 'competitive advantage' locates a number of interesting articles and case studies.

www.gartner.com Gartner's advanced search facility allows you to locate survey information on a huge range of topics. A great deal of content is free, although you must register to access the information.

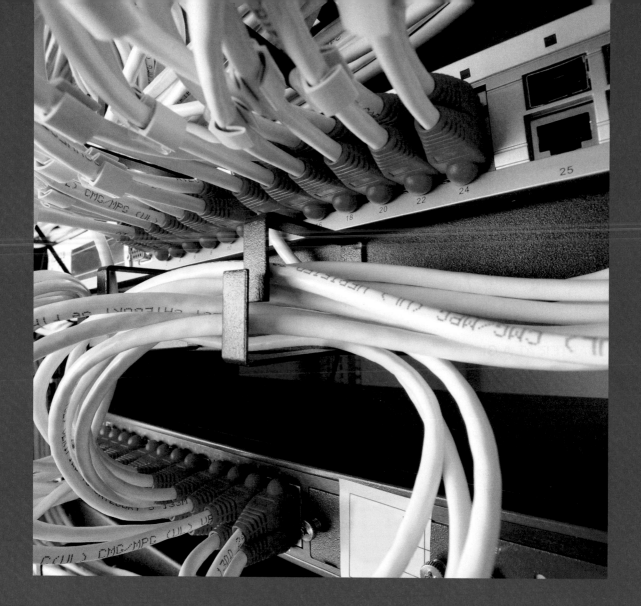

LINKS TO OTHER CHAPTERS

Chapter 1   considers the need for data for managerial decision making.

Chapter 4   focuses on database software applications.

Chapter 5   provides a detailed view of networks and communications.

Chapter 6   describes functional information systems and applications-specific software, providing a view of how computer hardware and software can be used to support specific business activities.

Chapter 8   contains a review of techniques for evaluating BIS from different suppliers which can also be applied to software.

Hardware and software

CHAPTER AT A GLANCE

MAIN TOPICS

FOCUS ON . . .

CASE STUDIES

LEARNING OUTCOMES

After reading this chapter, you will be able to:

- categorise the type of computer system that a business uses;
- recognise the different components of a computer;
- explain the purpose of software applications in different categories;
- describe the features found in a variety of modern applications software packages;
- identify some of the advantages and disadvantages associated with a variety of common applications;
- describe some of the ways in which applications software supports the activities of a business organisation.

MANAGEMENT ISSUES

Whilst it is unnecessary for managers to have an in-depth knowledge of computers, it is important for them to have an understanding of modern technology. Such an understanding can help to make sure that managers communicate with suppliers and apply technology effectively to an organisation. From a managerial perspective, this chapter addresses the following areas:

- Learning the characteristics of input, output and storage devices will allow managers to select the correct equipment for a given application.
- An increased understanding of computers will help managers to see how technology can be used to improve existing business processes and identify potential applications.
- All major organisations make use of common applications, such as word processing and spreadsheet software. An understanding of the factors involved with selecting these applications is required by all managers.
- An understanding of the range of software applications available will help managers to see potential applications relevant to a given organisation or industry.
- An understanding of recent developments in the software industry, such as the emergence of XML, will help managers to develop long-term plans for the organisation's use of technology.

INTRODUCTION

The aim of this chapter is to provide readers with a basic grasp of the often complex and technical language used to describe the computer hardware which is part of information systems. A knowledge of this language is necessary to help business users communicate with technical staff when discussing their requirements for new systems. An appreciation of how the different components of a computer interact is also useful when you are trying to understand problems that occur with hardware.

This chapter also provides an overview of the common software packages used in business. The material addresses two separate themes: a review of the features common to a range of modern software applications, and the way in which software can be used to support the business activities of an organisation. The chapter focuses on general-purpose applications software, such as word processors and spreadsheets, which is sometimes referred to as 'productivity software'. Database software is covered later (in Chapter 4), as is software for specific business applications (see Chapter 6).

COMPONENTS OF A COMPUTER SYSTEM

Some of the concepts explained in earlier chapters can be used to explain the notion of a computer system. A system was described (in Chapter 2) as a collection of interrelated components that work together towards a collective goal. It was also said that business information systems (BIS) can be defined as systems whose purpose is to convert data into information. We can think of a **computer system** as consisting of a number of interrelated components that work together with the aim of converting data into information. In a computer system, processing is carried out electronically, usually with little or no intervention from a human user. The components of a computer system include hardware and software which are both considered in this chapter.

Computer system

Interrelated components including hardware and software that work together with the aim of converting data into information.

Computer hardware

Hardware describes the physical components of a computer system. The hardware of a computer system can be said to consist of different elements whose relationship is shown from a systems theory perspective in Figure 3.1. Data are input, then processed according to software instructions, then output to the screen, for example, as information. Information that needs to be stored permanently will be placed in storage. This chapter is structured by describing the options available for each of these elements and assessing the criteria used for purchase decisions. The main components of a computer system, shown in Figure 3.1, can be conveniently grouped as follows:

Hardware

The physical components of a computer system: input devices, memory, central processing unit, output devices and storage devices.

Input device

Hardware used to enter data, information or instructions into a computer-based information system.

Central processing unit (CPU)

The processor found in a computer system that controls all of the computer's main functions and enables users to execute programs or process data.

- **Input devices.** Input devices are used to capture or enter data into the computer. Before data can be used within a computer system, it is usually necessary to convert them into a format that supports processing by computer. Most data are held in *human-sensible form*, that is, in a format that makes them directly accessible to human beings. A bank statement, for example, contains text and numbers that are relatively easy for a human to understand. However, such data are almost meaningless to the electronic components of a computer system. Input devices convert data into a form that makes them *machine-sensible*.

- **Central processing unit or processor.** The central processing unit (CPU) performs processing by carrying out instructions given in the form of computer programs. In a personal computer, the CPU is usually housed within the tower (or base unit) to which the mouse, keyboard and monitor are attached.

Figure 3.1 Basic hardware components of a computer system

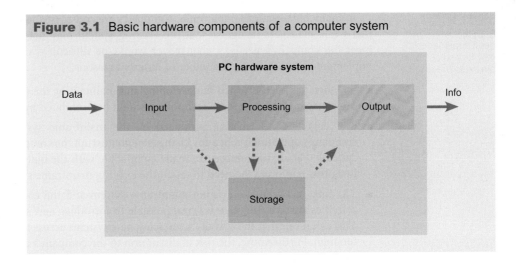

Memory

A temporary means of storing data awaiting processing, instructions used to process data or control the computer system, and data or information that has been processed.

- Primary storage or **memory**. Memory is used as a temporary means of storage data and instructions. Memory is used to store:

  (a) data awaiting processing,

  (b) instructions loaded from software which are used to process data or control the computer system,

  (c) data or information that has been processed.

Storage devices

A permanent means of storing data and programs until they are required.

- **Storage devices**. Storage devices provide a means of storing data and programs permanently until they are required. As an example, a program can be stored on a hard disk drive until it is needed. When the program is activated, it is transferred from the storage device into the computer's memory. When the program has ended or is no longer needed, it can be removed from memory so that other programs or data can be used.

Output devices

Translate the results of processing – output – into a human-readable form.

- **Output devices**. Output devices translate the results of processing – output – into a human-readable form. The results of a calculation, for example, might be displayed on a screen or sent to a printer. An output device may also transfer data requiring further processing to a storage device.

MAJOR CATEGORIES OF COMPUTERS

We can begin to understand more of the technology by looking at the ways in which computers themselves can be categorised. A traditional view of computer technology suggests three basic categories of computer: mainframe, minicomputer and microcomputer. We will briefly examine the characteristics of each category, in order to understand more of how industry makes use of computer technology.

Mainframe

Mainframe

Mainframes are powerful computers used for large-scale data processing.

A traditional view of **mainframe** computers saw them as large, extremely powerful machines designed for large-scale data-processing activities. The use of mainframe computers in industry, once responsible for the multi-billion-dollar revenues of companies such as IBM, Tandem, Amdahl and Hitachi, has declined steadily over the past four decades. Advances in technology have enabled smaller, less expensive systems to compete with mainframes in terms of speed and power. A modern personal computer, for example, could be considered many times more powerful than one of the very earliest mainframe systems.

Legacy system

A system which has been superseded by new technologies or business practices.

In many organisations, mainframe computers are considered legacy systems, meaning that while managers recognise that the existing system may not be entirely adequate to meet the company's needs, a changeover would be difficult – or even impossible – to implement. This can be for a number of different reasons:

- So much has been invested in developing and maintaining the mainframe system that a move towards more modern technology would be prohibited by the costs involved.

- The data and information produced by the mainframe system are critical to the company's operations. Since any changes might disrupt the company's activities, any new systems that are introduced are made compatible with the older mainframe system. In turn, this reinforces the need to retain the existing mainframe system.

- The links between the existing mainframe system and the company's major business activities are so strong that it is not possible to introduce new systems a little at a time. This can mean that the cost of introducing new systems across the entire organisation is too high. Furthermore, the risk of disruption to the company's activities may be so high that it is considered unacceptable.

Over the past few years, a solution to some of the problems associated with legacy systems has appeared in the form of virtual computing. Virtual computing is described in more detail later on.

Activity 3.1 Legacy systems

Using the Internet as a resource, find a case study that illustrates some of the problems that can result when companies are forced to retain legacy systems. Alternatively, find a case study that illustrates some of the benefits that can be achieved by replacing legacy systems. You may find an industry publication such as *Computer Weekly* (www.computerweekly.com) a useful source of information.

CASE STUDY 3.1

Mainframes are thriving in a cloud world

By Paul Taylor

When Mark Twain heard that his obituary had been published in the New York Journal he reportedly uttered the immortal line, 'the reports of my death are greatly exaggerated'.

The same might be said of the mainframe computer whose demise has been predicted for decades, but still thrives as the reliable core processing workhorse for many industries.

I asked Kris Manery, senior vice-president and general manager of Compuware, an IT services firm that has spent 30 years helping corporate customers achieve optimal performance and value from their mainframe investments, to help explaing how companies are ensuring the mainframe keeps pace with the expanding demands of today's information-hungry customers. Here is an edited version of our conversation.

Q. How has the mainframe market changed over the past few years?

First, some perspective. When the mainframe was introduced, it was designed to support a heavy workload of data-intensive back end processes. This technology is sometimes referred to as a system of record. The number of end users directly accessing the mainframe was small, and performance [speed] was a secondary concern.

Then the world changed: the growth of personal computers, the emergence of the World Wide Web, and now the mobile device explosion. With millions of end users needing to access data, and actively interact with it in real-time, new technologies emerged to handle the load.

The big change occurred when the standalone mainframe needed to accommodate an ever-increasing data demand from these external systems fed by the web, smartphones, tablets and other devices.

This demand is growing so fast and the number of transactions rising so quickly that it is necessary for IT teams to understand how web and mobile applications impact the mainframe and how the mainframe, in turn, affects the end-user experience.

Q. What are the demands that today's web and mobile applications are placing on the mainframe?

The mainframe is known for its ability to process large amounts of data securely and efficiently. But the volume of data requests coming from PCs, tablets, smartphones and other devices is staggering. These demands are expensive because the more 'CPU cycles' – [a measure of processing power] – a mainframe uses, the higher the cost.

In addition, mainframe hardware upgrades, while sometimes necessary, are very costly and should be delayed as long as possible. Our recent global survey of chief information officers, showed that MIPS [millions of instructions per second] costs are increasing on average by 21 per cent year-over-year, with 40 per cent of respondents claiming that consumption is becoming out of control.

The types of data that mainframes crunch have also changed. In the early days, most data were simple applications such as contact information and bank balances. Today's applications are much more complex and often involve continuous user interaction.

It is equally challenging to ensure the performance of these applications. End users – whether consumers or businesses – expect lightning-fast response times and 100 per cent availability. Anything less, and consumers start abandoning websites and business users can't get critical information in time.

Q. Could you give me an example of a company or industry and how it has adapted the mainframe to its evolving needs?

While nearly every major industry uses mainframes, a good example is financial services, specifically banking. Decades ago, only a handful of corporate personnel needed to access the mainframe's data. Then that data became available to bank tellers, but still the number of users was small.

Next came ATM machines, and suddenly thousands of users per minute needed access. Of course, the web opened up the flood gates, and now mobile devices with complex apps are commonplace. People need more than the ability to view bank balances; they also expect to make transfers, pay bills, scan and deposit checks, or buy stocks. Since one of the great attributes of a mainframe is its flexibility, corporations have been able to adapt mainframes for these multiple uses.

But as the variety and complexity of today's applications grow, companies are realising that a mainframe is no longer the 'isolated citizen' it once was. The mainframe is an integral part of a larger application delivery chain, a complex system which stretches from the data centre all the way to the end user's screen and back.

With this holistic view, companies realise it's not just the mainframe that requires ongoing management and optimisation. All the distributed systems feeding into the mainframe need to be finely-tuned to avoid undue stress on the overall system or on the mainframe itself.

So the mainframe division of a company IT department must adapt by constantly weeding out inefficiencies in the system while adjusting for an ever-increasing data load. The best teams know how to resolve performance problems quickly, reduce MIPS costs, postpone hardware upgrades and accelerate time-to-market for the new applications necessary to keep them ahead of the competition.

Q. What are the specific challenges your clients face to keep their mainframe investments relevant or efficient?

In addition to the external pressures I have outlined, there are several internal issues companies are grappling with. I've already referenced one of them: the siloing of the mainframe. Ovum analyst Tony Baer has used the term 'two alien worlds' to describe how isolated a company's mainframe team typically is from the rest of the IT department.

Because of the complexity of today's application delivery chain, and the interdependency of each component, this isolationism no longer works. When something breaks, you don't want finger-pointing between teams; you want answers and a quick solution.

A related problem is the lack of a unified view of the entire application delivery chain, from inside the mainframe and out to the distributed systems interacting with end-users. Managing triage across all these interconnected systems is a complex, time-consuming challenge. Traditionally when a problem or inefficiency is discovered, it could take days or even weeks to pinpoint the source.

Then there is what has become known as the mainframe knowledge gap: 68 per cent of chief information officers recently surveyed say their in-house teams no longer have the legacy knowledge to maintain mainframe applications. Many mainframe experts are baby-boomers who are now retiring in large numbers.

Q. Can mainframes 'keep up' with changes in today's technology?

Absolutely. Mainframes are flexible, secure, and no system can compete with their reliability. A new generation of models is better designed to handle today's challenges. The more relevant question is 'at what cost?'

Ultimately companies buy mainframes because of their cost efficiency and performance. When an application's CPU consumption is rising or its response times are not meeting users' real-time expectations, the cost savings of these systems suffer, either because MIPS costs are rising and forcing hardware upgrades or because customers are not being adequately served.

'Keeping up' is a process of carefully tuning mainframe applications. By understanding the new workloads with which the mainframe must contend, companies can overcome the surprises of degraded service, rising costs or unplanned hardware upgrades.

Q. Where will the mainframe be in five or 10 years time?

The mainframe has powered some of the world's most significant IT advancements – from man's first visit to the moon to today's explosive use of mobile ecommerce. Today and into the future, it will remain a cornerstone of enterprise IT and continue to support the world's most critical activities. It may not be the sexy new kid on the block, but its inherent efficiency, security and reliability still make it an easy choice for corporations.

QUESTION

What are the reasons for the continued use of mainframe computers?

Minicomputers and servers

Minicomputer

Minicomputers offer an intermediate stage between the power of mainframe systems and the relatively low cost of microcomputer systems.

The **minicomputer** combines some of the characteristics of the mainframe computer and the microcomputer. Today, they are often referred to as *servers* by companies such as Sun and Hewlett-Packard. This can be somewhat confusing since personal computers are also used as servers in some systems. Different types of server may have different functions, such as managing a network or hosting a database. Further information on how different types of servers are used in business is given later (in Chapter 5).

Microcomputers

Microcomputer

Microcomputers are considered less powerful than minicomputers and mainframes, but are more flexible and relatively inexpensive to purchase.

Client/server

The client/server architecture consists of client computers such as PCs sharing resources such as a database stored on a more powerful server computer.

IBM-compatible

The modern personal computer found in most business organisations, developed from a family of personal computers launched by IBM in the early 1980s.

The **microcomputer** makes use of more modern technology to provide relatively powerful computing facilities at low cost. A microcomputer is now sometimes referred to as the 'client' machine which receives services and data from a 'server' machine. This **client/server** architecture is a common type of communications structure. Some of the major characteristics of the microcomputer are as follows:

- In physical size a microcomputer is far smaller than a minicomputer.

- Microcomputers are widely used and generally provide the best price to performance ratio of all types of computer.

- Since microcomputers are inexpensive, they are more accessible than mainframes or minicomputers. A typical microcomputer will be within the means of a small business or an individual.

- Microcomputers are extremely flexible and are considered general-purpose machines capable of being used for a wide variety of applications. However, they are generally seen as being unsuitable for applications involving large volumes of data processing such as transaction processing (Chapter 6).

- Microcomputers are considered easier to use than mainframes or minicomputers. Users require little technical knowledge and can be trained quickly and at low cost.

- Technical and non-technical users are able to develop applications quickly and easily.

In industry, several types of microcomputer are in common use. The **IBM-compatible** or personal computer (PC), is considered the standard for general business use. The

Apple Macintosh

A family of personal computers produced by Apple Computers.

Apple Macintosh or iMac is often used for professional desktop publishing applications, such as the production of newspapers. **Workstations**, such as those produced by Sun, are typically used in the area of computer graphics. Typical applications include computer-aided design (CAD) and animation.

TYPES OF MICROCOMPUTERS

Workstation

A powerful terminal or personal computer system, usually used in specialised applications, such as computer-aided design (CAD).

Desktop computer

Intended for office use to support the day-to-day activities of an organisation's employees.

Tablet

A portable computing device normally equipped with a touch screen and/or a stylus. Tablets usually come with 17.5 cm (7 inch) or 24.5 cm (10 inch) screens and commonly use Google's Android, Apple's iOS or Microsoft's Windows RT operating system.

Portable computer

A self-contained computer with integrated power supply, keyboard, pointing device and visual display unit to facilitate carrying.

Notebook

A small portable computer, which is approximately the size of an A4 sheet of paper.

Netbook

One of the smallest types of portable computer, weighing less than 3 lb (1.4kg) and with a screen measuring 10 inches (25 cm) or less.

Desktop computers

As its name suggests, the **desktop computer** is intended for office use and supports the day-to-day activities of an organisation's employees. Desktop computers are often referred to as PCs (Personal Computers). These machines tend to be placed in a fixed location and connected permanently to items such as printers, scanners and other devices. At present, the desktop computer is the most common type of microcomputer and is found in the majority of organisations. However, in recent years **tablet** computers have started to become very popular and sales are predicted to overtake sales of desktop computers and laptops by 2015.

Desktop computers tend to have a modular design, that is, they are made up of components that can be removed or replaced individually. This means that repairs can be carried out quickly and easily. Since components are relatively inexpensive, it is possible to upgrade desktop machines at low cost. Many expansion devices can be fitted internally, protecting the device from accidental damage and helping to reduce its cost.

Portable computers

The **portable computer** is largely self-contained, featuring its own power supply, keyboard, pointing device and visual display unit. Modern portables tend to weigh very little and fit easily into a briefcase. Portable computers are often described as 'laptops' 'notebooks,' or 'netbooks'. A **notebook** (also termed a laptop) is approximately the size of an A4 writing pad. Netbooks are intended to be small and very light so that they are easy to carry around all day. Typically, a netbook will weigh less than 3 lb (1.4 kg) and will have a screen measuring 10 inches (25 cm) or less. More recently, ultrabooks and chromebooks have started to appear and are rapidly replacing the traditional netbook for both consumer and business applications. In fact, many manufacturers have discontinued production of netbooks in order to concentrate on these newer variants. In general, **ultrabooks** are thin and light portable computers with long battery life and solid state storage devices (SSDs). These devices typically feature Intel processors and are compatible with mainstream operating systems and software, such as Microsoft Windows. **Chromebooks** are also thin and light and have long-lasting batteries. However, they tend to have limited storage and less powerful processors than those found in ultrabooks and traditional laptop computers. Chromebooks are based on Google's relatively new Chrome operating system and make heavy use of Internet services, especially online storage. Chromebooks are considered relatively inexpensive and are rapidly growing in popularity.

A **tablet computer** is a portable computer integrated into a flat screen and primarily operated by touching the screen. They have become particularly popular since the introduction of the Apple iPad in 2010. Tablet computers are discussed in more detail later.

Ultrabook

A thin and light portable computer with long battery life and typically fearturing an Intel Processor. Ultrabooks and their variants are seen as the successors to netbooks

Chromebook

A thin and light portable computer with long battery life and limited storage. Chromebooks are based on Google's Chrome operating system and rely heavily on Internet services.

Tablet computer

A portable computer integrated into a flat screen and primarily operated by touching the screen.

Docking station

A docking station allows a portable computer to be connected to the company network and also provides access to a conventional monitor and keyboard.

Stylus

A simple device used with touch sensitive screens. A typical stylus is made of metal or plastic and is shaped like a pen. A *smart stylus* is used for more sophisticated applications.

Some typical applications for portable computers include:

- Collecting data from a number of different locations. Salespeople, for example, might record order details and other information as they visit different clients.

- Remote working. Portable computers allow users to work in a variety of different locations and situations, for example an employee travelling to work might use a portable so that they can complete a task that had been started in the office. Many portable computers are capable of being connected to a **docking station**, a desktop network access point that also provides a conventional monitor and keyboard. This allows 'hot-desking' which is popular for workers who are not regularly in the office.

- Communications. Many portable computers contain telecommunications facilities that can be used to send and receive information in a variety of forms. A manager, for example, might compose and send e-mail messages whilst travelling.

Although they are undoubtedly useful, some common criticisms of portable computers include:

- Portable computers often have a limited battery life, sometimes offering only as little as two hours of continuous use before the battery needs to be recharged.

- The limited expansion capacity of a portable computer means that it is often not possible to install additional devices, such as DVD drives. Expansion is often achieved by connecting devices externally through various ports.

- Many users find portable computers unsuitable for anything more than occasional use. Poor display units, small keyboards and clumsy pointing devices can sometimes make prolonged use of a portable computer very uncomfortable.

Tablet PC

Much of this section also applies to smartphones and other mobile devices.

Various factors have allowed tablet computers to become popular within a very short time. Previously, tablet computers were niche products, often created for specialised applications involving data collection in the field. Such devices typically came in three formats: as a single unit combining a touchscreen, battery and other hardware; as a convertible notebook, where the screen swivels or folds back to hide the keyboard; or as a touchscreen unit with a detachable keyboard. Often, tablet computers used a **stylus** to enter commands and data. Usually based on bulky PC technology, devices tended to have limited battery life and made use of the Windows operating system.

In 2010, Apple launched the first version of the iPad tablet to great acclaim. Compared to previous tablet computers, the iPad was light, had a long battery life and a high quality display. In addition, the tablet used Apple's iOS operating system, designed to make the device easy to operate for all users, including children. In the same year, Google launched the Android operating system under an Open Source licence, meaning that it could be distributed and modified free of charge. Android was specifically designed for touchscreen devices, making it ideally suited to mobile phones and tablet computers. An important feature of Android was its modest hardware requirements, making it possible to produce such mobile devices at low cost. Samsung, HP, Sony, Google, Lenovo, Asus and many other manufacturers quickly adopted Android and began to produce a wide variety of tablets in order to gain a share of a rapidly expanding market.

By 2013, Gartner reported that more than 120 million tablets were being sold annually, with sales likely to more than double within 2–3 years. In terms of market share, Strategy Analytics reported that Android tablets accounted for approximately 67 per cent of the market while the iPad accounted for 28 per cent. In the smartphone market, Strategy Analytics estimated more than 200 million Android smartphones were being sold each quarter, accounting for more than 80 per cent of the overall market. To put these figures in context, it was estimated that total sales of tablets would exceed sales of desktop computers by early 2014.

Modern tablet computers are typically offered in two sizes though many variations are available. Smaller modes have screens measuring approximately 17.5 cm (7 inches) while larger models have screens measuring around 24.5 cm (10 inches). Although the majority of tablets run the Android operating system, other operating systems are also available, including Apple's iOS and Microsoft Windows RT.

Many people consider e-book readers to be an offshoot of the tablet computer. This is because many e-book readers use similar hardware coupled with customised versions of the Android operating system. Examples include the Amazon Kindle Fire range of readers and the Barnes & Noble Nook series.

An important development in relation to the popularity of tablet computers has been the introduction of **app stores**. An app store provides an online marketplace where users can find, purchase, download and install new software quickly and easily. Services such as *Google Play* also allow users to purchase content, such as books, music and movies. These services provide users with a streamlined experience, allowing them to choose, pay for and receive items quickly and conveniently. In order to make use of an app store, a user must normally open an online account that is linked to each of the devices he owns, one or more online payment systems and any other relevant services, such as subscriptions to online publications. The online account can be managed from any Internet-enabled device and provides a way of integrating the individual services the user subscribes to. *Google Play*, for instance, keeps track of what software is installed on each of a user's devices and even advises when an application is not compatible with a particular device. As more devices become Internet-enabled, it is quickly becoming possible to link them together, often using a tablet as a controller. As an example, owners of **smart TVs** (televisions capable of connecting to the Internet and running applications) can use a tablet as a sophisticated remote control, even sending content from the tablet directly to the screen or controlling a video game using the tablet's touch screen. Sophisticated tablets feature a variety of **sensors** and input devices that open up many new potential uses. The sensors available on Android tablets, for example, can be divided into three main categories:

- motion sensors, such as accelerometers, gravity sensors and gyroscopes;
- environmental sensors for measuring temperature, air pressure, humidity, and so on;
- position sensors for measuring the location of the device.

Sensors can be used in combination with other on-board devices, such as cameras and GPS receivers, to perform many complex tasks. Such tasks range from monitoring the weather to helping drivers keep a safe distance from the vehicles in front of them.

Tablets have also encouraged hardware and software companies to look at making it easier to interact with devices. Touch sensitive screens have developed to support multi-touch commands, enabling users to control devices more easily with one hand. Pinch-to-zoom, for instance, lets users increase or decrease the size of an image by making a pinching motion on the screen. On-screen keyboards for entering text have also become more sophisticated. *Swype* is a text entry method that allows users to enter words without having to press each letter individually. Instead, the user moves a finger (or stylus) across all of the letters making up the word. The device determines the word that was 'swiped' when the user lifts his finger from the keyboard. Swype uses a number of other methods to minimise the number of taps the user needs to make when entering text. As an example, it automatically enters spaces between words so that the user does not need to.

Other common ways of interacting with tablets include voice commands, air gestures and eye tracking. *Voice commands* allow users to perform various actions hands-free, making them particularly useful during activities such as driving. More sophisticated tools provide a way of entering relatively large amounts of text without typing. A good example is *Siri*, which can be thought of as an intelligent personal assistant and is described by Apple: 'Siri lets you use your voice to send messages, schedule meetings, make phone calls and more. Ask Siri to do things just by talking the way you talk. Siri understands what you say, knows what you mean and even talks back.'

App store

An online store allowing users to buy software applications instantly, usually directly from the device they are using.

Smart TV

A television capable of connecting to the Internet and running simple applications, such as games. Additional peripherals, such as web cameras, can often be connected to Smart TVs, making them capable of using services such as Skype.

Sensors

Devices allowing aspects of the environment to be measured. A light sensor, for instance, can be used to detect when it is night-time or if the case covering a phone or tablet is closed.

Air gestures allow users to control their devices without having to touch the screen. As an example, users might scroll through a document or web page by moving a hand up and down above the screen of the device.

Eye tracking is a fairly new development that makes use of the front camera on a device to follow the user's eye movements. This allows the device to respond to the user's actions. 'Smart Pause', for instance, pauses the playback of a video if the user looks away and resumes playing when he looks at the screen again.

The capabilities of tablets and other mobile devices are growing rapidly thanks to advances in areas such as battery technology and mobile processors. With regard to processing power, for example, even fairly inexpensive devices can now easily match the desktop computers of less than a decade ago. This has allowed *convertible tablets* to become mainstream products, allowing users to choose between the portability of a tablet, the additional features of a laptop computer and the comfort of a desktop computer as circumstances dictate. Docking a tablet to a suitable keyboard produces a functional a laptop computer, often with additional battery power and other features. The same tablet might also be connected to a docking station that allows a standard keyboard, monitor and other devices to be attached.

Many of the facilities offered by tablets require them to interact with other devices and services. For this reason, many tablets offer Bluetooth, Wi-Fi and mobile Internet connectivity. When mobile phone capabilities are added, the distinction between a tablet and a smartphone starts to become blurred. Distinctions have become even more difficult to make as tablet screens have shrunk and smartphone screens have grown. Samsung's *Note* range of smartphones, for example, feature screens comparable in size to a small tablet. This type of device has become known as a **phablet**, a hybrid combining the features of a smartphone and a tablet.

The low cost, portability, ease of use and good connectivity of tablets make them ideal for applications and environments where it has traditionally been difficult to introduce technology. In remote areas of developing nations, for instance, tablets provide young people with valuable educational opportunities. Allowing teachers to use the Internet, for instance, instantly provides these communities with access to millions of educational resources, ranging from lesson plans to free text books. Tablets are seen as particularly useful in areas with unreliable electricity supplies, or where Internet access by landline is limited. In recent years, they have been widely used to support relief efforts following natural disasters.

Phablet

A hybrid device combining the features of a tablet and a smartphone. Phablets usually have screens slightly smaller than a tablet's but larger than a typical mobile phone.

m-Health

Mobile health (or m-Health) is the name given to the use of mobile devices to support medical services. Devices such as tablets and smartphones have many health related applications, ranging from simple record keeping to remote diagnosis. While some applications require tablets to be outfitted with special hardware devices, such as additional sensors, many take the form of standard software-only 'apps'.

Many applications use a device such as a tablet as a means of capturing and storing medical information. Home users, for example, might use a tablet to monitor and record information related to conditions such as high blood pressure or diabetes. On a larger scale, nursing staff might record information about a number of patients so that it can be reviewed by a doctor later on. Tablets can also be used to support diagnosis of conditions. As an example, a health care worker in a remote location can take a photograph of a patient's injury then transmit this to a doctor located a long distance away. The doctor can form an opinion of how best to treat the patient and send the information back to the health care worker, who then provides the treatment and monitors the patient further. In this way, it becomes possible to treat relatively large numbers of people, possibly located in different remote areas, with limited resources.

As well as treating illness or injury, mobile devices can also be used to perform health screening. Typical uses might include testing for colour blindness or hearing loss. There are also many applications that use a question-and-answer format to help people evaluate their own health or help medical staff identify common conditions.

The sensors featured on tablets and similar devices can also be used to support health-related tasks. As an example, the camera and flash on a smartphone or tablet can be used as a cardiograph; the user's heart rhythm is calculated from pictures taken of his fingertips. In a similar way, the built-in microphone found on most devices can be used as a fetal heart rate monitor, allowing medics and anxious parents to listen to the heartbeat of an unborn child. With the addition of extra sensors, even more tests can be carried out. Such sensors are relatively inexpensive and allow a tablet to monitor patient body temperature, breathing, pulse, blood sugar, and so on.

Finally, it is worth mentioning the use of mobile technology for reference and training, especially in areas where the support of specialists and a fully equipped hospital may not be available. Devices equipped with a mobile Internet connection can provide an instant reference tool or can deliver – and assess – basic knowledge and skills. Some examples of applications include: reference guides to common medications, revision tools for those about to take medical exams, simulations designed to teach how to interpret ECG readings and animated tutorials showing how to use medical equipment correctly.

While m-Health developments will undoubtedly benefit people all around the world, many people are concerned about the potential for harm that arises when people self-diagnose or rely too heavily on information found via the Internet. As an example, there have been many cases where people have died after deciding to rely on online information instead of seeking medical help. Many people have also died as a result of self-medicating after researching medical information online. A 2013 survey by *The Information Standard* in the UK found that approximately four in ten people put off visiting a doctor after using the Internet to self-diagnose. Of those who eventually visited a doctor and obtained a professional diagnosis, almost one in six were told they had a 'lucky escape'.

INPUT DEVICES

Input devices (Figure 3.2) are used to enter data or instructions. 'Device' is used in this context to refer to an individual piece of hardware with a specific function. The mouse and the keyboard are examples of input devices. Before looking at some of the devices available, it is worth making some observations:

- It should be noted that modern computers make use of a wide variety of input devices since data flowing in to the organisation may take a number of different forms.

- The choice of an input device will often depend upon the quantity of data to be entered. Entering data on a small scale is normally carried out by human operators, using a number of familiar input devices, such as the mouse or keyboard. However, large-scale data input may require the use of more specialised input devices. In many cases, a **direct capture** device will be used to acquire and store data automatically. Generally, the data are captured at the source and stored with little or no human intervention. Data obtained from sensors on a production line, for example, might be stored and then processed automatically.

Direct capture

A method of acquiring and storing data automatically with little or no human intervention.

- A computer-based information system will seldom make use of only a single input device. Even a typical personal computer will often feature several different methods for data entry, such as keyboard, mouse, joystick and microphone.

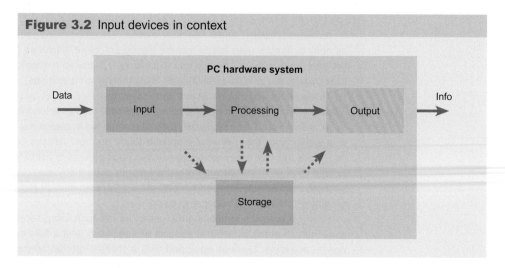

Figure 3.2 Input devices in context

There is a wide variety of types of input device; note the business applications of the following.

Keyboard/keypad

The keyboard remains the most common input device and its basic design has remained largely unchanged for more than a century.

A common criticism of the keyboard is that inexperienced users find it difficult and uncomfortable to use. In answer to this, new keyboard designs have appeared that attempt to make them easier to use. **Natural (or ergonomic) keyboards** have the keys arranged so that users can locate them more quickly and easily and is shaped to make prolonged use more comfortable.

Mouse

Computers featuring a **graphical user interface (GUI)** often require the use of a **mouse** or other **pointing device**. Although there are many different kinds of mouse, all use the same basic method of operation: moving the mouse over a flat surface causes a corresponding movement to a small pointer on the screen. The operating system software (Chapter 3) translates direction and rate of movement of the mouse to movement of the on-screen cursor.

Stylus and graphics tablet

Devices with touchscreens, such as smartphones, tablets and some laptop computers, often allow the use of a *stylus*. A traditional stylus appears similar to a pen and offers more precision than a fingertip. A stylus often replaces a mouse where space is limited or a small screen is being used. Many recent devices have started to include a *smart stylus*, a stylus that offers more functionality and features when coupled with the right hardware and software. Samsung's S Pen, for instance, offers features like 'Easy Clip', where the stylus can be used to draw around part of picture so that it can be cut, copied or manipulated in other ways.

Applications involving graphics, such as drawing packages, often involve **graphics tablets** (sometimes called *drawing tablets* or *digitizers*). With a graphics tablet, a stylus is used to draw an image onto a pressure-sensitive flat surface, just like using a pencil and paper. The image is shown on the computer's screen as the user works. Graphics tablets can also be used to replace other pointing devices, like the mouse. Tablets are often used instead of drawing directly onto a touch sensitive screen because they usually offer greater precision and flexibility. As an example, a graphics tablet makes it easy to trace drawings or diagrams. Graphics tablets are also useful for entering text in languages where characters are often drawn, e.g. Chinese.

Natural keyboard

Keys are arranged so that users can locate them more quickly and easily in a way that makes prolonged use more comfortable.

Graphical user interface (GUI)

Allows the user to control the operation of a computer program or item of computer hardware using a pointing device, such as a mouse, by selecting options from icons and menu options.

Mouse

A pointing device found on most modern personal computers.

Pointing device

An input device that allows the user to control the movement of a small pointer displayed on the screen that is used to select options.

Graphics tablet

Consists of a stylus and a flat drawing surface. The stylus is used to draw images onto the tablet. As the user works, the image is copied to the computer's screen.

Trackball

Trackball

A trackball is a pointing device that is controlled by rotating a small ball with the fingertips or palm of the hand.

A **trackball** is a pointing device that is controlled by rotating a small ball with the fingertips or the palm of the hand. Moving the ball causes corresponding movement to a small pointer on the screen. Buttons are used to select items in the same way as with the mouse. Trackballs are often used when space is limited; in portable equipment they are often used to replace a mouse.

Joystick

The joystick is one of the most common input devices available and is primarily used for leisure activities, such as playing computer games. There are, however, a number of more serious applications for joysticks, in areas such as medicine and engineering. We also include game controllers in this section, such as those supplied with games consoles.

Optical scanner

Optical scanner

An input device used to capture graphics and text from printed documents.

The **optical scanner** is now widely used in business for capturing graphics and text from printed documents. Images captured in this way are normally incorporated into word processing or desktop publishing documents or are part of workflow management systems (Chapter 6).

Optical character recognition (OCR)

Software that attempts to recognise individual characters.

Optical scanners can also be used to perform data entry by converting printed documents into text files that can be used by word processing packages and other programs. **Optical character recognition (OCR)** involves using software that attempts to recognise individual characters. As a scanned image is processed, the program creates a text file containing all of the characters recognised. This file can then be edited further using a word processor, text editor or some other suitable program since recognition is not always 100 per cent accurate. For example, the letter 'i' is sometimes recognised as 'l'.

Optical scanners often form the basis for document image processing (DIP) systems. A DIP system allows users to convert paper documents into their electronic equivalents. This makes it easier to organise, store and process large numbers of documents. Typical applications for DIP systems are found in areas such as medicine, insurance and law. For instance, hospital records are often stored electronically, allowing medical staff to access them via a network from anywhere in the hospital.

Optical mark recognition (OMR)

Detection and recognition of simple marks made on a document.

A variation on optical character recognition is **optical mark recognition (OMR)**, which involves detecting and recognising simple marks made on a document.

Mini case study | Optical mark recognition

Public examinations, such as the GCSE qualifications that students take at school, often involve a multiple-choice paper. Students record their answers on a special sheet, usually by filling in small boxes corresponding to their choices.

The answer sheet used by students is a special document that has been prepared so that it can be used with an optical mark reader. The size and position of the boxes on the sheet, for example, have been designed so that the optical mark reader can process the sheet quickly and accurately.

The optical mark readers used by examination bodies are almost completely automatic and are able to deal with hundreds of answer sheets each hour. However, although this simplifies the process of marking the papers from the many thousands of examinations sat each year, problems can still arise. Common problems include equipment breakdowns, damaged answer sheets and answer sheets that have been completed incorrectly.

Figure 3.3 Examples of different formats for bar codes

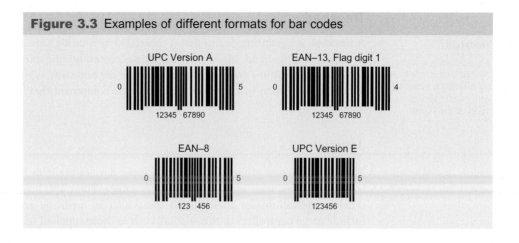

Bar code reader

A **bar code** (Figure 3.3) is a means of displaying a unique identification number as a series of thick and thin lines. The sequence and width of the lines in the bar code can be translated into a sequence of digits. Bar code numbers are normally produced according to a specific method. The **universal product code**, for example, is a standard method for creating and using bar codes.

A **bar code reader** measures the intensity of a light beam reflected from the printed bar code to identify the digits making up the unique identification number. The digits making up the identification number are also printed at the foot of the bar code.

The most common example of the use of the bar code reader in industry is the supermarket checkout. However, bar codes are also used in a variety of other situations including manual inspection and update of stock levels on inventory control systems; identification of patients in hospitals by bracelets to enable retrieval of patient information; bar codes on magazines and newspapers are used to record sales of particular titles, which helps vendors, distributors and publishers to monitor trends and plan possible promotions.

Many industry experts believe that bar codes will eventually be replaced by RFID (Radio-frequency identification) tags. These are often called *smart bar codes* and are small, fairly inexpensive tags that can be attached to a wide variety of objects. The information stored on each tag is transmitted when a request is received from an electronic reader. Depending on the power source used by the tag, the reader can be located from a few metres to a few hundred metres away. RFID has many applications, ranging from monitoring components as they move through a production process, to locating lost livestock. As an example, supermarkets have been experimenting with RFID for a number of years with the aim of eliminating the need for customers to pack and unpack their groceries at the checkout. Using RFID tags, as a customer walks past a special scanner, every item in the basket or trolley can be automatically identified and the total cost calculated. While such technology is likely to bring significant benefits to the retailing industry, there remain many problems to resolve.

Activity 3.2   Advantages and disadvantages

What are some of the disadvantages of printed bar codes and what are some of the advantages of RFID tags? Use the Internet as a resource and try to find at least three examples of each.

Touch screen

The **touch screen** is a transparent, pressure-sensitive covering that is attached to the screen of the monitor. Users make selections and control programs by pressing onto the screen. Although touch screens are simple to use, they are comparatively expensive to produce, especially at large sizes. However, touch screens have become popular as a means of controlling many different devices, from smartphones to kitchen appliances.

Leaving aside tablets, smartphones and touch-enabled computers, common business applications for touch screens include interactive kiosks and bookings systems. An **interactive kiosk** allows a user to purchase items or browse through a list of products by pressing buttons or other controls shown on the screen. Such kiosks are often found in banks, music stores, supermarkets and large catalogue stores. Many bookings systems, such as those used by airlines, theatres and travel agents, also make use of touch screens.

Video capture card

The **video capture card** records and stores video sequences (motion video) when connected to a digital video camera or other device. Video capture devices are often used for security applications, such as CCTV. The device can be connected to multiple of CCTV cameras, automatically capturing, combining and storing video on a digital video recorder. This reduces the storage space needed to keep large amounts of video and makes it easier to review the data quickly.

Microphone/sound card

A **sound card** can be used to capture sound, music and speech from a variety of sources. Sound can be captured at a very high quality; even the most inexpensive sound cards are capable of producing results at CD quality. A business application is the use of **voice recognition** software to dictate text directly into a word processing document. In many cases, a special microphone is required in order to ensure that the user's voice is not obscured by background noise. In addition, the software used normally requires 'training' so that it can adapt to a user's accent or the way in which they pronounce particular words. Even with this training, recognition rates seldom exceed 95 per cent, so some modifications are usually required after recognition. Voice recognition packages also provide limited control over a graphical user interface, for example allowing people to control a web browser or a word processing program.

The addition of a sound card and CD or DVD device provides a computer with **multimedia** facilities.

Advances in **Voice over IP (VoIP)** technology now allow users to make and receive telephone calls via the Internet. Services such as *Skype* allow users to make free or low-cost calls using a microphone or headset connected to a PC. It is also possible to buy special telephone handsets that connect directly to a computer. The very latest handsets connect directly to a hub, allowing users to make and receive calls without needing the computer to be switched on.

Web camera

Web cameras (webcams) allow the real-time capture of images and sound. The information captured by a webcam is usually compressed so that it can be transmitted via the Internet. This enables three basic applications: video e-mail, video conferencing and webcam monitoring.

Video e-mail (v-mail) involves sending an e-mail message to which a video clip has been attached. The video clip is usually accompanied by a viewer program that runs when the user clicks on a button or link in the e-mail message. V-mail is not in common use because of concerns related to security and because other methods, such as VoIP, offer more functionality.

Video conferencing allows a group of users to communicate with each other simultaneously. Each person taking part in the conversation is able to see and hear the other participants in real-time. Many applications provide a range of additional features that support collaborative working, such as shared whiteboards.

Webcam monitoring involves setting up one or more webcams to watch a given person or place. The images captured by the camera can be viewed at a web site using a normal browser. As an example, a number of static webcams continuously broadcast images from the UK road system in order to manage traffic jams, accidents, and so on. Images from almost 1,000 cameras around the London region can be seen by the public via the BBC (see **http://www.bbc.co.uk/travelnews/london/trafficcameras**). When used with appropriate motion detection software, a webcam can also be used to replace a CCTV system. This has the advantage that images from the camera can be viewed from any location via a browser. If the software detects movement, it can automatically begin recording images to hard disk and will even alert security staff by sending an instant message, e-mail or text message.

MICR

Magnetic ink character recognition (MICR)

Capture and recognition of data that have been printed using a special magnetic ink.

Magnetic ink character recognition (MICR). This involves capturing data that have been printed using a special magnetic ink. This technology is normally associated with the banking industry, especially cheque processing. Some of the details on a cheque, such as the cheque number, are printed in a special typeface using magnetic ink. The shape of each character means that it can be recognised by its magnetic field. As the use of cheques declines, it is likely that many organisations will also move away from MICR.

Selecting input devices

It is important to select an appropriate means of data entry in order to ensure that any computerised system works as efficiently as possible. The collection of data on a very large scale, for example, usually requires an approach that involves automating the process as far as possible. When selecting keyboard and mouse for a new PC, although these are provided as standard, it may be worth paying extra for superior quality versions to reduce the risk of repetitive strain injury (RSI). However, the selection of an input device is usually based upon three basic criteria: volume, speed and accuracy.

Volume

Some input devices are unsuitable for dealing with large volumes of data. An electricity company, for example, would be unlikely to use manual data entry methods to record the details of payments made by customers. Instead, these data would be collected using more sophisticated methods, such as optical mark recognition (OMR) or optical character recognition (OCR). On the other hand, a small business dealing with far fewer transactions might prefer to enter data using the keyboard as an input device.

Speed

If large volumes of data need to be entered, speed and accuracy may be important considerations for many business applications. It would be unrealistic, for example, to enter text into a word processor using only the mouse. Similarly, the electricity company mentioned earlier would be unlikely to employ data entry clerks in order to record payment details – OCR and OMR can be many thousands of times faster than manual data entry methods.

Accuracy

In some business applications it is essential to ensure that data entry is completely accurate. In engineering, for example, sensing devices are often required to measure components with an accuracy of plus or minus 0.01 cm. Obviously, if there are any errors in the data recorded this may mean that components need to be scrapped.

In many cases, it may be acceptable if an input device generates a certain number of errors. This is often referred to as the **error rate** and the acceptable level will vary according to the input device being used and the business application. Optical character recognition, for example, is generally considered a comparatively unreliable means of entering data. At present, a typical OCR software package may have an error rate of between 5 and 10 per cent.

Error rate

The frequency of errors which occur when using an input device to recognise patterns.

Other criteria

Other considerations when selecting an input device might also include:

- *Complexity of data*. Some methods are unsuitable for entering data of a complex nature. In many cases, data may need to be interpreted or altered before they are entered. In entering a letter into a word processor, for example, a secretary may need to interpret shorthand notes or alter words and phrases as the document is typed.
- *Cost*. Although some methods offer high levels of speed and accuracy, an organisation may be unwilling or unable to purchase the hardware and software required. In such cases an alternative means of data entry may be required.
- *Frequency of data entry*. Some types of data entry may be carried out on an infrequent or ad hoc basis. In these cases, the acquisition of new or specialised input devices may not be justifiable.

Activity 3.3	Selecting input devices

Using the criteria described in this section, select the most suitable type of input device to perform these functions:

- entry of an application for a loan, received on a paper form, into an operational system for processing loan applications;
- entry of details of a house into a system for estate agents;
- entry of details collected in a ward visit by a hospital consultant;
- a field map from a geologist's survey into a mapping system.

OUTPUT DEVICES

Output devices (Figure 3.4) display the results of computer processing. Before looking at some of the devices available, it is worth making some observations:

- The output produced by some devices is temporary in nature. A display shown on a monitor, for example, is lost when a new image is shown or the computer system is switched off. On the other hand, a report produced on a printer is more permanent and may last for many years.
- Some forms of output may be used as the input for another process. Photographs, sounds and video sequences, for example, might be combined during the production of a training package or demonstration programme.
- Business organisations have a wide range of requirements in terms of the form of the information they produce. These requirements mean that there are a large variety of specialised output devices available.

Figure 3.4 Output devices in context

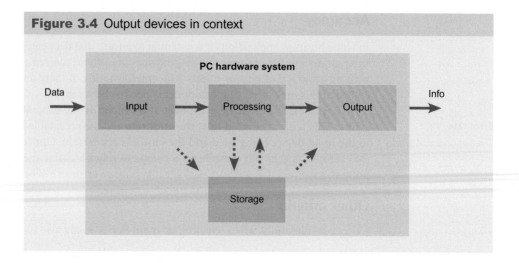

- A computer-based information system will seldom make use of only a single output device. Even a typical personal computer will often feature several different output devices, such as monitor, sound card and printer.

Display devices

The most common output device is almost certainly the *monitor* that is attached to all personal computer systems.

Most modern monitors feature a Liquid Crystal Display (LCD), making them more reliable and energy efficient than their predecessors. Better energy efficiency can be obtained if LEDs (Light Emitting Diodes) are used to provide the backlight needed to illuminate the display. The latest OLED (Organic Light Emitting Diode) technology does not need a backlight, allowing for better quality images and thinner screens. While all modern monitors are essentially liquid crystal displays, they may sometimes be known as LED or OLED monitors, depending on the technology being used.

The monitor has several advantages over other forms of output device:

- Information can be shown instantly with only a negligible delay between the information becoming available and its being displayed. In addition, the monitor is one of only a small number of devices that allows users to view the progress of an activity as it occurs.

- As standard components of a computer system, monitors are relatively inexpensive to purchase, repair or replace.

- The monitor is particularly suited to displaying certain kinds of information, for example charts and graphics.

- The cost of using the monitor as an output device is very low. Unlike printers, for example, a monitor does not require consumables, such as paper. In turn, this means that wastage does not occur.

Another way of producing a large display for presentations is by making use of a **data or video projector**. A computer system can be connected directly to a projector so that output is directed to a projection screen.

Video projector

A computer system can be connected directly to a projector so that output is directed to a projection screen.

Plotter

A plotter uses a number of different coloured pens to draw lines upon the paper as it moves through the machine.

Printers and plotters

Since many users are involved in selecting printers these are described in a separate section. A **plotter** uses a number of different coloured pens to draw lines upon the paper as it moves through the machine. Although capable of producing characters, the quality of the text created is often very poor. Plotters are primarily used to create technical drawings, such as engineering diagrams and to record the progress of continuous monitoring. In recent years, the use of plotters has declined as large inkjet printers have become more accessible.

Other output devices

In addition to the items described in this section, a wide variety of other output devices are also available. Some examples include the following:

- *Sound.* In addition to music and sound output via speakers, a sound card can be used to output information in a variety of other forms. Two common examples are voice annotations and speech synthesis.

- *MIDI devices.* The ability to link devices to a personal computer via **MIDI (musical instrument digital interface)** connections allows users to send information directly to one or more musical instruments.

- *Microfilm.* **Computer output to microfilm (COM)**, also known as 'computer output microform', is often used to archive large quantities of information for future reference. Information is processed via a personal computer and sent directly to a device that produces microfilm negatives. COM has largely been replaced by more modern document image processing systems, which tend to be less expensive to operate and offer more flexibility in terms of how information can be used.

MIDI (musical instrument digital interface)

MIDI connections allow users to control musical instruments or synthesise any sounds or effects required in order to play the music.

Computer Output to microfilm (COM)

Information is processed via a computer and sent directly to a device that produces microfilm negatives.

Selecting output devices

The selection of an inappropriate output device can incur unnecessary costs and lead to a variety of other problems. Some of the factors that should be considered when selecting an output device include appropriateness, permanence, speed, response time and cost.

Appropriateness

An output device should be appropriate to the type of information produced as the result of a business process. A plotter, for example, provides an efficient means of producing large technical diagrams, but would not be an appropriate way of printing a business letter.

Permanence

It is often necessary to make a permanent record of the results of a given activity, for example an organisation will normally retain a copy of a business letter sent to a client.

Response time

Many activities require constant and immediate feedback. The user of a word processor, for example, needs to see the results of their actions at all times – in other words, the **response time** between action and feedback must be very small.

Response time

The time it takes to respond to an action. For instance, the delay between pressing a key on the keyboard, and a letter appearing on the screen. The same term can also refer to the time it takes for a maintenance provider to fix a problem.

Speed

In many applications, the speed of the output device can be of critical importance. As an example, consider a mailmerge operation, where personalised letters are produced by inserting the names and addresses of customers into a standard document. Although generating each letter may take only a matter of seconds, printing each copy can take considerably longer. The time taken to complete the process will depend heavily on the speed of the output device: the slower the device (in this case, the printer), the longer the overall time taken to complete the task.

Cost

The operating costs of certain output devices can be extremely low. The monitor, for example, costs relatively little to purchase, maintain and operate. However, other output devices, for example printers, incur costs each time they are used.

Activity 3.4 | **Selecting output devices**

Using the criteria described in this section and using numerical specifications, select the most suitable type of screen output device and configuration to perform these functions:

- a business analyst involved in using a spreadsheet to model a company's financial performance;
- a student using a PC to produce assignments;
- a web site designer;
- a personal assistant to the director.

FOCUS ON... | **PRINTERS**

In this section we describe the main types of printer used for business and home use and criteria for selecting them.

Laser printer

Laser printer

A laser is used to charge sections of a rotating drum which is then used to print using toner powder achieving a combination of speed with high print quality.

In a laser printer, a laser is used to charge sections of a rotating drum. The pattern of charged and uncharged areas on the drum corresponds to the image that will be printed. As the drum rotates, particles of dry toner powder are picked up. Heat is used to transfer the toner powder to the paper.

Some advantages of the laser printer are as follows:

- *Print quality*. Laser printers are capable of producing documents at a quality appropriate for business correspondence.
- *Speed*. A typical laser printer will be able to print at a rate of up to 45 pages per minute or more. This compares well against other printing methods, for example a typical inkjet printer may only be capable of printing 20 pages per minute.
- *Volume*. Laser printers are normally capable of dealing with large volumes of work. Manufacturers often provide ratings for their printers that describe the typical workload appropriate for a given model. Laser printers are capable of a workload of 5000 pages or higher per month, with some models capable of 30,000 copies per month.
- *Noise*. Laser printers are almost completely silent in operation.

However, laser printers also suffer from a number of disadvantages:

- *Cost of printing*. The cost of printing via a laser printer is considered high. One reason for this is that all documents – including drafts – are usually printed at a high quality. In addition, unlike other types of printer, laser printers usually need relatively expensive components replacing at regular intervals.
- *Colour printing*. Although colour laser printers are available and have fallen in price significantly in recent years, they remain expensive to use and maintain. Expensive colour toner, for instance, may mean print costs of up to £0.30 per page. Despite this, the

increased availability of colour laser printers – and inkjet printers – means that they have largely replaced other forms of colour printing, such as wax printers.

- *Cost*. Laser printers are considered relatively expensive to purchase, operate and maintain in comparison with other types of printer.

Inkjet printer

Although initially considered expensive and unreliable, inkjet printers have rapidly gained acceptance and are now found in many organisations and homes. Changes in technology have resulted in models that are inexpensive to purchase, reliable in operation and capable of excellent results.

An **inkjet printer** uses a print-head containing 50 or more small nozzles. Each nozzle can be controlled individually by electrostatic charges produced by the printer. Characters are formed by squirting small droplets of ink directly onto the paper. Bubble jet printers work in a similar manner but transfer the character by melting the ink droplets onto the paper.

Some advantages of inkjet printers include:

- *Cost*. Inkjet printers can be purchased at low cost and are relatively inexpensive to operate.
- *Reliability*. Since inkjet printers have very few moving parts, they are considered reliable and robust.
- *Colour printing*. Inkjet printers provide a relatively inexpensive means of printing in colour at an acceptable quality.
- *Versatility*. Inkjet printers are able to produce a variety of different documents, including overhead transparencies, cards, labels and envelopes.
- *Noise*. Inkjet printers are almost completely silent in operation.

Some of the disadvantages of inkjet printers include the following:

- *Permanence*. The ink used by some printers is not waterproof, meaning that documents can become smudged or blurred easily. In addition, some inks fade over time or with exposure to bright sunlight.
- *Print quality*. Printing at the highest possible quality requires the use of special paper. This increases the cost of printing significantly.
- *Speed*. Although considerably faster than older technologies, inkjet printers are still unable to compete with laser printers in terms of speed. Colour printing can be particularly slow, with some models taking 6–8 minutes to produce a single page.

Inkjet printer

An inkjet printer uses a print-head containing 50 or more small nozzles that squirt ink onto paper by varying electrostatic charges produced by the printer.

Multi-function devices (MFDs)

In recent years manufacturers have started to develop new printers that offer additional functions such as scanning, faxing and photocopying. These printers, called *multi-function devices (or MFDs)*, often come with an automatic document feeder, allowing them to scan, copy or fax as many as fifty pages at a time.

MFDs hold many attractions for business users, including low purchase cost, space-saving designs and new features, such as low-cost colour photocopying. Sophisticated models also offer network features, such as a built-in Wi-Fi connection, or bundled software for controlling print queuing. As might be imagined, tremendous cost savings can result from replacing numerous printers, scanners, photocopiers and fax machines with a smaller number of MFDs, especially in environments where facilities like photocopying are not used frequently.

However, MFDs also have a number of disadvantages. For instance, if the device breaks down users lose access to all of its functions and work may grind to a halt. In network environments, there may also be problems when users compete for access to the device, especially if different people want to use different functions, such as printing or photocopying. Finally, many MFDs are designed for home users or small businesses, making them unsuitable for dealing with large volumes of work.

Despite these issues, MFDs have slowly increased in popularity since 2000 and new models are released regularly. Manufacturers producing MFDs include Hewlett-Packard, Epson, Canon, Xerox, Brother and Samsung.

Selecting a printer

A number of factors should be considered when selecting a printer for business use. The aim should be to acquire equipment that meets the business needs of the organisation and ensures high print quality at minimum cost. Some of the factors that should be considered include printing costs, print quality, speed, volume, any requirement to print in colour, and paper handling. Each of these factors is described in the following sections.

Printing costs

Cost per page

Figures refer to the costs of consumables such as ink and replacement components (toner cartridges, drums and so on).

The cost of printing is normally described in terms of cost per page. Two separate figures are usually given for the cost per page: the typical cost of a page containing only text and the typical cost of a page containing a large graphic image.

The cost per page provides a simple means of determining the overall running costs of a given printer. The figures given usually refer to the costs of *consumables* such as ink and replacement components (toner cartridges, drums and so on).

In general, laser printers and inkjet printers have slightly higher costs per page than other types. However, this is largely due to the fact these printers print at very high qualities. The cost per page tends to rise dramatically when printing in colour is carried out. In some cases, the cost per page can increase by a factor of more than ten.

Print quality

Dots per inch (DPI)

This describes the number of individual dots that can be printed within a space of one square inch.

Print quality is normally measured in dots per inch (dpi). This describes the number of individual dots that can be printed within a space of one square inch. Quality is normally compared with professional typesetting equipment used to produce a book or magazine. A typeset document is normally produced at a quality of between 1200 and 1500 dpi. However, since business documents seldom need to be produced to this standard, the typical 600 dpi quality provided by a laser printer is considered acceptable for business correspondence, reports and other documents.

Paper handling

Many organisations require the capability to print on envelopes, labels and card. In general, only inkjet and laser printers offer this facility. In addition, some laser and inkjet printers have special paper feeders that allow batches of envelopes or labels to be printed at a time.

The quantity of paper that a printer can hold is also an important factor when selecting a business printer for workgroup printing since a large paper capacity will reduce the need to refill the printer constantly.

Colour printing

At present, inkjet printers offer the best compromise between print quality and cost when producing documents in colour. Although other printers, such as colour laser printers, are capable of producing better results, printing costs can be prohibitive.

Volume

The volume of printing that will be carried out using a particular printer has implications for running costs, maintenance costs and reliability. Manufacturers often provide ratings for their printers that describe the typical workload appropriate for a given model. This value is often called the printer's **duty cycle** and is usually described in terms of **pages per month**. An inkjet printer, for example, might be described as appropriate for home use where the average monthly workload is likely to be less than 1000 pages per month. A laser printer might easily achieve volumes of 5000 pages per month or more.

Duty cycle

When referring to printers, this describes the typical monthly workload in terms of the number of pages printed.

Pages per month (ppm)

Manufacturers often provide ratings for their printers that describe the typical workload appropriate for a given model.

A common problem experienced by organisations using inkjet printers concerns increased printing costs. Many organisations acquire inkjet printers so that they have the facility to print documents in colour. In many cases this is seen as a facility that will be used infrequently, for specific documents on specific occasions. However, employees often overuse this facility, even printing internal and draft documents in colour. The result is often twofold: printing costs increase dramatically (sometimes by a factor of up to 20) and the working life of the printer is reduced significantly.

Speed

The speed of a printer can have a major impact on the work carried out within an organisation. Delays in printing documents can promote bottlenecks within administrative processes and are wasteful in terms of labour power. As an example, consider a household or motor insurance company. Such companies often print documents on demand, for example, a motor insurance quotation may be printed as the customer waits at the service counter. Clearly, printing the document quickly and efficiently has implications for customer service and company image.

Printing speeds are usually measured in **pages per minute (ppm)**. Typical examples of printing speeds are 12–20 ppm for an inkjet and 20 ppm and above for a laser printer.

Pages per minute (ppm)

A simple means of measuring the speed of a printer.

Primary storage

Data and instructions are loaded into memory such as random access memory. Such storage is temporary.

| Activity 3.5 | Selecting printers |

Using the criteria described in this section, select the most suitable type of printer for these applications:

- a student on a business course with a limited budget;
- a shared workgroup printer for ten people;
- proofing magazines;
- printing duplicate copies of invoices.

STORAGE DEVICES

Storage devices (Figure 3.5) are used to store programs, data awaiting processing and the information resulting from computer processing. Storage devices are categorised as **primary storage** when the data are loaded into computer memory or **secondary storage** when the data are stored on a separate device where the information will be retained even if the machine is switched off. This distinction is similar to that between human short-term and long-term memory.

Secondary storage

Floppy disks and hard disks are secondary storage which provides permanent storage.

Figure 3.5 Storage devices in context

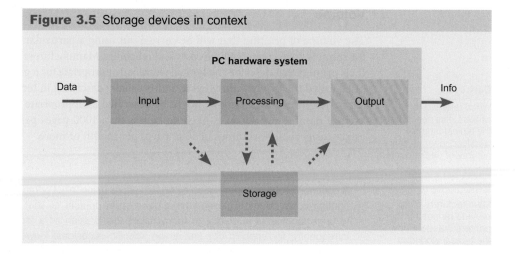

Units of data measurement

The capacity of a storage device is often measured in terms of kilobytes, megabytes and gigabytes. The following may help readers to understand these units.

- A **bit** is a single binary digit and represents a 0 (zero) or a 1. The bit is the smallest unit of measurement.
- A **byte** is made up of eight bits and represents a value between 0 and 255. A byte can be thought of as the amount of space required to hold a single character.
- A **kilobyte (kb)** is approximately 1000 bytes, or the equivalent of 1000 characters.
- A **megabyte (Mb)** is approximately 1000 kb, or the equivalent of one million characters.
- A **gigabyte (Gb)** is approximately 1000 Mb, or the equivalent of one billion characters.
- A terabyte (TB) is approximately 1000 Gb

The list below puts these numbers in context:

1. One character such as 'a'?

   A byte

2. *A typewritten page?*

   2 kilobytes (kilobyte = 1000 bytes)

3. *A low-resolution photograph?*

   100 kb (kilobyte = 1000 bytes)

4. *The complete works of Shakespeare?*

   5 megabytes (megabyte = 1,000,000 bytes)

5. *A standard CD-ROM?*

   700 megabytes (megabyte = 1,000,000 bytes)

6. *A pickup truck filled with documents?*

   1 gigabyte (gigabyte = 1,000,000,000 bytes)

7. *The works of Beethoven in digital audio format?*

   50 gigabytes

Bit

A single binary digit representing a 0 (zero) or a 1.

Byte

Made up of eight bits and represents the amount of space required to hold a single character.

Kilobyte (kb)

Approximately 1000 bytes, or the equivalent of 1000 characters.

Megabyte (Mb)

Approximately 1000 kb, or the equivalent of one million characters.

Gigabyte (Gb)

Approximately 1000 Mb, or the equivalent of one billion characters.

8. *50,000 trees made into paper and printed as documents?*

   terabyte (terabyte = 1,000,000,000,000 bytes)

9. *The printed collection of the US Library of Congress?*

   0 terabytes (terabyte = 1,000,000,000,000 bytes)

10. *All* printe*d material?*

    200 petabytes (petabyte = 1,000,000,000,000,000 bytes)

11. *All words ever spoken by human beings?*

    5 exabytes (exabyte = 1,000,000,000,000,000,000 bytes)

12. *Words possibly spoken by all beings in the Universe?*

    Zettabyte = 1,000,000,000,000,000,000,000 bytes

    Yottabyte = 1,000,000,000,000,000,000,000,000 bytes

Source: Roy Williams of Caltech.

Secondary storage – hard disks

Hard disk

A magnetic medium that stores data upon a number of rigid platters that are rotated at very high speeds.

Hard disk drives are a standard feature of a modern personal computer. They are used to store the computer's operating system, application software and data.

These are usually referred to as the 'C: drive' on PCs. On servers, network drives based on hard disks are typically denoted by a letter in the range F to Z.

A hard disk drive stores data upon a number of rigid platters that are rotated at very high speeds. Since the magnetic read/write heads float above the surface of the platter at a distance of a few microns, the drive mechanism is enclosed within a vacuum to protect against dust and other contaminants.

The major advantages of the hard disk drive are as follows:

- Hard disk drives tend to have large storage capacities, with typical capacities varying from 160 Gb to more than 3TB, easily capable of holding billions of pages of text.

Hybrid disk drive

A hard disk drive that contains a small amount of flash memory that can be used to speed up intensive tasks such as loading the operating system.

- A hard disk drive is considered a fast means of storing and retrieving data, for example a modern drive can be hundreds of times faster than a DVD drive. New **hybrid drives** have a relatively small amount of flash memory that can be used to speed up operations such as loading the operating system.

- The hard disk drive is a standard component of a personal computer system. As such they are relatively inexpensive to purchase or replace.

The major disadvantages of the hard disk drive are as follow:

- Hard disk drives are seen as delicate devices that are easily damaged. They are particularly susceptible to damage from sudden shocks and excessive vibration.

- In general, a hard disk drive is considered to be a fixed part of a computer system and is not portable. However, it should be noted that portable hard disk drives exist and are relatively inexpensive.

Flash drive

A flash drive is a portable storage device that connects to a computer via a standard USB port. Flash drives have no moving parts, so are reliable and robust.

Secondary storage – flash memory

Data are stored in flash memory, in an EEPROM (electrically erasable programmable read-only memory) chip that can retain its contents for as long as ten years before it begins to degrade. Since the **flash drive** appears to the operating system as a removable drive, users can copy, move or delete files just as if they are working with a hard disk. Like a rewritable disc, data can be written or erased many times and the drive can be locked to prevent files from being erased accidentally. Flash memory is in two main forms of a memory card (as used in a digital camera) and as a USB drive. USB drives connect to a personal computer via a standard USB port and require no special software to work.

Flash memory offers a number of advantages in that it is relatively inexpensive to buy and offer storage capacities of up to 128 Gb and beyond. Since it has no moving parts, it is robust and is considered extremely reliable. The use of a USB connection means that data can be transferred to and from a USB drive at high speed. In addition, flash memory requires no power supply and is portable between different operating systems and hardware.

A modern variation on the hard disk drive is the solid state drive (SSD), which uses flash memory to replace the mechanical parts found in a typical hard disk drive. Such drives operate much faster than an equivalent hard disk drive and are considered more robust. However, large capacity SSDs are considered expensive and unnecessary for routine office tasks.

Secondary storage – optical discs

Optical disc

The data on an optical disc are encoded as a series of dips and raised areas. Optical discs come in two main formats of compact discs (CD) and digital versatile discs (DVD).

The data on an optical disc are encoded as a series of dips and raised areas. These two states represent binary data – the same number system used by microprocessors. The player shines a laser beam onto the surface of the disc and measures the light that is reflected back. The intensity of the light that is reflected back enables the player to distinguish individual binary digits.

Optical discs come in two main formats. Compact discs (CD) typically store 700 Mb of data. Digital versatile discs (DVD) offer higher storage capacities, typically 4.7 Gb per side.

Primary storage – memory

Computer memory can take a number of different forms and is found within many of the devices that go to form part of a computer-based information system. Computers, printers, graphics cards, modems and many other devices all make use of various kinds of memory 'chips'. Although relatively expensive, memory is the fastest form of storage available.

There are two broad categories of computer memory: volatile and non-volatile. The contents of volatile memory are lost when the power to the device is switched off. On the other hand, non-volatile memory retains its contents until changed in some way.

Volatile memory

Anything held in memory is lost once the power to the computer system is switched off.

Non-volatile memory

Non-volatile memory retains its contents until altered or erased.

A digital camera is just one device that makes use of non-volatile memory. The memory found in a personal computer is considered volatile, that is, anything held in memory is lost once the power to the computer system is switched off. However, non-volatile memory retains its contents until altered or erased. Typically, non-volatile memory is housed in a small expansion card that can be inserted into a special slot on a digital camera, tablet computer or other device.

Random access memory (RAM)

RAM is used as volatile, working storage by a computer, holding instructions and data that are waiting to be processed.

Read-only memory (ROM)

The contents of ROM are fixed and cannot be altered. ROM is non-volatile.

Random access memory (RAM) is used as working storage, holding instructions and data that are waiting to be processed. The contents of RAM are volatile, that is, any data held are lost when the power to the computer system is switched off. A typical computer system will feature 4Gb, 8Gb or more of RAM. In general, the more RAM a computer system is equipped with, the faster it will operate and the more powerful it will be in terms of the complexity of the programs it can run. RAM is also found in a number of other devices, for example in a printer RAM is used to store an image of the document to be printed.

The contents of read-only memory (ROM) are fixed and cannot be altered. ROM is also non-volatile, making it ideal as a means of storing the information needed for a device to function properly. In a computer system, for example, the basic information needed so that the computer can access disk drives and control peripherals is stored in ROM. This prevents users from accidentally deleting or altering information essential to the computer's operation.

Some other forms of computer memory include the following:

EPROM (erasable programmable read-only memory)

This is a form of ROM memory that retains its contents until changed using a special device known as a 'burner'.

- An **EPROM (erasable programmable read-only memory)** is a type of ROM that retains its contents until they are changed using a special device (known as a 'burner').

- SDRAM (synchronous dynamic random access memory) is a common form of RAM found in many personal computers. New machines, however, make use of DDR SDRAM (double-data-rate synchronous dynamic RAM) which is roughly twice as fast as SDRAM. At present, the latest machines use variations on DDR memory that offer even higher performance known as DDR 3.

- CMOS, NMOS and PMOS memory are used as semi-permanent means of storage in a variety of different devices. Similar to EPROMs in many ways, a major difference is that no special device is needed to alter the contents of the memory. As an example, this kind of memory is generally used in computer systems as a means of storing any special settings needed to control the operation of the computer or a peripheral. This approach allows users to add or remove devices quickly and easily.

It is worth highlighting the wide range of ways in which computer memory is used. In a domestic environment, for example, one might find memory chips in television sets, satellite receivers, DVD recorders, burglar alarm systems, alarm clocks, washing machines, microwave ovens, hi-fi equipment and a variety of other devices.

In terms of a computer-based information system, the following examples illustrate the range of applications to which computer memory can be put:

- In a modem, ROM is used to store the commands used to control communications and any special settings the user has specified.

- In a laser printer, special ROM cards can be used to expand the printer's range of typefaces. Additional RAM can also be added to speed up printing or allow the printing of more complex documents.

Cache memory

Used to improve performance by anticipating the data and instructions needed by the processor. The required data are retrieved and held in the cache, ready to be transferred directly to the processor when required.

- In a computer system, **cache memory** is used to improve performance by anticipating the data and instructions that will be needed by the processor. The required data are retrieved and held in the cache, ready to be transferred directly to the processor when required. By removing the need for data to be retrieved from the computer's much slower main memory (RAM), the overall speed of the system is improved. The *hit rate* describes how often a correct prediction has been made in terms of the data needed by the processor. In general, the higher the hit rate, the greater the increase in performance.

- Another form of cache memory used on a PC is the virtual memory created on the hard disk when the RAM capacity is exceeded. Once too many programs are running in the RAM, additional temporary storage on the hard disk is used. This is cache or virtual memory. Note that although this enables the PC to continue operating, it slows considerably since accessing the virtual memory on the hard disk is significantly slower than accessing the primary RAM. This indicates the importance of investing in sufficient RAM to avoid the need to use the slower virtual memory.

Selecting storage devices

The selection of a storage device will normally be based upon speed, storage capacity and cost. However, the importance of these factors will vary according to the function being performed, for example speed might be considered of little importance when making a backup of data overnight. Table 3.1 summarises some of the characteristics of several typical storage devices.

Table 3.1 Comparison between storage media and devices

Storage medium	Speed	Cost	Capacity	Permanency
Magnetic tape	Very slow	Very low	Very high	No
Hard disk drive	Very Fast	Low	Very high	No
CD-ROM	Slow	Low	Low	Yes
Flash Memory	Fast	Medium	Low	No
Memory	Very fast	High	Low	No/yes

Speed

Many of the tasks carried out by a computer-based information system require large quantities of data to be processed quickly and efficiently. In many cases, the overall time taken to complete an action will depend upon the speed of the storage device used.

Access time

The average time taken to locate a specific item of data.

The speed of a storage device is usually measured in terms of its **access time** (sometimes known as 'seek time') and data transfer rate. The access time refers to the average time taken to locate a specific item of data. Access times are normally given in milliseconds, for example a typical hard disk drive might have an access time of 9 ms or faster.

Data transfer rate

The rate at which a device is able to read continuous blocks of data.

The **data transfer rate** describes how quickly the device is able to read continuous blocks of data. This figure is normally expressed in terms of kilobytes or megabytes. A typical data transfer rate for a CD drive, for example, might be given as 4.8 Mb per second, whilst a hard disk drive might achieve transfer rates of 60 Mb per second or higher.

Capacity

The storage capacity of a given device will be measured in kilobytes, megabytes or gigabytes, for example a standard CD has a storage capacity of 700 Mb. Some storage devices, such as a hard disk drive, will have a fixed storage capacity whilst others will use removable media that provide an almost unlimited amount of data storage. In general, a fixed storage device will operate faster than one that uses removable media. In addition, many applications generate large data files that cannot be stored conveniently on removable media. A database file, for example, can easily exceed the capacity of a CD, DVD or other kind of removable disk.

Cost of storage

Cost per megabyte

A simple means of gauging the costs associated with a given storage device.

The costs associated with storage devices are normally given in terms of **cost per megabyte**. In some cases, the cost per megabyte is based upon the cost of the hardware, in others it is based upon the cost of media. Two simple examples should help to make this clearer:

- A hard disk drive has a fixed capacity, so the cost per megabyte can be calculated by simply dividing the cost of the hard drive by its storage capacity.
- A DVD-RW drive uses removable media with a capacity of approximately 4Gb. The cost per megabyte would be calculated by dividing the cost of a single DVD-R disc by 4000.

Given the ever-increasing storage capacities of storage media, it is often appropriate to measure the cost per *gigabyte* rather than cost per megabyte.

Other factors

A number of other factors should be taken into consideration when selecting a storage device. Amongst these are the following:

- The *reliability* of a storage device can be an important factor in many circumstances, for example a hardware failure might prevent all access to important business data.

Furthermore, errors introduced when storing or reading data might also have serious consequences. For example, a small error on a magnetic tape cartridge might lead to the loss of all of the data held on the cartridge. For most hardware devices, including storage devices such as hard disk drives, reliability is often measured in terms of **mean time between failures (MTBF)**. This describes the average time that the device can operate before failure; the longer the MTBF, generally the more reliable the device.

■ *Permanence* of storage is important if there is a need to protect data from being deleted or altered. A more permanent form of storage can also be desirable if the data held are unlikely to change often. Reference materials, for example, are often distributed on CD or DVD.

■ It may often be necessary to take *security* measures to prevent data from being stolen or damaged. Flash drives, for instance, can be transported easily from one location to another. Whilst this can provide added security, it can also increase risk of theft. Fixed devices, such as hard disk drives, are less vulnerable but also less versatile.

Mean time between failures (MTBF)

This is a measurement of the reliability of a given device. The longer the MTBF, generally the more reliable the device. Figures for MTBF are quoted for a wide variety of devices, ranging from hard disk drives to monitors.

Activity 3.6   Hardware selection

Using the criteria described in this section, select the most suitable type of storage device (with numerical specifications) to perform these functions:

■ a backup device for a student working on their dissertation;
■ a backup device for a designer transferring large files between their home and work offices;
■ a graphic designer who requires large graphics to be held in memory;
■ web pages on a web server.

PROCESSORS

Processor

Uses instructions from software to control the different components of a computer.

The central processing unit (CPU) – or **processor** (Figure 3.6) – found within a computer consists of two components: a *control unit* and an *arithmetic logic unit* (ALU). The control unit fetches instructions from software that has been loaded into memory, decodes them and then executes them. The control unit controls the operation of all hardware, including all input/output operations. The ALU carries out arithmetical calculations, for example addition, and can also make comparisons between values. An often-used analogy is to compare the processor to the human brain – which has a similar control function over the other parts of the body. The brain controls bodily function according to stimuli monitored by different sensory organs of the body. The analogy is not entirely appropriate since the human brain is of course a very complex part of the human system, also containing permanent and volatile memory functions for example!

Clock speed

Measured in MHz (megahertz, or millions of pulses per second). The clock speed is governed by a quartz-crystal circuit.

Bus width

Describes how many pieces of data can be transmitted or received at one time by the bus connecting the processor to other components of the PC.

The speed of a processor will depend upon a number of different factors. Two such factors are clock speed and bus width. The **clock speed** determines how many instructions per second the processor can execute. The **bus width** describes how many pieces of data can be transmitted at one time. In both cases, the higher the value, the more powerful the processor. Clock speed and bandwidth values can be helpful when attempting to compare processors in order to select the most appropriate. For example, clock speeds for the Pentium range of processors have varied from 60 MHz in early versions through to several GHz in more recent versions. However, clock speeds are not always a reliable measure of speed or efficiency. Some of AMD's processors, for example, operate at slower clock speeds than Intel's but offer similar – and sometimes – superior overall performance.

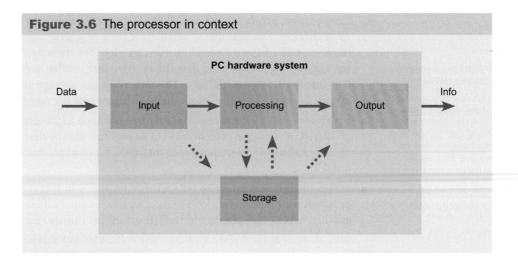

Figure 3.6 The processor in context

Most IBM-compatible personal computers are based upon a series of processors manufactured by Intel and several of its competitors. In recent years, Intel has faced increased competition from rivals such as AMD. Competitors such as AMD manufacture processors that are compatible with various Intel processors but they tend to market them at lower prices. The FX processors manufactured by AMD, for example, are broadly equivalent to Intel's Pentium and i-Series processors.

> Intel's first microprocessor, the 4004, ran at 108 kilohertz (108,000 hertz), compared to the Pentium 4 processor's initial speed of 1.5 gigahertz (1.5 billion hertz). If automobile speed had increased similarly over the same period, you could drive from San Francisco to New York in about 13 seconds.
>
> Source: Intel processor museum (**www.intel.com**)

It is important to recognise that not all aspects of performance of a computer are governed by the processor. As a general rule, the faster the processor, the faster and more efficient the computer. However, referring back to the section on virtual memory, RAM capacity, hard disk speed and graphics cards can also have a significant impact on overall system performance.

Multi-core processor

The latest CPUs combine two or more cores (processors) within a single physical device.

Multi-core processors

The latest generation of processors from manufacturers such as Intel and AMD contain two or more processors (cores) combined within a single physical unit. This arrangement can provide significant performance improvements depending on a various factors. As an example, most software is not designed to share processing tasks between multiple processors and so does not take advantage of the processor's ability to process several instructions at the same time. In general, each core provides a performance improvement amounting to between 50 and 80 per cent of a single processor. In other words, a dual-core processor will not operate twice as fast as a machine with a single processor – it will run only 50 to 80 per cent faster.

Multi-core processors are attractive to business buyers for several reasons:

- They are compatible with existing systems. This can make upgrades more cost-effective than replacing equipment, even if the upgrade process requires other components to be replaced.

- Multi-core processors are relatively inexpensive, adding little to the cost of a new system.

- Multi-core processors enable *virtual computing*, which is described in the next section.
- Multi-core processors consume less power than earlier CPUs and generate less heat. This makes systems cheaper to operate and more environmentally friendly.

Accelerated processing unit (APU)

Describes a processor that typically incorporates an additional GPU, removing the need for a separate graphics card while providing other benefits, such as reduced power consumption and performance improvements.

Graphics processing unit (GPU)

Describes circuitry integrated into a new form of processor, the APU. The GPU removes the need for a separate graphics card.

A recent development has been the introduction of accelerated processing units (APU), processors that typically incorporate an additional graphics processing unit (GPU). The addition of a GPU often removes the need for a separate graphics card while providing other benefits, such as reduced power consumption and performance improvements. For industry, APUs can significantly reduce the initial purchase cost of a computer as well as running costs. As an example, AMD's range of APUs is found in many low-cost systems intended for routine office work.

With the increase in popularity of mobile computing devices, such as tablets and smartphones, there has been growing demand for low cost, powerful processors with very low power consumption. This demand has been met by companies such as ARM Holdings, a British designer of RISC (reduced instruction set computing) processors. RISC processors use a simplified set of instructions that can be executed more quickly than the more complex instructions used by traditional processors. This allows some tasks to be carried out faster, including common tasks performed by smartphones, tablets and other mobile devices. Many of the mobile devices in use today are based around the *Cortex* series of processors designed by Arm Holdings.

Green computing

Green computing

Adopting policies and procedures to ensure resources are used as efficiently as possible so that environmental impact is minimised.

Building systems that use less power is important as companies begin to adopt policies and procedures supporting green computing. Green computing is sometimes known as green ICT, energy efficient computing or sustainable computing. While there are some differences between these terms, many people see them as being interchangeable. Green computing involves using resources as efficiently as possible with the aim of minimising any environmental impact. As an example, encouraging staff to switch off PCs at the end of the working day reduces costs and helps to reduce damage to the environment. The Carbon Trust estimates that a typical PC costs around £45 per year to run. Switching it off when it is not being used can reduce the cost to less than £10. Imagine the potential savings in the UK alone, where approximately 10 million PCs were sold in 2013.

Virtual computing

Virtual machine (VM)

A computer with sufficient memory and storage space can be used to emulate an entire computer system in software. Each VM behaves exactly the same as a physical computer and can be used in the same way.

Multi-core processors are considered responsible for the rise in popularity of virtual computing. Virtual computing involves simulating a complete computer system in software. The virtual machine (VM) behaves exactly the same as a physical computer system and can be used in the same way.

In general, virtual machines are implemented using a software package such as *VMware Workstation* or *Microsoft Virtual PC*. The software manages the computer's resources, reserving processor time, memory (RAM), hard disk space and other physical resources for the VM. Each VM runs its own operating system and applications, using the reserved RAM and hard disk space to store any programs and data. As an example, when the VM is created the user is asked to specify how much hard disk space to reserve for it. On a computer with 340 Gb of hard disk space, the user might reserve, say, 100 Gb. The reserved space will no longer be accessible to the host computer but the VM will 'see' its own 100 Gb hard disk drive (labelled 'C:'). Eventually, the user will be able to install an operating system and software onto the virtual drive and use it just like a physical unit. The software used to create the virtual machine also allows other physical devices to be treated as if they are part of the VM. For example, the VM will be able to access DVD drives, network cards, modems, printers, USB ports and other devices.

A single physical computer can host several virtual machines at the same time and each VM will be entirely independent of any other. However, on a machine with a single processor, performance will decrease as more virtual machines are hosted. This is because the processor must share its time between the VMs. On the other hand, there will be less of an impact on a multi-core machine because each VM can be assigned its own processor.

An entire VM – including operating system, software and the contents of memory – can be saved to a disk file called a *snapshot*. This facility provides two important benefits. First, VMs are portable and can be transferred from one computer system to another. Second, snapshots can be used as backups, enabling the entire VM to be restored to a prior state within a matter of minutes.

The main benefits associated with virtual computing include:

- The ability to run multiple operating systems allows software developers to develop and test applications on a single machine.
- Organisations can adopt a standardised computing environment by deploying VM snapshots. Installations and upgrades will be quicker and users will not be prevented from accessing any specialised software or hardware they need for one-off tasks.
- Data can be transferred between different operating systems quickly and easily.
- Users can bring their systems with them wherever they go. As an example, a user can use a VM to bring their entire desktop – including documents and data files – home at the weekend.
- The ability to use multiple operating systems means that VMs can be created to emulate legacy systems. This means that it is no longer necessary to maintain outdated equipment. In addition, a VM often runs more quickly than the legacy system being emulated, saving a great deal of time and potentially removing the need to migrate to a new, faster system.
- VMs can be used to handle network applications; a single physical computer can create a virtual network environment that includes client, server and database virtual machines.
- VMs can maximise the use of computing resources. As an example, several computers that are being underutilised can be replaced by a single computer running a number of VMs.

Case Study 3.2 demonstrates the benefits of virtual computing

CASE STUDY 3.2

Hertz reaps virtualisation rewards

By Paul Taylor

It may sound like something out of a sci-fi novel or Star Trek movie, but there are solid business reasons for companies to 'virtualise' their IT infrastructure.

By virtualising their servers (transforming a physical server using software into one or more virtual machines), companies can make better use of IT resources and react faster to changing demands.

Hertz International, the vehicle rental company, faced the choice of either refreshing its existing server and PC infrastructure at 1,000 sites across Europe at considerable expense, or implementing newer technologies.

'With 5,000 PCs to manage, the cost of technology was a constant battle,' says Paul Bermingham, vice-president of IT services, who is in charge of Hertz's global IT.

'Due to the nature of our business, the operational infrastructure is highly complex and dispersed,' he says. 'This puts a lot of pressure on our IT system and our ability to keep spiralling IT costs under control, while offering employees the technology services they require to do their jobs well.'

In addition to centralising its servers and reducing support costs, Hertz wanted to simplify its complex desktop infrastructure, improve Payment Card Industry (PCI) compliance and security systems, reduce power consumption and improve user experience.

After reviewing its options, Hertz decided to use EMC's VMware software to virtualise its servers and replace its legacy desktop devices with 'zero-client' terminals supplied by Dell's Wyse Technology unit.

'By virtualising our server and desktop estate with VMware, we were able to cut costs and free up resources to focus innovation and customer service, while dramatically simplifying our IT infrastructure and transforming how we support over 1,000 desktops in our service centre in Dublin,' says Mr Bermingham.

By simplifying its IT infrastructure, Hertz was able to cut help-desk calls by a third (giving the IT team more time to work on new services) and cut power costs by 10 per cent.

But one of the greatest benefits is that Hertz can now scale its computing requirements up and down according to demand. For example, its main office in Scotland experiences a rapid increase in demand during the British Open and Ryder Cup tournaments, while holiday destinations such as Italy and France see peaks in demand across the summer.

Using the virtualisation software, IT can anticipate and meet demand using virtual desktops instead of having to set up new physical PCs. Feedback from employees has been highly positive, with many describing it as a 'quantum leap' in technology for the company.

Upgrading and rolling out software packages has also become far simpler because the IT team no longer has to visit every PC and laptop individually. So far, Hertz has virtualised over 300 desktop applications through VMware ThinApp, which has helped the company standardise applications across devices and improve application speeds.

Compliance (with PCI) has also increased; (antivirus) patch management – a key factor in keeping corporate IT systems secure – is now done through servers rather than PCs, meaning that software is always up to date.

New uses can also be added quickly and, once plugged in, they will have instant access to the latest software and applications without needing support from an engineer. In addition, since everything is held centrally in the European Shared Services data centre in Dublin, security risks are considerably reduced.

'While this started off as a European project, the wider international Hertz network and franchisees have become interested in rolling out VDI as well and we are currently looking into how we can extend it to countries including China, Australia and New Zealand,' says Mr Bermingham. 'It is great to see something we developed in our Dublin Innovation Centre recognised as having the potential to be rolled out across the globe.'

Hertz is also considering extending virtualisation to encompass voice and video services. 'VMware has enabled us to build extremely strong foundations to realise even greater benefits, as we add more and more services and extend the research of the programme internationally,' says Mr Bermingham. 'This is only the start for us.'

Source: Tayor, P. (2013) Hertz reaps virtualisation rewards. *Financial Times*. 1 June.
© The Financial Times Limited 2013. All Rights Reserved.

QUESTION

Discuss the advantages of virtual computing.

Activity 3.7   Selecting processors

Since this book was published, the clock speed of processors will have increased significantly. Using a site that reviews hardware such as CNet (**www.cnet.com**) or ZDNet (www.zdnet.com) select the best processor specifications for:

- an entry-level 'cheap and cheerful' basic PC;
- a high-end PC for a graphics designer;
- a web server.

FOCUS ON...   MANAGING TECHNOLOGICAL CHANGE

A major difficulty for companies wishing to apply information systems to help their businesses is how often technology changes. The speed of this change occurs through the competitiveness of the IT industry. If the leading vendors do not introduce new products, they can quickly be overtaken by smaller companies, or even startups: witness the speed at which Microsoft moved from being a small player to toppling IBM as one of the world's leading software companies or the speed with which Facebook and Google became two of the largest companies in the world.

Moore's law

Gordon Moore, co-founder of Intel, predicted in 1965 that the transistor density of semiconductor chips would double roughly every 18 months. This prediction has actually happened as we have moved from different generations of processors, such as from 8086 to 80286 and through to the Pentium 4.

The problem of change refers to hardware, software and entire business information systems, but it is perhaps best evidenced by the speed in change of processors. Improvements in processing power are indicated by *Moore's law*.

Alongside this increase in the capacity and speed of processors, the capacity and speed of primary RAM storage and secondary magnetic disk storage have also increased dramatically, allowing larger, more complex, software to be run. The hardware improvements have permitted more complex software to be built, and this in turn requires newer hardware, since software designers tend to design new systems for the fastest machines available. To some extent, the speed of change in other hardware and software is governed by the rate at which processing power increases.

20,000,000 is the number of times cheaper that computing grew, between 1940 and 2000, according to David Mowery, economic historian at University of California, Berkeley.

How do these technical changes affect a business? Many managers would answer that they result in unnecessary expense and disruption. While this may be true, managers do not have to adopt the latest technologies if they do not believe that they are delivering benefits. So why are new technologies adopted? The reason may often be fear: fear that if your competitor has upgraded to the latest Intel version, or Windows or business system, then they may have a competitive advantage. If you perceive that your competitor has, or may develop, a competitive advantage, then this is a powerful incentive to invest in new systems.

Much of this investment cycle may be driven by uncertainty and the fear of falling behind. Industry figures seem to suggest that companies overestimate the benefits that new systems can give them and underestimate the risk of project failure. The productivity paradox, which was popularised by Strassman (1997), seemed to suggest that there is little or no correlation between a company's investment in information systems and its business performance measured in terms of profitability or stock returns (see Chapter 13 for further discussion).

Techniques for dealing with technological change

There is a continuum of approaches for how managers deal with technological change. The approaches are informed by considering the typical pattern for the diffusion of innovation summarised by Rogers (1983). Figure 3.7 illustrates a typical curve for adoption of any innovation by consumers or businesses, whether it be a new processor, a new form of storage such as DVD, or a new business concept such as e-business. One adoption approach is to be an early adopter, who always tries to be the first to make use of new technologies to gain a competitive advantage. The second is to use a more conservative 'wait-and-see' approach

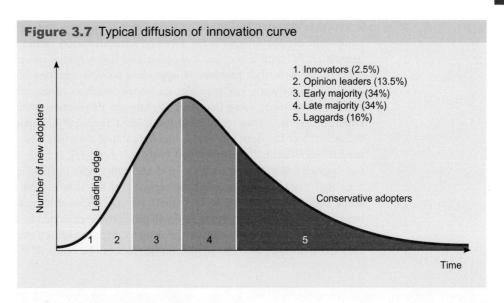

Figure 3.7 Typical diffusion of innovation curve

and not use new technology until its benefits have been successfully demonstrated by other companies in your sector. Of course, there is a continuum here and most companies would seek to position themselves somewhere between the two extremes.

The problem with being an early adopter is that the leading edge of development is often also referred to as the 'bleeding edge' of technology due to the risk of failure. New systems may have many bugs, may integrate poorly with the existing system or may simply not live up to their promise. The counterargument to this is that, although the risks of adoption are high, so are the rewards, since you may gain an edge on your rivals. American Airlines gained a considerable advantage over its rivals when it first introduced the SABRE customer reservation system. Similarly, the banks that first introduced new techniques such as auto-teller machines and phone banking facilities also managed to increase market share. The examples in the box show people and organisations that have been too conservative – not envisaging the benefits of new hardware or technology approaches.

Reported quotations from conservative technology adopters

'This "telephone" has too many shortcomings to be seriously considered as a means of communication. The device is inherently of no value to us.'

Western Union internal memo, 1876.

'Who the hell wants to hear actors talk?'

H.M. Warner, Warner Brothers, 1927.

'I think there is a world market for maybe five computers.'

Thomas Watson, chairman of IBM, 1943.

'There is no reason anyone would want a computer in their home.'

Ken Olson, Founder of DEC, 1977.

Keeping pace with PC software and hardware

There is a tendency for hardware vendors to retain their entry-level price as technology improves. For $1000 or £1000 the specification that is available has increased dramatically over the past five years. Yet this price bracket seems to be that most commonly used in business adverts. The result of this is that a business manager may over-specify the equipment needed for end-users. Does an administration assistant really need the latest-generation PC with a very fast processor and full memory complement for simple word processing? A further problem is upgrading to new versions of operating systems and applications software. For example, a company such as Microsoft needs to produce new versions of software every few years to maintain its revenue stream. The question for the business user is, do we really need these latest versions? Companies will often find that the benefits of the new software are marginal and the costs and disruption of upgrading may be significant. Remember that costs will not only include upgrading the software, but upgrades to hardware such as RAM and processors to run the new software, and also training for staff. Some people have argued that the slow uptake of Windows 8 is due to many companies choosing to keep their existing software because they perceive that the benefits are likely to be marginal and will probably be exceeded by the costs. Effectively, the argument is that organisations are choosing to 'skip' one or more versions of Windows until they feel that some new and significant benefits can be realised.

CATEGORIES OF SOFTWARE

Software

A series of detailed instructions that control the operation of a computer system. Software exists as programs that are developed by computer programmers.

Systems software

This form of software manages and controls the operation of the computer system as it performs tasks on behalf of the user.

Operating system (OS)

Software that interacts with the hardware of the computer in order to manage and direct the computer's resources.

Software can be defined as a series of detailed instructions that control the operation of a computer system. Software exists as *programs* which are developed by computer programmers. Software is less tangible than hardware – the instructions that make up a program are translated into binary instructions (a series of 0 and 1 digits) for the processor hardware.

There are two major categories of software: systems software and applications software. Managers purchasing new BIS have to specify their requirements for both categories. Figure 3.8 illustrates the major categories of information systems software.

Systems software

Systems software manages and controls the operation of the computer system as it performs tasks on behalf of the user. Systems software consists of three basic categories: operating systems, development programs and utility programs.

Operating systems

The operating system (OS) interacts with the hardware of the computer by monitoring and sending instructions to manage and direct the computer's resources. Figure 3.9 indicates

Figure 3.8 Categories of computer software

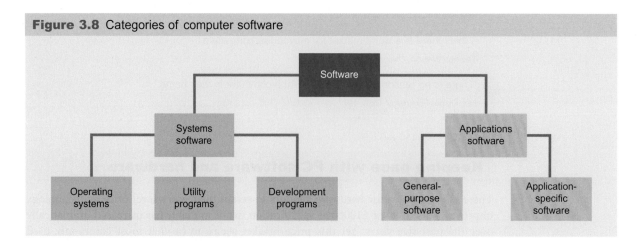

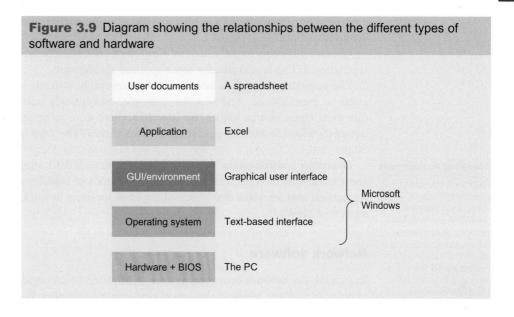

Figure 3.9 Diagram showing the relationships between the different types of software and hardware

the relationship between the operating system, the hardware and other types of software for a typical computer system. The components can be considered as different layers, with information being passed between the layers as the user interacts with the application. The operating system functions as an intermediary between the functions the user needs to perform, for example a spreadsheet calculation, and how these translate to and from the hardware in the form of responding to mouse clicks and displaying information on the screen. Older operating systems, such as Microsoft DOS, can be described as being text-based, whilst more modern operating systems, such as Windows 8, use a GUI (graphical user interface) operating environment. When a PC first starts, the BIOS stored in ROM is used to start the operating system loading.

The basic functions of the operating system include: allocating and managing system resources, scheduling the use of resources and monitoring the activities of the computer system. Examples of these functions include the following:

- controlling access to storage devices, for example disk drives;
- coordinating and controlling peripheral devices, for example printers;
- allowing users to input data and issue instructions, for example by allowing data to be entered via the keyboard;
- coordinating and controlling the operation of programs, for example by scheduling processor time;
- managing the computer's memory;
- performing file management and access control, for example by allowing certain users to create, view or delete files;
- dealing with errors, for example by displaying a message to the user if a fault is detected within a hardware component.

Operating systems can be controlled by either a text-based or a graphical interface. A text-based interface uses a **command line interpreter (CLI)** to accept instructions from the user. MS-DOS (Microsoft Disk Operating System) and some versions of Linux are examples of operating systems that use a CLI.

A **graphical user interface (GUI)** allows users to enter instructions using a mouse. The mouse is used to issue instructions using menus and icons. The term **WIMP** (windows, icons, mouse and pull-down menus) is often used to describe this kind of

Command line interpreter (CLI)

Passes instructions from a user to a computer program in the form of brief statements entered via the keyboard.

Graphical user interface (GUI)

Provides a means for a user to control a computer program using a mouse to issue instructions using menus and icons.

WIMP

Windows, icons, mouse and pull-down menus (WIMP) is often used to describe a GUI environment.

environment. Examples of operating systems using a GUI are Windows 8 and some versions of Unix.

Operating systems for PCs such as Windows 8 are normally 'bundled' when a computer is purchased. This is also true for some applications software.

The popularity of mobile devices has seen several new touch-based operating systems come to prominence. Android, for example, was quickly adopted by manufacturers due to its Open Source nature. By late 2013, there were more than one billion Android devices worldwide and the operating system's share of the smartphone market exceeded 80 per cent.

Operating environments describe programs intended to simplify the way in which users work with the operating system. Early versions of Windows, for example, provided a graphical user interface that removed the need for users to work with the more complex aspects of MS-DOS.

Network software

In general, the **network operating system (NOS)** used by an organisation will provide the majority of facilities required to support workgroup computing. For example, the NOS will allow a network manager to define a group of users as belonging to a particular workgroup. Some of the typical services provided by the NOS include:

- A centralised storage space can be created on the network system for the exclusive use of workgroup members.
- The security features of the NOS can be used to restrict access to documents and other data by those outside of the workgroup.
- The workgroup can be given network privileges that allow individual members access to resources and facilities that are not normally available to others. For example, many organisations with only limited Internet and e-mail facilities restrict access to key members of staff.

NOS are now often integrated with operating systems such as Microsoft Windows 8 and UNIX. However, older systems still exist that use third-party software such as Novell Netware in conjunction with earlier versions of Microsoft Windows.

Network operating software is described in more detail later (in Chapter 5).

Utility programs

Utility programs provide a range of tools that support the operation and management of a computer system. Programs that monitor system performance or provide security controls are examples of utility programs.

Development programs

Development programs allow users to develop their own software in order to carry out processing tasks using programming languages.

Programming languages can be described in terms of their historical position in the development of computer programming systems. Table 3.2 shows how programming languages have become more accessible to business users over time.

Applications software

Applications software can be defined as a set of programs that enable users to perform specific information-processing activities. Applications software can be divided into two broad categories: general-purpose and application-specific.

Operating environment

Programs intended to simplify the way in which users work with the operating system. Early versions of *Windows*, for example, provided a graphical user interface that removed the need for users to work with the more complex aspects of MS-DOS.

Network operating system (NOS)

This describes the software needed to operate and manage a network system.

Utility programs

Utility programs provide a range of tools that support the operation and management of a computer system.

Development programs

Allow users to develop their own software in order to carry out processing tasks.

Applications software

A set of programs that enable users to perform specific information processing activities that may be general-purpose or application-specific.

Table 3.2   The development of different programming languages

Generation	Characteristics and advantages	Main disadvantages
First generation	Early computer systems were programmed using machine language that consisted of strings of binary digits.	Programs were considered expensive to develop as they took extremely long periods of time to design, code and test.
Second generation	Assembly language represented an attempt to simplify the process of creating computer programs. Symbols and abbreviations were used to create sequences of instructions. An assembler or low-level language was used to translate a completed assembly language program into the machine code required by the computer.	Relatively slow for certain tasks, such as those involving large-scale data processing. Remained difficult to create large or complex programs using assembly language.
Third generation	Provided a more natural means of developing programs by enabling users to create programs made up of English-like statements. Such programming languages are still in use today and are known as 'high-level languages'. Languages such as COBOL, Fortran, C++ and Java allow users to develop programs quickly and easily.	Resulting applications were sometimes slow and inefficient.
Fourth generation	A drive towards even greater ease of use has resulted in the development of new programming systems designed to allow even non-technical users to develop their own applications. The focus of such tools as Microsoft Visual Basic. NET is on ease of use and the rapid development of applications, especially interactive, web-based applications. Examples of common programming tools include report generators, query languages and application generators.	Some programming knowledge is still necessary.
Fifth generation	Developments in this area may result in programming systems that accept a spoken question from a user and then generate a computer program intended to produce the required information.	Artificial intelligence techniques are still not sufficiently developed to make this a practical reality.

General-purpose applications

General-purpose applications are programs that can be used to carry out a wide range of common tasks. A word processor, for example, is capable of producing a variety of documents that are suitable for many different purposes. This type of application is often referred to as **productivity software** since it helps improve the efficiency of an individual.

The next sections in this chapter will describe the use of some general-purpose applications software in more detail for each of these business tasks that are carried out in an office:

Productivity software

This describes a category of computer software that aims to support users in performing a variety of common tasks.

- *Document production and graphics software.* This involves the creation of various internal and external documents, including letters, reports, invoices, notes and minutes of meetings. Various types of software can be used to support these activities, including text editors, word processors and desktop publishing packages.

- *Spreadsheets – software for processing numerical information.* All organisations require the means to store, organise and analyse numerical data. The spreadsheet program represents the most common means of carrying out these tasks.

- *Databases – software for storage and retrieval of information.* All organisations require the means to store, organise and retrieve information. Electronic database packages represent the most common means of carrying out these tasks. (Databases are covered in Chapter 4.)
- *Multimedia software.* Multimedia involves the user interacting with a computer using media such as text, sound, animation and video. Its main business applications are computer-based training and customer service in retail applications.
- *Software for using the Internet.* This describes activities involving internal and external communications. Significant examples include electronic mail (e-mail) and the use of web browsers to find information on the World Wide Web.
- *Management applications of productivity software.* Software for personal information management and team working.

Application-specific software

Application-specific software comprises programs intended to serve a specific purpose or carry out a clearly defined information processing task. Software designed to carry out payroll processing or manage accounts are examples of application-specific programs.

Application-specific packages such as software for use in the accounting or marketing function or enterprise resource planning software used across the organisation are described later (in Chapter 6).

Activity 3.8	The interaction between hardware and software

Develop an explanation of the purpose of and interaction between hardware, systems software and applications software to someone who is unfamiliar with them. To help the explanation use an example based on the creation of a spreadsheet to calculate wages based on hours worked and refer to Figure 3.9 earlier. Start your description with when the PC is first switched on.

DOCUMENT PRODUCTION SOFTWARE

Word_processor

Provides the ability to enter, edit, store and print text and layout different elements of a document.

Desktop publishing

Is concerned with the overall appearance of documents, placing a great deal of emphasis on features that provide control over the layout and presentation of a document.

One of the most common activities in a business organisation is the production of documents for internal or external use. Internal documents, such as an inter-office memo, are generally used to support communications within an organisation. External documents, such as a sales brochure, are generally used to support communications with customers, suppliers and other agencies.

The requirements for internal and external documents are often very different. The appearance of an internal document, for example, is seldom important since the document's main purpose is to convey information quickly and efficiently. However, since the appearance of an external document can have an impact on an organisation's image and reputation, a great deal of emphasis is often placed upon presentation.

Activity 3.9	Internal and external documents

Internal documents can include inter-office memos, reports and summaries, such as minutes of meetings. External documents can include invoices, sales brochures and correspondence. Using these examples, identify some of the other characteristics of internal and external documents. Are any of the characteristics identified common to both internal and external documents?

Document management

Involves managing documents such as company procedures, letters from customers or invoices from suppliers which are circulated to people throughout an organisation.

Paperless office

Describes the office environment of the future where paper documents are redundant and have been replaced by their electronic counterparts.

Office automation systems

By attempting to automate many of the activities carried out within a typical office, organisations seek to improve efficiency, reduce costs and enhance internal communications. Computer-based information systems used in this way are generally referred to as office automation systems.

A modern view of document production views technology used in three basic ways: word processing, desktop publishing and document management.

- **Word processing** is concerned with entering or editing text, with emphasis on the *content* of the document. Word processing allows the production of simple documents but gives more limited control over layout, compared with desktop publishing.

- **Desktop publishing** is concerned with the overall *appearance* of documents, placing a great deal of emphasis on features that provide control over the layout and presentation of a document.

- **Document management** involves managing documents such as company procedures, letters from customers or invoices from suppliers which are circulated to people throughout an organisation. Over time, the distinctions between different categories of document production software have become blurred. A modern word processor, for example, will often have much of the functionality of a desktop publishing program. Similarly, many desktop publishing packages now have sophisticated text editing features and no longer rely on users preparing the different elements of a document in advance. Document management can help to improve the efficiency of various administrative processes, particularly those concerned with storing, finding and retrieving information. Note that the paperless office is a concept that has been suggested for more than 30 years, but has failed to materialise in many organisations. Computer-based information systems used in this way are generally referred to as office automation systems. Applications of these systems and the software used to support them are described later (in Chapter 6).

Word processing

A word processor provides the ability to enter, edit, store and print text. In addition, word processing packages allow users to alter the layout of documents and often provide a variety of formatting tools.

CASE STUDY 3.3

Business life – rise of the paperless meeting

By Alexandra Stevenson

Once upon a time, Gerhard Roggeman would have disagreed with the saying that it is better to travel than to arrive. As a director on the board of a clutch of international companies, he spends much of his work life travelling and much of that travel time weighed down by thousands of pages of board meeting paperwork.

His burden will be a familiar one for many executives and company secretaries – one London-listed company recently even had to helicopter documents to a director located on an island off the coast of Australia.

Since Apple's iPad ushered in the age of the tablet in 2010, however, it has become easier to convince board members – many of whom are barely acquainted with a laptop, to consider a portable digital.

'It is a huge progress in technology,' says Mr Roggeman, who now uses his iPad for board meetings at Resolution,

the insurance consolidation vehicle, and Deutsche Börse. 'It really facilitates my job.'

As directors begin to swap wads of documents for tablet devices, stuffy boardrooms stacked with papers are turning into scenes more akin to science-fiction films. According to Diligent, a digital solutions business, its clients include 20 FTSE 100 that now use iPads in their board meetings – including Barclays, retailer Kingfisher and Weir Group, a pumps and valves manufacturer. The tablets are mainly used with apps that allow companies to consolidate boardroom documents into 'virtual boardbooks'.

Edis-Bates Associates, a consultancy, found that 40 per cent of 150 London-listed companies surveyed last year were using electronic means to distribute board meeting documents. 'It is all changing at a tremendous pace,' says Jon Edis-Bates, the company's principal consultant.

'The iPad was the real trigger,' says Paul McKenna, company secretary at insurance company Standard Life, which has been using virtual iPad boardbooks since September. Its adoption for board meetings was recommended by one of its directors, William Black, who had already been using his own iPad for board meetings at the Bank of Canada. Since then, Standard Life has equipped four of its boards and 43 committees across the world with the devices.

Lonmin, a FTSE 250 platinum producer, first began looking at digital solutions in 2006. But it was not until last year that the board made the switch to using digital boardbooks at meetings. 'There was a hell of a lot more room on the table,' says Rob Bellman, Lonmin's company secretary as he recounts the first fully digital board meeting. 'There just aren't the piles of paper there used to be.'

Others argue that any tablet-enabled boardroom revolution should be about more than saving space and eliminating paperwork. 'The potential is there for the technology to help give the board better knowledge of the company,' says Didier Cossin, professor of finance at IMD. The devices, he says, are currently being used in a static way rather than a tool for managing and exploiting information. 'It's just posting documents, which I don't think is the best use for the technology.'

David Yoffie, professor at Harvard Business School, is equally sceptical about whether adoption of tablet devices and virtual boardbooks has fundamentally changed the way boards operate. '[Change] may come as people find ways to take advantage of the technology, but today it's just an e-reader and, at least on the boards that I sit on, if it's just an e-reader it doesn't really change the underlying dynamics going on in the boardroom.'

Boards will have to wait for that shift to happen. 'I had some board members who used the iPad during a meeting to take pictures – one who took a picture of the guy in front of him who was angry,' recalls Prof Cossin, who sees such initiatives as having the potential to make the board room more transparent.

He also points out a possible drawback: board documents compiled for digital consumption can tend to be lengthier than those compiled on paper with a mind to the constraints of space and weight.

'With new iPads coming in, people are swamped with documents which can be highly inefficient in terms of governance because you can overwhelm them with documents,' he says.

A growing number of companies have cropped up to offer digital solutions for boardroom meetings. These include California-based BoardVantage, Diligent, and Projectplace.

Several companies and institutions have also introduced virtual boardroom applications for their clients, such as Nasdaq OMX, Computershare, the Institute of Chartered Secretaries and Administrators, Perivan and Thomson Reuters.

Diligent, which provides an iPad app and software to help companies compile virtual boardbooks, saw licence revenues for digital software increase to $6m in the fourth quarter of 2011, from $500,000 in 2008. 'We reached that tipping point in the second half of last year in the UK,' says Simon Small, a company executive. 'It became more of a conversation in the corporate community driven by the fact that iPads had been out for a year.'

Directors Desk, a US company that was bought by Nasdaq OMX in 2007, now has 20,000 users. It offers an online platform for Nasdaq-listed companies to upload documents to share with board members and executives.

However, it has not all been smooth sailing for the company, which last year was the target of hacking that compromised a handful of Fortune 500 companies. The attacks, which are being investigated by the Federal Bureau of Investigation and the National Security Agency, underline a major vulnerability for companies who choose to place market sensitive information on digital platforms and devices.

Tom Kellermann, vice president at cybersecurity company Trend Micro, says that just because these products are encrypted, it does not mean that they are safe.

'It shows arrogance on the part of the world's corporate elite to assume they will build an infrastructure that other individuals cannot break into,' he says. 'They are rushing to create this efficiency and access to capabilities without doing their due diligence on securing that infrastructure,' he adds.

One headhunter notes how, in an effort to strengthen security, some companies have equipped directors with iPads that they can use only for that particular board. As a result, directors sitting on the boards of different companies can face a high-tech variant of the original problem – but instead of clutching a pile of papers they have to carry a stack of different iPads.

Working accessories

The advent of iPads is something many directors enthuse about but they are largely still being used as e-readers only.

While the technology is still fairly basic, there are applications designed to make their working lives easier. These range from the basic, such as sticky notes, alerts and book tabs, to more inventive functions, such as private annotations, the ability to circle text in red and a briefcase that allows users to organise documents.

Win Chime, deputy company secretary at Network Rail, says these tools have produced one unexpected change in the boardroom dynamic. 'There is often a bit of competition [between directors] now about who has the best features,' she says.

Evaluate the use of digital boardbooks for company meetings.

Overview

Early word processors produced effects, such as bold or italics, by inserting special codes into the text. This made it difficult to see how the finished document would appear until it was printed. One of the most important features of a modern word processor is the provision of a WYSIWYG display (pronounced 'wizzywig'), where What You See Is What You Get.

Features of a word processor

The sheer range of features provided by a typical word processing program is a reflection upon the diverse requirements of modern business organisations. Many features are underutilised because many packages are so 'feature-rich' it is difficult to know which features are available (an example is shown in Figure 3.10). This section is intended to give a brief overview of features available so that the terms used are familiar when encountered in business.

Editing

The process of entering or correcting text.

1. *Editing.* All word processing programs allow users to enter, edit, copy, move and delete text. The process of entering or correcting text is known as editing.

Figure 3.10 Microsoft's Word for Windows showing the use of a document map

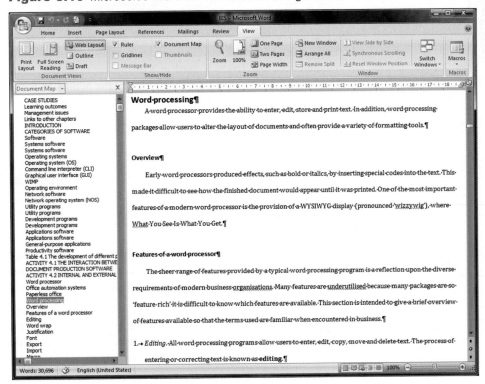

Source: Screenshot frame reprinted by permission from Microsoft Corporation.

2. *Text alignment.* As users type text and move towards the end of a line, the program automatically moves to the beginning of a new line. The spacing between words and characters is also adjusted so that the appearance of the text is improved. This is known as **word wrap**.

A word processor allows the user to control text alignment, that is, the layout of the margins on the page. Text alignment is often called **justification**. Text that is flush with the left margin but has a ragged right margin is known as *left-justified* (sometimes also known as 'unjustified'). Text that is flush with the right margin but has a ragged left margin is known as *right-justified*. Text that is flush with both margins is *fully justified* (it is said to have *full justification*).

> This paragraph is left-justified. Note that the text is flush with the *left* margin but has a ragged *right* margin. In contrast, the text in this book is *fully justified*.
>
> This paragraph is right-justified. Note that the text is flush with the *right* margin but has a ragged *left* margin. In contrast, the text in this book is *fully justified*.

3. *Block operations.* All word processing packages allow users to manipulate blocks of text in a number of ways. Once a block of text has been marked, it can be moved, deleted, copied or formatted. One powerful feature of a word processor is the ability to *cut and paste* blocks of text. A marked block can be removed from a document (cut) but held in the computer's memory. One or more copies can then be pasted into a new position in the same document (paste). This can be used to move whole sections of a document from one place to another or to make several copies of a block of text.

4. *Search and replace.* Programs such as Word for Windows allow the user to search an entire document for a specific word or phrase. Once the text has been located, it can be deleted or replaced with something else. This is called a search and replace operation. Text can be replaced *globally*, where every occurrence of the specified text is replaced automatically, or *with confirmation*, where the user is asked whether or not to replace each piece of text as it is found.

5. *Text formatting and style.* Most word processing packages allow users to specify the style, font and point size of text. *Style* refers to text effects such as bold, italics and underlined. The typeface used in a document is normally referred to as the **font**. The size of the characters used is referred to as the *point size*. For example, text in the body of a document may be 10 point and headings 14 point. There are 72 points to a vertical inch. Heading styles can be standardised for each document within a company to achieve standard communications.

> This text uses the *Arial* font, which is similar to the Helvetica styles used for newspaper headlines.
>
> `This text uses the Courier font found on typewriters.`

The word processor allows users to specify the layout of the pages in the document. *Page layout* is normally performed by setting the sizes of the top, bottom, left and right margins of the page and by selecting the size of the paper that will be used.

6. *Headers and footers.* A header is a piece of text that will appear at the top of every page of the document. Headers are typically used to print a chapter heading or title at the top of each page. A footer appears at the bottom of each page. Footers are typically used to print page numbers at the bottom of every page.

7. *Mailmerge.* Packages such as Word for Windows allow sets of personalised letters to be produced by merging information taken from a separate data file with a standard

Word wrap

In a word processor, as users type text and move towards the end of a line, the program automatically moves to the beginning of a new line.

Justification

In a word processor, the alignment of text with the left and right margins can be controlled by specifying the justification.

Font

The typeface used in a document is normally referred to as the font. The size of the characters used is referred to as the point size.

document. For example, a database could be used to hold the names and addresses of a number of business clients. A standard letter could be produced with blanks where the name and address of the client are meant to appear. When the mailmerge process begins, each name and address would be inserted in the document and printed. Mailmerge is not restricted to names and addresses; any kind of data can be merged into a standard document. This allows mailmerge to be used for applications ranging from the production of invoices to personalised newsletters.

8. *Import and export.* Many word processors allow documents to be opened or saved in a number of formats. The process of saving a file in a format compatible with another package is known as **exporting**. The process of loading a file created with another package is known as **importing**.

Export

The process of saving a file in a format compatible with another software package is known as exporting.

Import

The process of loading a file created with another package is known as importing.

Most modern word processing packages allow users to incorporate graphics and tables of figures into their documents. As an example, Word for Windows can import pictures from a range of sources. Some of the most common picture file formats are GIF, PNG, WMF, JPG, TIFF and PCX.

9. *Language tools.* Almost every major package now supports *spellchecking, grammar checking* and a *thesaurus* function. Many recent word processing programs offer an *autocorrect* feature that attempts to correct spellings as the user types. Common misspellings such as entering 'teh' instead of 'the' are detected and changed automatically by the program.

10. *Drawing tools.* Many packages provide a variety of drawing tools, allowing users to add lines, shapes or graphic files to their documents.

11. *Tables.* Packages allow users to produce tables containing a specified number of rows and columns. Tables created in this way often provide some of the functionality of a spreadsheet program, although this functionality is usually limited.

Macro

A sequence of instructions that can be used to automate complex or repetitive tasks.

12. *Programming applications.* A **macro** is a sequence of instructions that can be used to automate complex or repetitive tasks. Macros can be used to emulate a sequence of keys pressed on the keyboard or can be programmed so that they can carry out more complicated processes. For example, a company name and address could be prepared as a macro. Modern packages often feature entire progra mming languages that can be used to handle extremely complex tasks. Word for Windows, for example, contains Visual Basic for Applications – a complete implementation of the Visual Basic programming language which is available in all the Microsoft Office programs described in this chapter.

Activity 3.10   Word processing

We have described some of the key features of a word processor. How should the owner–manager of a small business with 10 staff using word-processor software ensure they work efficiently to produce good-quality standard internal and external documents?

GRAPHICS PACKAGES

Traditionally, graphics packages have been divided into three basic categories: drawing (or paint) packages, design packages and presentation software. However, it has become common to include two other categories of graphics software: diagramming packages and photo-editing programs.

Drawing programs

Paint programs serve the same purpose as a sketchpad and enable users to produce drawings using a variety of different techniques.

A combination of tools allows users to create drawings made up of freehand lines and regular shapes. Amongst the tools available are:

- A palette of drawing tools can be used to mimic the effects of drawing with different materials including pens, spray cans, brushes and charcoal.
- Selection tools can be used to copy, erase or resize sections of a drawing.
- Painting tools let users apply shading and colours to areas or shapes.
- Text tools allow users to add text to a drawing. Users can specify the typeface, size, colour and style of the text.
- Special tools provide a range of sophisticated features. A colour replacement tool, for example, can be used to change one colour for another within a specific section of the image.

One of the distinctions that can be made between drawing packages involves the type of image that can be produced. In general, paint packages are said to produce bit-map images whilst drawing packages are said to create vector images.

A bit map image is made of up of small dots (*pixels*) arranged in a grid. The finer the grid, the higher the resolution of the image. A newspaper photograph, for example, might offer a resolution of 100 dpi, whilst a photograph reproduced in a textbook might have a resolution of 1200 dpi. Although bit map images are suited for certain types of images, such as photographs, they suffer from two main disadvantages. First, the overall quality of the image cannot be maintained if it is resized. Secondly, bit map images can require a great deal of storage space, depending on the number of colours contained in the image and its resolution.

Vector graphics are made up of shapes, rather than individual dots. Mathematical formulae determine the size, position and colour of the shapes that make up a given image. Since far less information needs to be recorded about the contents of a vector image, they require comparatively little storage space. In addition, vector images can be resized with great precision and without loss of quality. Since it can be difficult to produce highly detailed images, vector graphics are often used for diagrams and relatively simple drawings.

Diagramming software

The need to produce a wide variety of business-related charts and diagrams has resulted in the emergence of numerous diagramming packages. Aimed at business users, the majority of these packages assumes little technical knowledge and rely on menus, icons and palettes of tools in order to construct diagrams.

In order to produce a chart or diagram, users select shapes and symbols from a library of pre-prepared materials. The libraries used by these programs are often called *stencils* or 'stamps', reflecting the idea that users are not expected to draw each required shape manually. Having arranged a number of shapes in order, users can then add text, lines and other elements to complete the diagram.

Diagramming programs such as Visio tend to offer a wide range of stencils from which users can select, and additional ones can be obtained from various sources. All packages cater for a range of common business diagrams, such as flow charts, office layouts, organisational charts, network diagrams, project timelines and block diagrams.

Photo-editing software

Photo-editing packages

Photo-editing packages enable users to capture, view and edit scanned images.

Filter

In a spreadsheet or database, a filter can be used to remove data from the screen temporarily. Filters do not alter or delete data but simply hide any unwanted items.

The growth in the use of optical scanners and video capture devices has resulted in a need for tools that can be used to edit and manipulate photographic images. **Photo-editing packages** enable users to capture, view and edit scanned images.

Although the majority of photo-editing programs provide many of the features found in paint packages, most provide more sophisticated tools intended especially for use with scanned images. Two typical examples are:

- Capture features enable a user to acquire images directly from an optical scanner or digital camera attached to the computer system, removing the need for the user to control two separate programs.

- **Filters** can be used to apply a range of special effects to an image. As an example, filters can be used to sharpen a blurred image or alter brightness and contrast.

SPREADSHEETS

Spreadsheet

A program designed to store and manipulate values, numbers and text in an efficient and useful way.

Modelling

Modelling involves creating a numerical representation of an *existing* situation or set of circumstances, whilst simulation involves *predicting* new situations or circumstances.

What if? analysis

This describes the ability to see the predicted effect of a change made to a numerical model.

Goal seeking

In a spreadsheet, goal seeking describes a way of automatically changing the values in a formula until a desired result is achieved.

Spreadsheet packages are used for a variety of different purposes. Some examples include the following:

- *Financial applications.* Common applications include the production of cashflow forecasts, accounting statements, invoices, purchase orders, sales orders, quotations, managing expenses and project management.

- *Modelling and simulation.* In general, **modelling** involves creating a numerical representation of an *existing* situation or set of circumstances, whilst *simulation* involves *predicting* new situations or circumstances. In both cases, a *model* is produced that provides a numerical representation of the situation or circumstances being studied. A cashflow forecast, for example, is a numerical model that attempts to predict the financial state of a business over a given period of time. Once a model has been constructed, it can be manipulated so that users can see how changes to parts of the model influence the whole. As an example, a user might change the level of sales in a cashflow forecast to see how overall profit and loss would be affected. This ability to manipulate models is often referred to as **what if? analysis** and is considered one of the spreadsheet's most powerful features.

- *Statistical analysis.* All spreadsheet programs provide a wide range of tools that can be used to analyse numerical information in a number of ways. Two simple examples can be used to illustrate the range of facilities available.

   (a) **Goal seeking** describes a way of automatically changing the values in a formula until a desired result is achieved. As an example, a user might enter a formula that calculates the profit made on sales of various items. Goal seeking could then be used to calculate the level of sales needed to produce a specified level of profit.

   (b) Many programs offer a *descriptive statistics* feature which can be used to generate various summaries relating to a block of data. The spreadsheet performs a simple analysis and creates a set of descriptive statistics automatically. The results are presented in table format and include values such as maximum, minimum, mean, average, standard deviation, sum, count and variance.

We use the plural *formulas* to distinguish those used by spreadsheets from traditional mathematical formulae.

All modern spreadsheet programs originate from the original Visicalc program launched in 1979 by Bricklin, Frankston and Fylstra. The program was originally created as a means of carrying out repetitive calculations for the Harvard Business School. Although created for the Apple II computer system, the program rapidly gained in popularity and became one of the best-selling software products of all time.

The interest shown in the Visicalc package prompted the Lotus Development Corporation to develop a version of the program for IBM-compatible computer systems. The release of Lotus 1–2–3 in 1982 is often credited as being responsible for the widespread acceptance of personal computers in business.

> Both Visicalc and Lotus 1–2–3 are often held as being the first *killer apps*. This term describes a program that offers a service so valuable that the purchase of a computer system is warranted in order to be able to use the software. More recently, the same term has begun to be used to describe an application that is superior to all similar products.

Spreadsheet features

Spreadsheet

A program designed to store and manipulate values, numbers and text in an efficient and useful way.

Worksheet

An individual area or sheet for entering data in a spreadsheet program.

We can describe a **spreadsheet** as a program designed to store and manipulate values, numbers and text in an efficient and useful way. As with word processors, we give a brief refresher of the terms used to describe spreadsheets:

1. *Worksheets and cells.* The work area in a spreadsheet program is called the **worksheet**. A worksheet is a grid made up of *cells*. Each cell is uniquely identifiable by its horizontal (row) and vertical (column) coordinates. A cell can contain text, numbers or a formula that relates to information held in another cell. For example, a cell could contain any of these pieces of data:

> 127
>
> 'Cash Flow Forecast'
>
> +A12 (a reference to another cell)

Figure 3.11 shows how a worksheet is organised. Cell coordinates are traditionally given in the form of column–row, for example the very first cell in a worksheet is A1, in column A and row 1.

One of the most important features of a spreadsheet is its ability to update the entire worksheet each time a change is made. For example, imagine that the cell at B4 contains information based on the contents of the cells at B2 and B3. Changing the contents of B2 and B3 causes the computer to update the worksheet, placing a new value in B4 automatically.

Formula

In a spreadsheet, a formula is a calculation that is entered by the user and performed automatically by the spreadsheet program.

Function

In a spreadsheet, a function is a built-in command that carries out a calculation or action automatically.

2. *Formulas.* Another important feature of the spreadsheet is that users can manipulate the contents of cells using formulas. A **formula** is a calculation that is entered by the user and performed automatically by the spreadsheet program. They are denoted to the spreadsheet by starting with =, + or@. Formulas can be used to manipulate the values held in cells by referring to their coordinates. An example is given in Figure 3.11; if B2 holds 2 and B3 holds 4, then placing the formula = B2 + B3 in B4 can be interpreted as 'take whatever is in B2 (in this case, 2), add it to the contents of B3 (in this case, 4) and place the result in B4' – giving a result of 6 in B4.

3. *Functions.* A spreadsheet **function** is a built-in command that carries out a calculation or action automatically. As an example, in Microsoft Excel, the AVERAGE function returns the average of a series of numbers.

Figure 3.11 Organisation of a spreadsheet worksheet showing example formula

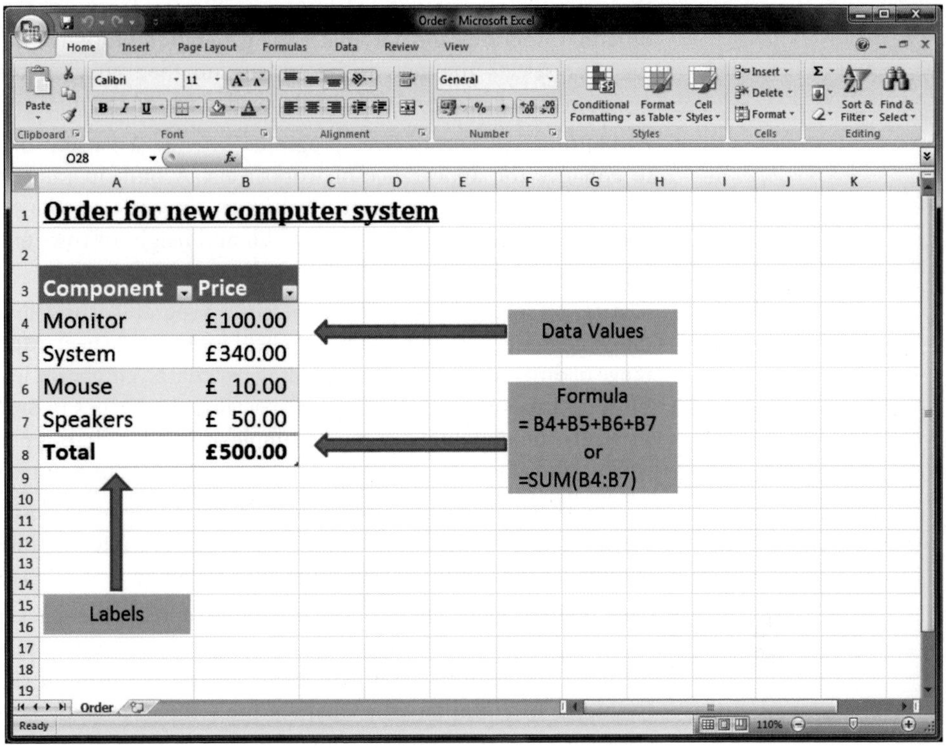

Source: Screenshot frame reprinted by permission from Microsoft Corporation.

4. All spreadsheet programs contain a number of built-in functions that can be used to simplify the construction of a worksheet. Functions are normally divided into categories so that users can locate them easily. Some typical categories include:

- *Date and time.* These allow users to perform calculations dealing with dates, for example a user might wish to calculate the number of working days between two dates.

- *Database.* Typical functions include the ability to sort rows or columns into a specified order. Although spreadsheet programs are clearly unable to offer the functionality of a specialised database program, all programs offer the basic functions of queries, filters and sorting.

- *Financial.* These provide a variety of financial and accounting functions, such as the ability to calculate loan repayments based on factors such as the interest rate and the amount borrowed.

- *Logical.* These allow users to create formulas that perform calculations according to whether or not specific conditions have been met. As an example, a worksheet used to create invoices might generate a different total according to whether or not the customer is required to pay VAT.

- *Lookup and reference.* These provide a range of functions that can be used to create more sophisticated worksheets. As an example, a user might wish to create a formula that looks up a value from a table.

- *Mathematics.* These include mathematical functions, such as factorials, exponential numbers, square roots and trigonometric functions

- *Statistical.* These allow users to produce statistical information, such as frequency distributions.

5. *Automatic features.* Many programs allow users to enter part of a formula, completing the rest of it automatically. The *autosum* feature, for example, is found in a number of different programs and automates the generation of totals. In order to use this feature, the user selects the cells to be added and then chooses the autosum feature. The program then generates the formula needed to add the numbers together automatically.

6. *Formatting.* All spreadsheet programs provide a variety of tools that can be used to enhance the appearance of worksheets. A built-in range of *numeric formats*, for example, allow users to display values as currency or to a fixed number of decimal places. Users may also adjust the width and height of rows and columns, use different typefaces and make use of shading, colour and lines.

7. *Charts.* An integral feature of spreadsheet programs is the ability to create a variety of different charts based upon the data held in the worksheet. Modern programs provide a range of different chart types, including bar charts, pie charts, line graphs and area charts. Most packages also offer a range of specialist chart types in order to cater for users with particular requirements. A good example of a such a chart type is the *combination chart* which can be used to show two or more sets of data in a single diagram.

 The charts created by spreadsheet programs are often described as *live* or *dynamic*, meaning that if the data in the worksheet are altered, the chart will be updated automatically in order to reflect the changes made.

8. *Data analysis tools.* The majority of modern spreadsheet packages contain a number of tools designed to automate common data analysis tasks. These tools remove the need for users to memorise complex formulae and perform all calculations automatically. Examples of common data analysis tools include: analysis of variance, correlation, covariance, *t*-test, *z*-test and regression.

9. *Import and export.* Spreadsheet programs are able to deal with data drawn from a variety of different sources. In many cases, files produced by other packages can be imported directly into a worksheet with no loss of data. Similarly, spreadsheets also allow data to be exported in a variety of different formats.

 Occasionally, it may be necessary to convert data into a form that can be used by the spreadsheet program. A common file format used to transfer data between spreadsheet packages and other programs is known as comma-separated (or -delimited) values (CSV). A CSV file is a simple text file made up of items enclosed within quotation marks and separated by commas. The use of commas and quotation marks enables the spreadsheet program to identify individual items.

10. *Workbooks.* Early spreadsheet programs allowed users to work with only a single worksheet at a time. In order to make use of information stored on a different worksheet, special commands were needed to access the disk file containing the data required. This often resulted in applications that were unnecessarily complex, slow to operate and prone to errors.

Modern packages enable a user to organise groups of worksheets within a single workbook. In addition, several workbooks can be opened at the same time. This facility allows users to carry out large or complex tasks more easily and quickly. Two examples may help to make this clearer:

- An organisation wishes to analyse monthly sales data. The data for each month can be stored on separate worksheets within a single workbook. Although the data held on each worksheet can be analysed separately, users can also employ special formulas and functions to examine the workbook as a whole. The total sales for the year, for example, could be obtained by using a formula that adds together the monthly totals taken from each worksheet in the workbook.

- An organisation uses two workbooks to store data on sales and expenses respectively. The data from both workbooks can be combined within a third workbook to produce

Comma-separated values (CSV)

A simple text file made up of items enclosed within quotation marks and separated by commas in order to assist conversion between programs.

Workbook

In a spreadsheet program, this describes a collection of worksheets.

information related to profitability. Only the third workbook needs to be open in order to carry out any calculations required, but all three workbooks can be open simultaneously if required.

An important feature of modern spreadsheet packages is the ability to create views on the data held in a worksheet or workbook. The use of views enables users to focus on specific sections of the worksheet by displaying data in a predetermined way. As an example, a manager might wish to view only the summary information held in a worksheet. In order to cater for this, a view could be created that displays only the required information, hiding all other data from sight.

As mentioned earlier, once a worksheet has been constructed it can be used to perform what if? analysis by changing some of the values stored. The task of keeping track of the changes made to the worksheet can be simplified by making use of *scenarios*. The user begins by constructing the basic model to be used for the analysis and stores it under a given name. The worksheet can then be altered repeatedly until the user obtains results they consider important. Each time a new set of results is obtained, the user can save these by storing the worksheet as a new scenario. They can then continue to alter the worksheet or can restore the original data to begin a new analysis. After the analysis has been completed, the user can access any of the scenarios stored and compare these to the original worksheet.

The sheer size of the workspace available to a spreadsheet user means that functions providing quick and efficient navigation are essential.

Although the capacity of a spreadsheet program will be limited by available memory and storage space, a typical workbook can contain 256 worksheets and a typical worksheet can contain 16,384 rows by 256 columns. This means that a worksheet can contain up to 4,194,304 cells and that a workbook can contain up to 1,073,741,824 cells.

MANAGEMENT APPLICATIONS OF PRODUCTIVITY SOFTWARE

Productivity software is general-purpose applications, aimed at supporting users in performing a variety of common tasks. In addition to the productivity applications such as word processors and spreadsheets, more specialist management applications are also possible. Office software such as Microsoft Office combines software both for document creation and for data analysis with team-working tools such as shared diaries. Such packages are now also intended to support knowledge management (Chapter 1) with built-in facilities or through integration with other software.

Managing time and projects

One of the principal activities of a business organisation is managing resources so that tasks are completed as quickly and efficiently as possible. It can be argued that the most important organisational resources are the skills and abilities of employees. For this reason, a major category of business applications is devoted to maximising the use of employee time. This type of software can be subdivided into a number of other categories:

- *Packages for managing tasks and projects.* These programs allow managers to schedule tasks, allocate resources and monitor progress. Typical applications include project management programs and scheduling software. How they are applied is described later (in Chapter 9).

■ *Packages for individual time management and organising personal information.* These programs help managers to make more effective use of their time by helping them to schedule appointments, organise meetings and record important information. Typical applications include personal information managers (PIMs) and contact management software.

Personal information manager (PIM)

A program that allows users to store, organise and retrieve personal information.

■ A **personal information manager (PIM)** can be thought as an electronic personal organiser. The program allows users to store, organise and retrieve personal information such as appointments, personal expenses, telephone numbers and addresses, reminders and to-do lists. Generally, a PIM is made up of several individual applications that are linked together by a menu system.

Contact manager

This describes a software application that can be used to maintain lists of information relating to customers, suppliers and other important individuals or organisations.

■ **Contact managers** can be used to maintain lists of information relating to customers, suppliers and other important individuals or organisations. Such programs are commonly used by sales organisations to assist in building and maintaining business relationships between customers and individual members of staff.

■ *Network software.* This describes the software used to establish workgroups on an organisation's network system. The programs used provide the basic infrastructure for workgroup computing.

■ *Scheduling software.* This describes programs that help to organise the activities of the workgroup. Typical applications include calendars, scheduling programs and workflow software.

A *workgroup* can be defined as a group of individuals working together on a given task. Each member of the workgroup will be attached to the organisation's network system so that tasks can be organised and information can be shared with other members.

Presentation packages

Interactive presentations are commonly used for a number of purposes including staff training and briefings and as sales tools. Presentation software enables users to create, edit and deliver presentations via a computer system. An example is the Microsoft PowerPoint application (Figure 3.12). At a simple level, presentations can consist of nothing more than a series of simple *slides* displayed on a computer monitor. More sophisticated presentations can incorporate multimedia, such as video sequences, and can allow users to interact with the material presented. Although primarily concerned with the creation of slides, many programs also support the creation of speaker notes, handouts and overhead transparencies.

MULTIMEDIA SOFTWARE

Multimedia software

Uses text, sound, animation or video to interact with the user.

Multimedia is the term used to describe software which (together with appropriate hardware) can interact with the user through text, sound, animation or video.

Multimedia software is most common in home computers, but also has business applications. These include training courses and product promotions that are distributed on CD or via the Internet. Multimedia and computer-based training (CBT) have been demonstrated to be more effective than simple presentations since studies show we remember:

■ 10 per cent of what we see;

■ 30 per cent of what we see and hear;

■ 50 per cent of what we see, hear and do (through interaction or role-plays).

Multimedia functions can be incorporated into both general-purpose software and application-specific software. For example, a word processor or e-mail can incorporate

Figure 3.12 Microsoft's Powerpoint for Windows

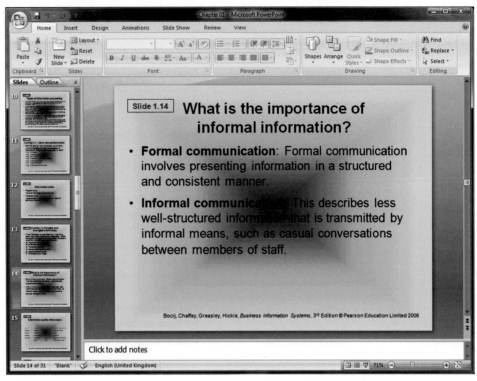

Source: Screenshot frame reprinted by permission from Microsoft Corporation.

Information kiosk

A multimedia system usually integrated with a touch screen to provide information for retail or community applications such as libraries or local government.

multimedia elements such as a commentary or video from a manager who has reviewed a document. Multimedia is also used for **information kiosks**. These are used for retail applications in shops or supermarkets. They usually consist of a PC mounted in a stand which is accessed by a touch screen and will often make use of multimedia. They have the appeal that they can be consulted when sales staff are not available, and they are used to provide information rather than giving a 'hard sell'. Some stores have started to use kiosks as a way of processing customer transactions more quickly and easily. Some stores, for example, use kiosks that not only provide information about products and services, but also allow customers to check the availability of stock and order items instantly.

Before turning to look at software for communications and the Internet, it is worth considering some of the business issues related to purchase and use of software applications. (Chapter 7 looks at approaches towards the acquisition of software and services in general, whilst Chapter 14 looks at outsourcing as a means of obtaining software and services at reduced cost.)

SOFTWARE FOR USING THE INTERNET

Internet

A global network system made up of many smaller systems.

The networking concepts behind the **Internet**, a description of how it functions, and how it has developed as a business tool are reviewed later (in Chapter 5). Here we introduce the main types of personal user software that are used to access the Internet – the web browser and e-mail.

Table 3.3 Applications of different Internet tools

Internet tool	Summary
Electronic mail or e-mail	Sending messages or documents, such as news about a new product or sales promotion between individuals.
Internet relay chat (IRC)	This is a synchronous communications tool that allows a text-based 'chat' between different users who are logged on at the same time. Becoming popular as a means of providing customer support in some industries.
Usenet newsgroups	A collection of more than 100,000 online 'forums' used to discuss topics such as a sport, hobby or business area. Traditionally accessed by special newsreader software, can now be accessed via a web browser.
FTP file transfer	The file transfer protocol is used as a standard for moving files across the Internet. FTP is available as a feature of web browsers that is used for downloading files such as product catalogues. Also used to update HTML files on web sites by uploading.
Gophers, Archie and WAIS	These tools were important before the advent of the web for storing and searching documents on the Internet. They have largely been superseded by the web which provides better searching and more sophisticated document publishing.
Telnet	This allows remote access to computer systems. Often used by technical support staff to test or configure equipment.
World Wide Web	Widely used for publishing information and running business applications over the Internet.

Internet-access software applications

Over its lifetime, many tools have been developed to help find, send and receive information across the Internet. Web browsers used to access the World Wide Web (WWW) are actually one of the most recent applications. These tools are summarised in Table 3.3. In this section we will briefly discuss the relevance of some of the more commonly used tools to the modern organisation. The other tools have either been superseded by the use of the World Wide Web or are of less relevance from a business perspective. Note that many of the other tools such as e-mail, IRC (see Table 3.3) and newsgroups, that formerly needed special software to access them, are now available through web browsers across the WWW.

Electronic mail or e-mail

Electronic mail (e-mail)

The transmission of a message over a communications network.

E-mail is well known as a method of sending and receiving electronic messages. It has been available across the Internet for over 40 years. E-mails are typically written and read in a special mail reader program that in a large company is often part of a groupware package such as Lotus Notes, Microsoft Exchange or Novell Groupwise. Smaller companies or individuals may use lower-cost or free mail programs such as Microsoft Outlook Express. A relatively recent innovation is the use of web sites which provide free e-mail facilities and do not require any special software other than a web browser.

Activity 3.11 E-mail

What are the benefits of web-based e-mail services, like those offered by Yahoo! and MSN, for home users? Why are companies unlikely to use these services for business purposes?

E-mail is now vital as a method of communicating internally and externally with customers, suppliers and partners. Since many e-mails are received and sent by companies, management of e-mail is a major management issue for the e-business. For example, 2013 figures from the Radicati Group (**http://www.radicati.com**) suggest that 100 billion business-related e-mail messages are sent every day.

For Dutch electronics company Philips International 110,000 users within the firm create 7 million e-mails and 700 Gb of data a week. A large company with an average of 8000 corporate e-mail users spends more than £1 million a year as users try to find and retrieve old e-mail messages, often from archives.

E-mail management involves developing procedures and using systems to ensure that inbound and outbound e-mails are processed efficiently. **Inbound e-mail** should be routed to the correct person or processed automatically. As an example, a message from a customer to a company requesting information such as product specifications or quotations could be dealt with automatically by an autoresponder or mail-bot. These programs can identify key words or phrases in an e-mail message and react accordingly. A message sent to products@companyrname.com or containing the word 'catalogue' could automatically trigger a response containing a price list or product catalogue. **Outbound e-mail** may be used on an ad hoc basis or as part of a standardised method of keeping customers informed, such as through a regular e-mail newsletter. Managing inbound and outbound e-mail is an important issue for customer service delivery.

In a business organisation, e-mail can be used to support both internal and external communications. Examples of two typical applications for e-mail are as follows:

- *Internal communications.* Many organisations use e-mail instead of internal memos or telephone calls. One of the advantages of using e-mail in this way is that messages are stored automatically until the user comes to access them. In addition, a great deal of information, such as the date and time of the message, can be included in the message automatically.

- *Teleworking.* It is estimated that approximately 3.1 million people work from home in the UK, representing around 2.5 per cent of the workforce. Worldwide, a 2012 poll by Reuters found that one in five people telecommute. E-mail enables people to stay in contact with clients, colleagues and employers. In addition, it allows **teleworkers** to send or receive work-related materials quickly and easily via e-mail or other methods. Teleworking is considered further later (in Chapter 17).

Advantages of e-mail

Some of the major advantages of e-mailcan be summarised as follows:

- *Speed.* E-mail messages can be transmitted very quickly. A typical message containing 15,000 words, for example, can be transmitted in under a second. As a means of communication, e-mail is considered extremely fast, with some messages able to reach their destinations in minutes.

Since e-mail is considered to be an extremely fast method of communication, users often use the derisory term 'snail mail' to refer to the conventional postal system.

- *Cost.* The cost of sending or receiving messages is considered very low. Hundreds of messages can be sent or received for the cost of a brief telephone call, making e-mail far cheaper than the postal service. Broadband provides an 'always on' e-mail service capable of sending and receiving thousands of messages daily for a relatively small monthly fee. For this reason, many companies have adopted e-mail marketing strategies.

- *Multiple copies.* E-mail allows multiple copies of the same basic message to be created and transmitted. Using some of the functions of the directory, groups of people can be

Inbound e-mail

E-mail received from outside the organisation such as customer and supplier enquiries.

Outbound e-mail

E-mail sent from the company to other organisations.

Teleworker

A teleworker is a person who works from home, using technology as a means of communicating with employers, clients and other persons.

Alias

The process of sending e-mail messages to specific individuals or groups of users can be simplified by making use of an alias or nickname.

contacted by assigning an **alias** (sometimes known as a *nickname*), for example the name of a department might be used as an alias for all of the people working there.

- *Auditing.* Even the simplest e-mail package will provide a number of features that allow users to *audit* their messages. Most programs allow users to keep copies of any messages they produce, automatically marking them with the date and time they were sent.

- *Sharing data.* E-mail messages can be used to transmit data files to other users. Files can be *attached* to messages and transmitted in the usual way. All types of data can be sent in this way including word processor files, spreadsheet data, graphics and database files.

- *Multimedia.* Most e-mail packages allow users to include multimedia elements in their messages. Messages can include a variety of different elements including graphics, video, hyperlinks to information on the Internet, and sound files.

- *Groupwork.* E-mail supports groupwork and remote working.

Disadvantages of e-mail

Some of the major disadvantages of e-mail can be summarised as follows:

- *Routeing.* E-mail messages seldom take the most direct route to their destinations. A message sent from Manchester to London, for example, might travel through Leicester, Birmingham and Nottingham before reaching its final destination. This can lead to a number of difficulties:

  (a) the time taken to receive the message can be long. Services such as Skype are increasingly used to overcome this deficiency but this raises other issues, such as security concerns;

  (b) there are more opportunities for the message to become lost or garbled;

  (c) there are more opportunities for messages to be intercepted.

- *Cost.* In order to send or receive e-mail, organisations must have access to the correct hardware and software. Although appropriate hardware and software is inexpensive nowadays, there are a number of additional costs, such as subscriptions to services, that may make e-mail expensive or unsuitable for use in some industries.

- The average office worker spends approximately two hours each day dealing with e-mail (Mail Online, 31 July 2012).
- Research from Atos Origin claimed that 'the average employee spends 40per cent of their working week dealing with internal emails which add no value to the business' (*The Guardian*, 17 December 2012).
- The average cost of providing e-mail access staff ranges between £5000–£10,000 per employee per year (Jackson, 2011).
- Research from Mimecast (**www.mimecast.co.uk**) found that 11 per cent of 'work' e-mails are personal, 7 per cent are spam and only 14 per cent are critically important. The remainder are work-related but not considered of high importance.
- A 2013 study by the University of Glasgow reported by Prevention (**http://www.prevention.com**) reported that 80 per cent of work e-mail is unnecessary.

Spam

Unwanted messages, such as advertisements, are received by most e-mail users. The act of sending out these messages is usually called spamming.

- *Technical issues.* Since using an e-mail service requires a certain level of technical knowledge: novice users may find it difficult to operate the hardware and software involved. This can place a burden on an organisation in terms of training and technical support requirements. E-mail services can be outsourced to reduce this problem.

- *Spam.* Unwanted messages, such as advertisements, are received by most e-mail users. The act of sending out these messages is usually called **spamming**. Dealing with unwanted or unnecessary e-mail messages can place a great burden on an organisation's resources.

Trustwave (**https://www.trustwave.com/support/labs/spam_statistics.asp**) publishes a regularly updated Spam Statistics page. In early 2014, the site reported that 64 per cent of all e-mail is spam. Other figures suggest that 94 billion spam e-mails are sent each day. Research from Rao and Reiley (2012) has estimated that some $20 billion is spent each year on dealing with spam, with a further $6 billion being spent on anti-spam software.

- *Security*. Unless encrypted, e-mail messages can be intercepted relatively easily. This makes e-mail unsuitable for sending confidential information unless special precautions are taken.

Features of an e-mail package

File attachment

E-mail messages can be used to transmit data files to other users. Files can be attached to messages and transmitted in the usual way.

Online

When a user is connected to their Internet account, usually by a modem link, they are said to be online.

Offline

When a user is not connected to their Internet account, they are said to be offline.

1. **Attachments.** Although messages sent by e-mail are usually composed of text alone, additional files can be 'attached' to an e-mail message so that users can send programs, data files and other materials with their messages.

2. *Composition tools.* E-mail messages can be composed online or offline. They can also be posted immediately (immediate delivery) or can have delivery deferred. All packages provide an editor that allows users to enter the text of a new message. More sophisticated programs will have many of the features of a word processor, for example spell-checking.

3. *Viewing tools.* All e-mail programs are designed to collect new messages and allow users to view them on the screen. All modern programs also allow users to print the contents of a message or copy the text into another program, such as a word processor.

4. *Filters.* Filters provide the ability to mark messages for special attention. A filter searches for key words or phrases in a message. Any messages matching the filter conditions can be dealt with automatically. Filters can be used to: highlight messages for special attention, delete messages automatically, copy or move messages to another location or reply to incoming messages automatically. Filters are particularly important for dealing with spam and can have a significant impact on staff productivity. As an example, Bill Gates, founder of Microsoft, was sent four million spam e-mails every day. However, his e-mail filtering software was so efficient that he actually only received ten junk e-mails (Source: The Tesh Media Group, **www.tesh.com**). Companies often use filtering software on their e-mail servers to remove as much unwanted e-mail as possible before forwarding any remaining messages to users. This means that all e-mail messages are filtered twice; once when they are received by the company's server and once when collected by the user's e-mail software.

5. *Management tools.* In addition to filters, most packages provide facilities for archiving, copying, moving, deleting and grouping messages. Mail boxes can be created to hold messages from certain people or concerning a particular subject.

In recent years, companies have become aware that a great deal of valuable information is held within the e-mail messages employees store on their personal computers. It has also become necessary to store certain e-mail messages for business and legal reasons. As an example, many organisations use e-mail instead of paper for receipts, invoices, orders and even contracts. The need to store messages in a form that allows them to be searched and retrieved easily has caused many companies to invest heavily in e-mail archiving systems.

Address book

A way of grouping e-mail addresses in a similar way to a phone book.

Signature file

Information such as an address and phone number that can be automatically added to the end of an e-mail message.

6. *Encryption.* Many programs provide the facility to encode (encrypt) messages so that only the intended recipients can read them.

7. *Managing addresses.* An alias usually consists of a description and the e-mail addresses of those grouped under the alias. Groups of aliases can be stored within the address book tool found within most e-mail packages. The address book enables users to create, delete, edit and organise aliases.

8. *Signature files.* A signature file contains information that can be automatically added to the end of an e-mail message. The signature file is normally a simple text file that can

be created or edited using a text editor or similar program. Most e-mail programs allow users to have a number of different signature files.

The World Wide Web and web browsers

World Wide Web (WWW)

Interlinked documents on the Internet made up of pages containing text, graphics and other elements.

Hypertext Markup Language (HTML)

WWW pages are mainly created by producing documents containing HTML commands that are special tags (or codes) to control how the WWW page will appear when displayed in a web browser.

Web browser program

Enables users to navigate through the information available and display any pages of interest.

Hypertext

A hypertext is a document containing highlighted words or phrases that represent links to other documents activated by clicking the mouse.

The World Wide Web, or 'web' for short, is a medium for publishing information on the Internet in an easy-to-use form. If we take the analogy of television, then the Internet would be equivalent to the broadcasting equipment such as masts and transmitters, and the World Wide Web is equivalent to the content of different TV programmes. The medium is based on a standard document format known as HTML (Hypertext Markup Language) which can be thought of as similar to a word-processing format. It is significant since it offers *hyperlinks* which allow users to readily move from one document to another – the process known as 'surfing'.

The World Wide Web (WWW) is accessed using a web browser. Since they have been designed for ease of use, WWW pages feature sections of text that include hypertext links and graphics. Figure 3.13 shows the Microsoft Explorer web browser being used to access a typical web site. Other web browsers include Opera, Firefox and Mozilla.

Features of a web browser

The interface used by a web browser makes use of hypertext linking techniques. A hypertext is a document that includes highlighted words or phrases. These highlighted sections represent *links* to other documents or sections of the same document. Clicking the mouse above one of these links causes it to be activated. A link can be used to move to another document, transfer a file, view a section of video, listen to a sound file or carry out a number of other actions.

Figure 3.13 Web browser being used to access Google

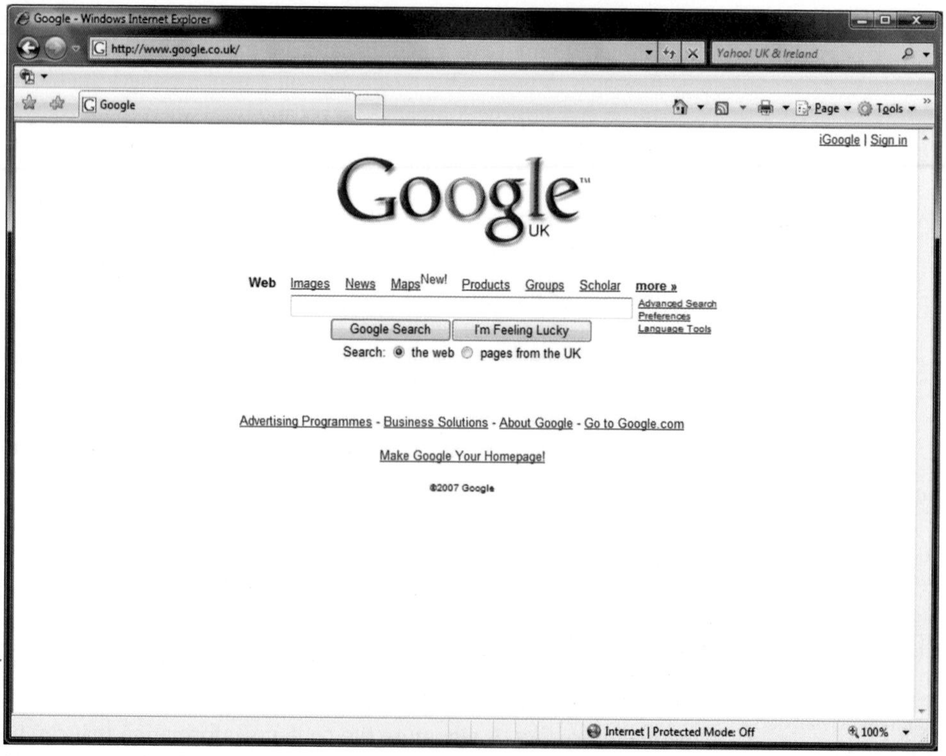

Source: Screenshot frame reprinted by permission from Microsoft Corporation.

As users move through a hypertext document, their actions are recorded automatically by the program being used. Users can access the *history* of their movements and jump backwards or forwards through all of the documents they have viewed.

All web browsers provide users with a variety of tools that enable them to navigate through often complex collections of WWW pages. Some of the most common tools include:

- *Navigation buttons.* These enable users to move backwards and forwards through the list of pages previously viewed. Additional command buttons include:

  (a) *Stop.* This cancels the action currently being taken.

  (b) *Home.* Users are able to designate a specific WWW page as a 'home page' which is displayed each time the web browser runs. The user can return to the home page at any time by using the appropriate command button. Some browsers allow users to specify multiple home pages, making it easy to keep track of several web sites at a time. This can be very useful, for instance, when monitoring web sites belonging to competitors.

  (c) *Search.* Many pages provide access to search engines that can be used to locate specific information on the Internet. This command causes the web browser to load a WWW page that provides access to one or more search engines.

- *History.* All web browsers maintain a list of pages previously viewed by the user. The user is able to display the list and can revisit any of the pages previously viewed.

- *Address bar.* Users are able to enter the location of a WWW page or file via the address bar.

- *Multiple tabs.* The latest generation of web browsers allows users to open a number of pages at the same time. Pages are organised using tabs and can be managed individually or in groups.

- *Extensions.* The browser's functionality can be extended by installing small files that add new features. As an example, a user might install a translation tool that automatically translates foreign-language web pages into English.

- *Integrated tools.* Many browsers include a variety of additional tools for handling tasks related to e-mail, scheduling and time management, security, and so on.

In order to increase the speed and efficiency with which a web browser functions, a temporary storage space is used to store copies of any pages that the user has viewed. If the user returns to a given location, the web browser retrieves the required page from the temporary storage space, rather than transferring a fresh copy from a remote computer. The use of a cache in this way improves the speed with which previously viewed pages can be displayed.

> The transmission of information across the Internet is often described as being based around either pull or push technology. **Pull technology** describes information sent out as a result of receiving a specific request, for example a page is delivered to a web browser in response to a specific request from the user. **Push technology** describes information that is sent without a user specifically requesting it, for example a customised news service received by subscribing to a channel or e-mail.

All web browsers allow users to maintain a directory of WWW sites. The directory will enable users to add, edit, delete and organise addresses in the form of bookmarks.

As organisations seek to apply the Internet to business applications, renewed emphasis has been placed on matters concerning security and privacy. As an example, many users and organisations cite security concerns as a reason for not taking up developments such as e-commerce. In order to address these concerns, many web browsers now provide a range of

---

Search engine

Key words are entered to locate information stored on the Internet.

Cache

A temporary storage space is used to store copies of any pages that the user has viewed for rapid access if the user revisits a site.

Pull technology

Information sent out as a result of receiving a specific request, for example a page is delivered to a web browser in response to a specific request from the user.

Push technology

Information that is sent without a user specifically requesting it, for example a customised news service received by subscribing to a channel.

Bookmarks

All web browsers allow users to maintain a directory of WWW sites. The directory will enable users to add, edit, delete and organise addresses in the form of bookmarks.

security features that can be used alone or in combination to offer varying levels of security. Some common features include the following:

- *Digital ID.* A digital ID provides a means of confirming the identity of a specific user through the use of a small data file called a personal certificate. The certificate contains encrypted information relating to the user's identity. Since the user's web browser is able to transmit or receive personal certificates, they are able to verify the identity of a third party or confirm their own identity to that party. Personal certificates can also be used within e-mail packages.

- *Certificates.* A site certificate contains information regarding the identity of a particular site on the Internet. As with personal certificates, the site certificate is encrypted to protect the information it contains. Web browsers automatically maintain a list of certificates concerning sites designated as being trustworthy by the user or organisation. When the web browser accesses a given site on the Internet, the corresponding certificate is checked to ensure the authenticity of the site. If the information in the certificate is invalid or out of date, a suitable warning is issued.

- *Ratings.* Many browsers support the use of ratings in order to restrict access to inappropriate content, for example pornography. The majority of ratings schemes are voluntary and are based on four basic criteria: language, nudity, sex and violence. When a web browser is used to access a site belonging to a given scheme, the site's ratings are checked against the list of criteria set within the browser. If a site does not meet the criteria specified within the browser, access to the site is denied.

- *Applets.* WWW pages can contain small programs that are activated when a page is accessed. Such programs can take a variety of forms and can include complete, self-contained applications known as applets. As an example, a page may have been created to display an animation sequence by activating an appropriate applet after the page has finished loading. Although such programs are generally considered harmless, they can represent a potential security risk to an organisation or individual. As a result, all web browsers provide control over the operation of any applets embedded in a WWW page.

A plug-in is a small program or accessory that can be used to extend a web browser's capabilities. For example, a number of different plug-ins exist that allow a web browser to display video or animation sequences.

The use of plug-ins offers two main advantages. First, users are able to select which plug-ins they require and can install only those needed to meet a specific requirement. This acts to reduce storage space requirements and prevents unnecessary or unwanted changes being made to the user's computer system. Secondly, the functionality of some plug-ins can be extended to the user's computer system as a whole. From the point of view of a company hosting the web page they have the major disadvantage that their customer will not be able to view the content unless they go through the process of downloading and setting up the plug-in.

All modern web browsers are capable of executing special commands that have been embedded within the body of a WWW page. These scripts can be used to control the appearance of the page or can provide additional facilities, such as on-screen clocks and timers.

Many scripts are produced using a special programming language known as Java. Java, a derivative of the C++ programming language, can be used to create small applications that run when users display a WWW page or activate a control shown on the screen. One of the major advantages of Java is that applications are *platform-independent*, meaning that they can be used with any system equipped with the correct software. This allows applications created using one particular kind of system to work on other systems without modification.

Other common scripting languages include Javascript, VBScript and PHP.

A brief introduction to HTML

Many web browsers provide facilities that allow users to construct their own WWW pages using a special authoring language known as Hypertext Markup Language (HTML). HTML pages are made up of two elements: tags and content. Tags describe the

HTML (Hypertext Markup Language)

HTML is the language used to create web pages and documents. The HTML code used to construct pages has codes or tags such as <TITLE> to indicate to the browser what is displayed.

characteristics of the page and how to display the content. Tags are usually paired; the first tag is called the *opening tag*, the second is called the *closing tag*. As an example, all HTML documents begin with a <HTML> opening tag and end with a </HTML> closing tag. These tags indicate to a web browser that everything between them is formatted as HTML. As a further example, the snippet of code below specifies that everything following the <B> opening tag should be displayed in bold type until the </B> closing tag is encountered:

This <B>bold</B> but this is not.

HTML pages are usually made up of several sections, some of which are not intended to be shown on the screen. For instance, the HEAD element contains information describing the document, such as the name of the author or a description of the page, while the BODY element contains the actual content of the page.

<HTML> tag	Denotes an HTML document.
<HEAD> tag	The header part of an HTML document containing titles, meta tags and scripts.
<TITLE> tag	The text that appears in the browser title bar.
<BODY> tag	The main part of an HTML document containing content.
Comment tag <!– –>	Used to document code; text does not appear in browser.

HTML code	Browser display
<HTML>	Welcome to the web site of BIS 5E
<HEAD>	
<TITLE>BIS</TITLE>	
</HEAD>	
<BODY> <!-Main content starts here->	
Welcome to the web site of the <B>BIS 5E</B>	
</BODY>	
</HTML>	

Extensible markup language (XML)

Since 1999 a great deal of attention has been paid to the use of the extensible markup language (XML) for business applications. Both HTML and XML share SGML (standard generalised markup language) as a common ancestor. However, whilst HTML is used primarily for the creation of WWW pages, XML is intended to serve a wider variety of applications. In simple terms, XML is a data description language that allows documents to store any kind of information. The 'extensible' part of XML refers to an ability to create new language elements (or whole new languages) using standard XML elements. An XML document created using one application can be used with other programs without the need to convert it or process it in any other way.

The nature of XML means that it is ideal for applications that require information to be shared between business organisations. For example, many organisations have already adopted XML as a core element of their EDI systems. Since XML documents are easily transferred between operating systems and applications software, XML lends itself to applications that include web portals, e-commerce, e-procurement, m-commerce, mobile Internet, groupwork and database development.

Some of the advantages of XML include the following:

- XML is supported by a wide range of existing applications. All modern web browsers, for example, support XML. This means that XML documents can be created and distributed without the need to purchase or install additional software.
- A large number of development packages already feature support for XML. Such packages range from conventional programming languages, such as Visual Basic, to web authoring software, such as Front Page.
- XML is extremely flexible. If a feature does not exist, it can be created and added to the 'core' language. This enables XML to be used for an extremely wide range of purposes, from controlling the content of a web page to sophisticated database applications.
- XML can be used across a wide range of technologies. In terms of information technology, XML can be used across different processors and operating systems with little difficulty. This means, for example, that the same basic material can be used on Windows computers, UNIX systems and even WAP mobile phones.
- Since XML allows extremely flexible data structures to be created, it can be used to work with any existing legacy data owned by an organisation.
- XML is considered simpler to use than alternatives such as SGML.
- XML files are often compatible with many existing applications that are based on SGML (although the reverse is not necessarily true).

Many large organisations have already begun to adopt applications that use XML as a medium for storing and transmitting data. Furthermore, as organisations move towards distributed computing, using the Internet to enable communications, we are likely to see an even greater emphasis placed on the use of XML.

| Activity 3.12 | Web addresses |

Using the simple web-page design tools included with packages such as Internet Explorer and Netscape Navigator, produce a simple web page containing your CV. If possible, make use of colour, different typefaces, graphics, horizontal lines, bullet points and other features. When you have created the page, save it and then view it from within the web browser. View the source for the web page so that you can see how the design of your page has been translated into HTML.

Web 2.0

Web 2.0

Describes a new generation of applications and services that allows Internet users to communicate, share information and do business in new ways.

The term **Web 2.0** describes a new generation of applications and services that allows Internet users to communicate, share information and do business in new ways. The term was coined by Tim O'Reilly (**www.oreilly.com**) and Dale Dougherty in 2004 after they noted that many of the companies that had survived the dot-com collapse at the turn of the century seemed to share certain characteristics. They also noted that today's most successful Internet companies had a very different approach to those of the dot-com time. In order to distinguish between these approaches, they began to call the older approach Web 1.0 and the newer one Web 2.0.

Tim O'Reilly's 'official' definition (see http://radar.oreilly.com/archives/2005) of Web 2.0 is:

Web 2.0 is the network as platform, spanning all connected devices; Web 2.0 applications are those that make the most of the intrinsic advantages of that platform: delivering software as a continually-updated service that gets better the more people use it, consuming and remixing data from multiple sources, including individual users, while providing their own data and services in a form that allows remixing by others, creating network effects through an 'architecture of participation', and going beyond the page metaphor of Web 1.0 to deliver rich user experiences.

1. *The web as platform.* The Internet is seen as a platform for creating and running applications. Applications are delivered to users through a web browser. Example: Google provides a range of services via any web browser – users can search the Internet, edit documents, schedule appointments, pay for goods and send e-mail.

2. *Harnessing collective intelligence.* Users are encouraged to contribute their knowledge and experience ('the wisdom of crowds'). Wikipedia is an online encyclopedia that allows anyone to add or edit entries.

3. *Data is the next Intel Inside.* Every significant Internet application to date has been based around a specialised database. Ownership or control of a database can confer competitive advantage. Example: companies such as NavTeq and TeleAtlas supply map data for the web mapping services such as MapQuest, Google Maps and MSN Maps & Directions.

4. *End of the software release cycle.* Applications should be continuously updated. Example: the database used by any major search engine, such as Google, must be constantly updated in order to ensure that users receive accurate results.

5. *Lightweight programming models.* Such models encourage users to participate, foster innovation, reduce development times and effort and result in more flexible applications. Example: the Google Desktop Search API (Application Programming Interface) is available free of charge and allows users to develop simple search tools quickly and easily.

6. *Software above the level of a single device.* Applications should be portable and not limited to a single platform, such as a PC. Example: Windows Media Player is available across a variety of devices and operating systems.

7. *Rich user experiences.* Applications should have interactive, user-friendly interfaces that make it easy to perform tasks. Example: GMail provides sophisticated features, like voice mail, but remains easy to use.

Web 2.0 technology

Rich Internet Applications (RIAs)

RIAs are web applications that combine enhanced user interfaces with the power and functionality of desktop programs.

Some of the principles behind Web 2.0 have been associated with particular forms of technology. O'Reilly's 'rich user experiences', for example, are often associated with rich Internet applications (RIAs). RIAs are web applications that combine enhanced user interfaces with the power and functionality of desktop programs. Typically, programs run within the user's browser but save and retrieve any data that are needed from a server. As an example, Google Docs allows users to create and edit word processing documents, presentations and spreadsheets. The application runs via the user's web browser but documents and other data, such as user settings, are stored on Google's servers.

In general, RIAs can be said to have three typical characteristics:

1. RIAs do not require installation and run via a web browser. This enables RIAs to run under any operating system – all that is required is a web browser and an Internet connection.

2. Applications run within a secure environment called a *sandbox*. This limits the application's access to system resources and is intended to improve security.

3. Applications are created using specialised development tools and techniques such as Ajax, Adobe Flash, Flex, OpenLaszlo and Silverlight.

Some of the tools and technologies associated with RIAs include the following:

- Ajax (Asynchronous Javascript + XML). This is a combination of technologies that is used to make applications seem faster and more responsive. It is achieved by changing the way a web page is updated by a browser. Instead of reloading the entire page, only the parts of the page that need to be updated are refreshed. As an example, on a page with a news ticker showing the latest headlines, the headlines can be updated in real time without needing to reload the whole page.

- Adobe Flash (formerly Macromedia Flash) is a multimedia authoring tool that is typically used to add interactive content to web pages. Flash applications are distributed as 'movies' and can include music, graphics, animations and streaming video. Interactivity is added using a scripting language called ActionScript. Some programmers are uncomfortable working with the Adobe Flash Professional development environment and prefer to use an alternative development system, Adobe Flex, to create Flash movies.

- OpenLaszlo is an open-source development system made up of the LZX programming language and the OpenLaszlo Server. LZX allows applications to be created using Javascript and XML. Programs can be compiled as Flash movies or run via a Java servlet. A servlet is a program written in Java that runs on a web server and can produce dynamic pages.

- Silverlight is a relatively new development from Microsoft and aims to compete with Adobe Flash. Silverlight is a run-time system used to run RIAs created using any of the programming languages compatible with the.NET system including Visual Basic, C++, C# and others.

- Open Web APIs (Application Programming Interface – see Chapter 6) provide ready-made libraries of functions that simplify the creation of applications. An 'open' API has been made available to developers free of charge and without restriction. As an example, the Google Maps API 'allows you to create innovative online mapping applications and helps integrate maps and geo-coding into your websites'.

Key Web 2.0 applications

Web 2.0 emphasises what is sometimes called the 'social Internet', a range of applications that encourage greater collaboration and interaction among Internet users. Such applications transform users from passive consumers of third-party content into content producers. Applications commonly associated with Web 2.0 include the following.

Blog (web log)

A blog (web log) can be thought of as an online journal or diary.

A Wiki

A Wiki is a software application that allows the creation of collaborative web sites.

Social bookmarking

Social bookmarking allows Internet users to manage lists of bookmarks that can be shared with other people.

A blog (web log) can be thought of as an online journal or diary. Blogs are often hosted on a third-party web site, such as Blogger (**www.blogger.com**). An important feature of a blog is the ability for readers to leave comments on individual entries. Some of the most popular blogs, such as those posted by celebrities, can attract thousands of readers. Blogging is an extremely popular pastime; at this writing, the Technorati search engine was tracking 112 million blogs.

A Wiki is a software application that allows the creation of collaborative web sites. Users can create, edit and delete pages on the site using any web browser. The content on the site is usually organised in a structured manner with menus, hyperlinks and search tools allowing users to find specific pages. Perhaps the best-known example of a Wiki is Wikipedia, a free online encyclopedia that allows anyone to create or edit entries.

Social bookmarking allows Internet users to manage lists of bookmarks that can be shared with other people. Lists are usually stored online so that they can be accessed from any location and can be shared more easily. One of the best-known social bookmarking sites is del.icio.us (**https://delicious.com**). This site introduced the concept of *tags*, one word descriptions that can be applied to groups of bookmarks. More than one tag can be assigned to a bookmark and users can search for interesting sites by specifying one or more tags. As social bookmarking sites have matured, they have started to offer new services, such as *web annotation*. This allows users to add notes to a web page without altering the content of the page, something like writing notes in the margin of a book. Multimedia sharing describes a range of services that allow users to share photographs, video and other media. Facebook (**www.facebook.com**), for example, allows users to publish photographs, video and articles that can be shared with other users.

Social networking web sites allow members to create online profiles that can be linked to those of other members. Profiles can contain various elements, including music, blog entries, video clips, photographs and *blurbs*, pages with titles such as 'About Me', 'Who I'd Like To Meet' and so on. Sites such as Facebook provide a variety of features intended to encourage members to interact with one another, such as shared message boards.

RSS (Really Simple Syndication) is a specification for publishing documents that contain regularly updated content, such as news stories. An item published in RSS format is called a *feed* (or channel) and can be read using an up-to-date web browser or a program called an RSS reader (sometimes also called a 'feed reader'). It is possible to combine several feeds together automatically using a program called an *aggregator*. Readers can subscribe to one or more feeds so that they can retrieve the latest information that has been published. As an example, most newspapers publish their headlines in RSS format. As new headlines replace older stories, the RSS feed is continually updated. When a reader accesses the RSS feed, the software being used automatically checks for the latest information, then retrieves the newest headlines and a summary of each story. Clicking on a headline automatically retrieves and displays the full story. RSS automates the process of keeping track of the content published on one or more web sites. Although typically used for news headlines, it can be used to syndicate any content that changes frequently, such as blogs and podcasts. In business, RSS can be used for a variety of purposes, such as advising customers of special promotions or publishing share prices.

Podcasting involves distributing media files via the Internet in the same way as RSS feeds. Most podcasts are audio files that have been saved in MP3 format so that they are compatible with media players, such as iPods, and personal computers. Like RSS feeds, users can subscribe to channels they are interested in and can automatically download new content when it becomes available.

Mashups are web applications that combine data from several sources in order to create an entirely new service or application. The term is derived from the music industry where it describes the process of producing a new song by mixing two or more existing pieces. The data used to create a mashup is typically obtained from a third party, such as Microsoft or Google. Some companies provide APIs that simplify the process of obtaining and using data. An example of a typical mashup is *Goggles*, a flight simulator that makes use of data from Google Maps.

Web 2.0 implications for business

Adapting to Web 2.0 requires fundamental changes to the way in which we approach the use of the Internet for business. There are two main ways in which Web 2.0 alters the business environment and the way organisations interact with customers and other parties. First, the richer social environment created by Web 2.0 applications changes the way people use the Internet, including how they respond to advertising and how they shop. Second, RIAs enable customary ways of doing business to be replaced with new, innovative approaches.

One of the biggest challenges faced by companies has been in finding ways to harness the power of social networks for business purposes. Before Web 2.0, using the Internet was a largely solitary pastime and involved little interaction with other people. Users tended

---

Social networking web sites

Social networking web sites allow members to create online profiles that can be linked to those of other members.

RSS (Really Simple Syndication)

This is a specification for publishing documents that contain regularly updated content, such as news stories. An item published in RSS format is called a *feed* and can be read using an up-to-date web browser or a program called an RSS reader.

Podcasting

Podcasting involves distributing media files via the Internet in the same way as RSS feeds

Mashups

Mashups are web applications that combine data from several sources in order to create an entirely new service or application.

to be passive, responding to content produced by others and often using only a relatively small number of sites and services. Today, Internet users are seen as *content producers*, contributing their knowledge, experience and views to a large body of material that is constantly growing and changing. As an example, sites such as Wikipedia rely completely upon ordinary Internet users to create the content that attracts visitors to the site. Users have also become more active in their use of the Internet, now spending most of their time interacting with others through social networking sites, such as Facebook, Twitter, LinkedIn, Pinterest, Tumbler and Instagram.

CASE STUDY 3.4

Cloud is silver lining for German online bank Fidor

By Jane Bird

A bank that pays its customers for 'liking' it on Facebook or uploading an instructional video about buying life assurance on YouTube might sound unlikely. But this is precisely what Munich-based Fidor Bank is doing.

Its founders have created an online bank with a full range of products, no branches and a 'community' of 250,000 people who exchange opinions, advice and comments. Some 50,000 of them are fully-fledged account holders.

They can discuss financial topics online, much as they previously might have done while queueing at an ATM, says Matthias Kröner, chief executive. Active participants can earn cash bonuses by answering money questions, sharing saving tips and rating financial advisers.

Fidor Bank, which received its licence in 2009, offers services that would be impossible in a bricks-and-mortar institution, such as executing a loan in 20 seconds and managing virtual currencies such as Bitcoin and those used in internet games.

Cloud computing has made it possible to create such an innovative service by letting the bank form partnerships with third-party providers without having to invest in costly infrastructure, Mr Kröner says.

'If we had tried to do everything on our own, we would never have got off the ground. It would have been too time-consuming and expensive.'

For example, Fidor Bank was the first bank in Germany to let customers buy currency online, and to make payments and view balances in a variety of currencies. It did this by partnering with The Currency Cloud – a multicurrency, regulated ewallet.

'By connecting to a variety of exchange rate providers and payment networks, The Currency Cloud ensures our users always receive the best and lowest cost conversion and payment service possible,' says Mr Kröner.

Customer currencies are stored in a single account and money can be withdrawn from ATMs. Because The Currency Cloud processes currency exchange directly, Fidor Bank does not need to hold currency itself, so is not exposed to foreign exchange risk.

Mike Laven, chief executive of The Currency Cloud, says such cloud-based partnerships are the future of financial services, which will be increasingly turned into components and assembled like Lego. 'Fidor would have taken 18 months to build a foreign exchange payment system on its own, whereas with us it took two weeks,' Mr Laven says.

Cloud computing in the form of social networks has also helped Fidor Bank's marketing. Being a relatively small institution, with much shallower pockets than established banks, it has depended on word of mouth via social media to expand.

'We don't have a big advertising budget, and in the beginning it was very hard work spreading the word,' says Mr Kröner. 'But in January 2010, we set up chat rooms on social media platforms such as Twitter, Facebook, YouTube and Xing, and awareness of Fidor went viral.'

The chat rooms are effectively 'digital pedestrian areas' where people go shopping, says Mr Kröner. 'It is like showing we have a shop in 'Facebook street'. Before becoming customers, people can ask others what we are like – our people, our management, and whether we're incentivising staff to rip customers off, or whether we are providing fair banking.'

The chat rooms also provide a forum for people to discuss money issues. 'There are not many places where people can do this online,' says Mr Kröner.

People can earn €50 by creating a 'user-help-user' video on YouTube that is accepted and uploaded by Fidor Bank. The current account interest rate goes up by 0.1 of a percentage for every 2,000 people who add a Fidor Bank 'like' to their Facebook profile.

Some people might think cloud computing and banking are not a good match because of security concerns. This is a mistake, says Mr Laven. 'Cloud-based services can provide very high levels of security, conform to regulations, and offer best practice in areas such as encryption.'

 Source: Bird, J. (2014) Cloud is silver lining for German online bank Fidor. *Financial Times*. 28 January.
© The Financial Times Limited 2014. All Rights Reserved.

QUESTION

What are the potential benefits in the use of cloud computing for banking services?

As Internet users have become more sophisticated, businesses have found that traditional approaches to advertising are no longer appropriate and have looked for new methods to adopt. Amongst these new methods have been viral marketing, affiliate marketing and Google's AdWords system. **Viral marketing** uses word-of-mouth to spread awareness of a product or service amongst Internet users. One of the earliest and best-known examples of a viral marketing campaign is attributed to Hotmail. At start-up, the company needed to attract a large number of new users very quickly. This was accomplished by adding a footer to every message sent from a free Hotmail e-mail account saying 'To get your FREE email account go to www.hotmail.com'. Viral marketing is popular with advertisers because it is inexpensive and is capable of reaching a large audience very quickly. As an example, film and television companies often use viral marketing to promote new films or shows. Recent campaigns considered to be highly effective include those for series such as Big Brother, True Blood, Arrested Development and movies such as *Cloverfield, The Dark Knight, Pacific Rim and X-Men Days Of Future Past*.

Affiliate marketing involves paying Internet users a small sum each time traffic is directed towards a merchant's web site. Some schemes pay a commission each time a sale is made either directly by the affiliate or as a result of the affiliate directing a visitor to the merchant's web site. Affiliate marketing differs from viral marketing in that affiliates are paid according to their performance. Different mechanisms can be used to direct Internet users to a merchant's site but a common technique involves the use of click-throughs. These are small advertisements that take users to another web site when they are clicked on. Click-throughs are often placed on sites hosting blogs or other content that is likely to attract a large number of visitors. A good example of affiliate marketing is Amazon's affiliate scheme. Under this scheme members modify their web sites to display small adverts in prominent positions. Each advert describes a book or other product that is relevant to the content of the page. Whenever a visitor clicks on the advertisement, he or she is taken to a page on the Amazon web site that allows the item to be bought. Affiliates earn a commission from each sale made in this way.

Google AdWords represents an entirely new way of advertising via the Internet. Whenever a search is carried out via Google, a series of sponsored links is shown next to the search results. The links shown depend upon the search terms used and advertisers pay to associate keywords with their advertisements. Competition between advertisers means that popular keywords cost more to 'own' than keywords that are used less frequently. Many companies use AdWords as their sole means of advertising and invest large amounts of time and money in determining the most cost-effective keywords for their particular products or services. Companies also invest heavily in *search engine placement*, particularly the process of altering the content of a web site so that it appears within the first set of results returned by a search engine for a given set of keywords. A great deal has been written about Google AdWords and its impact on business. However, in brief, many people feel that AdWords has been successful because the advertisements shown are unobtrusive and do not alter the quality of the results returned by the search engine. In addition, the effectiveness of

Viral marketing

Viral marketing uses word-of-mouth to spread awareness of a product or service amongst Internet users.

Affiliate marketing

Affiliate marketing involves paying Internet users a small sum each time traffic is directed towards a merchant's web site.

Google AdWords

Google AdWords is whenever a search is carried out via Google, a series of sponsored links is shown next to the search results. The links shown depend upon the search terms used and advertisers pay to associate keywords with their advertisements.

keywords (and their cost to advertisers) is determined by what people actually search for; new trends or fashions will result in some keywords becoming more or less popular. This means that advertisers pay for the service according to results and can control how much is spent on advertising.

The examples given here show that the Internet and Web 2.0 have changed the ways in which companies market their products and services. These forces have also made companies reconsider some of the basic ideas underlying their businesses. For many companies, responding to the changes brought about by Web 2.0 involves the adoption of new approaches, some of which seem at odds with long-established customs.

A good example of this involves the concept of the 'long tail', an idea popularised by Chris Anderson in an article written for *Wired* in 2004. Traditional bricks-and-mortar retailers have always faced the problem of making the best use of limited shelf space. This has resulted in a tendency to stock a limited range of products, restricting customer choice to those items considered most popular. Music retailers, for instance, devote most of their display space to albums from well-known, established artists or music that is currently in the charts. Another problem, according to Anderson, is that bricks-and-mortar retailers tend to think in terms of serving a relatively small, local population. This means that retailers must stock items they feel will be 'hits' in order to produce a profit. This is because any niche markets that might be served will be very small and are unlikely to generate a profit.

Anderson's view is that the Internet removes both of the restrictions faced by retailers. First, there are no limits on the number of items that can be stocked by a business that operates via the Internet. iTunes, for instance, advertises more than 6 million songs. Second, the global market served by the Internet means that even a niche market is likely to generate a significant number of sales. As an example, movie rental company Netflix rents more than 100,000 Bollywood titles each month.

The 'long tail'

Bricks-and-mortar retailers tend to serve a relatively small, local population and stock items they feel will be 'hits' in order to produce a profit. The Internet removes both of these restrictions faced by retailers and allows them to serve the 'long tail' of customers. This is because there are no limits on the number of items that can be stocked by a business that operates via the Internet. and the global market served by the Internet means that even a niche market is likely to generate a significant number of sales

Companies serving niche markets can generate significant profits providing they follow three basic rules:

Rule 1: Make everything available.

Rule 2: Cut the price in half. Now lower it.

Rule 3: Help me find it.

Web 2.0 tools and techniques make it easier to follow Anderson's rules by helping companies create sophisticated web sites such as those operated by Amazon, iTunes and Netflix. Such sites make it easy for users to browse through the products on offer and locate items of interest. As an example, Amazon has a feature that creates a list of recommended books based on items the user has previously bought or looked at on the site. The site also makes use of customer opinions by allowing visitors to post reviews of books or create lists of recommended reading. Companies also have the ability to create innovative applications by making use of Web 2.0 technologies. As an example, Google provides APIs that allow the creation of RIAs that include AdWords functionality, while Amazon helps developers create applications that make use of its payment services.

| **Activity 3.13** | **Web 2.0** |

1. Find two examples for each of the rules proposed by Chris Anderson.
2. List the advantages of Google AdWords for small businesses.
3. 'The "long tail" is good for retailers and good for customers.' Discuss.

Content management systems

Content management system (CMS)

A software application intended to help users create and manage sophisticated web sites quickly, easily and without any technical knowledge

Content management systems (CMS) enable users to create and manage sophisticated web sites quickly, easily and without any technical knowledge. Most programs feature a number of built-in tools intended to simplify common tasks, such as adding, editing and removing content. In addition, most programs are designed to allow groups of users to work on content items at the same time.

The majority of CMS are component-based, meaning that users can extend the system's functionality by installing additional components (called 'extensions'). As an example, a user might install a message board or guestbook by downloading the necessary components from a library of extensions.

CMS are designed to simplify the management of very large web sites. They are particularly suited to managing sites where large numbers of contributors regularly create and edit content. Many leading CMS are distributed as open-source or are based on open-source products. Some of the best-known applications include Joomla, Drupal and PHP-Nuke. The open-source CMS web site (**www.opensourcecms.com**) enables users to test every major package before installing one.

| **Activity 3.14** | **Different software types** |

To check your knowledge of the different types of software introduced in this chapter (and Chapter 4), match the descriptions of software above with the specific types of software below.

Software descriptions
1. Allows you to create and edit company reports.
2. Finds information for an assignment from the World Wide Web.
3. The use of icons, bars, buttons and other image displays to get things done.
4. Sends information to a computer user in another country.
5. Creates and displays a worksheet for analysis.
6. Manages and supports the maintenance and retrieval of structured data.
7. Manages and supports telecommunications on a network of computers.
8. Detects and removes viruses.
9. A program or set of programs that controls the computer hardware.

Software types
(a) Spreadsheet; (b) graphical user interface (GUI); (c) operating system; (d) a search engine such as Google accessed through a web browser; (e) Norton Anti-Virus Kit; (f) word processor; (g) e-mail package; (h) Novell Netware (a network operating system); (i) relational database management system (RDBMS).

FOCUS ON... SOFTWARE DISTRIBUTION MODELS

This section looks at alternative models of software distribution including open source and application service providers.

Open source

Open source

This describes a type of computer program where the source code has been made freely available to the general public and where there are no restrictions on how the software can be used, modified or redistributed.

Open source is a generic term used to describe software that is supplied to users completely free of charge and without restrictions limiting how it is used, modified or redistributed. In general, the source code for the program is freely available and users can modify it as they see fit.

Open-source projects are usually developed using a community approach, meaning that any individual or company can take part in the development process. Projects are normally managed by committees and all development work is sub-ject to formal peer review. Large projects may involve thousands of individual developers and dozens of large companies, all working on individual aspects of the software.

Many open-source projects use specialised project management software to coordinate the efforts of developers. As an example, SourceForge (**www.sourceforge.net**) is a web site that provides open-source projects with their own miniature web sites containing a range of management tools, such as a tracking system to manage bug reports, support requests and requests for new features.

Supporters of open source argue that software developed in this way tends to be robust, secure and flexible. Programs are more secure, for example, because many thousands of developers may have helped to test them and deal with any problems found. In addition, since many thousands of developers may be working on a given project at any time, security problems tend to be discovered and corrected very quickly – sometimes in a matter of hours.

Apart from the obvious attraction of cost, many organisations adopt open-source software because it gives their own development projects a head start. As an example, a company developing a PIM or scheduling application might save thousands of hours in development time by making use of the code behind the open-source *Sunbird* calendar program.

Some of the benefits of open-source software include:

- A wide variety of applications is available free of charge.

- Problems, such as security flaws, tend to be discovered and repaired very quickly.

- In general, the software available is of very high quality.

- It is often possible to customise software to meet specific requirements quickly and at low cost. Companies adopting open source gain the benefit of many thousands of development hours for little or no cost.

- Companies can retain ownership of any improvements or modifications made to the software.

Some disadvantages associated with open source include:

- It can be difficult to keep software up to date since some applications change almost daily.

- Support services, such as training, are sometimes costly or difficult to obtain.

- There are sometimes compatibility issues, particularly with regard to the file formats.

- The quality of some applications is variable; some applications may be badly written and may require a great deal of time and effort to modify.

- Some software licences require companies to release any improvements made to the software back to the open-source community. In some cases, this has implications regarding competitive advantage; competitors might gain the benefit of a company's investment in improving the software for little or no cost.

Some people argue that the operation of the Internet depends upon open-source software. This is why.

Most blogs, forums and portals are produced using content management systems. The most popular content management systems are based around open-source systems, such as Wordpress, Joomla and Drupal. These systems use scripting languages to generate the pages they display. The most popular scripting languages used are PHP and Java, which together account for around a third of all scripts and which are both open source. The pages produced by content management systems are sent to users by a web server. The world's most popular web server is Apache, an open-source program that serves almost half of all web sites. Finally, the pages served by Apache are viewed within a web browser, such as Firefox or Chrome, which, after Internet Explorer, are the world's most popular browsers and are open source.

Table 3.4 illustrates the variety of open-source applications available to business users. As shown, all major software categories are covered.

It was mentioned earlier that open-source software is supplied without any real restrictions on its use. This is because the use of the software is governed by a software licence that is considered very permissive. There are several other types of software licence that allow organisations to obtain programs free of charge or at low cost. Table 3.5 describes common software licences that enable organisations to acquire free or inexpensive software. However, note that there may be subtle differences in a particular software licence that place significant restrictions on how a program (and its source code) may be used. As an example, a company that has invested a great deal in modifying an application may choose to recover some of that investment by selling the software to others. This would be acceptable under an open-source software licence, but unacceptable under a GNU General Public License.

Table 3.4 Common applications and open-source alternatives

Application	Open-source alternative
Web browser, e.g. Internet Explorer	Firefox or Chrome
Word processing and office software, e.g. Microsoft Office	Apache Open Office, Libre Office
Database, e.g. Microsoft Access or SQL Server	MySQL or Borland Interbase
Web server, e.g. Microsoft Internet Information Server (IIS)	Apache
Media player, e.g. WinAmp	Media Player Classic
Operating system, e.g. Windows 8	Linux variant, e.g. Ubuntu
Scripting language, e.g. VBScript	PHP
Development tool, e.g. Visual Basic	Java

Table 3.5 Common software licences allowing organisations to obtain software free or charge or at low cost

Open source	There are no restrictions limiting how software/materials can be used, modified or redistributed. The source code for an application is always provided.
GNU General Public License (GNU GPL)	Software/materials can be used freely but any improvements must be released as free software. Software distributed under a GNU GPL licence is sometimes described as *copylefted*.
Public domain	Software/materials are not copyrighted and can be used, modified or redistributed without any restrictions. Although a working application may be provided, its source code may not be available.
Shareware	Software/materials are supplied on a 'try before you buy' basis. The software may be used without charge for a trial period. After the trial period, the user must purchase the software or stop using it.
Creative commons	Software/materials are distributed free of charge under a flexible licence that enables the originator of the software to control various conditions, such as whether or not the software can be used for commercial purposes.

Application service provider (ASP)

Application service provider (ASP)

A company that supplies software and services to a client organisation over a network, usually the Internet.

Software as a Service (SaaS)

A software distribution model where users access software and data via a network, such as the Internet, using a web browser.

Under this model, an **application service provider (ASP)** supplies software and services to a client organisation over a network, usually the Internet. Users access software and data via a web browser. This type of approach is often described as **on-demand software or Software as a Service (SaaS)**. This is because software is downloaded automatically as users come to need particular features. As an example, if a user chooses to edit a word processing document, the browser will automatically download and install a simple word processing component. ASPs have a number of common features:

- The ASP owns and operates the application.
- The ASP owns and operates the servers used to provide the service.
- The ASP employs the staff who operate and maintain the application and servers, and who provide support.
- The service makes the application available via the Internet; users can access their data from almost any location.
- The service is paid for on a per-use basis or by a regular fee.

For organisations, some of the advantages of using ASPs include:

- Initial (startup) costs are low and installation is quick.
- Operating costs are very low and are predictable.
- Hardware and software requirements are very low; all that is needed is an Internet connection and a computer or terminal capable of running a web browser.
- All necessary software and hardware is maintained and kept up-to-date by the ASP.
- The ability to access programs and files from almost any location allows staff to work more flexibly and productively.
- The ASP assumes responsibility for the security and integrity of data.
- Existing ICT resources are freed and can be directed elsewhere.

Although the benefits of ASPs are undoubtedly attractive, they also have a number of disadvantages. Some of the most significant include:

- The organisation becomes dependent upon the Internet; all work will stop if the organisation loses its access to the Internet.

- The ASP takes control of the organisation's data; the data will be at risk if the ASP has inadequate security or poor backup procedures.

- Adopting an ASP may require the organisation to change working practices; the organisation changes to meet the requirements of the system, not the other way around.

- Although startup costs are low, long-term costs may be very high. As an example, the cost of renting an application for an extended period of time may exceed outright purchase costs.

Software as a Service has seen renewed interest because of major changes in the computing industry. As software sales have started to decline, many software developers have attempted to reposition themselves by becoming service organisations and adopting business models similar to those used by organisations such as Sun Microsystems and Red Hat. As an example, various versions of Sun Microsystem's Java programming language are available as open source or free of charge. The company earns an income from the software by marketing a range of complementary services and products including hosting, training and software development.

SUMMARY

1. A computer system consists of a number of interrelated components that work together with the aim of converting data into information. In a computer-based information system, processing is carried out electronically, usually with little or no intervention from a human user.

2. Hardware is the physical components of a computer system. The hardware of a computer system can be said to consist of input devices, memory, central processing unit, output devices and storage devices.

3. Major categories of computers include mainframes, minicomputers and microcomputers.

4. The main hardware components of a computer system are the following:

   - Input devices are used to enter data, information or instructions.
   - Output devices display the results of computer processing.
   - Storage devices are used to store programs, data awaiting processing and the information resulting from computer processing.
   - The processor, which is used to execute software instructions and perform calculations.

5. A personal computer consists of a number of components, including: microprocessor (CPU), graphics card, motherboard and casing.

6. Software can be defined as a series of detailed instructions that control the operation of a computer system. There are two major categories of software: systems software and applications software.

7. Systems software manages and controls the operation of the computer system as it performs tasks on behalf of the user. Operating systems interact with the hardware of the computer at a very low level in order to manage and direct the computer's resources.

8. Applications software can be defined as a set of programs that enable users to perform specific information processing activities. Applications software can be divided into two broad categories: general-purpose productivity software and application-specific.

9. Productivity software describes general-purpose applications that aim to support users in performing a variety of common tasks. In business organisations, productivity software is often used to reduce the time needed to complete routine administrative tasks, such as producing documents or organising meetings. Computer-based information systems used in this way are generally referred to as 'office automation systems'.

10. The three main types of productivity software are:

- A word processor provides the ability to enter, edit, store and print text. In addition, word-processing packages allow users to alter the layout of documents and often provide a variety of formatting tools.
- Spreadsheet programs are designed to store and manipulate values, numbers and text in an efficient and useful way.
- Databases (Chapter 4).

11. The Internet provides a variety of opportunities for organisations to carry out business activities. These include competitor research, product research, customer support, advertising and promotion, and e-commerce. The World Wide Web (WWW) is a part of the Internet that can be accessed using a web browser. A web browser provides the means to search for and retrieve information quickly and easily.

12. E-mail (electronic mail) can be defined as the transmission of a message over a communications network. Messages can be entered via the keyboard or taken from files stored on disk. E-mail programs provide the ability to create, edit, organise, transmit and receive e-mail messages.

13. Office automation systems consist of five basic categories: electronic publishing systems, electronic communications systems, electronic meeting systems, image processing systems and office management systems.

14. Management applications consist of personal information managers (PIMs), project management software, contact managers and groupware applications.

15. Alternative models of software distribution include open source and application service providers. Open source describes software that is supplied to users completely free of charge and without restrictions limiting how it is used, modified or redistributed. Application service providers provide software on a rental basis; customers are charged a regular fee or on a per-user basis.

EXERCISES

Self-assessment exercises

1. In addition to 'Smart Pause', describe at least three other features offered by devices with eye tracking technology.

2. In terms of developing more powerful tablets, why are advances in battery technology just as important as advances in microprocessor technology?

3. Which type of printing technology is best suited to the production of the following documents?

(a) a business letter
(b) a program listing
(c) a chart or diagram, printed in colour
(d) an internal memorandum
(e) an engineering diagram.

4. Which input device is best suited to the following tasks?

(a) entering the details of bank cheques
(b) entering data from multiple-choice test papers
(c) entering data from labels or price tags
(d) entering a diagram, picture or photograph
(e) entering the text of a letter.

5. Describe some of the major characteristics of mainframes, minicomputers and personal computers.

6. How can network computers help to reduce the cost of ownership?

7. List at least three common pointing devices.

8. What is the meaning of each abbreviation or acronym listed below? Provide a brief explanation for each of the items listed.

    (a) MICR   (f) OCR
    (b) RAM   (g) COM
    (c) BIOS   (h) PDA
    (d) CD-ROM   (i) ROM
    (e) CPU   (j) DVD

9. What are some of the benefits of flash drives?

10. Produce your own definitions of the following terms:

    (a) software
    (b) operating system
    (c) graphical user interface
    (d) productivity software
    (e) personal information manager.

11. Describe the different approaches to file processing. What are the major characteristics, advantages and disadvantages of each?

Discussion questions

1. Will network computers and thin clients make personal computers obsolete? Using relevant examples, make a case for one side of this argument.

2. You intend to purchase a personal computer to help with your studies. You have decided to create a weighted ranking table to help you choose a suitable system. What criteria should be used for selection and how should each item be weighted?

3. Despite still being functional, an obsolete computer system is of little value to a business organisation. Organisations should continually upgrade or replace systems in order to keep abreast of changes in technology. Make a case in favour of or against this argument.

4. 'The results from search engines cannot be relied upon.' Carry out any additional research you need in order to discuss whether or not you think this statement is true.

5. Why do you think XML is considered to be of great importance to business organisations?

Essay questions

1. How is convergence affecting home entertainment and personal communications?

2. You have been asked to produce a guide to buying a personal computer by a fellow student on your course. The student has a budget for hardware of £1000. Avoiding technical terms as far as possible, produce a guide that addresses the following:

    (a) Produce a detailed specification for a personal computer system. You should describe the system in terms of the input, output and storage devices needed. Justify any choices made and explain any technical terms used.

(b) Select at least two computer systems that meet the requirements specified. Evaluate each of the systems in turn and make a recommendation to the student.

(c) Provide a realistic costing for the chosen system. Ensure that any ongoing costs are included.

3. Voice recognition systems have begun to gain popularity with both business and home users. However, such systems still suffer from a number of limitations that restrict their overall effectiveness. Conduct any research necessary to produce a report that addresses the following tasks:

(a) Provide an overview of voice recognition technology and describe how such systems operate.

(b) Provide a balanced view of the advantages, disadvantages, strengths and limitations of voice recognition systems.

(c) Explain some of the uses to which voice recognition systems can be applied. Pay particular attention to the business applications for this technology.

4. Select two competing software packages as the basis for a detailed comparison. Produce a report that addresses the following tasks:

(a) Using relevant examples, describe the major features of each package.

(b) Considering the range of features offered by each package, indicate how these might be of benefit to a business organisation.

(c) Which package would be more likely to meet the needs of a business organisation? Provide a detailed rationale for your choice.

5. Conduct any required research and produce a report that addresses the following tasks:

(a) Provide an overview of how organisations can conduct business transactions over the Internet.

(b) Discuss the advantages and disadvantages of using the Internet as a business tool.

(c) Issues related to security are of great concern to many organisations. Discuss the major security problems faced by organisations conducting business over the Internet.

6. As a student, you are required to produce essays and reports containing graphics, diagrams and charts. You may also be required to take part in seminars and presentations. As your course progresses you are likely to recognise a need to store information obtained through research. Produce a report that addresses the following areas:

(a) Considering the tasks described above, identify a range of applications software that can be used to support your studies.

(b) Discuss the ways in which the applications you have identified can help to improve your studies or enhance the quality of your work.

(c) Identify and discuss any other ways in which the applications identified may be of benefit.

7. Discuss the use of specialised software for the Internet in terms of its value to business organisations. Refer to applications such as meta-search engines and intelligent agents in your response.

8. What are the challenges and benefits of RFID technology for supermarkets? Illustrate your response with appropriate examples.

Examination questions

1. A small business organisation wishes to purchase a number of personal computers and has issued a tender document to a number of suppliers. Using relevant examples, provide an overview of the technical, support and cost issues that should be considered when evaluating supplier proposals.

2. A modern supermarket will make extensive use of technology to support all of its activities. Considering an organisation such as ASDA or Sainsbury's, describe the range of input,

output, storage and processing devices that might be used within a typical branch. For each item identified, provide a brief description of its purpose and any benefits gained from its use.

3. Considering a typical IBM-compatible personal computer, you are required to:

   (a) Identify the main components of a personal computer system. For each item identified, provide a brief description of its purpose.
   (b) Using relevant examples, describe some of the methods that can be used to assess the performance and quality of key components.
   (c) In addition to the initial cost of the personal computer itself, a number of other expenses are likely to be incurred. Using relevant examples, provide an overview of these additional costs.

4. Interest in commercial uses for the Internet has grown rapidly over the past five years. You are required to carry out the following tasks:

   (a) Using relevant examples, describe the range of business applications to which the Internet can be applied.
   (b) Using relevant examples, discuss the costs, technical problems and organisational issues associated with making use of the Internet as a business tool.
   (c) Using relevant examples, discuss the potential benefits to an organisation of using the World Wide Web as a business tool.

5. You have been approached for advice by the manager of a small company. The manager wishes to purchase a number of software packages in order to improve the productivity of staff. Prepare a guide that can be used by the manager when selecting appropriate applications.

6. Groupware improves productivity, enhances communication and reduces costs. Using relevant examples, provide a balanced discussion of this statement.

7. How can mobile devices, such as tablets, support relief work following a natural disaster?

References

Anderson, C. (2004) *The Long Tail*. Wired.com. Available online at: www.wired.com/wired/archive/12.10/tail_pr.html

Rao, J. M. and Reiley, D.H. (2012) 'The Economics of Spam', *Journal of Economic Perspectives*, 26, 3, 87–110

Rogers, E. (1983) *Diffusion of Innovations*, 3rd edition, Free Press, New York

Strassman, P. (1997) *The Squandered Computer*, Information Economics Press, New Haven, CT

Further reading

Mueller, S. (2013). *Upgrading and Repairing PCs*, 21st edition, QUE, Indianapolis, IN. Although comprehensive and highly detailed, this book is fairly easy to follow, even for non-technical readers. Chapter 2 provides an overview of the components of a PC. Chapter 3 describes processors in detail. Chapter 6 describes computer memory. Chapter 9 describes hard disk drives, while Chapter 11 looks at optical storage, such as CD and DVD. Chapter 16 describes input devices in detail.

Parsons, J. and Oja, D. (2013) *New Perspectives on Computer Concepts 2014*, 16th edition, Thomson Course Technology, Boston. Although some of the material might be considered a little lacking in depth, this book is very easy to read and beautifully presented. Chapter 2 covers computer hardware, especially processors and memory. There are also sections on storage devices and input/output devices.

Web links

www.dell.com Dell is one of the world's leading manufacturers of personal computers.

www.hp.com Hewlett-Packard is one of the world's largest manufacturers of personal computers, laser printers and inkjet printers.

www.intel.com The Intel web site holds a great deal of information concerning microprocessors. Intel manufacture the Pentium II and Pentium III range of processors.

www.amd.com AMD manufactures the Athlon series and other processors.

www.nvidia.com NVidia is responsible for an extremely popular range of graphics cards. The site contains information on the cards themselves, as well as other useful snippets, such as which software products are supported.

http://foldoc.org/ Online dictionary of computing.

www.ask.com A generic search tool that allows questions to be asked in plain language. Ideal for asking questions such as 'How do hard disks work?'

www.howstuffworks.com A great deal of general material but contains relevant features on microprocessors, the Internet and more.

www.whatis.com This site is effectively a glossary giving succinct definitions of terms relating to hardware and software.

www.tomshardware.com Despite the name, this site is a detailed well-laid-out site giving detailed reviews on areas such as RAM and hard disks.

www.wired.com Wired is one of the oldest and most respected titles to provide up-to-date news on technology and related subjects.

www.21stcentury.co.uk Online publication covering all areas of science and technology.

www.fastchip.net/howcomputerswork/p1.html An online book by Roger Young offering an extremely detailed and technical tutorial describing how microprocessors work.

www.irt.org Articles on web-related technology, such as CGI, PHP, SSI, etc.

www.tutorialfind.com/tutorials Access to a wide range of tutorials on a wide range of subjects including hardware, operating systems, programming and web development.

www.pcwebopaedia.com An online encyclopedia of computer-related acronyms and terms. Each entry is accompanied by a concise explanation and additional web links.

www.hotfiles.com ZDNet provides access to a large library of software including shareware, freeware and commercial (demonstration) packages.

www.microsoft.com Microsoft are the world's largest software company. Use this site to locate information on products such as Windows (all versions), MS Office, Internet Explorer and Visual Basic.

LINKS TO OTHER CHAPTERS

Databases and business intelligence

CHAPTER AT A GLANCE

LEARNING OUTCOMES

After reading this chapter, you will be able to:

- understand the use of database application software;
- describe the need for business intelligence systems;
- understand the concept of a data warehouse and describe alternative architectures for a data warehouse;
- explain the process of data mining;
- describe business analytics techniques such as OLAP, cube analysis and visualisation tools.

MANAGEMENT ISSUES

In Chapter 1, a central role of BIS was described as supporting the manager's work by providing the information he or she needs in order to make decisions. Business intelligence involves the capture, storage, processing and delivery of information in a timely manner to assist decision making. From a managerial perspective, this chapter addresses the following areas:

- The role of databases for storage and sharing of information in the organisation.
- The use of a data warehouse which is a special database or data repository that has been prepared to support decision making.
- The use of data mining which is used to find patterns in data that can be used to predict future behaviour.
- The use of business analytics tools to produce on-demand reports and graphical output for decision making.

INTRODUCTION

This chapter covers the use of database application software which stores information in an organised way so that specific items can be selected and retrieved quickly. Business intelligence systems, which are derived from executive information systems (EIS) (see Chapter 6), generally focus on providing timely information at a strategic level in large organisations with large data sets. The major elements of a business intelligence system are a data warehouse that holds the data, data mining techniques for extracting data and business analytics tools for reporting data analysis to the user.

DATABASES

Prior to the introduction of electronic database systems, almost all of the information an organisation needed to store was organised using manual filing systems. Typical methods included filing cabinets and card index records. Although manual filing systems are still used widely today, electronic databases are also commonplace and are considered to provide a number of important benefits to business organisations. Since databases are so important in storing data for information systems the analysis and design need to create databases is covered extensively later (in Chapters 10 and 11).

We can understand more about electronic databases by first considering the disadvantages of manual filing systems. Some of the most common disadvantages include:

- The way in which information is organised largely determines the uses to which it can be put. For example, if a list of customers is stored in alphabetical order by name, it becomes difficult to view customers by location.
- It is often difficult to retrieve specific items of information quickly.
- It might not be possible to add, amend or delete the information held in a manual record without creating a new copy of the record.
- It is sometimes difficult to classify information so that it can be stored in the correct location. This can make it difficult to locate specific items at a later date.
- If the information is used regularly by a number of different individuals or departments, multiple copies of manual files may need to be maintained. This is a major information management problem since a number of difficulties arise from the duplication of data. Some examples include:

  (a) Extra expense is incurred in terms of the additional storage space and labour power required to maintain files.

  (b) Changes made to one set of files may not be reflected in all copies. This can mean that some files contain outdated information, whilst others may contain new or additional details.

  (c) If a standardised filing system is used, this may not suit the needs of all users. On the other hand, the use of different filing systems creates problems in maintaining files and locating information.

The use of an electronic database can remove all of the difficulties outlined above. We can suggest that an electronic database offers the following advantages:

- A database will allow users to organise information in a variety of different ways. The initial order in which records are placed is often unimportant, as information can be reorganised quickly and easily. This allows an organisation to maximise its usage of the information it holds.

- The powerful search facilities provided by electronic database programs can be used to locate and retrieve information many thousands of times faster than by manual methods.

- An electronic database provides facilities for users to add, amend or delete records as required. Additional features simplify data entry and assist in managing the information held. As an example, adding groups of similar records can be simplified by making multiple copies of an existing entry. Each copy can then be edited as needed. This removes the need for the data entry operator to enter the details of each record in full.

- Sophisticated indexing features mean that the same basic information can be stored under a number of different categories. This provides great flexibility and allows users to locate, retrieve and organise information as needed.

- Databases used throughout a company are usually accessed by many different users across a network system. Some of the advantages of this approach include:

   (a) Since the unnecessary duplication of information is minimised, the costs involved in maintaining records are reduced, although often separate databases can give rise to similar problems from those of duplicated paper records.

   (b) Any changes made to the information held in the database are reflected to all users, ensuring consistency at all times.

   (c) Although information is held in a structured manner, the database software will normally provide sufficient flexibility to meet the different requirements of individual users and departments.

Database

A collection of related information stored in an organised way so that specific items can be selected and retrieved quickly.

To summarise, a **database** can be defined as a collection of related information. The information held in the database is stored in an organised way so that specific items can be selected and retrieved quickly. A database need not involve the use of technology – examples of manual databases include telephone directories, address books, diaries and card index files.

Business-level advantages of databases

The main business benefits of databases derive from the way that databases are designed for sharing information. They are superior for:

- *multi-user access* – allowing different people in the business access to the same data simultaneously, such as a manager and another member of staff accessing a single customer's data;

- *distributed access* – users in different departments of the business can readily access data;

- *speed* – for accessing large volumes of information, such as the customers of a bank, only databases are designed to produce reports or access the information rapidly about a single customer;

- *data quality* – sophisticated validation checks can be performed when data are entered to ensure their integrity;

- *security* – access to different types of data can readily be limited to different members of staff. In a car dealership database, for example, the manager of a single branch could be restricted to sales data for their branch;

- *space efficiency* – by splitting up a database into different tables when it is de-signed, less space is needed, as will be seen in the section on normalisation (Chapter 11).

Despite the many advantages of databases, there are certain information management applications where other software, such as spreadsheets, are more appropriate. For instance, in some cases it is:

- easier and faster to create a spreadsheet structure;

- easier and faster to enter data using facilities such as auto-filling the months;

- easier to perform numeric modelling;
- easier and faster to produce total and average sales summary data.

An overview of the types of database

Approaches to the design of electronic databases include file processing databases, database management systems, relational database management systems, object-oriented databases and network and hierarchical databases. The following provides a brief overview of each of these approaches.

File processing databases

Early data processing systems were based around numerous files containing large amounts of data related to daily business transactions. As a result, many organisations found themselves in a position where they held large amounts of valuable data but were unable to maximise their use of them. A major problem stemmed from the fact that the data held were often stored in different formats, for example completely different structures might be used to store details of sales and purchases. In order to make use of these data, it was usually necessary to create specialised computer programs, often at great expense.

Flat-file database

A self-contained database that only contains one type of record – or table – and cannot access data held in other database files.

This type of database is sometimes described as having a flat file structure. A flat-file database can be described as being self-contained since it contains only one type of record – or *table* – and cannot access data held in other database files. A free-form database allows users to store information in the form of brief notes or passages of text. Each item held can be placed within a category or assigned one or more key words. Information is organised and retrieved by using categories or key words.

A modern variation on free-form databases is the hypertext database. In a hypertext database information is stored as series of objects and can consist of text, graphics, numerical data and multimedia data. Any object can be linked to any other, allowing users to store disparate information in an organised manner.

A good example of a free-form database is the help files found within most software packages. An example of a hypertext database is the pages available via any given site on the World Wide Web.

Free-form database

Allows users to store information in the form of unstructured notes or passages of text. Information is organised and retrieved by using categories or key words.

Hypertext database

Information is stored as series of objects that can consist of text, graphics, numerical data and multimedia data. Objects are linked, allowing users to store disparate information in an organised manner.

Database management system (DBMS)

One or more computer programs that allow users to enter, store, organise, manipulate and retrieve data from a database.

Database management systems

The introduction of database management systems altered the way in which organisations managed their data resources. Although data were still held separately from the programs that made use of them, this new approach offered greater flexibility whilst reducing development and operating costs. Some of the major characteristics of the database management system (DBMS) approach included:

- Programs included a range of general-purpose tools and utilities for producing reports or extracting data. This meant that comparatively little development was needed in order to undertake new tasks.

- The availability of general-purpose tools enabled non-technical users to access data. Users were able to analyse data, extract records and produce reports with little support from technical staff.

- The use of a DBMS encouraged organisations to introduce standards for developing and operating their databases. As an example, many organisations developed standards governing the structure of any new data files created.

We will now review the main types of database management system.

Relational database management systems

Relational database management system (RDBMS)

An extension of a DBMS that allows data to be combined from a variety of sources.

The popularity of the **relational database management system (RDBMS)** approach grew from a need to share data resources across the entire organisation. In the past, it had been normal to concentrate resources in a small number of specific areas. For example, an organisation's accounting and stock control functions often dealt with the largest number of business transactions and were seen as having the greatest need of the organisation's information technology resources. In the same way, these functions were also seen as having the greatest need of the organisation's data resources. However, as companies aimed to become more efficient and reduce costs it became essential to ensure the widest possible access to organisational data resources. In addition, organisations were also beginning to receive increased demands for information from users and managers.

The RDBMS approach can be seen as an extension of the DBMS approach with the additional benefits to be gained by sharing data across an organisation and the ability to combine data from several different sources. As an example, it is possible to reduce stockholding costs by linking together an organisation's production and stock control functions. Such an approach would allow stock levels to be adjusted continuously by examining production levels. In this way, stocks of raw materials can be increased or decreased according to actual usage. In the same way, production scheduling might be improved by inspecting stock levels at regular intervals.

Relational databases

Data are stored within a number of different tables with each dealing with different subjects that are related (linked) using key fields.

Relational databases enable data to be stored within a number of different tables. They are the most widely used type of database. Separate record designs can be used to store data dealing with different subjects. For example, a database used for stock control might use separate record designs to store information concerning items stocked, reorder levels and supplier details.

Record key

Identifies a specific record within a database, usually takes the form of a number or code and will be different for each record in the database.

The tables within a relational database can be linked together using one or more **record keys**. As mentioned earlier, all database records must contain a unique record key that can be used to identify a specific record. In a relational database, this is often called the **primary key**. However, records can also contain other keys to help locate data stored in another table. The record keys contained in each table can used to establish one or more **relationships** between tables. By using record keys in combination – a **compound key** – it is possible to retrieve data from several tables at once. Note that a field used to locate information in another, related table is often called a **foreign key**.

Primary key

The tables within a relational database can be linked together using one or more record keys. All records must contain a unique record key called the primary key.

Figure 4.1 illustrates how records can be linked together using record keys. The diagram illustrates a simple relational database containing two tables: one holding details of an employee's pay, the other holding personal information, such as the employee's address. The database is to be used to generate pay slips for all employees. In order to accomplish this, the DBMS would carry out the following actions for each record in the Personal Details table:

Relationship

In a relational database, data can be combined from several different sources by defining relationships between tables.

1. Locate a record within the Personal Details table. The unique primary key can be used to identify a specific employee.

2. Extract any information required from the Personal Details record, such as the employee's name and address.

Compound key

In a relational database, it is possible to retrieve data from several tables at once by using record keys in combination, often known as a compound key.

3. The secondary key identifies a unique record in the Pay Details table. Since the secondary key in the Personal Details table matches the primary key in the Pay Details table, the DBMS can locate the specific record required.

4. The information required from the Pay Details table is extracted and the pay slip is printed.

A more detailed explanation of database terminology is provided later (in Chapter 11).

Foreign (secondary) key fields

These fields are used to link tables together by referring to the primary key in another database table.

Object-oriented databases

Object-oriented database

The database is made up of objects combining data structures with functions needed to manipulate the object or the data it holds.

An **object-oriented** approach to database design employs the concept of reusable objects in order to develop sophisticated or complex applications. An *object* combines data structures with any functions needed to manipulate the object or the data it holds. As an example, an

Figure 4.1 An example of how key fields are used to link information from different database tables

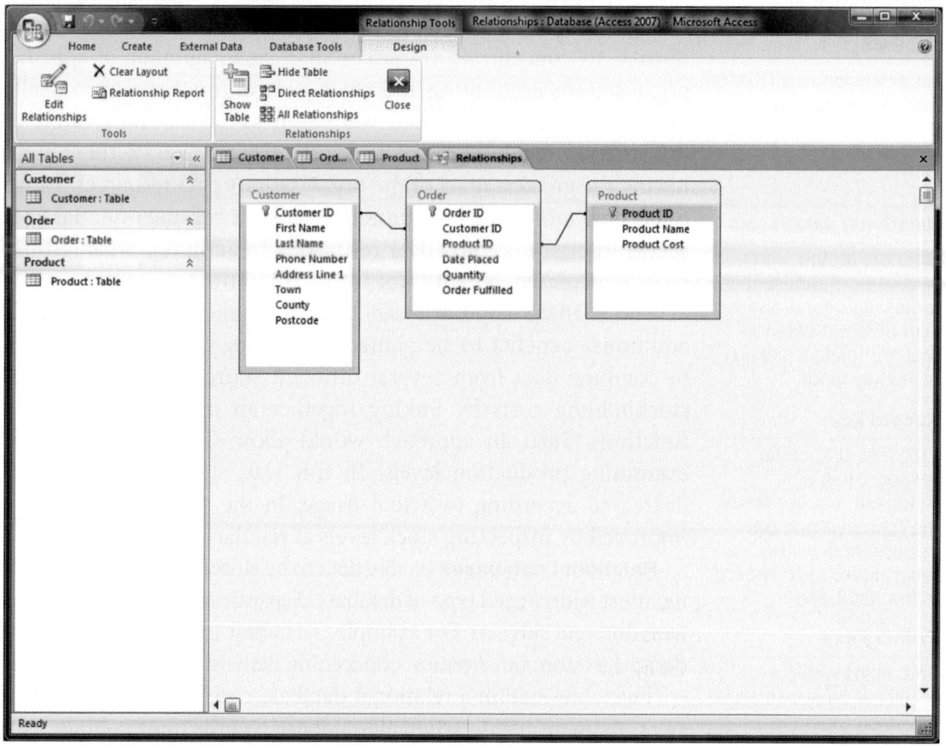

Source: Screenshot frame reprinted by permission from Microsoft Corporation

object called Employee might be created to store details of staff. The object would contain a data structure that allowed basic details such as name, address, age, etc. to be stored. In addition, the object would also contain facilities that allow various actions to be performed, such as changing an employee's address.

This object-oriented approach offers several important advantages:

■ Since objects are self-contained, they are easy to manage, for example changes can be made to an individual object without necessarily altering any other part of the system.

■ New objects can be created quickly and easily from existing ones. Continuing with the example given previously, the Employee object might be used as the basis for a new object entitled Manager. Only minor changes would be needed to complete the new object since it would already share most of the features of Employee.

■ Objects can be copied or transferred into new systems with little difficulty. Since the object already contains any functions needed to make use of it, it can be used immediately within the new system.

Network and hierarchical databases

Mention of these types of databases is included for completeness. These are alternatives to the relational model and were its competitors in the 1980s. In the 1990s, the vast majority of business applications became RDBMS-based, but with object-oriented techniques being used increasingly. The network or hierarchical model may be used for some high-performance applications such as data warehouses (although many of these are based on RDBMS).

Using database software

All database programs enable users to create and edit tables or record structures. In addition, all packages allow users to enter, modify, delete, sort and extract records. The majority of packages also enable users to print data in a variety of different formats. Microsoft Access is the best-known database used on the PC (Figure 4.1) and is mainly for personal or departmental use by a small number of users. Where databases are used by a large number of users, they are hosted on a mainframe or on a Unix or Microsoft Windows Server. These databases for 'mission-critical' applications include Oracle, Informix, Sybase, Microsoft SQL Server and IBM DB2.

The majority of modern database programs support the creation of relational databases containing several linked tables. Although tables can be used in isolation, they can also be used to combine together information drawn from one or more other tables.

Many programs also provide the ability to link tables together automatically. Microsoft Access, for example, provides an interactive facility to analyse one or more tables and create any required relationships.

All major database programs enable users to create and modify data entry forms. A data entry form provides a convenient means of viewing, entering, editing and deleting records.

An index stores information concerning the order of the records in the database. The index lists the locations of records but does not alter the actual order in the database. This can be made clearer by using the index of a book as a simple analogy: the index allows users to find a specific piece of information quickly and easily, regardless of how the material in the book is organised.

Indexes are commonly used to increase the speed at which records can be located or sorted. Multiple indexes can be created so that the records in the database can be sorted in a variety of ways.

All modern database programs provide a range of sophisticated security features. Examples of some of the most common features available include:

- *Encryption*. Data can be encoded so that they appear meaningless until decoded. Passwords provide control over the encryption and decryption process.

- *Recovery*. Many programs contain tools that allow damaged database files to be repaired. In the event that a file cannot be repaired, additional tools may be available that allow users to retrieve as much data as possible from the damaged file.

- *Passwords*. Access to specific files or tables can be restricted through the use of passwords. Several passwords can be used to limit what parts of the database different users can view or alter. As an example, a data entry clerk might be assigned a password that prevents changes being made to the structure of a table or the format of a report.

All major database packages allow users to generate a wide variety of *reports*. Many programs are capable of creating simple reports automatically. In addition, many programs allow users to perform calculations and other actions as the report is produced. This enables additional information, such as subtotals, to be calculated and included in the report whenever required.

A query enables a user to locate, sort, update or extract records from the database. Users design a query by specifying the conditions that must be met in order for a record to be selected. In many programs, the creation of a query is an interactive process, where users respond to a series of questions in order to generate the required design.

There are two basic types of query: selection queries and update queries:

- A *selection query* can be used to locate and display any records meeting a set of specified conditions. None of the data held in the database are altered; any records not meeting the conditions set are simply hidden from view temporarily.

- An update query (sometimes known as an 'action query') can be used to modify records in a variety of ways. Records are selected for alteration according to a set of conditions specified by the user. Common actions performed by update queries include:

Data entry form

In an electronic database, a data entry form provides a convenient means of viewing, entering, editing and deleting records.

Index

Stores information concerning the order of the records in the database. The index lists the locations of records but does not alter the actual order of the database.

Query

Extracts data according to a set of conditions specified by the user.

Update query

An update query can be used to change records, tables and reports held in a database management system.

(a) updating values held in fields, for example by carrying out a calculation;

(b) deleting any records no longer required;

(c) appending new records to the database;

(d) generating new tables containing selected records or summary information.

Structured Query Language (SQL)

A form of programming language that provides a standardised method for retrieving information from databases.

Filter

In a spreadsheet or database, a filter can be used to remove data from the screen temporarily. This allows users to work with a specific group of records. Filters do not alter or delete data but simply hide any unwanted items.

It is worth noting that the majority of database programs make use of a special **Structured Query Language (SQL)** in order to create queries. SQL is described in more detail in a moment.

A **filter** allows users to view the information held in a database in a variety of ways. Filters can be used to sort data into different orders, display only selected fields or display only selected records. In many ways, filters can be thought of as combining some of the features of both indexes and selection queries. It is worth noting that filters do not alter any of the data held in the database.

Structured Query Language (SQL) provides a standardised method for retrieving information from databases. Although traditionally used to manage large data-bases held on mainframes and minicomputers, it has become a widely used and popular tool for personal computer database packages. One of the reasons for this popularity is that SQL supports multi-user databases that operate across network systems.

SQL programs are created by producing a series of statements containing special key words. The example below shows a simple SQL query designed to search the Student Record table and display records for students with a Last Name of 'Jones'.

SELECT DISTINCTROW [Student Record].[Last Name]

FROM [Student Record]

WHERE (((([Student Record].[Last Name])='Jones'));

Users are often unaware that queries created using the interactive design tools provided by many modern database packages are converted into SQL programs before being executed. In Microsoft Access, for example, a mouse is used to design a query on the screen. However, the query is translated into equivalent SQL statements before it is executed.

In common with many other types of application software, most modern database packages include a *macro language* or a programming tool that can be used to handle extremely complex tasks.

The majority of modern database programs contain a number of tools designed to automate common *data analysis* tasks. The ability to generate charts and graphs, for example, is a common feature amongst programs.

Database programs are able to deal with data drawn from a variety of different sources. In many cases, files produced by other packages can be *imported* directly into a database with no loss of data. In addition, some programs are capable of producing table designs automatically, based on the content of the file being imported.

The ability of a database program to *export* data in a variety of formats is used extensively in a variety of applications. Mailmerge operations, for example, often make use of data drawn from customer records held in an organisation's sales database.

Activity 4.1	Forms, queries and reports

Using a package such as Microsoft Access, create a simple database that can be used to store the names and addresses of your friends and colleagues. Make sure that the database includes the following features:

- a simple data entry form that can be used to add, edit or delete records;
- at least one query, for example a query to list all people living in a certain city;
- at least one report, for example a report to show the telephone number of every person listed in the database.

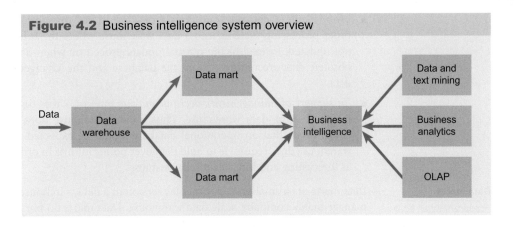

Figure 4.2 Business intelligence system overview

BUSINESS INTELLIGENCE

Business intelligence

A general term that describes a range of techniques and technologies used to gather, store and analyse information from a variety of sources in order to improve decision making within the organisation.

Business intelligence (BI) systems are needed due to the vast amounts of data now held in organisational information systems and the need to extract useful information from these in the form of patterns and trends, and present the information in a understandable way to decision makers. Although this role has many similarities with the use of management information systems (i.e. decision support systems, information reporting systems and executive information systems) described in Chapter 6, BI systems generally focus on providing timely information at a strategic level in large organisations with large data sets (hence the need for a data warehouse, described later). BI systems also generally provide indirect support for particular decisions rather than the decision specific orientation of decision support systems.

Figure 4.2 shows the main elements of a business intelligence system. Data is gathered from various sources and then held in a special database repository termed a data warehouse in order to support decision making in the organisation. Repositories of data focused on departmental or subject areas are termed 'data marts'. Data mining is a type of analysis that aims to identify patterns in the data that can be used to predict future behaviour. Business analytic tools are used to conduct analysis of the data held in the data warehouse using reporting and querying tools.

DATA WAREHOUSES

Data warehouses

Large database systems containing current and historical data that can be analysed to produce information to support organisational decision making

Data warehouses are large database systems containing current and historical data that can be analysed to produce information to support organisational decision making.

William Inmon (2005) is often known as the father of the data warehouse. He defines a data warehouse as:

A subject-oriented, integrated, time variant, and non-volatile collection of data in support of management's decision making process.

It is worth considering each of the characteristics of the definition in more detail:

- 'Subject-oriented' – examples of subjects that are commonly held in data warehouses for analysis are customers and products. Data are held by subject only containing information relevant for decision support.

- 'Integrated' – an important principle of data warehouses is that information is collected from diverse sources within an organisation and brought together to enable integrated analysis. This means differences in aspects such as name and units definitions of data need to be addressed by the data warehouse.

- '*Non-volatile*' – data are transferred from operational information systems such as sales order processing systems into a data warehouse where the information is static – it is not updated. Instead of the normal update procedure when data are changed, the old, obsolete data are removed from the database and the 'changed' data recorded as new data.

- '*In support of management's decision making process*' – this final point emphasises the purpose of the data warehouse. Thus a data warehouse does not necessarily contain current data that an operational database would be expected to require. What a data warehouse does require is to hold data over points in time in order to allow analysis such as forecasting and long-term relationships.

Data marts

These are small-scale data warehouses which do not aim to hold information across an entire company, but rather focus on one department.

Data marts are a smaller, departmental version of a data warehouse which may be easier to manage than a company-scale data warehouse. Data marts do not aim to hold information across an entire company, but rather focus on one department. A data warehouse can consist of many data marts supporting different (smaller) operations.

The largest data warehouse

Sun Microsystems and software vendor BMMSoft have designed the world's largest data warehouse, capable of handling 1 petabyte – 1m gigabytes – of data. It is not a working system, as no one yet needs that sort of data-crunching capability. The largest commercial data warehouse known is that of Wal-Mart and is half that size.

Source: Extract from 'HP extends iPaq mobile devices range' by Geoff Nairn, *Financial Times*, 19 September 2007.

Mini case study

How to get rid of 'devil customers'

The cost of customer acquisition in many industries can be high, but some large retailers are investing in computer systems to help them get rid of customers. These systems identify 'devils' – unwanted customers who cost the retailers money. 'In all retail businesses there is a segment of customers which is unprofitable, and often this is far larger than expected,' said Tony Stockil, chief executive of retail consultancy Javelin Group. 'This varies by industry, and in some cases this segment may be as large as 20 per cent of the entire customer base.'

Devil consumers' behaviour ranges from the legal to the fraudulent. At one end of the scale are devils who only visit a store to buy loss leaders. At the other end are criminals who carry out scams such as buying an item to get a valid receipt, then stealing the same item and returning it for a refund using the original receipt. Other devil activities include wardrobing – the practice of buying an expensive item of clothing such as a cocktail dress, wearing it for one night with the labels tucked out of sight, and returning it the next day for a refund; pack attacks – damaging the packaging of an article on display in the hope of buying it later at a discount; and excessive returning, which may involve buying the same item of clothing in many different sizes and colours with the intention of returning all but one item after a few days.

Excessive or fraudulent returning is a huge problem in the US, where it is estimated to cost retailers $16bn annually. 'Wardrobing is an especially big problem for large retailers,' said David Jones, president of New York based loss prevention consultancy Cost Benefit Consultants. 'In the US it's not unusual to get people who make hundreds of purchases from a store every year and then return them all,' he said.

To combat this, some American retailers are turning to a data warehouse service, operated by a California-based company called The Return Exchange, to identify customers carrying out wardrobing or fraudulent returns. Every time a return is made, relevant transaction data and customer identity information from a driver licence or other ID card is sent to The Return Exchange where it is stored in its database. By analysing large samples of customer returns data, the company helps retailers recognise the mark of a devil: specific patterns of returns behaviour that indicate excessive returning or return fraud.

When a customer takes an item to a store to return it, that customer's previous return history at that store – which includes the number, frequency and value of returns that have previously been made – is examined to see if it matches the profile of a devil. If so, the retailer can decide whether the customer should be given a warning or refused a return. Devil customers who are consistently refused returns are thus forced either to change their habits and become profitable customers, or take their unprofitable custom elsewhere.

British high street retailers are far more restricted in the type of personal information they can store, but they can still spot devil behaviour by analysing data captured at the sales tills. Retailer John Lewis uses software from London-based loss prevention vendor IntelliQ to sift through transactions carried out at all of its shops. 'We have business protection teams who identify the sorts of bad things that criminals do, and the software allows us to look at millions of transactions and identify suspicious ones that match the modus operandi of these criminals,' says Peter Kaye, John Lewis's head of business protection. 'An experienced investigator can see what's happening and say "Yes, that transaction is fraud", or "this one is suspicious".'

Many large retailers are also adopting software that produces barcoded till receipts. These make it harder for customers to manufacture or copy receipts, or to use them to return the same goods more than once.

But sometimes, low tech solutions can be the best way to avoid acquiring devil customers in the first place. 'A number of the largest mail order companies in the UK sell on credit, so assessing accurately if a customer is creditworthy or not is key,' says Javelin's Tony Stockil. 'One of the many things a company might look at is whether a credit application is filled out in pencil or pen. The use of a pencil is a good indicator that the customer may not be creditworthy.'

Source: Rubens, P. (2007) How to get rid of 'devil customers'. *Financial Times*. 13 June. © The Financial Times Limited 2007. All Rights Reserved.

Data warehousing

Data warehousing

The process of creating and maintaining a data warehouse.

Along with the special characteristics of a data warehouse is the process of creating and maintaining that data warehouse, referred to as **data warehousing**. Figure 4.3 indicates the major steps in the data warehousing process. It can be seen that there are three main elements to the data warehousing process. Firstly the data warehouse takes information from internal

Figure 4.3 The data warehousing process

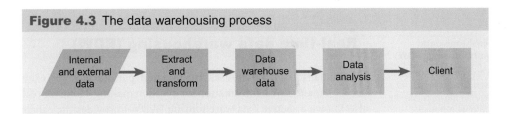

and external sources such as operational systems which record sales or transactions with customers. Data can come from sources such as legacy databases holding historical data (see Chapter 3), operational systems such as enterprise resource planning systems (ERP) (see Chapter 6), electronic point-of-sale (EPOS) data from customer transactions (see Chapter 6), data from electronic data interchange (EDI) systems (see Chapter 5) and RFID tags (see Chapter 5). Data is then extracted from these databases and transformed into a suitable form to be placed in the data warehouse using software known as ETL (see below).

Extraction, transformation and load (ETL)

An important part of the data warehousing process is the requirement to transfer data from a variety of sources, put the data in a relevant format and place them in the data warehouse repository. **ETL software** extracts data from one or more databases, transforms that data into a suitable format for the data warehouse and loads that data into the data warehouse. This involves processing the source data according to business rules defined within the data warehouse. These rules can include definitions of data attributes and calculation methods. Part of the advantage of the data warehouse approach is that rules can be applied to data in a consistent way within the enterprise data warehouse. ETL software can be developed by the organisation but due to its complexity it is usually purchased from an ETL software provider such as Tibco, Oracle, Microsoft or IBM.

Extraction, transformation and load (ETL) software

Extracts data from one or more databases, transforms that data into a suitable format for the data warehouse and loads that data into the data warehouse.

Data warehouse architecture

The configuration of the system that undertakes the data warehousing process previously outlined can actually take a number of forms depending on the current information systems infrastructure and the organisational requirements of the data warehouse. The objectives and capabilities of management can also lead to compromise when considering the implementation of enterprise-wide systems. Ekerson (2003) provides four options to build a data warehouse (see Figure 4.4):

- Data mart centric. Data are linked to users through independent data marts. This provides a relatively easy implementation in technical and organisational terms but lacks an enterprise-wide view of the organisation's data and can lead to inconsistencies of data across data marts.

- Virtual, distributed, federated. This consists of linking users directly to data sources through the use of middleware (see Chapter 11). Whilst providing integration of systems there may be performance and data quality issues using this approach.

- Hub-and-spoke data warehouse. This links users to dependent data marts, which are then linked to an enterprise data warehouse which in turn is linked to organisational data sources. This provides the ability for customisation to user needs through the use of dedicated data marts but can lead to redundancy of data and relatively high operational costs of running both data marts and the data warehouse.

- Enterprise data warehouse. This links users directly to a data warehouse which is linked in turn to data sources. This provides a single and thus consistent view of the data across the enterprise. It does require leadership from senior management in order to implement an enterprise-wide solution.

Real-time data warehousing (RDW)

The capability to load and process data as events happen into the data warehouse.

Real-time data warehousing (RDW)

Traditionally data warehouses are updated periodically, for example weekly, to provide decision makers with information for decision making. However real-time data warehousing, also known as active data warehousing (ADW) provides the capability to load and process

Figure 4.4 Alternative architectures for data warehousing

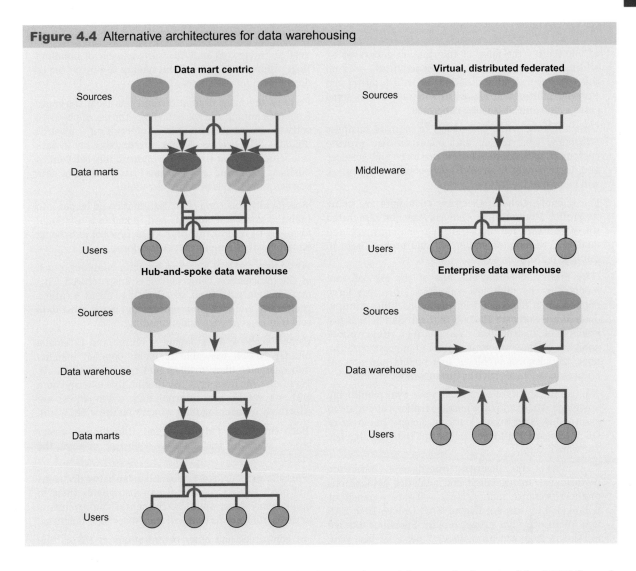

data as events happen into the data warehouse. This permits the use of the RDW for real-time operational decisions such as process flow performance which require current as well as historical data. Although RDW widens the type of decisions that can be assisted by data warehousing systems there are disadvantages to this approach. On problem is the technical difficulty in extracting and transforming real-time data. Another issue is the inconsistency in results of queries which are constantly updated, for example report statistics may differ for different personnel during a working day depending on the report viewing time.

CASE STUDY 4.1

Big data put under the spotlight as never before

By Paul Taylor

Data are the raw materials of this age of information, whether in such structured form as ATM transactions and till receipts, or unstructured such as trends on social media feeds and sites.

Business intelligence and data mining and warehousing applications enable companies to gain insights from information that has mostly been generated internally. Modern analytic techniques, including examinations of 'big data' – the mass of information generated by all kinds of commercial and other activities – expand this concept by asking questions of both internal and external information almost as soon as, and in some cases even while, it is being generated.

Companies are using these tools to improve business efficiency, spot trends and opportunities, provide customers with more relevant products and services and, increasingly, to predict how people, or machines, will behave in the future.

For example, General Electric's customers are using its Proficy Monitoring & Analysis Suite, an integrated set of software for industrial data management and analytics, to monitor equipment and process data to improve performance.

GE's Proficy Historian HD, one of the six software modules in the suite, lets companies store very large data sets in a Hadoop cluster (many machines running open-source software Hadoop that can handle massive amounts of unstructured data) and then run advanced analytics on huge amounts of data to improve performance, troubleshoot problems, and predict and prevent failures in machines such as turbines or jet engines.

'We use the software ourselves in our own monitoring and diagnostics centres to manage trillions of dollars in asset value,' said Brian Courtney, general manager of GE Intelligent Platforms' Industrial Data Intelligence Software group.

The market for business intelligence, corporate performance management and analytics applications and performance management software – much of it provided by the 'big five' of SAP, Oracle, IBM, SAS and Microsoft – has grown rapidly. Spending totalled $12.3bn in 2011 and grew about 7 per cent last year, according to research company Gartner.

Many companies use business intelligence software to provide their senior executives, sales staff and other managers with access to key performance indicators such as costs, sales and margins.

Among the leading trends in the market for business intelligence software is the increasing call for screen-based visualisation tools, such as dashboards, to make financial and other data more accessible to executives on the road via smartphones and tablets.

'We saw a new way to engage with people and democratise data,' says Quinton Alsbury, founder of Roambi, which provides mobile business intelligence visualisation software for iPhones and iPads.

Pret A Manger, the sandwich retailer, uses Roambi in the UK to augment its traditional business intelligence software and has provided 70 field and regional managers with iPads. Staff can carry out stock takes while they are on the move instead of leafing through a 200-page paper file, or they can monitor kitchen production while standing on the shop floor.

Similarly, SiSense's Prism 10X software is designed for companies that have outgrown Microsoft Excel and

need an integrated analytics suite capable of handling huge volumes of data without having to rely on the IT department for assistance.

Perhaps the most dramatic trend has been the move from data mining and warehousing – the use of powerful software to interrogate stored information – towards big data. 'The origins of data warehousing lay in data sets which, at that time, were immediately relevant to business problems,' says Duncan Ross, director of data science at analytics provider Teradata.

'Specifically, this comprised data that could be put into tables of rows and columns and linked in a relational form.' By its nature, this limited the types of data being stored mostly to highly structured forms.

While they are still a part of big data analytics, much of the information being tapped is unstructured. This may include data from social media, about weather, geography, mobility, from sensors and many other data sets that can enhance understanding.

Using Facebook data, Japanese online and catalogue retailer Nissen was able to glean detailed insights into customer likes, dislikes and buying motivations. Teradata's Mr Ross says: 'By linking this external data with its established internal data, [companies] are effectively broadening their window on the wider world.

'Each time more data are added, this window grows larger, affording the business a clearer view of the market.

'This allows them to test ideas and make better decisions and predictions. Crucially, it can also enable them to break away from small, incremental improvements towards innovations that will transform their business.'

For companies and other organisations at the cutting edge of big data analytics, the main goal is to be able to use the intelligence gleaned from analysing large volumes of information to predict and anticipate future trends.

Leading US banks such as Wells Fargo and Bank of America, consumer goods companies such as Coca-Cola and 3M, and retailers including Walmart are all using big data analytics to improve the running of their business models and to anticipate changes in demand before they actually occur.

Scott Schlesinger, senior vice-president and head of business information management for the technology consultancy Capgemini in North America, says: 'Predictive analytics can turn poor business decisions, made using haphazard guesswork, into well thought out and successful business decisions that improve performance.'

He also warns that to use predictive analytics tools well, an organisation must first know what information it needs, and devise 'a proper information and business process strategy that drives and [delivers] efficiencies across the organisation'.

Eddie Short, head of data and analytics at management consultancy KPMG, sounds a similar cautionary note. 'Three years ago, some commentators suggested that data would become the new currency of business, almost on a par with capital and labour,' he says.

'Since then, information has clearly moved to the core of most organisations' operations, but questions remain about how to extract real value because the journey from traditional business analytics to [data becoming a] business enabler requires organisations

to fundamentally rethink how they collect, analyse, distribute and monitor data,' Mr Short adds.

'In my view, three years from now it will be the businesses that have answered these questions by combining their hunger for data with an appetite to match it with the needs of their businesses that will win the day and become masters of their own data.'

 Source: Taylor, P. (2013) Big data put under the spotlight as never before. *Financial Times*. 26 June.

QUESTIONS

1. Define the term 'big data'.

2. Compare data mining and big data analytics.

DATA MINING

Data mining

In its broadest sense is a process that uses statistical, mathematical, artificial intelligence and other techniques to extract useful information from large databases.

Data mining in its broadest sense is a process that uses statistical, mathematical, artificial intelligence and other techniques to extract useful information from large databases. Under this wide definition most types of data analysis can be classified as data mining. In its original definition data mining is used to identify patterns or trends in the data in data warehouses which can be used for improved profitability. Rather than asking direct questions such as 'Who are the top 20 per cent of our customers?', more open questions will be asked such as 'What are the characteristics of the top 20 per cent of our customers?' Through understanding customers better, their needs can be better met. Particular data mining techniques include the following.

Identifying associations

This involves establishing relationships about items that occur at a particular point in time, for example a shopping basket analysis by a chemist revealed an association of shoppers who purchase condoms and foot powder. It is not clear how this information can be used.

Identifying sequences

This involves showing the sequence in which actions occur (e.g. path or click-stream analysis of a web site).

Classification

This involves analysing historical data into patterns to predict future behaviour, for example identifying groups of web site users who display similar visitor patterns. Classification is distinct from clustering in that at least some of the classes are previously known. Classification is often used to classify new data into previously defined classes by learning the pattern of the data within the current classes. Classification can be implemented using techniques such as neural networks (Chapter 6) or decision trees (Chapter 1).

Clustering

This involves finding groups of facts that were previously unknown, for example, identifying new market segments of customers or detecting e-commerce fraud. Cluster analysis sorts attributes such as people or events into groups (i.e. clusters) in which the degree of association between the items within the cluster is strong and across clusters is weak. Cluster analysis may be undertaken using methods such as statistical techniques, neural networks (Chapter 6) and genetic algorithms. Cluster analysis can proceed from either placing all items in the analysis in one cluster and breaking this into separate clusters (divisive) or placing all items in separate clusters and joining the clusters together to make new clusters (agglomerative).

Modelling

This involves using forecasting and regression analysis to predict sales (e.g. using sales histories to forecast future sales).

Text mining

Text mining

Text mining is the application of data mining to text files. Text mining aims to find previously hidden patterns in text within and between documents

Text mining is the application of data mining to text files. Text held in documents will normally be unstructured in terms of its content and text mining aims to find previously hidden patterns in text within and between documents. A text mining system consists of an information retrieval system that queries and finds text within a variety of document formats such as word processor and PDF format. These documents may exist on a variety of platforms such as emails, web pages and text files. An information extraction system then analyses and processes the text. This entails mapping information from unstructured data into a structured format using techniques such as reducing the text to a list of terms and weights. Data mining methods such as cluster analysis can then be performed on the structured text data.

Web mining

Web mining

Data mining applications that are being developed to analyse information from the web.

Because of the size and popularity of the web many data mining applications are being developed to analyse information from the web and these are classified under the term **web mining**. Extraction of information from web pages specifically is termed *web content mining* and involves reading and analysing data from web pages. As much of web content is textual then text mining techniques may be used to analyse the data. A further technique of web mining is to analyse information from the links within the web documents and this is termed *web structure mining*. For example the popularity of a document may be judged by a count of the number of links to that document from other documents. This is one of the attributes used to rank web pages for search engines such as Google. Finally *web usage mining* extracts information from usage data relating to web page visits and web page transactions. This includes **clickstream analysis** which is the analysis of user behaviour gathered as they visit web pages. Information on the background of users or when users visit a site can be used to target advertisements and marketing campaigns or to provide information for cross-marketing of alternative products. Sites such as Amazon and Expedia use information gathered on previous customer behaviour to recommend products and services that they might be interested in. The web-based grocery store Ocado suggests to customers supplementary grocery products at checkout, based on their previous and current grocery orders.

Clickstream analysis

Analysis of user behaviour gathered as they visit web pages.

CASE STUDY 4.2

Making business intelligence work

By Bryan Cruickshank of KPMG

Everybody knows that in business, the winners are those that outperform the market.

Recent research (conducted in partnership with Cambridge University) demonstrated that good decision-making can improve the average performance of a company by more than five per cent. As a result it is clear that effective Business Intelligence is what will separate the market leaders from the rest of the pack.

Business Intelligence – or BI – is not a new concept. For decades, businesses have been combing through their available data in order to make better and more accurate business decisions. Today, modern BI is characterised by a set of methodologies, processes, architectures, and technologies that transform mountains of raw data into meaningful and useful information.

In effect, BI aims to improve decision-making by providing business leaders with rich and valuable insights into their business and a holistic view of their actual performance, which is then usually presented in user-friendly reports and progress dashboards. The market has grown substantially in the past decade (some analysts already put the global market at an astounding US$100bn), with many software vendors active in the sector, largely led by the traditional ERP (Enterprise Resource management) vendors and a host of small boutique shops.

Unfortunately – despite the maturity of the market – most BI initiatives ultimately fail to deliver any real value. Indeed, half of all executives interviewed said they did not trust the quality of their information, and nine out of ten admitted that their BI capabilities were not living up to their expectations.

Those that can get it right, therefore, stand to reap a significant competitive advantage. For most, the first step is aligning BI capabilities to strategy. With only 23 per cent of respondents reporting that their BI initiatives were driven by business strategy, many organisations are expending unnecessary energy and resources creating reports that ultimately provide little strategic value.

It is important to recognise that BI is not just about obtaining and analysing data, but rather ensuring that data is credible, easily accessible, and is presented in an intelligent and meaningful way to the right people, at the right time for them to make the right decisions.

To be successful, BI programs face three main challenges:

■ Data volumes are increasing. A recent report in the Economist magazine highlighted the sheer scope of the issue: where organisations globally were holding a mere 150 Exabytes (or 150bn Gigabytes) of data in 2005, that number has ballooned to an estimated 1,200 Exabytes today. Leading retailer Wal-Mart, for example, now captures and processes data from well over a million transactions per hour.

■ The value has broadened. BI systems of the past were largely engineered to facilitate the reporting and analysis of internal data such as the monitoring of stock levels and the development of financial forecasts. Today, however, business leaders are increasingly looking to BI systems to enable their people to make insightful decisions based on rich and reliable data from across the organisation.

■ Silos must be broken. To be of any real value, information also needs to be managed across organisational boundaries. This has led market leaders to reconsider the way they approach, implement and manage their BI systems, in order to develop a common, enterprise-wide view of their data. Far from a simple technical challenge, this will necessitate an organisational rethink about how to properly manage data and – in some cases – structural changes that will lead to better data flow overall.

Underpinning this change is the recognition that BI systems are a pervasive business tool, drawing on and serving a broad cross-section of the organisation. Successful BI program development and governance demands a multi-functional team, led by the business and supported by IT, and driven by a single-minded objective of delivering the data that provides the most value across the entire organisation.

Recent advances in technology have also substantially changed the environment for BI, as significant improvements in both data-warehousing and the related analytical software have enabled businesses to achieve an unprecedented level of insight and analysis into their organisations.

At the same time, many organisations have found that a decade of M&A activity, globalisation and ad-hoc technology implementations has resulted in a complex web of back-end systems and disparate data warehouses that do not always operate together effectively. Without a solid foundation of compatible and integrated systems, BI initiatives will never achieve their expected value or results.

Simply put, BI should never be viewed as a simple technology-led 'plug and play' business application. Making BI work requires businesses to create (and reinforce) a common view of their data, aligning outputs to business strategy, while ensuring the proper data and fundamentals exist to deliver the information that provides the most value to the business.

Bryan Cruickshank is the Global Leader for KPMG's Technology Advisory Practice where he focuses on helping clients cut through the complexity of their IT decisions to uncover sustainable business value. Mr. Cruickshank can be reached at bryan.cruickshank@kpmg.co.uk.

 Source: Cruickshank, B. (2010) Making business intelligence work. *Financial Times*. 6 October.

QUESTIONS

1. Define the term 'business intelligence'.
2. What are the challenges to implementing a successful business intelligence capability?

BUSINESS ANALYTICS

Business analytics (BA)

Refers to various approaches to data-driven analysis.

Business analytics (BA) is a term that is used to describe various approaches to data driven analysis including reporting tools such as OLAP and visualisation tools such as dashboards. For example the SAS Analytics software (**www.sas.com/technologies/analytics**) covers the following areas:

- *Statistics* – use statistical data analysis to drive fact-based decisions.
- *Data and text mining* – build descriptive and predictive models and deploy results throughout the enterprise.
- *Data visualisation* – allows users to interact with graphs to clarify results and take action.
- *Content categorisation* – categorises content, which is then used to create metadata and trigger business processes.
- *Forecasting and econometrics* – analyse and predict outcomes based on historical patterns and apply statistical methods to economic data, problems and trends.
- *Operations research* – applies techniques such as optimisation, scheduling and simulation to achieve the best result.
- *Model management and deployment* – streamline the process of creating, managing and deploying analytical models.
- *Quality improvement* – identifies, monitors and measures quality processes over time.

Thus business analytical tools cover a wide range of techniques that includes data mining, text mining and web mining which are discussed earlier in this chapter. Various BA reporting tools such as OLAP and cube analysis, and BA visualisation tools such as dashboards and scorecards, will now be discussed.

Mini case study

Traders' tools turn tables on dodgy deals

By Brooke Masters

Set a thief to catch a thief, the adage goes. When it comes to catching insider traders, the UK financial watchdog hasn't gone quite that far, but it is turning to trader's tools.

Under the leadership of Patrick Spens, a former Citigroup and hedge fund manager, the market monitoring division of what is now the Financial Conduct Authority has launched a data-based attack on suspicious trading.

First the FCA stepped up the pressure on City banks and brokers to do a better job of getting information to the regulator both about ordinary trades and those that looked suspicious.

Under UK law, banks and brokers must report every single transaction in a regulated security to the FCA every day. But many groups fell short of their responsibilities until the watchdog fined Barclays and eight other companies a combined £8m and forced them to go back and re-report everything they had missed.

Now the watchdog gets 13m detailed transaction reports every day with details of who bought, who sold and for how much. It is thought to be the most comprehensive regulatory database in the world.

Next Lord Spens, who has a hereditary title, stepped up the pressure on banks and brokers to live up to their duty to flag up unusual trading. After much prodding of companies, the watchdog also received 1018 'suspicious transaction reports' last year, nearly double the previous total.

But data are only as good as the ability to interpret it, so the FCA hired a team of quantitative analysts and set them to work writing algorithms. Some of these 'technologists' come from industry; others have PhDs in maths or statistics. Bolstered by the latest in high-end analytics servers as well as commercial surveillance software from Nasdaq OMX, the quants are writing programmes to comb the transaction data alongside news feeds to identify timely trades and unusual patterns.

For Lord Spens, who oversaw the building of Citi's trading algorithms a decade ago, the FCA's task is a familiar one.

'Using experience born from trading algorithms intellectually is no different from looking for abusive behaviour in the markets. Both rely on huge data sets where you are looking for patterns and anomalies,' he says.

The quants represent a small share of the 60-person market monitoring programme and their special project budget is in the millions of pounds. They have been at work for close to 18 months now and their programmes are being gradually introduced into a variety of securities markets.

It is still early days, but the efforts are starting to bear fruit with a stream of alerts that are probed for obvious explanations – such as a news report or a matching trade that makes clear the lucky one was a hedge. The rest are then referred on to the enforcement division for possible investigation.

Over time, Lord Spens predicts, the surveillance system will only get better as the results from the computers are compared with the STRs sent in by the companies.

'By marrying the algorithms with the STR's received we can self-police the quality of STR submissions and create a virtuous circle of surveillance,' he says.

Enforcement cases take years – several City professionals first arrested with great fanfare in 2010 won't go on trial until September 2014.

But knowing someone is watching appears to be having a deterrent effect. Suspicious trading before UK mergers and acquisitions fell to the lowest level in more than a decade last year.

 Source: Masters, B. (2013) Traders' tools turn tables on dodgy deals. *Financial Times*. 10 July.
© The Financial Times Limited 2013. All Rights Reserved.

OLAP (Online analytical processing)

Refers to the ability to analyse in real time the type of large data sets stored in data warehouses.

Multidimensional data

Data broken down in analysis for a data warehouse into dimensions such as time period, product segment and the geographical location. Dimensions are broken down into categories. For time these could be months, quarters or years.

OLTP (online transaction processing)

OLTP systems process large quantities of repetitive transactions conducting simple manipulations.

Online analytical processing (OLAP)

Online analytical processing (OLAP) refers to the ability to analyse in real time the type of large data sets stored in data warehouses. 'Online' indicates that users can formulate their own queries, compared to standard paper reports. The originator of OLAP, Dr E. Codd, defines it as the dynamic synthesis, analysis and consolidation of large volumes of multidimensional data. An example of a popular OLAP software application is shown in Figure 4.5.

OLAP should not be confused with OLTP (online transaction processing). OLTP systems process large quantities of repetitive transactions conducting simple manipulations, whilst OLAP examines many data items in complex relationships. OLAP can be implemented on a relational database structure when it is termed *ROLAP (relational OLAP)* and the query

Figure 4.5 Screen display of IBM Cognos Enterprise software

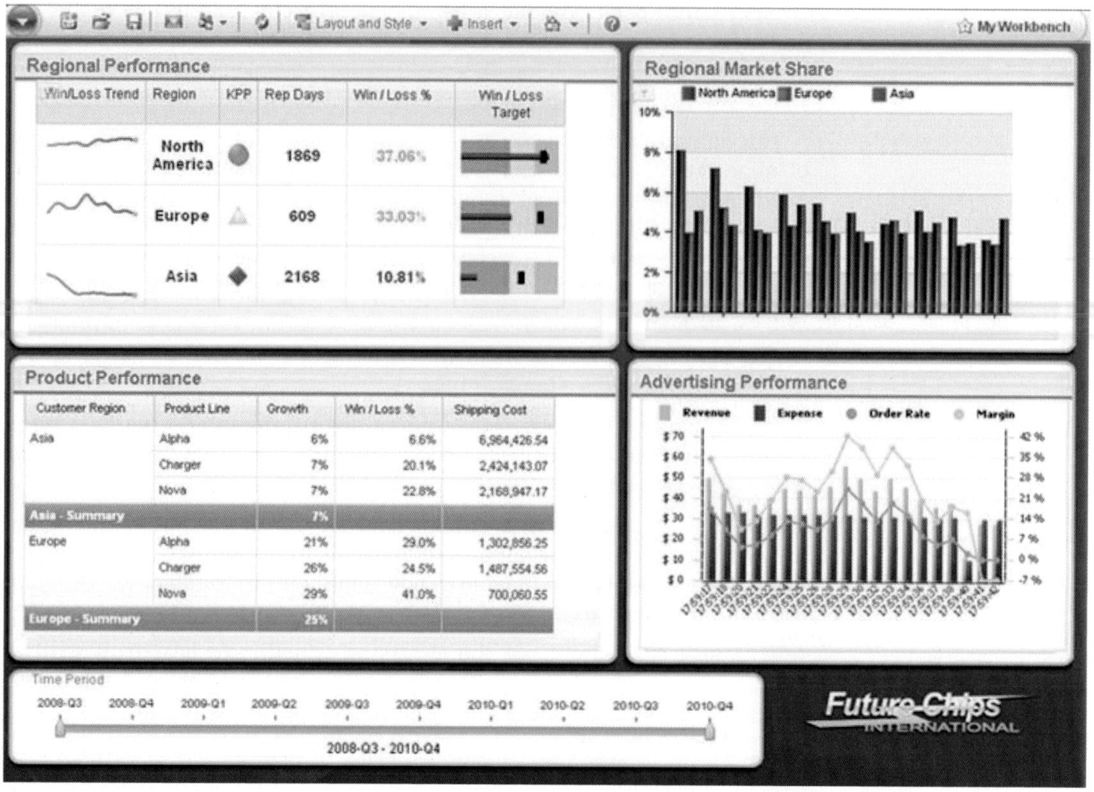

Source: IBM Cognos Enterprise screenshot, courtesy of International Business Machines Corporation, © 2014 International Business Machines Corporation.

language SQL (see earlier in this chapter) can be used to interrogate the data. Alternatively OLAP can be implemented using a multidimensional database when it is termed *MOLAP (multidimensional OLAP)*. OLAP queries can produce both routine reports that are generated automatically and periodically, for example weekly sales figures, and ad-hoc reports which are created in response to some event. An event can be triggered by a fall in sales volume or by a user request for specific information.

Data cube

A data cube is a two-dimensional, three-dimensional or higher–dimensional view of the data in which each dimension in the cube represents an attribute such as sales or products and each cell in the cube represents a measure such as sales of a product in a particular month.

Cube analysis

A range of approaches such as sorting, pivoting and filtering that can be used to interrogate the data within the cube.

Cube analysis

Data in a multidimensional database are broken down for analysis into a number of chosen dimensions. For example for sales data the common dimensions are time period, product types and geographic location. Dimensions can be then broken down into categories. For example, for time these could be months, quarters or years. Usually a multidimensional database is formed from data held in a data warehouse specifically for multidimensional analysis. The form of the data used in the multidimensional database is termed a **data cube**. A data cube is a two-dimensional, three-dimensional or higher–dimensional view of the data in which each dimension in the cube represents an attribute such as sales or products and each cell in the cube represents a measure such as sales of a product in a particular month.

Slice-and-dice

Rearranging data so that they can be viewed from different perspectives.

Cube analysis is a range of approaches such as sorting, pivoting and filtering that can be used to interrogate the data within the cube. Thus cube analysis uses software tools to allow users to **slice-and-dice** a cube of data to observe subsets of the data in any way they like.

Data warehouse analysis techniques for describing multidimensional data

Example: A car sales data warehouse

Information collected on transactions can often be broken down in different ways. Say that we have data on car sales. We can break this information down by:

- time car was sold;
- model;
- location at which sold;
- salesperson;

and so on. This type of breakdown is vital for marketing staff to assess the performance of advertising campaigns, sales staff and dealerships. Problems in sales of particular models or particular staff can be identified and then rectified.

Whenever we break information down in this way we are identifying the different *dimensions* of the data. There are usually three common dimensions:

- time period;
- product or market segment;
- geographic location where the product was sold (or where consumers originate).

The example in Figure 4.6 shows how these three dimensions form a cube, with each individual cube effectively representing one combination of data. The small cube represents all four-wheel-drive vehicles in quarter 1 of 1998 sold into a particular postal sector.

When designing data warehouses, each dimension and its division into categories can be shown on a diagram, as in Table 4.1.

Figure 4.6 Example of multidimensional data cube for vehicles sales

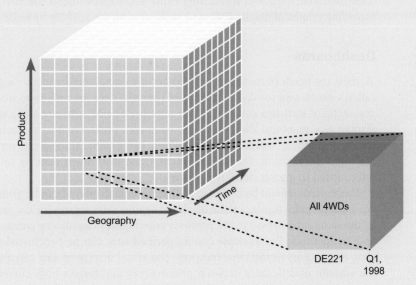

Table 4.1 Designing a data warehouse

		Dimensions				
	All time periods (85)	All locations (4306)	All products (35)	Age groups (8)	Economic groups (6)	Genders (3)
Categories	Year 5	Regions 6	Segments 5	8	ABC1 C2DE 6	3
	Quarter 20	Postal areas 200	Models 30			
	Month 60	Postal districts 1500	(Paint colours 100)			
		Postal sectors 2000	(Plus competitor segments)			
		Dealerships + DARs (plus sales staff not shown) 300 × 2				

Measures: Forecast sales, Budget sales, Actual sales, Budget variance (calc), Forecast variance (calc), Market share. For each of 6 measures, number of data items are: 85 × 4306 × 35 × 8 × 6 × 3 = 1.8 billion. Assume 4 bytes per item, 6 × 4 × 1.8 billion = approx. 40 gigabytes.

Note that measures such as sales figures and market share, which are all broken down into the different dimensions, are shown along the bottom of the table. This table can also be used to assess the information storage requirements.

Visualisation tools

In order to facilitate better and easier understanding of data, software that provides a visual representation of data is available. Applications such as spreadsheets, dashboards, scorecards and geographical information systems can be utilised as visualisation tools.

Spreadsheets

The ability of spreadsheets to create a variety of different charts which are updated automatically in response to changes in data is covered earlier (in Chapter 3). In conjunction with their statistical and forecasting capabilities spreadsheets are particularly useful are providing graphical displays of trends such as sales for analysis by organisations.

Dashboards

Dashboard

A graphical interface to assist people to understand performance measurement information.

To meet the needs of managers who do not use computers frequently a graphical interface, called a **dashboard** (or digital dashboard) permits decision makers to make sense out of the avalanche of statistics collated by any enterprise-wide software application. A dashboard display is a graphical display on the computer presented to the decision maker which includes graphical images such as meters, bar graphs, trace plots, text fields to convey real-time information. Dashboards incorporate drill-down features to enable data to be interrogated in greater detail if necessary.

Dashboards should be designed so that the data displayed can be understood in context. For example sales figures can be displayed against sales figures for the previous time period or the same time period in the previous year. Figures can also be compared against targets and competitors. For example quality performance can be benchmarked against best-in-class competitors in the same industry. The visual display of data can also be used to show the amount of difference between performance and targets both currently and the trend over time. Visual indicators such as traffic lights can be used to show when performance has fallen below acceptable levels (red light), is a cause for concern (amber light) and is acceptable (green light). An example of a dashboard display is shown in Figure 4.7.

Figure 4.7 Example of a dashboard

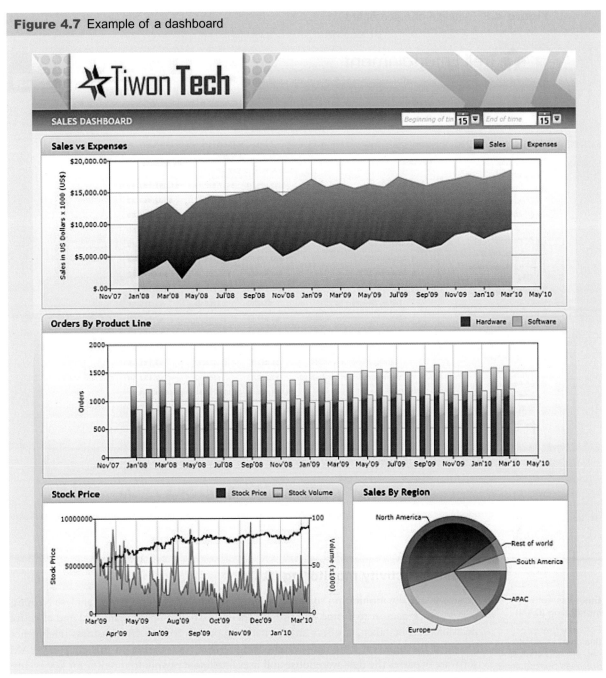

Source: http://www.dashboardinsight.com/articles/digital-dashboards/fundamentals/a-closer-look-at-scorecards-and-dashboards.aspx

Scorecard

A graphical interface
to assist people to
understand a summary
of performance over
time. Associated with
the balanced scorecard
strategy tool.

Scorecards

Whilst dashboards are generally considered to measure operational performance, scorecards provide a summary of performance over a period of time. Scorecards are also usually associated with the concept of the balanced scorecard strategy tool (Chapter 13) and examine data from the balanced scorecard perspectives of financial, customer, business process and learning and growth. An example of a scorecard display is shown in Figure 4.8.

Figure 4.8 Example of a scorecard

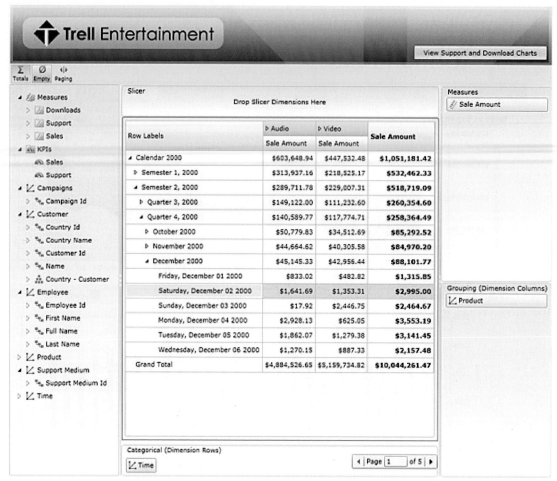

Source: http://www.dashboardinsight.com/articles/digital-dashboards/fundamentals/a-closer-look-at-scorecards-and-dashboards.aspx

Business activity monitoring (BAM)

Business activity monitoring (BAM)

Software that is designed to monitor, capture and analyse business performance data in real time and present them visually in order that rapid and effective decisions can be taken.

Intelligent agent (IA)

Software that performs a specific task, based on rules and knowledge stored in a knowledge base.

Business activity monitoring software is designed to monitor, capture and analyse business performance data in real time and present them visually in order that rapid and effective decisions can be taken. It offers an alternative approach to real time business intelligence provided through real time data warehousing (RDW) (see earlier in this chapter). BAM software bypasses the data warehouse and uses intelligent agents to monitor for key events. These events are then processed according to the three levels of implementation of Alert and Dashboard, Automatic Response and Predictive and Adaptive.

Alert and Dashboard. These systems capture data from various applications and internal and external data sources, which are then filtered and analysed to provide an alert of unusual performance. The use of dashboard displays to convey information for decision making are covered in a previous section in this chapter.

Automatic Response. In a standard Alert and Dashboard system any decisions made on the basis of the information supplied by the BAM are made using traditional telephone, e-mail or alternative communication systems. Automatic Response systems add the ability to automatically handle business exceptions. They could do this, for example, by matching any exceptions with a repository of known error fixes and then initiating an appropriate business process which can trigger a number of automated and manual events.

Figure 4.9 Oracle business activity monitoring (BAM) software

Source: http://www.oracle.com/technetwork/middleware/bam/loanflow-098007.html

Predictive and Adaptive. This implementation of BAM, not only provides alerts in response to exception events, but also suggests alternative actions which could be taken and allows the exploration of future scenarios based on alternative responses. Business process simulation (BPS) (Chapter 12) could be used to both predict future events and help explore future scenarios. In addition adaptive systems can adapt to and learn from changing business conditions.

Figure 4.9 provides an example of BAM software.

Geographical information systems (GIS)

Geographical information system (GIS)

Uses maps to display information about different geographic locations such as catchment areas or branches. They are commonly used for performance analysis by marketing staff.

A **geographical information system (GIS)** uses maps to display information about different areas. They are commonly used for performance analysis by marketing staff. Performance of distribution channels such as branches can be shown by colour-coding them. Colour-coded areas on the map can be used to show variation in the demand of customers for products or the characteristics of people living in different areas, such as average disposable income. Figure 4.10 shows an example of the application of a GIS. The locations of banks are shown – the dark areas indicate where the bank is performing well and lighter areas where the bank is underperforming. The performance ratio here can be thought of as market share. Marketing analysts can review this in an attempt to correct problems in areas of underperformance, for example there appears to be an opportunity in the south of the area to open a new branch.

Figure 4.10 The traditional approach to defining markets by primary trade area is outdated. Finding that elusive boundary where a customer goes to one store rather than another is challenging. GIS can help.

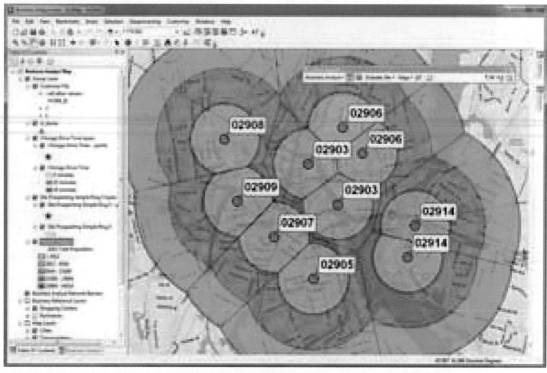

Source: http://www.esri.com/news/arcuser/0611/localization-not-location.html

CASE STUDY 4.3

After 160 years, the value of maps is starting to be appreciated

By Dr Richard Waite

Maps are not just pretty things. They can transform businesses and save lives.

The classic example of this occurred nearly 160 years ago when John Snow used a map to plot the deaths from a cholera outbreak in London. At the time nobody knew what caused this disease, but conventional wisdom blamed a nebulous concept of "miasma" in the air. John Snow wasn't convinced.

So he plotted the locations of the deaths on a map and discovered a strong correlation between the deaths and a water pump in Soho's Broad Street. He thus found compelling evidence that cholera was spread via contaminated water and not through the air.

The final proof came when he removed the handle of the pump in the Broad Street well. The deaths stopped almost immediately.

John Snow's work was a precursor to what we now know as Geographic Information Systems (GIS). He pioneered a technique so powerful that even now its full potential for transforming businesses is only just beginning to be appreciated.

More and more businesses are realising that location plays a vital role in all aspects of their operations. Something like 80 per cent of business data has a geographical context and 70 per cent of all local authority services are location dependent.

Customers, suppliers, workforces, field assets, vehicles, depots and branches all have a location. Increasingly, many of these locations are dynamic; they move in real time and need to be tracked.

Managing and leveraging location information can allow an organisation to increase its revenues (or increase its outcomes in the public sector) through satisfying a growing demand for location dependent services, while at the same time improving efficiencies and reducing costs by targeting resources based on location and through optimising the use of mobile resources.

For example optimising vehicle routes can reduce journey times, allow more deliveries per round, minimise carbon footprint or guarantee delivery times.

The key to delivering these benefits is GIS, but not GIS as we have known it. The true benefits of managing location intelligence are only gained if GIS is deployed across an organisation, linking all its IT systems and underpinning all of its operations.

This is why GIS is starting to be recognised for what it really is, an enterprise technology, rather than a specialist, back office technology.

Historically many applications of GIS have been about recording fixed, physical assets, such as cables and pipes in utility companies or roads, street lights and buildings in local authorities. It has been used for mapping and in many people's minds, GIS equates to digital mapping. GIS has been seen as a tool for geographers and cartographers.

But this severely underestimates the power of GIS, the power of spatial analysis.

With a GIS, previously unthinkable questions can be answered, hidden patterns and trends can be revealed and operations can be optimised based on location, but only if all of the data is 'geo-referenced', i.e. location is built into the data. This is why GIS has to be enterprise-wide.

But to deliver this change in the use of GIS and to achieve the benefits of implementing GIS at the enterprise level will require nothing less than a paradigm shift. In fact, two paradigm shifts.

First, the power of GIS and location data needs to be understood and valued and then put at the heart of a business. The CEO and CFO need to understand the benefits that GIS can deliver to their business. GIS needs to be recognised as an enterprise technology and implemented across a business, rather than in isolated pockets.

Only by underpinning a business with location intelligence, can the real benefits be achieved. This is the first paradigm shift: treating GIS as a core enterprise system.

Second, business processes need to change to become location driven.

As an example, utility companies carry out preventative maintenance of field assets, based on the anniversary of their installation date. A maintenance crew will visit one sub-station and ignore another one 100 yards away, but come back to the second sub-station in a month, when its turn is due.

Many business processes are time driven, but if they were location driven, huge efficiencies could be gained. In this case, both sub-stations could be maintained in one visit, thus saving considerable time and travel costs.

This is the second paradigm shift that is required, from time-based to location-based business processes.

So the power of GIS is starting to be recognized, but realising the growth and efficiency benefits that this power can deliver will require change. There will need to be a major shift in how location intelligence is perceived and a fundamental change in how many business processes are operated. If we can make these paradigm shifts, we can transform so much of our world, in a way that would have made John Snow proud.

Dr Richard Waite is managing director of ESRI (UK), a California-based global software development and services company providing GIS software and geodatabase management applications.

QUESTION

What are the benefits of Geographic Information Systems (GIS)?

Mini case study Using GIS to identify road traffic accident locations

One of the activities of the police service in the UK is to attend road traffic accidents (RTA). It was found that two aspects of performance of the system for reporting road traffic accidents required particular attention. The need to speed process execution was seen as essential to provide a faster and more efficient service to vehicle drivers. In particular there is a need to provide UK government agencies with accident statistics within four-weeks of the incident. The second aspect of performance which required improvement was the need to reduce the relatively high staffing cost associated with the process. The total cost of traffic police staff is relatively high as their on-costs need to include the purchase and maintenance of a police patrol vehicle. There is also a need for extensive administrative support at locations across the area covered by the Police Force.

In the proposed computerised RTA reporting system the attending officer completes paper-based forms as before but this information is promptly converted to digital form using a document image processing (DIP) system. This is achieved by a combination of image capture and data recognition through a facsimile link. Data recognition systems, such as optical character recognition (OCR) are used to process information that is entered in a structured format, such as options selected using a ticked box format. Image capture is used in the following ways. Documents are stored as images to enable input bureau staff to validate the OCR scanned data. Images which cannot be interpreted by data recognition software, such as hand drawn sketches of the RTA scene are stored for later retrieval. Images of text such as officer written notes can be entered by input bureau staff, saving officer time. Once in digital format the documents can be delivered electronically preventing data duplication and enabling faster distribution. Physical documents are held in a central repository for reference if needed.

The proposed computerised system also incorporates a geographical information system (GIS) in order to improve the accuracy of the recorded location details of the RTA. Currently location details are based on a written description of the RTA by an officer which leads to inconsistent results. The current location description by the officer is usually acceptable for city incidents where nearby street intersections and other features can be used to pinpoint a location. However on long stretches of road it is often difficult to pinpoint an exact spot. This is important because of the need to accurately pinpoint areas with high accident rates for road safety measures (e.g. road humps) and speed camera placement. Further inaccuracies can also occur when the officer description is converted by the local council using an UK Ordnance Survey (OS) map grid reference which is only accurate to 200 yards.

In this proposal each officer is issued with a portable digital map on which to indicate the RTA location. This information is transmitted by a mobile link to a geographical information system (GIS) which provides accurate location analysis of both injury and non-injury incidents using the geocode system. The geocode system is a network of grids covering the UK which allow a location to be assigned within a $10m^2$ area. The GIS system will combine the accident location analysis with data relating to the location of pelican crossings, traffic lights, street parking and anything else that might contribute to accidents or affect schemes being proposed. Along with data on details on road conditions at the time of the accident this information will help determine a prioritised list of road safety improvement measures.

Source: Adapted from Greasley (2004).

SUMMARY

1. A database can be defined as a collection of related information.

2. The data in a database are organised by fields and records. A field is a single item of information, such as a name or a quantity. A record is a collection of related fields.

3. The information held in an electronic database is accessed via a database management system (DBMS). A DBMS can be defined as one or more computer programs that allow users to enter, store, organise, manipulate and retrieve data from a database.

4. A relational database can consist of numerous record designs – tables – and can combine information drawn from several tables. A key field can be used to identify individual records within an electronic database or to create relationships between different tables.

5. Business intelligence systems are needed due to the vast amounts of data now held in organisational information systems and the need to extract useful information from this in the form of patterns and trends, and present it in a understandable way to decision makers.

6. In a business intelligence system, data are gathered from various sources and then held in a special database repository termed a data warehouse in order to support decision making in the organisation. Repositories of data focused on departmental or subject areas are termed data marts.

7. Data mining is a type of analysis that aims to identify patterns in the data that can be used to predict future behaviour.

8. Business analytic tools are used to conduct analysis of the data held in the data warehouse using reporting and visualisation tools.

EXERCISES

Self-assessment exercises

1. In an electronic database, what are the differences between queries and filters?

2. Describe the major components of business intelligence.

3. Describe the data warehousing process.

4. What is data mining and how can it bring benefits to a business organisation?

5. Compare and contrast OLAP and OLTP.

Discussion questions

1. How is a data warehouse different from a database?

2. What are the benefits of data warehouses?

3. Compare and contrast scorecards and dashboards.

4. What is clickstream analysis?

5. Identify applications for text mining.

Essay questions

1. Describe the elements of a dashboard.

2. Describe the ETL process.

3. Describe four alternative architectures for data warehousing

4. What is the role of data marts when an organisation has an existing data warehouse?

Examination questions

1. What are the benefits of data mining?

2. What are the advantages of a real-time data warehouse?

3. Evaluate the concept of business activity monitoring (BAM).

4. Describe the types of OLAP.

5. What are the benefits of a geographic information system (GIS)?

References

Ekerson, W. (2003) 'Four ways to build a data warehouse', *What Works: Best Practices in Business Intelligence and Data Warehousing*, 15, 46–49

Greasley, A. (2004) 'A redesign of a road traffic accident reporting system using business process simulation', *Business Process Management Journal*, 10, 6, 636–44

Inmon, W.H. (2005) *Building the Data Warehouse*, 4th edition, John Wiley and Sons, Chichester

Further reading

Davenport, T.H. and Harris, J.G. (2007) *Competing on Analytics*, Harvard Business School Press, Boston, MA.

Davenport, T.H. and Kim, J. (2013) *Keeping up with the Quants: Your guide to understanding and using analytics*, HBR Press, Boston, MA.

Turban, E., Sharda, R. and Delen, D. (2013) *Decision Support and Business Intelligence Systems*, 9th edition, Prentice-Hall, Englewood Cliffs, NJ.

Web links

Business intelligence

www.businessintelligence.ittoolbox.com Offers discussion forum and resources on BI topics.

www.information-management.com *Information Management* magazine. Has articles on BI and data warehousing.

http://www.tomdavenport.com Web site of a business analytics guru.

Geographical information systems

http://www.mapinfo.co.uk Pitney Bowes MapInfo web site.

Software vendors

http://www-01.ibm.com/software/analytics/cognos/enterprise/index.html IBM Cognos Enterprise web page.

www.datawarehousing.com Link to the IBM InfoSphere Data Warehouse web page.

http://www.microsoft.com/bi/ Microsoft BI web page.

http://www.oracle.com/us/solutions/business-analytics/business-intelligence/overview/index.html Oracle BI web page.

http://www.sap.com/uk/solutions/sapbusinessobjects/index.epx SAP Business Objects BI web page.

www.sas.com SAS Analytics web page.

http://www.teradata.com/t/active-enterprise-intelligence/ Teradata BI web page.

LINKS TO OTHER CHAPTERS

The chapter focuses on the physical components of networks and how they can be structured.

Chapter 1   describes the qualities of the business information shared and transported via networks.

Chapter 3   covers software for network management including network operating systems, and also software that makes use of networks such as groupware and e-mail.

Chapter 6   reviews business applications of Internet-based networks.

Networks, telecommunications and the Internet

CHAPTER AT A GLANCE

LEARNING OUTCOMES

After reading this chapter, you will be able to:

- specify which components of a communications system are necessary to exchange information within and between businesses;
- explain the basic components and terminology of networks, including the Internet;
- identify the benefits available through the introduction of computer networks;
- identify the advantages and disadvantages of the client/server architecture in comparison with traditional approaches;
- explain the broad implications of the Internet on the marketplace.

MANAGEMENT ISSUES

As organisations become increasingly dependent on networking technologies, managers need to be aware of the business benefits of deploying and updating networks and the risks if they are mismanaged. A basic grasp of the terminology is required for discussing networks with solution providers. From a managerial perspective, this chapter addresses the following questions:

- What are the business benefits of networks?
- What are the basic concepts and terminology associated with the Internet and other networks?
- How does the Internet change marketplace structures?
- How are network components selected?

INTRODUCTION

For the modern organisation to operate effectively, the links connecting its people and their computers are vital. The network links provide the channels for information to flow continuously between people working in different departments of an organisation, or in different organisations. This allows people to collaborate much more efficiently than before the advent of networks when information flow was irregular and unreliable. These links also allow hardware such as printers and faxes to be shared more cost-effectively.

As with many aspects of technology, jargon is rife when describing the different parts of and types of network. As an example of the many three-letter acronyms (TLAs), networks of different scales are referred to as LAN, WAN, MAN, VAN, and VPN! Here, we will try to filter out the jargon to highlight the terms you need to know when understanding and specifying information systems for a business.

In this chapter, we trace the use of computer networks from the global network of the Internet through to small-scale networks. We look at the components that form a network and how to specify a suitable architecture for the modern business.

We will see here that most medium and large businesses already use internal company networks and the Internet – the business case is clear, but many smaller businesses are still considering the need for internal or external networks. For this reason, we start by examining the business case for implementing networks and some of the management problems involved with implementing and running networks. Selecting the right solutions for telecommunications becomes ever more important as businesses become more reliant on electronic communications. As new networking technologies become available, companies have to evaluate the benefits against the cost of implementation and running these new technologies. Some of the main telecommunications issues currently, which are highlighted in this chapter, are selecting higher-speed broadband communications to connect to the Internet and the use of wireless networking using technologies like 'Wi-Fi' and '4G'.

COMPUTER NETWORKS

What are computer networks?

Computer network

A computer network can be defined as a communication system that links two or more computers and peripheral devices and enables transfer of data between the components.

Local-area network (LAN)

A computer network that spans a limited geographic area, typically a single office or building.

We can describe the links that transfer information between different parts of an information system on different scales. At the smallest scale, links are etched in silicon between the different components of a microchip. At a larger scale, all the components of a PC, such as the hard disk and main processor, are connected by internal cables. In this chapter, we consider links at a larger scale still, that is, between computers and other hardware devices such as printers, scanners and separate storage devices. These links between computers and other hardware form a computer network.

A **computer network** can be defined as: 'a communications system that links two or more computers and peripheral devices and enables transfer of data between the components'.

As we shall see, computer networks are themselves constructed on different scales. Small-scale networks within a workgroup or single office are known as **local-area networks (LANs)**. Larger-scale networks which are national or international are known as **wide-area networks (WANs)**. The Internet is the best-known example of a wide-area network.

Wide-area networks (WANs)

Networks covering a large area which connect businesses in different parts of the same city, different parts of a country or different countries.

Telecommunications

The method by which data and information are transmitted between different locations.

Telecommunications

On a national or global scale, communications technology such as satellite and micro-wave transmissions are important in linking businesses. To transfer information electronically, companies create **telecommunications** systems. These systems consist of both the hardware and the software necessary to set up these links. Telecommunications enable a business that operates from different locations to run as a single unit. This means that the same information and control structures do not need to be repeated at each company office. Instead, information can be managed centrally and control maintained from a central location. As well as improving internal communications in a company, telecommunications also allow companies to collaborate using electronic data interchange or web-based e-procurement with partners such as suppliers. Similarly, customers can transact with the company using the Internet.

What are the business benefits of networks?

Networks are vital to a business. They are important for the cost savings and improved communications that arise from an internal network. Beyond this, they are truly vital, because they help a business reach out and connect with its customers, suppliers and collaborators. Through doing this a company can order new raw materials more rapidly and cheaply from its suppliers and can keep in touch with the needs of its customers.

Figure 5.1 indicates the links that may exist between different partners. In some industries, such as the travel industry, travel agents and suppliers (such as the airlines) have made use of telecommunications links for over 25 years. In other sectors, however, most communications have been over the phone or in person, until more recently. The potential for e-business has been made possible by the use of the Internet technologies to reduce the cost and complexity of linking companies.

When computers and telecommunications are integrated, they can provide many advantages. Take the simple example of a humble e-mail sent to a customer or colleague. This costs only a few pence and can be sent to any location in the world immediately. As well as the low cost and fast delivery, it can be integrated to work with the users' other information needs, perhaps by supplying a spreadsheet as an attachment.

Figure 5.1 Communications links between different stakeholders in an industry

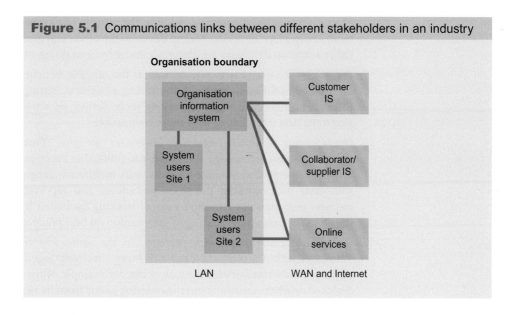

We will now look at the benefits that networks provide in more detail.

1. *Reduce cost compared to traditional communications.* Costs can be reduced in various ways depending on the type of communication required. If information has to be sent to another location, the cost of sending is very low compared to using a letter or even a fax. If face-to-face communication is needed to exchange information or solve a problem, then the traditional approach would be to jump into a car or onto a plane. Telecommunications now make this less necessary. Meetings can be conducted by conferencing, which not only includes video conferencing, but also sharing ideas through writing on whiteboards or running shared software. Money is saved on transport and accommodation but, perhaps more significantly, the time it takes for people to travel to the meeting is also saved.

2. *Reduce time for information transfer.* The benefits of shorter times for messages to arrive are obvious, but more subtle benefits can also occur through the rapid transfer of information. It is now possible for the global company to operate 24 hours a day by taking advantage of people working in different time zones. If someone is working on a product design in New Zealand, for example, they can dispatch it for review in Europe at the end of their working day. The review can then be conducted in Europe while the other team members are asleep and will be ready for review the next morning. Using this simple method product designs could be accelerated significantly. Customer service queries can also be turned around more quickly through the use of telecommunications.

3. *Enable sharing and dissemination of company information.* Opportunities to share information are lost when it is locked in a filing cabinet or stored on an individual's PC. By placing information on a server, either as a file or within a database, it can be made accessible to all departments that need it and the flow of information in the company is improved. This has proved to be one of the big benefits of intranets. A company selling through agents worldwide can provide information such as prices or technical specifications over an intranet. This information is always up to date, as there is no delay while price lists are reproduced and transported to the agents. Of course, this approach also helps in reducing costs.

4. *Enable sharing of hardware resources such as printers, backup, processing power.* An obvious benefit of setting up a network is that it enables the cost of equipment such as printers, faxes, modems or scanners to be shared between members of a workgroup. Printers are the most obvious item that can be shared within a business. Workgroup printers may be shared between small teams of three or four or up to twenty or so people, but a more powerful printer would be required in the latter case. For a printer shared by many people, it is usual to use a print server to schedule the jobs and store them while they are pending. Through storing information on a server, the security of the users' data can be increased by attaching a tape or optical backup device to the server and performing regular backups. Other administrative tasks are also made easier by centralising more complex equipment.

5. *Promote new ways of working.* As well as the tangible benefits, introducing networks can facilitate a different approach to running a business. Setting up an internal network makes it possible to use group-working tools. Setting up a wide- area network makes electronic data interchange with suppliers possible.

6. *Operate geographically separate businesses as one.* Through using wide-area communications technology, it is possible to rationalise the operations of a company that originally operated as separate business units in different geographic locations, perhaps with their own working practices, procedures and reporting mechanisms. Linked business units can use common ways of working facilitated by video conferencing as shown in the case study. Sharing of information on best practices can also occur.

7. *Restructure relationships with partners.* In the same way that different groups or businesses within a company can work more effectively together, different companies can also collaborate better. This may occur, for example, when new products are being designed or when a manufacturer is ordering goods from its suppliers.

Table 5.1 A summary of the key advantages and disadvantages of network technology

Advantages	Disadvantages
1. Lower transaction costs due to less human input	1. Overreliance on networks for mission-critical applications
2. Improved sharing of information and hardware resources	2. Cost of initial setup and administration
3. Reduced costs through sharing hardware and software	3. Disruption during initial setup and maintenance
4. Reduced time for communication compared with traditional methods postal mail	4. Reduced security due to more external access points to the network on wide-area networks and the Internet
5. Increased security of data which are backed up on file servers. Increased security through restricting access via user names and passwords	

To balance against the many benefits, there are, of course, disadvantages with introducing networks. The main disadvantages are:

1. The initial setup cost may be high, and there may be a considerable period before the costs are paid off.

2. When implementing or updating the network there may be considerable practical difficulties. Deploying cabling can be very disruptive to staff doing their daily work.

3. In the long term, companies become reliant on networks, and breaks in service can be very disruptive. For this reason investment in network maintenance is vital.

4. Security is reduced through introducing a network, since there are more access points to sensitive data. Data may also be intercepted when they are transferred from one site to another.

Despite these disadvantages, most companies still proceed with implementation and take care to reduce the risks of disruption and security breaches. In doing so, further costs will be introduced. Table 5.1 summarises the advantages and disadvantages of networks.

NETWORK COMPONENTS

In this section we examine how to specify the often confusingly named components that are necessary to setting up a network. We start by looking at the client/server architecture of the modern information system and why this has been adopted by businesses. We will then examine each of the components in turn and look at how they fit together and the important factors in their selection.

Client/server

The client/server architecture consists of client computers such as PCs sharing resources such as a database stored on more powerful server computers.

The client/server model of computing

The **client/server** architecture consists of client computers such as PCs sharing resources such as a database stored on more powerful server computers. Processing can be shared between the clients and the servers.

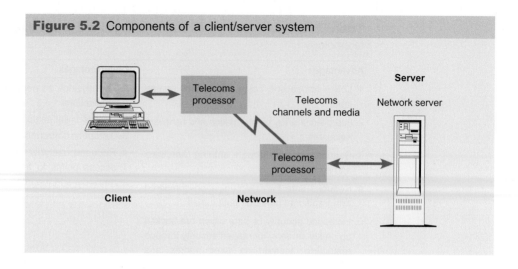

Figure 5.2 Components of a client/server system

Client/server architecture is significant since most modern networked information systems are based on this structure. The client/server model involves a series of clients, typically desktop PCs, which are the access points for end-user applications. As shown in Figure 5.2, the clients are connected to a more powerful PC or server computer via a local-area network within one site of a company, or a wide-area network connecting different sites and/or companies. The network is made up of both telecommunications processors to help route the information and the channels and media which carry the information.

The server is a more powerful computer that is usually used to store the application and the data shared by the users. When a user wants to run a program on a PC in a client/server system, the applications, such as a word processor, will usually be stored on the hard disk of the server and then loaded into the memory of the client PC, running or 'executing' on the processor of the client. The document the user creates would be saved back to the hard disk of the server. This is only one alternative. One of the benefits of client/server is that there are many choices for sharing the workload between resources. The system designers can decide to distribute data and processing across both servers and client computers, as described in Chapter 11. There we also explain how different functions can be partitioned between client and server and the merits of using 'thin' or 'fat' clients, applications on the former being smaller and easier to maintain.

- To summarise, the main components of a client/server system shown in Figure 5.2 can be defined as follows:

- Client software is the interface by which the end-user accesses the software. It includes both the operating system, such as Windows 8, and the applications software, such as word processors. Increasingly, web-based browsers are being used as clients on a company intranet.

- Server software is used to store information, administer the system and provide links to other company systems. Again, this may be a web server or a database server.

- The application development environment provides interactive programming tools to develop applications through the application programming interface (API) of the package.

- The infrastructure or plumbing of the system. This is based on local- and wide-area networking techniques and consists of the telecommunication processors and media.

Why use client/server?

The adoption of the client/server architecture was part of a trend to 'downsize' from large mainframes with arrays of user terminals which had limited functionality. This latter type of architecture was widespread in businesses during the 1970s and 1980s. The client/server model represented a radically new architecture compared to the traditional, centralised method of a mainframe, with its character-based 'dumb terminals' which dated back nearly to the birth of computers. Rather than all the tasks involved in program execution (other than display) occurring on the mainframe, client/server gives the opportunity for them to be shared between a central server and clients. This gives the potential for faster execution, as processing is distributed across many clients.

Cost savings were originally used to drive the introduction of client/server. PC-based servers were much cheaper than mainframes, although the client PCs were more expensive than dumb terminals. The overall savings were dramatic. These savings were coupled with additional benefits of ease of use of the new clients compared with the older terminals. The clients used new graphical user interfaces which were easier to use thanks to a mouse, and the graphics could improve analysis of business data. Customisation of the client is also possible – the end-user is empowered through being able to develop their own applications and view data to their preference. With queries occurring on the back end, this reduces the amount of network traffic that is required. Centralised control of the user administration and data security and archiving can still be retained.

With these advantages, there are also a host of system management problems which were not envisaged when client/server was first adopted. These have been partly responsible for the reduced costs promised with this 'downsizing' not materialising. To some extent there is now a backlash, in which the new 'network-centric' model is being suggested as a means of reducing these management problems. These disbenefits include:

1. *High cost of ownership*. Although the purchase price for a PC is relatively low, the extra potential for running different applications and modifications by end-users means that there is much more that can go wrong in comparison with a dumb terminal. More support staff are required to solve problems resulting from the complex hardware and software. The annual cost of ownership of a PC is estimated by the Gartner Group using their total cost of ownership (TCO) measure. The issue of reducing the 'total cost of ownership' is considered further in Chapter 16.

2. *Instability*. Client/server technology is often complex and involves integrating different hardware and software components from many different companies. Given this, client/server systems may be less reliable than mainframe systems.

3. *Performance*. For some mission-critical applications, a smaller server cannot deliver the power required. In a travel agency business, for example, this will give rise to longer queues and poorer customer service. For this reason, many banks and travel agents have retained their mainframe-based systems where performance is critical. The use of a PC can also cause delays at the client end, as the screen takes a long time to redraw graphics compared to a teletext terminal.

4. *Lack of worker focus*. Although PCs can potentially empower end-users, the freedom of choice can also lead to non-productive time-wasting, as users rearrange the colours and wallpaper on their desktop rather than performing their regular tasks!

Despite these difficulties, the compelling arguments of ease of use and flexibility of client/server still remain. The empowerment of the end-user to develop their own applications and to use and share the data as they see fit is now considered to be the main benefit of client/server.

Servers

A server is a powerful computer used to control the management of a network. It may have a specific function such as storing user files or a database or managing a printer.

Servers

Servers are vital to an information system, since they regulate the flow of information around the network in the way that a heart controls the flow of blood around the body. Network servers run the network operating system (NOS), the software that is used to manage the network, and are often used to store large volumes of data. The server and NOS together perform the following functions:

- *Maintain security* – access to information in files is restricted according to the user name and password issued to users of the network.

- *Sharing of peripheral devices* connected to the network, such as printers and tape drives. These are often attached directly to the server.

- *Sharing of applications* such as word processors, which do not then need to be stored on the hard drive of the end-user's computer. The cost of buying applications can be reduced through buying a 'site licence'.

- *Sharing of information* – access to this data is maintained by the NOS and it is stored within the hard drive of a server as files or as part of a database.

Both applications and data can be managed better when they are stored on a managed server. It is easier to audit who uses which applications and to ensure the security of the data. Data quality can also be managed more effectively.

For the larger network of perhaps 20 people or more, the functions described above may be split between several servers to share the load. There may be a separate file server, print server, password server and database server. In very large companies there will be many servers used for data storage. These will all be linked by the network to ensure that the data are accessible by everyone. They will also be responsible for ensuring through a process known as **replication** that the same version of data exists on different servers. With the use of many servers, an opportunity exists to spread the computing workload across these servers rather than overloading a single central machine, which is what happened in the days of the mainframe. The sharing of functions across several computers is known as 'distributed computing'.

Computing blade servers are unique computers, often dedicated to a single application, and the facilities they lack are provided either within the chassis, or, particularly with storage, over a network. The chassis and included blade servers may require a substantial initial investment in hardware and implementation for a business but bring advantages in space, power consumption, cable reduction, reliability, and economy of scale that may offer considerable longer term benefits.

The different types of server are summarised in Table 5.2.

When creating an information system, there are a number of critical functions which must be designed in to the server. These are important requirements which must be checked with server vendors, database vendors and operating systems vendors. They are:

- *Performance*. The server should be fast enough to handle all the requests from users attached to the network. A margin should be built in to accommodate future growth in users and network traffic. This means specifying a suitable amount of memory, a fast hard disk and, less importantly, a fast processor.

- *Capacity*. When initially specified, the hard disk capacity should be large enough that it will not need to be upgraded in the near future.

- *Resilience/fault tolerance*. If there is a problem affecting the hardware, such as a power surge or a problem with the hard disk, it is important that the whole network does not 'crash' because of this. Preventive measures should be taken, such as installing an uninterruptible power supply or running two disks in parallel (disk mirroring or RAID – redundant array of inexpensive disks).

- *Clustering* is used to spread the load across different servers, so improving reliability and performance. It involves linking several servers together via a high-speed link such as fibre-optic cabling. This can enable parallel processing, where tasks are shared between processors, and also storage mirroring, where duplicate copies of data are stored on different servers to improve performance and reduce the risk of one server failing.

Replication

Ensures that the versions of data stored on different servers are consistent. Software is used to check changes made to data on each server. Changes are transmitted to all other servers.

Table 5.2 Types of server

Type of server	Purpose
Network	Contains functions to manage the network resources and control user access
File	This term is sometimes used to refer to network server functions. It can also indicate that users' files such as documents and spreadsheets are stored on the network server
Print	Dedicated print servers have a queue of all documents for which print requests have been made, often combined with file or network servers
Fax	Used to route incoming and outgoing faxes received and sent from the user's desktop
Mail	Stores and forwards e-mail messages
Database	Used to store data and provide the software to process data queries supplied by users, often accessed by Structured Query Language (SQL)
Application	Used to store programs such as spreadsheet or bespoke applications run by end-users on their PCs. This removes the need to store each application on every user's hard disk
Communications	Manages connections with other networks in a WAN configuration. Sometimes known as 'gateways' and attached to other gateway devices such as routers and firewall servers
Blade	A computer configuration where elements such as power, cooling, storage are largely provided in an outer housing or chassis. The chassis provides these services to a number of specialised, stripped down motherboard units – the blade servers – each one a complete computer or service device containing only vital processing and storage elements.

Servers can be specified as powerful PCs running an operating system such as Windows NT or Novell Netware, or they can run the UNIX operating system, from companies such as Sun, IBM or Hewlett-Packard.

End-user computers or terminals

The access points for users of a network are known variously as clients, nodes, workstations or, most commonly, just PCs. It is best to use the term 'client PC', as this helps distinguish clients from servers which may also be PC-based. To work on the network each client must have networking software such as Novell Netware or TCP/IP installed (see later section). Of course, a physical connection to the network is also required. For a PC on an office LAN, this is provided by a *network interface card* in one of the PC's slots. The card is then attached to the network cabling. For a PC at home which is linked to the Internet, the network card is replaced by a modem.

Data communications equipment or telecommunications processors

As well as the physical cables that link the computers, there are also other important components of the complete telecommunications system that have to be purchased by a business. These are the pieces of hardware that are used to link the servers and clients and different networks together. These devices can be thought of as connectors located between client computers and servers. Collectively, these processors can be called telecommunications

Dial-up networking (DUN)

Dial-up networking software allows users to access a network at a remote location via a modem.

Remote location

Remote location describes a means of accessing a network from a distant location. A modem and specialised software allows users to send and receive information from home or an office when travelling.

Modem (modulator– demodulator)

A modem is a communications device that allows users to access ordinary telephone lines.

Analogue

Analogue data are continuous in that an infinite number of values between two given points can be represented.

Digital

Digital data can only represent a finite number of discrete values.

ISDN (integrated services digital network)

ISDN represents a standard for communications that allows data transfer rates of 64 kpbs. An ISDN telephone line provides two separate 'channels', allowing simultaneous voice and data transmissions.

ADSL (asymmetric digital subscriber line)

A communications technique for making use of existing telephone lines to provide very high data-transfer rates.

Satellite communications

A communications link via satellite. The satellite dishes can be fixed or mobile.

connectors or gateways, but they are usually referred to by their specific names, such as hubs, multiplexers, bridges and routers. In a company that needs to use gateway devices, a specialist is required to maintain them. Modems and network interface cards also fit into this category.

Communications devices

The following are options for connecting telecommunications equipment.

- **Dial-up networking (DUN)** facilities allow users to access a network at a remote location via a modem. The **modem (modulator–demodulator)** works by converting data between digital and analogue form. The modem receives analogue data (for example as transmitted via an analogue telephone line) and converts these into digital data so that the computer can make use of them. Similarly, the modem converts outgoing digital data into an analogue signal before transmitting them.

- Digital telephone exchanges support an **integrated services digital network (ISDN)** standard that allows data transfer rates of 64 kbps. An ISDN telephone line provides two separate 'channels', allowing simultaneous voice and data transmissions or combined to give a transmission rate of 128 kbps. Since ISDN lines transmit digital data, a modem is not required to make use of the service. Instead, a special terminal adaptor (often called an 'ISDN modem') is used to pass data between the computer and the ISDN line.

- **Asymmetric digital subscriber line (ADSL)** services makes use of existing telephone lines to provide very high data-transfer rates. ADSL or DSL is usually simply referred to as 'broadband' Internet access when offered by ISPs for home and small-business users across their phone lines. Although the bandwidth offered by such services is usually shared by a number of users, ADSL offers many of the benefits associated with ISDN and the potential of data transfer rates of up to 24 Mbps. ADSL is known as 'asymmetric' since it offers different speeds for download and upload of data. A range of different options are available for ADSL Internet packages from 512 kbps download. Up to 24 Mbps download is possible across some telephone lines. Variations on ADSL include Annex M which can more than double upload speeds and Annex L which can increase the range of coverage.

- **Satellite communications** systems can be used to receive data at very high speeds in remote locations. Such systems are used to beam back news stories from remote locations. The satellite dishes can be fixed or mobile, for example fixed to a car roof.

- **Cable modems** make use of the fibre-optic cables that have been installed by cable television companies such as Virgin Media. Services tend to be restricted to heavily populated areas, such as cities and large towns. Cable modems offer very high data-transfer rates, up to a maximum of 100 Mbps.

As more individuals and organisations gain access to high-speed services (known as **broadband services**, as opposed to traditional 'narrowband' services), data transfer speeds are more commonly measured in terms of thousands (kbps) or millions (Mbps) of bits per second. The standard ADSL broadband speed when it was first introduced was 512,000 bps, 512 kbps or 0.512 Mbps and it requires a specific *ADSL modem*. However, as we will see below, providers have introduced a range of speeds by limiting this speed to enable them to offer a range of packages.

Options for consumer broadband services

Competition in the marketplace amongst broadband providers has caused a great increase in the Internet access options available for consumers and small businesses. While broadband was originally introduced as an 'always-on' connection, some Internet service providers (both ADSL and cable companies) have offered lower-speed options while others have capped usage at a fixed number of hours per month or put limits on the amount of data transferred. For example, in 2011, one cable company offered four levels of speed (10Mb,

Cable modem

These devices allow users to make use of the fibre-optic cables that are installed by cable television companies. They offer very high data transfer rates, up to a maximum of 100 Mbps.

Baud

A simple means of measuring the performance of a modem or other device. Data transmission rates can also be expressed in bits per second (bps). In general, the higher the baud rate or bps value, the faster and more efficient the device.

Broadband

A relatively high-capacity, high-speed transmission medium such as cable.

20Mb, 50Mb and 100Mb) with unlimited downloads and another provider offered 20Mb with a 2Gb monthly usage allowance or 20Mb with unlimited monthly usage.

Given the complexity of choice, several Internet services have been created to compare the offerings (Google 'compare broadband'). For example, visit Broadband Checker (**www.broadbandchecker.co.uk**) to find out the latest choices in your area or see thinkbroadband (**www.thinkbroadband.com**) for a wide range of suppliers. The choices in selecting business broadband for small business users are similar to those for home users.

What is behind the rapid adoption of consumer broadband?

What has been most significant in the new millennium is the growth in adoption of broadband services. Ofcom (**http://media.ofcom.org.uk/facts/**) showed that by 2013 75 per cent of adults in the UK have broadband (fixed and mobile) services with an average speed of 12.0 Mbit/s. Some 55 per cent of adults with an home Internet connection use social networking sites such as Facebook.

Hubs

Hubs are used to connect up to 20 PCs to a network in a convenient way using patch cables (which look similar to phone cables and sockets) running between the back of each PC and the hub. The hub may then be attached to a server or a backbone connection leading to the server.

Bridges and routers

These are used to connect different LANs and transfer data packets from one network to the next. They can be used to connect similar types of LAN. They also offer filtering services to restrict local traffic to one side of the bridge, thus reducing traffic overall. Routers can select the best route for packets to be transmitted and are also used on the Internet backbones and wide-area network to achieve this. Although these devices used to be distinct, they are now produced as hybrids which share functions.

Companies attached to the Internet usually use a router as a gateway to attach their internal network to the Internet. This is often combined with a 'firewall', which is intended to reduce the risk of someone from outside the company gaining unauthorised access to company data. (Firewalls are described in more detail in Chapter 15.)

Repeaters

Over a long transmission distance, signal distortion may occur. Repeaters are necessary to increase transmission distances by regenerating signals and retransmitting them.

Data service units and channel service units

These devices are used to connect to digital communications lines by converting signals received from bridges, routers and multiplexers.

| **Activity 5.1** | **Transmission of data through different hardware and network components** |

Describe the order in which a message passes from one piece of hardware to the next when a home user in the UK sends an e-mail via the Internet to someone in a large corporation in the USA. You should refer to the following terms:

- mail server;
- client PC;

- modem;
- hub;
- network cable;
- network card;
- gateway server (telecommunications processor);
- router.

Treat the Internet transmission as a single stage.

Telecommunications channels

Telecommunications channels

The media by which data are transmitted. Cables and wires are known as guided media and microwave and satellite links are known as unguided media.

Telecommunications channels are the different media used to carry information between different locations. These include traditional cables and wires known as *guided media*, and wires and more recent innovations such as satellite and micro-wave which are *unguided media*.

We will now examine the benefits and applications of these different media. When doing this, the main factors that need to be considered are the physical characteristics, data transmission method, performance and cost.

Characteristics of guided media

The main types of cabling used in LANs are based on copper cabling. Data are transmitted along this by applying at one end a voltage, which is received at the other. A positive voltage represents a binary one and a negative voltage represents a binary zero. There are three main types of cabling used in networks:

- *Twisted-pair* cabling consists of twisted copper wire covered by an insulator. The two wires form a circuit over which data can be transmitted. The twisting is intended to reduce interference. Shielding using braided metal may also be used to reduce external interference. A cable may have more than one pair, such as category 5 cable generally known as CAT5. CAT5 consists of four twisted pairs inside an outer insulating cover. The cable is used for many applications such as computer networking, telephony, low-voltage power distribution and home automation applications such as movement detectors and transmission of high-definition television. CAT5 can support network speeds up to 1 Gbps.

- *Co-axial* cable consists of a single solid copper core surrounded by an insulator and a braided metal shield. 'Co-ax' can be used to connect devices over longer distances than twisted-pair. It is possibly best known as the means used to connect an antenna to a television set. Co-axial can be used for transmission speeds up to 500 Mbps. There are different grades of co-ax available, with a standard named CT100 suitable for transmission of digital TV around the home. CT125 offers even better performance.

- *Fibre-optic* cable consists of thousands of fibres of pure silicon dioxide. Packets are transmitted along fibre-optic cables using light or photons emitted from a light-emitting diode at one end of the cable; detection is by a photo-sensitive cell at the other end. Fibre-optic cables give very high transmission rates since the cable has very low resistance. This is well known as a method by which cable TV is delivered to homes. Fibre optic transmission rates can be as much as 100 times greater than those of co-axial. They are also much smaller and lighter than co-axial or twisted-pair cabling. Other advantages are that they have a much lower data error rate than other media and are harder physically to 'tap' into and thus offer greater security.

Characteristics of unguided or wireless media

For wide-area network cables are still commonly used, but they are being superseded by the use of unguided media. This method uses signals transmitted through air and space from a transmitter to a receiver. It tends to be faster than wired methods. Wireless transmissions can be used for different business applications at different scales:

- *Wireless infra-red transmission* can be used for sending data between a portable PC or personal digital assistant (PDA) and a desktop computer. Laser printers can receive documents for printing via wireless infra-red transmission from desktop or laptop computers that do not need to be connected to the printer.

- *Wireless transmission* can also be used locally to form a wireless LAN. Here a microwave or narrowband radio transmitter and receiver may be used to connect different buildings. Wireless LANs are often used across college campuses. They have the benefit that the cost of laying cabling is not incurred. This makes them particularly suitable where it is not clear whether a link is needed in the long term.

- *Microwave transmission* can be used to beam information through the atmosphere. The maximum distance that can separate microwave transmitters is 45 km, since the signal follows a straight line and the curvature of the earth limits transmission distance. This can make microwave an expensive method of transmitting data, but the cost can be reduced if it is combined with satellite methods.

- *Satellite transmission* operates at two orbit levels, high orbit at 22,300 miles in a geostationary orbit and at a lower orbit. Messages are sent from a transceiver at one location on the earth's surface and are bounced off the satellite to another transceiver. Because of the distances involved, this can give a time delay of up to a quarter of a second, which is evident in interviews conducted by satellite. A range of frequencies can be used. Satellite applications include television, telephone and data transmission.

- Both guided and unguided media use a number of transmission schemes such as OFDM in order to improve their efficiency. Orthogonal frequency-division multiplexing (OFDM) is used in applications such as digital television and audio broadcasting, wireless networking and broadband internet access.

Orthogonal frequency-division multiplexing (OFDM)

A technique used for transmitting data over guided and unguided media.

Network operating systems

The final component that is needed to make all the other components work in unison is a network operating system (NOS). This is systems software necessary to control the access to and flow of information around a network and provides the following functions:

- access control or security through providing user accounts with user names and passwords;
- file and data sharing of data stored on a database server or file server;
- communication between users via e-mail, diary systems or workgroup software such as Lotus Notes;
- sharing of devices, enabling, for example, the backup to tape of data on the server, or printer sharing.

Network operating system (NOS)

The software necessary to control the access to and flow of information around a network.

The most widely used NOS for a PC-based LAN are Novell Netware and IBM LAN Manager. However, NOS features are now being built into standard operating systems such as Microsoft Windows, and this is increasingly being adopted by companies. For UNIX-based servers the NOS is a component of the operating system. UNIX is used by many medium and large companies operating servers from companies such as Sun Microsystems, Hewlett-Packard and IBM. It is often thought to offer better stability than Windows NT since it is a long-established NOS.

NETWORK TYPES

This section describes a variety of network types that cater for short-range, medium-range and long-range communication implemented using guided and unguided media.

Personal-area networks (PAN)

Bluetooth

A wireless standard for transmission of data between devices over short ranges (less than 10 metres).

A personal-area network (PAN) can be implemented using the **Bluetooth** wireless technology. Bluetooth is used for short-range data transmission between devices and thus can be used to create a small-scale network. Bluetooth is the popular name for the 802.15 wireless networking standard defined by the Institute of Electrical and Electronics Engineers (IEEE). Applications of Bluetooth include wireless keyboards and beaming data between a PDA and a desktop or a laptop and a printer. A popular application of Bluetooth which makes use of its low power needs is the use of wireless headphones. Transmission distances between Bluetooth-enabled devices were initially limited to 10 metres, but can now be up to 100 metres, so there is now the option for using the technology for networking like Wi-Fi. Bluetooth 2 offers transmission speeds of up to 3 Mbps, Bluetooth 3.0 (introduced in 2009) offers 24 Mbps and Bluetooth 4 was introduced in 2010.

It has been suggested that use of Bluetooth for business purposes represents a security risk through a process known as 'bluesnarfing'. An example of this often referred to is that, if you so wished, you could go to an airport passenger lounge and scan the diaries or contacts on passengers' different laptops, phones or PDAs.

Ultra-wideband (UWB)

A wireless standard for high-speed transmission of data between devices over short ranges (less than 10 metres).

Ultra-wideband (UWB) allows the transfer of data up to 2 Gbps over around 10 metres. The technology could be used to connect electronic devices in the house such as PC, printer, scanner, monitor, MP3 player, DVD player and digital camera and so eliminate unsightly cabling. UWB is at present little used due to a lack of agreement on standards and the need to keep transmission power low so as not to interfere with 3G.

Local-area network (LAN)

Local-area network (LAN)

A computer network that spans a limited geographic area, typically a single office or building.

A **local-area network (LAN)** consists of a single network segment or several connected segments that are limited in extent, hence local. A network segment defines a group of clients that are attached to the same hub or network interface card linked to a single server. The term 'local' can be interpreted in different ways. LANs are usually limited to a company occupying a single building, but could equally connect several buildings across a larger company site. Faster, higher-capacity links such as fibre-optic cables connecting different LANs or network segments are sometimes referred to as 'backbones'. Such networks may just have a single server if the company is of fewer than, say, 20 people. Larger companies with hundreds of employees are very likely to have several central servers and possibly departmental servers also. A LAN is used to share computer resources between different members of a company or workgroup. For example, a printer sharer allows several computers to be attached to a single printer, thus reducing costs. Manual printer sharers are controlled by turning a dial to indicate which computer will be used to send data to the printer. Automatic printer sharers detect any data sent to the printer and configure themselves accordingly.

A simple network that links three PC workstations with a shared server and printer is shown in Figure 5.3. This is an example of a LAN that might serve a workgroup or a small company. Here the computers and the printer are the main components of the network, with the cables and network cards forming other components. We will explain servers in more detail later. For now, consider them as a more powerful computer that is used to store data and help the other PCs communicate. The final component needed to make the

Figure 5.3 A small workgroup network connecting a single server to three PCs and a laser printer

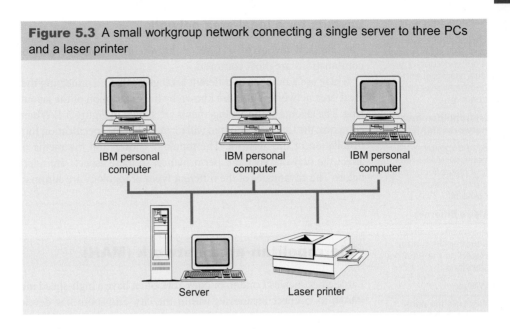

network function, which is not shown on the diagram, is the communications software that enables all the components to work together.

A small-scale or workgroup network gives the following benefits by enabling:

- workers to share common information which is typically stored on the server;
- communication between workers, perhaps through e-mail or a shared diary system;
- sharing of various facilities such as printing, hard disk storage or software applications on the server.

The capability to share devices and applications also gives the additional major benefit of cost reduction.

Wi-Fi is the shorthand often used to describe a high-speed wireless local-area network. Most Wi-Fi networks use a standard IEEE protocol known as 802.11 a, b or g. The 802.11a variant offers speeds up to 54 Mbps at 5 GHz. The 802.11b and 802.11g variants both operate at a frequency of 2.4 GHz and are thus compatible. 802.11b offers speeds up to 11 Mbps and 802.11g offers speeds up to 54 Mbps. The 802.11n standard aims to achieve transmission speeds above 100 Mbps and a recent development is the 802.11ac standard which aims to deliver speeds above 500 Mbps.

Wi-Fi is widely deployed in an office or home environment where it removes the need for cabling and adds flexibility. Note that this increased usage has security limitations since Wi-Fi encryption is limited and communications can potentially be intercepted or 'sniffed' by anyone in the vicinity with appropriate scanning software.

For WLANs additional hardware is needed. For example, home users need to buy a wireless router (sometimes with firewall software included) which connects to the Internet and shares the Internet and local network access with all PCs in the house which contain wireless cards to receive the signal. Other devices can also be used; for example, music or video streamed from the Internet can be played on appropriate devices. Transmission is limited in home applications to around 100 m line-of-sight.

Hotspots consist of access points positioned in a strategic spot in a public place to provide wireless coverage for a specific area. This allows employees and customers access to the Internet from their laptops or other mobile devices without the need to connect using a wire. In 2012 it was estimated that over 16,000 public Wi-Fi hotspots where available in the UK (**http://stakeholders.ofcom.org.uk/market-data-research/other/telecoms-research/ broadband-speeds/infrastructure-report-2012/**).

Wi-Fi ('wireless fidelity')

A high-speed wireless local-area network enabling wireless access to the Internet for mobile, office and home users.

Hotspot

An access point positioned in a strategic spot in a public place to provide wireless coverage for a specific area.

Network topology

The physical layout of a LAN is known as a network topology. Bus, star, ring and combinations are most common.

Metropolitan-area networks (MAN)

A metropolitan-area network (MAN) refers to a network covering a city or university campus.

Metro Ethernet

A network covering a metropolitan area based on the Ethernet standard.

WiMax

WiMax is the name given to the IEEE 802.16 wireless standard which allows an access range of up to 30 miles at speeds of up to 75 Mbps.

Layouts for a local-area network

The physical layout of a LAN is known as a network topology. Bus, star, ring and combinations are most common.

There are a number of different arrangements for connecting the clients to the server in a local-area network. These are known by the description of the layout or topology: bus, star or ring. The layouts of the arrangements are shown in Figure 5.4. When building a network for a company, the topology adopted will form part of the specification for the company performing installation of the network. The topology chosen and the media used to implement it will affect the network cost and performance, so these aspects are referred to in the description below. The advantages of the different types of topology are summarised in Table 5.3.

Metropolitan-area network (MAN)

Large cities such as London or New York often have a high-speed metropolitan-area network (MAN) to connect businesses within the city. Singapore has developed the concept of the 'intelligent island' in which businesses of the city are connected by a very high-speed network.

A MAN can be implemented using a Metro Ethernet which is a network based on the Ethernet standard for computer communications over a network. Alternatively a MAN can be implemented using WiMax (Worldwide Interoperability for Microwave Access) which is

Figure 5.4 Local-area network topologies

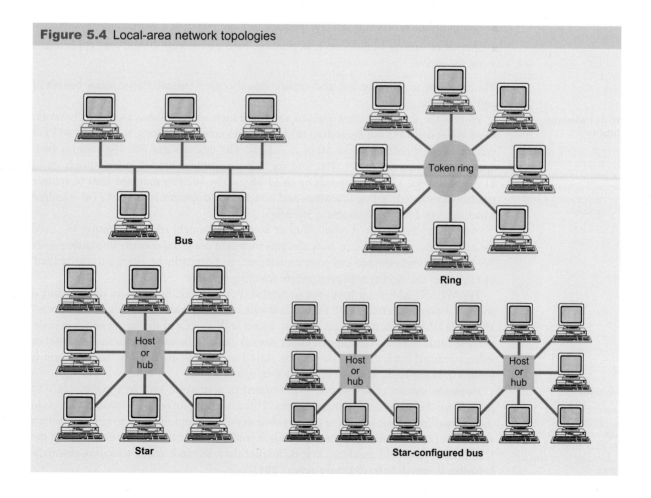

Table 5.3 Summary of the characteristics, advantages and disadvantages of the main local-area network topologies

Topology	Characteristics	Advantage	Disadvantage
Bus or linear	Simple. Based on co-axial Ethernet cable, e.g. twisted pair 10 Base-T	Easy to install and manage for small workgroup	Breaks in the cable disrupt the whole network
Star	Each PC is connected via a cable to a central location. Each PC is not usually connected directly to the server, but via a hub	Provides protection from cable breaks	Dependent on central host
Ring	A continuous ring of network cable, e.g. token ring. The word 'token' refers to a packet of data which is passed from one node to the next	Suitable for large data volumes and mission-critical applications	Higher initial cost and time for installation

the name given to the IEEE 802.16 wireless standard. WiMax can also be used for 'last mile' wireless broadband access as an alternative to cable connections.

Wide-area network (WAN)

Networks covering a large area which connect to businesses in different parts of the same city, different parts of a country or different countries.

Wide-area network (WAN)

These are large in extent and may connect offices in different parts of the same city, different parts of a country or even different countries (Figure 5.5). The **WAN** will connect many servers at each site. When we connect from a PC at one site to a server at another site, we talk about connecting to a 'remote' server across a WAN. If there is a large international

Figure 5.5 A wide-area network (WAN)

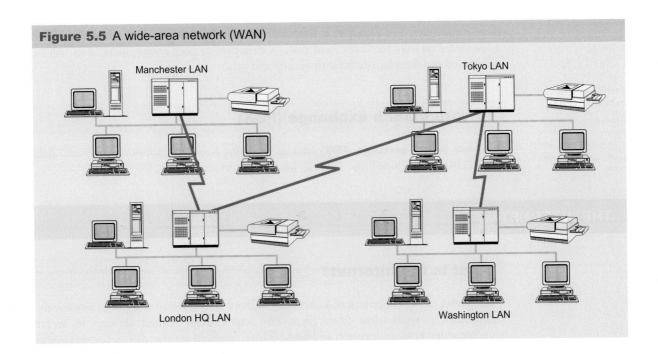

coverage, it will be referred to as a 'global network'. If the WAN enables communication across the whole company, it is referred to as the 'enterprise network' or 'enterprise-wide network'. Companies usually pay for their own 'leased lines' or communications links between different sites. Virtual private networks and value-added networks, which are described later, provide cheaper alternatives where the communications links are shared.

Often the network used to connect remote sites is the public telephone, referred to as POTS or 'plain old telephone system'. A company can also lease private or dedicated lines from a telecommunications supplier to connect sites, or can set up links using microwave or satellite methods.

Value-added networks (VANs)

Value-added networks (VAN)

Value-added networks (VANs) give a subscription service enabling companies to transmit data securely across a shared network.

Virtual private network (VPN)

A data network that makes use of the public telecommunication infrastructure and Internet, but information remains secure by the use of security procedures.

Value-added networks (VANs) are so named because they allow a company to minimise its investment in wide-area communications while still receiving all the benefits this can bring. The cost of setting up and maintaining the network is borne by the service provider, which then rents out the network to a number of companies. This works out more cheaply than if a company had leased its own point-to-point private lines, but it is not as secure.

A similar concept to VAN is **virtual private networks (VPNs)**. These are data networks that make use of the public telecommunications infrastructure and Internet, but information remains secure by the use of what is known as a 'tunnelling protocol' and security procedures such as 'firewalls', which are described in Chapter 15. A virtual private network can again be contrasted with a system of owned or leased point-to-point lines that can only be used by one company.

Peer-to-peer networking

Peer-to-peer network

A simple type of local-area network which provides sharing of files and peripherals between PCs.

A **peer-to-peer network** is a simple type of local-area network which provides sharing of files and peripherals between PCs. The same principle can be used on a larger scale – online music sharing systems are peer-to-peer.

'Peer-to-peer' refers to the capability of any computer on a local-area network to share resources, in particular files and peripherals, with others. It is particularly appropriate for small workgroups where central control from a server is less necessary. Windows provides these capabilities. For example, a user can, with permission, share across the network a file stored on another user's hard disk. With a peer-to-peer arrangement, data will be distributed and therefore difficult to backup and secure.

Private branch exchange (PBX)

Enables switching between phones or voice and data using existing telephone lines.

Private branch exchange (PBX)

A **private branch exchange (PBX)** enables switching between phones or voice and data using existing telephone lines. This can be used for printer sharing, for example.

THE INTERNET

What is the Internet?

The **Internet** allows communication between millions of connected computers worldwide. Information is transmitted from client PCs whose users request services to server computers that hold information and host business applications that deliver the services in

Figure 5.6 Infrastructure components of the Internet

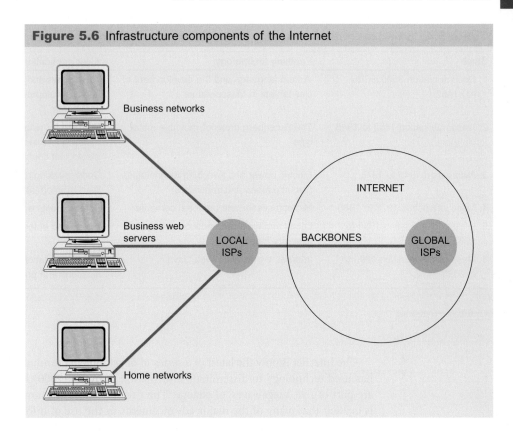

The Internet

The Internet refers to the physical network that links computers across the globe. It consists of the infrastructure of network servers and communications links between them that are used to hold and transport information between the client PCs and web servers.

Internet service provider (ISP)

A provider enabling home or business users a connection to access the Internet. They can also host web-based applications.

Backbones

High-speed communication links used to enable Internet communications across a country and internationally.

response to requests. The Internet is a large-scale client/server system. By June 2012 it was estimated that, worldwide, there were over 2.4 billion Internet users or 34 per cent of the world's population (**http://www.internetworldstats.com/stats.htm**). The client PCs within homes and businesses are connected to the Internet via local **Internet service providers (ISPs)** which, in turn, are linked to larger ISPs with connection to the major national and international infrastructure or backbones (Figure 5.6). In the UK, at the London Internet Exchange in the Docklands area of east London, a facility exists to connect multiple **backbones** of the major ISPs within the UK onto a single high-speed link out of the UK into Europe and through to the rest of the world. These high-speed links can be thought of as the motorways on the 'information superhighway' while the links provided from ISPs to consumers are equivalent to slow country roads.

A variety of end-user tools are available to exchange information over the Internet – web browsers and e-mail are the best known. As we will see in the next section, although the Internet has existed for around 30 years, it is only since the early 1990s, when the web browser was first widely adopted, that the use of the Internet by business has grown dramatically.

Development of the Internet

The simplest way in which the Internet can be described is as a global network system made up of smaller systems. The history and origin of the Internet as a business tool is surprising since it has taken a relatively long time to become an essential part of business. The Internet was conceived by the Defense Advanced Research Projects Agency (DARPA), an American intelligence organisation, in 1969. The Internet began to achieve its current form in 1987, growing from systems developed by DARPA and the National Science Foundation (NSF). See Gillies and Cailliau (2000) for a detailed description of the history of the Internet.

Table 5.4 Six stages of advances in the dissemination of information

Stage	Enabling technology	Killer applications and impact
1. Documentation 3500 BC to AD 1452	Written language and the development of clay tablets in Mesopotamia	Taxes, laws and accounting giving rise to the development of civilisation and commerce
2. Mass publication 1452 to 1946	The Gutenberg press of movable metal type	Demand for religious and scientific texts resulting in scientific advances and ideological conflicts
3. Automation 1946 to 1978	Electric power and switching technologies (vacuum tubes and transistors)	Code breaking and scientific calculations. Start of information age
4. Mass interaction 1978 to 1985	Microprocessor and personal computer	Spreadsheets and word processing
5. Infrastructuralisation 1985 to 1993	Local- and wide-area networks, graphical user interfaces	E-mail and enterprise resource planning
6. Mass communication 1993 to c. 2005	Internet, World Wide Web, Java	Mass information access for communications and purchasing

Source: Based on Kampas (2000).

The Internet is only the latest of a series of developments through which the human race has used technology to disseminate information. Kampas (2000) identifies ten stages that are part of five 'megawaves' of change. The first six stages are summarised in Table 5.4. It is evident that many of the major advancements in the use of information have happened within the last hundred years. This indicates that the difficulty of managing technological change is likely to continue. Kampas goes on to speculate on the impact of access to lower-cost, higher-bandwidth technologies.

Business and consumer models of Internet access

Business-to-consumer (B2C)

Commercial transactions are between an organisation and consumers.

Business-to-business (B2B)

Commercial transactions are between an organisation and other organisations.

It is useful to identify e-business opportunities in terms of whether an organisation is using the Internet to transact with consumers (**business-to-consumer – B2C**) or other businesses (**business-to-business – B2B**).

Business-to-business transactions predominate over the Internet, in terms of value, if not frequency. Figure 5.7 helps explain why this is the case. It shows that there are many more opportunities for B2B transactions than B2C, both between an organisation and its suppliers, together with intermediaries, and through distributors such as agents and wholesalers with customers. Additionally there is a higher level of access to the Internet among businesses than among consumers, and a greater propensity to use it for purchasing.

Table 5.5 gives examples of different companies operating in the business-to-consumer (B2C) and business-to-business (B2B) spheres and also presents transactions where consumers transact directly with consumers (C2C). It has been suggested that employees should be considered as a separate type of interaction through the use of intranets – this is sometimes referred to as employee-to-employee or E2E. Other types of transactions, such as government, have also been defined.

Disintermediation

The removal of intermediaries such as distributors or brokers that formerly linked a company to its customers.

The role of the Internet in restructuring business relationships

The relationship between a company and its suppliers and customers shown in Figure 5.4 can be dramatically altered by the opportunities afforded by the Internet. This occurs because the Internet offers a means of bypassing some of the channel partners. This process is known as **disintermediation** or 'cutting out the middleman'.

Figure 5.7 B2B and B2C interactions between an organisation, its suppliers and its customers

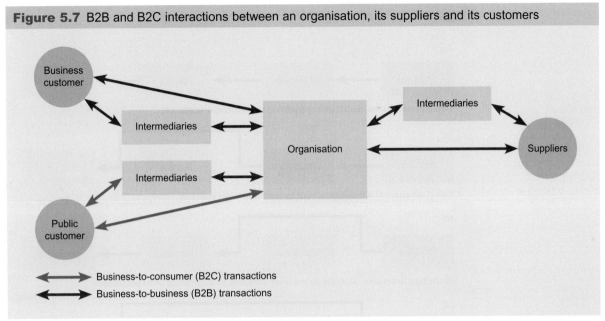

Business-to-consumer (B2C) transactions

Business-to-business (B2B) transactions

Table 5.5 Examples of types of transactions between businesses and consumers

Transaction type	Example
B2B	Car leasing (www.nationwidevehiclecontracts.co.uk)
	Construction resources (www.constructionplus.co.uk)
B2C	Expedia travel (www.expedia.co.uk)
	Flights (www.qantas.com)
C2C	Advice on trips (www.tripadvisor.co.uk)
	Auction site (www.ebay.co.uk)

Figure 5.8 illustrates disintermediation in a graphical form for a consumer distribution channel. Further intermediaries such as additional distributors may occur in a business-to-business market. Figure 5.8(a) shows the position where a company markets and sells it products by 'pushing' them through a sales channel. Figures 5.8(b)(c) and (d) show three different types of disintermediation in which the retailer (b), wholesaler (c) or the wholesaler and retailer (d) are bypassed, allowing the producer to sell and promote direct to the consumer. The benefits of disintermediation to the producer are clear – it is able to remove the sales and infrastructure cost of selling through the channel. Some of these cost savings can be passed on to the customer in the form of cost reductions.

At the start of business hype about the Internet in the mid-1990s there was much speculation that widespread disintermediation would see the failure of many intermediary companies as direct selling occurred. However, although sales at amazon.co.uk continue to increase this has not led to the demise of bookshops such as Waterstones. Disintermediation can be a powerful force however, for example the travel industry has seen a major shift from the use of travel agents offering packaged flight and hotel bookings to consumers dealing directly with flight providers (for example easyJet, RyanAir, Bmibaby, Jet2, British Airways) and to a lesser extent Internet-based hotel providers (for example **www.shangri-la.com**, **www.hyatt.com**).

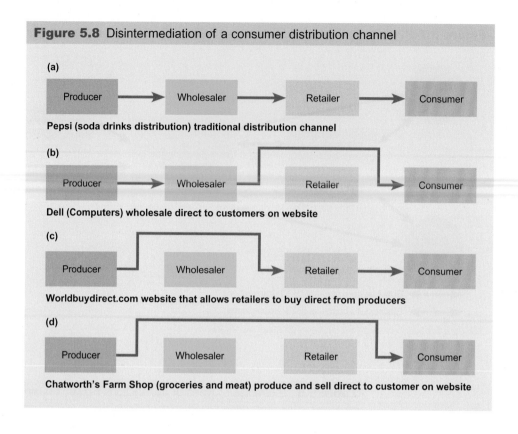

Figure 5.8 Disintermediation of a consumer distribution channel

(a)

Producer → Wholesaler → Retailer → Consumer

Pepsi (soda drinks distribution) traditional distribution channel

(b)

Producer → Wholesaler → Retailer → Consumer

Dell (Computers) wholesale direct to customers on website

(c)

Producer → Wholesaler → Retailer → Consumer

Worldbuydirect.com website that allows retailers to buy direct from producers

(d)

Producer → Wholesaler → Retailer → Consumer

Chatworth's Farm Shop (groceries and meat) produce and sell direct to customer on website

---

Re-intermediation

The creation of new intermediaries between customers and suppliers providing services such as supplier search and product evaluation.

In fact, although disintermediation has occurred, the creation of new intermediaries between customers and suppliers, termed **re-intermediation**, has also occurred. For example, in the travel industry sites such as Tripadvisor (**www.tripadvisor.com**) provide information regarding destinations and hotels and then provide links to hotel providers.

What are the implications of re-intermediation for the e-commerce manager?

First, it is necessary to make sure that your company, as a supplier, is represented with the new intermediaries operating within your chosen market sector. This implies the need to integrate, using the Internet, databases containing price information with those of different intermediaries.

Secondly, it is important to monitor the prices of other suppliers within this sector (possibly by using the intermediary web site for this purpose).

Thirdly, it may be appropriate to create your own intermediary, for example DIY chain B&Q has set up its own intermediary to help budding DIYers, but it is positioned separately from its owners.

Activity 5.2   Re-intermediation in practice

Purpose

To provide an example of the services provided by 'cybermediaries' and explore their viability as businesses.

■ Visit the Kelkoo web site (**www.kelkoo.co.uk**), shown in Figure 5.9, and search for this book, a CD or anything else you fancy. Explain the service that is being offered to customers.

Figure 5.9 Kelkoo.com, a European price comparison site

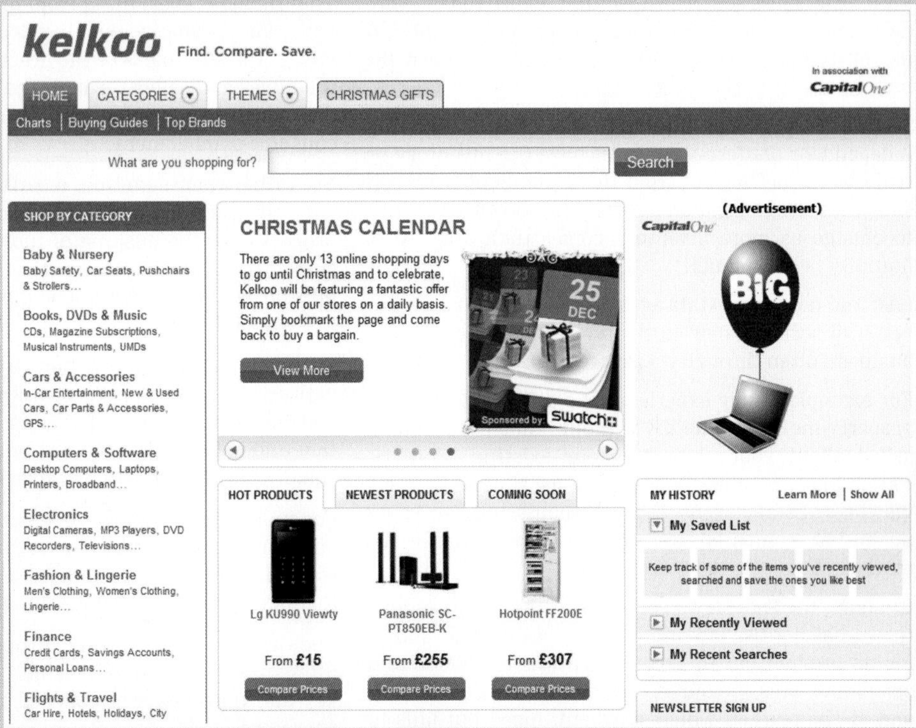

Source: www.kelkoo.com

- Write down the different revenue opportunities for this site (some may be evident from the site, but others may not; write down your ideas also).
- Given that there are other competing sites in this intermediary category such as PriceRunner (**www.pricerunner.com**), assess the future of this online business using press releases and comments from other sites such as Moreover (**www.moreover.com**).

CASE STUDY 5.1

Death of a matchmaker

By Izabella Kaminska,

Today we live in a world where almost anything can be bought or sold directly through an internet platform. The role of the middleman – from retailer to broker and even financier – is being hit on all fronts. And yet somehow the estate agent model, which depends on matching buyers and sellers, withstands.

It is, to say the least, a puzzle.

Before I go on I should declare an interest. I've started to think about selling my London flat, which has made me wonder: do I really need an agent to help me in that process in this day and age of online platforms?

Also, how easy would it be to arrange a private sale? And why on earth aren't more people selling without the middleman?

The more I think about it, the more I struggle to understand how the estate agent model has managed to defy technology's disruptive influence. Why would anyone pay a commission when an internet listing can open just as big a market door?

My suspicion is that, for now, the estate agent's lingering presence relates to three things.

First, the mass-sell websites that exist today were designed to complement rather than disrupt the old model. Simply speaking, they make it very hard for individuals to market properties.

Second is platform liquidity and choice. Existing independent platforms don't yet have the inventory or scale to attract buyers from the incumbent mass-sell sites that still depend on agents. This, however, stands to change as more inventory comes their way. Also, liquidity begets liquidity.

Last and not least, estate agents themselves are getting better at securing new stock and capturing continuing business, often through ever more aggressive tactics.

For example, in my experience it's difficult to make a property inquiry in the UK without immediately being asked about your plans for your existing property. Valuations are presented almost as a condition for viewings. Estate agents have a reputation for being pushy but, compared with the last time I was in the market, they seem more desperate.

In short, the industry's response to the technological threat has not been to improve service and desirability for its product but to become more monopolistic and cartel-like. This, of course, comes at the cost of the low-end of the market, which stays entrapped but fails to benefit from the clubby relationships still offered to the high-end part of the market.

While it's true that these tactics have been successful thus far, I'm not sure they will be enough to withstand the trend towards disintermediation. It seems inevitable that the independent sites will gain critical mass eventually.

The real shame is that, in the interim, the industry has failed to recognise that it must evolve if it is to avoid being fully digitised. Evolution lies in recognising that the future is about more than just sourcing inventory or matching. People may have the power to market properties directly but they still desire all the indirect services associated with expertise and convenience.

That includes everything from drawing up plans, managing appointments, opening doors, fielding questions and, at the later parts of the process, hand-holding both the buyer and seller through the transaction process – one which can involve complicated chains that need constant management.

Yet rather than adapting, agents have become fixated with protectionist tactics focused on capturing new properties or the pushing of mortgages and finance to customers. And this is exactly the sort of thing that puts off would-be clients. The industry would do better if it responded more creatively.

For example, imagine a new type of model focused entirely on convenience, local knowledge, prospecting and the hand-holding of clients. Or, perhaps a model that understands that the cost burden should be shared equally between seller and buyer?

For many years the estate-agent market prided itself on being localised, specialised and fragmented. If you wanted to buy in Richmond, you had to go to the area to talk to local specialist agents directly.

Looking for and selling property was a labour-intensive process, one in which local knowledge was key and liquidity was guarded by a handful of local operators.

Property websites understandably changed the rules of the game. Market access was no longer linked to local specialists. Searches became quicker, deeper and further reaching. Buyers got more choice, sellers got access to ever wider audiences.

But rather than embracing this new field, the industry has seemingly stumbled at the last hurdle. Rather than turning itself into a market facilitator and gate opener, it's stubbornly stuck to the role of gatekeeper and inventory guardian.

The problem with closed gates, of course, is that people will always find ways around them. I, for one, have already been tempted to jump the fence.

 Source: Kaminska, I. (2013) Death of a matchmaker. *Financial Times*. 22 February.
© The Financial Times Limited 2013. All Rights Reserved.

QUESTION

Discuss the barriers to disintermediation in the estate agency business.

Intranets and extranets

Intranet

A private network within a single company using Internet standards to enable employees to share information using e-mail and web publishing.

The majority of Internet services are available to any business or consumer that has access to the Internet. However, many e-business applications that access sensitive company information require access to be limited to favoured individuals or third parties. If information is limited to those inside an organisation, this is an intranet. If access is extended to some others, but not everyone beyond the organisation, this is an extranet. The relationship between these terms is illustrated in Figure 5.10. Extranets can be accessed by

Figure 5.10 The relationship between intranets, extranets and the Internet

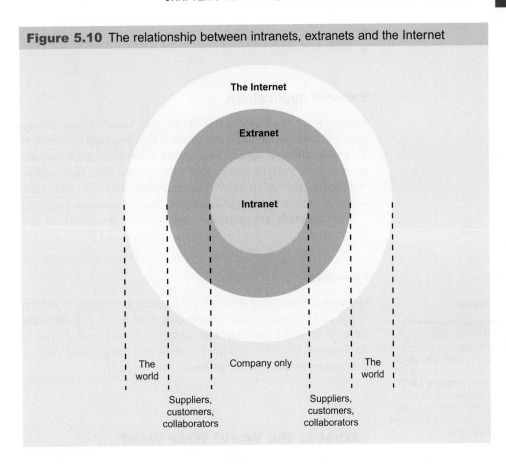

Extranet

Formed by extending the intranet beyond a company to customers, suppliers and collaborators.

authorised people outside the company such as collaborators, suppliers or major customers, but information is not available to everyone with an Internet connection – only those with password access. Note that the term 'intranet' is sometimes loosely used to refer to an extranet.

Intranet applications

Intranets are used extensively for supporting the marketing function. They are also used to support core supply-chain management activities as described in the next section on extranets. A marketing intranet has the following advantages:

- reduced product lifecycles – as information on product development and marketing campaigns is rationalised we can get products to markets faster;
- reduced costs through higher productivity, and savings on hard copy;
- better customer service – responsive and personalised support with staff accessing customer information via the web;
- distribution of information through remote offices nationally or globally.

Intranets are also used for sharing these types of information:

- staff phone directories;
- staff procedures or quality manuals;
- information for agents such as product specifications, current list and discounted prices, competitor information, factory schedules and stocking levels – all this information normally has to be updated frequently and can be costly;

- staff bulletin or newsletter;
- training courses.

Extranet applications

Extranets are used extensively to support supply chain management as resources are ordered from suppliers and transformed into products and services delivered to customers. To enable different applications within a company, such as a sales ordering system and an inventory control system that interoperate with each other and databases in other companies, requires an internal company intranet to be created that can then communicate across an extranet with applications on another company intranet.

The case study 'get control of your web site' describes how the distinction between the locations of applications for intranets, extranets and public web sites in becoming smaller.

Firewalls

Firewall

A specialised software application mounted on a server at the point where the company is connected to the Internet. Its purpose is to prevent unauthorised access into the company from outsiders.

Firewalls are necessary when we are creating an intranet or extranet to ensure that outside access to the confidential information does not occur. Firewalls are usually created as software mounted on a separate server at the point where the company is connected to the Internet. Firewall software can then be configured to only accept links from trusted domains representing other offices in the company.

What is the World Wide Web?

World Wide Web

The most common technique for publishing information on the Internet. It is accessed through web browsers which display web pages of embedded graphics and HTML/XML-encoded text.

Hyperlink

A method of moving between one web-site page and another, indicated to the user by an image or text highlighted by underlining and/or a different colour.

The **World Wide Web**, introduced in Chapter 3, provides a standard method for exchanging and publishing information on the Internet. The medium is based on standard document formats such as HTML (Hypertext Markup Language) which can be thought of as similar to a word-processing format such as that used for Microsoft Word documents. This standard has been widely adopted because:

- it offers **hyperlinks** which allow users to readily move from one document or web site to another – the process known as 'surfing';
- HTML supports a wide range of formatting, making documents easy to read on different access devices;
- graphics and animations can be integrated into web pages;
- interaction is possible through HTML-based forms that enable customers to supply their personal details for more information on a product, perform searches, ask questions or make comments.

It is the combination of web browsers and HTML that has proved so successful in establishing widespread business use of the Internet. The use of these tools provides a range of benefits including the following:

- It is easy to use since navigation between documents is enabled by clicking on hyperlinks or images. This soon becomes a very intuitive way of navigation which is similar across all web sites and applications.
- It can provide a graphical environment supporting multimedia which is popular with users and gives a visual medium for advertising.
- The standardisation of tools and growth in demand means information can be exchanged with many businesses and consumers.

Web browsers and servers

Web browsers are software used to access the information on the WWW that is stored on **web servers**. Web servers are used to store, manage and supply the information on the WWW. The main web browsers are Microsoft Internet Explorer, Mozilla Firefox, Google Chrome, Apple Safari and Opera. Browsers display the text and graphics accessed from web sites and provide tools for managing information from web sites.

Web servers

Store and present the web pages accessed by web browsers.

Protocol

The Internet functions using a series of standard protocols which allow different computers to communicate with each other.

Web browsers communicate with web servers in the following way. A request from the client PC is executed when the user types in a web address, clicks on a hyperlink or fills in an online form such as a search. This request is then sent to the ISP and routed across the Internet to the destination server using the mechanism described in the section on **protocols**. The server then returns the requested web page if it is a **static** (fixed) **page**, or if it requires reference to a database, such as a request for product information, it will pass the query on to a database server and will then return this to the customer as a **dynamically created web page**. Information on all page requests is stored in a **transaction log file** which records the page requested, the time it was made and the source of the enquiry.

FOCUS ON...   HOW THE INTERNET WORKS – INTERNET STANDARDS

Static web page

A page on the web server that is invariant.

Dynamically created web page

A page that is created in real time, often with reference to a database query, in response to a user request.

Transaction log files

A web server file that records all page requests from site visitors.

We have introduced the general terms and concepts that describe the operation of the Internet and World Wide Web. In this section we look in more detail at the standards that have been adopted to enable transfer of information. Knowledge of these terms is useful for anyone involved in the management of e-commerce since discussion with suppliers may involve them.

Networking standards

Internet standards are important since they are at the heart of definitions of the Internet. According to Leiner et al. (2003), on 24 October 1995 the Federal Networking Council unanimously passed a resolution defining the term 'Internet':

> 'Internet' refers to the global information system that – (i) is logically linked together by a globally unique address space based on the Internet Protocol (IP) or its subsequent extensions/follow-ons; (ii) is able to support communications using the Transmission Control Protocol/Internet Protocol (TCP/IP) suite or its subsequent extensions/follow-ons, and/or other IP-compatible protocols; and (iii) provides, uses or makes accessible, either publicly or privately, high level services layered on the communications and related infra-structure described herein.

TCP/IP

The transmission control protocol is a transport-layer protocol that moves data between applications. The Internet protocol is a network-layer protocol that moves data between host computers.

TCP/IP development was led by Robert Kahn and Vince Cerf in the late 1960s and early 1970s and, according to Leiner et al. (2003), four ground rules controlled Kahn's early work on this protocol. These four ground rules highlight the operation of the TCP/IP protocol:

- Distinct networks would be able to communicate seamlessly with other networks.

- Communications would be on a best-effort basis, i.e. if a data packet didn't reach the final destination, it would be retransmitted from the source until successful receipt.

- Black boxes would be used to connect the networks; these are the gateways and routers produced by companies such as Cisco and 3Com. There would be no information retained by the gateways in order to keep them simple.

- There would be no global control of transmissions, these would be governed by the requester and sender of information.

It can be seen that simplicity, speed and independence from control were at the heart of the development of the TCP/IP standards.

The data transmissions standards of the Internet such as TCP/IP are part of a larger set of standards known as the open systems interconnection (OSI) model. This defines a layered model that enables servers to communicate with other servers and clients. When implemented in software, the combined layers are referred to as a 'protocol stack'. The seven layers of the OSI model are:

Open systems interconnection (OSI) model

A layered model of data transmission standards that enables servers to communicate with other servers and clients.

- *Application*. This layer is not the application itself, such as the web browser. Instead, it provides functions for privacy, messaging and file transfer.

- *Presentation*. This layer includes data-transfer protocols such as SMTP, HTTP and FTP.

- *Session*. This layer is so called since it manages session and connection coordination. It sets up, coordinates, and terminates conversations, exchanges and dialogues between the applications at each end of a communications channel. As such, the session layer is specific to each presentation-layer type such as SMTP, HTTP or FTP.

- *Transport*. This layer ensures the integrity of data transmitted, i.e. are all data transmitted? Examples include the Internet transmission control protocol and Novell SPX.

- *Network*. Defines protocols for opening and maintaining links between servers. This layer handles the routeing of the data (sending it in the right direction to the right destination on outgoing transmissions and receiving incoming transmissions at the packet level). The network layer does routeing and forwarding. The best-known network layers are the Internet protocol (IP) and Novell IPX.

- *Data link*. Defines the rules for sending, receiving and acknowledging information exchange at the level of 1s and 0s.

- *Physical layer*. Low-level description of physical transmission methods such as ISDN, ADSL and co-axial cables.

The postal service is a good analogy for the transmission of data around the Internet using the TCP/IP protocol. Before we send mail, we always need to add a destination address. Likewise, the IP protocol acts as an addressed envelope that is used to address a message to the appropriate IP address of the receiver.

The Internet is a packet-switched network that uses TCP/IP as its protocol. This means that, as messages or packets are sent, there is no part of the network that is dedicated to them. This is like the fact that when your letters and parcels are sent by post they are mixed with letters and parcels from other people. The alternative type of network is the circuit-switched network such as phone systems where the line is dedicated to the user for the duration of the call. Taking the analogy further, the transmission media of the Internet such as telephone lines, satellite links and optical cables are the equivalent of the vans, trains and planes that are used to carry post. In addition to the transmission media, components of the network are also required to direct or route the packets or messages via the most efficient route. On the Internet these are referred to as 'routers' or 'hubs', and are manufactured by companies such as Cisco and 3Com. The routers are the equivalent of postal sorting offices which decide the best route for mail to take. They do not plan the entire route of the message, but rather direct it to the next router that seems most appropriate given the destination and current network traffic.

IP address

The unique numerical address of a computer.

Packets

A packet is a formatted unit of data. A packet contains both the data the user is sending or receiving (user data) and control information which provides information that the network needs to deliver the user data, for example the source and destination addresses of the data.

Some addressing information goes at the beginning of your message; this information gives the network enough information to deliver the packet of data. The IP address of a receiving server is usually in the form 207.68.156.58, which is a numerical representation of a better-known form such as www.microsoft.com. Each IP address is unique to a given organisation, server or client, in a similar way to postal codes referring to a small number of houses. The first number refers to the top-level domain in the network, in this case.com. The remaining numbers are used to refer to a particular organisation.

Once the Internet message is addressed, the postal analogy is not so apt since related information is not sent across the Internet in one large message. For reasons of efficiency, information sent across IP networks is broken up into separate parts called packets. The information within a packet is usually between 1 and 1500 characters long. This helps to route information most efficiently and fairly with different packets sent by different people gaining equal priority. The transmission control protocol, TCP, performs the task of splitting up the original message into packets on dispatch and reassembling it on receipt. Combining TCP and IP, you can think of an addressed IP envelope containing a TCP envelope which in turn contains part of the original message that has been split into a packet.

The HTTP protocol

HTTP (hypertext transfer protocol)

HTTP or hypertext transfer protocol is a standard that defines the way information is transmitted across the Internet between web browsers and web servers.

HTTP, the hypertext transfer protocol is a standard used to allow web browsers and servers to transfer requests for delivery of web pages and their embedded graphics. When you click on a link while viewing a web site, the web browser you are using will request information from the server computer hosting the web site using the HTTP protocol. Since this protocol is important for delivering the web pages, the letters http:// are used to prefix all web addresses. HTTP messages are divided into HTTP 'get' messages for requesting and web page and HTTP 'send' messages. The web pages and graphics transferred in this way are transferred as packets, which is why web pages do not usually download smoothly, but come in jumps as different groups of packets arrive.

The inventor of HTTP, Tim Berners Lee, describes its purpose as follows (Berners Lee, 2000):

> HTTP rules define things like which computer speaks first, and how they speak in turn. When two computers agree they can talk, they have to find a common way to represent their data so they can share it.

Uniform resource locators (URLs)

Uniform (universal) resource locators (URLs)

A web address used to locate a web page on a web server.

Web addresses refer to particular pages on a web server which is hosted by a company or organisation. The technical name for web addresses is **uniform or universal resource locators (URLs)**. URLs can be thought of as a standard method of addressing similar to postcodes that make it straightforward to find the name of a site.

Web addresses are usually prefixed by 'http://' to denote the http protocol that is explained above. Web addresses always start with 'http://', so references to web sites in this book and in most promotional material from companies omit this part of the URL. Indeed, when using modern versions of web browsers, it is not necessary to type this in as part of the web page location since it is added automatically by the web browser. Although the vast majority of sites start with 'www', this is not universal, so it is necessary to specify this.

Web addresses are structured in a standard way as follows:

http://www.domain-name.extension/filename.html

Domain names

The domain name refers to the name of the web server and is usually selected to be the same as the name of the company, and the extension will indicate its type. The extension is known as the global top-level domain (gTLD). There are also some 250 country-code top-level domains (ccTLD).

Some common gTLDs are:

- .com represents an international or American company such as www.travel-agency.com
- .co.uk represents a company based in the UK such as www.thomascook.co.uk
- .ac.uk for a UK university (e.g. **www.aston.ac.uk**)
- .org.uk or .org are for not-for-profit organisations (e.g. **www.greenpeace.org**).

The 'filename.html' part of the web address refers to an individual web page, for example 'products.html' for a web page summarising a company's products. When a web address is typed in without a filename, for example www.bt.com, the browser automatically assumes the user is looking for the home page, which by convention is referred to as index.html. When creating sites, it is therefore vital to name the home page index.html. The file index.html can also be placed in sub-directories to ease access to information. For example, to access a support page a customer would type **www.internic.net.**

Note that gTLDs are continuously under review by Icann, the Internet Corporation for Assigned Names and Numbers (**www.icann.org**). Available are.biz for business,.name to be used by individuals,.museum,.pro for professionals,.aero for aviation,.coop for cooperatives and.info. Some of the proposed gTLDs refused included '.sex', '.shoes', '.kids' and '.xxx'. The introduction of these names, while increasing choice where.com names have already been assigned, may make finding the URL of a company more difficult – it may less often be sufficient to take the name of the company and add '.com'. According to another view, existing companies such as Amazon will attempt to register with the new domain such as '.biz' which will not help to increase the availability of gTLD names.

Icann is involved in domain name arbitration. Its first case involved an individual who offered the name WorldWrestlingFederation.com to the World Wrestling Federation. The WWF won since it was considered the individual was 'cybersquatting'. In another case, Penguin books stated that it had a claim to www.penguin.org which had been registered by an individual. But in this case the company lost since the respondent argued convincingly that he was known as Penguin and his wife as Mrs Penguin!

Domain name registration

HTML (Hypertext Markup Language)

HTML is a standard format used to define the text and layout of web pages. HTML files usually have the extension .html or .htm.

XML or eXtensible Markup Language

A standard for transferring structured data, unlike HTML which is purely presentational.

If a company wants to establish a web presence they need to register a domain name that is unique to them. Domain names can be registered via an ISP or at more favourable rates direct from the domain name services:

- InterNIC – **www.internic.net**. Registration and information about sites in the .com, .org and .net domains.
- Nominet – **www.nominet.org.uk**. This is the main co.uk site.

Web page standards

The main web page standards (introduced in Chapter 3) are HTML (Hypertext Markup Language) and, for data exchange, XML (eXtensible Markup Language).

FOCUS ON... MOBILE OR WIRELESS ACCESS DEVICES

The characteristics that mobile or wireless connections offer to their users is that they provide ubiquity (can be accessed from anywhere), reachability (their users can be reached when not in their normal location) and convenience (it is not necessary to have access to a power supply or fixed-line connection). In addition to these obvious benefits, there are additional benefits that are less obvious: they provide security – each user can be authenticated since each wireless device has a unique identification code; their location can be used to tailor content and they provide a degree of privacy compared with a desktop PC – looking for a new job on a wireless device might be better than under the gaze of a boss! The case study 'Ubiquity will be a hard state to reach' examines the mix of mobile, wireless and fixed connections that are being used in order to provide the maximum coverage of Internet services to the world population.

In addition to offering voice-calls, mobile phones have increasingly been used for e-mail and text messaging, using the short messaging service (SMS) standard. During 2011 it was estimated that there were over 5.9 trillion SMS messages exchanged worldwide! Traffic is expected to increase to 9.4 trillion by 2016 (**http://mobithinking.com/mobile-marketing-tools/latest-mobile-stats/c#mobilemessaging**). To allow the transmission of sound, images and video, as well as text, the multimedia messaging service (MMS) has been established. This allows the transmission of formatted text, images in formats such as JPEG and GIF, audio in formats such as MP3 and video in MPEG format. Unlike the SMS standard which limits the size of messages to 160 bytes there is no limit to the size of messages using MMS. During 2011 it was estimated that there were over 1.6 trillion MMS messages exchanged worldwide. (**http://mobithinking.com/mobile-marketing-tools/latest-mobile-stats/c#mobilemessaging**). Whilst mobile phone users can create and send their own MMS messages, perhaps the biggest use of MMS is likely to be companies sending MMS messages to customers. For example, a company could send visitors an MMS map to help them find its office. Other possible applications include weather reports, news and sport bulletins, etc. Internet access by phone is also becoming increasingly popular.

Short messaging service (SMS)

The standard for sending text messages by mobile phone.

Multimedia messaging service (SMS)

The standard for sending multimedia messages by mobile phone.

High-speed mobile services

In 1999 the first of a new generation of mobile phones such as the Nokia 7110 were introduced; these offered the opportunity to access the Internet. They are known as wireless application protocol or WAP phones or, in more common parlance, web-enabled or Internet phones. What these phones offer is the facility to access information on web sites that has been specially tailored for display on the small screens of mobile phones.

In 2001 new services became available on GPRS (General Packet Radio Service), sometimes referred to as 2.5G. This is approximately five times faster than the 2G devices using the GSM (global system for mobile communication) standard used for most mobile voice calls. GPRS is an 'always-on' service which is charged according to usage. The display is still largely text-based and based on the WAP protocol.

In 2004 a completely new generation of 3G services based on the UMTS wireless technology became available, offering a maximum practical download speed of 384 kbps (although 2 Mbps is possible) and an upload speed of 64 kbps. So 3G is approximately six times faster than GPRS. 3G allows rapid delivery of video and images with 'always-on' web browsing and permits MMS messages to be sent (although small MMS messages can be sent even with second generation networks using GPRS).

In the UK, auctions in 2000 for the licence to operate on these frequencies exceeded £20 billion – such was the perceived importance of these services to the telecommunications companies. You can read the historic document giving the background to 3G and these auctions at: **www.ofcom.org.uk/static/archive/spectrumauctions/3gindex.htm**.

In 2012 Ofcom allowed EE, the owner of the Orange and T-Mobile networks, to use its existing bandwidth to launch fourth-generation (4G) mobile services. The group aims to cover 70 per cent of the UK by 2013 and 98 per cent by 2014. 4G aims to give consistently faster and more reliable service for video and music streaming, mobile gaming, and sending emails with large attachments.

Wireless application protocol (WAP)

WAP is a technical standard for transferring information to wireless devices, such as mobile phones.

GPRS (General Packet Radio Service) (2.5G)

Improved digital (GSM) standard for mobile devices.

3G

Digital standard for mobile devices featuring always-on broadband internet availability.

4G

Digital standard for mobile devices featuring faster speeds for applications such as video and music streaming.

CASE STUDY 5.2

Americans turning off TV and on to digital devices

By Emily Steel in New York

The amount of time people in the US spend consuming digital media is set to overtake hours spent watching television for the first time this year, marking a significant tipping point in the shift away from traditional forms of media.

The average adult will spend five hours and nine minutes a day online or consuming other types of digital media this year, an increase of 38 minutes, or 16 per cent, compared with 2012, according to new estimates from eMarketer.

The amount of time spent watching TV is projected to fall by seven minutes to four hours and 31 minutes.

In another pivotal change, mobile devices such as smartphones and tablets will overtake the computer as the primary means of consuming digital media. The amount of time people spend using mobile devices to surf the web will increase by nearly an hour to two hours and 21 minutes, compared to one hour and 33 minutes in 2012.

Meanwhile, hours spent using a desktop PC or laptops for internet-related activities will fall by eight minutes, from two hours and 27 minutes in 2012 to two hours and 19 minutes.

The change in consumer behaviour is already shaking the foundations of the advertising business.

Google reported a larger than expected drop in advertising rates during the most recent quarter because of the shift to mobile, where ad rates are typically cheaper. By contrast, Facebookshares have soared after the company last week reported better than expected mobile ad revenues.

This week, Publicis and Omnicomannounced a $35bn tie-up, which will create the world's largest advertising and marketing services group. Executives are pitching the deal, the largest in the history of the ad industry, as a way to create a technology and digital media-driven advertising company for the future.

'The objective was not to do a deal to be bigger,' said Maurice Lévy, the chief executive of Publicis. 'The objective is to drive the key issues of the future of this industry.'

Yet advertising dollars still lag behind consumer behaviour. While marketers are steadily shifting their budgets to follow how people are spending their time, ad spending on television is far greater than on digital media.

Marketers are set to spend $205bn on television commercials worldwide this year compared to the $116.8bn they are expected to spend on digital ads, according to eMarketer.

QUESTION

What are the implications of the switch from television to digital media?

FOCUS ON...   EDI

Electronic data interchange (EDI)

The exchange, using digital media, of structured business information, particularly for sales transactions such as purchase orders and invoices between buyers and sellers.

Transactional e-commerce predates PCs and the World Wide Web by some margin. In the 1960s, **electronic data interchange (EDI)** and **electronic funds transfer (EFT)** over secure private networks became established modes of intra- and inter-company transaction. The idea of standardised document exchange can be traced back to the 1948 Berlin Airlift, where a standard form was required for efficient management of items flown to Berlin from many locations. This was followed by electronic transmission in the 1960s in the US transport industries. The EDIFACT (Electronic Data Interchange for Administration, Commerce and Transport) standard was later produced by a joint United Nations/European committee to facilitate international trading. There is also a similar X12 EDI standard developed by the ANSI Accredited Standards Committee.

Electronic funds transfer

Automated digital transmission of money between organisations and banks.

Clarke (1998) considers that EDI is best understood as the replacement of paper-based purchase orders with electronic equivalents, but its applications are wider than this. The types of documents exchanged by EDI include business transactions such as orders, invoices, delivery advices and payment instructions as part of EFT. There may also be pure information transactions such as a product specification, for example engineering drawings or price lists. Clarke (1998) defines EDI as:

> the exchange of documents in standardised electronic form, between organisations, in an automated manner, directly from a computer application in one organisation to an application in another.

DTI (2000) describes EDI as follows:

> Electronic data interchange (EDI) is the computer-to-computer exchange of structured data, sent in a form that allows for automatic processing with no manual intervention. This is usually carried out over specialist EDI networks.

It is apparent from these definitions that EDI is one form, or a subset, of electronic commerce. A key point is that direct communication occurs between applications (rather than between computers). This requires information systems to achieve the data processing, data management associated with EDI, and integration with associated information systems such as sales order processing and inventory control systems.

Internet EDI

Use of EDI data standards delivered across non-proprietary IP networks.

Internet EDI enables EDI to be implemented at lower costs since rather than using proprietary, so-called *value-added networks (VANs)*, it uses the same EDI standard documents but using lower cost transmission techniques through *virtual private networks (VPNs)* or the public Internet. Internet EDI also includes EDI-structured documents being exchanged by e-mail or in a more automated form using FTP.

Virtual private networks can be used to enable remote workers such as sales representatives or teleworkers to access a company network and access customer databases and file servers, thus making them more productive by giving the information they need in real time. Such VPNs are not only for large organisations, but smaller organisations can use them. For example, a medium-sized company with five travelling sales representatives could access customer data and product information in 'real time' while meeting clients in different parts of the country. Traditionally, this would have been achieved through connecting a laptop via a phone line, but this is not practical in clients' offices. Today, laptops with wireless data transmission cards can be used to access the company network from anywhere that has access. Alternatively a VPN can be used to access company data using smaller mobile devices such as Pocket PCs and personal digital assistants using WAP or 3G wireless transmission which were described earlier in this chapter.

Benefits and limitations of EDI

The benefits of EDI are the same as those for Internet-based electronic commerce between organisations. The benefits of using EDI to streamline business processes include:

- more rapid fulfilment of orders. Reduced lead times are achieved through reduced times in placing and receiving orders, reduced times of information in transit and integration with other processes;
- fewer errors in data entry and less time spent by the buyer and supplier on exception handling;
- reduced costs resulting from reduced staff time, material savings such as paper and forms and improved inventory control.

Early EDI solutions were expensive to implement. Despite efforts to create national and international standards for document formats, they were based on proprietary technologies which tended to lock a company into that supplier since each EDI link tended to be set up specifically for a single supplier and buyer. This made it difficult to switch the connection to another supplier. If a company was multi-sourcing rather than single-sourcing then separate EDI standards might be needed for each supplier. Internet EDI tends to reduce these disadvantages.

Although EDI was established before Internet-based e-commerce became wide-spread, it appears to have a future. The volume of Internet EDI is increasing rapidly and revision of EDI standards to be compatible with XML should guarantee its continued use.

FOCUS ON... VOICE OVER IP (VoIP)

Voice over IP (VoIP)

Voice data are transferred across the Internet – it enables phone calls to be made over the Internet.

Voice over IP (VoIP) can be used for transmitting voice over a LAN or on a wider scale. You will remember that IP stands for Internet protocol and so VoIP enables phone calls to be made over the Internet. IP enables a single network to handle all types of communications needs of an organisation, i.e. data, voice and multimedia. VoIP (pronounced 'voyp') is proving increasingly popular for reducing the cost of making phone calls both within an office and between offices, particularly internationally. In the longer term it will also be used by major telecommunications companies such as AT&T and BT to replace their existing voice networks with IP networks.

In addition to the cost-reduction benefits, other benefits include:

- *click-to-call* – users click the number they want from an on-screen directory to call.
- *call forwarding and conferencing* to people at other locations.
- *unified messaging* – e-mails, voicemails and faxes all integrated into a single inbox.
- *hot-desking* – calls are routed to staff wherever they log in – on-site or off-site.
- *cost control* – review and allocation of costs between different businesses is more transparent.

To implement VoIP several options are available to managers:

1. *Peer-to-peer.* The best-known peer-to-peer solution is Skype which is free to download and Skype-to-Skype (PC-to-PC) calling is free. A service called SkypeOut enables calls to landlines or mobile phones at a reduced cost compared to traditional billing. This service is only really suited to smaller businesses, but could be used in larger businesses for some staff who call abroad frequently to bypass the central system. Skype also offers two premium services, SkypeIn and Skype Voicemail. SkypeIn customers can purchase a personal number to receive incoming calls from a fixed or mobile line, and can manage incoming messages with Skype Voicemail.

2. *Hosted service.* This principle is similar to hosted software from application service providers (ASPs). Here, a company makes use of a large centralised IP-based system shared between many companies. This potentially reduces costs, but some companies might be concerned about outsourcing their entire phone directory.

3. *Complete replacement of all telephone systems.* This is potentially costly and disruptive in the short term, but new companies or relocating companies may find this the most cost-effective solution.

4. *Upgrading existing telephone systems to use VoIP.* Typically, the best compromise for existing companies.

CASE STUDY 5.3

Asian mobile chat apps challenge Western dominance

By Ben Bland in Jakarta, Nguyen Phuong Linh in Hanoi and Simon Mundy in Seoul

Popular mobile chat services are posing a threat to traditional operators, write FT reporters

Nguyen Tung Lam, a 16-year-old high school student in Hanoi, uses Japanese mobile messaging service Line to chat with his girlfriend because she 'likes the cute icons such as the teddy bear and bunny'.

Doan Nguyen Trang, another Vietnamese teenager, prefers South Korea's KakaoTalk app because it is promoted by a wildly popular Korean boy band.

'I use KakaoTalk because Big Bang also use it and they are number one; I love them,' says the 14-year-old.

KakaoTalk, Line and WeChat, a mobile messaging app developed by China's Tencent, are spending tens of millions of dollars on television advertising, online promotions and celebrity endorsements as they fight for the attention of tech-savvy southeast Asian teenagers.

With a population of 600m people, a fast-growing middle class and fast-rising smartphone sales, southeast Asia has become the front line in a battle for mobile phone users that is threatening the traditional dominance of mobile phone network operators, global internet companies such as Facebook and Google and now-struggling handset maker BlackBerry.

Like their western rivals, KakaoTalk, Line and WeChat allow users to send free messages through mobile internet connections but their playful, teen-friendly style has set them apart, driving them to the top of many app download charts.

'When you use Asian mobile chat apps such as KakaoTalk or Line, you have a certain sense of joy and fun communicating with your loved ones, whereas western apps focus more on pure functionality,' says Le Hong Minh, chairman of VNG Corporation, Vietnam's leading internet company.

KakaoTalk sparked the Asian mobile messaging revolution when it launched in 2010, but it has been overtaken by Line which this month crossed the 200m user threshold, two years after its inception – an accomplishment that took Facebook and Twitter more than five years.

'Facebook and Google definitely see these mobile messaging apps as a threat,' says Mark Ranson, an analyst at technology research company Ovum.

BlackBerry, long dominant in Indonesia because of its free Messenger service, is losing ground due to growing competition from the Asian chat apps that can be downloaded to any smartphone.

Sales of smartphones in southeast Asia have surged in the past few years because of rising incomes and the advent of cheaper, often Chinese-made phones that sell for as little as $50.

Southeast Asians bought 44m smartphones in the 12 months to April, a rise of 60 per cent on the previous year, according to GfK, a market research group.

'Southeast Asia is like Korea three or four years ago,' says Lee Sir-goo, joint chief executive of KakaoTalk. 'If you think about Korea, KakaoTalk really took off when these smartphone devices were first being sold [in large numbers].'

Like Samsung, Hyundai and other South Korean companies, KakaoTalk has been benefiting from the widespread popularity of South Korean music and TV shows in Asia.

Along with WeChat and Line, which is based in Japan but owned by NHN, a South Korean internet company, it tailors its marketing strategies in each of the big emerging Asian markets including India, Indonesia, the Philippines and Vietnam. That is a markedly different approach from US-based Google and Facebook, which tend to eschew traditional TV and billboard advertising and localisation in favour of building homogenous global communication products such as email and instant messaging.

Mr Ranson says the rise of these Asian messaging apps shows the limits of the 'one-size fits all' approach, even as Facebook hits back with its own enhanced messaging services.

'If you're really serious about breaking into new markets, you need to customise and listen to local users,' he says. 'But for a massive company like Facebook, it's hard to listen to people in every country.'

The three apps are free to download and the companies say they are focusing on attracting new users rather than making profits at this early stage.

They are also keen to expand beyond the region. Line's strongest markets are in Indonesia, Japan, Taiwan and Thailand but the app also has 10m users in Spain.

And the revenues are starting to flow, through sales of 'stickers' – stylised icons for user profiles – and add-ons for free games.

Line reported revenue of Y5.82bn ($58.9m) in the first quarter of 2013 in its first public results, while KakaoTalk had its first profitable year last year, reporting revenue of $42m and a net profit of $6.5m.

Whichever companies survive and thrive, VNG's Mr Minh believes the rapid success of KakaoTalk, Line and WeChat presages the emergence of Asian internet companies that will challenge the dominance of the US online pioneers.

 Source: Bland, B. et al. (2013) Asian mobile chat apps challenge Western dominance. *Financial Times*. 1 August.
© The Financial Times Limited 2013. All Rights Reserved.

QUESTION

Discuss the challenges for companies such as Facebook of operating in a global market for mobile phone services.

SUMMARY

1. Computer networks are built on different scales, from those limited to a single location (LAN) to national or international wide-area networks known as WAN. Table 5.6 summarises the different types.

2. Most PC-based networks are based on a client/server architecture in which there are a number of PC clients that share resources and communicate via a more powerful server computer. Client/server networks can be arranged in a number of different topologies, such as bus, star and ring.

Table 5.6 Summary of the applications of different scales of network

Scale of network	Description	Business application
Peer-to-peer	A simple network enabling sharing of files and devices	Small company or local workgroups in a single department
Local-area network	One or several servers accessed by client computers and used for sharing peripheral devices such as printers	Network at a single company site
Wide-area network	LANs at different sites are linked via leased lines which will often use microwave or satellite transmission	National company with several offices or multinational company; company wanting to perform EDI with its suppliers
Internet	A global arrangement of wide area networks	Companies needing to communicate with many other companies via e-mail or accessing web servers

3. The main components of a network are the server and client computers which are linked to peripheral devices such as printers. The hardware is connected by guided media such as cables or, on a larger scale, unguided satellite and microwave. Telecommunications processors or gateways are required to translate information as it is passed from the hardware devices to the media. A network operating system such as UNIX, Windows NT or Novell Netware is necessary to control the hardware and provide facilities such as security and file and printer sharing.

4. Through using networks, companies can exchange information more rapidly and reduce costs by removing the need for human resources. The advantages of faster communication are not only internal, but extend to improving links with customers, suppliers, collaborators and even competitors.

5. The Internet is a global communications network that is used to transmit the information published on the World Wide Web (WWW) in a standard format based on Hypertext Markup Language (HTML) using different standard protocols such as HTTP and TCP/IP.

6. Companies deliver e-business services to employees and partners through web servers which are often hosted at third-party companies known as Internet service providers (ISP). Web servers will be linked to applications servers, database servers and legacy applications to deliver these services.

7. Consumers and business use these e-business services through web browser software with connections to the Internet also managed by an ISP through which they can access web servers.

8. Intranets are private networks used inside companies to share information. Internet-based tools such as e-mail, FTP and the World Wide Web are all used as the method of sharing this information. Not all Internet users can access intranets since access is restricted by firewalls and password controls. Extranets are similar to intranets, but they are extended beyond the company to third parties such as suppliers, distributors or selected customers.

9. Standards to enable delivery of information include:

   ■ communications standards such as TCP/IP and HTTP;
   ■ text information standards such as HTML, XML and WML;
   ■ graphical information standards such as GIF and JPEG;
   ■ multimedia standards such as Shockwave, Flash and streaming audio and video.

EXERCISES

Self-assessment exercises

1. Specify the components required for a client/server-based LAN for a company of 10 people.

2. Distinguish between a local-area network (LAN) and a wide-area network (WAN).

3. What are the main business benefits delivered by a local-area computer network?

4. What are the main components of a telecommunications system?

5. What is the purpose of a network operating system?

6. What is the difference between the Internet and the World Wide Web?

7. Describe the two main functions of an Internet service provider (ISP). How do ISPs differ from applications service providers?

8. Distinguish between intranets, extranets and the Internet.

9. Describe the standards involved when a web page is served from a web server to a user's web browser.

Discussion questions

1. Do you think that the introduction of client/server systems has been worthwhile to businesses?

2. There are many possible benefits of company-wide networks. Is it possible for them to be achieved without changing working practices?

3. Discuss the merits and disadvantages of locating company e-business services inside a company, in comparison with outsourcing to an ISP or ASP.

Essay questions

1. You are a newly installed IT manager in a company with 100 staff. You want to convince the directors of the benefits of adopting a local-area network across the whole company. How would you present your case?

2. Explain the benefits that a company deciding to downsize to a client/server architecture as part of its IT strategy could derive. What management initiatives will be necessary to ensure that the introduction of the new system is a success?

3. You are consultant to a small retailer interested in setting up a transactional e-commerce site. Create a summary guide for the company about the stages that are necessary in the creation of a web site and the management issues involved.

Examination questions

1. Name three ways in which installing a local-area network can reduce costs. Explain how this is achieved.

2. Which features would you need to specify for a company network for a company of 100 people working at a single site?

3. Computer networks exist on different scales. Distinguish between the following types:

   (a) local-area network;
   (b) wide-area network;
   (c) metropolitan-area network;
   (d) value-added network.

4. Explain, with the aid of diagrams, the difference between the following network topologies:

   (a) star;
   (b) bus;
   (c) ring.

5. Distinguish between the following different types of servers:

   (a) network;
   (b) applications;
   (c) database.

6. What are the advantages of the following types of media? Is each more likely to be found in a local- or wide-area network?

   (a) copper cable;
   (b) fibre-optic;
   (c) satellite;
   (d) microwave.

7. Networked communications in business occur through wide-area networks and local-area networks.

   (a) How do the two types of network differ?
   (b) What is the difference between a local-area network and an intranet?

8. You have been tasked with arranging Internet access for other employees in your company. Summarise the hardware and software needed.

9. How would you explain to a friend what they need to purchase to access the World Wide Web using the Internet? Explain the hardware and software needed.

10. Explain the term 'electronic data interchange'. What is its relevance to companies now that the Internet is widely used for data exchange?

References

Berners Lee, T. (2000) *Weaving the Web. The Past, Present and Future of the World Wide Web by its Inventor*, Orion Publishing, London

Clarke, R. (1998) Electronic Data Interchange (EDI): An Introduction, http://www.rogerclarke.com/EC/EDIIntro.html

DTI (2000) *Business in the Information Age – International Benchmarking Study 2000*, Department of Trade and Industry, UK

Gillies, J. and Cailliau, R. (2000) *How the Web Was Born*, Oxford University Press, New York

Kampas, P.J. (2000) 'Road map to the e-revolution', *Information Systems Management Journal*, 17, 2, March, 8–22

Leiner, B., Cerf, V., Clark, D., Kahn, R., Kleinrock, L., Lynch, D., Postel, J., Roberts, J. and Wolff, S. (2003) *A Brief History of the Internet*. Published by the Internet Society at www.isoc.org/internet/history/brief.shtml continuously updated document)

Further reading

Berners Lee, T. (2000) *Weaving the Web. The Past, Present and Future of the World Wide Web by its Inventor*, Orion Publishing, London. A fascinating, readable description of how the concept of the web was developed by the author.

Gillies, J. and Cailliau, R. (2000) *How the Web Was Born*, Oxford University Press, New York. Another readable book on the whole history of the Internet.

Krotoski, A. (2013) *Untangling the Web: What the Internet is doing to you*, Faber and Faber, London. Discussion of the effect of the internet on our social world.

Laudon, K. and Laudon, J. (2007) *Essentials of Business Information Systems*, 7th edition, Prentice Hall International, London. A summary of how telecommunications are used in business is given in Chapter 9.

Web links

www.gartner.com Reports on aspects such as total cost of ownership.

www.internet2.edu Information on the Internet2 project.

www.isoc.org/internet/history/brief.shtml A brief history of the Internet. Updated history by key players in its design – Barry M. Leiner, Vinton G. Cerf, David D. Clark.

http://networking.ittoolbox.com Guidelines, articles on developments in networking technology.

www.rosettanet.org Organisation promoting exchange of B2B data.

www.howstuffworks.com Good explanations with diagrams of many Internet and networking technologies.

http://searchnetworking.techtarget.com Part of the whatis.com service, specifically providing definitions and explanations of networking technology.

www.xml.com XML resources.

Wireless media

www.bluetooth.com Information on the Bluetooth standard.

www.totaltele.com Industry news and the latest adoption levels for wireless and telecoms.

www.text.it Promotion of text messaging services for business and consumers.

www.wi-fi.org The trade body with information on wi-fi.

LINKS TO OTHER CHAPTERS

Enterprise and functional BIS

LEARNING OUTCOMES

After reading this chapter, you will be able to:

- identify and describe the major components of an enterprise system;
- appreciate the importance of transaction processing systems, process control and office automation systems to the operational management of a business;
- appreciate the importance of decision support, information reporting and executive information systems to decision making in the organisation;
- assess the potential for using business information systems in different parts of an organisation.

MANAGEMENT ISSUES

From a managerial perspective, this chapter outlines the use and importance of BIS in relation to operational and management decision levels and covers how they are applied at an enterprise and functional business level.

INTRODUCTION

The value of business information systems (BIS) to an organisation is dependent on how the hardware, software and network technologies described in the previous chapters are applied to support the organisation's objectives. This is achieved through deployment of specific business applications that support different organisational processes and functions. Earlier (in Chapter 2) business information systems are categorised into *operations* and *management* systems which can be implemented as either *enterprise* or *functional* business systems.

This chapter considers enterprise systems in general and the major types of enterprise systems, namely enterprise resource planning (ERP), supply chain management (SCM), customer relationship management (CRM) and supplier relationship management (SRM). BIS applications are then reviewed as *operational* information systems which include transaction processing systems and those used for manufacturing and office automation, and *management* information systems which include decision support systems used for tactical and strategic planning. Finally, we will briefly review how different types of software are used in different functional areas of a business, such as finance and accounting, human resources and marketing.

ENTERPRISE SYSTEMS

Enterprise systems

Enterprise systems aim to support the business processes of an organisation across any functional boundaries that exist within that organisation

Enterprise systems (ES) aim to support the business processes of an organisation across any functional boundaries that exist within that organisation. They use Internet technology to integrate information within the business and with external stakeholders such as customers, suppliers and partners. The main types of enterprise system are enterprise resource planning (ERP) which is concerned with internal production, distribution and financial processes, customer relationship management (CRM) which is concerned with marketing and sales processes, supply chain management (SCM) which is concerned with the flow of materials, information and customers through the supply chain, and supplier relationship management (SRM) which is concerned with sourcing, purchasing and the warehousing of goods and services. Other types of ES include product lifecycle management (PLM), financial management and human capital management. Figure 6.1 shows a selection of enterprise applications available from the SAP software vendor.

The main reason for implementing an ES is explained by Figure 6.2. It compares an Enterprise application with the previous company arrangement of separate data silos and applications (sometimes known as 'information islands') in different parts of the company. The problem of information silos arose as BIS selection became devolved, with the end-users in individual departments making their own BIS purchasing decisions. This often led to separate BIS applications from different vendors in different departments, often with poor data transfer between applications.

Characteristics of an enterprise system

An enterprise system (ES) is characterised by a cross-functional process view of an organisation. The ES will contain a set of defined business process designs, or process blueprints, covering areas such as procurement, production and fulfilment. The second major characteristic of an ES is that it uses a centralised database structure that enables integration of data across the organisation.

Figure 6.1 Enterprise applications from SAP

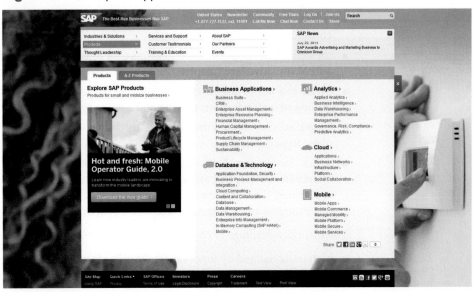

Source: www.sap.com

Figure 6.2 Enterprise application in comparison to separate functional applications

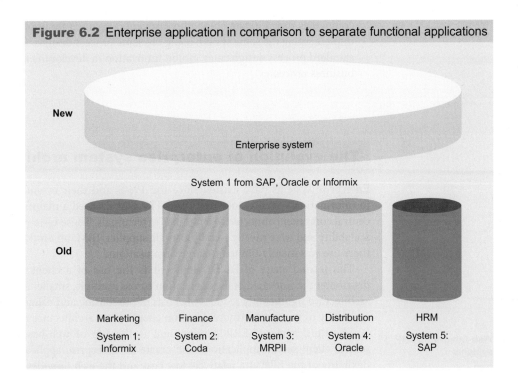

The benefits of the ES approach include:

- integration of organisational processes resulting in increased efficiency and quality of customer service;
- the defined business process blueprints contained in the ES can be used as a template for a BPM initiative (see Chapter 12);
- better sharing of information within the organisation due to integration of modules leading to better decision making and a more agile organisation;
- simplified support and maintenance through a single supplier rather than dealing with many legacy systems;
- use of 'best-of-breed' ES solution applied by other companies. These are applications offered by vendors that are seen as providing excellent functionality within their area of application. These solutions are usually specific to one process and have evolved from departmental applications, for example a procurement system.

The main disadvantage of ES systems are:

- high costs charged by suppliers for what is a large complex system;
- implementation of the major organisational change required by these systems – a major planning, training and development effort is needed to successfully introduce a system that will radically change both the information systems and business processes of the organisation;
- the business usually has to change its processes or way of working in order to fit the ERP **process blueprint**. For example, the ES supplier SAP has over 1000 detailed business activities defined in its model, such as 'post an accounting entry'. Thus competitor companies can mitigate competitive advantage gained by implementing an ES by also implementing the same system using the same process designs. In addition, the use of ES standard process designs may inhibit innovation in developing new ways of undertaking business processes.

Process blueprint

A standardised process design for an organisational process.

The evolution of enterprise system architecture

Enterprise systems have existed since the 1960s and their evolution reflects the changes in information systems since that time. The first ES used a mainframe architecture with a central computer connected to a number of terminals. These systems were expensive, lacked scalability and were mostly sold by a single supplier, IBM, up until the 1980s. Consequently there use was mainly limited to large organisations.

The second stage of ES development is the use of a client server architecture that distributes the workload of the application across multiple, smaller applications servers. This architecture significantly reduces the costs of purchasing and using an ES and improves the scalability of the system (more detail on client server architecture is given in Chapter 11).

Web-integrated ERP systems

ERP systems which use the web to provide a platform for ERP application development and provide a standardised architecture for communication of ERP based information across organisations.

The third stage of ERP development is the use of web-based systems to integrate several client-server applications and create an enterprise application. This increases the flexibility of the ERP at a relatively low cost and the web provides a standard platform for integration of applications across organisations. These systems can be referred to as **web-integrated ERP systems**. These systems make use of service oriented architecture (SOA) which enables the integration of many different client server systems together. By using web services an organisation can integrate several client-server applications and create an enterprise composite application (called a 'mashup' – see Chapter 3). This increases the flexibility of the ES at a relatively low cost. More detail on web services and SOA is given later (in Chapter 12).

Implementing enterprise systems

A framework for implementation of an ES may be linked to the approach of business process management (BPM). This identifies business processes as adding value to products and services; work gets done by people through business processes while the role of technology is to support those processes. ERP systems may lack process models that explain business operations and so BPM provides methods to automate or improve activities and tasks for particular business purposes. (BPM is covered in more detail in Chapter 12.)

In common with other investment decisions that managers have to make in terms of people and equipment, it is important that decisions are based on achieving strategic objectives. It is unlikely that one ES software supplier will provide all the most up-to-date and relevant application software for a particular company. If alternative software is available that may provide a competitive advantage then a decision to forgo the advantages of integration may have to be taken. It should also be considered that the main reason for ES, in terms of achieving integration of systems, can usually be achieved at a price, in terms of the cost of writing integration software. The major choice facing an organisation is to renew IT systems in a number of 'big bangs' with the installation of detailed specified major systems or to develop systems that contain a mix of new and old (legacy) systems in a more incremental manner. Either of these choices may make sense and can incorporate the advantages of the other.

Owing to the high cost and complexity of ES solutions, until recently only medium or large companies could afford the software and the consultants, which often cost millions of pounds. Smaller companies are, however, being increasingly targeted by ES vendors.

CASE STUDY 6.1

ERP: A convincing case must be made before investment

By Jessica Twentyman

Finance software that captures every transaction a company conducts and automatically routes it to the correct ledger is at the heart of every enterprise resource planning (ERP) system.

Implemented well, these complex software suites – which also include applications for manufacturing, logistics, human resources and customer relationship management – can make a chief financial officer's life easier, by automating otherwise time-consuming manual processes and streamlining financial reporting.

Implemented poorly, however, they can quickly become a CFO's worst nightmare, blowing a hole in the company budget and leaving staff struggling to perform day-to-day duties.

After more than 20 years of ERP implementations, the disaster stories keep coming.

Last year, for example, Ingram Micro, an IT distributor, reported two consecutive quarters of profit shortfalls, which it blamed on problems in its Australian operations implementing an ERP system from SAP, a software group. In the US, ERP software specialists

Epicor and Lawson are both facing lawsuits from disgruntled customers over failed projects that they say led to substantial cost overruns.

While there are plenty of success stories too, an annual survey released this month by Panorama Consulting Solutions, an ERP specialist, suggests that some of the blame for failures lies with customers who fail to identify project costs and potential savings – both of which are clear areas of responsibility for the CFO.

Panorama Consulting surveyed 246 companies from 64 countries worldwide over the course of 2011, and found that in 50 per cent of cases, at least 50 per cent of expected benefits from an ERP implementation were not realised.

More than half of ERP projects (56 per cent) went over budget and nearly one in three organisations said they had yet to recoup project costs.

The report suggests that better business cases are needed for ERP investments. "A business case captures potential costs savings and establishes a baseline," it says.

"While organisations want to know when they will realise the total cost of a project, a good organisation will capitalise on the ERP system. Not only should a company calculate its breakeven point, but also its overall return on investment," it continues.

That view is echoed by Andrew Meade, UK and Ireland lead for finance and enterprise performance at Accenture, a consultancy.

While the CFO's role should include working with the chief information officer on the business case and project costs relating to an ERP implementation, he says, they should also "set the tone for the rules of the design and build of the ERP system", so the strategy is based on both "real business needs and business affordability".

That means that, from the start, CFOs need to take a careful view of the business as a whole – a view that extends beyond their own department.

Employees in the finance function are likely to be among the main users of the system, certainly, but the needs of employees elsewhere also need to be taken into account.

At Selecta Biosciences, a start-up pharmaceutical company that develops vaccines, David Siewers, the CFO, has been able to develop the company's ERP strategy from scratch.

When he chose a cloud-based ERP system from NetSuite, a seller of on-demand business software, he was mindful of the fact that, as Selecta grows, it is likely to require additional modules to the finance applications now in place.

"Finance applications drove this selection, but the ability to add HR software or sales software was a key factor in my choice," he says.

"From the start, I knew that I didn't want to be replacing the ERP system further down the line." The cloud computing approach, with its subscription-based model of payment, he says, means Selecta only pays for the applications it uses at any given time.

But what approach should CFOs take, who are working in companies that already have ERP systems in place?

According to a 2011 report from Gartner, an IT market analysis company, these CFOs should take a step back from automatically approving a hefty annual budget for upgrades and improvements.

"Specifically, we recommend that CFOs interrupt the annual default administrative ERP project funding trend, by placing a two-year moratorium on funding fresh ERP-based finance and HR solution additions, upgrades, enhancements and so forth if their organisations have already completed [these] within the past two years," writes Ken McGee, a Gartner analyst.

That moratorium does not need to be absolute, he adds – but only the most robust appeal should be allowed to override it.

The message is clear: just because an implementation was successful, that does not mean the system should go on making large claims on a budget.

QUESTION

How can an organisation ensure the financial success of an ERP investment?

Types of enterprise systems

Enterprise resource planning (ERP) systems are enterprise systems which support processes within an organisation. These processes include procurement, product development, manufacturing and sales. An ERP system can be extended to service processes across organisations with the addition of enterprise systems such as supply chain management systems (SCM). These cover processes such as warehousing, transportation and supply network collaboration. Customer relationship management (CRM) systems cover marketing, sales and service. Supplier relationship management (SRM) systems cover sourcing, contract management, supplier collaboration and procurement. These different types of enterprise systems are now discussed in more detail.

Enterprise resource planning applications (ERP) software

Provides functions for managing business areas such as production, distribution, sales, finance and human resources management.

Enterprise resource planning (ERP) systems

Enterprise Resource Planning (ERP) systems offer a single solution from a single supplier with integrated functions for major internal processes such as production, distribution, sales, finance and human resources management. Three core ERP processes are procurement, fulfilment and production. The activity of procurement will be used as an example of the use of an ERP system.

The procurement process

The role of procurement is to acquire all the materials needed by an organisation in the form of purchases, rentals, contracts and other acquisition methods. The procurement process also includes activities such as selecting suppliers, approving orders and receiving goods from suppliers. The term *purchasing* usually refers to the actual act of buying the raw materials, parts, equipment and all the other goods and services used in operations systems. However the procurement process is often located in what is called the purchasing department. Figure 6.3 outlines the main steps in the procurement process and the role of the functional areas of operations, purchasing and suppliers in the process.

The procurement process begins with the department requiring the goods or services issuing a purchase requisition which authorises the purchasing function to buy the goods or services. The requisition will usually include a description of what is to be purchased, the amount to be purchased and a requested date for delivery. Other information provided will be the account to which the purchase cost will be charged, the delivery address and the approval of an appropriate person of the transaction. The purchasing department will receive the request and prepare a 'request for quotation' document to a suitable supplier or suppliers. The quotation will require a price, any other payment terms such as quantity discounts, a delivery date and any other conditions stipulated by the supplier. When a supplier has been chosen then they are issued with a purchase order which represents a legal obligation by the buyer to pay for the items requested. The purchase order will usually include information

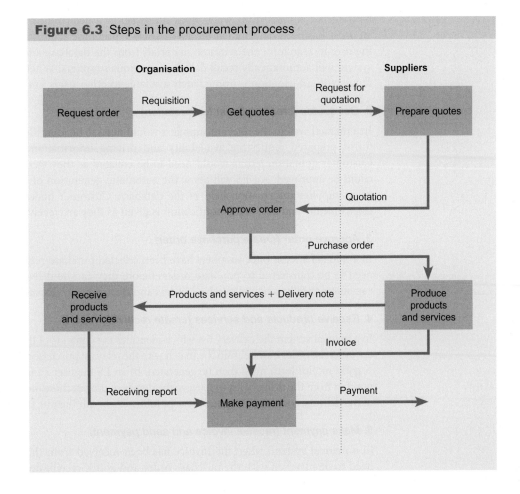

Figure 6.3 Steps in the procurement process

specifying the item to be purchased, its price and delivery date. The supplier will then produce the goods or service and deliver them to the relevant department and provide an invoice form requesting payment. When the organisation is satisfied the good or services and the invoice details are satisfactory a payment will be issued to the supplier.

The role of the ERP system in the procurement process

The ERP system will make the procurement process more efficient by supporting the execution of the process, capturing and storing data generated by the process steps and providing information that can be used to monitor process performance.

The execution of the process is supported by using the ES to store relevant data and documents in a common database. This eliminates the need to re-enter data at different stages of the process and means documents can be quickly and easily created and stored. Process execution is also supported by providing automatic notification of tasks that need completing by staff involved in the process. For example after a purchase requisition is received the purchasing department can be alerted to send requests for quotations from potential suppliers. The processes involved in the procurement process are now discussed in more detail to outline differences between the manual and ES approaches.

1. Request order (create purchase requisition)

In a manual system, physical checks of stock would need to be made to ascertain whether a purchase of new materials is necessary. Then forms would need to be gathered that covered information such as previous purchases of items and lists of potential suppliers. Using the ES will enable a display of the supply of inventory at any time so the need to make a purchase requisition can be made. If necessary the purchase requisition process can be triggered automatically when stock drops below a determined level. Once the need for an order has been determined the ES displays a 'purchase requisition' screen which allows the user to search for the required materials from the database and allocate suppliers. The system will automatically recall details of previous suppliers. When complete the purchase requisition information is immediately available to other users in the organisation.

2. Get quotes (create request for quotation)

In a manual system the relevant suppliers would need to be identified and customer inquiry forms prepared requesting availability and pricing information for the relevant items. Customer quotation letters would need to be collated as they were received before orders could be approved. An ES will allow the automatic generation of customer inquiry letters using supplier information held in the database. Customer quotations are then received electronically and automatic notification is given as they are received.

3. Approve order (create purchase order)

In a manual system once suppliers have been selected purchase requisition information will need to be transferred to purchase orders before they can be delivered to suppliers. An ES can automatically generate purchase orders and electronically dispatch them to the suppliers.

4. Receive products and services (create receiving report)

In a manual system the delivery list which identifies the contents of the shipment and contains the purchase order number must be match with the relevant purchase order from the paper files. A good receipt form must then be generated. In an ES the user simply enters the purchasing number from the delivery list to retrieve the details of the purchase order and to allow checking of the delivery contents. The goods receipt information can then be stored on the database.

5. Make payment (receive invoice and send payment)

In a manual system, when the invoice has been received from the supplier, then this will need to be matched with the purchase order and goods receipt document before payment can be authorised and sent. Using an ES, an invoice can quickly be generated and cross-checking of purchase order, goods receipt and invoice amounts is undertaken automatically. Any payment terms can be allocated by the system and payment can be made electronically to the supplier's bank account.

Supply chain management (SCM) systems

Supply chain

This consists of the series of activities that moves materials from suppliers, through operations to customers.

Upstream suppliers

Suppliers that supply the organisation with goods or services.

The **supply chain** consists of the series of activities that moves materials from suppliers, through the organisation to customers. Each product or service will have its own supply chain, which may involve many organisations in processing, transportation, warehousing and retail. A representation of the structure of a supply chain is shown in Figure 6.4.

Activities on the input side to the organisation are termed 'upstream' or 'supply side' and are divided into tiers of suppliers. **Upstream suppliers** that supply the organisation directly are termed 'first-tier' and suppliers that supply first-tier organisations are termed 'second-tier' and so on. Examples of upstream suppliers are component and sub-assembly suppliers.

Figure 6.4 The structure of a supply chain

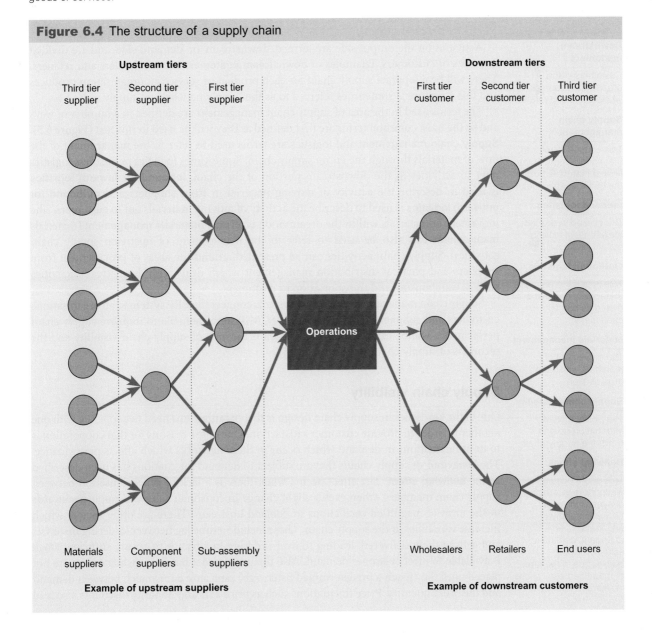

Figure 6.5 Terms used to describe the management of the supply chain

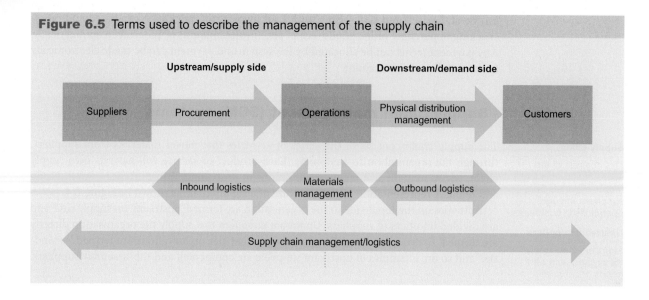

Activities on the output side are termed 'downstream' or 'demand side' and are divided into tiers of customers. Examples of **downstream customers** are wholesalers and retailers. There will be a separate supply chain for each product or service an organisation produces and this structure is sometimes referred to as the 'supply network' or 'supply web'.

The terms used in the area of supply chain management are defined in a number of ways and so the most common terms are first defined as they will be used in this text (Figure 6.5). **Supply chain management** and logistics are terms used to refer to the management of the flow of materials through the entire supply chain. Some-times logistics or business logistics refer to activities in the downstream portion of the chain. **Inbound (or inward) logistics** is used to describe the activity of moving material in from suppliers and **outbound (or outward) logistics** is used to describe the activity of moving materials out to customers. The movement of materials within the organisation is termed **materials management** (materials management can also be used to refer to the management of upstream supply chain activities). Supply chain activities can be presented around the areas of procurement from suppliers and physical distribution management which deals with downstream activities such as warehousing and transportation to customers.

Supply chain management enterprise systems connect the ERP system to an organisation's customers and suppliers. Two areas where SCM systems are able to improve supply chain performance will be examined. The first area is the area of supply chain visibility and the second is of supply chain integration.

Supply chain visibility

One of the key issues in supply chain design is that organisations need to cooperate with one another in order to provide customer satisfaction. One of the reasons for that cooperation is to limit fluctuations in demand which occur in these networks which affects performance. The behaviour of supply chains that are subject to demand fluctuations has been described as the **bullwhip effect**. The effect occurs when there is a lack of synchronisation between supply chain members, when even a slight change in consumer sales will ripple backwards in the form of magnified oscillations in demand upstream. There are other factors which increase variability in the supply chain. These include a time lag between ordering materials and getting them delivered, leading to over-ordering in advance to ensure sufficient stock is available to meet customer demand. Also the use of order batching (when orders are not placed until they reach a predetermined batch size) can cause a mismatch between demand and the order quantity. Price fluctuations such as price cuts and quantity discounts also lead

Downstream customers

Customers of the organisation such as wholesalers and retailers.

Supply chain management

This is used to refer to the management of the flow of materials through the entire supply chain

Inbound logistics

This is used to describe the activity of moving material in from suppliers.

Outbound logistics

This is used to describe the activity of moving materials out to customers.

Materials management

The movement of materials within the organisation.

Supply chain visibility

The ability to view information up and down the supply chain.

Bullwhip effect

This effect occurs when there is a lack of synchronisation between supply chain members. Even a slight change in consumer sales will ripple backwards in the form of magnified oscillations in demand upstream to more demand variability in the supply chain as companies buy products before they need them. In order to limit the bullwhip effect certain actions can be taken.

The major aspect that can limit supply chain variability is to share information amongst members of the supply chain and so improve supply chain visibility. In particular it is useful for members to have access to the product demand of the final seller, so that all members in the chain are aware of the true customer demand. Enterprise systems can be used to connect to organisations within a supply chain and so information, generated by systems such as electronic point-of-sale (EPOS) systems which are used by retailers to collect customer demand information and RFID technologies (Chapter 5) which can be used to track inventories, can be transmitted to warehouses and suppliers further down the supply chain. If information is available to all parts of the supply chain it will also help to reduce lead times between ordering and delivery by using a system of coordinated or synchronised material movement.

CASE STUDY 6.2

Managing the supply chain

By Ronald Teijken

For many, managing the supply chain can seem an overwhelming prospect; most complex manufacturers receive more than 50 per cent of their business, both demand and supply, from international markets.

Although many now accept that 'visibility' – the ability to view a process – is key, there is still a lack of integration with partners across the supply chain. Studies by Sterling Commerce last year found that in the UK, France and Germany, many manufacturers, including large and global companies, lack integration with their business partners.

Without this integration there is no information. Without information it is impossible to achieve visibility. IT departments often struggle to provide support but it actually costs more not to know what is happening across the supply chain because it can lead to non-compliance and in some cases inefficient supply chains can lose revenue.

So, who determines what makes a successful supply chain? More importantly, what are the critical success factors and are they achievable or merely theoretical perfections?

Inventory levels

A key element of any supply chain strategy is to examine inventory levels and to understand where efficiencies can be gained. Using visibility to improve inventory management is critical for any manufacturer operating across multiple geographies and channel partners.

Traditional inventory optimisation strategies tend to approach the issue from only one perspective – examining inventory locations in isolation and not considering how they relate to the wider inventory network across multiple trading partners and multiple geographical locations.

In many cases manufacturers have outsourced warehousing operations to Logistics Service Providers. But in the context of the overall supply chain, it is important to integrate all information about inventory in order to make the right decisions. Unfortunately, many manufacturers still lack the systems to be able to achieve this level of visibility.

Supplier visibility and communication

Extending visibility to the complex fulfilment aspect of any supply chain is often a challenge. Understanding the relationships between perhaps thousands of suppliers with differing process models, relationships and technology levels can appear daunting, and that is before you even think about process and technology integration across multiple IT systems and architectures.

Despite this however, many industry leaders are investing significant time and resources into extending visibility globally. For most complex manufacturers, more than 50 per cent of their business is global and in order to remain competitive they need they need to have a global approach to issues including improving supplier visibility.

Real time availability over a global network

As orders are placed into suppliers, a manufacturer typically no longer has the ability to retain a linked view, especially over a global network. Linking the original order (the demand) to the purchase order (supply) can open up the supplier's ability to share stock allocations and availability. This in turn enables the manufacturer to be more responsive and perhaps re-distribute orders in the event of availability issues.

Co-ordinated single orders across multiple suppliers, systems and the internal supply chain (Distributed Order Management)

Because many manufacturers continue to work across different systems, it is hardly surprising that quite often there is a lack of co-ordinated orders across multiple suppliers. Linking orders across a global supply chain can in turn unlock other cost savings and efficiencies for the manufacturer.

Beginning with the original sales order from a distributor for a complex item, a manufacturer can break the order down into its related components which may in turn be fulfilled from multiple suppliers in multiple geographies. If the manufacturer has a global visibility system in place, they can consistently monitor progress of these component orders, regardless of the fulfilment route, in relation to the original order.

But to achieve this requires carefully timing production and responding to exceptions quickly and in a measured way in order to reduce disruption and order delays.

Order tracking and management

Because demand is often driven through multiple channels, it is necessary to consolidate all these channels into one picture. Unfortunately in many cases, orders are often logged and tracked as separate information. Without a full picture, companies cannot make the right decisions to fulfilling orders from customers across the whole supply chain.

Investment in integration and cross-enterprise order management systems to track orders and fulfilment can deliver considerable cost savings in traditional supply chains, which cannot be achieved by traditional enterprise resource management and/or manufacturing execution systems.

Responsiveness through diversion

As all supply chain professionals know, supply chains are run by exception. No matter how efficient or effective your planning, the unexpected often happens.

While planning is necessary, a flexible fulfilment strategy is critical to enable a supply chain to respond quickly in the event of disaster or change.

Aside from the usual factors driving change within a distribution network, companies sometimes go out of business or are acquired. When this happens, orders have to be diverted to new facilities, geographies and trading partners, preferably without completely re-writing the order management systems and processes. Because some glitches are only temporary, the network also needs to be flexible and responsive enough to switch back once the issue is solved.

Coping with single source products in a global distribution network

Often the headache of single source products and distributing fulfilment efficiently can be solved by improving visibility and inventory management. Understanding how the inventory is distributed across the network, by country, business unit and trading partner, can make it simpler and more cost effective to fulfil orders from existing supplies in a neighbouring region or facility, rather than ordering more from the single source. Because single source products tend to be expensive, this simple step can represent significant cost savings and process efficiencies.

What underlies all of the above strategies is the ability to link supply and demand outside the traditional four walls of the enterprise. They also require companies to implement processes, integrate systems and maintain collaborative relationships that leverage improved supply chain visibility.

Ultimately, integration with your B2B community is the smart way to do business. It can support the achievement of full visibility of your supply chain and provide the opportunity to calculate where financial savings can be made and where efficiency can be increased.'

Ronald Teijken is in charge of manufacturing operations for Sterling Commerce across Europe, The Middle East and Africa.

 Source: Teijken, R. (2011) Managing the supply chain. *Financial Times*. 8 February.
© The Financial Times Limited 2011. All Rights Reserved.

QUESTION

Why is visibility key to a successful supply chain?

Supply chain integration

ERP systems provide integration of processes across functional areas within the organisation. SCM systems extend this integration across organisations within the supply chain. One way of looking at supply chain integration decisions is to use the technique of value-chain analysis (Chapter 2) which views the decision in terms of which set of activities (e.g. design, assembly) should be undertaken, rather than from the viewpoint of products or services. This approach allows consideration of the fact that the outsourcing of one product or service may have cost implications for other products and services which are produced

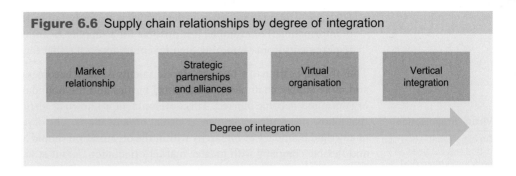

Figure 6.6 Supply chain relationships by degree of integration

using the same resources. However, value chain analysis aims to configure activities in order to minimise cost, given a firm's competitive strategy, and not specifically define where (i.e. inside or outside the firm) activities should occur. This decision will need to be made within the constraints of the financial resources available to the organisation in acquiring supply chain elements and the challenge of the coordination of activities within the supply chain. The different degrees of integration in the supply chain are now discussed (Figure 6.6).

Market relationships

In this relationship each purchase is treated as a separate transaction and the relationship between the buyer and seller lasts as long as this transaction takes. There can be some additional arrangements around this relationship such as the use of ES to share information, combining orders in a single delivery to reduce transportation costs, agreements on packaging standards to improve materials handling and other factors. A **market relationship** does have a number of advantages in that it permits flexibility in that suppliers can be changed or discontinued if demand drops or a supplier introduces a new product. Other advantages include the use of competition between suppliers to improve performance in aspects such as price, delivery and quality. However, there can be disadvantages in this arrangement in that either side can end the relationship at any time. A supplier withdrawal requires the often lengthy task of finding a new supplier. From a supplier perspective the withdrawal of a buyer may cause a sudden drop in demand on the operations facility, leading to disruption and idle resources.

Market relationships

Here each purchase is treated as a separate transaction and the relationship between the buyer and seller lasts as long as this transaction takes.

Strategic partnerships and alliances

When an organisation and supplier are trading successfully they can decide to form a strategic alliance or **strategic partnership**. This involves a long-term relationship in which organisations work together and share information regarding aspects such as planning systems and development of products and processes. There may also be agreement on such aspects as product costs and product margins. The idea of a partnership or alliance is to combine the advantages of a marketplace relationship which encourages flexibility and innovation with the advantages of vertical integration which allows close coordination and control of such aspects as quality. Some factors may mitigate against the formation of a partnership. For instance, for low-value items the use of a partnership may not be worthwhile. Also a company may not want to share sensitive information or lose control of a particular product or process.

Strategic partnerships and alliances

This involves a long-term relationship in which organisations work together and share information regarding aspects such as planning systems and development of products and processes.

The virtual organisation

The form of an organisation's relationship within its supply chain is increasingly being affected by developments in e-business systems which can form a part of an Enterprise System. Evans and Wurster (1997) describe how information can impact the value chain in three ways:

- *Reach* – a business can share information with more stakeholders or gain a larger audience at a relatively low cost.
- *Customisation* – information can be more readily tailored for sharing with a large number of partners.

■ *Dialogue* – interaction between the parties is two-way rather than the traditional push of information. For example, it is possible for a supplier to anticipate a retailer's product requirements from examining their inventory forecast rather than awaiting a faxed order.

Thus the implication of e-business developments is that it becomes easier to outsource more and more supply chain activities to third parties and the boundaries between and within organisations become blurred. This development is known as *virtualisation* and companies that follow this route are known as **virtual organisations**. The objective is that the absence of any rigid boundary or hierarchy within the organisation should lead to a more responsive and flexible company with greater market orientation. Kraut et al. (1998) suggest that the features of a virtual organisation are:

■ Processes transcend the boundaries of a single form and are not controlled by a single organisational hierarchy.

■ Production processes are flexible with different parties involved at different times.

■ Parties involved in the production of a single product are often geographically dispersed.

■ Given this dispersion, coordination is heavily dependent on telecommunications and data networks.

E-business can also be used to alter the supply chain structure by bypassing some of the tiers using a process known as 'disintermediation and re-intermediation', the creation of new intermediaries between customers and suppliers in the supply chain (see Chapter 5).

Vertical integration

Complete integration is achieved by an organisation when it takes ownership of other organisations in the supply chain. The amount of ownership of the supply chain by an organisation is termed its 'level' of **vertical integration**. When an organisation owns upstream or supply-side elements of the supply chain is termed 'backward vertical integration'. Ownership of downstream or demand-side elements of the supply chain is termed 'forward vertical integration' (see Figure 6.7).

Virtual organisation

An organisation is which e-business is used to outsource more and more supply chain activities to third parties so that the boundaries between and within organisations become blurred.

Vertical integration

The amount of ownership of the supply chain by an organisation.

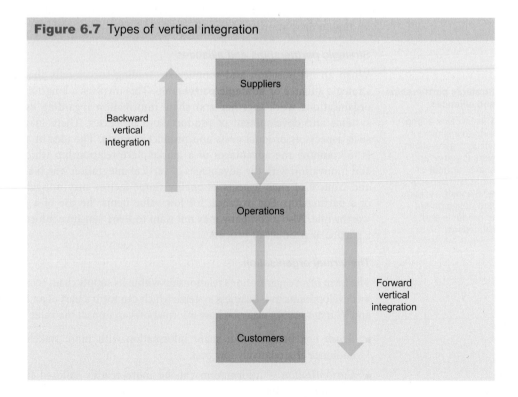

Figure 6.7 Types of vertical integration

There are a number of factors that need to be taken into account when deciding the amount of vertical integration that is appropriate for an organisation. First, the amount of vertical integration that can feasibly be undertaken will be dependent on the financial resources of the organisation. It is unlikely that smaller firms will be able to own large sections of the supply chain, but even large organisations may find this difficult. For example, a car manufacturer may source an engine for a new car from a third party rather than invest millions of euros in developing a new design. Apart from cost, the time taken to acquire supply chain capabilities may be a barrier. It may also be felt that resources used for vertical integration could be better spent elsewhere (R&D or marketing for example). Finally, an organisation needs to consider that it is unlikely that it will be able to undertake all the activities in the supply chain well and may leave certain aspects to specialist suppliers.

Even if the organisation has the capability to undertake further activities in the supply chain it may not make sense to take ownership of them. The virtual organisation concept using e-business systems described earlier, may allow efficient coordination of supply chain activities without the need for ownership of them. Disadvantages of non-ownership of supply chain elements include the potential high cost of switching partners, loss of intellectual property which may provide the competitive advantage of the firm, and the termination of partnerships if the strategic interests of the supply chain partners diverge.

Mini case study

The supply chains that could bind unsuspecting managers

By Stefan Stern

Emma Maersk – and I don't think she would mind me saying this – is a very big girl indeed. She's as wide as a motorway. And at almost 400 metres in length and 60 metres in height she is probably the largest container ship the world has ever seen. When the Emma Maersk docked in Felixstowe in the south-east of England this month the sighs of relief from retailers, manufacturers and parents should have been audible all over the planet. Christmas, in the UK at least, had not been cancelled. An amazing 45,000 tonnes of Chinese manufactured goods have now been safely unloaded and despatched to shops and warehouses across the country. This is what it looks like when supply chains work. But the story does not always have such a happy ending. Globalisation has led to the development of longer and at times more precarious supply chains. The drive for efficiency has often seen companies rationalise the number of suppliers they use, leaving them more dependent on a smaller array of partners. As for suppliers, they find themselves under constant price pressure, with less slack or tolerance in the system. The suppliers' relationship with their customers is frequently less 'sticky' than it was in the past. There is the permanent risk of being substituted should problems – delays or quality concerns – arise. Supply chains, in other words, are both leaner and meaner than they used to be. And some observers suggest that this leaves many businesses exposed to much greater risks than perhaps they realise.

 Source: Stern, S. (2006) The supply chains that could bind unsuspecting managers. *Financial Times*. 28 November (abridged version).
© The Financial Times Limited 2006. All Rights Reserved.

Customer relationship management (CRM)

Systems that are designed to integrate the range of information systems that contain information regarding the customer

Customer relationship management (CRM) systems

CRM systems connect the ERP system to its customers and cover the whole process by which relationships with customers are built and maintained. CRM systems are designed to integrate the range of information systems that contain information regarding the customer.

These include applications such as customer details and preference databases, sales order processing applications and salesforce automation. The idea is to acquire customers, retain customers and increase customer involvement with the organisation.

CRM systems are built around a database and when this database is accessed by employees and customers using a web site the technology is often referred to as e-CRM. Common applications which would be integrated in a CRM system include:

- *Customer data collection.* This can include personal details such as age, sex and contact address, also a record of purchase transactions undertaken in terms of factors such as location, date, time, quantity and price. This information can be used by call centre staff to improve and tailor their services to individual customers.

- *Customer data analysis.* The captured data allow the categorisation and targeting of customers according to criteria set by the firm. This information can be used to improve the effectiveness of marketing campaigns.

- *Salesforce automation.* The entire sales cycle from lead generation to close of sale and after-sales service can be facilitated using CRM.

The technology must support all of these applications through whatever communications channel the customer and employee use. Communication channels include face-to-face, mail, phone and e-mail as well as web-based interaction. As with other technologies the implementation of CRM is a choice between attempting to integrate a number of legacy (existing) systems such as sales order processing and choosing a single-vendor supplier such as for ERP. Single-vendor systems from suppliers such as SAP and Oracle are able to provide better integration and thus potentially better customer service. However, they are relatively expensive to install and one firm is unlikely to supply the best-in-class applications in all aspects of the CRM implementation.

Supplier relationship management (SRM)

Supplier relationship management (SRM)

This refers to all the activities involved with obtaining items from a supplier, which includes procurement, but also inbound logistics such as transportation and warehousing.

SRM systems connect an organisation's ERP system to its suppliers and refers to all activities involved with obtaining items from a supplier, which includes procurement, but also inbound logistics such as transportation, goods-in and warehousing before the item is used.

Procurement is an important aspect of SRM as the cost of materials can represent a substantial amount of the total cost of a product or service. The use of process technology such as flexible manufacturing systems (FMS) (see later in this chapter) has meant a reduction in labour costs and thus a further increase in the relative cost of materials associated with a manufactured product. This means that the control of material costs becomes a major focus in the control of overall manufacturing costs for a product. A further issue that has increased the importance of procurement is that the efficient use of automated systems requires a high quality and reliable source of materials to be available. This is also the case with the adoption of production planning systems such as JIT which require the delivery of materials of perfect quality, at the right time and the right quantity.

Another aspect of supplier relationship management is the choice of supplier, but before choosing a supplier, the organisation must decide whether it is feasible and desirable to produce the good or service in-house. Buyers in purchasing departments will regularly perform a make-or-buy analysis to determine the source of supply. Often goods can be sourced internally at a lower cost, with higher quality or faster delivery than from a supplier. On the other hand suppliers who focus on delivering a good or service can specialise their expertise and resources and thus provide better performance. Strategic issues may also need to be considered when contemplating the outsourcing of supplies. For instance internal skills required to offer a distinctive competence may be lost if certain activities are outsourced. It may also mean that distinctive competencies can be offered to competitors by the supplier. If a decision is made to use an external supplier, the next decision relates to the choice of that supplier. Criteria for choosing suppliers for quotation and approval include price, quality and delivery performance.

SRM also encompasses the area of warehousing. When producing a tangible item it is possible to provide a buffer between supply and demand by holding a stock of the item. Many organisations have specific locations to hold this stock, termed a warehouse or distribution centre. Most warehouses are used to hold a stock of incoming raw materials used in production or hold finished goods ready for distribution to customers. Warehouses are also used to store work-in-progress items or spares for equipment. Because of the need to process goods and services through the supply chain as quickly as possible to serve customer demand, warehouses are not simply seen as long-term storage areas for goods, but provide a useful staging post for activities such as sorting, consolidating and packing goods for distribution along the supply chain. One of the major issues in warehouse management is the level of decentralisation and thus the number and size of the warehouses required in inventory distribution. Decentralised facilities offer a service closer to the customer and thus should provide a better service level in terms of knowledge of customer needs and speed of service. Centralisation, however, offers the potential for less handling of goods between service points, lower control costs and lower overall inventory levels due to lower overall stock levels being required.

SRM can achieve significant savings and other benefits which directly impact the customer including faster purchase cycle times leading to a need for less material in inventory and less staff time spent in searching and ordering products and reconciling deliveries with invoices. Savings also occur through automated validation of pre-approved spending budgets for individuals or departments, leading to fewer people processing each order, and in less time. SRM also enables greater flexibility in ordering goods from different suppliers according to best value. A major benefit of SRM is the integration of the many information systems that are used to cover different parts of the SRM process.

Perhaps the major barrier to the use of SRM is in the difficulty of linking systems with suppliers whose systems may be incompatible or non-existent. It may be that small firms may find themselves increasingly excluded by buyers due to their lack of investment in the required information technology infrastructure.

OPERATIONS INFORMATION SYSTEMS

Operations information systems (OIS)

These are used for the tasks involved in the daily running of a business.

Operations information systems are used for the tasks involved in the daily running of a business. Their performance is often vital to an organisation and they are sometimes described as *mission-critical* or *strategic* information systems. We consider three types of operational systems:

1. *Transaction processing systems (TPS)*. These are used to manage the exchange of information and funds between a company and third parties such as customers, suppliers and distributors.

2. *Office automation systems (OAS)*. OAS are used to manage the administrative functions in an office environment and are often critical to service-based industries.

3. *Process control systems*. These are important in manufacturing industries for controlling the manufacture of goods.

Transaction processing systems (TPS)

Manage the frequent external and internal transactions such as orders for goods and services that serve the operational level of the organisation.

Transaction processing systems (TPS)

Transaction processing systems (TPS) perform the frequent routine external and internal transactions that serve the operational level of the organisation. Examples of these transactions include:

- customers placing orders for products and services from a company, such as making a holiday booking;

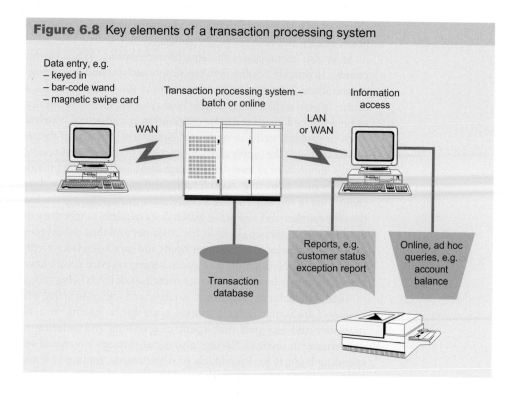

Figure 6.8 Key elements of a transaction processing system

- a company placing orders with a supplier for components from which to make its products;
- payment for goods or services received by a third party;
- a customer visiting a supermarket to shop (see the mini case study on retail applications of TPS by Sainsbury's);
- a customer ringing a call centre of a bank to pay their bills;
- a withdrawal of money from an auto-teller machine (ATM).

Although the functions undertaken by the TPS are routine and repetitive, they usually perform a vital function in the organisation.

Figure 6.8 shows the typical components of a transaction processing system. Data are usually input by being keyed in to on-screen data entry forms such as those used when orders are placed by phone. For retail applications, customer transactions are recorded through bar-code technology.

Transactions will typically occur across a local-area network within a retail branch or bank environment, with real-time processing and data transfer occurring across a wide-area network with a central mainframe computer. Sometimes data on transactions such as loyalty card purchases are stored locally in the supermarket on a local server in real time and then uploaded by a batch system (when the store is closed) to head office. This arrangement is shown in Figure 6.9. Other information such as supply requests may be transmitted on demand in real time. Links with suppliers occur through EDI, which is described in Chapter 5.

There are two main types of transaction systems in operation. Batch systems, as the name suggests, collect information on transactions in batches before it is processed at times of lower transaction rates (such as overnight). Real-time systems process information immediately. These are two design alternatives compared in Chapter 11.

Information from the transaction processing system is accessed in the branch and in the head office using online reporting, for example to find stock availability, or by offline

Figure 6.9 Network architecture for a retail transaction processing system

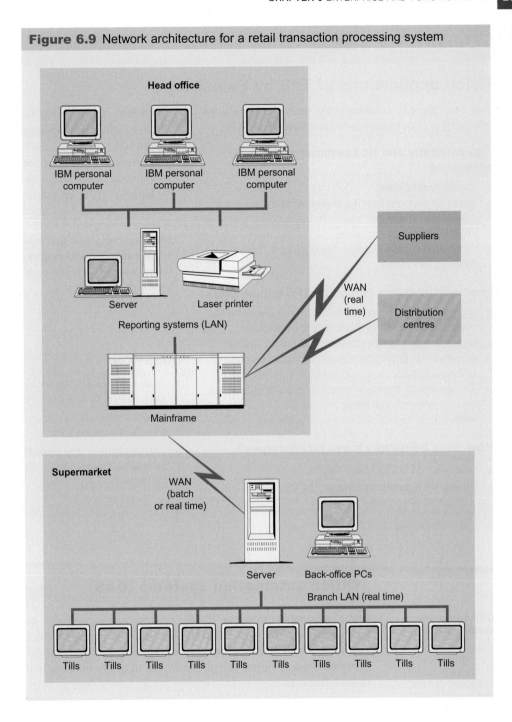

reporting, where information is stored in a separate system for detailed analysis. This is the approach used for data warehouses, which are described in Chapter 4.

Because the TPS give direct contact with customers and suppliers beyond the boundary of an organisation, if they fail it becomes immediately apparent to the organisation's customers (think about the consequences of a failure of an airline reservation system!). Therefore these are often mission-critical systems which must be reliable and secure. Another reason for such applications being mission-critical is that data captured by the TPS are used to monitor the performance of the organisation.

The Sainsbury's case study shows that for some organisations there will be many TPS in operation which have become essential to the needs of the organisation.

CASE STUDY 6.3

Retail applications of TPS by Sainsbury's

This case study of UK retailer Sainsbury's considers the different ways in which a retailer may make use of TPS.

The company and its customer service objectives:

- 17,000 commodities;
- aim is for no more than five commodities to be unavailable at any one time
- order lead time 24–48 hours;
- distribution centres manage deliveries of 11 million cases to 335 stores.

How is Sainsbury's helped by TPS technology?

- Improved customer service through more choice, lower prices, better quality of produce and full shelves.
- Improved operational efficiency by automatic links to suppliers and better information on product demand and availability.
- Assessment of the effectiveness of product promotions through availability of better information.
- Marketing through customer loyalty schemes.

How does Sainsbury's use technologies?

- At the till – EPOS and EFTPOS.
- On shelves – auto-price-changing LCDs.

- On trolleys – 'self-scanning systems'.
- At home – direct wine sales from the Internet Barclay Square site.
- At warehouses – EDI links between stores, warehouses, suppliers and banks.
- For banking – TPS are vital to providing customer statements and cash withdrawals.
- In the marketing department – the effectiveness of marketing campaigns and loyalty card schemes can be assessed using information on transactions stored in data warehouses. This type of system is covered in more detail in Chapter 4.

QUESTIONS

1. Draw a diagram summarising the links between all the parties who access Sainsbury's TPS.
2. What benefits will Sainsbury's gain compared to the time before the introduction of TPS?
3. Can you think of any problems with using TPS so extensively? What can be done to counter these problems?

Office automation systems (OAS)

Office automation systems (OAS)

Are intended to increase the productivity of office workers. Examples include groupware, workflow and general-purpose applications such as word processors and spreadsheets.

Office automation systems (OAS) are information systems intended to increase the productivity of office workers. Examples include groupware, workflow and general-purpose applications such as word processors and spreadsheets. Mission-critical applications such as groupware and workflow can be considered to be key for supporting the internal processes of the e-business.

Laudon and Laudon (2010) state three critical organisational roles for office automation systems:

- They coordinate and manage the work of local, professional and information workers within the organisation.
- They link the work being performed across all levels and functions of the organisation.
- They couple the organisation to the external environment, including to its clients and suppliers; when you call an organisation, you call an office.

These roles emphasise the fact that the office should be seen as more than a typing area but rather as a centre for the exchange of organisational knowledge. Activities undertaken in offices include document management, collaborative work and the management of project activities.

Personal OAS technologies have been introduced elsewhere (see Chapter 4). These applications included desktop publishing (DTP), for producing, for example, drafts of promotional marketing material such as brochures and flyers; personal information managers (PIM), for managing tasks and contacts; and project management software, to assist the management and control of projects. In this section we focus on groupware and workflow management systems, which are most significant in office automation systems, involving teams of people. They are the cornerstone of many 'in-side e-commerce' e-business systems.

Groupware

Groupware

Software that enables information and decision making to be shared by people collaborating within and between businesses.

Groupware is software that enables information to be shared by people collaborating on solving problems. This could include activities such as the scheduling and running of meetings, sharing documents and communicating over a distance. Groupware assists teams of people in working together because it provides the 'three Cs' of communication, collaboration and coordination:

- *Communication* is the core groupware feature which allows information to be shared or sent to others using electronic mail. Groupware for conferencing is sometimes known as 'computer-mediated communication' (CMC) software.

- *Collaboration* is the act of joint cooperation in solving a business problem or undertaking a task. Groupware may reduce some of the problems of traditional meetings, such as finding a place and a time to meet, a lack of available information or even dominance by one forceful individual in a meeting. Groupware improves the efficiency of decision making and its effectiveness by encouraging contributions from all group members. As a result, the study of groupware is known as 'computer-supported collaborative work' (CSCW).

- *Coordination* is the act of making sure that a team is working effectively and meeting its goals. This includes distributing tasks to team members, reviewing their performance and perhaps steering an electronic meeting.

Synchronous

When people exchange information simultaneously as is the case with real-time chat or a telephone conversation this is said to be synchronous.

Asynchronous

When collaborators send messages that can be accessed at a later time these are said to be asynchronous. Asynchronous exchange occurs with e-mail and discussion groups.

When people exchange information simultaneously, as is the case with real-time chat or a telephone conversation, this is said to be **synchronous**. When collaborators send messages that can be accessed at a later time, these are said to be **asynchronous**. Asynchronous exchange occurs with e-mail and discussion groups.

A further reason that groupware has become a useful business tool is that it can be used for collaboration within and between companies when face-to-face contact is impossible. Employees can continue to communicate and work on joint projects even when they are in different locations or in different time zones. The asynchronous use of groupware is one of its key benefits. When considering the benefits of collaborative systems, it is useful to categorise them according to the quadrant in which they lie on a grid showing how people can work together in time and space (Table 6.1).

Software applications associated with groupware are summarised in Table 6.2.

Normally, applications such as electronic calendars and e-mail are purchased as separate software packages. However, some software provides an integrated package of groupware

Table 6.1 Different uses of collaborative systems classified in time and space

	Synchronous	Asynchronous
Same location	Same time, same place example: meeting support software	Different time, same place example: workflow systems
Different location	Same time, different place example: video conferencing	Different time, different place example: e-mail and discussion groups

Table 6.2 Main groupware functions

Groupware function	Application
E-mail and messaging	E-mail, electronic forms processing
Document management and information sharing	Improved information dissemination
Collaborative authoring	Team development of documents
Conferencing	Text conferencing, video conferencing, whiteboarding
Time management	Calendar and group scheduling
Groupware management and decision support	Remote and distributed access facilities including replication and access control
Ad hoc workflow	Loosely coupled collaboration
Structured workflow	Structured management of tasks

functions. One such package is Lotus Notes, which is based on a database that allows the sharing of text, graphics, sound and video data. The system can run on a local-area network (LAN) or a wide-area network (WAN) and so allows information to be shared over distance. Communication between users is automatically logged by Notes for reference. This facility can be used to increase customer service by retrieving previous interactions between organisation members and customers in a variety of formats in response to a customer request. The other main integrated groupware packages are Novell Groupwise and Microsoft Exchange. These are similar to e-mail software in that they have an inbox of messages (Figure 6.10), but they also provide calendar and worklist facilities and document management.

The use of groupware applications has been revolutionised by the adoption of intranets as part of the move to e-business. Many groupware products are now available through web browsers that enable, for example, e-mail to be sent and reviewed.

Document imaging processing (DIP)

Document imaging processing (DIP)

DIP systems are used in industry to convert printed documents into an electronic format so that they can be stored, organised and retrieved more easily.

DIP systems attempt to alleviate the problems caused by paper-based systems, including the cost of handling large amounts of paperwork and the time wasted searching for paper documents. DIP systems convert documents (and images) into a digital format which allows storage, retrieval and manipulation of the document on computer. The document is converted using a scanner which can be either handheld and passed over a document, or a flat-bed type where a document is placed on a glass sheet and a scanner reader passes under it. It is then indexed and stored on high-capacity magnetic or optical storage. The main components of a DIP system are shown in Figure 6.11.

Workflow management systems (WFMS)

Workflow management (WFM)

Systems for the automation of the movement and processing of information in a business according to a set of procedural rules.

Workflow management (WFM) is defined by the Workflow Management Coalition as:

the automation of a business process, in whole or part during which documents, information or tasks are passed from one participant to another for action, according to a set of procedural rules.

Workflow systems are used to automate business processes by providing a *structured* framework to support the process. Workflows help manage business processes by ensuring that tasks are prioritised to be performed:

as soon as possible;

by the right people;

in the right order.

Figure 6.10 Universal inbox of Novell Groupwise groupware product

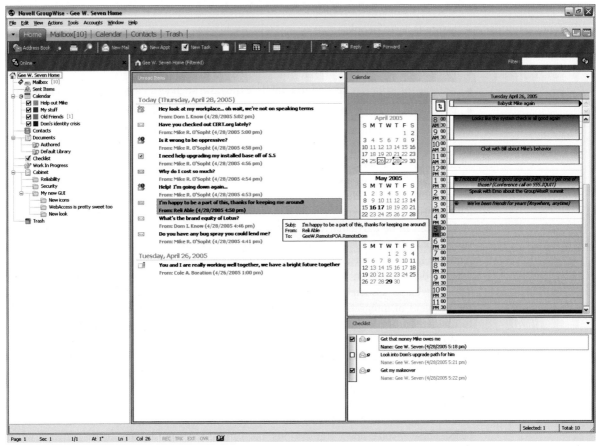

Source: Screenshot – Universal inbox of Novell GroupWise email/groupware product. Copyright © 2005 Novell, Inc. All Rights Reserved.

Figure 6.11 Components of a document image processing system

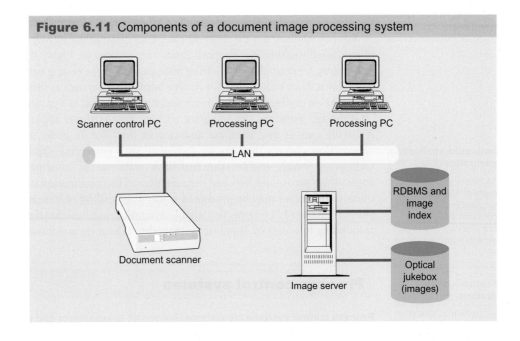

This gives a consistent, uniform approach for improved efficiency and better customer service. Workflow software provides functions to:

- assign tasks to people;
- remind people about their tasks which are part of a workflow queue;
- allow collaboration between people sharing tasks;
- retrieve information needed to complete the task, such as a customer's personal details;
- provide an overview for supervisors of the status of each task and the team's performance.

Workflow and groupware systems are often used to support re-engineering. BPR (business process re-engineering) is discussed in detail later (in Chapter 12). Today, these workflow systems are typical of e-business systems.

Workflow is usually used in conjunction with DIP technology to improve efficiency by automatically routeing documents to the correct person to deal with them. Each person is given a list of tasks or documents on which to work, from what is known as the 'workflow queue'.

WFMS can be particularly effective when they replace a large paper-based system, and substantial amounts of time can be saved by eliminating lengthy searches for documents. Another improvement area is for customer service applications, such as at a call centre when a document can be called up instantaneously in response to a customer request. The drawbacks associated with the technology include the expense of installation and the problem of integration with existing computer network systems. In order to gain the full benefits from WFMS, it is also necessary to re-engineer or redesign the paper-based workflow in order to avoid simply automating inefficient processes.

WFM is most closely associated with large companies such as banks and insurance companies which deal with a large number of complex, paper-based transactions. These transactions need to be dealt with in a structured way and use structured or production workflow systems to manage them.

Small and medium companies are making increasing use of workflow for administrative tasks. These involve fewer transactions and can be managed by less costly software which is based on an e-mail system. Example applications for this administrative or forms-based workflow include authorisation of travel claims or holidays or payment of an invoice. In the latter example, the details of the invoice could be typed into the workflow system by a clerk. The workflow system will then forward the details of the invoice to a senior manager for authorisation. When this has occurred, the authorised invoice will automatically be sent back to the clerk for payment. This process will occur entirely electronically through routeing of forms.

Figure 6.12 illustrates the different categories of workflow software according to the degree of structured working they support. *Production* systems are highly structured and are used in call centres, for example, for assessing insurance claims or issuing new policies. *Administrative* workflow is more widely used, for routine administration such as processing a travel claim. *Ad hoc* workflow overlaps with groupware applications, such as in a group design of a new product.

Although workflow can integrate with existing business applications to exchange data it usually uses its own database and custom interface. In order to increase the flexibility of workflow systems they can be combined with enterprise application integration (EAI) technology which enables the real-time exchange of information between different applications across and between organisations. The combination of workflow and EAI and other technologies may be promoted under the heading of business process management (BPM) (Chapter 12) systems that enable dynamic cross-functional processes to be modelled responding to events in disparate systems throughout the organisation.

Enterprise application integration (EAI)

Technology which enables the real-time exchange of information between different applications within and between organisations.

Process control systems

Systems that report to employees who are very close to a specific activity.

Process control systems

Process control systems are systems that report to employees and supervisors who are very close to a specific activity. They are particularly associated with the support and control of manufacturing processes. Traditionally, information systems for operations management

Figure 6.12 Classification of different types of workflow systems

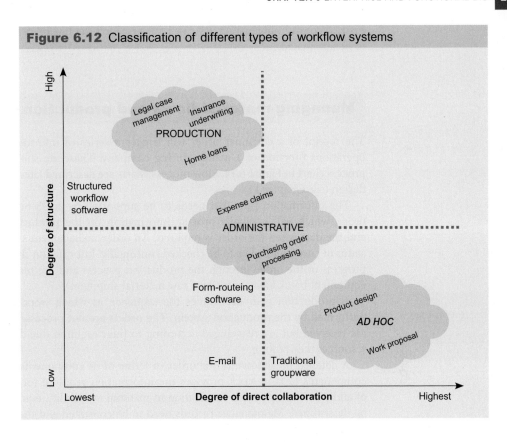

were thought of in terms of automation of *repetitive*, uniform products such as foodstuffs on a production line. While this was true when information systems were first introduced, there is a strong trend to specialised tailoring of products or *mass customisation* to an individual customer's needs.

Figure 6.13 shows the three main types of production facility that information systems can be used to support:

- *Repetitive.* Production-line-type systems producing a standard product such as the Model T Ford car (this is the equivalent of packaged software).

- *Job shop.* Production of individual 'jobs' for individual customers according to their specific requirements (this is the equivalent of bespoke software).

- *Batch.* Intermediate between the two, a batch of identical products produced before changing the production setup for the next batch of systems.

Figure 6.13 Development of manufacturing in terms of volume of production and variety of product

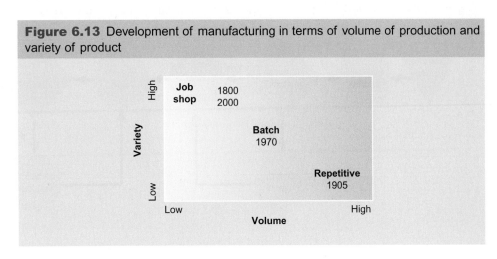

Process control information systems have provided the flexibility to enable all three types to be automated.

Managing material flows and production management

The receipt of a customer order will trigger a series of information flows through the operations function of a manufacturing company. These are shown as a simplified flow process chart in Figure 6.14. Flow process charts are described later in the context of system design (see Chapter 11).

The information flow that needs to be supported by an IS begins with the customer order, which will normally provide information on the product required, the quantity and the date when the order is required. An order management system should enable the status of customer orders to be checked continually. Information should be available on the progress of the order through the production process and the reason for any delays (e.g. equipment breakdown, awaiting a raw material shipment).

A production plan determines the sequence in which work generated by orders is performed by the production system. The orders are not processed in the order that they are received but are rearranged according to their required due dates and the amount of resources they require.

A detailed breakdown of the order in terms of its components and an examination of components held in stock provides the information required for activating the ordering of additional components. In addition to material availability, equipment availability must be determined. Maintenance records need to be consulted and the equipment may not be available due to routine maintenance or breakdown. Also, special tools may be required to process a particular component.

Scheduling concerns the order and quantity of components that are processed through the production system on a day-to-day or operational basis. In order to form a schedule, information on labour availability and the routeing of the order through the system is required. Scheduling issues are usually considered under the three main types of production system that are put into the context of variety and volume in Figure 6.13: repetitive, job shop and batch.

When the goods have passed through the production process they are held as finished goods inventory. Information on finished goods inventory is used to form a shipping schedule for delivery to customers (in service operations, storage of the finished service is not usually feasible).

Figure 6.14 Simplified flow process chart for a production management system

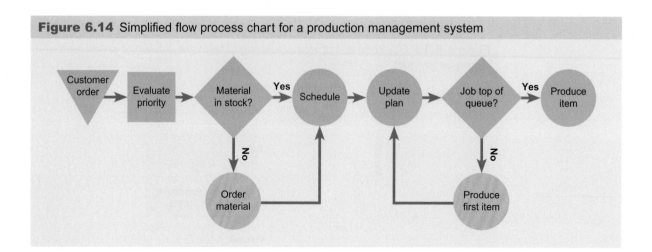

Materials management

Three approaches to materials management will be described. Materials requirements planning (MRP) aims to ensure that just the right amount of each item is held at the right time in order to meet the needs of the manufacturing schedule. Just-in-time (JIT) production uses a 'pull' mechanism that provides a trigger when demand occurs and then attempts to supply that demand. Optimised production technology (OPT) focuses on the system bottleneck, that is, the production stage with the lowest level of capacity which is the limiting factor on the speed of the flow of goods to the customer.

MRP requires information from three main sources. The master production schedule (MPS) identifies what products are needed and when they are needed based on customer orders held and a forecast of future demand. The bill of materials (BOM) file provides a list of the components required to create each product, and the inventory status file (ISF) provides information on the current stock level of each component. From this information, the MRP system will indicate when an order should be placed.

The JIT approach implements a 'pull'-type system called the 'kanban' production control system. The idea is that parts are requested in the system only when needed by 'pulling' them from the subsequent operation that requires more work. To implement this system, a kanban (Japanese for 'card' or 'sign') is used to pass through the production system information such as part identification, quantity and the location of the next work centre. The kanban authorises the production and movement of material through the pull system.

The OPT system is based on the identification of bottlenecks within the production process. The idea is that the output of the whole production process is determined by the output of the bottleneck machine. Thus the bottleneck should pace production and determine the amount of work done at non-bottleneck resources.

Product/service design and development

Good design of products and services is an essential element in satisfying customer needs. The success of the design process is primarily dependent on the relationship between the marketing, design and operations functions of the organisation. Information requirements are:

- market research to evaluate customer needs;
- demand forecasts;
- component costings;
- technical specification of the product.

In order to reduce time to market for new designs, the concept of concurrent design can be implemented. This replaces the traditional sequential design process when work is undertaken within functional business areas. Instead, the contributors to the design effort work together as a team (groupware can assist in this). This means improved communications and enables different stages of the design process to occur simultaneously. Another concept is design for manufacture (DFM), which aims to improve design and reduce costs through such techniques as simplification, standardisation and modularisation of the product design (Greasley, 2013).

Facility design

Facility design concerns how capacity will be supplied by the organisation to meet market demand, that is, it involves the design of production facilities, often using CAD/CAM software which is defined below. Information requirements are:

- external sources on the state of competition and risks associated with not undertaking a task in-house;
- facility location needs to consider long-range demand forecasts and information on the cost of land, the availability of appropriately skilled labour, transportation links and the quality of local education and training services.

Materials requirements planning (MRP) software

Materials requirements planning (MRP) software

Used to plan the production of goods in a manufacturing organisation by obtaining components, scheduling operations and controlling production.

Materials requirements planning (MRP) software is used to plan the production of goods in a manufacturing organisation by obtaining components, scheduling operations and controlling production. Dedicated MRP software provides input screens, a database and reporting facilities required of a production system. Information required by the system includes the master production schedule which states what needs producing, the bill of materials or component list and the inventory status file (ISF) giving the current component stock levels. A typical structure for an MRP system is shown in Figure 6.15. For large numbers of components a computerised system is essential. The MRP system will automatically generate a series of purchase orders for components along with the timing of their release to the production process, in order to ensure that customer-order due dates are met. A development of the MRP system termed 'MRP II' integrates the information system with other functional areas in the business such as finance and marketing, for instance the incorporation of cost data through integration with the financial accounting system.

Computer-aided design (CAD)

Computer-aided design (CAD)

Provides interactive graphics that assist in the development of product and service designs. Connects to a database allowing designs to be recalled and developed easily.

CAD provides interactive graphics that assist in the development of product and service designs. It also connects to a database, allowing designs to be recalled and developed easily.

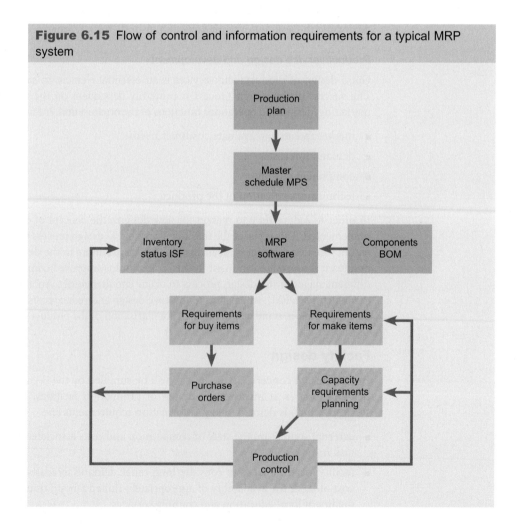

Figure 6.15 Flow of control and information requirements for a typical MRP system

Computer-aided manufacture (CAM)

CAM involves the use of computers, directly to control production equipment and indirectly to support manufacturing operations. Direct CAM applications link a computer directly to production equipment in order to monitor and control the actual production process. An example is a computerised numerical control (CNC) machine which reads instructions for making parts from tape or disk. Indirect CAM applications include MRP, quality control and inventory control systems.

CAD/CAM

The successful design of a component must consider not only design issues in achieving customer requirements, but also the ability of the production system to manufacture the design. CAD/CAM systems improve the design process by enabling information exchange between the CAD and CAM systems by using a common database containing information on items such as component lists, routeings and tool design.

Computer-integrated manufacture (CIM)

CIM aims to integrate information for manufacturing and external activities, such as order entry and accounting, to enable the transformation of a product idea into a delivered product at minimum time and cost. CIM incorporates design activities such as CAD/CAM and operational activities such as MRP, FMS and inventory control. One of the main challenges in the implementation of CIM is integrating equipment from different manufacturers on a common network. In order to overcome this a data communication standard, called Manufacturing Automation Protocol (MAP), has been evolved. CIM covers all aspects of the overall process of production in a business. Its aims, through process automation, are to simplify production processes and product design, automate using robots and process control computers and integrate inventory holding and stock control and costings through the accounting information system.

Flexible manufacturing systems (FMS)

Each such system is a group of machines with programmable controllers linked by an automated materials handling system and integrated by an information system that enables a variety of parts with similar processing requirements to be manufactured. FMS are most suited to batch production systems which have intermediate amounts of variety and volume of output. The system aims to use computer control to produce a variety of output quickly.

MANAGEMENT INFORMATION SYSTEMS

Management information systems were introduced earlier (in Chapter 2) where they were defined as systems providing feedback on organisational activities and supporting managerial decision making. Basic decision-making theory was also introduced earlier (in Chapter 1). Here we will consider the application of MIS from a decision-making perspective. We consider three types of management information systems:

1. *Decision support systems (DSS).* These provide information and models in a form to facilitate tactical and strategic decision making.

2. *Information reporting systems (IRS).* These provide pre-specified reports for day-to-day decision making.

3. *Executive information systems (EIS).* These provide senior managers with a system to analyse, compare and highlight trends to help govern the strategic direction of a company.

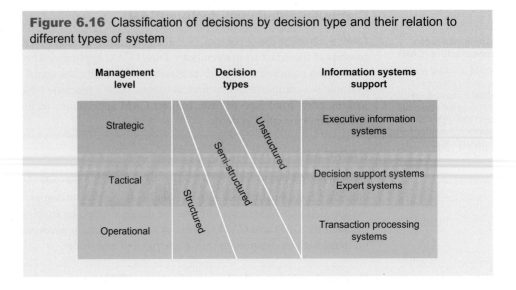

Figure 6.16 Classification of decisions by decision type and their relation to different types of system

Decision types

The identification of problems according to their degree of structure dates back to Garry and Scott-Morton (1971), but it still provides a useful framework for defining decision types. Figure 6.16 indicates that at the operational level, structured decisions predominate and these are commonly supported by TPS. Decision support systems are mainly used to support the tactical, semi-structured decisions that need to be made as part of the evaluation and planning of the business. Executive information systems are targeted at strategic decision making, which often involves unstructured decisions.

It should be noted that there is considerable overlap between strategic and tactical and structured and unstructured. Similarly, there is overlap between the types of systems used to support these different levels. For example, decision support systems can also be used in a strategic capacity or in an operational capacity.

Decision support systems

Decision support systems (DSS)

Provide information and models in a form to facilitate tactical and strategic decision making involving semi-structured and unstructured decisions.

Decision support systems (DSS) provide information and models in a form to facilitate tactical and strategic decision making. When used by teams of people to make decisions, they are sometimes known as GDSS or group decision support systems. They are information systems that support management decision making by integrating:

- company performance data;
- business rules based on decision tables;
- analytical tools and models for forecasting and planning;
- an easy-to-use graphical user interface.

They are often developed by end-users and are departmental rather than corporate systems. DSS tend to be used for ad hoc queries rather than regular reporting. The technology varies particularly rapidly in this area and the newest developments such as data warehouses attest to this. They are frequently used as a marketing tool, with applications such as:

- forecasting sales through geodemographic analysis;
- optimising distribution networks, using a model to select the best retail locations;
- optimising product mixes.

Sprague (1980) suggests the following main objectives for a DSS:

1. The DSS should provide support for decision making, but in particular semi-structured and unstructured decisions.
2. The DSS should not focus on a single level of management decision making, such as tactical. Rather, it should integrate across all levels in recognition of the overlap between operational, tactical and strategic decisions.
3. The DSS should support all phases of the decision-making process outlined above.
4. The DSS should be easy to use.

Watson and Sprague (1993) identify three main components in a decision support system. These are:

1. *Dialogue.* This component is used for achieving interaction with the user so they can formulate queries and models and review results. Essentially, it is the user interface. It is often difficult to devise an effective user interface for a DSS since there is a trade-off between simplicity and flexibility. Simplicity is needed since some managers may not be frequent users of decision support systems. Flexibility is required to allow a range of different questions to be asked and to enable data to be displayed in different ways. The problem is that as more flexibility and options are built into the system, it becomes more difficult to use.
2. *Data.* Data sources are, of course, critical to DSS. Information may need to be collected from a range of sources such as operational systems (for sales performance), financial accounting systems (for financial performance), or document sources such as internal documents or those available on the Internet. Note that changes or additions to data are made using the database systems organising the data and not by the DSS dialogue itself.
3. *Model.* The model component provides an analysis capability for the DSS. A financial model, for example, may predict for given inputs what the future profitability of a company will be if it continues on the present course.

There is a bewildering array of terms used to describe software developed to help solve unstructured and semi-structured problems. These include business intelligence (BI) systems (see Chapter 4), artificial intelligence, expert systems and neural networks. All of these types of software have the same broad aim – to assist decision making by using software to mimic the way decisions are made by experts in their own field.

Artificial intelligence (AI)

Artificial intelligence (AI)

The study of how computers can reproduce human intelligence.

Artificial intelligence (AI) is the term given to research into how computers can reproduce human intelligence. Many of the terms above, such as expert systems and neural networks, are specialist areas of artificial intelligence from which business applications have been produced. Further business applications of AI include voice recognition and security applications such as retinal scanning.

A useful method of considering different types of DSS is to consider the different types of problem they can solve (Luconi et al., 1986). The problems are considered in terms of four elements:

- the data;
- the problem-solving procedures;
- the goals and constraints;
- the flexibility of strategies among the procedures.

The types of problem are:

- Type I problems are structured in all of the four elements above.
- Type II problems have some incomplete data and partly understood goals and constraints.
- Type III problems are those in which rules can be defined in a knowledge base and the software can then solve problems of a similar type.
- Type IV problems have aspects of both Type II and Type III problems.

Which types of DSS can be used for solving these types of problems? Type I problems are usually incorporated into operational systems as part of the program logic and do not require a specific DSS. Type III problems can be solved by a classical expert system and Types II and IV require a hybrid approach, which may involve modern techniques such as data mining, neural networks and genetic programming as described by Goonatilake and Khebbal (1995). We will now consider some of these types of system in more detail.

Expert systems

Expert systems are used to represent the knowledge and decision-making skills of specialists so that non-specialists can take decisions. They encapsulate the knowledge of experts by providing tools for the acquisition of knowledge and representation of rules and their enactment as decisions. They need to contain information relevant to taking the decision. This is often referred to as the *knowledge base* and includes the rules on which the decisions are based. An important distinction between expert systems and other information systems that are used for decision making is that the suggested actions are not based only on rules and algorithms. Instead, they also use heuristic techniques that may involve searching through different 'rules of thumb' that recommend the best action. The different rules are applied using a separate module of the expert system, known as the *inference engine*.

The relationship between these different components of the expert system is shown in Figure 6.17. The *user interface* program, sometimes referred to as the 'expert system shell', is used to build rules and ask questions of the system.

Applications of expert systems include:

- gold prospecting;
- medical diagnosis;
- credit decisions and insurance underwriting;
- product design, management and testing.

Expert systems

Used to represent the knowledge and decision-making skills of specialists so that non-specialists can take decisions.

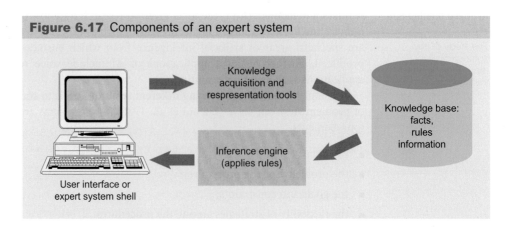

Figure 6.17 Components of an expert system

Knowledge acquisition and respresentation tools

Knowledge base: facts, rules information

Inference engine (applies rules)

User interface or expert system shell

In medicine, expert systems have recorded some success in diagnosing illnesses that might not have been recognised by doctors because of their obscurity. In a medical expert system such as MYCIN which was used to identify the treatment for blood disorders, the symptoms of a condition are entered into the expert system, which then compares them with all the known symptoms of different ailments in a knowledge base and gives a diagnosis. The knowledge base consists of facts or expert knowledge, in this case the symptoms and also a series of rules that match the symptom to the problem.

Expert systems are used quite widely in the financial services industry for assessing the risk of investing in a particular share or futures market or in personal finance or issuing a loan. For example, if a customer wants a loan they will give personal details about their employment history and where they have lived, and an expert system will assess what the credit risk is based on this pattern of behaviour in their existing customer base. The degree of sophistication of this risk assessment could vary from assessing the individual on a series of rules or a more advanced system using neural networks. The rules-based approach might state, for example, that credit cannot be issued if an individual has not lived in a particular location for less than six months over the last five years or if the amount of the loan is greater than 10 per cent of their salary. With a neural network approach, the software would learn from the history of previous customers what characteristics represented a bad credit risk and assess according to these criteria.

Neural networks

Neutral networks

Systems that use a similar process to biological intelligence to learn problem-solving skills by 'training' or exposure to a wide range of problems.

Neural networks are systems that use a similar process to biological intelligence to learn problem-solving skills by 'training' or exposure to a wide range of problems. The learning occurs through interactions between nodes, which are similar to the neurons of the brain. Neural networks work in a similar way to brain neurons, which gives them the capacity to learn through exposure to different patterns. For example, a neural network could be used for a photofit application if it learnt the characteristics of different types of people. As an example of the way in which neural networks can be applied to business applications, consider a bank processing Visa credit card transactions. Of all the transactions that occur, a proportion will be fraudulent. By learning from past transactions, both legal and fraudulent, a neural network will be able to predict the likelihood of fraud on an account. Barclays Bank installed such a system in the UK in 1997, and it was soon recognising over £100,000 of fraudulent transactions each month.

Information reporting systems (IRS)

Information reporting systems

Systems that provide information in the form of predefined reports for day-to-day decision-making needs.

Information reporting systems, also referred to as *management information systems*, produce reports that have been defined in advance for day-to-day decision-making needs. There are two main types of report that these systems produce:

- *Periodic reports*. These are predefined reports that are required by decision makers at regular intervals. Examples include a monthly financial statement and a weekly sales analysis.

- *Exception reports*. These are reports produced only when required. They can be generated automatically by the information system when a performance measure moves outside a predefined range. Examples include sales falling below a certain level and customers exceeding their credit limits. Exception reports can also be generated manually when a decision maker does not want to wait until the next scheduled periodic report or the information is only occasionally required.

Executive information systems (EIS)

EIS or executive support systems (ESS) provide senior managers with a system to assist them in taking strategic and tactical decisions. Their purpose is to analyse, compare and highlight trends to help govern the strategic direction of a company. A typical application would be to monitor the organisation's performance against changes in the external environment such as competitor actions.

EIS are intended as decision support tools for senior managers. Since these strategic decisions are based on a wide range of input information, they always need to be well integrated with operational systems in a business. This integration may be difficult in firms with many incompatible systems but ESS are a logical extension of the integration provided by the enterprise systems described earlier in this chapter.

Some important features of EIS are:

- They provide summary information to enable monitoring of business performance. This is often achieved through measures known as 'critical success factors' or 'key performance indicators' (KPIs). These will be displayed in an easy-to-interpret form such as a graph showing their variation through time. If a KPI falls below a critical preset value, the system will notify the manager through a visible or audible warning.

- They are used mainly for strategic decision making, but may also provide features that relate to tactical decision making.

- They provide a drill-down feature which gives a manager the opportunity to find out more information necessary to take a decision or discover the source of a problem. For example, a manager with a multinational manufacturing problem might find from the EIS that a particular country is underperforming in production. He could then drill down to see which particular factory was responsible for this.

- They provide analysis tools.

- They must be integrated with other facilities to help manage the solving of problems and the daily running of the business. These include electronic mail and scheduling and calendar facilities.

- They integrate data from a wide variety of information sources, including company and external sources such as market and competitor information. This may be provided from Web sources.

- They have to be designed according to the needs of managers who do not use computers frequently. They should be intuitive and easy to learn.

EIS are often associated with a graphical interface called a dashboard which are covered elsewhere (see Chapter 4).

DEPARTMENTAL APPLICATIONS

In the final section of this chapter we will review how information systems can be used in key departments in the organisation: the human resources, marketing and finance functions. These examples have been chosen since they usually require application-specific software.

Human resource management (HRM) information systems

Human resource management (HRM) is about ensuring that the employees of the organisation have the required skills and tools in order to meet its strategic goals. The management of an organisation's human resources is critical to its success. The development of an organisation's human resources is particularly important in a service company, where employees are more likely to be required to provide customer contact. Human resource decisions and information systems support will be required both within the central human resource function and by managers of the functional areas of the business. Organisations need a supply of trained and qualified personnel in order to achieve their goals. Human resource management (HRM) is about ensuring that the employees of the organisation have the required skills and tools in order to meet its strategic goals.

Objectives of HRM software

The main role of HRM software is to act as a storage and retrieval system maintaining large volumes of data on employee and job specifications. These data will be required for applications such as routine reports for government agencies, information for recruitment and selection, and more sophisticated forecasting models for workforce planning.

Information needs for human resources systems

The main activities of the HR function and the information needed to support them are:

- *Job analysis and design*. HR systems need to contain job descriptions describing the purpose, tasks and responsibilities of that job and job specifications describing the skills, knowledge and other characteristics required of workers in order to undertake the tasks specified in the job description.
- *Job management*. This includes recording of employee development through appraisals, training, salary and benefits planning. The government will also require human resource information to be available from all organisations to comply with laws governing such areas as health and safety legislation, equal opportunities regulations and employee sickness history.
- *Recruitment*. In large organisations workflow systems are used for managing the thousands of applications for jobs. Such systems will help structure interviewing and in sending out letters.

Software for HRM information systems

A database provides a central feature of HRM systems and will contain information on such areas as name, address, job title and attendance for each employee in the organisation and other information required to construct job description and applicant files. With this information it should be possible to use a database management system to match applicant and current employee details to a job specification. The database could also be used in areas such as the identification of training needs and producing details of employees for government agencies. Unfortunately, some HR databases have been constructed within the HR function and are not compatible with such areas as payroll. This leads to problems of duplication and ensuring that data are up to date. Small companies could develop their own databases, but more often small, medium and large companies will buy an off-the-shelf package based on a database.

An example of an HRM database

Single *record* per employee in main employee table. *Fields* within the employee *table* to include:

- surname, forename, next of kin;
- date of birth;

➡

- address;
- National Insurance number;
- position – job description;
- department;
- salary;
- tax code;
- start date.

Links to other tables:

- training records;
- assessment/performance appraisal details;
- payroll.

The terms table, field and record were introduced earlier (in Chapter 4). Database design is discussed further later (in Chapters 10 and 11).

Marketing information systems

The word *marketing* has two distinct meanings in terms of modern management practice. It describes:

1. The range of specialist marketing functions carried out within many organisations. Such functions include market research, brand/product management, public relations and customer service.

2. An approach or concept that can be used as the guiding philosophy for all functions and activities of an organisation. Such a philosophy encompasses all aspects of a business. Business strategy is guided by an organisation's market and competitor focus and everyone in an organisation should be required to have a customer focus in their job.

The modern marketing concept unites these two meanings and stresses that marketing encompasses the range of organisational functions and processes that deliver products and services to customers and other key stakeholders, such as employees and financial institutions. Increasingly, the importance of marketing is being recognised both as a vital function and as a guiding management philosophy. Marketing has to be seen as the essential focus of all activities within an organisation.

Given the importance of marketing to an organisation, many companies make use of information systems to assist in mission-critical activities such as customer sales – sell-side e-commerce is a major component of e-business. The benefits of this type of transactional e-commerce system have been described in earlier sections.

In this section we will mainly consider information systems that are used within the marketing department to assist in running the marketing function.

Marketing information systems

Support decision making at the operational, tactical and strategic levels necessary to manage the marketing function.

Marketing information systems support decision making at the operational, tactical and strategic levels. At the operational level, distribution information systems and telemarketing systems offer assistance in day-to-day activities and provide information to areas such as inventory and customer credit systems. Tactical marketing systems provide assistance in such areas as product pricing and sales management information systems. At the strategic level, information from sales forecasting, marketing research and competitive tracking systems helps management plan and develop new products.

Telemarketing software

This software is designed to dial the telephone numbers of potential customers automatically, based on customer files maintained in a database. The software will also allow notes to be stored on customer requests, generate follow-up letters and display information gathered on the customer for reference as the call is taking place. Telephone call centres use computer-integrated telephony (CIT) to sell direct product lines such as insurance and personal finance. CIT is also used to provide customer service via help-desk and advice services. The software can be integrated with a workflow system that provides automatic management of customer requests (e.g. automation of activities such as letter generation). Using historical data, the software can also be used to predict workload levels over time and thus aid management in workforce planning.

Accounting information systems

Accounting information system

Provides functions for the numerous financial activities that take place in any organisation.

Accounting information systems are used for the financial activities that take place in any organisation. These include the operation of sales order processing systems, payroll, budgeting and reporting of the financial condition of the organisation. Other functions include the management of capital investment and general cashflow management.

Operational accounting systems focus on daily recording of business transactions, that is, the flow of funds through an organisation. All businesses require this basic information. In larger businesses these systems will be linked to other operational functions, such as sales order processing and inventory.

Management accounting systems enable planning and control of business finance. These are sometimes referred to as 'financial information systems' and will be linked to executive information systems.

Application areas for accounting information systems

Most companies use an integrated accounting system that covers a number of application areas, as shown in Figure 6.18. The essential modules are accounts receivable, accounts payable and the general ledger. Many companies will look to extend these to related areas such as sales order processing and payroll.

- *Sales order processing (SOP).* This system is particularly important, as it records sales transactions and supplies documents to other areas such as stock control and manufacturing. There might also be links to payroll to calculate such elements as bonus payments to salespeople on receipt of a customer order. The accounts receivable system contains customer information such as sales made, payments made and account balances for overdue payments. These can be used to halt the extension of further credit until the balances have been cleared. The system may also be searched to identify customers who have purchased certain items – a list of them is then used as the basis for a mailing list for promotional purposes. The accounts payable system contains information regarding the firm's creditors (as opposed to customers for the accounts receivable). The system provides information on which a schedule of supplier payments can be made and thus ensures that payments can be made as late as possible (to optimise cashflow) without losing discounts offered from suppliers for prompt payment.

- *Inventory.* This system maintains stock levels by recording when stock is used for sales orders. A reorder point (ROP) system will generate an order for stock once the level of a stock item falls below a certain number of units. Other time-based systems will replenish stocks after a predetermined time interval.

Figure 6.18 Modules of a standard accounting system, plus additional purchasing, sales order processing and payroll modules

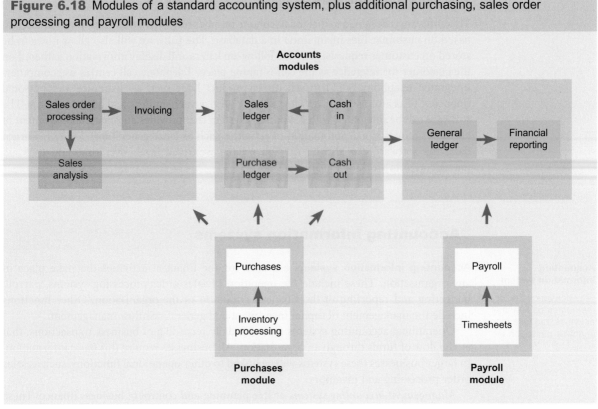

- *Payroll.* This system processes payments to employees, including deductions for such items as National Insurance and income tax. Many organisations will have electronic links to banks for direct deposit to employee accounts rather than issuing pay cheques.

- *Budgeting systems.* Budgets are an important control tool for management. A predetermined budgeted amount is periodically compared to the actual expenditure and any difference noted as a variance. This comparison of allocations (budgeted amounts) against actuals (amounts spent or received) can be reported to management. The identification of a variance will normally instigate a discussion and may lead to corrective action being taken to eliminate any adverse variance. Budgets for areas or departments can be aggregated or brought together to form a functional or organisational budget statement for higher-level decision making.

- *Cashflow reporting.* A major cause of business failure is inadequate cash reserves to keep the organisation functioning. Cashflow reporting is necessary to keep track of the organisation's cash reserves. Cash is needed for working capital (day-to-day expenses) and for the purchase of long-term assets such as plant or machinery. A cashflow report will contain a running total of the cash balance from information on cash inflows and outflows for each reporting period. An adverse cash position may necessitate the deferring of a planned acquisition. The report can be used as a planning tool by incorporating different cost and revenue scenarios and studying the results.

- *Capital budgeting system.* The financial system should contain tools that allow for the evaluation of capital spending plans. Major investments are compared to the financial return that the organisation could have gained from placing the cash in a bank account and accruing interest. The investment evaluation may also inform the decision to buy or lease equipment. Financial measures often used to assess an investment include net present value (NPV), internal rate of return (IRR) and payback period.

- *Financial analysis system.* Financial analysts use a variety of performance measures to gauge the financial position of an organisation. These include such measures as the current ratio, inventory turnover and earnings per share (Dyson, 2010). An information system can be used to generate these values automatically using figures stored in a database of such items as current assets and current liabilities.

- *Forecasting systems.* By projecting budget statements into the future, an organisation is able to forecast its potential financial state. These forecasts will need to incorporate economic and market forecasts in order that sales and cost data can be estimated.

Spreadsheets

Owing to their flexibility in numerical analysis and the incorporation of built-in facilities for statistical and numerical analysis, spreadsheets are an ideal medium in which to conduct financial analysis. For instance, a budget or cashflow forecast can be compiled by the addition of relevant items under income and expenses headings. If a spreadsheet template is constructed, consisting of the headings for the relevant items to be included, it is simply a matter of the user entering the appropriate amounts into the spreadsheet cells. Cashflow forecasts are an essential financial statement in any business. Bank managers can be forewarned of the probable requirement for overdraft facilities. The forecasts are of particular importance to startup businesses where they can be used to support applications for additional funding from potential money lenders.

Once the cashflow statement has been entered, any values can easily be changed and the spreadsheet cell values will be updated to reflect the new cash position.

Accounting packages

A vast number of accounting software packages are available which can produce invoice statements, monthly budget statements and other financial items needed to run a small or medium-sized organisation. The requirements for accounting information systems will differ from other types of system in which issues such as ease of use and performance will usually be considered important. In accounting systems, accuracy and reliability are paramount.

Financial modelling packages

While accounting packages tend to be restricted to operational systems, financial modelling packages are also available for decision making at the strategic and tactical levels of an organisation. These provide the following types of facilities for strategic planning:

- corporate financial forecasting models;
- merger and acquisition strategy.
- Facilities for tactical planning include:
- annual budgets – cashflow, capital, tax planning;
- new product assessments – ROCE (return on capital employed).

They can also be used for operational financial management issues such as:

- funds management – cash and securities, shares;
- cost accounting and project cost monitoring;
- tax accounting.

Systems to provide these functions tend to be available as modules of the high-end accounting packages. Such software allows the decision maker to hold financial models of the organisation in order to construct 'what-if?' analysis. It has the advantage of providing more guidance than a spreadsheet does on building financial models.

SUMMARY

1. Enterprise systems aim to support the business processes of an organisation across any functional boundaries that exist within that organisation. Examples of enterprise systems are enterprise resource planning (ERP), customer relationship management (CRM), supply chain management (SCM) and supplier relationship management (SRM).

2. ERP provides functions for managing internal business areas such as production, distribution, sales, finance and human resources management.

3. SCM provides functions for the management of the flow of materials through the supply chain.

4. CRM systems are designed to integrate the range of information systems that contain information regarding the customer.

5. SRM provides functions to manage all activities involved with obtaining items from a supplier, including procurement, and also inbound logistics such as transportation and warehousing.

6. Operations information systems are often critical to the success of a business, since their efficiency directly affects customer experience, profitability and cashflow. Operational systems include:
   - transaction processing systems for managing transactions such as customer orders, supplier purchases and payment;
   - office automation systems such as groupware and workflow systems, which enable office workers to collaborate on administration and customer service;
   - process control systems for manufacturing.

7. Decision support systems are tools for assisting decision making at tactical and strategic levels within an organisation. The main tools available are:
   - business intelligence software such as executive information systems (EIS) and data warehouses;
   - expert systems which enable non-specialists to take unstructured decisions outside their area of expertise;
   - neural networks that learn problem-solving skills by exposure to a wide range of problems.

8. Business applications have traditionally served the departmental areas of an organisation, such as:
   - human resources;
   - accounting;
   - marketing and sales.

EXERCISES

Self-assessment exercises

1. What is the difference between an enterprise system and an enterprise resource planning (ERP) system?

2. Evaluate the role of transaction processing systems in an organisation.

3. How can information systems support the manufacturing process?

4. Explain how decision support systems can support different parts of an organisation.

5. Describe the purpose of workflow management and groupware.

6. Which information systems tools can be used to support the marketing function?

Discussion questions

1. Discuss the concept of customer relationship management (CRM).

2. 'Workflow systems are currently mainly in large organisations. This is likely to remain the case.' Discuss.

3. Neural networks, fuzzy logic and genetic programming are some of the latest artificial intelligence ideas. Are they likely to remain lab-based products, or is there potential for their use in industry?

Essay questions

1. Evaluate the different levels of integration in supply chain management (SCM).

2. Review the changing tools available for decision making at a strategic level within the organisation. What does this mean for senior managers?

3. Was the promise of expert systems in the 1980s delivered in the 1990s? Justify your answer.

4. How must transaction processing systems be managed, given their mission-critical role in many organisations?

Examination questions

1. How can workflow software and groupware assist in re-engineering an organisation?

2. What special precautions need to be taken when using IT for managing human resources?

References

Dyson, J.P. (2010) *Accounting for Non-accounting Students*, 8th edition, Financial Times Prentice Hall, Harlow

Evans, P. and Wurster, T.S. (1997) 'Strategy and the new economies of information', *Harvard Business Review*, September

Garry, A.G. and Scott-Morton, M. (1971) 'A framework for Management Information Systems', *Sloan Management Review*, 12, 55–70

Goonatilake, S. and Khebbal, S. (1995) 'Intelligent hybrid systems: issues, classifications and future directions', in S. Goonatilake and S. Khebbal (eds) *Intelligent Hybrid Systems*, John Wiley, New York

Greasley, A. (2013) *Operations Management*, 3rd edition, John Wiley, Chichester

Kraut, R., Chan, A., Butler, B. and Hong, A. (1998) 'Coordination and virtualization: The role of electronic networks and personal relationships', *Journal of Computer Mediated Communications*, 3, 4

Laudon, K.C. and Laudon, J.P. (2011) *Management Information Systems: Managing the Digital Firm*, 12th edition, Macmillan, Upper Saddle River, NJ

Luconi, F.L., Malone, T.W. and Scott-Morton, M. (1986) 'Expert systems: the next challenge for managers', *Sloan Management Review*, 27, 3–14

Sprague, R. (1980) 'A framework for the development of decision support systems', *MIS Quarterly*, 4, 4

Watson, H.J. and Sprague, R.H. (1993) 'The components of an architecture for DSS', in R.H. Sprague and H.J. Watson (eds) *Decision Support Systems: Putting Theory into Practice*, 3rd edition, Prentice-Hall, Englewood Cliffs, NJ

Further reading

Greasley, A. (2013) *Operations Management*, 3rd edition, John Wiley, Chichester. Provides more details on process control systems.

O'Brien, J.A. and Marakas, G. (2011) *Management Information Systems*, 10th edition, McGraw-Hill Irwin, Boston, MA.

Turban, E., Sharda, R. and Delen, D. (2010) *Decision Support and Business Intelligence Systems*, 9th edition, Prentice-Hall, Englewood Cliffs, NJ.

Web links

Enterprise systems

www.oracle.com, **www.sap.com**, **www.infor.com** Major suppliers of enterprise systems.

www.supply-chain.org The Supply Chain Council. Numerous papers and news items regarding supply chain management.

Workflow

www.wfmc.org This Workflow Management Coalition site contains extensive technical papers explaining how workflows are defined. It also contains introductory papers on the purpose and components of workflow systems.

www.bpmfocus.org BPM-Focus (BPMF) is a new member network formed by the recent merger of Enix Consulting and WARIA (Workflow and Reengineering International Association). The new organisation extends the traditional services offered by Enix and WARIA through a range of educational services focused around the BPM arena.

www.aiim.org The Enterprise Content Management Association is a source for helping individuals and organisations understand the challenges associated with managing documents, content, records, and business processes.

Introduction to Part 2

Part 2 focuses on how business information systems are acquired and built. An understanding of building BIS is important to users and managers who are responsible for, or are involved in, a systems development project. Such managers need to understand the activities involved in different stages of systems development to help plan the project or work with the developers of the system. They will also need to be aware of the alternatives for sourcing IS such as buying a pre-written off-the-shelf system or a specially written bespoke system, in order to decide which is best for their company or department.

To build a good-quality BIS, a company will follow a process that has defined stages with clear objectives and deliverables at each stage. Part 2 describes the typical activities involved when a new system is built. These stages form what is commonly referred to as the *systems development lifecycle* (SDLC):

- *initiation*: a startup phase that usually occurs in response to a business problem or opportunity;
- *feasibility*: an attempt to determine whether the proposed systems development will be viable;
- *systems analysis*: to determine what the system is required to do;
- *systems design*: to specify how the system will deliver the stated requirements;
- *systems build*: the design is transformed into a physical system by programming, testing and creation of databases;
- *systems implementation and changeover*: the organisation moves from installing and testing the information system to operating in a live business environment;
- *review and maintenance*: the success of the system is measured against the original requirements, and modifications are made over its lifetime.

Note that as errors are found, or new requirements arise, it is necessary to revisit previous stages. Iterative models such as the spiral model are used to show the cyclical nature of system development where several prototypes are built; this involves repeating the analysis, design and build phases.

The unique nature of systems development projects, which is in part due to the speed of technological and business change and the iteration referred to above, makes it very difficult to develop a system that satisfies the three key constraints:

1. Does it meet the requirements of the business and end-users?
2. Is it delivered on time?
3. Has it been produced within the allocated budget?

Part 2 involves reviewing each stage of the SDLC systematically to consider what action can be taken to ensure the project objectives are met.

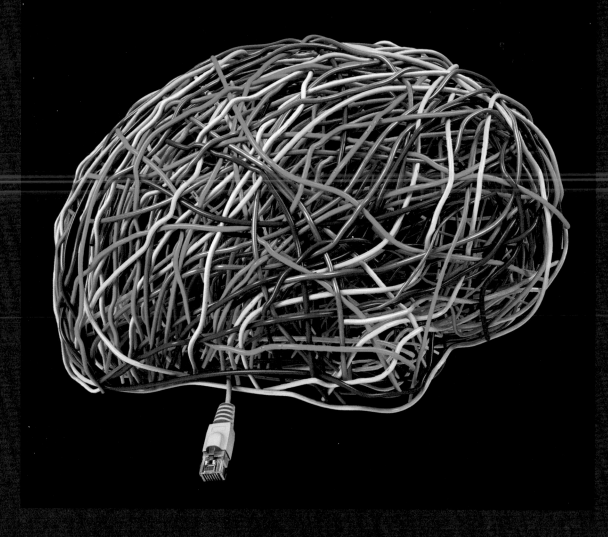

LINKS TO OTHER CHAPTERS

This chapter provides a framework for all subsequent chapters in Part 2.

An introduction to acquiring and developing BIS

CHAPTER AT A GLANCE

MAIN TOPICS

CASE STUDIES

LEARNING OUTCOMES

After reading this chapter, you will be able to:

- evaluate the different alternatives for acquiring BIS;
- distinguish between the typical stages involved in building BIS;
- explain the purpose of each stage in building a system;
- select the best alternative type of approach or methodology for building a BIS.

MANAGEMENT ISSUES

Managers need to select the optimal method for introducing a new BIS once an opportunity is identified. From a managerial perspective, this chapter addresses the following questions:

- What are the alternatives for systems acquisition and how is the most suitable approach selected?
- What alternative models are there for the different stages for introducing a BIS? Which is most appropriate?
- Which activities need to occur at each stage for the project to be successful?

INTRODUCTION

This chapter provides the foundation for subsequent chapters in Part 2 by taking a broad look at the main activities involved in acquiring and building new business information systems. The word 'acquire' is used deliberately here, since 'development' implies the writing of bespoke software for a business information application. However, since many business applications can be purchased off the shelf without the need for any detailed design or programming activity, 'acquisition' more precisely defines the process we are going to outline here.

This chapter will start by reminding ourselves about the business rationale for information systems. We will then consider, in broad terms, alternative approaches to the acquisition of new computer-based information systems, ranging from creating new bespoke systems through to purchasing off-the-shelf applications.

BIS acquisition

The process of evaluating and implementation for a BIS.

Systems development lifecycle (SDLC)

Any information systems project follows a logical series of development phases. These are known as the systems development lifecycle.

SDLC stages

Initiation, feasibility study, analysis of business requirements, systems design, system build and implementation and, finally, review and maintenance.

BIS acquisition describes the method of obtaining an information system for a business. The main choices are off-the-shelf (packaged), bespoke (tailor-made) applications developed by an in-house IT department or a software house, and systems that are end-user-developed (i.e. by non-IS/IT professionals).

We will then review the traditional **systems development lifecycle (SDLC)**, sometimes known as the 'waterfall model' of systems development within the specific context of bespoke software development. This defines the different **SDLC stages** involved in developing a new system. Any BIS project follows a logical series of development phases. Typical stages are: initiation, feasibility study, analysis of business requirements, systems design, system build and implementation and, finally, review and maintenance. The stages will be summarised in this chapter in preparation for a more detailed description in subsequent chapters. The analysis of bespoke software development will also incorporate some of the different methodologies for building systems such as rapid applications development (RAD).

From bespoke development, we will move on to consideration of factors affecting the acquisition of packaged software, and in particular software selection factors. We will also consider how the traditional systems development lifecycle applies to the purchase of packaged software and where the key differences lie when compared with bespoke software development.

Finally, while end-user computing is addressed in more detail (in Chapter 16), we will look briefly at user-developed applications where information systems are developed by IS users for their own or their department's usage in the context of the steps of the SDLC that apply.

HOW AND WHY ARE INFORMATION SYSTEMS ACQUIRED?

Organisations spend significant sums on information systems and it is important to understand the business context within which information systems are acquired. Earlier (in Chapters 1 and 2) we looked at a number of topics including:

- the qualities of 'good' information to support effective decision making;
- the business environment, both internal and external, and the ability of information systems to impact positively on it;
- the information needs of managers at different levels of an organisation and how this results in different categories of business information system;
- how BIS can produce a strategic advantage for an organisation.

Figure 7.1 demonstrates that an organisation's information systems needs are driven by business strategies and policies which in turn are driven by both the internal and external business environment.

Figure 7.1 Drivers for information systems acquisition

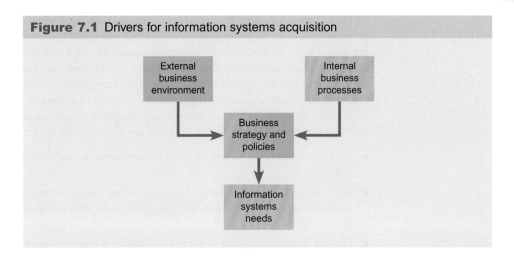

An organisation's business strategy will determine where the business is going, and why. This in turns creates 'demand' for information and the applications software that can provide it. What remains is the need to acquire, implement and manage these solutions and this is the stimulus for the software acquisition process.

Whilst many texts deal admirably with the range of tools and techniques available to the systems analyst for bespoke systems development to meet these needs, there is a tendency to forget that bespoke development is only one method of software acquisition. In fact for many businesses, especially small and medium-sized enterprises, bespoke applications development is not a viable option because of the costs and practical difficulties involved. It is necessary, therefore, to begin by looking at the range of acquisition methods and consider which is most appropriate for the needs of a particular business.

There are three main methods for acquiring the information system necessary to support a particular business need. These are bespoke development, off-the-shelf software and end-user development. Figure 7.2 summarises these three alternatives.

Bespoke development

An IS is developed 'from scratch' by an IS professional to suit the business requirements of the application.

1. Bespoke development

Bespoke development is the term for when an information system is developed 'from scratch' by one or more information systems professionals to meet the business requirements of the application.

Figure 7.2 An example of a typical evaluation of alternatives for BIS acquisition

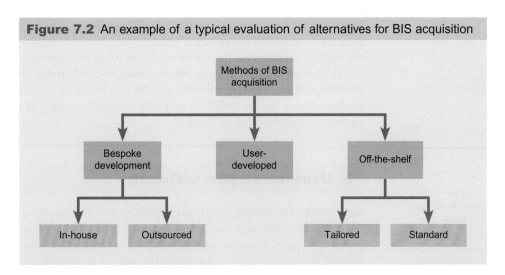

Here a new BIS will be developed from scratch by a team of information systems professionals. The IS professionals will either work for the business, in which case we refer to this as 'in-house' bespoke development, or for a third party such as a software house, in which case we say that the software development has been 'outsourced'. Bespoke development has the benefit of producing software tailored to the precise requirements of the business. There is also the benefit that the creation of a bespoke information system may confer specific competitive advantage since competitor organisations do not have the same software solutions. On the downside, there are a number of difficulties:

- *Expense*. Bespoke development is the most expensive way of developing new information systems.

- *Time*. Bespoke development, especially when using formal structured development methodologies, is notorious for time overruns, with delays of months or years not uncommon.

- *Quality*. Bespoke software is not usually free from bugs; software bugs can range from the trivial to the catastrophic, the latter often attributable to poor analysis of requirements.

2. Purchasing 'off-the-shelf' software

Off-the-shelf purchase

An acquisition method that involves direct purchase of a pre-written application used by more than one company.

Off-the-shelf purchase of packaged software is an acquisition method that involves direct purchase of a pre-written application used by more than one company.

This type of software is pre-written and is available for a whole variety of hardware platforms from PCs to mainframes. Off-the-shelf software is written to offer a broad functionality that will suit a wide range of different businesses. This broad range of functions has the benefit of fitting the requirements of a large number of businesses. It also may offer too many features for any particular business, which may then feel that it is paying for things it will not use. At the same time, it may require businesses to process information in a particular way that is at odds with the way they normally do business. Alternatively, a certain off-the-shelf software package may not offer sufficient features. For example, a well-known accounting package in the UK only offered an eight-character code for the customer's order number, though it would appear that some 50 per cent of UK companies use longer order number codes. The major benefit, however, of off-the-shelf software packages is their low cost when compared with acquiring bespoke software with the same level of functionality. In addition, because packaged software has been developed for a commercial market, it is less likely to suffer from the bugs that afflict bespoke software.

In a *tailored off-the-shelf package*, pre-written software is purchased from a supplier, but it is possible to configure it to be specific to the company by altering software code as required for the customer as well as enabling the customer to define (within the limits set by the package vendor) how the software will run using pre-written configuration parameters. A standard off-the-shelf package may be similarly configurable, whilst in a *component off-the-shelf package*, different modules may be purchased from different suppliers and built together. Visual Basic controls for graphing is a good example of a component that can be added to an off-the-shelf application.

3. User-developed software

User-developed software

Software written by non-IS professionals, i.e. the business users.

User-developed software is software written by non-IS professionals, i.e. the business users.

Senn (2004) estimated that 50 to 75 per cent of all computing applications will be classed as end-user applications (as distinct from institutional applications) and that many of these systems will be developed by end-users (i.e. non-IT professionals).

Enterprise resource planning or institutional applications are those that affect general corporate activities, cut across more than one department or functional area, or systems that involve organisational data held in corporate databases. Examples include accounting systems, sales order processing systems and materials requirements planning.

End-user applications are more limited in scope. Applications may be departmental or personal in nature and are usually output- or report-oriented rather than input-driven. These applications may either be written by IT professionals or by the end-users themselves. If the latter is the case, they are often referred to as *user-developed applications*.

User-developed applications may be simple (e.g. a spreadsheet or a small PC database) or less commonly they may be more sophisticated (e.g. a production planning system based on sales forecast data from several branches of the same organisation). Such applications are typically for individual or departmental use, although in the case of the second example the system may have company-wide relevance. The main benefit of end-user-developed software is that it is normally used by those who develop it, and so the requirements are not subject to mistranslation or the provision of over-sophisticated solutions. The negative side to this is that in some cases inappropriate software development tools might be used (such as complicated spreadsheets instead of the construction of a database). A further significant concern with end-user development is that software may be riddled with bugs as a consequence of corner-cutting (poor or non-existent design, little or no testing, or no documentation). The end-user development approach is described in more detail later (in Chapter 16).

There are also a number of hybrid approaches to acquisition. A group of organisations in the same business or activity area may have information systems requirements that individually may be very expensive to develop. A solution may be for a bespoke system to be developed by a third party, which allows the development costs to be spread among all the organisations involved. Good examples here are a university student records system and various systems used in police forces across the UK.

Similarly, an off-the-shelf package may provide 80 per cent of the required features, but others may need to be added through some bespoke development by either IS/IT professionals or by end-users.

Hybrid approaches to systems acquisition

The approaches to systems acquisition described above are not mutually exclusive to a given project or within an organisation. Where the software is generic to all businesses, as is the case with systems software and office productivity packages, off-the-shelf software will be purchased. Where the business has more specific needs and wishes to achieve a competitive advantage, bespoke and tailored approaches to acquisition will be used. With e-business systems there is often a need to integrate in-house legacy systems and systems purchased from different vendors. This uses a building block approach of different components including data sources that are integrated together. This is referred to as **enterprise application integration (EAI)**, and achieving this is a significant challenge facing project managers and systems designers.

Enterprise application integration (EAI)

Software used to facilitate communications between business applications including data transfer and control.

Factors affecting software acquisition

There are a number of factors that will influence the choice of acquisition method. Three critical ones are time, cost and quality considerations.

If an organisation has a pressing problem that requires a new information system quickly, it is probable that a package or tailored package will be sought. Similarly, an organisation that needs a 'quality systems solution' may well consider the packaged software route, especially if its requirements are straightforward.

Table 7.1 An evaluation of alternatives for BIS acquisition

Acquisition option	Delivery time	Cost	Quality: bugs	Quality: fits business needs
Bespoke in-house	Poor	Poor	Poor	Good
Bespoke software house	Good	Very poor	Medium	Medium
End-user development	Poor	Medium	Poor	Good
Tailored – off-the-shelf	Good	Good	Good	Medium
Standard – off-the-shelf	Very good	Very good	Very good	Poor

The different acquisition options have different strengths when considered in terms of the three critical criteria. Table 7.1 shows how the alternatives compare in terms of these three criteria. Quality of the delivered product is considered from two respects: the number of bugs or errors found and the suitability of the software in meeting the requirements of the business user. Note that good quality in terms of the number of bugs that typically occur for packaged software may coincide with poor quality in terms of the business fit.

The benefit of packaged software occurs because the cost of developing and debugging the software is shared between more than one company. This results in lower costs and fewer bugs than bespoke development for a single company. The use of packaged software by more than one company is also its greatest weakness, since its features must suit the typical company. As a consequence, it may not meet the needs of an individual company.

Other factors affecting software acquisition include the following:

- *Organisation size.* A small or medium-sized business will inevitably have relatively limited resources for the purchasing of information systems and information technology (IS/IT). This suggests that there will be a tendency for such organisations to favour the purchase of off-the-shelf packages or possibly end-user applications development.

- *In-house IS/IT expertise.* Where little in-house IS/IT expertise exists, either in the form of IS/IT professionals or experienced end-users, there will be a need to use third parties in the acquisition of new business information systems. These may include software vendors for off-the-shelf software packages, the use of consultants and/or software houses. Precisely what form of third party is used will depend on the other factors discussed here.

- *Complexity of the required information system.* Where a business information system requirement is particularly complex, or for an unusual application not available as a packaged solution, it is possible that one may view bespoke software (either developed in-house or by a third party) as the only viable solution. However, complexity does not necessarily equate to 'uniqueness'. For example, one could regard a materials requirements planning system or a complete accounting system as complex, but many packages exist for a variety of hardware platforms. Therefore, complexity is not necessarily an indicator that an off-the-shelf package should be ruled out.

- *Uniqueness of the business or business area to be supported.* The higher the degree of uniqueness that exists in the area to be supported, the less likely it is that a suitable off-the-shelf package can be found. This is clearly an indicator, therefore, for bespoke development of some kind. As before, we must not confuse uniqueness with complexity. It may well be feasible for a non-IS/IT specialist to develop a solution using tools available to end-user developers. Of course, if the required system is complex and also carries a high degree of uniqueness, then bespoke development by IS/IT professionals is probably the best acquisition method.

- *IS/IT expertise among end-users.* A certain degree of IS/IT literacy and expertise is necessary if end-users are to be able to develop information systems. In addition, such

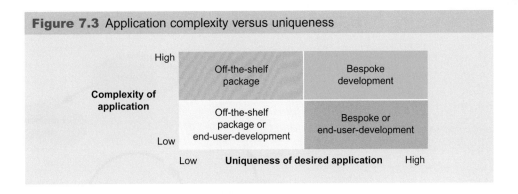

Figure 7.3 Application complexity versus uniqueness

literacy is desirable when selecting suitable off-the-shelf packaged software, as it can help the business focus more clearly on its precise requirements from both a functional and a technological perspective. If an organisation has little end-user IS/IT expertise of its own, but has its own IS/IT department, it will be very much dependent on solutions provided by IS/IT professionals with or without third-party support.

■ *Linkages with existing applications software.* Where new business software needs to integrate very tightly with existing information systems, there is a higher probability that at least some bespoke development work will need to be done to integrate the two systems. Also, a high degree of integration may imply that the new information system has to be developed in a bespoke fashion in order to achieve the desired level of integration. Having said that, many software vendors supply packages for different business areas which integrate very well with each other.

By looking at combinations of the above, it is possible to come up with a 'best-fit' acquisition method. Figure 7.3 illustrates the relationship between the complexity of the required application (as driven by the business needs) and the uniqueness of the application under consideration. The reader should note that bespoke development may be performed either by in-house IS/IT specialists or by a third party.

Similar relationships can be established with other pairs of selection acquisition factors. For example, when comparing the expertise of end-users in developing applications with the complexity of the desired application, a relatively simple information system may need professional IT staff involvement if the end-users do not have sufficient IS/IT capability.

SOFTWARE ACQUISITION AND THE SYSTEMS DEVELOPMENT LIFECYCLE

The systems development lifecycle (SDLC) model was developed and launched by the National Computing Centre in the UK in 1969. Until then, the emphasis in systems development was on programming. It was recognised, however, that many systems being developed at that time failed to meet user needs, because they were either functionally inadequate or too inflexible to meet changing business needs. The SDLC approach recognises that systems are developed in a series of steps or phases and that each phase needs to be completed before the next one commences. Recognition is also given to the fact that the programming activity (part of the build phase) should only commence once user requirements have been determined and the system design produced. Figure 7.4 illustrates the normal steps found in the systems development lifecycle.

Within the diagram it will be noted that in addition to the lifecycle phases, the concepts of project management and change management have been added. This reinforces the notion that information systems projects do not take place by chance, but that they must be managed carefully.

We will now summarise the basic steps that most systems development projects follow.

Figure 7.4 The systems development lifecycle (SDLC)

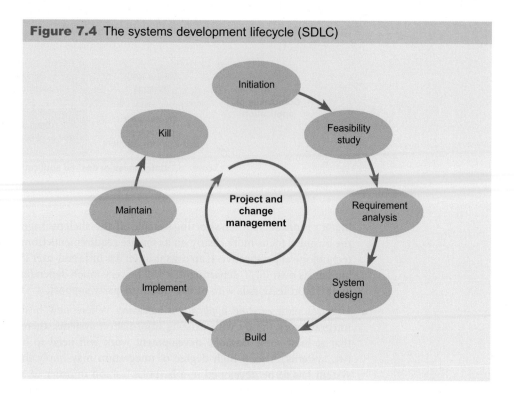

The startup phase in an IS development project. Its aims are to establish whether the project is feasible and then prepare to ensure the project is successful.

Initiation phase context

Input: creative thought and/or systematic evaluation of IS needs. Output: idea for initiation of a new information system.

Feasibility assessment

An activity at the start of a project to ensure that the project is a viable business proposition. The feasibility report analyses the need for and impact of the system and considers different alternatives for acquiring software.

Feasibility assessment context

Input: idea for initiation of a new information system. Output: feasibility report and recommendation to proceed.

Initiation (Chapter 8)

The **initiation phase** is the initiation or startup phase and is the first phase in an information systems development project. Its aims are to establish whether the project is feasible and then prepare to ensure the project is successful. The **initiation phase context** is:

Input: creative thought and/or systematic evaluation of IS needs.

Output: idea for initiation of a new information system.

The initiation phase contains the stimulus from which the need to develop a new BIS arises. This stimulus may come about as a result of some external event such as a change in legislation, or it may arise from a desire internally to develop an information system that better supports the business needs of the organisation. The source of this initiation process may be one of the following:

- *Managing director or other senior management.* Systems initiated from this point are likely to have the support necessary for successful development.

- *Information systems department.* A system may be initiated here as part of the organisation's overall IS/IT strategy; to maximise the chances of success the system will still need high-level management support.

- *Functional business area.* A system initiated here will be competing for attention with all other development projects then being undertaken; often an organisation will have a steering committee to decide on development priorities.

Feasibility assessment (Chapter 8)

Feasibility assessment is the activity that occurs at the start of the project to ensure that the project is a viable business proposition. The feasibility report analyses the need for and impact of the system and considers different alternatives for acquiring software. The **feasibility assessment context** is:

Input: idea for initiation of a new information system.

Output: feasibility report and recommendation to proceed.

The feasibility assessment can be considered to be part of the *initiation phase*. It will establish whether a computer-based information system fits certain feasibility criteria. Three criteria are usually cited:

1. It must be established whether the information system is *technically feasible*. To be technically feasible, either the technology exists or it can be created to support the required system.

2. To be *economically feasible*, an information system must generate more in the way of benefits than the cost needed to produce it. One of the problems here is that benefits are often difficult to quantify in monetary terms, while costs are far easier to estimate.

3. Assuming that a proposed information system is both technically and economic-ally feasible, an assessment must be made of whether the project is *operationally and organisationally feasible*. By operationally feasible, we mean that the system must be capable of performing within the required speed, volume, usability and reliability parameters. Also, to be feasible for the organisation, the proposed information system must either be capable of running alongside work patterns or existing work patterns must be capable of being adapted or re-engineered to run alongside the new information system. Organisational feasibility will involve a review of how the potential users' skill sets and attitudes will affect the system.

Part of the feasibility process may be the invitation to tender for some or all of the information system elements. These may include application software, hardware, communications technology or systems software. Different alternatives from different vendors will then be assessed.

The output from this step (and, therefore, the input to the next step of the model) is a stage review and a feasibility report, which will recommend either that the project proceeds or that the project is reassessed in some way.

Systems analysis (Chapter 10)

Systems analysis

The capture of the business requirements of a system from talking to or observing end-users and using other information sources such as existing system documentation. Defines *what* the system will do.

Systems analysis context

Input: terms of reference in feasibility report describing outline requirements. Output: detailed requirements specification summarising system functions. Supported by diagrams showing the information flow and processes that are required.

Systems analysis is the capture of the business requirements of a system from talking to or observing end-users and using other information sources such as existing system documentation. The **systems analysis context** is:

Input: terms of reference in feasibility report describing outline requirements.

Output: detailed requirements specification summarising system functions. Supported by diagrams showing the information flow and processes that are required.

Once a proposed information system is agreed to be feasible, it is necessary to carry out the detailed work of assessing the precise requirements that the intended users have for the new system. Note that the *systems analysis* step is sometimes referred to as the 'requirements determination' step or the 'systems study' step. There are three main tasks within this phase.

First, it is necessary to gain an understanding of how the *current* information system (computerised or paper-based) works. Second, a diagrammatic model of the current system workings is produced to ensure that IT professionals and system users are in agreement. Finally, a set of requirements for the new information system is produced. The requirements specification will define:

- the features that the new system is required to contain (for example, the ability for end-users to be able to design their own reports);

- the scope of the system under consideration (for example, is the system intended for just one functional area of the business or is it to embrace all business activities?);

- the intended users of the new system;

- system performance standards, including response times, batch processing times (if required) and reliability needs;
- environment requirements such as physical working environment, operating system and hardware on which the system will run.

In this last task, it may be desirable to produce another diagrammatic model, this time of the *required* information system.

If at any point it is discovered that the requirements of the system as articulated by the prospective users appear to be unfeasible in some way, it will be necessary to revisit the feasibility step and perform an additional analysis of the possible options.

The output from this step in the model will be a user requirements analysis document which details *what* the proposed system must do.

Systems design (Chapter 11)

Systems design

Defines *how* the system will work in key areas of user interface, program modules, security and database structure and transactions.

Systems design context

Input: requirements specification.
Output: detailed design specification.

The **systems design** phase defines how the system will work in key areas of user interface, program modules, security and database transactions. The **systems design context** is:

Input: requirements specification.

Output: detailed design specification.

The input to this stage is a breakdown of the requirements that the proposed information system is to deliver. The task of the systems design stage is to convert those requirements into a number of design alternatives from which the best will be selected. The design step therefore deals with *how* the proposed information system will deliver what is required.

Some texts and methodologies make a distinction between 'systems design' and 'detailed design'. Systems design is broader in scope and will deal with such matters as:

- choosing an appropriate database management system;
- establishing general systems security standards;
- deciding on methods of system navigation (e.g. menu systems and graphical user interfaces);
- general standards for printed report production;
- screen design standards for input and output;
- data capture requirements;
- data storage requirements.

System build

Describes the creation of software by programmers. It involves writing the software code (programming), building release versions of the software, constructing and populating the database and testing by programmers and end-users. Writing of documentation and training may also occur at this stage.

System build context

Input: requirements and design specification.
Output: working software, user guides and system documentation.

Detailed design, on the other hand, will result in a blueprint for individual system modules which will be used in the system build phase that follows. Detailed design will further define some of the aspects of system design referred to above.

If at any point during the design step it becomes obvious that the requirements as presented in the analysis step do not have a design solution (e.g. because of conflicting or incomplete requirements), it will be necessary to revisit the analysis step and determine more precisely what the new information system is to do in those particular respects.

System build (Chapter 12)

System build is the creation of software by programmers. It involves writing the software code (programming), building release versions of the software, constructing and populating the database and testing by programmers and end-users. Writing of documentation and training may also occur at this stage. The **system build context** is:

Input: requirements and design specification.

Output: working software, user guides and system documentation.

The term 'build' is one that we shall be using in addition to the more usual and ambiguous term 'implementation' which is found in many texts and methodologies. This step embraces three substeps: physical database construction, programming and testing.

Physical database construction involves the conversion of the database design from the previous step into the required tables and indexes of a relational database. The programming substep involves the construction of computer code that will handle data capture, storage, processing and output. In addition, it will be necessary to program various other operational attributes of the required system (e.g. those that stem from control design). Alongside and subsequent to the programming substep, various forms of testing will take place.

The output from the build stage will be an information system that has been tested and is available for final data conversion or take-on and live operation.

If during the build phase it appears from testing that the system does not meet the original requirements as determined during the analysis step, then it will be necessary to revisit the design step to see whether any errors were made in interpreting the systems requirements. If the design brief was correctly interpreted but the system still contains errors in the delivery of the perceived requirements, it will be necessary to revisit the analysis to determine the systems requirements more precisely.

System implementation and changeover (Chapter 12)

System implementation

Involves the transition or changeover from the old system to the new and the preparation for this such as making sure the hardware and network infrastructure for a new system are in place; testing of the system; and also human issues of how best to educate and train staff who will be using or affected by the new system.

System implementation context

Input: working system, not tested by users. Output: signed-off, operational information system installed in all locations.

System implementation covers practical issues such as making sure the hardware and network infrastructure for a new system are in place; testing of the system; and also human issues of how best to educate and train staff who will be using or affected by the new system. Implementation also involves the transition or change-over from the old system to the new. The **system implementation context** is:

Input: working system, not tested by users.

Output: signed-off, operational information system installed in all locations.

This step in the waterfall model deals with preparing for and making the change from old to new information systems. As one might expect, the systems implementation step is fraught with difficulties. Here, it will be discovered whether all the previous steps have combined to deliver an information system that does what the users actually want and that also works properly. Data will be converted from old information systems or directly entered into the new database. Finally, the new system will become operational straightaway, or in phases, or after a period of parallel running. If errors are encountered at the live running stage it may be possible for the system to continue in operation while the errors are corrected. Alternatively, it may be necessary to suspend the operation of the new system while the most significant errors are fixed. Such error correction may require any of the previous steps to be revisited, depending on the nature and severity of the error(s).

It will be clear from this short discussion that the later in the systems development process errors are discovered, the higher is the cost of putting them right. The worst-case scenario is probably for a system to have reached the live running stage only for it to be discovered that the required system was never really feasible in the first place.

Review and maintenance (Chapter 12)

Once an information system is operating under live running conditions, it will be inevitable that changes will be required over time. The maintenance phase involves two different types of maintenance. The first, known as 'unproductive maintenance', stems from errors or oversights in the original systems development which, while not preventing the system operating to an acceptable level, are still necessary to correct for it to conform with the original specification. The second form of maintenance involves the addition of new

Post-implementation review

A meeting that occurs after a system is operational to review the success of the project and learn lessons for the future.

features and facilities that extend the scope and functionality of the information system. In the early days, these may take the form of 'nice-to-haves' or 'bells and whistles' which were not deemed to be essential to the system at changeover time. Over the longer term, the system will be adapted and modified to meet changing business requirements. An activity known as the **post-implementation review** should also be undertaken. This should take place about six months after the system changeover and should review what was planned for the information system against what actually happened. Lessons learned from this exercise will be extremely valuable when the next system is developed.

BESPOKE DEVELOPMENT

The evidence from project failures has implied that traditional structured methodologies such as the SDLC have a tendency to deliver systems that arrive too late and therefore no longer meet their original requirements. Traditional methods can fail in a number of ways:

- *A gap of understanding between users and developers.* Users tend to know less about what is possible and practical from a technology perspective, while developers may be less aware of the underlying business decision-making issues which lie behind the systems development requirement.

- *Tendency of developers to isolate themselves from users.* Historically, systems developers have been able to hide behind a wall of jargon, thus rendering the user community at an immediate disadvantage when discussing IS/IT issues. While some jargon may be necessary if points are to be made succinctly, it is often used to obscure poor progress with a particular development project. The tendency for isolation is enhanced by physical separation of some computer staff in their own air-conditioned computer rooms. Developers might argue in their defence that users also have their own domain-specific jargon which adds to the problem of deciphering requirements.

- *Quality measured by closeness of product to specification.* This is a fundamental difficulty – the observation that 'the system does exactly what the specification said it would do' hides the fact that the system may still not deliver the information that the users need for decision-making purposes. The real focus should be on a comparison of the deliverables with the requirements, rather than of deliverables with a specification that was a reflection of a perceived need at a particular point in time.

- *Long development times.* A glance back at the previous section on the SDLC will reveal that the processes of analysis and design can be very laborious and time-consuming. Development times are not helped by the fact that an organisation may be facing rapidly changing business conditions and requirements may similarly be changing. There is a real risk of the 'moving goal-posts' syndrome causing havoc with a traditional approach to systems development.

- *Business needs change during the development process.* This is alluded to above. A method is needed where successive iterations in the development process are possible so that the latest requirements can be incorporated.

- *What users get isn't necessarily what they want.* The first a user may see of a new information system is at the testing or training stage. At this point, it will be seen whether the system as delivered by the IS/IT professionals is what the user actually needs. An appropriate analogy here is the purchase of a house or car simply on the basis of discussions with an estate agent or a garage, rather than by actually visiting the house or driving the car. It is unlikely that something purchased in this way will result in a satisfied customer and there is no reason to suppose that information systems developed in a similar way will be any more successful.

Rapid applications development (RAD)

A method of developing information systems which uses prototyping to achieve user involvement and faster development.

Prototyping

A prototype is a preliminary version of part of a framework of all of an information system which can be reviewed by end-users. Prototyping is an iterative process where users suggest modifications before further prototypes and the final information system is built.

Not only is there pressure from end-user management for faster systems development, IS/IT departments themselves increasingly recognise the need to make more effective use of limited human resources within their departments while at the same time quickly delivering systems that confer business benefits. All this is in a climate of rapid business change and, therefore, rapidly changing information needs. Rapid applications development (RAD) is a possible solution to these problems and pressures. This uses prototyping to involve users and increase development speed.

Rapid applications development (RAD) is a method of developing information systems which uses prototyping to achieve user involvement and faster development.

Prototyping produces a preliminary version of part or a framework of all of an information system which can be reviewed by end-users. Prototyping is an iterative process where users suggest modifications before further prototypes and the final information system are built.

Case Study 7.1 illustrates the benefits that can be derived from an RAD approach. It also hints at some disadvantages, such as the lack of a methodology to support RAD which can lead to a casual approach to a project. A later section on the Dynamic Systems Development Methodology shows how this deficiency is being made good.

CASE STUDY 7.1

Lloyds Bank Insurance Services applies RAD

When marketing people spot a business opportunity, it is often IT people who have to think and act the fastest.

Systems have to be put in place that meet the stipulated deadline, that work first time, and that fulfil the expectations of users. Otherwise the opportunity could be lost forever.

That was the situation facing the computer team at Lloyds Bank Insurance Services when a new product called MUDI (Mortgage Unemployment Disability Insurance) required a telesales quotation system that had to be fully operational by October 2nd.

Yet it was already mid-August when David Jacklin, IT Development Manager, LBIS, was informed of the need for a new application. It was a moment he remembers well. 'I faced the classic dilemma of no available resource within my team and an immovable deadline', he recalls.

However, in spite of that initial reaction and against some unexpected odds, the race against time was won. The insurance broker's objective was achieved with the help of a hard-working software house, a development environment toolset, and a fast-track approach called RAD (Rapid Application Development). In fact, the entire development took just five weeks.

Reason for the urgency at the LBIS headquarters in Haywards Heath, West Sussex was a government decision to amend the rules relating to the payment of mortgage cover out of social security in the event of a house-owner being made redundant. This opened a new insurance window which the company was determined to exploit.

LBIS, a subsidiary of Lloyds Bank and Abbey Life, is a firm of independent brokers dealing in life assurance, pensions and general insurance. Annual turnover is £100 million and 800 people are employed at Haywards Heath and six regional offices. A significant proportion of the company's business is generated through a business unit called Lloyds Bank Insurance Direct.

This is essentially a telemarketing organisation based in Bournemouth. About 70 per cent of its business comes via branches of Lloyds Bank, where advisors take an enquirer's details and ring LBID for a quote. The remaining 30 per cent is from people responding to direct mail of advertisements and telephoning in direct.

A simple version of MUDI was, in fact, available at the bank branches. But there were no facilities for accurate underwriting and anyone taking up the policy paid a straight £6.50 per £100 of cover (i.e. if the monthly mortgage payment was £300, the premium was £19.50). The new system would incorporate a complex screen replacing the existing simple paper form, providing the flexibility to quote premiums appropriate to the enquirer ranging from £4.40 to £9.40 per £100 of cover.

But first the new system had to be built. There already existed another application at Bournemouth – BIQS (Building Insurance Quotations Service) – but this ran under DOS, so what would almost certainly be a Windows system could not merely be tagged on.

Jacklin and his team had been looking at development toolsets and the RAD concept earlier in the summer. They had been particularly attracted by a RAD specialist, MDA Computing, and had already met the Croydon-based software house at the end of July.

Suddenly, with the new business-critical requirement looming, the need for RAD became urgent. 'We had no hesitation going back to MDA. They obviously knew what they were talking about and we were in urgent need of a system', says Jacklin. ➡

Some of the main attractions of RAD included the delivery of a workable first version within a very short time-scale, testing that is integrated within the development cycle, flexibility of the specification, and user involvement throughout the whole process.

Within days, Jacklin and his colleagues had agreed with MDA the RAD methods to be used. The software house underlined the need for an appropriate development environment, and recommended Enterprise Developer. This versatile toolset from Symantec had all the advanced features of a second generation client/server development system, and this was precisely what the LBIS team sought.

Such systems are repository-based and scaleable, and – specially important according to Jacklin – are driven by business rules so that future changes are easily made as business needs change. MDA evaluates every tool that comes on to the client/server market and felt that Enter-prise Developer offered the best set of second generation facilities.

Next step was a demonstration of the Symantec toolset at MDA, 'The demo convinced us. We had looked at other development tools but they did not seem meaty enough for our needs. And although MDA had never built anything with Enterprise Developer they were clearly keen to do so.' Following that demo and an agreement of project scope, work began on August 24th.

The key requirement was for a front-end system that would enable telesales staff at 30 screens to capture a caller's details and generate an immediate MUDI quotation. The system would be in Windows 3.1 and GUI based, essentially a classic PC LAN application. It would run a Compaq server using Novell.

However, MDA's first task was systems analysis. At the early stage, LBIS had not formulated all their needs – not even the design of the 'forms' that would appear on the screen. So MDA used RAD techniques to work out what the requirements would be, and spent three days at LBID in Bournemouth prototyping the forms on screen using Enterprise Developer. The software house also had to allay fears, among a user-team with little experience of Windows, about mouse-driven systems.

In order to get the project started, the use of a Watcom database was assumed. However, following discussions within LBIS, it was decided that for strategic and operational support reasons the use of Oracle was preferred.

MDA had to accommodate a new database in already tight development cycle. The ability to adapt to the fresh circumstances and still deliver the system on time was a big tribute to the software house's RAD methods and the Symantec toolset. (In fact, there were minor compatibility problems which disappeared when LBIS upgraded to Enterprise Developer 2.5 at the beginning of November.)

The system was delivered in the last week of September for final testing in readiness to go live the following Monday. By then, LBIS's own technical team had adjusted the BIQS system so that the telesales people could flip to it from MUDI, depending on the caller's needs, with a simple keyboard Alt/Tab depression.

On 'live' day, the telesales team processed 200 customer quotations with scarcely a hitch. Jacklin, MDA and Symantec had every right to feel pleased with themselves. A business need had demanded IT support, and that support was implemented on time.

Now the end-users, equipped with telephone headsets, enter personal details which affect ratings, such as sex, post code and occupation, on to a GUI screen. The quotation then appears on the same screen. There are five other, supporting screens labelled status, comments, letter print, rating and search for existing customer.

A happy Jacklin concludes, 'Here was a software house that gave us what we needed. They were always confident they could do something with Enterprise Developer and within time. There was no slippage despite it being their first real use of the Symantec product and despite the change in database midway through. I think that says something for Enterprise Developer too. And we went live on the big day.

'We like RAD and we shall use it again. In a market-oriented organisation like LBIS, we always have a need to react to business changes quickly, and I suspect that within 18 months we could need a system to handle all six of our insurance products.'

He adds, 'The system has allowed LBIS to launch a more competitive product than would otherwise have been possible, and we have sold more than we would have done. It had to be in at the right time or we would have missed the boat. From a technical point of view, it forced us to go to Windows which was always our eventual intention. All this, and the system will pay for itself before Christmas!'

Source: www.dsdm.org

QUESTIONS

1. Why and how did the company choose the RAD approach used for this project?

2. What disadvantages of the RAD method can you identify from the study?

3. Do you think that Lloyds can be confident that future RAD projects will be successful?

Since modern systems development using prototyping is an iterative approach, the sequential model defined in Figure 7.4 is a simplification of the actual process. Figure 7.5 gives a more realistic representation of systems development. It is apparent that all the phases within the SDLC are still present, but that the activities of analysis, design, test and review repeat within the prototyping phase.

Figure 7.5 The role of prototyping within the systems development lifecycle

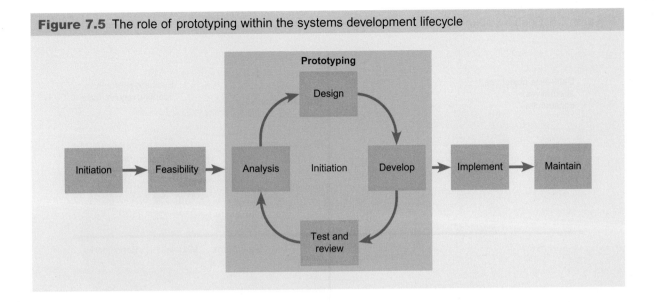

The spiral model

Spiral model

An iterative systems development in which the stages of analysis, design, code and review repeat as new features.

The **spiral model** is an iterative systems development model developed by Boehm (1988) which incorporates risk assessment.

The spiral model was developed in recognition of the fact that systems development projects tend to repeat the stages of analysis, design and code as part of the prototyping process. Each spiral consists of four main activities, as shown in Figure 7.6. The activities are:

1. *Planning* – setting project objectives, defining alternatives.
2. *Risk analysis* – analysis of alternatives and the identification and solution of risks.
3. *Engineering* – equivalent to the build phase of the SDLC with coding and testing.
4. *Customer evaluation* – testing of the product by customers.

It can be seen from Figure 7.6 that the model is closely related to RAD, since it implies iterative development with a review possible after each iteration or spiral, which corresponds to the production of one prototype or incremental version.

Before the first spiral starts the requirements plan is produced, so it can be seen that the spiral model does not detail the initiation and analysis phase of the SDLC, focusing on design and build.

Although the spiral model has not been applied widely in industry, proponents of this model argue that it includes the best features of both the classic SDLC and the prototyping approach. It also adds validation of requirements and design, together with risk analysis, which is often overlooked in RAD projects.

Agile and lean software development

Lean software development

Lean software development is an approach to software development where software is developed and deployed in small and useful feature sets which work incrementally.

Whilst the spiral model may not have been widely adopted un industry and commerce, two of the more recent developments appear to be making some inroads into the commercial domain. Mary and Tom Poppendieck (2003) originally set out seven principles behind **lean software development** and provided 22 toolkits or best practice guides to underpin them. These principles have been refined and can now be summarised as follows:

- *Eliminate waste* – this can be achieved by concentrating on the 20 per cent of the software features that deliver 80 per cent of the system's value, reducing requirements

Figure 7.6 Boehm's spiral model of systems development

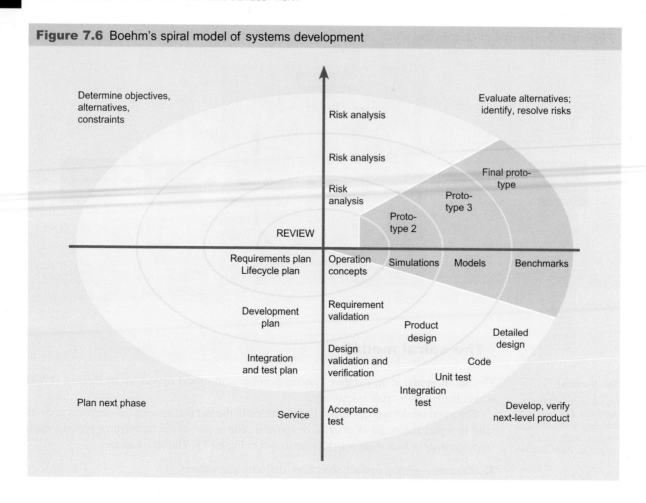

churning (moving goalposts) by delaying detailed software specifications and ensuring that development processes allow organisational boundaries to be crossed easily by eliminating buffers between functional business areas.

- *Create knowledge* – teams should adopt a scientific approach to selecting alternatives by establishing hypotheses, testing them and creating concise documentation; everyone should follow current best-known practice in standards while being actively encouraged to challenge and improve the standards; performance should become predictable through the development of an organisation's capacity to respond to the future as it unfolds.

- *Build quality in* – here, testing forms a key aspect of the approach by adopting a test-driven approach to software development where automated unit and user acceptance tests are built in.

- *Defer commitment* – the key elements of this principle include the abolition of the idea that a complete system specification is a good way to start a systems development project; in addition, the system architecture should be able to support the addition of any feature at any time, options should be left open for as long as possible and irreversible decisions should be delayed to the 'last responsible' moment so that as much can be learned as possible before commitment.

- *Deliver fast* – the objective here is to eliminate the buffers that slow things down by aggressively limiting the size of lists, queues and 'things in process' so that the organisation can limit the work it is undertaking to its capacity to deliver; it is claimed that rapid delivery, high quality and low cost are fully compatible and that companies can enjoy cost advantages and be more attuned to their customers' needs when they compete on the basis of speed.

- *Respect people* – this principle enshrines the view that the most sustainable competitive advantage comes from having thinking and engaged people mutually committed to achieving a common goal.

- *Improve the system* – here, measurement forms an important element including the measurement of process capability with cycle times and the measurement of team performance with delivered business value; in addition there should be a focus on the entire value stream from customer request to deployed software and the complete product should be delivered, not just the software.

In summary, the lean approach to software development emphasises what is essentially an incremental approach to software development where software is developed and deployed in small and useful feature sets which work incrementally. This 'feedback-driven' approach to software development is in contrast to the traditional waterfall model where software development proceeds in a series of discrete steps, each of which should be completed before the next one can proceed and where project plan is based on a series of forecasts about what is likely to happen at each stage of the development project.

If lean software development relates primarily to an overarching philosophy behind software development, then agile software development tends to relate more to the software engineering aspects of systems development. The term 'agile methods' has been around since 2001 and today encompasses a number of agile software development methods including:

- Adaptive Software Development (ASD);
- Agile Unified Process (AUP);
- Scrum;
- Dynamic Systems Development Methodology (DSDM).

DSDM is dealt with in more detail below. Of the other methods mentioned, it is worth discussing AUP in a little more detail. AUP is a simplified version of the Rational Unified Process (RUP). As with RUP, there are four phases in the development cycle:

1. *Inception* – this is where the initial scope of the project is identified including a potential architecture for the system, and the obtaining of initial project funding and stakeholder acceptance. A business case must be established along with an initial risk assessment and project description.

2. *Elaboration* – a model describing the business problems to be solved is developed alongside 'use case' descriptions (sequences of events that, taken together, lead to a system doing something useful).

3. *Construction* – the key task here is in building working software on a regular, incremental basis which meets the highest-priority needs of project stakeholders; the bulk of the coding takes place in this phase and in larger projects, several construction iterations may be developed in an effort to divide the project components as defined by the 'use cases' manageable segments that produce demonstrable prototypes.

4. *Transition* – finally, the software products move from the software development area to the end-user where activities such as training of the end-users and maintainers and beta testing (see Chapter 12) of the system to validate it against the end-users' expectations take place; the product is also checked against the quality criteria as set in the inception phase.

In summary, lean software development and agile methods are complementary and together they provide an alternative to the traditional waterfall model. Whilst it would be unwise to say that one approach is better than the other, it is fair to say that as organisations increasingly seek to compete using the speed with which they are able to respond to their customers, then the pressure to develop and implement software solutions rapidly in order to maintain competitive advantage may tip the balance towards more widespread adoption of these newer development methods.

CASE STUDY 7.2

Use of waterfall v. agile methods at Mellon Financial

Mellon Financial's shift to agile software development is part of an emerging trend. 'Every investment bank and hedge fund I've spoken to is looking at agile', says Sungard's Chapman. A relatively new term, agile development is based on iterative development – developing software in small, manageable chunks that can be modified as requirements change, yet using a disciplined software delivery mechanism.

Historically, the software development approach used throughout Wall Street has been the 'waterfall' method, which calls for strict, lengthy analysis and documentation of requirements. For a one-year project, for example, three to six months might be spent on needs analysis. 'The business people are expected to define 100 percent of their requirements up front before the project even starts', Chapman says. 'People get stuck in this analysis paralysis– they spend months and months trying to define what they want.'

Another three to six months can be devoted to soft-ware design, then the actual program finally is written. 'Inevitably what happens is requirements change, integration becomes very difficult and all the risky software development happens at the end of the development effort', Chapman explains. 'The waterfall approach has a horrible track record of delivery.'

Agile software development is designed to deliver software more quickly yet maintain high quality. In agile methods, every two or four weeks, businesspeople get a small amount of code to review and the opportunity to change the requirements. 'Imagine a hedge fund where traditionally a new credit derivatives trading system would take a year to build using the waterfall approach, with businesspeople writing six months' worth of documentation versus using an agile approach, where some of the system is delivered in two weeks, and it's OK if you change your mind', Chapman says. 'For the hedge funds particularly, agile is an extraordinarily good fit because the portfolio managers want to get things done quickly.'

But not every project lends itself to short iterations, Chapman concedes. 'On Wall Street it's not so easy because there are a lot of other systems you need to integrate with', he says. 'But I think there are parts of agile you can use on every project to improve it.'

Agile development has three levels: developer, project and enterprise. 'Nobody on Wall Street is using agile at the enterprise level', Chapman says. 'A lot of education needs to take place within the banks – it's going to take some time. But I think every project could gain some benefit from trying to break down the project into more-manageable chunks that can be delivered in a more iterative and agile way.'

Agile methods even improve software quality, Chapman contends, because they emphasize testing. Agile methods encourage developers to do their own testing, often requiring them to write the tests before they write any code and to develop automated testing routines for the programs they deliver.

'Agile development approaches and CMMI are compliant with each other – you can use CMM and CMMI to make agile software development better', Chapman adds. On the other hand, he asserts, trying to use CMM and CMMI on top of waterfall development approaches will just weigh projects down with bureaucracy and paperwork.

Source: www.wallstreetandtech.com/advancedtrading/showArticle.jhtml?articleID=199601961&cid=RSSfeed_TechWeb accessed via www.computing.co.uk

QUESTIONS

1. What does the observation that 'requirements change, integration becomes very difficult and all the risky software development happens at the end of the development effort' suggest about the traditional waterfall approach to software development with respect to system design?

2. Do you think there are any dangers in trying to take short cuts around the traditional approach to systems design?

Dynamic Systems Development Methodology (DSDM)

Dynamic Systems Development Methodology (DSDM)

A methodology that describes how RAD can be approached. The latest version is named DSDM Atern.

The ideas behind RAD have been around for several years, but a methodology that encapsulates its principles has only recently emerged. In the UK, an organisation known as the DSDM Consortium has put together a set of underlying principles. These are given in full below, together with a commentary provided by the consortium. In total, DSDM (Dynamic Systems Development Methodology) has nine key principles, as shown in the following box.

The nine principles of the Dynamic Systems Development Methodology (DSDM)

1. *Active user involvement is imperative.* DSDM is a user-centred approach. If users are not closely involved throughout the development life-cycle, delays will occur as decisions are made. Users no longer sit outside the development team acting as suppliers of information and reviewers of results but are active participants in the development process.

2. *DSDM teams must be empowered to make decisions.* DSDM teams consist of both developers and users. They must be able to make decisions as requirements are refined and possibly changed. They must be able to agree that certain levels of functionality, usability, etc. are acceptable without frequent recourse to higher level management.

3. *The focus is on frequent delivery of products.* A product-based approach is more flexible than an activity-based one. The work of a DSDM team is concentrated on products that can be delivered in an agreed period of time. This enables the team to select the best approach to achieving the products required in the time available. By keeping each period of time short, the team can easily decide which activities are necessary and sufficient to achieve the right products.

4. *Fitness for business purpose is the essential criterion for acceptance of deliverables.* The focus of DSDM is on delivering the business functionality at the required time. The system can be more rigorously engineered later if such an approach is acceptable. Traditionally the focus has been on satisfying the contents of a requirements document and conforming to previous deliverables, while losing sight of the fact that the requirements are often inaccurate and the previous deliverables are flawed.

5. *Iterative and incremental development is necessary to converge on an accurate business solution.* DSDM allows systems to evolve incrementally. Therefore the developers can make full use of feedback from the users. Moreover partial solutions can be delivered to satisfy immediate business needs. Iteration is inherent in all software development. DSDM recognises this and, by making it explicit, strengthens the use of iteration. When rework is not explicitly recognised in a development life-cycle, the return to previously 'completed' work is surrounded by controlling procedures which slow development down. Since rework is built into the DSDM process, the development can proceed more quickly during iteration.

6. *All changes during development are reversible.* Backtracking is a feature of DSDM. However in some circumstances it may be easier to reconstruct than to backtrack. This depends on the nature of the change and the environment in which it was made.

7. *Requirements are baselined at a high level.* Baselining high-level requirements means 'freezing' and agreeing the purpose and scope of the system at a level which allows for detailed investigation of what the requirements imply. Further baselines can be established later in the development.

8. *Testing is integrated throughout the lifecycle.* Testing is not treated as a separate activity. As the system is developed incrementally, it is also tested and reviewed by both developers and users to ensure that the development is moving forward; not only in the right business direction, but that it is technically sound. Early in DSDM, the testing focus is on understanding the business needs and priorities. Towards the end of a project, the focus is on assuring users and developers that the whole system operates effectively.

9. *A collaborative and co-operative approach between all stakeholders is essential.* The nature of DSDM projects means that low-level requirements are not necessarily fixed when the developers are originally approached to carry out the work. Hence the short-term direction that a project takes must be quickly decided without recourse to restrictive change control procedures. When development is procured from an external supplier, both the vendor and the purchaser organisations should aim for as efficient a process as possible while allowing for flexibility during both the pre-contract phase and when the contracted work is carried out.

Source: www.dsdm.org

Avison and Fitzgerald (2006) outline an approach to rapid applications development which embraces many of the principles outlined above. For them, the RAD approach:

- is based on evolutionary prototyping rather than the traditional lifecycle approach;
- identifies key users and involves them in workshops at the early stages of development;
- obtains commitment from the business users;
- requires the use of CASE (computer-aided software engineering) tools for system building.

Typical RAD activities include:

- joint requirements planning (JRP) to determine high-level management requirements;
- joint applications design (JAD) using prototyping tools to explore processes, interfaces, screens, reports, dialogues etc., which are then developed and modelled using entity modelling, dataflow diagrams, action diagrams and function decomposition diagrams;
- transformation of user designs to detailed design and code generation, often with the assistance of CASE tools;
- a cutover phase involving more testing, functional-level training, training for organisational change and adaptation, conversion, parallel running and, finally, live running.

The result of the rapid applications development approach should be new information systems that more closely meet the requirements of the intended users, not least because the requirements will not have changed significantly over a relatively short development timescale.

The following general points can be made regarding bespoke development:

- Bespoke development is much more expensive than alternative software acquisition methods – the software that is produced is unique and must be tailored to the precise needs of the users.
- The time taken to develop a new, bespoke computer-based information system is significantly longer than the period needed to purchase an off-the-shelf software package. That said 'rapid applications development' claims to reduce substantially the time taken to develop bespoke software.
- There will be situations where bespoke development provides the only realistic way of producing the required software – high degrees of organisational or application uniqueness or the need to integrate a new information system very tightly with existing applications are common reasons for this.

PURCHASE OF AN OFF-THE-SHELF PACKAGE

The traditional waterfall or SDLC model as described above was discussed in the context of a system that is being acquired using a bespoke development approach. However, as we have seen, there are methods of information system acquisition that do not require the development of bespoke solutions. For packaged software, that application of the SDLC stages would typically be as follows.

- *Initiation.* This step clearly applies regardless of the acquisition method: there must be some kind of stimulus which creates the notion that a computer-based information system is needed to respond to a business opportunity or problem.
- *Feasibility.* Again, this step must be followed. Indeed, it is during the feasibility step that an investigation will be undertaken into the technical aspects of the required system and a make-or-buy decision will be made. A 'buy' decision indicates that a solution is probably available off the shelf; a 'make' decision indicates that a bespoke solution is probably required because of a combination of factors, as discussed above.

■ *Analysis*. This is as important a step in the acquisition of off-the-shelf software as it is in building bespoke software solutions. System requirements must be determined and catalogued so that they can be compared with the features offered by the package. Many packages can be configured in different ways to meet the different needs of customers. With complicated systems or those that offer a wide range of functionality, the configuration process can be a demanding one and may require actions by end-users, the organisation's IS department, the package vendor or any combination of these. Part of the analysis exercise, therefore, will be to determine the extent to which a software package may be configured to meet the organisation's needs.

■ *Design*. It is here that significant differences are found when compared with bespoke software design. An off-the-shelf package will have been designed with many different businesses in mind and will offer a range of features to satisfy most requirements. The 'how' aspect of software acquisition has, therefore, already been determined and the system subsequently built. The task for the purchaser of an off-the-shelf package is to compare the design features required (e.g. menu systems, database design or user interface design, ease and scope of configuration) against those offered by different packages.

■ *Build*. With an off-the-shelf package, the system has already been built by the vendor. As part of the feature set offered by a package, there may be an ability to customise aspects of the software product by setting certain parameters. For example, an accounting package may be set up either to interface with a sales order processing system from the same vendor, or to offer the ability to interface with a package offered by another supplier or with a bespoke system. There will also need to be a testing phase where all the relevant features of the package are run in a simulated live environment. This might, for example, be done in parallel with existing information processing activities.

■ *Implementation/changeover*. As with a bespoke software solution, data will have to be converted or entered from old computer- or paper-based information system. One of the benefits of purchasing off-the-shelf software is that the product should be free from major bugs and errors. The purchaser should be confident, therefore, that the software product will work as specified from the outset.

■ *Maintenance and review*. Maintenance and enhancements of the software will differ from those in a bespoke solution. Whereas bespoke software can be enhanced over time by the developer (either in-house or by a third party), an off-the-shelf package will differ in a number of ways. Enhancements to the package will normally be made available by the vendor as a new release. Sometimes it is possible for a business organisation to build its own enhancements or 'add-ons' to the package. There is a danger that such bespoke amendments to standard packages may be lost if the organisation buys a new release of the software. In addition, maintenance is usually covered by a separate maintenance agreement after the original guarantee period. There may be differential pricing depending on whether the maintenance agreement is to cover simply 'bug fixing' or whether it is to entitle the user to the latest version of the software at no or little additional cost. As with the bespoke solution, a post-implementation review should be undertaken.

Software selection criteria for packaged software

There is no doubt that by following a structured sequence of steps when acquiring a software package the probability of a successful implementation will be increased. However, package selection and purchase is also governed by an additional set of software selection criteria. Sahay and Gupta (2003) have produced a comprehensive analysis of both primary and secondary drivers as they apply to software selection. Although they were researching with particular reference to business supply chain solutions, their findings can be applied just as well in a generic way. *Primary drivers* are those that form a set of essential requirements, which, if not met, mean that the software solution will not be suitable for the organisation. These primary drivers, in descending order of importance are:

- *Features.* This refers to the software features and functionality of the package under consideration. Aspects such as availability and functionality of modules, ability to integrate with existing applications, speed of operation when up and running, implementation time, portability of the package to other hardware platforms and operating system environments.

- *Technology.* Here, the software acquisition team needs to consider the compatibility of the solution under consideration with existing hardware, operating systems, database management systems, Internet, networking and e-commerce setups. Sahay and Gupta also consider that a high level of technology support for business integration is essential.

- *Support and services.* Of particular importance with packaged software is support for day-to-day operational requirements. This means that problems with any software module or group of modules must be dealt with by the software vendor through their technical maintenance function. Aspects such as pre-sales support (for example to assist with hardware and networking configuration before purchase and implementation), automated support (remote identification, diagnosis and fixing of software problems), software documentation, user guides and manuals and training are also important components of this driver. Version support is also an important consideration, since older versions of software will cease to be supported after a certain period of time.

- *Cost.* Software vendors have different approaches to the pricing of their products. The organisation that is purchasing the software package will typically want to meet their qualitative and quantitative requirements as quickly as possible and at the lowest possible cost. Therefore, software vendors tend to offer the basic package and a low cost, but charge much higher sums for additional hardware, software modules or special equipment. The charging mechanisms also vary from vendor to vendor. Some will charge per module, others per user, and many a combination of the two. In addition, the purchaser will be expected to pay an annual maintenance fee (typically 20% of the purchase price), planning, implementation and installation costs, plus any upgrade costs when new versions of the software are released.

- *Customisation.* Each organisation that purchases a software package will have slightly different requirements. Some of these can be taken care of through con-figuration options within the standard software package. Other, more specialised, needs may possibly only be met through the provision of customised versions of the software. Some software vendors will offer customised versions, while others will not. Customisation can make a software package a better fit with business needs, but the costs can be high. In particular, it must be remembered that any customisation will have to re-applied in subsequent software releases, at extra cost.

The secondary drivers identified by Sahay and Gupta (2003) are those requirements that are less important and non-essential in nature, but which add value to the customer. These drivers will differ in importance from purchaser to purchaser, and some may be as important as the primary drivers for some purchasers.

- *Vendor strength.* When purchasing a software package from a vendor, it is important to know how strong the vendor is in terms of their financial position, number and quality of their personnel, the vendor's understanding of the business and market in which the purchaser operates and the vendor's experience in this area. Lack of vendor support when problems arise and insufficient product development can leave the purchaser at a considerable operational and competitive disadvantage.

- *Vendor vision.* This is linked with the previous driver insofar as the prospective package purchaser will be interested in how the vendor intends to improve the software product and expand the market for it. In some cases, vendor and purchaser will work closely together in order to develop the product further: the vendor ends up with a superior product, while the purchaser may be able to negotiate a lower purchase price.

- *Industries covered.* Some vendors will focus on a very narrow market segment while others will aim their products at a wider audience. This could be of particular importance to an organisation that operates in many markets and that needs a software package that will operate across a number of sectors.

- *Other drivers.* Included under this broad heading are such factors as ease of use, versatility, flexibility, responsiveness, error handling and security issues. Some of these factors may be such that they appear as primary drivers (e.g. as a feature of the software product.

These drivers, both primary and secondary, will ultimately have their expression in the set of software requirements and desirable design features as noted in the analysis and design elements of the SDLC. In addition factors such as cost and functionality may also be a feature of the feasibility study – i.e. can a package be purchased that meets the organisation's economic, technical, operational and organisational feasibility constraints?

USER-DEVELOPED APPLICATIONS

User-developed software

Software written by non-IS professionals, i.e. the business users.

User-developed applications (software) 'should' be developed in line with the steps normally covered during the bespoke development process. The main difference is that end-user-developed applications are usually on a much smaller scale than those developed for corporate use. However, many of the tools and techniques associated with large-scale corporate bespoke development still have a role, albeit a more limited one, in end-user-developed information systems. As before, each step in the waterfall model will be discussed separately. The advantages and disadvantages of end-user development are described in detail later (in Chapter 16).

- *Initiation.* The stimulus for end-user information system development will typically come from a personal or departmental requirement which can be satisfied by employing easy-to-use end-user development tools. Such systems may be standalone with no linkages to any other end-user or corporate system, or they may use databases and database extracts from corporate information systems (perhaps with additional database tables created by the user) and manipulate the data in order to produce information not previously made available. In the latter case, the data may already exist in the corporate database, but the processing necessary to produce the information has not been included as a core part of the application.

- *Feasibility.* Part of the feasibility exercise is for the user to be sure that the necessary and appropriate end-user development tools exist or can be acquired in order to proceed with the development. A second aspect is an analysis of the cost involved in end-user-developed software: while an end-user is producing software, their 'normal' tasks either remain undone or have to be done by someone else. Therefore, end-user applications development needs to be justified on economic grounds.

- *Analysis.* One of the benefits is that an end-user need not present information systems requirements to an IS/IT specialist for subsequent development. This therefore reduces the risk of mistranslating information systems requirements and increases the probability that the developed system is what the user actually wants. The end-user may still find it useful to apply some of the tools associated with the analysis phase such as those discussed later (in Chapter 10) , although clearly they will be used on a much smaller scale.

- *Design*. End-user-developed software has a tendency to be developed more on a 'trial and error' basis than through the use of formal design techniques. When it works well, this can result in the faster development of applications software. The downside is that poor design may result in a system that at best does not work quite as it should and at worst a system that actually results in incorrect information being produced. Incorrect information can have various results, ranging from short-term irritation to corporate decision-making errors with large financial consequences. One of the most useful tools in end-user design is entity relationship modelling, which should be used in conjunction with logical and physical database design. The probability is that if the database design and associated data validation rules are correct, then the system is more likely to produce the information that is required.

- *Build*. Recent improvements in the availability of inexpensive development tools such as Visual Basic for the PC have made it much easier for the end-user developer to build systems without recourse to difficult programming techniques. As end-user development is now much easier than it was previously, emphasis can be placed on the functionality which the system is to offer. Also, development times are speeded up, and this provides for the effective use of iterative prototyping in this step.

- *Implementation/changeover*. This step is less critical than for company-wide information systems. Data are either locally generated or extracted from central databases, where it can be assumed that the data are validated and verified as correct. In fact, the term 'changeover' is probably not a good one in this context – 'live running' may be a better one. It is quite possible that an end-user-developed system is capable of producing useful information even before it becomes a 'live' product. A risk is that end-user-developed software may not have been tested sufficiently thoroughly and this raises an important question of the management of such software. We will deal with this later (in Chapter 16).

- *Maintenance and review*. All software has to be maintained in some way. In many respects, the maintenance of end-user-developed software is more problematic than for other forms of software acquisition. This is because end-user-developed systems are often not documented and they may employ obscure techniques in their construction.

End-user development is discussed in more detail later (in Chapter 16).

CASE STUDY 7.3

Lascelles Fine Foods

Lascelles Fine Foods (LFFL) is a fictitious example of a long-established company operating in the food industry. The company has its administrative headquarters in Ashville and manufactures on an adjacent site. All customer deliveries are from the Ashville-based warehouse. In addition, LFFL purchases finished and semi-finished food products from other manufacturers which it then finishes before resale.

The company has enjoyed steady growth in recent years and is now seeking to capitalise on the current fashion for quality and healthy food products. LFFL's

Source: Thinkstock photos

turnover is £16 million with net profitability of 6.3 per cent of turnover. It is hoping to gain a competitive edge by providing quality food products which meet all present and anticipated quality standards and to this end will be applying for BS5750 accreditation within the next six months. It is hoping to increase turnover by 10 per cent per year after inflation over the next five years and increase net profitability to 9 per cent of turnover over the same period.

LFFL's main operations are divided into four main areas:

- sales and marketing;
- warehousing and distribution;

- manufacturing;
- finance.

All information recording and internal communication is paper based and relies on a range of preprinted documents which are then used as appropriate.

The sales department

LFFL has a diverse customer base, ranging from small health food shops to major supermarket chains. Orders can be one of two types: standard orders placed in advance for delivery in a specific week or priority orders placed for immediate delivery.

Orders are placed either directly through sales office 'account handlers' or through field sales persons (each customer has one sales person). Each customer is allocated an account handler who acts as the main liaison point within LFFL. Besides receiving orders, the account handler is responsible for cash collection, ensuring satisfactory progress of the order and handling day-to-day queries. Customers are also placed into sales categories based on geographic location, volume of business and type of customer (e.g. specialist store vs supermarket chain). The sales director is apt to change his mind about which category a customer is in and which category means what.

Order processing

Once an order is taken, it is recorded on a preprinted order form. One copy is retained by the sales department and two copies are sent to warehousing and distribution.

Warehousing and distribution sort all order forms into date order. When an order is due to be delivered, products are picked from the warehouse and loaded into the appropriate vehicle.

When an order is delivered, it is accompanied by a consignment note and an invoice. The customer is required to check the delivery against the invoice and note any errors on the consignment note. The delivery driver returns with a signed copy of the consignment note and if any errors are noted a corrected invoice is sent to the customer.

Warehousing and distribution

LFFL stores finished products, bought-in products and raw materials in the warehouse. The warehouse is divided into three areas:

- the general zone, comprising a high-rise bulk storage area with a floor-level picking area;
- the cool zone, comprising low-level storage at 2 to 4°C;
- the frozen zone, with temperatures held to −18°C.
- In addition to their role in the order processing cycle, other activities are also performed:
- internal warehouse movements from high-rise locations to ground-level areas and vice versa;
- receiving products and raw materials from suppliers and returned products from customers;
- issuing raw materials to manufacturing in response to submitted requisition forms;
- receiving finished products from manufacturing and any unused raw materials.

Information about quantities of finished goods and raw materials in stock is recorded in a card file, which has to be searched manually for the appropriate entry when updating is required.

Manufacturing

Manufacturing ranges in complexity from simple repackaging of bulk-purchased materials to complex mixing and cooking activities.

Recipes are recorded on 7″ by 5″ cards and include details of the required ingredients as well as the processing which is to take place.

Finance

LFFL's finance department is divided into three areas:

- *accounts payable* – when LFFL makes purchases, suppliers will invoice them; LFFL uses a manual purchase ledger to manage these accounts;
- *financial accounting* – management of all monies flowing in and out of the company together with compliance with legal accounting requirements;
- *management accounting* – internal accounting information necessary to manage the business more effectively.

The accounts receivable area is handled by the account handlers who use a manual sales ledger and make a weekly return to the finance department on the state of their customers' accounts.

Specific business issues

There are a number of specific issues which relate to the activities of each department. These are detailed below.

Sales

- The status of an order cannot easily be determined without pestering the warehouse.
- Many customer complaints occur due to delivery of wrong products, orders delivered too late, incomplete orders and faulty products.
- Warehousing does not deliver the most important orders first – small orders are often given priority over larger orders from major retailers.
- Orders often cannot be delivered on time because manufacturing produces too late and in insufficient quantity.

Warehousing and distribution

- Many items have a limited shelf life – warehousing often fails to rotate the stock properly.
- Actual stock levels are rarely in step with the recorded stock levels – this may be due to pilfering, poor update of stock records or both.

- The sales department often accepts priority orders for products which are not in stock.
- Manufacturing bypasses the normal requisition procedures and simply takes raw materials as required – it also often fails to return unused materials to warehousing.

Finance

- The sales returns from the account handlers are often incomplete.
- There are several bad debts which cannot be recovered – this is attributed to poor credit control procedures.
- Management accounting is very difficult due to a general lack of accurate information from other departments.
- Financial accounts are often published late due to lack of accurate information.

Manufacturing

- Warehousing is slow to respond to requests for raw materials, thus necessitating correct procedures being bypassed (especially when the sales department is applying pressure).
- Lack of accurate forecasting makes it difficult for production to be planned ahead and adequate supplies of raw materials to be secured.

General

- There is a rapid turnover of staff, especially in the sales area where the pressure from customers can be in-tense. In addition, field sales personnel are apt to make promises which cannot be kept and new sales personnel are often thrown in at the deep end with little formal training for their jobs.
- There is a high level of sickness in the warehousing and distribution area, due mainly to inadequate provision of lifting equipment.
- There is a perceived lack of management and technical support which has resulted in a general lowering of morale.

Future plans

The managing director, Clive Moor, has indicated that he would like to replace the existing paper-based systems with 'computers of some kind'. With such a move, he is hoping to improve on the communication of information at all levels in the organisation. However, Mr Moor knows little about computer hardware or applications software except that it seems to cost rather a lot.

In order to proceed with the computerisation programme, Mr Moor has asked the following senior managers to produce a plan:

- Paula Barlow – finance director;
- Terry Watson – sales and marketing director;
- Peter Jackson – manufacturing operations director;
- Frances Clarke – warehousing and distribution director.

However, these directors have varying degrees of enthusiasm for the project, together with a desire to minimise the risk of damage or exposure within their own departments. One of the key decisions which must be made will be how LFFL acquires the necessary applications software. One option will be to hire relevant IT staff and build bespoke applications, while another will be to purchase off-the-shelf packages. Yet another option will be for end-users to develop their own applications. This last option may prove awkward, since there is very little IT expertise among the end-users.

QUESTIONS

1. Which method(s) of business systems software acquisition would you recommend to LFFL? Explain and justify your answer.

2. Assuming that LFFL decides to go down the route of purchasing off-the-shelf packages, what steps do you recommend it takes to ensure that the applications which are selected meet their requirements?

SUMMARY

1. Acquisition refers to the approach for sourcing BIS. Alternative acquisition methods include:

   - *off-the-shelf* – purchased from a software vendor;
   - *bespoke* – 'built from scratch';
   - *end-user-developed* – self-explanatory.

   Complex and organisation-wide BIS such as e-business systems often require hybrid sourcing approaches and enterprise applications integration of different components from different vendors.

2. A useful model for the stages of a BIS acquisition project is the systems development lifecycle model (SDLC). The stages described in later sections of Part 2 are:

   - *initiation* – identification of opportunity or problem to be solved by BIS;
   - *feasibility* – assessing cost–benefit and acquisition alternatives;

- *analysis* – assessing the user and business requirements;
- *design* – producing a specification for the approach of producing a structure for the BIS;
- *build* – coding, documenting, data migration, testing;
- *implementation* – installation, testing, changeover;
- *maintenance and review* – live system review and update.

3. End-user development tends to neglect the feasibility, analysis, design and testing phases. The design and build phases are relatively insignificant for off-the-shelf acquisition.

4. The classic SDLC model of system acquisition has experienced problems of insufficient user involvement – leading to poor delivery of business-user requirements and a protracted lifecycle which may also result in loss of competitive advantage or budget overruns.

5. RAD and prototyping approaches encapsulated in lean and agile approaches to software development and as illustrated in the Dynamic Systems Development Methodology (DSDM) are aimed at solving the problems of the stage models. The key characteristics of this approach are an iterative approach with frequent delivery of prototypes coupled with user involvement throughout the project.

EXERCISES

Self-assessment exercises

1. Explain what the main similarities and differences are between bespoke development and end-user development.

2. Why would a small business be more constrained in its choice of software acquisition method than a large one?

3. What are the main differences between the analysis and design steps of the traditional waterfall model of systems development?

4. What are the main components of the system build stage?

5. Explain how the application of the waterfall model differs between (a) the purchase of an off-the-shelf package and (b) an end-user-developed application.

6. Briefly review the main advantages and disadvantages of bespoke development when compared with off-the-shelf packages.

Discussion questions

1. 'The rise of rapid applications development is mainly a response to the failure of traditional systems development methodologies to deliver the right system at the right price and at the right time.' Discuss.

2. 'End-user applications development would be far less popular if central IS/IT departments did not have such a large applications development backlog.' Discuss.

Essay questions

1. What do you believe to be the main differences between large and small organisations in deciding the best approach for information systems acquisition?

2. In what circumstances do you think that rapid applications development would be (a) appropriate and (b) inappropriate when carrying out systems analysis and design?

3. Is the end-user development approach to business software development something which you think should be encouraged, or do you believe that applications software for business is best left to information systems professionals?

4. Compare and contrast the traditional waterfall model with lean and agile approaches to software development with particular emphasis on the ability to deliver business value.

Examination questions

1. Explain the terms 'bespoke development', 'off-the-shelf package' and 'end-user computing'. Illustrate your answer with some of the reasons cited in favour of each of these methods of application software acquisition.

2. Give three advantages usually associated with prototyping.

3. During a bespoke development project, the systems development lifecycle will include a number of steps from requirements analysis, design and system. Which of these steps is relevant to an off-the-shelf system? Which activities might be involved?

4. Explain how the spiral model of systems development which can be applied to RAD differs from the traditional waterfall model. Which do you believe represents the best method of developing information systems?

References

Avison, D.E. and Fitzgerald, G. (2006) *Information Systems Development: Methodologies, Techniques and Tools*, 4th edition, Blackwell, Oxford

Boehm, B. (1988) 'A spiral model of software development and enhancement', *IEEE Computer*, 21, 5, May, 61–72

Poppendieck, M. and Poppendieck, T. (2009) *Leading Lean Software Development*, Addison-Wesley, Upper Saddle River, NJ

Sahay, B.S. and Gupta, A.K. (2003) 'Development of software selection criteria for supply chain solutions', *Industrial Management and Data Systems* 103, 2, 97–110

Senn, J. (2004) *Information Technology: Principles, Practices and Opportunities*, 3rd edition, Prentice-Hall, Englewood Cliffs, NJ

Further reading

Curtis, G. and Cobham, D. (2008), *Business Information Systems: Analysis, Design and Practice*, 6th edition, Financial Times Prentice Hall, Harlow.

Kendall, K.E. and Kendall, J.E. (2013) *Systems Analysis and Design*, 9th edition, Prentice-Hall, Englewood Cliffs, NJ.

Martin, R.C. (2011) *Agile Software Development: Principles, Patterns and Practices*, Prentice-Hall, Upper Saddle River, NJ.

Poppendieck, M. and Poppendieck, T. (2009) *Leading Lean Software Development*, Addison-Wesley, Upper Saddle River, NJ.

Tudor, D.J. and Tudor, I.J. (2010) *The DSDM Atern Student Workbook*, Galatea Training Services, Rochdale.

Web links

www.sei.cmu.edu Carnegie Mellon Software Engineering Institute.

www.computerweekly.com *Computer Weekly* is a good source of case studies of different acquisitions approaches and problems of project management.

www.yourdon.com Ed Yourdon's web site is a good collection of up-to-date papers about problems of information systems development from one of the gurus of software development.

www.research.ibm.com/journal The *IBM Systems Journal* and the *Journal of Research and Development* have many cases and articles on analysis and design related to e-business concepts such as knowledge management and security.

LINKS TO OTHER CHAPTERS

The chapter focuses on the startup phase of systems development projects.

Chapter 7 describes alternative acquisition methods such as bespoke and off-the-shelf development.

Chapter 9 describes how to manage a project to ensure that the quality of the system is maintained throughout the project.

Chapter 13 also considers cost–benefit analysis in relation to the overall investment that a company makes in IS rather than individual systems. Critical success factors for the new system are described in more detail. Outsourcing of information systems development and management is also described.

Initiating systems development

CHAPTER AT A GLANCE

MAIN TOPICS

FOCUS ON . . .

CASE STUDIES

LEARNING OUTCOMES

After reading this chapter, you will be able to:

- explain the importance of conducting a structured initiation phase for a BIS project;
- identify typical tangible and intangible costs and benefits associated with the introduction of an information system;
- apply different techniques to select the most appropriate options from different software, hardware and supplier alternatives;
- describe the importance of contracts to a successful outcome to information systems projects.

MANAGEMENT ISSUES

The senior management team sponsoring a new BIS must ensure that the project is (a) necessary, i.e. will contribute to business performance, and (b) that it is managed effectively. The initiation and feasibility phase of the systems development lifecycle is directed at achieving these two aims. From a managerial perspective, this chapter addresses the following questions:

- How should we assess the feasibility of a project?
- What are the stages and techniques that can be applied to assess feasibility?
- How can the return on investment of a BIS project be assessed?
- How can we manage the risks associated with IS projects?

INTRODUCTION

Initiation or startup phase

The first phase in an information systems development project. Its aims are to establish whether the project is feasible and prepare to ensure the project is successful.

Feasibility study

The activity that occurs before the requirements determination stage of a systems development project to ensure that the project is a viable business proposition. The feasibility report analyses the need for and impact of the system and considers different alternatives for acquiring software.

Successful completion of information systems is challenging – many information systems projects fail. Often these projects overrun in time or budget, or they do not deliver the benefits expected (see section 'Why do projects fail?' in Chapter 9 for more details on information systems project failure).

Failure to achieve success often occurs if the very first initiation or startup phase of the project is poorly managed. This chapter describes all the activities that need to occur at the start of a project to minimise the risk of failure later.

The initiation phase is the first phase in an information systems development project. An information systems project is typically initiated as a response to internal and/or external demands in an organisation's environment.

A feasibility study will typically follow the initiation phase. It is designed as a preliminary investigation intended to establish whether a business opportunity or problem can be solved through introducing a new information system. It is often also referred to as defining the 'terms of reference' for the project.

This chapter will consider the two stages separately. First, we will look at the reasons why an information systems project might be initiated, and then we will analyse those elements that make up a typical feasibility study. Provided that a proposed development project can demonstrate that the various feasibility elements can be satisfied, further work on software acquisition can then proceed.

REASONS FOR PROJECT INITIATION

Figure 8.1 summarises the context for the initiation phase of a systems development project. The stimulus for such a project may come internally from within the organisation or externally from outwith it, or from a combination of the two.

From an internal perspective, the initiation point may lie within one or more individual functional area within the organisation (such as accounting or marketing). The initiation point may also be as a consequence of a need to integrate different functional parts of the organisation more effectively.

From an external perspective, the project initiation may be in response to one or more external entities that lie outside the organisation. Sometimes, an organisation has no choice but to meet the requirements as set out by an external body (such as a government agency). An organisation may also place itself at a competitive disadvantage if it does not meet the requirements of a customer or supplier (for example by not trading electronically).

An information systems project, therefore, may either be in response to a problem or opportunity that arises in the internal and/or external organisational environment or simply as a result of necessity in order to meet legal or other obligations.

When a company is considering the benefits that can arise through implementing an information system, there are a number of possible reasons why an information systems project might be initiated:

1. *Capability.* A new information system can provide a new capability to achieve something that has not previously been possible. For example, creating online grocery sales through a web site gives a new sales channel capability. Information systems can also be enhanced to improve an existing capability where capacity has become limited. For example, business expansion may produce workloads with which current systems cannot cope – a growing company may find that its existing systems can no longer handle the quantity of orders received. An improved capability can be provided by increasing the amount of storage of an existing system or upgrading the software to a version with new features.

Figure 8.1 Sequence of main activities involved with project initiation

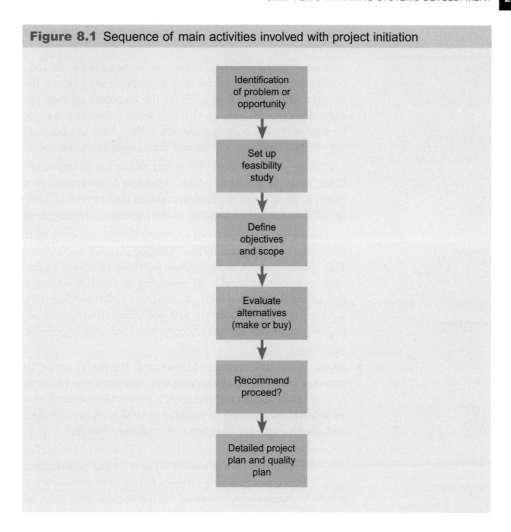

2. *Cost savings.* Cost reduction is often the key driver for the introduction of new systems. This factor is relatively easy to quantify and is readily understood by the managing director and finance manager. Different aspects of quantifying cost are given in the section on cost–benefit analysis. For a new banking system cost reduction can be measured by modelling the cost savings per transaction – each transaction between a customer and staff over the phone or in a branch can cost several euros, but for an online system these staff costs are zero.

3. *Improved internal information flows.* Well-established organisations with a long history of using computer-based information systems may have developed their software portfolio in a piecemeal manner over many years. As a result, the installed legacy systems may not have the linkages necessary to facilitate efficient and effective communication within and between different functional areas of the organisation. This is one of the reasons, therefore, why many organisations turn to enterprise systems of the type discussed in Chapter 6.

4. *Improved external information flows.* In addition to an organisation's internal value chain, there is also the external value chain to consider and, in particular, the relationship between the organisation and its customers, suppliers and channel partners. For example, a company wishing to purchase computer hardware may be more likely to use a supplier that gives accurate stock levels and delivery information on their web site so that there is an increased level of certainty that the right products

will be delivered on time. Order tracking through the supplier's delivery partner will also enhance the buying process.

5. *Improved customer service.* Customer service can be enhanced indirectly: a company could purchase an improved sales order processing system that reduces the time taken to order and deliver a product to the customer or 'free up' staff time to deal with more difficult customer service problems. Customers are also more likely to respond favourably to an organisation when they have confidence in the accuracy of the information held about them and their business transactions.

6. *Legislation changes.* These are a fact of life for all organisations and provide one of those 'must-do' situations where legislative requirements must be complied with. For example, many countries have introduced data protection laws that may trigger changes to software needed to conform to the legislation's requirements.

7. *Responsiveness.* Organisations are increasingly competing on the basis of the speed with which they can respond to the changing internal and external business environment. This means that an organisation's portfolio of computer-based information systems must not only be capable of providing appropriate information from both internal and external sources (such as accurate market intelligence), but must also enjoy a sufficiently flexible hardware and software infrastructure so that enhancements and improvements can easily be incorporated into the organisation's information systems portfolio.

8. *Reach.* While this overlaps with some of the points above, this factor recognises that potential customers and suppliers can exist anywhere in the world. Therefore, by using Internet and extranet technologies, it is possible to extend an organisation's value chain such that it can broaden its range of possible suppliers (thus potentially reducing costs) and also its customer base (thus in-creasing revenues).

9. *Control.* Control can be improved through better information delivery for managers. A sales manager who has weekly reports on the performance of his or her salesforce is in a better position to exercise control than a manager who receives the figures monthly. Similarly, an internal budget holder will have much better control over their income and expenditure if they have access to real-time financial accounting information.

10. *Competitive advantage.* If information systems can give a company the edge over its rivals through the benefits above, a competitive advantage may be achieved. For example, supermarket Tesco (www.tesco.com) was one of the first in its sector to introduce a home shopping service – it has a far greater market share in the online world than for its physical stores. First-mover advantage means, therefore, that rivals will find it difficult to win back customers already using these services who are partially locked-in to the system and they may take several years to catch up. However, some such as Nicholas Carr of the Harvard Business School argue that competitive advantage is transitory as competitors copy innovation (Carr, 2003).

An alternative indication of the need for a new system is to ask: *What would be the consequence of not having the proposed information system?*

Activity 8.1   Benefits of BIS

Select a company or organisation with which you are familiar. Rank in order of importance the benefits that developing a new BIS, such as an e-commerce system, could deliver to the business or a particular department. You should give an explanation of why you have placed each benefit factor where you have. If you are completing a class activity you can compare the different systems by placing the benefits side-by-side on a whiteboard.

THE FEASIBILITY STUDY

The different parts of a feasibility study are commonly categorised as *organisational feasibility, economic feasibility, technical feasibility and operational feasibility*. These factors will usually be reviewed for each of the possible solutions that have been proposed. The alternative solutions may be from different hardware or software vendors, or they may be different technical solutions that have been proposed by systems integrators or internal development teams.

In this section we will review each type of feasibility in turn. They are summarised in Table 8.1. The main focus will be on organisational and economic feasibility since these are most important as regards whether the IS project proceeds. Technical and operational feasibility usually address risks with the project which can be managed and as such these stages will not usually determine whether the project goes ahead or not.

Organisational feasibility

Organisational feasibility

Reviews how well the solution meets the needs of the business and anticipates problems such as hostility to the system if insufficient training occurs. (Considers the effect of change, given a company's culture and politics.)

Organisational feasibility considers how closely the solution will match the needs of the organisation and identifies problems that may arise in this area. The most important aspect of organisational feasibility is consideration of how well the proposed system fits in with the company's overall business and IS strategy. Often the desirability of a system will be compared to other competing systems.

Alignment of information systems with the business strategy

As part of benefits identification during assessment of economic feasibility, it is important to check that there is a strong alignment between the benefits that the new information system will provide and the overall business strategy. This is the top-down approach to IS strategy described later (in Chapter 13), where the mission and objectives of the company are translated into a portfolio of information systems required by the company.

Table 8.1 A summary of the different aspects of a feasibility study

Feasibility type	Scope	Question answered	Technique used to control
Organisational	Alignment of the system with organisational needs. Impact of system on organisational practice.	Will the system meet the business's needs and help improve its performance?	Critical success factors and key performance indicators. Change management.
Economic	Evaluation of the relative costs and benefits of the new system.	Will the costs outweigh the benefits?	Cost–benefit analysis. Return-on-investment and payback calculations.
Technical	Evaluation of possible technical problems and their solutions.	Will the system work efficiently?	Risk analysis. Capacity planning. Performance and availability modelling.
Operational	Evaluation of likely response to system by its users and management.	Will the system be accepted by end-users into their day-to-day work?	Risk analysis. Change management. Usability analysis.

An IT governance model for alignment of benefits with business needs

An example of an IT industry initiative to help deliver better alignment of IS with business needs is *COBIT*. COBIT is the widely adopted **IT governance** model for Control Objectives for Information and related Technology. More information on IT governance and COBIT is provided later (in Chapter 14).

Critical success factors

The use of **critical success factors (CSFs)** is valuable in helping to align new systems with business objectives. Critical success factors are those factors that determine whether business objectives will be achieved. Key performance indicators (KPIs) are then used to set targets for CSFs and assess whether these have been achieved. COBIT defines KPIs as 'the lead indicators that define measures of how well the IT process is performing in enabling the goal to be reached'. COBIT uses a three-level method of integrating CSFs and KPIs. An example of this approach is illustrated by Reicheld and Schefter (2000). They reported that Dell Computer has created a customer experience council that has researched key loyalty drivers or CSFs which determine whether customers will be retained by Dell as repeat customers. The business objectives and corresponding CSFs and KPIs are shown in Table 8.2.

BIS play a significant role in achieving CSFs since:

1. BIS are required indirectly to collect KPI data and report them throughout the organisation, so corrective action can be taken when targets are not achieved.

2. BIS may be used to directly achieve the CSFs.

IT governance

Management of the processes to direct and control the enterprise use of IT in order to achieve the enterprise's goals by adding value while balancing risk versus return over IT and its processes.

Critical success factors (CSFs)

A performance measure which must be achieved in order for business objectives to be met.

Activity 8.2 | Critical success factors

Suggest how Dell Computer may use BIS to:

(a) collect and report the CSFs and KPIs in Table 8.2;

(b) achieve the business objectives and KPIs in Table 8.2.

After identification of CSFs during initiation, development of a system should be targeted specifically at meeting KPIs at all SDLC phases. For example, the analysis stage will question which functionality, data inputs and outputs the system requires to meet these objectives. The testing stage will involve benefits-based testing to check that the system has the features to deliver the intended benefits.

The impact of the system on the organisation

Organisational feasibility will also involve a review of how the potential users' skill sets and attitudes will affect the system. Problems may include resistance to change from end-users,

Table 8.2 Relationship between loyalty drivers and measures to assess their success at Dell Computer

Business objective	Critical success factor	KPI
1 Improve order fulfilment	Ship to target	Percentage of systems that ship on time exactly as the customer specified
2 Increase product performance	Initial field incident rate	Frequency of problems experienced by customers
3 Enhance post-sale service	On-time, first-time fix	Percentage of problems fixed on the first visit by a service representative who arrives at the time promised

particularly those who don't have experience of using computer systems. If resistance to change from staff is anticipated, then steps should be taken to ensure that this does not happen. Such measures include training and educating staff by explaining why the system is being introduced (Chapter 12). If potential users are not familiar with using computers, then training must occur.

Organisational feasibility is a particularly important consideration for large-scale systems that will be deployed across an organisation. Examples are e-business and enterprise resource planning systems that substantially change working practices through re-engineering business processes. In these cases, the new system may affect the balance of power of different functional parts of the organisation. These implications should also be included as part of the organisational feasibility assessment. A new system may well also affect the communication channels and control mechanisms within an organisation and any detrimental effects on these should be established. Approaches to managing change associated with large systems is discussed further later in the chapter.

Economic feasibility

Economic feasibility

An assessment of the costs and benefits of different solutions to select that which gives the best value. (Will the new system cost more than the expected benefits?)

Economic feasibility is the analysis of the different costs and benefits of implementing the new system. It also assesses the relative importance of the new system in the comparison with other proposed systems (see coverage of portfolio analysis in Chapter 13 for further details). We will start by looking at different methods for assessing costs and benefits and then go on to look at how critical success factors and KPIs are devised during initiation as part of benefit identification to help align the outcomes of the project with business needs.

Assessing costs and benefits

Assessing costs and benefits of IS is not an exact science. A fundamental problem is that it is not easy to measure each benefit and cost accurately. Even where the benefits and costs are quantifiable, the figures used are only based on an estimate predicting several years into the future. This section outlines how cost–benefit analysis occurs at the start of a project to implement a new BIS.

All feasibility assessments for information systems development should include a cost–benefit analysis. Although this may seem obvious, some companies miss out this stage because other factors are driving the development such as the need to counter a competitor threat or respond to customer demand. The creation of e-commerce systems by banks is an example of this – here the cost of setup and maintenance may be greater than the revenue achieved through increased sales. The marketing manager may, however, want to proceed with such a strategic initiative to gain first-mover advantage as explained above and to gain experience aimed at ensuring success in the future when this form of channel becomes more widely used.

Tangible costs

A measure of cost can be calculated for each tangible cost.

Intangible costs

A monetary value cannot be placed on an intangible cost.

Tangible benefits

A definite measure of improvement can be calculated for each tangible benefit.

Intangible benefits

It is not possible to measure intangible benefits.

The business analyst undertaking a cost–benefit analysis will identify both **tangible and intangible costs and benefits**. When a cost or benefit is tangible, it is possible to set a definite numeric value against an item such as the cost of installing a new network. It is not possible to place a numeric value on intangible costs and benefits. Note that for some factors it may be difficult to establish whether the benefit is tangible or intangible. For example, although it is difficult to measure the benefit of general improvements in data quality, it would be possible to measure specific aspects of quality such as the time the new system takes to deliver information to the users.

Tangible costs are a measure of cost that can be calculated for each item of expenditure on BIS. For example, the purchase price of new hardware needed to run new software is a tangible cost. A monetary value cannot be placed on an intangible cost: the disruption and possible user resistance that will occur due to implementing a new system will have an effect on overall company performance, but they are difficult to measure.

A definite measure of improvement can be calculated for each tangible benefit. A reduction in cost per transaction system is an example of a tangible benefit for an online bank. It is not possible to measure an intangible benefit. For example, the improved decision-making capability provided by a decision support system would be difficult to cost.

Assessing costs

A range of costs must be included in the feasibility study. These include:

- hardware and software purchase costs;
- systems development staff costs if a bespoke or tailored solution is chosen;
- installation costs including cabling, physically moving equipment and bringing in new furniture to house the computers;
- migration costs such as transferring data from an existing system to the new system or running the new and original systems in parallel until the reliability of the new system is established;
- operating costs including maintenance costs of hardware such as replacing parts or upgrading to new versions of software. Staff costs in maintaining the hardware and software and trouble-shooting any problems must also be factored in. Operating costs may also include an environmental audit of the amount of energy and consumables used;
- training costs;
- wider organisational costs, for example redundancy payments, may need to be made if computerisation leads to loss of jobs.

Note that these costs include not only the initial cost of purchase, but also the ongoing maintenance costs. These are considerable for information systems and will often exceed the initial cost of purchase.

It is worth noting that there is a growing realisation that the cost of ownership of a software or hardware product is potentially much higher than the purchase cost. This is mainly due to the cost of trouble-shooting software bugs and hardware faults, phone support, installing upgrades and paying for support and/or upgrades from the vendor. The cost of ownership of the selected software and hardware combination should obviously also be factored into your cost–benefit analysis. The cost of training and education and documentation of staff should also be included with standard development costs of paying analysts and programmers.

Activity 8.3	Typical BIS costs and benefits

The following are examples of costs and benefits:

- software purchase cost;
- user resistance;
- reduction in working hours;
- improved decision making;
- hardware purchase cost;
- new working practices;
- sales increase;
- broader planning horizons;
- implementation costs;
- disruption during implementation;
- training costs;
- reduction in customer complaints;
- better data integration;
- reduction in maintenance costs;
- better data quality;
- hardware and software maintenance and consumable costs;
- reduction in inventory levels;
- better cashflow.

Assess where they should be in the grid below:

Costs		Benefits	
Tangible	Intangible	Tangible	Intangible

Assessing benefits

While information systems costs are relatively easy to identify, the benefits are harder to quantify since they are often intangible and will occur in the future. Benefits from a new system can be considered in terms of improvements to business processes and the quality of information used to support these processes. Common benefits include reduced costs of operating processes and greater efficiency leading to faster completion of tasks such as serving a customer.

Parker and Benson (1988) recommend a structured approach to identifying tangible benefits. This involves considering the cost of performing a business process *before* introduction of a new system and comparing this to the cost *after* implementation. Costs may include staff time, materials and equipment. This result will indicate either a tangible benefit through cost reduction or an added cost of using the new system.

Intangible benefits will include improvements to the quality of information, as described earlier (in Chapter 1). A new information system should enable information quality to be improved in some of the following ways:

- improved accuracy;
- improved availability and timeliness;
- improved usability (easier to understand and then act on information);
- improved utilisation;
- improved security of information.

Technical feasibility

Technical feasibility

Evaluates to what degree the proposed solutions will work as required and whether the right people and tools are available to implement the solution. (Will it work?)

Technical feasibility refers to the analysis of possible technical problems in the different solutions and who is appropriate to solve them. Technical feasibility can involve asking a series of questions to determine whether a computer system is the right tool for solving a problem. Some tasks may only be conducted using a human operator. The types of questions asked are:

- Can the system deliver the *performance* required? For example, an online banking solution may be required to deliver thousands of transactions a second.
- Will the system meet *availability* or *reliability* requirements? An online banking system should ideally be available 100% of the time, so what are the risks in terms of hardware, software and network errors that will prevent this? Service-level agreements (SLAs) with the hosting provider are usually used to control this.

- Does the system deliver the necessary level of *security*?

- Will there be *data integration* or *data quality* problems? Complex systems can fail due to the difficult of transferring data between different systems. Data quality needs to be managed in order for a system to deliver satisfactory outputs to end-users. This problem is best illustrated by the IT industry expression: 'garbage in, garbage out'.

- Can the system support the type of *decision making required* (particularly support for semi-structured or unstructured decisions)?

A technical feasibility assessment will aim to determine whether the proposed solution will work at all. In some cases, such as for an accounting system, there will be an obvious product that will fulfil the outline requirements. In others, such as for a specialised manufacturing facility, a fairly detailed analysis of requirements and a high-level design of the system may be necessary to assess alternatives before it is possible to decide on the feasibility. If this is the case then the initiation stage will be protracted and costly.

For simple applications, most problems will be technically feasible, the important question is 'How much will the solution cost?' Some solutions may be possible, but will require expensive hardware, software or development staff. So technical feasibility needs to be conducted before economic feasibility to assess these costs. Furthermore, to achieve technical feasibility is dependent on a sound approach to risk management which is described in more detail later in this chapter.

Operational feasibility

Operational feasibility

An assessment of how the new system will affect the daily working practices within the organisation. (Is the system workable on a day-to-day basis?)

Operational feasibility will review how the introduction of the new system will affect working practices on a day-to-day basis. For example, detailed estimates will be made of whether the system usability and response times are sufficient for the expected volume of customer transactions. With a customer-facing system such as the online banking solution, operational feasibility is very important since a difficult-to-use system will lead to customer use of the system lapsing after the first trial. For this reason, banks employ usability companies such as the Usability Company (www.theusabilitycompany.com) to reduce the risks that the system will be difficult to use or will not meet accessibility guidelines. There is close linkage between operational and organisational feasibility, and they are sometimes considered together.

RISK MANAGEMENT

Risk management

Aims to anticipate the future risks of an information systems project and to put in place measures to counter or eliminate these risks.

Risk management can be used at the start of a project to determine the level of risk and develop plans for reducing this risk – it is particularly important as part of assessing operational and organisational feasibility.

Baccarini, Salm and Love (2004) have produced an excellent analysis of the management of risks in information technology projects. They point out that existing literature identifies 27 common IT risks, grouped into seven broad categories. The impacts of these risk factors will differ, depending on the nature of the system being developed.

1. *Commercial and legal relationships.* These can include inadequate third-party performance where the contractor is unable to provide a solution that meets time, cost, quality and performance objectives; inadequate protection of software at the start of the project that may result in competitors taking advantage through copying, resulting in high litigation cost and loss of market potential; friction between clients and contractors where misunderstandings, unanticipated changes in the scope of the contract, missed or delayed delivery, or some other item of dispute may split clients and contractors into opposing camps.

2. *Economic circumstances.* Factors here can include changing market conditions where the business return on investment in IT can be eroded owing to changing consumer market conditions or advancements in software engineering (perhaps as a result of lengthy cycle times for software development); harmful competitive actions where competitors may build software solutions more quickly, with greater functionality at cheaper cost; software no longer needed because the software that is developed is prematurely terminated because its value or impact exceeds what management is prepared to absorb.

3. *Human behaviour.* Here, personnel shortfalls where work cannot be completed owing to insufficient staff and poor quality staff through lack of ability, training, motivation and experience of staff can be significant factors which can also have implications that extend to hardware, operating systems and database management systems selection as well as to other software.

4. *Political circumstances.* Unfortunately, political factors in the software acquisition process can play a significant role in the decision-making process. Aspects of this that are relevant here include situations where the corporate culture is not supportive of the project owing to hidden agendas, factions within the organisation, organisational culture under continuous change or threat of change, and other internal priorities; lack of executive support where the project is disrupted from achieving its objectives owing to management playing politics within and between departments or external agents – this can also lead to users not supporting the project if they perceive that there is a lack of top-level management sponsorship; politically motivated collection of unrelated requirements where a number of unrelated requirements are grouped in an all-encompassing project which becomes difficult to manage and make it meet its objectives.

5. *Technology and technical issues.* Again there are a number of risks that can occur from problems and errors within the software acquisition process. These can include: inadequate user documentation, meaning that users are unable to fully utilise the new information system as intended; application software perceived as not being fit for purpose because users believe that the software provided does not directly help them with completing day-to-day tasks, thus leading to low user satisfaction; poor production system performance due to the selected software architecture/platform not meeting the purpose for which it was intended, resulting in a system being released into production which is excessively slow or has major operational problems; technical limitations of the software solution are reached or exceeded during the development process resulting in time delays to the project while a work-around solution (if available) is determined – if a solution cannot be found the project will either be cancelled or restarted with a more viable technical solution; incomplete requirements where insufficient information has been obtained in the analysis phase, resulting in construction of a solution that does not meet project objectives; inappropriate user interface which fails to meet user requirements and expectations.

6. *Management activities and controls.* Over and above the political factors indicated above, there is a range of management factors that can significantly increase the risk of project failure. These include: an unreasonable project schedule and budget where the project is unable to realise its objectives owing to unrealistic restrictions placed on the project's budget, schedule, quality or level of performance; continuous changes to the requirements by a client can result in project delays unless a software development methodology such as DSDM or RUP is used where the change process is explicitly built in to the method; lack of agreed-to user acceptance testing and sign-off criteria where the project sign-off can be delayed owing to an unclear understanding of what constitutes final sign-off and solution delivery; failure to review daily progress, resulting in project slippage; lack of a single point of responsibility for project deliverables, resulting in the project's failing to meet its objectives; poor leadership where the project manager and/ or steering committee is not committed to solving problems and providing direction to

the project team; developing the wrong software functionality as a consequence of poor analysis, design or construction; lack of a formal change management process meaning that project progress is hindered owing to ad hoc changes to system specification without a formal review of technical and project impact.

7. *Individual activities.* There are two factors here of note: over-specification where the project team is focused on analysing and generating excessive levels of detail, thus losing sight of the project's objectives; unrealistic expectations where the functionality and benefits of the product are over-sold and the items promised for delivery to individuals may be unrealistic.

In summary, risk assessment will involve balancing the risks and costs likely to be incurred against the anticipated business benefits. As mentioned in Chapter 7, some approaches to software development such as DSDM or RUP are better at addressing some of the problems identified here. However, even the best methodology cannot compensate for poor management decisions and inadequate project control.

CASE STUDY 8.1

Recession reveals the dark side of advanced IT

By David Moschella

The role of computers in facilitating and compounding current economic turmoil has gone largely unmentioned (with one notable exception being a *Digital Business* article, 'The dog that bit its master', in March 2008).

Without computers, the extraordinary speed and volume of highly complex financial instruments and transactions would have been impossible. The combination of supercomputer-class hardware, complex software and mathematics led to mission-critical strategic trading systems that hardly anyone could understand.

The irony is that until everything fell apart, these systems and experts were seen as the crown jewels of investment banking and trading operations.

Financial institutions accepted unprecedented degrees of leverage in part because their computer models said it was OK. As these models initially seemed to work as advertised, too many executives eagerly bought into the absurd idea that, through the clever use of technology, one could all but eliminate investment risk, ignoring whatever warnings their internal experts may have raised.

When this wishful thinking inevitably imploded, these same systems also proved to be very difficult to turn off and unravel.

Are there lessons here for the rest of us? The financial services industry is not the only sector where system complexity is beginning to boggle or even overwhelm the human mind.

Think how many businesses today rely on complex, computer-based pricing, scoring, logistics, routing, occupancy, and simulation algorithms. Or how many sectors, such as nanotechnology, biotechnology, and robotics are being driven by scientists whose models

say that everything is OK (or, in the case of climate change, not OK). Or how many critical infrastructure systems such as the electrical grid, the internet, and much of the telecommunications system lack clear mechanisms of human governance and control.

We are now well into the early years of a phase that science fiction writers have imagined for decades, where more and more essential societal systems are controlled by machines whose complex workings no one person can fully understand, and which can be very difficult to repair, replace or even terminate should an unexpected crisis occur.

Where all this will lead is impossible to say, but we aren't far from a world where we will struggle to fly an aeroplane, conduct a transaction, design a product, or defend our countries without complex computer mediation.

While this sort of automation has many potential, even essential, advantages, it also creates new kinds of risks.

Our CIO clients typically say that, while all of this seems true and interesting, it isn't really their problem to solve. The traditional view of information technology risk has been a relatively narrow one: to make sure that systems are secure, available, and running as designed – challenges that are plenty tough already.

The actual purpose of a given system has, understandably, been seen mostly as a business issue. This attitude results in the curious fact that, from a traditional information systems perspective, the very computer systems that helped bring down the world economy were essentially operating as planned.

This begs the question as to who should be responsible. Most senior business executives lack the specialised knowledge needed fully to understand advanced business/IT applications.

But as we have seen, scientists and mathematicians often struggle to find the balance between the upside and downside of their work, especially in the middle of powerful political, career and financial pressures.

The result is today's unstable situation where much of our economy's most valuable intellectual property and most important infrastructure tends to lie outside the bounds of traditional business and IT risk assessment.

What to do? Barring radical societal changes, computer dependency will only rise over time.

Our research focuses on the implications of business/IT co-evolution, the idea that business and IT change are becoming inseparable and will increasingly require integrated management processes.

Looking ahead, we will need to think of risk management within a co-evolutionary framework that

encompasses both the still serious risks of traditional IT, and the new risks that come with complex business automation and control.

We need to come to grips with the fact that deterministic computer systems tend to generate surprising feedback loops, 'irrational' human behaviour, and all sorts of important, but unintended consequences.

This more expansive, co-evolving view of business/IT risk management is emerging as an exciting new field, with leadership opportunities for academics, business people and IT professionals alike.

The integration of business and IT will surely create fantastic opportunities for many years, but it will also create many new challenges and even dangers. For the IT industry, the lesson of the global financial crisis is clear: we need to control complex computer systems, lest they increasingly control us.

David Moschella is global research director for CSC's Leading Edge Forum

 Source: Moschella, D. (2013) Recession reveals the dark side of advanced IT. *Financial Times*. 24 July. © The Financial Times Limited 2012. All Rights Reserved.

QUESTION

What lessons does the case study have for the initiation of an IT project in the organisation?

Activity 8.4   A feasibility analysis for Lascelles Fine Foods

This activity is based on Case Study 7.3 where acquisition alternatives were considered for this company.

Produce a feasibility analysis of the alternative methods of acquiring application software as they relate to LFFL. You should pay particular attention to the operational, organisational, economic and technical feasibility of each one. You should conclude with a recommendation on how LFFL should best proceed to the next phase of the information systems acquisition process.

1. Identify risks, including their probabilities and impacts.

2. Identify possible solutions to these risks.

3. Implement the solutions, targeting the highest-impact, most-likely risks.

ACQUISITION CHOICES AND METHODS

Part of the feasibility stage is to decide on the method of acquisition. This will usually occur after the need and requirements for the system have been established. The make-or-buy decision will occur, and different suppliers of either off-the-shelf or bespoke solutions will be evaluated (as has been described in Chapter 7). The economic, technical and operational feasibility will be evaluated for each of the suppliers after a tender or request for proposals has been sent out to the suppliers. If a company decides to use a third party to develop its information systems or provide other IS services, this is known as *outsourcing* (Chapter 14). This is usually a strategic initiative which involves the outsourcing company in developing more than one system.

Example request for proposals for a BIS

Executive summary (two pages) – includes company description, acquisition mission statement, ROI requirement, preferred technology strategy, acquisition timing.

Administrative information (three pages) – includes procurement timeline, short-list requirements, proposal submission preparation guidelines, evaluation criteria checklist.

Business case (six pages) – includes business benefit, description of current operations, expectations, critical success factors.

Technical case (fifteen pages) – this section acts as an acceptance list for the buyer. Includes overview of current IS operations, expectations for the new IS operations, system functional specs, expected system response time, document management requirements, integration requirements, exception handling, hardware requirements, software requirements, mass storage specifications.

Management (three pages) – can be reserved for short-list vendors to complete. Includes system acceptance criteria, project management plan, site preparation plan, training plan and schedule, delivery and installation plan and schedule, systems maintenance plan, documentation (description and pricing), qualification and experience (number of installations etc.), customer references, financial report.

Agreement (one page) – asks for vendor's pricing breakdown, itemised by definitions, so you can easily compare vendor to vendor.

Summarising system requirements

Request for proposals (RFP)

A specification drawn up to assist in selecting the supplier and software.

If we decide to go ahead after the initial feasibility study, the next stage for a major implementation for a large organisation will be to issue an invitation to tender a document, brief or **request for proposals (RFP)**. The RFP is a specification drawn up to assist in selecting the supplier and software. An example structure of an RFP is shown in the box. The purchaser will fill in the first four sections and different vendors will fill in the last two sections. For a smaller company or system, alternative suppliers will also need to be assessed, but the effort spent on selection will be scaled down.

FOCUS ON... TECHNIQUES FOR COMPARING SYSTEMS

When purchasing a system, structured decision making is required to ensure that the best option is selected. Three simple methods for making product or supplier decisions are given below.

Feature checklist – first-cut exclusion

This is used initially to exclude products that are perhaps missing a key function or do not support the operating system you use. The humble feature checklist is the most easily applied and useful tool. The case study shows a typical checklist, which might be available in a magazine such as *PC Magazine* (www.zdnet.com), comparing three off-the-shelf software products.

Table 8.3 Five example scenarios for selecting a business intelligence system

Function to test	Scenario
1 Administration: add new user	How readily can a new user be added to the system or their personal details changed? How easy is it to set up the client (end-user) PC?
2 Compare actual against forecast sales	How easily can a user review the variance between actual and forecast sales and their trend through time?
3 Drill-down on a problem	If sales are down for one product line, how easy is it to identify the cause of that problem?
4 Export data	How easy is it to export part of the data for further analysis into a spreadsheet?
5 Configure data views	How easily can charts be customised to show a new KPI?

Feature checklist – detailed ranking

The main deficiency of simple checklists is that they do not attach relative importance to features. To extend them, give each feature a weighting of, say, between 0 and 100 points for each factor and then add up the scores for the different products. Activity 8.6 shows a detailed analysis using a range of factors to decide on which supplier to use.

Final selection using benchmarking

Once a company has narrowed down its selection of software using feature checklists to two or three contenders, a number of possibilities are available to make the final decision. These can be quite costly for both purchaser and supplier. First, it is possible to benchmark against other organisations that are performing similar tasks to you – what are their experiences, what performance is the software achieving, are they an independent reference site?

Second, if it is a large order, you can ask the suppliers to provide the software and test important functions using example process scenarios from a company, often including example data. Table 8.3 gives such scenarios for using a business intelligence product such as Cognos (www.cognos.com) introduced in Chapter 4. Often a comparison will not be meaningful unless a company's own data or processes are used as a basis for this scenario.

Mini case study | **Feature checklist for comparing three different groupware products**

Three products are compared according to:

- features provided;
- operating systems supported for the server platform;
- operating systems supported for the client (end) user.

These systems are compared using Table 8.4. Price for different options could also be shown in a table such as this, together with more detailed features, such as, does the e-mail have an address book for the whole company and does it support file attachments?

Table 8.4 Feature comparison for three groupware products

Criteria	Product A	Product B	Product C
Server platforms			
Windows XP Professional	Yes	Yes	Yes
Novell Netware	Yes	No	Yes
Linux	Yes	No	No
Client platforms			
Windows XP	Yes	Yes	Yes
MacOS X	Yes	No	Yes
Features			
E-mail	Yes	Yes	Yes
Scheduling	Yes	No	Yes
Document management	Yes	No	Yes
Internet access	Yes	No	Yes

From inspection of the table, it can be seen that Product A and Product C fulfil most of the criteria. Product B would be unsuitable for a company that had a range of existing computers running different operating systems. Since Products A and B are similar and cannot be distinguished using this table, a more detailed evaluation of these two could then occur after excluding Product B. A different example of a more detailed evaluation for a business system is described below.

Activity 8.5   Detailed weighted analysis of an ERP software decision

Table 8.5 shows an analysis for three products from different suppliers that were compared across many factors to establish which was most suitable. This type of detailed analysis is usually conducted when a new system costs tens or hundreds of thousands of pounds. The grand total shows that Supplier 3 is the clear winner.

Table 8.5 Detailed weighted analysis for ERP software

Decision criteria	Weighting factor	Supplier 1 score	Supplier 2 score	Supplier 3 score
A. General functionality				
Receive information	70	60	60	60
Verify cut quantity	70	30	40	80
Schedule operations	80	56	56	56
Monitor schedule execution	80	40	40	68
Verify shop data input	80	64	64	64
Verify parts loss reporting	70	28	56	56
Detect labour variances?	60	30	36	42
Provide real-time status	60	24	19	43
Provide capacity planning?	70	56	40	50
Calculate incentive pay	70	30	25	35
Provide needed flexibility	80	65	50	55

Decision criteria	Weighting factor	Supplier 1 score	Supplier 2 score	Supplier 3 score
Verify inventory data entry	60	42	42	42
Provide operation history	60	32	40	42
Provide security	90	30	36	36
A. Subtotal	1000	587	604	729
B. Technical considerations				
System reliability	100	56	56	56
Compatibility with other systems	100	56	56	56
Cross-module integration	100	45	70	65
Implementation time	100	45	70	65
Ease of customisation	100	60	48	56
B. Subtotal	500	262	300	298
C. Other considerations				
Cost	60	36	48	54
Service and support	90	45	50	57
Vendor vision	25	25	40	
Confidence in supplier	80	35	45	65
C. Subtotal	300	141	168	216
Grand total	1800	990	1072	1243

QUESTION

1. Review the different categories and the criteria within them. Do you think that the weighting factors are valid? Are there other factors that might apply for ERP software?
2. Look in detail at the values for each product. Comment on the basis for deciding on individual scores.
3. Given possible deficiencies in 1 and 2 above, comment on the suitability of this technique for making a decision. Would you use it and why? What would you do differently?

Which factors should be used when selecting systems?

When comparing software, cost is an obvious constraint on any purchase, but since this is often a fixed constraint, it is often best to evaluate software on other factors to narrow the choice and then decide finally on cost where contenders are similar in other respects. Eight important factors in deciding on systems are shown in the box. Note though, that from an internal perspective, an organisation needs to consider the skills base within the organisation to manage the application – this may exclude some functionally superior solutions for example. Complete Activity 8.6 to see how these factors can be applied in practice.

Eight key factors in selecting systems

Functionality

A term used to describe whether software has the features necessary to support the business requirements.

1. **Functionality**. Does the software have the features described to support the business requirements?
2. *Ease of use* for both end-users and initial setup and administration.

Compatibility

Software compatibility defines whether one type of software will work with another. For example, will a word processor run Windows 3.1 or Windows 95? Data compatibility defines whether data can be exported from one package and imported for use into another. For example, can a word-processor file from one package be used in another?

Interoperability

A general term used to describe how easily different components of a system can be integrated.

3. *Performance* for different functions such as data retrieval and screen display. If used in a customer-facing situation, this will be a critical factor.

4. *Compatibility* or *interoperability*. How well does your solution integrate with other products? This includes what you are using now and what you will be using based on your strategic direction.

5. *Security*. This includes how easy it is to set up access control for different users and the physical robustness of methods for restricting access to information.

6. *Stability or reliability of product*. Early versions of products often have bugs and you will experience a great deal of downtime and support calls; hence the saying 'never buy one dot zero' (Version 1.0).

7. *Prospects for long-term support of product*. If the vendor company is small or likely to be taken over by a predator, will the product exist in three years' time? Is the company responsive in issuing patches and new features for the product? Is the company forming strategic alliances with other key vendors which will improve the product's features and interoperability?

8. *Extensibility*. Will the product grow? Are the features available to accommodate your future needs? Are the features available in the initial purchase or will you have to integrate with software from another vendor? As a rule of thumb, it is best if you can single-source software, or use as few vendors as possible: the system will have greater reliability than making different modules interoperate.

Activity 8.6 | Comparing selection factors for different systems

Referring to the eight key factors for selecting software, discuss in a group, the order of importance of these factors for each of these different types of business information system:

- an accounting system;
- a system controlling a production line;
- a system for booking customers on to coach trips;
- a system to support investment in company shares;
- an HR management system.

Create a table comparing the different factors for each system. Explain similarities and differences.

Assessing products from different suppliers

Some businesses make the mistake of limiting an assessment of new software to its technical merits or features. This is unwise, since software purchase is a long-term commitment and a company is reliant on the support provided by the vendor. A small 'startup' company may provide a good range of features in its products, but it is likely to have fewer staff responsible for ensuring quality of the software and providing after-sales support. A further risk is that the vendor may fail or be taken over by a larger company and no support or upgrade versions will be available.

Contract negotiation

An appropriate contract is vital when outsourcing to a third-party systems development or any information systems function. This may include custom or bespoke software, amendments to off-the-shelf software and outsourcing or facilities management (FM). In essence, contracts define which activities should happen and when, and who is responsible for them. For example, the supplier should deliver Prototype 1 by 1 October, and review should be completed by 28 November. Both the customer and the suppliers benefit from a reduced risk of failure.

The value of having a well-defined contract is illustrated by failures that have occurred when they are not in place. For example, in the mid-1990s, the UK police terminated a fingerprint system development after two years in development, claiming £10 million in costs. The supplier, IBM, then counter-claimed £19 million on the basis of the client not having made their requirements clear. A protracted legal battle followed before agreement was reached.

Contracts should define the following main parameters:

1. business requirements and features of system;
2. deliverables such as hardware, software and documentation;
3. timescales and milestones for different modules;
4. how the project is managed;
5. division of responsibilities between different suppliers and the customer;
6. costs and method of payment;
7. long-term support of system.

Contracts are particularly difficult to establish for information systems projects for the following reasons:

- It is difficult to specify the requirements in detail at the outset of the project when the contract is signed. Varying functional requirements can lead to project overruns.
- Establishing acceptable performance at the outset is difficult because this depends on the combination of hardware and software.
- Many different suppliers are involved and it is often not clear where responsibilities for fixing problems may lie.
- After the project is finished, critical errors can potentially occur and a support contract is required to ensure that they are remedied rapidly.
- If a supplier's business fails, the system may be unmaintainable without the software program, which may need to be put into safe keeping with a third party in a source code escrow agreement.

Contents of a typical IS product contract

A typical contract will be made up of the following sections or schedules, as well as general clauses on confidentiality, intellectual property (who owns the rights to the software), indemnity, law and jurisdiction.

Schedule 1: Product specification and acceptance

This is usually the most involved section, since it will detail the features of the software and acceptance criteria. These will include the completion of all key features with an acceptable level of error and ensure that functions such as reporting occur rapidly enough.

Schedule 2: Input to project from client

This information is sometimes omitted since most activities are conducted by the provider. The activities essential to the completion of the project may include time for writing and reviewing requirements and prototypes; time for user acceptance testing (UAT); time for training; supply of test data; possibly supply of hardware and systems software (if purchased by buying department of company); support from internal IS function and project management.

Schedule 3: Services to be supplied by contractor

Each deliverable should be linked to a milestone and a specific payment to help avoid slippage in the project. Milestones should include deliverables from both client and supplier. Frequent monthly milestones should be set.

Schedule 4: Support of system and warranty

A service-level agreement should state how problems are 'escalated' within sup-pliers (passed up through the hierarchy so as to be resolved), and should define acceptable times for response according to the severity of the problem. The fault-logging system and contact points such as a helpdesk may also be defined.

Schedule 5: Project plan

An outline project plan showing key deliverables and milestones should be part of the contract. Responsibility for project management will be identified for both parties and regular meetings defined.

Schedule 6: Payment method

The two main methods of payment are fixed price, which tends to be favoured by the client since it has better visibility of costs, and time and materials, which is usually preferred by the supplier. Timing of payments should be tied into milestones (when they are known as 'phased payments'). Suppliers may prefer regular monthly payments. Penalty clauses or liquidated damages may be stipulated where the supplier loses part of its payment if it delivers late or risk and reward clauses which provide financial incentives if it delivers early.

CASE STUDY 8.2

Sedgemoor District Council
Quick availability of information increases efficiency and reduces costs

Sedgemoor District Council is improving the availability of information online to enhance customer service, increase the efficiency of accessing information and reduce data management costs. The council is now in a position to remove its planning department's legacy data management system (DMS), as it has completed migrating information to its electronic document and records management (EDRM) system, Trim Context from Tower Software.

Craig Wilkins, information systems manager at Sedgemoor District Council, says archived material for planning stretches from 1974 to 1995. 'It was in a proprietary DMS but it has been migrated to our EDRM system and been made available to the public online', he says.

'Dropping the DMS means we can improve efficiency and save about £7,000 annually on maintenance and server hardware. Making planning documents available online has also reduced the number of phone calls to the council.'

The aim is to replace paper-based systems and integrate all systems with the EDRM software to centralise the storage and management of all documents, and to remove legacy DMS applications. 'We now have a million records in the EDRM system out of 7.5 million documents. We have a variety of systems covering 14 different business areas and EDRM will underpin them all to attain availability of information accurately', says Wilkins.

'New documents go into the repository as well as archived data being migrated. We can scan documents into EDRM and recycle paper documents, reducing storage costs. We also aim to specify retention policies for data to improve information lifecycle management.'

The council has started to fully integrate its Goss iCM content management system with its EDRM software to assist in making data available via its web site.

As volumes of data multiply, the council has also installed a storage area network to support EDRM. 'We are scanning documents into the EDRM system and populating the back-office systems with metadata. We are having to key in metadata manually but the aim is to automate this process, perhaps through a barcode system, although there is a question over how much metadata a barcode can contain', says Wilkins.

Recently the council received confirmation that it is likely to be one of the first local authorities to comply with the Code of Connection requirements for connecting onto GCSx, part of the Government Connect programme to provide a common infrastructure for secure electronic transactions between local and central government. Other benefits include making council reports, agendas and minutes available online – and using Goss software in conjunction with EDRM to ensure the correct document versions are published online in each service area. The ultimate goal is for the EDRM system to make information readily available to support customer services through all access channels – the internet, face to face and by telephone, says Wilkins.

Source: Lisa Kelly, *Computing*, 11 October 2007, www.computing.co.uk/computing/analysis/2200923/case-study-sedgemoor-district

QUESTIONS

1. Given the intangible nature of some of the benefits from the new information systems, how might the council have gone about making the investment decision?

2. Analyse the initiation part of the project in terms of the internal and external factors driving the systems acquisition process.

SUMMARY

Stage summary: initiation

Purpose:	Determine viability of systems and technique used to acquire it
Key activities:	Feasibility study
Input:	Idea for new system or problem with existing system
Output:	Feasibility study, recommendation to proceed

The key characteristics and success factors for the initiation stage of systems development are as follows:

1. The initiation phase is the first stage of the system development lifecycle.

2. The initiation phase is generally considered to consist of two main activities: the generation of the idea for a new system and assessing the feasibility of introducing a new system. Feasibility assessment should occur for all projects, whatever the acquisition method.

3. Feasibility assessment will involve comparing different alternatives in terms of their:

   ■ *economic feasibility* – the cost–benefit analysis;
   ■ *technical feasibility* – evaluation of the merits of different alternatives in terms of practicality;
   ■ *operational feasibility* – will the system meet the needs of the business and end-users?
   ■ *organisational feasibility* – do the staff have the skills to use the system and how will their attitudes affect the acceptance of the system?

4. There is a range of financial measures for assessing the financial viability of a new system. These should take into account the time-varying nature of costs and benefits by using discounted cashflow techniques. Non-financial measures should not be neglected.

5. A contract for the supply of the system should be negotiated at the outset; this minimises the risk of project failure and provides adequate support for when the system becomes operational.

EXERCISES

Self-assessment exercises

1. What is the purpose of the initiation phase of a project?

2. What is meant by the terms 'intangible' and 'tangible benefit'?

3. Identify each of the following as tangible or intangible benefits or costs:

   (a) purchase of a server for data storage with a new information system;
   (b) reduced waiting time for customers when querying the progress of an order;
   (c) disruption caused by installation of a new company network;
   (d) reduced inventory holding period resulting from a new stock management system.

4. Summarise the differences between economic, operational, technical and organisational feasibility.

5. What do you understand by the term 'risk assessment' and how can it be applied to assist an information systems development project?

6. What is the purpose and outline contents of a 'request for proposal' or 'invitation to tender' document?

7. What are the key factors that a company will consider when choosing software from different suppliers?

8. What are the main items that should be specified in an information systems contract?

Discussion questions

1. To what extent is the failure of many information system projects a consequence of too little time being spent on the initiation stage?

2. 'The techniques that are available for comparing different software packages or systems from different suppliers must be applied rigorously.' Discuss.

Essay questions

1. Examine the main consequences for an information systems project if the initiation stage is omitted.

2. A company is intending to purchase accounting software for 100 staff and is considering three different packages. It is currently using a Microsoft Windows 2000-based application, but wants to move to using a Microsoft Windows XP Professional-based application. Give a full account of the factors it should consider when making the comparison. Which do you consider are the most important factors?

3. Risk assessment is a valuable tool for the project manager. What does this technique involve and which future risks might be identified at different stages in a systems development project?

4. Write a short feasibility or initiation report for a new e-commerce site or an enhancement to an existing site incorporating the elements of initiation referred to in this chapter. It can refer to a fictitious company, a small company you are familiar with, or a larger company whose sites you can visit. Your answer should not be limited to exploring economic, operational, organisational and technical feasibility, but should include all the aspects of initiation planning covered in this chapter.

Examination questions

1. What is the purpose of establishing the following types of feasibility:

   (a) operational;
   (b) organisational;
   (c) technical;
   (d) economic.

2. Give three reasons for a company's initiating an information systems project. Give a brief example of each.

3. Define information systems outsourcing.

4. Give examples of two tangible costs and two intangible costs that may be incurred during an information systems development project.

5. What are the most important factors you would consider when comparing alternative software packages?

References

Baccarini, D., Salm, G. and Love, P.E.D. (2004) 'Management of risks in information technology projects', *Industrial Management and Data Systems*, 104, 4, 286–95

Carr, N. (2003) 'IT doesn't matter', *Harvard Business Review*, May, 5–12

Parker, M. and Benson, R. (1988) *Information Economics: Linking Business Performance to Information Technology*, Prentice-Hall, Englewood Cliffs, NJ

Reicheld, F. and Schefter, P. (2000) 'E-loyalty: your secret weapon on the Web', *Harvard Business Review*, July–August, 105–13

Further reading

Birdoğan Baki, B. and Kemal Çakar, K. (2005) 'Determining the ERP package-selecting criteria – the case of Turkish manufacturing companies', *Business Process Management Journal*, 11, 1, 75–86.

Boehm, B. (1991) 'Software risk management: principles and practices', *IEEE Software*, 8, 1, January, 32–41. A detailed assessment of risks that occur at the level of software creation and refinement.

Verville, J. and Halingten, A. (2003) 'Analysis of the decision process for selecting ERP software: the case of Keller Manufacturing', *Integrated Manufacturing Systems*, 14, 5, 423–32.

Verville, J., Bernadas, C. and Halingten, A. (2005) 'So you're thinking of buying an ERP? Ten critical factors for successful acquisitions', *Journal of Enterprise Information Management*, 18, 6, 665–77.

Ziaee, M., Fathian, M. and Sadjadi, S.J. (2006) 'A modular approach to ERP system selection – a case study', *Information Management and Computer Security*, 14, 5, 485–95.

Web links

www.cio.com CIO.com for chief information officers and IS staff has many articles related to analysis and design topics.

http://www.isaca.org/Knowledge-Center/cobit/Pages/Overview.aspx Cases and specifications for the COBIT governance model for Control Objectives for Information and related Technology.

www.computerweekly.com *Computer Weekly* is a weekly IS professionals' trade paper with UK/Europe focus which has many case studies on practical problems of analysis, design and implementation.

www.research.ibm.com/journal *IBM Systems Journal* and the *Journal of Research and Development* have many cases and articles on analysis and design related to e-business concepts such as knowledge management, security.

http://www.datamation.com/ Has case studies on systems analysis and design specific to intranets.

www.gartner.com Gartner Group web site containing information on return on investment in IS projects.

LINKS TO OTHER CHAPTERS

The preparation of a preliminary project plan will occur during the initiation phase of a systems development project which was described in Chapter 8. After the project has been given the go-ahead, a more detailed project plan will be generated using the techniques described in this chapter. The project plan will specify the activities and the resources needed to complete the subsequent stages of the project lifecycle. These are analysis (Chapter 10), design (Chapter 11) and build and implementation (Chapter 12).

BIS project management

CHAPTER AT A GLANCE

LEARNING OUTCOMES

After reading this chapter, you will be able to:

- understand the main elements of the project management
  approach;
- relate the concept of project management to the creation of BIS;
- assess the significance of the different tasks of the project
  manager;
- outline different techniques for project management.

MANAGEMENT ISSUES

Managers need to ensure that their BIS projects will be completed
satisfactorily, whether they are directly responsible, or if the project
management is delegated to another person in the organisation, or
an external contractor. From a managerial perspective, this chapter
addresses the following questions:

- What are the success criteria for a BIS project?
- What are the attributes of a successful project manager?
- Which project management activities and techniques should be
  performed by the project manager for a successful outcome?

INTRODUCTION

Projects

Projects are unique, one-time operations designed to accomplish a specific set of objectives in a limited timeframe.

Projects are unique, one-time operations designed to accomplish a specific set of objectives in a limited timeframe. Examples of projects include a building construction or introducing a new service or product to the market. In this chapter we focus on providing the technical knowledge that is necessary to manage information systems projects. Large information systems projects like construction projects may consist of many activities and must therefore be carefully planned and coordinated if a project is to meet its objectives.

The three key objectives of project management are shown in Figure 9.1. The job of project managers is difficult since they are under pressure to increase the quality of the information system within the constraints of fixed costs, budget and resources. Often it is necessary to make a compromise between the features that are implemented and the time and resources available – if the business user wants a particular new feature, then the cost and duration will increase or other features will have to be omitted.

A major issue in IT project management is the determination of a realistic assessment of the costs and benefits of an IT project. This information is required when deciding whether to proceed with the project and for making a reasonable assessment of project success. This issue is discussed in Case Study 9.1.

While it is difficult to control and plan all aspects of a BIS development project, the chance of success can be increased by anticipating potential problems and by applying corrective strategies. The PRINCE2 methodology is reviewed since it is used to assist in the delivery of BIS projects to time, cost and quality objectives. Network analysis techniques are also reviewed in this chapter, since they can be used to assist project planning and control activities by enabling the effects of project changes to be analysed.

Figure 9.1 Three key elements of project management

Time

Project manager must negotiate for more time, more people or fewer features

Quality/features

Cost

CASE STUDY 9.1

Putting an all-inclusive price tag on successful IT

By Ron Barker

Failure to derive the expected benefits from IT systems is legendary. Yet organisations still fail to recognise or accept why this occurs and generally do little to address the root causes in any meaningful way.

The first place to look is the application of the Return on Investment (ROI) tool as the arbiter for benefits delivery and the subsequent plans for implementing the systems. An ROI is required by most organisations, but the tool is often applied without fully understanding all of the cost components (full disclosure).

By definition, IT projects tend to focus on dealing with the technical issues. It is these that get measured as the cost side of the change – usually the cost of hardware and software with some allowance for training. Typically, costs are grossly underestimated (often by 40 per cent or more) by failing to consider precisely those factors that are needed to deliver the return.

ROI is a technical measure taking expected returns and expected costs to determine the worth of the investment. The key word is 'expected'. The reality, of course, is that the ROI calculation is no more than a forecast, based upon someone's view of the costs and benefits. Realising the benefits forecast is where the hard work arises, there is often a drastic underestimate of the efforts required to 'make it happen'. The underestimates are generally in:

- ensuring compliance with the business strategy;
- aligning the people with the processes the business is changing to;
- ensuring that behaviours are commensurate with the required new ways of working.

This assumes processes are being changed – otherwise where are the benefits coming from? Which means there is an implicit assumption that people somewhere will be doing something differently. It is the need to ensure and facilitate this change that generates a high proportion of the total project costs. By including these costs some projects start to appear unprofitable. This, of course, is generally not in the interests of any systems suppliers. It may, however, stop some projects from getting off the ground and avoid some of the overspending we have seen in the past. If the way things are done in the business is being changed then there is a need to understand what that change means. There is a range of implementation approaches taken by companies including:

- simple ROI and the 'stuff it at 'em' approach that follows the principles of 'if we tell them what to do and give them a bit of training then they'll make it work';
- a considered approach that defines real business need and vision but then fails to communicate this through to the 'what's in it for me' messages and thereby does not connect with the users;
- development of a system that involves some users early and is well communicated to staff, but is not properly aligned to the organisation's strategy and owned by specific, accountable people in the business.

Quite often, once the decision to invest is made, technology projects are devolved to the IT department who are then responsible for overseeing through delivery and implementation. Often these technically focused people are poorly qualified to understand the business nuances and may not have the required communications skills. Over and above this, who looks at the changes required in human behaviour? Who is addressing the motivational issues that will get the right people doing the right things?

A framework can be proposed to improve chances of success. This is based around the simple model of People, Process and Technology (PPT) with the added element of environment or context (PPTE). Context is the first parameter to get right. How does the development proposed relate to the business strategy? What is the desired outcome for the development, in business benefit terms, so that we know what is to be delivered and why? After thinking through the application needs and functions, the next useful question is how is it to be delivered? This should be viewed as a problem that the business deals with rather than abdicating it to the IT group.

Costs can then be assessed in outline for the whole PPTE model. This may include some scenario planning work fully to appreciate the different ways that the system may work, and identify the best options, prior to getting the technologists involved. A full disclosure ROI can then be calculated that takes all benefits and PPTE costs into account. This should include all of the people costs for effective change, from ownership and visions through stakeholder buy-in, to positive, user-led adoption. Decisions to proceed are now likely to be better informed and can be done on all fronts of process, technology and people readiness, perhaps with the 'go' decision requiring people readiness to be assured.

Truer costs will be understood and the full implications of benefits will emerge. The business's responsible project owner will now have a budget that allows them to plan from concept to execution with holistic consideration of all PPTE elements. This will give positive adoption of systems that are pulled through by users who expect what they get and get what they expect. They will 'pull' the system through rather than having it shoved at them.

QUESTION

Discuss the difficulties in estimating the costs and benefits of an IT project.

THE PROJECT MANAGEMENT PROCESS

When undertaking a BIS project, the project manager will be held responsible for delivery of the project to the traditional objectives of time, cost and quality. Many BIS have the attributes of a large-scale project in that they consume a relatively large amount of resources, take a long time to complete and involve interactions between different parts of the organisation. To manage a project of this size and complexity requires a good overview of the status of the project in order to keep track of progress and anticipate problems. The use of a structured project management process can greatly improve the performance of IS projects, which have become well known for their tendency to run over budget or be late as stated earlier. The ubiquity of projects and the challenge of project management is outlined in the mini case study 'The key to ... project planning'.

Mini case study | The key to . . . project planning

By John Plummer

Projects equal pounds. Ever wondered what all those programme managers and project leaders do? Earn cash, it seems. According to project management training providers APM Group (**www.apmgroup.co.uk**) a quarter of the UK's GDP comes from projects.

A full-time job. Many companies reorganised over the past decade to chase the project pound, which has had a profound impact on staff. 'Projects are no longer "something extra",' says the website **www.chiefprojectofficer.com**, 'they are the way work gets done at an increasing number of companies, from small start-ups to the likes of Hewlett Packard.'

Get trained. As income from projects has grown, so too has the market in accredited project management qualifications. More companies are sending staff on courses such as Prince2 (**www.prince2.org.uk**), a project management methodology owned by the Office of Government Commerce.

Define your objectives. Every project begins with a plan. When will we start? What do we need? Can we do it alone, or do we need help? How long will it take? What will it cost? 'These are typical questions asked at the start of any project and the answers are the building blocks of project management,' says the Prince2 website.

Expect to change. Projects that don't evolve are the likeliest to wither so no matter how good your initial plan is, expect it to change. If you're running a project that has been outsourced to your company, consider inviting a customer on to the project team to keep them informed, involved in decisions and better motivated.

The advantages. 'Project management' may sound as sexy as the words 'Charles Kennedy lap-dancing', but don't be fooled. 'One of the advantages of working in projects is that you never know what you will be doing in six months,' says Andrew Delo at the project management advisers Provek (**www.provek.co.uk**). 'If you like uncertainty, it is an exciting environment.'

Source: Plummer, J. (2005) The key to ... project planning. *The Times*, 26 May.

Context: where in the SDLC does project planning occur?

Project managers need to control projects, and to achieve this they tend to use frameworks based on previous projects they have managed. The systems development lifecycle (SDLC) or waterfall model (introduced in Chapter 7) provides such a framework. The majority of project plans will divide the project plan according to the SDLC phases.

An *initial project plan* will usually be developed at the initiation phase (Chapter 7). This will normally be a high-level analysis that does not involve the detailed identification of the tasks that need to occur as part of the project. It may produce estimates for the number of weeks involved in each phase, such as analysis and design, and for the modules of the system, such as data-entry and reporting modules. If the project receives the go-ahead, a more detailed project plan will be produced before or as the project starts. This will involve a much more detailed identification of all the tasks that need to occur. These will usually be measured to the nearest day or hour and can be used as the basis for controlling and managing the project. The *detailed project plan* will not be produced until after the project has commenced, for two reasons:

1. It is not practical to assess the detailed project plan until the project starts, since the cost of producing a detailed project plan may be too high for it to be discarded if the project is infeasible.

2. A detailed project plan cannot be produced until the analysis phase has started, since estimates are usually based on the amount of work needed at the design and build phases of the project. This estimate can only be produced *once the requirements for the system have been established at the analysis phase*.

These points are often not appreciated and, we believe, are a significant reason for the failure of projects. Project managers are often asked to produce an estimate of the amount of time required to finish a project before the analysis phase, when insufficient information is at their disposal. Their answer should be:

> I can give you an initial estimate and project plan based on similar projects of this scale at the initiation phase. I cannot give you a detailed, accurate project plan until the analysis is complete and the needs of the users and the business have been assessed. A detailed estimate can then be produced according to the amount of time it is likely to take to implement the users' requirements.

Why do projects fail?

There has been a number of high-profile IT project failures in the UK public sector which underline the difficulties of IT project management. Despite these failures there are also a number of successes which generally receive less publicity. One reason for public-sector IT failures may be the sheer size and thus complexity of the projects. It is also difficult to compare performance with private-sector IT project performance as private companies are generally reluctant to disseminate knowledge regarding IT failures in order not to tarnish their reputation. Read Case Study 9.2 for more information on the success and failure of IT project management.

In general terms Lyytinen and Hirscheim (1987) researched the reasons for information systems projects failing. They identified five broad areas which still hold true today:

- *Technical failure* stemming from poor technical quality – this is the responsibility of the organisation's IS function.

- *Data failure* due to (a) poor data design, processing errors and poor data management; and (b) poor user procedures and poor data quality control at the input stage. Responsibility for the former lies with the IS function, while that for the latter lies with the end-users themselves.

- *User failure* to use the system to its maximum capability – may be due to an unwillingness to train staff or user management failure to allow their staff full involvement in the systems development process.

- *Organisational failure*, where an individual system may work in its own right but fails to meet organisational needs as a whole (e.g. while a system might offer satisfactory operational information, it fails to provide usable management information). This results from senior management's failure to align IS to overall organisational needs.

- *Failure in the business environment* can stem from systems that are inappropriate to the market environment, failure in IS not being adaptable to a changing business environment (often rapid change occurs), or a system not coping with the volume and speed of the underlying business transactions.

It is apparent that a diverse range of problems can cause projects to fail, ranging from technical problems to people management problems.

It is the responsibility of the project manager to ensure that these types of problems do not occur, by anticipating them and then taking the necessary actions to resolve them. This will involve risk management techniques, described in Chapter 8. Case Study 9.2 shows the type of problems that occur, the reasons behind them and advice for new project managers on how to manage projects successfully.

CASE STUDY 9.2

Project management: lessons can be learned from successful delivery

By Vanessa Kortekaas

The team behind Britain's most high profile infrastructure project in recent times says there was no 'magic ingredient' in its successful delivery, but having £9.3bn available is likely to have helped.

The construction of the Olympic park in east London was widely hailed as a success long before the first athlete set foot in it last month.

While the fate of a few key venues is still unclear, there is a strong consensus on the park's delivery. 'On time and under budget' is the most common appraisal batted around by politicians and Olympic organisers – though the latter description is not entirely accurate.

The success of the build has prompted some soul-searching about lessons that can be applied to future developments, partly to avoid repeats of projects that went wrong, such as Wembley Stadium.

'In reputation terms [the Olympic project] was an opportunity, clearly,' says Sir John Armitt, the man in charge of the body that built the park.

He says that the UK's reputation for major construction and infrastructure developments has always been high, but admits that Wembley 'didn't go so well'.

The fact that the world was watching and judging as the Olympic park was erected on top of former industrial wasteland added more pressure to get it right. 'The Olympic project is the most high profile project that you could imagine,' he says.

Sir John says successful programme management starts from the client, in this case the Olympic Delivery Authority, which he led. He says the ODA knew what it valued, balancing cost and quality, and made that clear to its suppliers.

'If you talk to the suppliers on the Olympics what they will say is that the ODA was an intelligent client, and a consistent client in contractual terms,' says Sir John. Consistency, he says, reinforced to suppliers what was expected of them.

The ODA oversaw the procurement of more than £6bn worth of contracts to deliver the Olympic park, and arguably its most important contract was with its delivery partner – CLM, a consortium that includes CH2M Hill.

But the creation and structure of the ODA itself was also key to the success of the project.

'One of the weakest points of London's bid originally was the sense that the UK, and London in particular, had such a range of agencies and bodies that would need to be corralled together to make anything happen,' says Tim Jones, a partner at Freshfields law firm who was heavily involved in the negotiations that spawned the ODA.

The ODA served as a 'single governmental interface' with planning authority, he says, removing the need for time-consuming negotiations with various local bodies.

It also assumed power for some aspects of Olympic transport and security. 'The ODA was where all those functions were really brought together,' says Mr Jones. Having a delivery partner enabled the relatively small ODA to function efficiently, he adds.

That sentiment is echoed in an ODA report on the project, which says having a delivery partner gave it 'flexibility and agility' and their partnership underpinned its success.

But not everything went to plan. Sir John says the impact of the financial crisis on delivering the athletes' village was the 'biggest challenge' the ODA faced during the construction period.

Both the village and the media centre had to be bailed out by the government.

'You couldn't get a sensible financial package out of the banks, so the decision was made to use contingency money to fund [the village] and then sell the asset as soon as we could after... to recover the money,' says Sir John.

Some £557m was recouped last year, when a Qatari-backed consortium bought half of the homes in the village and several plots of land in the Olympic park. Triathlon Homes had already paid £268m for 1,379 units, which are earmarked for affordable housing.

The contingency money that was drawn on for the village was available only because the Olympics budget was revised to £9.3bn in 2007, from an original estimate of £2.4bn. The ODA spent £6.8bn delivering the Olympic park.

The immovable deadline also drove the project. The opening ceremony was always going to happen on July 27, and frequent missions from the International Olympic Committee served as a potent reminder.

Cross-party support was another unique factor from which the build benefited. 'You don't always get that [support],' admits Sir John.

It is unclear whether local authorities would be willing to yield some elements of power again, under different circumstances.

Mr Jones is hopeful but unsure. 'They only agreed to do it that time because it was the Olympics and they all wanted this to happen,' he says. 'Maybe it is rather optimistic to suspect that you would get such support for another project, that people would actually surrender their power.'

 Source: Kortekaas, V. (2012) Project management: lessons can be learned from successful delivery. *Financial Times*. 19 August. © The Financial Times Limited 2012. All Rights Reserved.

QUESTION

Discuss the delivery of the Olympic Park in terms of time, cost and quality performance objectives.

Project organisation

In order that a project is clearly defined and meets its objectives it is important to define the roles of the staff involved and how those roles are organised within a particular project. The principal roles encountered in a project are outlined below. Note that these roles may be known by other names or be undertaken by more than one person or roles may be combined and allocated to a single person, depending on the organisational context and the size of the project.

Project sponsor

The project sponsor role is to provide a justification of the project to senior management. The role includes defining project objectives and time, cost and quality performance measures. The role also involves obtaining finance and appointing a project manager. The project sponsor is accountable for the success or failure of the project in meeting its *business* objectives.

Project manager

Appointed by the project sponsor the project manager role is to provide day-to-day management and ensure *project* objectives are met. This involves selection and management of the project team, monitoring of the time, cost and quality performance measures and informing the project sponsor and senior management of progress. In larger projects the project manager may delegate certain areas of the project (e.g. programming) to team leaders for day-to-day management.

Project user

The project user is the person or group of people who will be utilising the outcome of the information systems project. The user(s) should be involved in the definition and implementation of the system to ensure successful ongoing usage.

Other major roles that may be defined in the project include the following.

Quality manager

This role involves defining a plan containing procedures that ensure quality targets are met. Quality can be defined as 'conformance to customer requirements'. Total quality management (TQM) attempts to establish a culture that supports quality. The European Foundation for Quality Management (EFQM) has provided a model that allows an organisation to quantify its progress towards a total quality business. For more information on quality management in relation to IS projects see Cadle and Yeates (2007).

Risk manager

All projects contain some risk that the investment made will not achieve the required business objectives. Risk management has become increasingly important in providing processes that attempt to reduce risk in complex and uncertain projects (see Chapter 8 for more details on risk management).

In many situations the project is organised by the main roles of project sponsor, project manager and project user. However, in complex or larger projects other organisational bodies may be encountered. A *steering committee* brings together a variety of interested people such as users, functional staff (e.g. finance, purchasing) and project managers in order that all stakeholder views are taken into consideration. At a lower level *user groups* may be instituted to represent the views of multiple potential users.

STEPS IN PROJECT MANAGEMENT

Before the planning process can commence, the project manager will need to determine not only the business aims of the project but also the constraints under which they must be achieved. Major constraints include the overall budget for project development, the timescale for project completion, staffing availability, and hardware and software requirements for system development and running of the live system. These questions form the framework for the project and it is important that they be addressed at the beginning of the project planning process. It is usual, however, to only prepare detailed plans of the early stages of the project at this point.

The project management process includes the following main elements:

- estimate;
- schedule/plan;
- monitoring and control;
- documentation.

Estimation

Estimation allows the project manager to plan for the resources required for project execution through establishing the number and size of tasks that need to be completed in the project.

Estimation

Estimation allows the project manager to plan for the resources required for project execution through establishing the number and size of tasks that need to be completed in the project. This is achieved by breaking down the project repeatedly into smaller tasks until

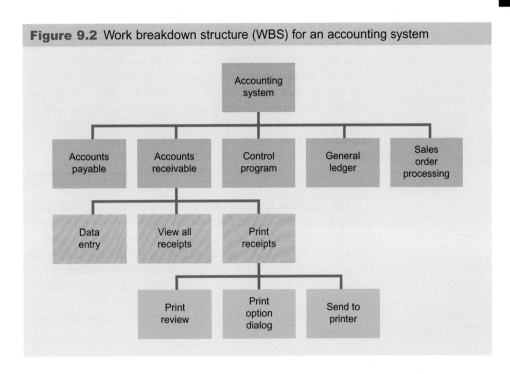

Figure 9.2 Work breakdown structure (WBS) for an accounting system

a manageable chunk of one to two days' work is defined. Each task is given its own cost, time and quality objectives. It is then essential that responsibility be assigned to achieving these objectives for each particular task. This procedure should produce a **work breakdown structure (WBS)** that shows the hierarchical relationship between the project tasks. It is an important part of estimation. Figure 9.2 shows how the work on producing a new accounting system might be broken down into different tasks. Work on systems projects is usually broken down according to the different modules of the system. In this example, three levels of the WBS are shown for the accounts receivable module down to its printing function. All the other five modules of the system would also have similar tasks.

At the start of the project in the initiation or startup phase, an overview project plan is drawn up estimating the resources required to carry out the project. It is then possible to compare overall project requirements with available resources.

Project constraints can be resource-constrained (limited by the type of people or hardware resources available) or time-constrained (limited by the deadline).

The next step, after the project has been given the go-ahead, is a more detailed estimate of the resources needed to undertake the tasks identified in the work break-down structure. If highly specialised resources are required (e.g. skilled analysts), then the project completion date may have to be set to ensure that these resources are not overloaded. This is a resource-constrained approach. Alternatively, there may be a need to complete a project in a specific timeframe (e.g. due date specified by customer). In this case, alternative resources (e.g. subcontractors) may have to be utilised to ensure timely project completion. This is a time-constrained approach. This information can then be used to plan what resources are required and what activities should be undertaken over the lifecycle of the project.

Effort time and elapsed time

When estimating the amount of time a task will take, it is important to distinguish between two different types of time that need to be estimated. **Effort time** is the total amount of work that needs to occur to complete a task. The **elapsed time** indicates how long in time (such as calendar days) the task will take (duration). Estimating starts by considering the amount of effort time that needs to be put in to complete each task. Effort time is then converted into

---

Work breakdown structure (WBS)

This is a breakdown of the project or a piece of work into its component parts (tasks).

Project constraints

Projects can be resource-constrained (limited by the type of people, monetary or hardware resources available) or time-constrained (limited by the deadline).

Effort and elapsed time

Effort time is the total amount of work that needs to occur to complete a task. The elapsed time indicates how long in time (such as calendar days) the task will take (duration).

elapsed time, which indicates how long the task will take through real-time measures such as months or days. Effort time does not usually equal elapsed time, since if a task has more than one worker the elapsed time will be less than the effort time. Conversely, if workers on a task are also working on other projects, then they will not be available all the time and the elapsed time will be longer than the effort time. An additional factor is that different workers may have different speeds. A productive worker will need less elapsed time than an inexperienced worker. These constraints on elapsed time can be formalised in a simple equation:

$$Elapsed\ time = Effort\ times \times \frac{100}{Availability\ \%} \times \frac{100}{Work\ rate\ \%}$$

The equation indicates that if the availability or work rate of a worker is less than 100 per cent, the elapsed time will increase proportionally, since availability and work rate are the denominators on the right-hand side of the equation. The equation will need to be applied for each worker, who may have different availabilities and work rates. These factors can be entered into a project management package, but to understand the principles of estimation better the activity on project planning should be attempted (see Activity 9.1 below).

From the example in the activity, it can be seen that several stages are involved in estimation:

1. estimate effort time for average person to undertake task;
2. estimate different work rates and availability of staff;
3. allocate resources (staff) to task;
4. calculate elapsed time based on number of staff, availability and work rate;
5. schedule task in relation to other tasks.

Cadle and Yeates (2007) provide the following techniques for estimating the human resource and capacity requirements for the different stages of an IS project:

1. *Estimating the feasibility study*. This stage will not usually be estimated in detail, since it will occur at the same time as or before a detailed project estimate is produced. The feasibility stage consists of tasks such as interviewing, writing up interview information and report writing in order to assess the financial, technical and organisational acceptability of the project. The estimate will depend greatly on the nature of the project, but also on the skills and experience of the staff involved. Thus it is important to keep records of previous performance of personnel for this activity in order to improve the accuracy of future estimates.

2. *Estimating analysis and design phases*. The analysis phase will typically involve collection of information about the operation of current systems and the specification of requirements for the new system. This will lead to the functional requirements specification, defining the new system in terms of its business specification. The design phase will specify the new computer-based system in terms of its technical content. This will need to take into account organisational policies on design methodologies and hardware and software platforms. In order to produce an accurate estimate of the analysis and design phases, it is necessary to produce a detailed description of each task involved. As in the feasibility stage, time estimates will be improved if timings are available for previous projects undertaken.

3. *Estimating build and implementation*. This stage covers the time and resources needed for the coding, testing and installation of the application. The time taken to produce a program will depend mainly on the number of coding statements required and the complexity of the program. The complexity of the coding will generally increase with the size of the program and will also differ for the type of application. A lookup table can be derived from experience to give the estimated coding rate dependent on the

complexity of the project for a particular development environment. This is discussed in more detail below.

Estimating tools

Statistical methods can be used when a project is large (and therefore complex) or novel. This allows the project team to replace a single estimate of duration with a range within which they are confident the real duration will lie. This is particularly useful for the early stage of the project when uncertainty is greatest. The PERT approach described later in this chapter allows optimistic, pessimistic and most likely times to be specified for each task – from these a probabilistic estimate of project completion time can be computed.

The most widely used economic model is the **constructive cost model (COCOMO)**, described by Boehm (1981) and first proposed by staff working at US consultancy Doty Associates. The constructive cost model is used to estimate the amount of effort required to complete a project on the basis of the estimated number of lines of program code. Based on an analysis of software projects, the model attempts to predict the effort required to deliver a project based on input factors such as the skill level of staff. A simplified version of the model is:

$$WM = C \times (KDSI)^K \times EAF$$

where WM = number of person months, C = one of three constant values dependent on development mode, $KDSI$ = delivered source lines of code $\times$ 1000, K = one of three constant values dependent on development mode, EAF = effort adjustment factor.

The three development modes or project types are categorised as organic (small development teams working in a familiar environment), embedded (where constraints are made by existing hardware or software) and semi-detached, which lies somewhere between the two extremes of organic and embedded. In order to increase the accuracy of the model, more detailed versions of COCOMO incorporate cost drivers such as the attributes of the end product and the project environment. The detailed version of the model calculates the cost drivers for the product design, detailed design, coding and unit test, and integration and test phases separately.

These techniques may take a considerable amount of time to arrive at a reasonably accurate estimate of personnel time required. However, since the build phase will be a major part of the development budget, it is important to allocate time to undertake detailed estimation.

The COCOMO method derives the time estimates it produces from an estimate of the number of lines of programming code to be written. A method of estimating the number of lines of code was developed by Alan Albrecht of IBM (Albrecht and Gaffney, 1983). **Function point analysis** is based on counting the number of user functions the application will have. It is possible to do this in detail after the requirements for the application have been defined. The five user function categories are:

1. number of external input types;

2. number of external output types;

3. number of logical internal file types;

4. number of external interface file types;

5. external enquiry types.

Each of these types of input and output is then weighted according to its complexity and additional factors applied according to the complexity of processing. The function point estimate can be compared to the function point count of previous completed information systems to give an idea of the number of lines of code and length of time that are expected.

Constructive cost model (COCOMO)

A model used to estimate the amount of effort required to complete a project on the basis of the estimated number of lines of program code.

Function point analysis

A method of estimating the time it will take to build a system by counting up the number of functions and data inputs and outputs and then comparing to completed projects.

Note that both the COCOMO and function point analysis techniques were developed before the widespread use of applications with graphical user interfaces, interactive development environments for 'graphical programming', rapid applications development (RAD) and client/server databases to store information. These new techniques have made it faster to develop applications and the original data sets and principles on which these models are based have been updated to account for this. In order to take account of developments in software and software development methodologies COCOMO II has been developed (Boehm et al., 2001).

Scheduling and planning

Scheduling is determining when project activities should be executed. The finished schedule is termed the *project plan*.

Resource allocation is part of scheduling. It involves assigning resources to each task. Once the activities have been identified and their resource requirements estimated, it is necessary to define their relationship to one another. There are some activities that can only begin when other activities have been completed. This is termed a *serial relationship* and is shown graphically in Figure 9.3.

The execution of other activities may be totally independent and thus they have a *parallel relationship*, as shown graphically in Figure 9.4. Here, after the design phase, three activities must occur in parallel before implementation can occur.

For most significant projects there will be a range of alternative schedules which may meet the project objectives.

For commercial projects, computer software will be used to assist in diagramming the relationship between activities and calculating network durations. From a critical path network and with the appropriate information, it is usually possible for the software automatically to generate Gantt charts, resource loading graphs and cost graphs, which are discussed later in the chapter. Project management software, such as Microsoft Project, can be used to assist in choosing the most feasible schedule by recalculating resource requirements and timings for each operation. The network analysis section of this chapter provides more information on project scheduling techniques.

Figure 9.3 Serial relationship of activities

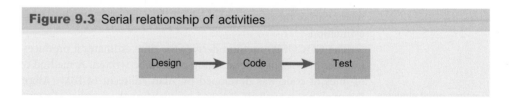

Figure 9.4 Parallel relationship of activities

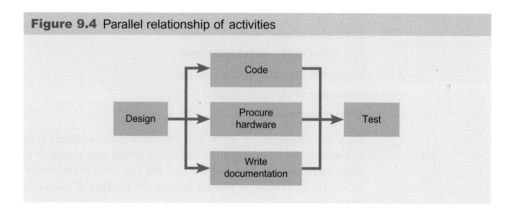

Activity 9.1   Project planning exercise

The scenario

You are required to construct a project plan for the following BIS development project. Your objective is to schedule the project to run in the shortest time possible. The plan should include all activities, the estimated, elapsed and effort time, and who is to perform each activity. In addition, it is necessary to indicate the sequence in which all the tasks will take place. The programs can be scheduled in any order, but for each program the design stage must come first, followed by the programming and finally the documentation.

Within the context of the exercise, you can assume that the detailed systems analysis has already been carried out and that it is now necessary to perform the design, programming and documentation activities. For the purposes of this exercise, we will not include the testing and implementation phases.

Present your project plan in the form of a Gantt chart (see Figure 9.10 later) showing each task, the sequence in which tasks will be performed, the estimated effort and elapsed time and the resource allocated to each task.

The activities

There are five programs in the system. Each has a different level of difficulty:

- Program 1   Difficult
- Program 2   Easy
- Program 3   Moderate
- Program 4   Moderate
- Program 5   Difficult

For each level of difficulty, the design, programming and documentation tasks take different amounts of effort time:

Design
- Easy programs   1 day
- Moderate programs   2 days
- Difficult programs   4 days

Programming
- Easy programs   1 day
- Moderate programs   3 days
- Difficult programs   6 days

Documentation
- Easy programs   1 day
- Moderate programs   2 days
- Difficult programs   3 days

Resources

In order to complete the project plan, you need to know what resources you have available. For each resource, there are two variables:

- *Work rate*. This describes the speed at which the resource works (i.e. a work rate of 1.0 means that a task scheduled to take one day should only take one day to complete satisfactorily; a work rate of 1.5 means that a task scheduled for three days should only take two days etc.).
- *Availability*. Each resource will be available for certain amounts of time during the week. 100% availability = 5 days per week, 50% availability = 2.5 days per week, etc.

In planning your project, work to units of half a day. For simplicity, any task which requires a fraction of half a day should be rounded up (e.g. 1.6 days should be rounded up to 2 days). Also, a resource can only be scheduled for one task at any one time!

Resource availability

System designer 1 (SD1)
- Work rate   1.0
- Availability   100%

Systems designer 2 (SD2)
- Work rate   1.5
- Availability   40%

Systems designer 3 (SD3)
- Work rate   0.5
- Availability   50%

Programmer 1 (P1)
- Work rate   2.0
- Availability   40%

Programmer 2 (P2)
- Work rate   1.0
- Availability   100%

Programmer 3 (P3)
- Work rate   0.5
- Availability   60%

Technical author 1 (TAI) (to do the documentation)
- Work rate   1.0
- Availability   60%

Technical author 2 (TA2)
- Work rate   0.5
- Availability   100%

Technical author 3 (TA3)
- Work rate   2.0
- Availability   40%

Tips

1. This exercise will be easier if you structure the information well. You could do this by producing three matrices for the design, programming and documentation tasks. Each of them should show across the columns three different tasks for easy, moderate and difficult programs. Each row should indicate how long the different types of workers will take to complete the task.

2. To calculate the length of elapsed time for each cell in the matrix, it is easiest to use this relationship:

$$\text{Elapsed time} = \text{Effort times} \times \frac{100}{\text{Availability \%}} \times \frac{100}{\text{Work rate \%}}$$

3. A calculator may help!

4. When drawing the Gantt chart, you may want to put your best people on the most difficult tasks, as you would on a real project.

Monitoring and control

When a project is under way, its objectives of cost, time and quality in meeting targets must be closely **monitored**. Monitoring involves ensuring that the project is working to plan once it has started. This should occur daily for small-scale tasks or weekly for combined activities. **Control** or corrective action will occur if the performance measures deviate from plan. It is important to monitor and assess performance as the project progresses, in order that corrective action can be taken before it deviates from plan to any great extent. Milestones (events that need to happen on a particular date) are defined so that performance against objectives can be measured (e.g. end of analysis, production of first prototype).

Computer project management packages can be used to automate the collection of project progress data and production of progress reports.

Achieving time, cost and quality objectives

As stated earlier, the project should be managed to achieve the defined objectives of time, cost and quality. The time objective is met by ensuring that the project is monitored in terms of execution of tasks within time limits. Corrective action is taken if a variance between actual and planned time is observed. The cost objective is achieved by the use of human resource and computing resource budgets and, again, variation between estimated and actual expenditure is noted and necessary corrective action taken. To ensure that quality objectives are met it is necessary to develop a quality plan which contains a list of items deliverable to the customer. Each of these will have an associated quality standard and procedure for dealing with a variance from the required quality level defined in the quality plan.

Project structure and size

The type of project structure required will be dependent on the size of the team undertaking the project. Projects with up to six team members can simply report directly to a project leader at appropriate intervals during project execution. For larger projects requiring up to 20 team members, it is usual to implement an additional tier of management in the form of team leaders. The team leader could be responsible for either a phase of the development (e.g. analysis, design) or a type of work (e.g. applications development, systems development). For any structure it is important that the project leader ensures consistency across development phases or development areas as appropriate. For projects with more than 20 members, it is likely that additional management layers will be needed in order to ensure that no one person is involved in too much supervision.

Reporting project progress

The two main methods of reporting the progress of a project are by written reports and verbal reports at meetings of the project team. It is important that a formal statement of progress is made in written form, preferably in a standard report format, to ensure that everyone is aware of the current project situation. This is particularly important when changes to specifications are made during the project. In order to facilitate two-way communication between team members and team management, regular meetings should be arranged by the project manager. These meetings can increase the commitment of team members by allowing discussion of points of interest and dissemination of information on how each team's effort is contributing to the overall progression of the project.

Documentation

Ensuring adequate project documentation is a key aspect of the role of the project manager. Software development is a team effort and documentation is necessary to disseminate design information throughout the team. Good documentation reduces the expense of maintenance after project delivery. Also, when members of the team leave the department or organisation, the coding they have produced must be understandable to new project members. Often a development methodology will require documentation at stages during the project in a specific format. Thus documentation must be an identified task in the development effort and a standard document format should be used throughout the project (this may be a standard such as BS 5750 or ISO 9001).

Documents that may be required include the following:

- *Workplan/task list.* For each team member a specified activity with start and finish dates and relevant coding standard should be defined.
- *Requirements specification.* This should clearly specify the objectives and functions of the software.
- *Purchase requisition forms.* Required if new software and hardware resources are needed from outside the organisation.
- *Staffing budget.* A running total of personnel costs, including expenses and subsistence payments. These should show actual against predicted expenditure for control purposes.
- *Change control documents.* To document any changes to the project specification during the project. A document is needed to highlight the effect on budgets and timescales of a change in software specifications.

FOCUS ON... A PROJECT MANAGEMENT METHODOLOGY: PRINCE2

PRINCE2 (published in 1996) is a process-based project management methodology based on PRINCE (published in 1989), which stands for Projects in Controlled Environments. The development of PRINCE2 involved a consortium of 150 European organisations and is a de facto standard used by the UK government and widely used by the private sector, both in the UK and internationally. The PRINCE2 method for managing projects is designed to help you work out who should be involved and what they are responsible for. It also provides a set of processes to work through and explains what information you should be gathering along the way.

The key features of PRINCE2 are:

- its focus on business justification;
- a defined organisation structure for the project management team;
- its product-based planning approach;
- its emphasis on dividing the project into manageable and controllable stages;
- its flexibility to be applied at a level appropriate to the project.

Thus the PRINCE2 methodology means managing the project in a logical organised way, following defined steps. The PRINCE2 methodology says that a project should have an:

- organised and controlled start, i.e. organise and plan things properly before leaping in;
- organised and controlled middle, i.e. when the project has started, make sure it continues to be organised and controlled;
- organised and controlled end, i.e. when you've got what you want and the project has finished, tidy up the loose ends.

Figure 9.5 PRINCE2 Process Model

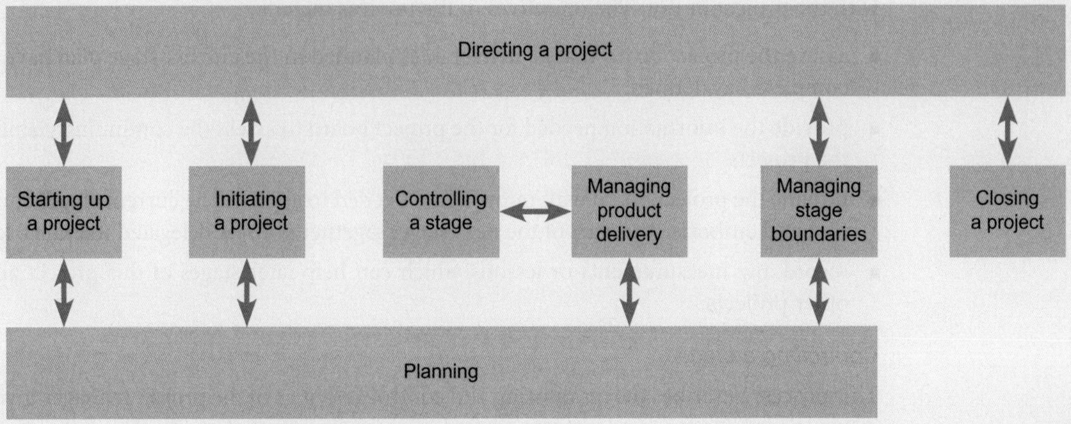

The PRINCE2 Process Model

In order to describe what a project should do when, PRINCE2 has a series of processes which cover all the activities needed on a project from starting up to closing down. The PRINCE2 Process Model (Figure 9.5) defines each process with its key inputs and outputs together with the specific objectives to be achieved and activities to be carried out.

Each element in the process model will now be described.

Directing a project

This process is aimed at the project board and involves the management and monitoring of the project via reports and controls from the startup of the project until its closure. Key processes for the project board are:

- initiation (starting the project off on the right foot);
- stage boundaries (commitment of more resources after checking results so far);
- ad hoc direction (monitoring progress, providing advice and guidance, reacting to exception situations);
- project closure (confirming the project outcome and controlled close).

Starting up a project

This is a pre-project process designed to ensure that the prerequisites for initiating the project are in place. The work of the process is built around the production of three elements:

- ensuring that the information required for the project team is available;
- designing and appointing the project management team;
- creating the initiation stage plan.

Initiating a project

The objectives of initiating a project include:

- agree whether or not there is sufficient justification to proceed with the project;
- establish a stable management basis on which to proceed;
- document and confirm that an acceptable business case exists for the project;
- agree to the commitment of resources for the first stage of the project.

Managing stage boundaries

This process provides the project board with key decision points on whether to continue with the project or not. The objectives of the process include:

- assure the project board that all deliverables planned in the current stage plan have been completed as defined;
- provide the information needed for the project board to assess the continuing viability of the project;
- provide the project board with information needed to approve the current stage's completion and authorise the start of the next stage, together with its delegated tolerance level;
- record any measurements or lessons which can help later stages of this project and/or other projects.

Controlling a stage

This process describes the monitoring and control activities of the project manager involved in ensuring that a stage stays on course and reacts to unexpected events. Throughout a stage there will be a cycle consisting of:

- authorising work to be done;
- gathering progress information about that work;
- watching for changes;
- reviewing the situation;
- reporting;
- taking any necessary corrective action.

Managing product delivery

The objective of this process is to ensure that planned products are created and delivered by:

- making certain that work on products allocated to the team is effectively authorised and agreed accepting and checking work packages;
- ensuring that the work is done;
- assessing work progress and forecasts regularly;
- ensuring that completed products meet quality criteria.

Closing a project

The purpose of this process is to execute a controlled close to the project. The process covers the project manager's work to wrap up the project either at its end or at premature close. Most of the work is to prepare input to the project board to obtain its confirmation that the project may close. The objectives of closing a project therefore include:

- check the extent to which the objectives or aims set out in the project initiation document (PID) have been met;
- confirm the extent of the fulfilment of the project initiation document (pid) and the customer's satisfaction with the deliverables;
- make any recommendations for follow-on actions;
- prepare an end project report;
- notify the host organisation of the intention to disband the project organisation and resources.

Planning

Planning is a repeatable process, and plays an important role in other processes, main ones being:

- planning an initiation stage
- planning a project
- planning a stage
- producing an exception plan.

PRINCE2 organisation

The following are the main project management roles in PRINCE2.

Project manager

The project manager is responsible for organising and controlling the project. The project manager will select people to do the work on the project and will be responsible for making sure that the work is done properly and on time. The project manager also draws up the project plans that describe what the project team will actually be doing and when they expect to finish.

Customer, user and supplier

The person who is paying for the project is called the customer or executive. The person who is going to use the results or outcome of the project is called the user. On some projects the customer and user may be the same person. The person who provides the expertise to do the actual work on the project is called the supplier or specialist. All these people need to be organised and coordinated so that the project delivers the required outcome within budget, on time and to the appropriate quality.

Project board

Each PRINCE2 project will have a project board made up of the customer (or executive), someone who can represent the user side and someone to represent the supplier or specialist input. In PRINCE2 the people are called customer, senior user and senior supplier respectively. The project manager reports regularly to the project board, keeping them informed of progress and highlighting any problems they can foresee. The project board is responsible for providing the project manager with the necessary decisions for the project to proceed and to overcome any problems.

Project assurance

Providing an independent view of how the project is progressing is the job of project assurance. In PRINCE2, there are three views of assurance: business, user and specialist. Each view reflects the interests of the three project board members. Assurance is about checking that the project remains viable in terms of costs and benefits (business assurance), checking that the users' requirements are being met (user assurance), and that the project is delivering a suitable solution (specialist or technical assurance). On some projects, the assurance is done by a separate team of people called the project assurance team, but the assurance job can be done by the individual members of the project board themselves.

Project management methodologies compared

In addition to PRINCE2 many other project management methodologies (as opposed to development process methodologies such as SSADM, JSD and STRADIS) exist, such as BPMM (www.bates.ca) and IDEAL (www.sei.cmu.edu/ideal). In addition, methodologies have been developed 'in-house' by companies for their own use or have been developed commercially and require a licence fee before more information is released.

Activity 9.2 An assessment of PRINCE2

An important function of a company's information systems manager is to review which methodologies should be employed to improve the quality of its systems development processes. Some methodologies may add a structure to a company process which improves its efficiency. Others may enforce restrictions which reduce the efficiency of the process and increase the cost and duration of the project.

You are a project manager in a company of 400 people. The company has a history of developing systems that meet the needs of the end-users well, but can sometimes be over six months late. The managing director has decided that the project will be conducted by internal IS development staff. Your role as the owner of the system in which the project will be implemented is to manage the project using other resources, such as the IS department, as you see fit.

QUESTION

From the information given in the preceding section and using any relevant books, decide whether to use a formal project methodology such as PRINCE2 or IDEAL or a different approach. Justify your answer, giving a brief evaluation of what you perceive as the advantages and disadvantages of the methodology.

A PROJECT MANAGEMENT TOOL: NETWORK ANALYSIS

Critical path

Activities on the critical path are termed critical activities. Any delay in these activities will cause a delay in the project completion time.

Critical path diagrams are used extensively during scheduling and monitoring to show the planned activities of a project and the *dependencies* between these activities. For example, network analysis will show that activity C can only take place when activity A and activity B have been completed. Once a network diagram has been constructed, it is possible to follow a sequence of activities, called a *path*, through the network from start to end. The length of time it takes to follow the path is the sum of all the durations of activities on that path. The path with the longest duration gives the *project completion time*. This is called the *critical path* because any change in duration in any activities on this path will cause the whole project duration to become shorter or longer. Activities not on the critical path will have a certain amount of slack time in which the activity can be delayed or the duration lengthened and not affect the overall project duration. The amount of *slack time* is the difference between the path duration the activity is on and the critical path duration. By definition, all activities on the critical path have zero slack. Note that there must be at least one critical path for each network and there may be several critical paths. The significance of the critical path is that if any node on the path finishes later than the earliest finish time, the overall network time will increase by the same amount, putting the project behind schedule. Thus any planning and control activities should focus on ensuring that tasks on the critical path remain within schedule.

Critical path network diagrams are sometimes called 'PERT charts', but the correct technical meaning of this term is detailed in a later section.

The critical path method (CPM)

Once the estimation stage has been completed, the project activities should have been identified, activity durations and resource requirement estimated and activity relationships identified. Based on this information, the critical path diagrams can be constructed using either the activity-on-arrow (AOA) approach or the activity-on-node (AON) approach. The issues involved in deciding which one to utilise will be discussed later. The following description of critical path analysis will use the AON method.

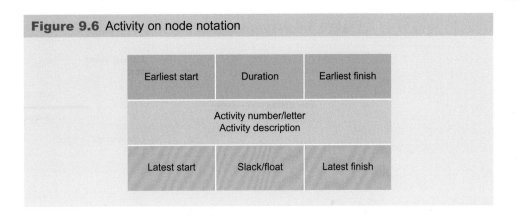

Figure 9.6 Activity on node notation

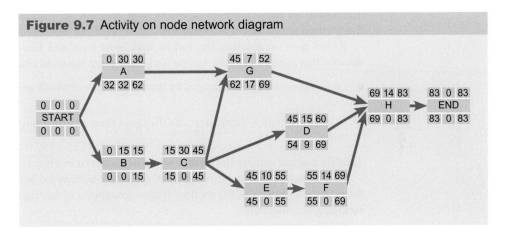

Figure 9.7 Activity on node network diagram

Critical path method (CPM)

Critical path diagrams show the relationship between activities in a project.

The **critical path method (CPM)** uses critical path diagrams to show the relationships between activities in a project.

The activity-on-node (AON) method

In an activity-on-node network, the diagramming notation shown in Figure 9.6 is used. Each activity task is represented by a node with the format shown in the figure. Thus a completed network will consist of a number of nodes connected by lines, one for each task, between a start and an end node, as shown in Figure 9.7.

The diagram illustrates *sequential activities* such as from activity B to activity C and *parallel activities* such as activities D, F and G. Once the network diagram has been drawn using the activity relationships, the node information can be calculated, starting with the earliest start and finish times. These are calculated by working from left to right through the network, in the 'forward pass'. Once the forward pass has been completed, it is possible to calculate the latest start and finish times for each task. This is achieved by moving right to left along the network, backward through time, in the 'backward pass'. Finally, the slack or float value can be calculated for each node by taking the difference between the earliest start and latest start (or earliest finish and latest finish) times for each task. There should be at least one (there may be more than one) critical path running through the network where each task has a slack value of 0. In Figure 9.7 the critical path can be stated as running through the activities B, C, E, F and H. Any delay to these critical activities will increase the current project duration of 83. The critical path represents the sequence of activities that takes the longest time to complete and thus defines the shortest time that the project can complete in. Activities not on the critical path have a slack time, for example activity A has a slack time of 32, which represents how late the activity can be without effecting the overall project duration.

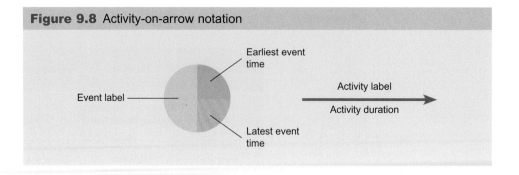

Figure 9.8 Activity-on-arrow notation

The activity-on-arrow (AOA) method

The format for the activity-on-arrow method will now be described. The symbols used in this method are as shown in Figure 9.8.

Rather than considering the earliest and latest start and finish times of the activities directly, this method uses the earliest and latest event times, as below:

- *Earliest event time* – determined by the earliest time at which any subsequent activity can start.

- *Latest event time* – determined by the latest time at which any subsequent activity can start.

Thus for a single activity the format would be as shown in Figure 9.9.

There has historically been a greater use of the activity-on-arrow (AOA) method, but the activity-on-node (AON) method is now recognised as having a number of advantages, including the following:

- Most project management computer software uses the AON approach.

- AON diagrams do not need dummy activities to maintain the relationship logic.

- AON diagrams have all the information on timings and identification within the node box, leading to clearer diagrams.

Gantt charts

Gantt charts

Show the duration of parallel and sequential activities in a project as horizontal bars on a chart.

Although network diagrams are ideal for showing the relationship between project tasks, they do not provide a clear view of which tasks are being undertaken over time and particularly of how many tasks may be undertaken in parallel at any one time. **Gantt charts** are used to summarise the project plan by showing the duration of parallel and sequential activities in a project as horizontal 'time bars' on a chart. The Gantt chart provides an overview for the project managers to allow them to monitor project progress against planned progress and so provides a valuable information source for project control.

Figure 9.9 Calculating event times for an activity-on-arrow network

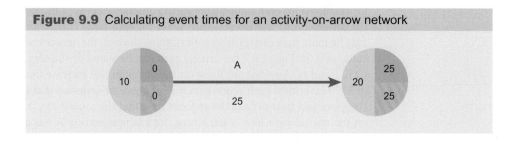

Figure 9.10 Gantt chart showing activities and milestones

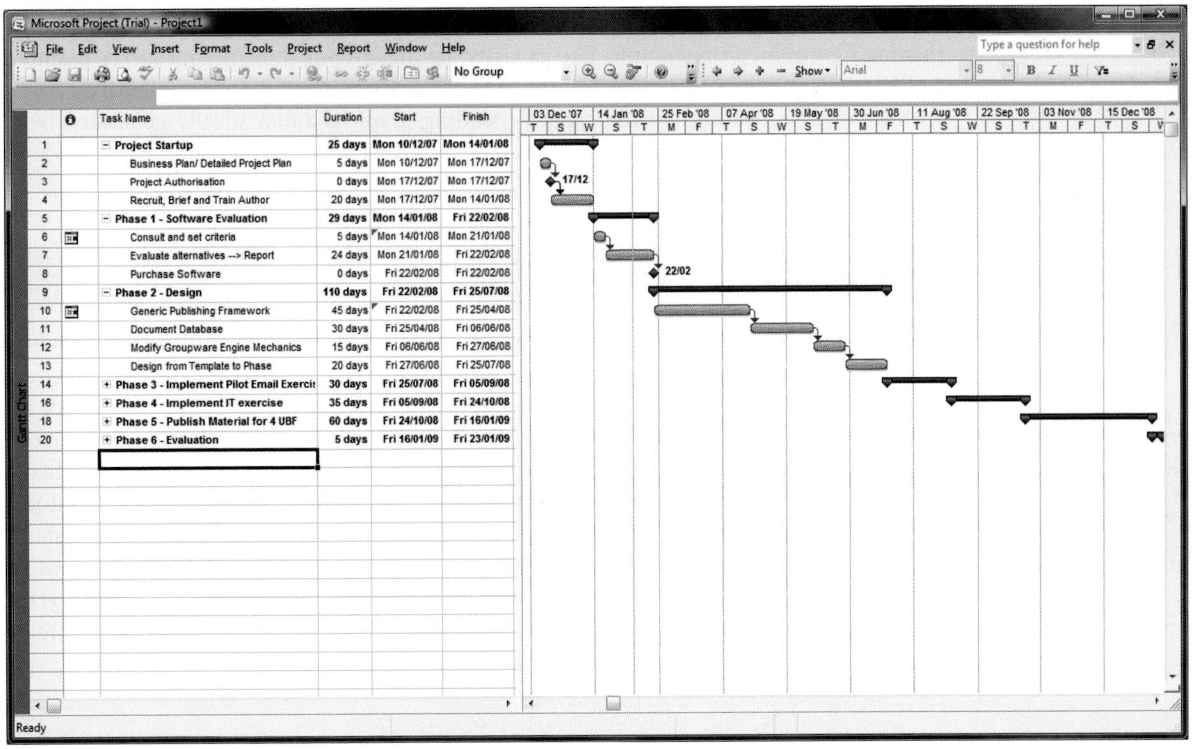

Source: Screenshot frame reprinted by permission from Microsoft Corporation

Figure 9.10 shows a typical Gantt chart produced using Microsoft Project. Note that some phases such as 'Phase 1 – software evaluation' have *subactivities* such as 'consult and set criteria' and 'evaluate alternatives – report'. Each of these subactivities has a certain number of days and a corresponding cost assigned to it. **Milestones** are activities that are planned to occur by a particular day, such as 'Purchase hardware by 17/06'. These are shown as triangles. They are significant events in the life of the project, such as completion of a prototype.

To draw a Gantt chart manually or using a spreadsheet or drawing package, follow these steps:

1. Draw a grid with the tasks along the vertical axis and the timescale (for the whole project duration) along the horizontal axis.

2. Draw a horizontal bar across from the task identifier along the left of the chart, starting at the earliest start time and ending at the earliest finish time.

3. Indicate the slack amount by drawing a line from the earliest finish time to the latest finish time.

4. Repeat steps 2 and 3 for each task.

If the network analysis is being conducted using project management software, then the Gantt chart is automatically generated from information in the network analysis.

Milestone

This denotes a significant event in the project such as completion of a prototype.

Capacity loading graphs

The basic network diagram assumes that all tasks can be undertaken when required by the earliest start times calculated from the node dependency relationships. However, resources required to undertake tasks are usually limited and the duration of an individual task or the number of parallel tasks may be limited. In order to calculate the capacity requirements of a project over time, the capacity requirements associated with each task are indicated on the Gantt chart. From this, a **capacity loading graph** can be developed by projecting the loading figures on a time graph. The capacity loading graphs show the resources required to undertake activities in a project. If the network analysis is being conducted using project management software, then the capacity loading graph is automatically generated from information in the network analysis.

Capacity loading graphs

Capacity loading graphs show the resources required to undertake activities in a project.

Project costs

The previous discussion has concentrated on the need to schedule and control activities in order to complete the entire project within a minimum timespan. However, there are situations in which the project cost is an important factor. If the costs of each project are known, then it is possible to produce a **project cost graph** which will show the amount of cost incurred over the life of the project. This is useful in showing any periods when a number of parallel tasks are incurring significant costs, leading to the need for additional cashflow at key times. In large projects it may be necessary to aggregate the costs of a number of activities, particularly if they are the responsibility of one department or subcontractor. As a control mechanism, the project manager can collect information on cost to date and percentage completion to date for each task to identify any cost above budget and take appropriate action without delay.

Project cost graphs

Show the financial cost of undertaking the project.

Trading time and cost: project crashing

Within any project there will be a number of time–cost trade-offs to consider. Most projects will have tasks that can be completed with an injection of additional resources, such as equipment or people. Reasons to reduce project completion time include:

- to reduce high indirect costs associated with equipment;
- to reduce new product development time to market;
- to avoid penalties for late completion;
- to gain incentives for early completion;
- to release resources for other projects.

Project crashing

Refers to reducing the project duration by increasing spending on critical activities.

The use of additional resources to reduce project completion time is termed **crashing** the project. The idea is to reduce overall indirect project costs by increasing direct costs on a particular task. One of the most obvious ways of decreasing task duration is to allocate additional labour to a task. This can be either an additional team member or through overtime working. To enable a decision to be made on the potential benefits of crashing a task, the following information is required:

- the normal task duration;
- the crash task duration;
- the cost of crashing the task to the crash task duration per unit time.

The process by which a task is chosen for crashing is by observing which task can be reduced for the required time for the lowest cost. As stated before, the overall project completion time is the sum of the task durations on the critical path. Thus it is always necessary to crash a task that is on the critical path. As the duration of tasks on the critical path is reduced, however, other paths in the network will also become critical. If this happens, it will require the crashing process to be undertaken on all the paths that are critical at any one time.

Project evaluation and review technique (PERT)

PERT replaces the fixed activity duration used in the CPM method with a statistical distribution which uses optimistic, pessimistic and most likely duration estimates.

The critical path method (CPM) described above was developed by the company Du Pont during the 1950s to manage plant construction. The PERT approach was formulated by the US Navy during the development of the Polaris submarine-launched ballistic missile system in the same decade (Sapolsky, 1972). The main difference between the approaches is the ability of PERT to take into consideration uncertainty in activity durations.

The PERT approach attempts to take into account the fact that most task durations are not fixed, by using a beta probability distribution to describe the variability inherent in the processes. The probabilistic approach involves three time estimates for each activity:

- *optimistic time* – the task duration under the most optimistic conditions;
- *pessimistic time* – the task duration under the most pessimistic conditions;
- *most likely time* – the most likely task duration.

As stated, the beta distribution is used to describe the task duration variability. To derive the average or expected time for a task duration, the following equation is used:

$$Expected\ duration = \frac{Optimistic + (4 \times Most\ likely) + Pessimistic}{6}$$

The combination of the expected time and standard deviation for the network path allows managers to compute probabilistic estimates of project completion times. A point to bear in mind with these estimates is that they only take into consideration the tasks on the critical path and discount the fact that slack on tasks on a non-critical path could delay the project. Therefore the probability that the project will be completed by a specified date is the probability that all paths will be completed by that date, which is the product of the probabilities for all the paths.

Project network simulation

In order to use the PERT approach, it must be assumed that the paths of a project are independent and that the same tasks are not on more than one path. If a task is on more than one path and its actual completion time was much later than its expected time, it is obvious that the paths are not independent. If the network consists of these paths and they are near the critical path time, then the results will be invalid.

Simulation can be used to develop estimates of a project's completion time by taking into account all the network paths. Probability distributions are constructed for each task, derived from estimates provided by such data collection methods as observation and historical data. A simulation then generates a random number within the probability distribution for each task. The critical path is determined and the project duration calculated. This procedure is repeated a number of times (possibly more than 100) until there are sufficient data to construct a frequency distribution of project times. This distribution can be used to make a probabilistic assessment of the actual project duration. If greater accuracy is required, the process can be repeated to generate additional project completion estimates which can be added to the frequency distribution.

Benefits and limitations of the network analysis approach

The main benefit of using the network analysis approach is the requirement to use a structured analysis of the number and sequence of tasks contained within a project, so aiding understanding of resource requirements for project completion. It provides a number of useful graphical displays that assist understanding of such factors as project dependencies and resource loading, a reasonable estimate of the project duration and the tasks that must be completed on time to meet this duration (i.e. the critical path), and a control mechanism to monitor actual progress against planned progress on the Gantt chart. It also provides a means of estimating any decrease in overall project time by providing extra resources at any stage and can be used to provide cost estimates for different project scenarios.

Limitations to consider when using network analysis include remembering that its use is no substitute for good management judgement in such areas as prioritising and selecting suppliers and personnel for the project. Additionally, any errors in the network such as incorrect dependency relationships or the omission of tasks may invalidate the results. The tasks' times are forecasts and are thus estimates that are subject to error. PERT and simulation techniques may reduce time estimation errors, but at the cost of greater complexity which may divert management time from more important issues. Also time estimates for tasks may be greater than necessary to provide managers with slack and ensure that they meet deadlines. Slack time that does exist may be 'wasted' by not starting activities until the last possible moment and thus delaying the project if they are not completed on time.

SUMMARY

1. Projects are unique, one-time operations designed to accomplish a specific set of objectives in a limited timeframe with a limited budget and resources.

2. Major roles in project organisation include the project sponsor, the project manager and the project user. The project sponsor provides a justification of the project to senior management. The project manager role is to provide clearly defined goals and ensure that adequate resources are employed on the project. The project user who will be utilising the system should be involved in the definition and implementation of the system.

3. The main elements in the project management process include estimate, schedule and plan, monitoring and control, and documentation.

4. A work breakdown structure splits the overall project task into a number of more detailed activities in order to facilitate detailed estimation of resources required.

5. Projects can be resource-constrained (limited by resource) or time-constrained (limited by the deadline).

6. Scheduling involves producing a project plan which determines when activities should be executed.

7. Once under way a project can be monitored against the defined objectives of time, cost and quality.

8. Documentation is essential in reducing the expense of project maintenance.

9. PRINCE2 is an example of a project management methodology. An example of a systems development methodology is RAD.

10. Critical path analysis shows the activities undertaken during a project and the dependencies between them. The critical path is identified by making a forward and then a reverse pass through the network, calculating the earliest and latest activity start/finish times respectively.

11. Gantt charts provide an overview of what tasks are being undertaken over time. This allows the project manager to monitor project progress against planned progress.

12. Capacity loading graphs provide an indication of the amount of resource needed for the project over time.

13. Cost graphs provide an indication of monetary expenditure over the project period.

14. Project crashing consists of reducing overall indirect project costs (e.g. by reducing the project duration) by increasing expenditure on a particular task.

15. To reduce the length of a project we need to know the critical path of the project and the cost of reducing individual activity times.

16. The PERT approach provides a method of integrating the variability of task durations into the network analysis.

EXERCISES

Self-assessment exercises

1. What are the main elements of the project management process?

2. What are the main project aims of the PRINCE2 methodology?

3. What information is required for the construction of a critical path diagram?

4. What information do the Gantt chart and the PERT chart convey?

5. Define the term 'critical path'.

6. What is the difference between effort time and elapsed time?

Discussion questions

1. Draw a Gantt chart for the following AON network (Figure 9.11).

2. 'One of the most difficult parts of project management is getting the estimates right.' Discuss.

Figure 9.11 Activity-on-node network

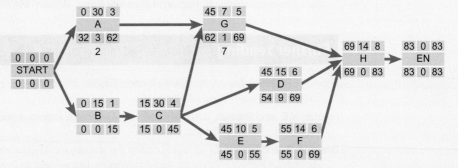

Essay questions

1. Explore the features of a project management computer package such as Microsoft Project. Evaluate its use in the project management process.

2. Compare the different alternatives that are available for the critical path method of network analysis.

3. What is the most effective method of estimating the duration of an information systems development project?

Examination questions

1. Evaluate the roles undertaken by people in a project organisation.

2. What are the main elements in the project management process?

3. Evaluate the use of the PRINCE2 project management methodology.

4. Explain the difference between portraying a project plan as a Gantt chart and as a PERT chart.

5. What is the importance of conducting monitoring and control when managing a project?

6. Why is it difficult and often impossible for a software project manager to balance the three constraints of time, budget and quality? You should relate your answer to two different aspects of the quality of the delivered information system.

7. What is the difference between elapsed time and effort time? How are the two factors related in terms of the availability and work rate of different staff? Describe this in words, or using an equation or an example.

References

Albrecht, A.J. and Gaffney, J. (1983) 'Software function, source lines of code and development effort prediction', *IEEE Transactions on Software Engineering*, SE-9, 639–48

Boehm, B.W. (1981) *Software Engineering Economics*, Prentice-Hall, Englewood Cliffs, NJ

Boehm, B.W., Abts, C., Winsor Brown, A., Chulani, S., Clark, B.K., Horowitz, E., Madachy, Cadle, J. and Yeates, D. (2007) *Project Management for Information Systems*, 5th edition, Financial Times Prentice Hall, Harlow

Lyytinen, K. and Hirscheim, R. (1987) 'Information systems failures: a survey and classification of the empirical literature', *Oxford Surveys in IT*, 4, 257–309

Sapolsky, H.M. (1972) *The Polaris System Development: Bureaucratic and Programmatic Success in Government*, Harvard University Press, Boston, MA

Further reading

Brooks, F.P. (1995) *The Mythical Man-Month: Essays on Software Engineering – Anniversary Edition*, Addison-Wesley, Reading, MA.

Fenton, N.E. and Bieman, J. (2014) *Software Metrics: A Rigorous and Practical Approach*, 3rd edition, PWS Publishers, London.

Garmus, D. and Herron, D. (2000) *Function Point Analysis: Measurement Practices for Successful Software Projects*, Addison-Wesley, Upper Saddle River, NJ

Greasley, A. (2013) *Operations Management*, 3rd edition, John Wiley, Chichester.

Hughes, B. and Cotterell, M. (2009) *Software Project Management*, 5th edition, McGraw-Hill, Maidenhead.

Kerzner, H. (2013) *Project Management: A Systems Approach to Planning Scheduling and Controlling*, 11th edition, John Wiley, New York.

Kerzner, H. (2013) *Project Management Metrics, KPIs, and Dashboards: A Guide to Measuring and Monitoring Project Performance*, 2nd edition, John Wiley, Chichester.

Lock, D. (2013) *Project Management*, 10th edition, Gower, Aldershot.

Maylor, H. (2010) *Project Management*, 4th edition, Financial Times Prentice Hall, Harlow.

Persse, J.R. (2007) *Project Management Success with CMMI: Seven CMMI Process Areas*, Prentice-Hall, Upper Saddle River, NJ.

Selby, R.W. (2007) *Software Engineering: Barry W. Boehm's Lifetime Contributions to Software Development, Management, and Research*, Wiley-Interscience, Huboken, NJ.

Web links

Web sites with further information on project management methodologies are as follows:

http://www.prince-officialsite.com/ PRINCE2 official site.

www.prince2.com website of ILX Group who offer PRINCE2 training.

www.bates.ca BPMM.

www.sei.cmu.edu/ideal IDEAL.

www.pmi.org Project Management Institute.

https://at-web1.comp.glam.ac.uk/staff/dwfarthi/projman.htm Dave Farthing's software project management web page has many links to project management resources.

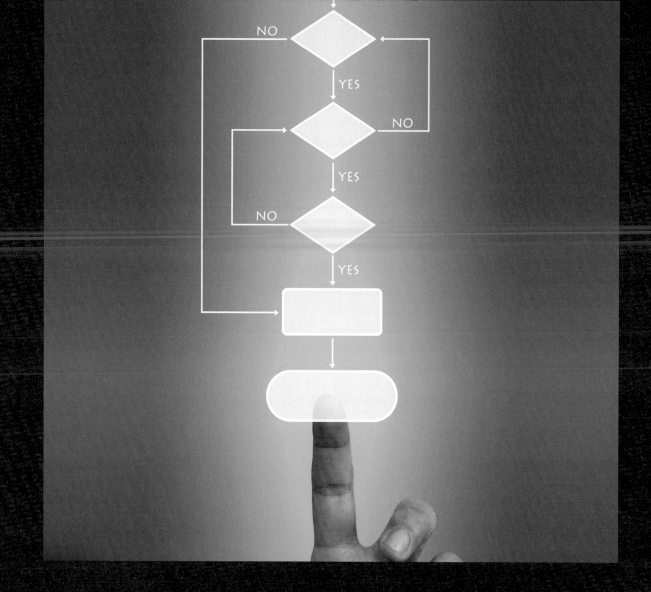

LINKS TO OTHER CHAPTERS

This chapter is directly related to Chapter 8, which describes the preceding stage of information systems development (initiation), and Chapter 11, which describes the next phase (systems design).

Systems analysis

CHAPTER AT A GLANCE

LEARNING OUTCOMES

After reading this chapter, you will be able to:

- define the importance of conducting the analysis phase to the
  overall success of the system;
- choose appropriate techniques for analysing users' requirements
  for an information system;
- construct appropriate textual descriptions and diagrams to
  assist in summarising the requirements as an input to the design
  phase.

MANAGEMENT ISSUES

Careful systems analysis must be conducted on each BIS project
to ensure that the system meets the needs of the business and its
users. From a managerial perspective, this chapter addresses the
following questions:

- Which different aspects of the system must be summarised in
  the requirements document?
- Which diagramming tools are appropriate to summarise the
  operation of the existing and proposed systems?

INTRODUCTION

Once it has been determined that it is desirable to proceed with the acquisition of a new BIS, it is necessary to determine the system requirements before any design or development work takes place. **Systems analysis** is about finding out *what* the new system is to do, rather than *how*. There are two basic components to the analysis process:

- *Fact-finding*. An exercise needs to take place where all prospective users of the new system should contribute to determining requirements;

- *Documentation*. Detailed systems design follows the analysis stage and it needs to be based on unambiguous documentation and diagrams from the analysis stage.

Systems analysis involves the investigation of the business and user requirements of an information system. Fact-finding techniques are used to ascertain the user's needs and these are summarised using a range of diagramming methods.

Factors that will influence the use of fact-finding techniques and documentation tools will include:

- *The result of the 'make-or-buy decision'*. Made during the feasibility stage, a 'make' decision where bespoke software is developed will need more detailed analysis than a 'buy' decision where packaged software is purchased off-the-shelf, especially when the results of the analysis process are fed into the design stage.

- *Application complexity*. A very complex system or one where there are linkages to other systems will need very careful analysis to define system and subsystem boundaries, and this will lead to use of more formal techniques when compared with a simple or standalone application.

- *User versus corporate development*. User development does not lend itself to extensive use of formal analysis tools. However, basic analysis is required and there are certain analysis tools that user developers can use that increase the probability of success. Similarly, where application development by IS/IT professionals occurs there will be a need for a more formal approach, especially where systems cut across functional boundaries.

Any errors in systems development that occur during the analysis phase will cost far more to correct than errors that occur in subsequent stages. It is therefore essential that maximum thought and effort be put into the analysis process if unanticipated costs are not to arise in the later stages of development.

IDENTIFYING THE REQUIREMENTS

The emphasis in this section will be on those methods typically used during the traditional systems development lifecycle approach to software development. However, it is recognised that lean and agile approaches to software development will focus on techniques that are particularly relevant to those methods. Therefore, these will be commented on later in the chapter in a 'Focus on' section.

The main purpose of the requirements determination phase of a systems development project is to identify those user requirements that need to be incorporated into the design of the new information system and that the requirements identified 'really' meet the users' needs. Therefore, the first task in analysis is to conduct a fact-finding exercise so that the information systems requirements can be determined. Unfortunately, as identified by Shi et al. (1996) and by Browne and Rogich (2001), there are a number of reasons why this is very difficult for many organisations:

- user limitations in terms of their ability to express correct requirements;

- lack of user awareness of what can be achieved with an information system (both in terms of under- and over-estimating an information system's capabilities;
- different interpretation of software requirements by different users;
- existence of biases amongst users so that requirements are identified on the basis of attitude, personality or environment rather than real business needs;
- requirements may overlap organisational boundaries (e.g. between different functional areas of the business) such that conflicts occur when identifying requirements;
- information requirements are varied and complex and this can lead to difficulties in structuring requirements so that they can be properly analysed;
- communication issues can result because of the complex web of interactions that exists between different users.

Nonetheless, while the task of requirements determination may be difficult, it must still be undertaken if the developed system is to have those features that the users and the organisation actually need. The methods an organisation uses in the analysis phase will depend, at least in part, on two factors:

- *Levels of decision making involved.* A new information system will be under consideration either to resolve a problem or to create an opportunity. In either case, the objective is to improve the quality of information available to allow better decision making. The type of system under consideration may include a transaction processing system, a management information system, a decision support system, a combination of these or some other categorisation of system (Chapter 6). So, for example, an information system that is purely geared towards the needs of management will require a different approach to fact-finding (for example, using one-to-one interviews with senior managers) from one that mainly involves transaction processing (for example, using observation of the existing process).

- *Scope of functional area.* A new information system may serve the needs of one functional business area (e.g. the HRM function), or it may cut across many functional areas. An information system that is restricted in scope may be faced with fewer of the problems that can affect new systems designed to meet the needs of many different areas. As before, the techniques of fact-finding may be similar, but how they are used and the findings presented may be radically different. Organisational culture, structure and decision-making processes will all have a part to play in selling the systems solution to all the affected parties.

Regardless of the scope and organisational levels involved, the objective of the fact-finding task is to gather sufficient information about the business processes under consideration so that a design can be constructed which will then provide the blueprint for the system build phase. We will now turn to a consideration of a number of fact-finding methods.

Although it might be thought that finding out the requirements for a system is straightforward, this is far from the case. Dissatisfaction with information systems is often due to the requirements for the information system being wrongly interpreted. Figure 10.1 shows an oft-quoted example of how a user's requirements for a swing might be interpreted, not only at the requirements analysis stage but throughout the project.

Interviewing

As noted by Browne and Rogich (2001), the most popular strategy likely to be adopted by an analyst is to use structured interviews with the people who will use the new system and to identify the procedures they follow in performing their tasks and also to identify the information they need to perform them. A successful requirements determination exercise

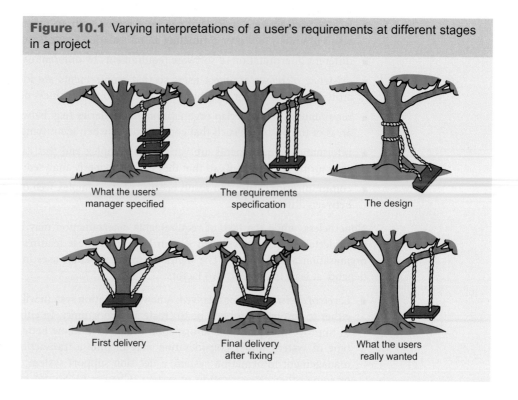

Figure 10.1 Varying interpretations of a user's requirements at different stages in a project

What the users' manager specified

The requirements specification

The design

First delivery

Final delivery after 'fixing'

What the users really wanted

will require the analyst to elicit from the users both their understanding of the current business environment and current information needs and flows and also a visualisation of the preferred future organisational environment and information needs. The difficulties associated with this have already been indicated above.

During interviewing, a range of staff are interviewed using structured techniques to identify features and problems of the current system and required features of the future system.

Success with this method involves careful planning, proper conduct of the interviews themselves and, finally, accurate recording of the interview findings. We can expand each of these to provide more detail.

Analysis technique – interviewing

Recommended practice: a range of staff are interviewed using structured techniques to identify features and problems of the current system and required features of the future system.

Planning

- Clear objectives need to be set to identify what needs to be achieved at the end of the interviewing process.

- Interview subjects must also be carefully selected so that the information gained will be relevant to the system being developed. For example, there may be little use in interviewing all the shopfloor workers in a manufacturing company if the system being developed is an executive information system (EIS) to assist with decision making at senior levels within the business. There may still be some merit in interviewing certain key personnel involved in operational decision making, since data produced may be useful in the proposed EIS.

- Customers should be involved in analysis if the use of a system affects them directly. For example, a customer of a phone-based ordering system or a telephone bank may well give an insight into problems of an existing system.

- The topics the interview is to cover need to be clearly identified and the place where interviews are to take place must be determined.

- Finally, it is necessary to plan how the interviews are to be conducted and the types of questions to be used.

Conduct

- The interviewer must establish a control framework for the interview. This will include the use of summarising to check the points being made and appropriate verbal and non-verbal signals to assist the flow of the interview.

- Interviewers must be good listeners. This is especially important when dealing with complex business processes which are the object of the systems development project.

- The interviewer must select a mix of open and closed questions which will elicit maximum information retrieval.

- Finally, the interview must be structured in an organised way. There are three main approaches to structuring an interview. The first is the '*pyramid structure*', where the interview begins with a series of specific questions and during the course of the interview moves towards general ones. The second is the '*funnel structure*', where the interviewer begins with general questions and during the course of the interview concentrates increasingly on specific ones. The third approach is the '*diamond structure*', where the interview begins with specific questions, moves towards general questions in the middle of the interview and back towards specific questions at the end.

Regardless of which approach is taken, it will still be necessary to document carefully the findings of the interview.

Interviews should use a mixture of open and closed questions. Open questions are not restricted to a limited range of answers such as Yes/No (closed questions). They are asked to elicit opinions or ideas for the new system or identify commonly held views among staff. Open questions are not typically used for quantitative analysis, but can be used to identify a common problem.

Closed questions have a restricted choice of answers such as Yes/No or a range of opinions on a scale from 'strongly agree' to 'strongly disagree' (Likert scale). This approach is useful for quantitative analysis of results.

Recording

During the course of the interview, the interviewer will need to make notes to record the findings. It may also be useful to draw diagrams to illustrate the processes being discussed. Some interviewers like to use a tape recorder to be sure that no points are missed. Whichever methods are used, the requirement is to record three main attributes of the system under consideration:

- *Business processes*. A business process exists when an input of some kind (raw materials, for example) is transformed in some way so that an output is produced for use elsewhere in the business.

- *Data*. Data will be acquired and processed and information produced as a con-sequence of carrying out business processes. Data must be analysed so that data acquisition, processing needs and information requirements can be encapsulated in the new information system.

- *Information flows*. Functional business areas do not exist in isolation from each other and neither do different business processes within the same business function. It is necessary, therefore, to identify how data and information within one business process are necessary for other business processes to operate effectively.

We will look at some relevant tools and techniques which help to record the findings later in this chapter.

As an information-gathering tool, interviews have a number of advantages and disadvantages. On the positive side they include:

- the ability to gather detailed information through a two-way dialogue;

- the ability for candid, honest responses to be made;

Open questions

Not restricted to a limited range of answers such as Yes/No (closed questions). Asked to elicit opinions or ideas for the new system or identify commonly held views amongst staff. Open questions are not typically used for quantitative analysis, but can be used to identify a common problem.

Closed questions

Closed questions have a restricted choice of answers such as Yes/No or a range of opinions a scale from 'strongly agree' to 'strongly disagree' (Likert scale). Approach is useful for quantitative analysis results.

- an open, spontaneous process which can lead to valuable insights, especially when open questions are used;

- responses that can easily be quantified, especially when closed questions are used;

- being one of the best methods for gathering qualitative data such as opinions, and subjective descriptions of activities and problems.

On the negative side, however, the following points can be made:

- The analyst's findings may be coloured by his or her perceptions of how other, similar, business operations work. Interviewers need to be especially skilled if this is to be avoided.

- The development of a new information system may represent a threat through the risk of deskilling, redundancy or perceived inability to cope with change. Interviewees may, therefore, not cooperate with the interview process, either by not taking part or by giving vague and incomplete replies.

- The interviewee may tell the analyst what he or she thinks should happen rather than what actually happens.

- An interview at lower organisational levels may not yield as much information as some other methods if staff in this area are not capable of articulating with sufficient clarity.

On balance, interviewing is an essential part of the information-gathering process. For maximum benefit, interviewing should be used in conjunction with other techniques, and we will turn to these now.

Questionnaires

Analysis techniques – questionnaires

Used to obtain a range of opinion on requirements by targeting a range of staff. They are open to misinterpretation unless carefully designed. They should consist of open and closed questions.

Questionnaires are used to obtain a range of opinion on requirements by targeting a range of staff. They are open to misinterpretation unless carefully designed. They should consist of both open and closed questions.

Questionnaires can be a useful addition to the analyst's armoury, but are not in themselves enough to gather sufficient information for the later stages of the systems development process. That said, questionnaires can be very useful when used with other fact-finding methods, either to confirm the findings obtained elsewhere or to open up possible further areas for investigation. Typically, they are used before more detailed questions by interview.

Successful questionnaires have a number of characteristics:

- The questions will be framed by the analyst with a clear view of the information that is to be obtained from the completed questionnaires.

- The target audience must be carefully considered – a questionnaire designed for clerical or operational personnel should not contain questions that are not relevant to their level of work.

- The questionnaire should only contain branching (e.g. 'if the answer to Question 3 was 'No', then go to Question 8') if it is absolutely necessary – multiple branches create confusion and may lead to unusable responses.

- Questions should be simple and unambiguous so that the respondent does not have to guess what the analyst means.

- Multiple-choice, Likert-scale-type questions make the questionnaire easier to fill in and allow the results to be analysed more efficiently.

- The questionnaire should contain the required return date and name of the person to whom the questionnaire should be returned.

Difficulties that can be encountered with questionnaires include:

- the inability of respondents to go back to the analyst to seek clarification about what a question means;
- difficulty in collating qualitative information, especially if the questionnaire contains open-ended questions;
- the inability to use verbal and non-verbal signals from the respondent as a sign to ask other or different questions;
- low response rates – these can be lower than 20 to 25 per cent when sent to other organisations or customers, which means that a large sample size is needed if the results are to carry any weight. Response rate is not such a problem with internal staff.

By contrast, the questionnaire process also has a number of benefits:

- When large numbers of people such as customers or suppliers need to be consulted, a carefully worded questionnaire is more efficient and less expensive than carrying out large numbers of interviews.
- Questionnaires can be used to check results found by using other fact-finding methods.
- The use of standardised questions can help codify the findings more succinctly than other tools.

In summary, questionnaires can have a useful role to play in certain circumstances, but they should not be used as the sole data-gathering method.

Documentation review

Analysis technique – documentation review

Uses information on existing systems such as user guides, or requirements specifications together with paper or on-screen forms used to collect information such as sales order forms.

Documentation reviews target information about existing systems, such as user guides or requirements specifications, together with paper or on-screen forms used to collect information, such as sales order forms. They are vital for collecting detail about data and processes that may not be recalled in questionnaires and interviews.

All organisations have at least some kind of documentation that relates to some or all of the business operations carried out. A documentation review can be carried out at a number of different stages in the analysis process. If carried out at the beginning of a requirements analysis exercise, it will help provide the analyst with some background information relating to the area under consideration. It may also help the analyst construct a framework for the remainder of the exercise, and enable interviews to be conducted in a more effective way since the analyst has some idea of current business practices and procedures. If document review is carried out later, it can be used to cross-check the actual business operations with what is supposed to happen. The kinds of documentation and records that can be reviewed include the following:

- instruction manuals and procedure manuals which show how specific tasks are supposed to be performed;
- requirements specifications and user guides from previous systems;
- job descriptions relating to particular staff functions which may help identify who should be doing what;
- strategic plans both for the organisation as a whole and the functional areas in particular, which can provide valuable background data for establishing broad functional objectives.

While documentation review can provide a very useful underpinning for other fact-finding tasks, there are still a number of problems:

- There can be a large quantity of data for an analyst to process. This is especially true in large organisations and it may take the analyst a long time to identify the documentation that is useful and that which can be ignored.

■ Documentation is often out of date. If there is an old computerised system, it is quite possible that the documentation has not been changed for years, even though the system may have changed considerably over that period. The same can be said for the documentation of activities and procedures.

Observation

Observation

Useful for identifying inefficiencies in an existing way of working either with a computer-based or a manual information system. Involves timing how long particular operations take and observing the method used to perform them.

Observation is useful for identifying inefficiencies in an existing way of working, with either a computer-based or a manual information system. It involves timing how long particular operations take and observing the method used to perform them. It can be time-consuming and the staff who are observed may not behave normally.

This fact-finding method involves the analyst in directly observing business activities taking place so that they can see what is *actually* taking place rather than looking at documentation which states what *should* be taking place. One of the benefits of observation is that the analyst can see directly how something is done, rather than relying on verbal or written communication which may colour the facts or be the subject of misinterpretation by the analyst. Other benefits include:

■ the ability to see how documents and records are actually handled and processed;

■ observation may give a greater insight into actual business operations than simple paper documentation;

■ identification of particular operations that take a long time;

■ the opportunity to see how different processes interact with each other, thus giving the analyst a *dynamic* rather than a *static* view of the business situation under investigation.

On the downside, there are a number of difficulties associated with the observation technique:

■ It is an extremely time-consuming exercise and therefore needs to be done as a supplementary rather than a principal fact-finding method.

■ While observation allows an organisation to be dynamically assessed, it still does not allow attitudes and belief systems to be assessed. This can be a very important issue if the proposed information system is likely to encounter resistance to change among the workforce.

■ Finally, there is the issue of the 'Hawthorne effect', where people tend to behave differently when they are being observed, thus reducing the value of the information being obtained. Of course, for the analyst, the problem is in determining whether those being observed are behaving differently or not!

This last effect was first noticed in the Hawthorne plant of Western Electrics in the United States. Here, it was noted that production increased, not as a con-sequence of actual changes in working conditions introduced by the plant's management, but because management demonstrated an interest in improving staff working conditions.

Despite these difficulties, it is desirable for the analyst to conduct at least some observation to ensure that no aspect of the system being investigated is overlooked.

Brainstorming

Brainstorming uses interaction within a group of staff to generate new ideas and discuss existing problems. It is the least structured of the fact-finding techniques.

Brainstorming

Brainstorming uses interaction within a group of staff to generate new ideas and discuss existing problems. It is the least structured of the fact-finding techniques.

This is the final fact-finding technique we will consider. The methods we have looked at so far are either passive or conducted on a one-to-one basis, or both. The brainstorming method involves a number of participants and is an active approach to information gathering. While the other methods allow for many different views to be expressed, those methods do not allow different persons' perceptions of the business processes and systems needs to be considered simultaneously. Brainstorming allows multiple views and opinions to be brought forward at the same time. If the proposed system's user community participates actively, it is more likely that an accurate view of current business processes and information systems needs will be reached.

Brainstorming sessions require careful planning by the analyst. Factors to consider include:

- which persons to involve and from which functional business areas;

- how many people to involve in the session – too few and insufficient data may be gathered; too many and the session may be too difficult to handle;

- terms of reference for the session – there may need to be more than one session to identify clearly areas of agreement and those that need further discussion;

- management involvement – a session for shopfloor workers, for example, may be far less successful if management personnel are involved than if they are not. It would be appropriate, however, for management groups to have their own brainstorming session so that tactical and strategic issues can be tackled rather than simply operational ones.

The main benefit of the brainstorming approach is that, through the dynamics of group interaction, progress is more likely to be made than from a simple static approach to information gathering. Brainstorming sessions, if they are handled properly, can result in the productive sharing of ideas and perceptions, while at the same time cultural factors, attitudes and belief systems can be more readily assessed. Also, when the outcomes are positive ones, a momentum for change is built among those who will be direct users of the new information system. Change management is therefore more easily facilitated.

The main danger of the approach is that in the hands of an inexperienced analyst, there is a risk that the sessions may descend into chaos because of poor structure, bad planning, poor control or a combination of all three.

However, if used properly, this fact-finding method can generate the desired results more quickly than any other information-gathering method. Even so, it still needs to be supplemented by one or more of the other methods discussed above.

Yeates and Wakefield (2004) explain how structured brainstorming can be used to identify different options for a new system. This technique involves the following stages:

- invite ideas which are written by individuals on separate sheets of paper or called out spontaneously and then noted on a whiteboard;

- identify similarities between ideas and rationalise the options by choosing those which are most popular;

- analyse the remaining options in detail, by evaluating their strengths and weaknesses.

It is important when brainstorming is undertaken that a facilitator be used to explain that a range of ideas is sought with input from everyone. Each participant should be able to contribute without fear of judgement by other members. When such an atmosphere is created, this can lead to 'out-of-box' or free thinking which may generate ideas of new ways of working.

Brainstorming and more structured group techniques can be used throughout the development lifecycle. Brainstorming is an important technique in re-engineering a business, since it can identify new ways of approaching processes. Taylor (1995) suggests that once new business processes have been established through analysis, they should be sanity-checked by performing a 'talk-through, walk-through and run-through'. Here, the design team will describe the proposed business process and in the talk-through stage will elaborate on different business scenarios using cards to describe the process objects and the services they provide to other process objects. Once the model has been adjusted, the walk-through stage involves more detail in the scenario and the design team will role-play the services the processes provide. The final run-through stage is a quality check in which no on-the-spot debugging occurs – just the interactions between the objects are described.

Once the analyst has completed the requirements investigation, it will be necessary to document the findings so that a proposal can be put forward for the next stage of the project. Some of the documentation tools discussed below may be used at the same time as the fact-finding process. For example, information flow diagrams may be used by the analyst to check with the end-user that points have been properly understood.

Pictures and brainstorming

Research has shown that new ideas and recall are improved by the use of pictures, which tend to prompt thought better than text. This point is well made by Buzan and Buzan (2010), who describe a technique known as 'mindmapping' to record information and promote brainstorming. Mindmaps are a spontaneous means of recording information which are ideally applied to systems analysis, since they can be used to record information direct from user dialogues or summarise information after collection.

Another graphical technique which is useful to the system analyst is the 'rich picture'. The rich picture is an element of the soft systems methodology described later in this chapter.

FOCUS ON... REQUIREMENTS DETERMINATION IN A LEAN OR AGILE ENVIRONMENT

As indicated earlier (in Chapter 7), the traditional waterfall approach to software development is by no means the only valid approach to software development, as the increasing adoption of lean and agile approaches bears witness. In the traditional waterfall model, requirements analysis results in a systems specification and a catalogue of user requirements which is then converted into a design specification. However, the emphasis in an agile development environment is on the frequent delivery of software products and the daily involvement of end-users in the software development process. Agile methodologies place an emphasis on delivering working code and downplay the importance of formal processes. It is suggested, therefore, that the software development process can adapt and react promptly to changes that occur in user requirements.

Lindstrom and Jeffries (2004) identify a number of reasons for failed information systems projects. Those relating to requirements determination include:

- requirements that are not clearly communicated;
- requirements that do not solve business problems;
- requirements that change prior to completion of the project.

There is also a tendency for stakeholders to ask for everything to be included in the software, regardless of how much it might be used, thus increasing development costs and maintenance budgets. He also claims that by trying to identify all the requirements up-front, the opportunity to develop and implement the most valuable and high-priority requirements is forgone, thus increasing the payback period for the system.

The requirements determination emphasis with agile methods is, therefore, on the frequent delivery of rapidly implementable software products, where a requirement can be built in a single product release iteration of two to four weeks (depending on the chosen methodology). Critics will claim that this approach results in impossible-to-estimate project costs since the entire project cannot be costed up front (the assumption being that requirements will evolve in response to frequent delivery of software products). However, proponents of agile methods point out that it is better for the customer to be able to call a halt once they have enough of what they need, rather than to embark on a lengthy development project only to discover that user requirements have changed in such a way that the delivery system is no longer fit for purpose.

DOCUMENTING THE FINDINGS

In this section we will concentrate on three main diagramming tools: information flow diagrams (IFDs), dataflow diagrams (DFDs) and entity relationship diagrams (ERDs). These techniques are used by professional IS/IT personnel, partly as documentation tools and partly as checking tools with the user community. It is important, therefore, for non-IS/IT personnel to understand the fundamentals behind these diagramming tools so that communication between functional personnel and IS/IT experts is enhanced. Furthermore, tools such as ERDs can be applied by end-users to assist them in developing their own personal or departmental applications. As well as these tools, the requirements specification will also contain a text description of what the functions of the software will be. We will consider this first, and then consider the documentation tools.

The requirements specification

Requirements specification

The main output from the systems analysis stage. Its main focus is a description of what all the functions of the software will be.

The **requirements specification** is the main output from the systems analysis stage. Its main focus is a description of what all the functions of the software will be. These must be defined in great detail to ensure that when the specification is passed on to the designers, the system is what the users require. This will help prevent the problem referred to in Figure 10.1.

The scope of the requirements specification will include:

- *Data capture* – when, where and how often. The detailed data requirements will be specified using entity relationship diagrams and stored in a data dictionary. Dataflow diagrams will indicate the data stores required.

- *Preferred data capture methods* – this may include use of keyboard entry, bar codes, OCR, etc. (it could be argued that this is a design point, but it may be a key user requirement that a particular capture method be used).

- *Functional requirements* – what operations the software must be able to perform. For example, for the maps in a geographic information system, the functional requirements would specify: the ability to zoom in and out, pan using scroll-bars and the facility to change the features and labels overlaid on the map.

- *User interface layout* – users will want access to particular functions in a single screen, so the requirements specification will define the main screens of an application. Detailed layout will be decided as part of prototyping and detailed design.

- *Output requirements* – this will include such things as enquiry screens, regular standard and ad hoc reports and interfaces to other systems.

One approach to documenting requirements is illustrated by the 'requirements catalogue' specified in SSADM (discussed in Chapter 7). Figure 10.2 illustrates a typical requirements catalogue entry.

The purpose of the requirements catalogue is to act as the repository of all requirements information. It can be used from the initiation stage when early thoughts are being gathered about the possible requirements, through to the design stage when user requirements may still be emerging (especially in such areas as system navigation and performance requirements).

Figure 10.2 Example of a requirements catalogue entry

REQUIREMENTS CATALOGUE ENTRY			
Source Credit Control Clerk	**Owner** Credit Control Manager	**Requirement ID** 5.9	**Priority** High

Functional Requirements

Link Sales Order Processing system in with accounting package so that online credit checking is an automatic process when new orders are being processed.

Non-functional requirements

Description	**Target Value**	**Acceptable range**	**Comments**
Response Time	Within 10 seconds	Within 20 seconds	
Service Hours	08:30 to 18:00 Monday to Friday		
Availability	97.5%	Above 92.5%	

Benefits

Will speed up order processing and enable account handlers to spend more time collecting cash rather than continually switching between computer systems when processing orders.

Comments / suggested solutions

Either provide a function key to perform the credit check function, or make it an automatic process when an order is entered. Do not allow order to be confirmed if credit check is failed.

Related documents

Required System DFD, process box 5.9

Related requirements

3.2. Improve cash collection process – more accurate sales ledger data
4.9. Reduce number of bad debts – link to improved aged debtors report

Resolution

3.2. Improve cash collection process – more accurate sales ledger data
4.9. Reduce number of bad debts – link to improved aged debtors report

There are three main aspects that need to be documented, usually from a user perspective:

- *Functional requirements* – consist of requirements that perform the activities that run the business. Examples include updating master files, enquiring against data on file, producing reports and communicating with other systems.
- *Non-functional requirements* – define the performance levels of the business functions to be supported. Examples include online response times, turn-round time for batch processing, security, backup and recovery.
- *Quantification of requirements* – refers to the need for a measure of quality if the benefits are to be properly evaluated. Examples might include reducing customer complaints by 75 per cent, reducing the value of unsold stock by 85%, or increasing online sales by 25 per cent.

Each entry in the requirements catalogue would typically consist of an A4 sheet that contains the details outlined above. Other elements such as requirements originator, date and links to other formal documentation would be included.

When reviewing the contents of a requirements catalogue, it is desirable to prioritise requirements so that the development effort concentrates on the most important features of the new system. For example, it is possible to categorise user requirements into three: the A list, the B list and the C list (or Priority 1 to 3). The A list should comprise all those requirements that the proposed system *must* support and without which it would not function. For example, an accounting system that does not produce customer statements may be seriously deficient. The B list would contain those requirements that are very desirable but are not vital to the successful operation of the system. For example, it may be very desirable for a sales order processing system to produce a list of all customers who have not placed an order for the last six months, but it is not essential. The C list would contain those things that are nice to have (the 'bells and whistles') but are neither essential nor very desirable. It might be nice in a stock control system, for example, if a screen 'buzzed' at the user if a certain combination of factors were present. However, this would not be classified as essential.

The requirements catalogue can be used to prioritise the 'very desirables' and the 'bells and whistles' so that at the design stage most attention can be paid to those items that are perceived as having the highest priority. It may be, however, that if a low-priority item is seen to be very easy to implement, and a higher-priority item less so, the lower-priority item would be included in the development in preference.

It may be that in the case of a 'very desirable but hard to implement' feature, a simpler item might be included as an imperfect substitute. This would be more readily apparent at the design stage and it may be necessary to revisit the requirements catalogue at this point and consult the functional personnel again.

Information flow diagrams

Information flow diagram (IFD)

A simple diagram showing how information is routed between different parts of an organisation. It has an information focus rather than a process focus.

The **information flow diagram (IFD)** is one of the simplest tools used to document findings from the requirements determination process. It is used for a number of purposes:

- to document the main flows of information around the organisation;

- for the analyst to check that they have understood those flows and that none has been omitted;

- for the analyst to use during the fact-finding process itself as an accurate and efficient way to document findings as they are identified;

- as a high-level (not detailed) tool to document information flows within the organisation as a whole or a lower-level tool to document an individual functional area of the business.

The information flow diagram is a simple diagram showing how information is routed between different parts of an organisation. It has an information focus rather than a process focus.

An information flow diagram has three components, shown in Figure 10.3. The ellipse in the diagram represents a source of information, which then flows to a destination location. In a high-level diagram, the source or destination would be a department or specific functional area of the business such as sales, accounting or manufacturing. In a lower-level (more detailed) diagram, one might refer to subfunctions such as accounts receivable, credit control or payroll (as you would normally find in an accounts department). The name of the source or destination should appear inside the ellipse. The source or destination is sometimes referred to as an 'internal' or 'external entity' according to whether it lies inside or outside the system boundary. The term 'entity' is used frequently when constructing entity relationship diagrams, and entities are described more fully later.

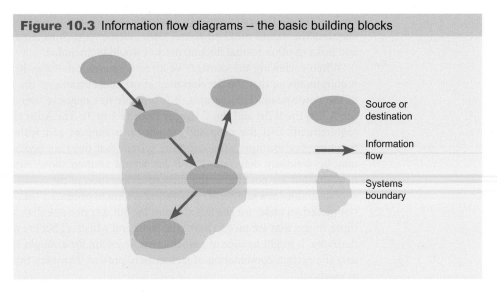

Figure 10.3 Information flow diagrams – the basic building blocks

Source or destination

Information flow

Systems boundary

Figure 10.4 An illustration of a simple information flow

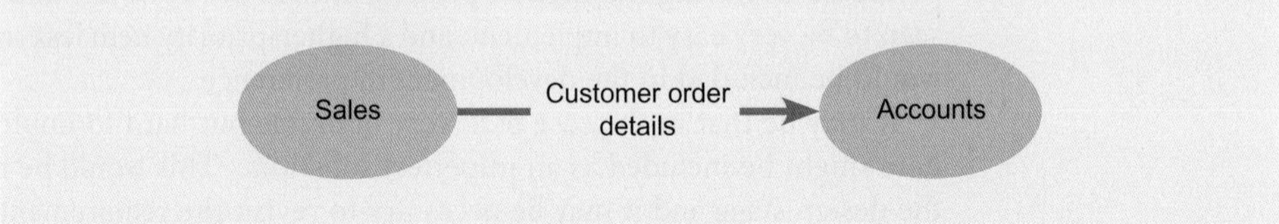

Sales — Customer order details → Accounts

The information flow, as represented by the arrowhead line, shows a flow of information from a source location to a destination. In an IFD the line should always be annotated with a brief description of the information flow. So, for example, if a sales department sends a customer's order details to the accounts department for credit checking, the resulting flow might look like Figure 10.4.

Sources or destinations lying within the system's boundary imply that this information will be used directly by the system. The concept of the system boundary is explained further in Case Study 10.1. This detailed example illustrates how an IFD could be used in practice.

CASE STUDY 10.1

IFD drawing – a student records system

Suppose that a university wished to move from a manual, paper-based student records system to one that was computerised. The analyst would need to create a clear picture of the required information flows to help the system designer with the blueprint for the proposed system. We include some sample narrative to demonstrate the possible result of an interview between the analyst and the head of admissions.

When a student enrols for the first time, they are required to fill in a form which has the following details:

- forename;
- surname;
- date;
- local authority;
- home address;

- term-time address;
- home telephone number;
- term-time telephone number;
- sex;
- course code;
- course description;
- module code (for each module being studied);
- module description (as above).

When the forms have been completed, they are passed to the student information centre. A series of actions follows:

- The student information centre (SIC) allocates the student a unique code number which stays with the student until they complete their studies.

- The SIC creates a card index of the student's details down to and including course description, plus the new student code number.
- The SIC also creates a list of all students belonging to each local education authority (LEA).
- The SIC sends the LEA list to the finance department, which then invoices the LEAs for the tuition fees relating to the students from their area.
- The SIC creates a study record card (SRC), giving the student details and the modules being studied.
- The SIC groups the SRCs by course and for each course sorts the cards into student name order; the SRCs for each course are then sent to the department that runs that course.
- Each department will take the SRCs for its courses and produce a number of class lists, based around the modules that the student is studying, which are then passed to the relevant module leaders.
- The SIC will issue the student with an enrolment form which the student can use to obtain a library card.
- Finally, the SIC will pass a list of all new students to the library and the students' union so that the library can issue students with library cards and the students' union can issue students with their NUS cards.'

It is necessary to translate the above into a series of information flows and also define the systems boundary (i.e. the line that separates what is in the system under consideration from what is outside it).

In order to be successful in drawing IFDs, it is helpful to follow a few simple steps, since an attempt to draw a diagram from scratch may prove a little tricky:

Step 1   List all the sources of information for the system under consideration (in other words, places where information is generated).

Step 2   List all the destinations (receivers) of information for the system under consideration.

Step 3   Make a simple list of all the information flows.

Step 4   For each of the information flows identified in Step 3, add the source and destination that relate to it.

Step 5   Draw the IFD from your list that you produced from 3 and 4.

Tips

1. When you have gained experience in doing this, Steps 1 and 2 can be ignored and Steps 3 and 4 can be combined.
2. An information source/destination can appear more than once on an IFD – it can help to eliminate lots of crossed lines (and crossed lines are best avoided since the annotations can look rather jumbled).
3. Use A4 paper, or larger, in landscape mode.

The result of your efforts should look something like this:

Step 1 (information generators)

- STUDENT
- SIC
- FINANCE
- DEPARTMENT

Step 2 (information destinations)

- STUDENT
- SIC
- LEA
- TUTOR
- LIBRARY
- STUDENTS' UNION

Step 3 (information flows)

- Student's personal and course information
- LEA list
- Invoices
- Students on course
- Class list
- Enrolment form
- List of all new students (times two)

Step 4 (adding sources and destinations to the information flows)

Generator	Flow	Destination
STUDENT	Student's personal and course information	SIC
SIC	LEA list	FINANCE
FINANCE	Invoices	LEA
SIC	Students on course	DEPARTMENT
DEPARTMENT	Class list	TUTOR
SIC	Enrolment form	STUDENT
SIC	List of all new students (1)	LIBRARY
SIC	List of all students (2)	STUDENTS' UNION
STUDENTS'	NUS card	STUDENTUNION
LIBRARY	Library card	STUDENT

Step 5 (the completed diagram)

It is almost certain that if you were to attempt this diagram your results would not be exactly the same. However, provided that all the flows are represented correctly and there are no crossed lines, the result will be perfectly acceptable. Also, note that the student appears twice on the diagram. This is not just because the student is important ➡

Figure 10.5 A simple, high-level IFD, excluding the system boundary

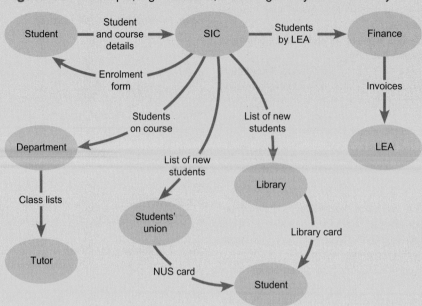

(which of course they are!), but because it helps avoid crossed lines (Figure 10.5).

What remains now is to consider the systems boundary. If this manual information system were to be replaced by a new computer-based information system, it would be necessary to identify what would be within the systems boundary and what would be external to the system and, hence, outside the system boundary. For the purposes of this example, we will make some assumptions:

- *Students* are external to the system – they provide information as an input to the system and receive outputs from the system but are not themselves part of it – students will, therefore, be outside the system boundary.
- The *student information centre* is clearly central to the whole system and, therefore, is an integral part of the system under consideration – the SIC will lie inside the system boundary.
- The *finance* area needs a further assumption to be made. Let us assume that the finance area operates a computer-based information system for its accounting records and that the proposed system is to interface directly with it; in this case, it would make sense to include the finance area inside the system boundary.
- Similarly, suppose that the *library* operates its own computerised lending system. In the new system, it may wish to use an interface between the student records system and its own system for setting up new students' details. Since the library system is a separate one and does not require development itself, we will place the library outside the system boundary.
- As with the library, we need to make an assumption about the students' union information systems. The students'

union may be able to use an interface file from the student record system to generate NUS cards automatically; but, as with the library, that system would lie outside the scope of the area under consideration. Therefore, we will place the students' union outside the system boundary.
- It is reasonable to assume that the *tutor* is only to receive outputs from the system rather than carry out any processing of the data; it is reasonable, then, for the tutor to lie outside the system boundary.
- Finally, the local education authority is physically external to the university as well as not being part of the university itself; the LEA should, therefore, lie outside the system boundary.

We can see the result of this analysis in the final IFD, with the system boundary included (Figure 10.6).

You will observe that there are three different types of information flow:

- the first crosses the system boundary from outside with its destination inside the boundary – it is thus an input to the system from the external environment;
- the second lies entirely within the system boundary and is, therefore, an output from one area in the system which then forms the input to another;
- the third begins inside the system boundary and its destination lies outside – it is, therefore, an output from the system into its external environment.

What we have now is a diagram that clearly identifies the context for the systems development under consideration. The diagram can be used by the analyst to check with the prospective system users that all areas have been covered. It also helps the user community build a picture of how a

Figure 10.6 The completed IFD, including the system boundary

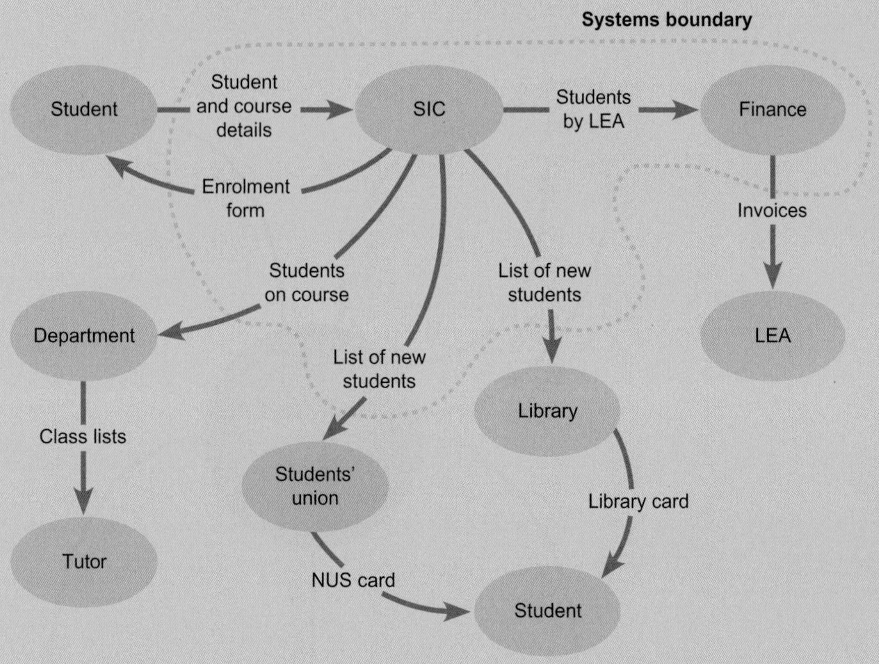

new computer system should help to make the processes more efficient. Two separate IFDs are often drawn:

1. System 'as-is' to identify inefficiencies in the existing system.
2. New proposed system to rectify these problems.

What is required is further work to identify the business processes and data needs for the proposed system and this is where the following tools come in.

Source: Simon Hickie, course notes

Context diagrams

Context diagrams

Simplified diagrams that are useful for specifying the boundaries and scope of the system. They can be readily produced after the information flow diagram since they are a simplified version of the IFD showing the external entities.

Context diagrams are simplified diagrams that are useful for specifying the boundaries and scope of the system. They can be readily produced after the information flow diagram since they are a simplified version of the IFD showing the external entities. They show these types of flow:

1. Flow crosses the system boundary from outside with its destination inside the boundary – it is thus an input to the system from the external environment.
2. Flow begins inside the system boundary and its destination lies outside – it is, therefore, an output from the system into its external environment.

The internal flows which lie entirely within the system boundary are not shown. Context diagrams provide a useful summary for embarking on dataflow diagrams and entity relationship diagrams, since they show the main entities. The main elements of a context diagram are:

- a circle representing the system to be investigated;
- ellipses (or boxes) representing external entities;
- information flows.

Figure 10.7 Context diagram for the student loan system described in Case Study 10.1

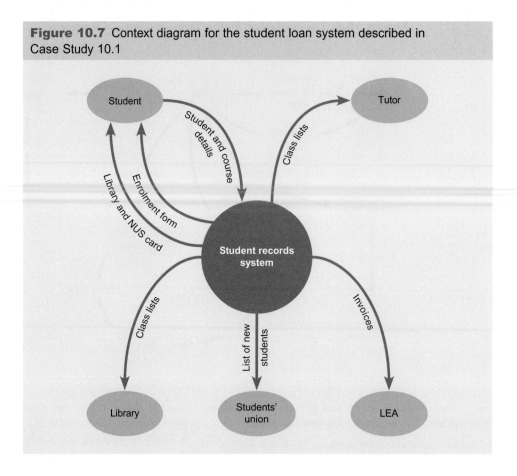

Figure 10.7 shows a context diagram for the student loan system described in Case Study 10.1.

Dataflow diagrams

Dataflow diagrams (DFDs)

Define the different processes in a system and the information that forms the input and output of the processes. They may be drawn at different levels. Level 0 provides an overview of the system with levels 1 and 2 providing progressively more detail.

Dataflow diagrams (DFDs) define the different processes in a system and the information that forms the input and output to the processes. They provide a process focus to a system. They may be drawn at different levels: level 0 provides an overview of the system with levels 1 and 2 providing increasing detail.

Dataflow diagrams of different types are one of the mainstays of many systems analysis and design methodologies. SSADM, for example, makes extensive use of DFDs, not only to document things as they are at the moment but also to document the *required* system. Whether the latter is really of any value is debatable. How-ever, as a tool to document processes, data or information flows and the relationships between them for an existing system (computerised or paper-based), they are extremely valuable.

Dataflow diagrams build on IFDs by adding two new symbols as well as subtly redefining others.

The diagram conventions in Figure 10.8 are those that are in most common use in Europe. Differing methodologies adopt different symbols for some items (such as a circle for a process), as you will see in some of the supplementary texts for this chapter.

Explanations of symbols

- *Sources and sinks* – an information source is one which provides data for a process and is outside the system boundary. A sink lies outside the system boundary and is a receiver of information. There is a clear distinction between the use of this symbol in the DFD

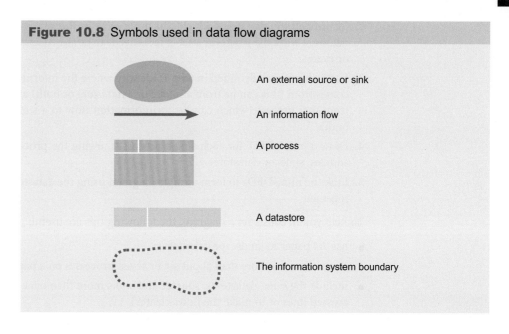

Figure 10.8 Symbols used in data flow diagrams

An external source or sink

An information flow

A process

A datastore

The information system boundary

and in the IFD that we looked at before, in that the symbol should not appear inside the system boundary.

- *Processes* – convert data into either usable information or data in a different form for use in another process. The data that enter a process can come either from a datastore (see below) or from an external source.

- *Datastores* – a datastore can either provide data as input to a process or receive data that have been output from a process. The amount of time that data would spend in a datastore can vary from a very short time (e.g. fractions of seconds in the case of some work files) to much longer periods (e.g. months or years in the case of master files).

- *Dataflows* – a dataflow describes the exchange of information and data between datastores and processes and between processes and sources or sinks. Note that in this context we are using 'data' in a broad sense (to include information) rather than in the narrow sense used earlier (in Part 1 of the book).

- *Systems boundary* – remains the same as for an IFD. It indicates the boundary between what lies inside the system under consideration and what lies outside.

Drawing dataflow diagrams

It is unfortunate that many texts actually contain errors in the DFD examples used. This is mainly through having 'illegal' information flows. In a well-constructed diagram, you will note the following:

- Data do *not* flow directly between processes – the data that enter a process will come either from a source or from a datastore, they cannot exist in a vacuum!

- Data do *not* flow directly between datastores – there must be an intervening process that takes the input data and converts them into a new form and outputs them to either a datastore or a sink.

- Data do *not* flow directly from a datastore to a sink, or from a source to a data-store – there *must* be an intervening process.

To draw a basic high-level DFD, there are five steps required:

1. Identify and list all *processes* which take place in the system under consideration. A process is an event where an input of some kind, from either a source or a datastore, is transformed into an output (the output being either to a sink or to a datastore).

2. Identify all the datastores which you think exist in the system under consideration. A datastore will exist wherever a set of facts needs to be stored about persons, places, things or events.

3. For each process identified in Step 1, identify where the information used in the process comes from (this can be from a *source* or a *datastore* or both) and identify the output(s) from that process (which can be an information flow to a sink or to a datastore or to both).

4. Draw a 'mini-DFD' for each single process, showing the process box and any relevant sources, sinks or datastores.

5. Link the mini-DFDs to form a single diagram, using the datastores to link the processes together.

To help you to construct a diagram, the following tips are useful:

■ use A4 paper in landscape orientation;

■ aim to have no more than about six or seven processes on a page (ten maximum);

■ include the same datastores, sources and sinks more than once if required (to eliminate crossed lines or to make the flows clearer).

Before working through the student records example introduced in the previous section, it is necessary to introduce the concept of 'levelling' in DFDs. For anything other than a very small system with a handful of processes, it would be almost impossible to draw a single diagram with all the processes on it. It is necessary, therefore, to begin with a high-level diagram with just the broadest processes defined. Examples of high-level processes might be 'process customer orders', 'pay suppliers' or 'manufacture products'. Needless to say, each of the processes described can be broken down further until all the fundamental processes which make up the system are identified. It is usual to allow up to three or four levels of increasing detail to be identified. If there are any more levels of detail than this, it suggests that the system is too large to consider in one development and that it should be split into smaller, discrete subsystems capable of separate development.

To illustrate the levelling concept and also to demonstrate how process boxes should be used, we will take the simple example of checking a customer order. At Level 1, the process box will appear as in Figure 10.9.

It is desirable to split this process up into smaller components. As an example, suppose the following are identified:

■ check customer credit limit – can the customer pay for the goods?

■ perform stock check – to see whether the desired goods are in stock;

■ create sales order – this may be a special order form that is needed for each order;

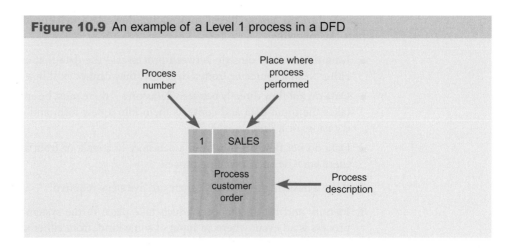

Figure 10.9 An example of a Level 1 process in a DFD

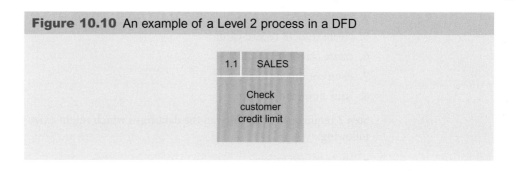

Figure 10.10 An example of a Level 2 process in a DFD

- send order to warehouse – the warehouse will need to pick the stock ready for delivery;
- dispatch customer order;
- invoice customer.

This will give us six new processes to record at the next level. The process box for the first Level 2 process would be similar to this (Figure 10.10).

Note that the process number is 1.1. This indicates that the process has been decomposed from the higher-level process numbered 1. Subsequent processes would be numbered 1.2, 1.3, 1.4, and so on. Also note that the process name begins with a verb. The choice of verb helps indicate more clearly the type of process that is being performed.

Suppose now that we still need to decompose the new process 1.1 further. For example, the credit check process may involve these steps:

- calculate order value;
- identify current balance;
- produce credit check result.

We need to present the new processes as Level 3 processes, since they have been decomposed from the higher Level 2 process. The first of these would be represented as in Figure 10.11.

The new processes would be numbered 1.1.1, 1.1.2 and 1.1.3. This approach to numbering allows each of the low-level processes to be easily associated with the higher-level process that generated it. Thus, for example, processes 3.2.1, 3.2.2 and 3.2.3 could be tracked back to process 3.2, and thence to process 3.

We will now return to the student enrolment example. We will concentrate on producing a Level 1 diagram for this procedure, although it will be clear that the example is a somewhat simplified one.

The first task is to identify all the processes which exist. Looking back to Figure 10.6, we can identify the following:

1. allocate unique student code;
2. create student card index;
3. create LEA list;

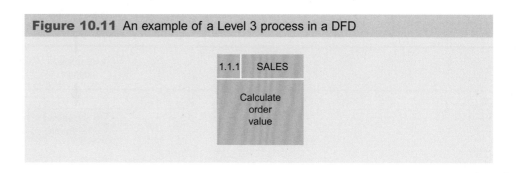

Figure 10.11 An example of a Level 3 process in a DFD

4. invoice LEA;

5. create student record card;

6. create class list;

7. issue enrolment form;

8. issue new students list.

Step 2 requires us to identify all the datastores which might exist. Our example reveals the following:

- student card index;
- LEA list;
- student record card;
- class list;
- new students list.

Step 3 requires us to construct a 'mini-DFD' for each of the eight processes identified above. We will restrict ourselves to the first three (see Figures 10.12, 10.13 and 10.14).

You will see from these figures that each of the processes we have considered has generated an output which forms an input to the next process. In the full diagram in Figure 10.15 you will see the complete picture, including all processes, datastores, sources and sinks. In this diagram, you will notice that the datastore 'card index file' appears more than once. This does not mean that there are two separate datastores with the same name, but that we have included it for a second time to make the diagram easier to draw. If we did not do this, there would have been either crossed lines or at least very tortuous ones. A system boundary is also included and you will note that sources and sinks lie outside the system boundary, while processes and datastores are inside. Many of the dataflows are inside the boundary, but you see where flows also cross the system boundary.

The final point to note is that a dataflow diagram is *time-independent*. This means that we are not trying to show the sequence in which things happen, but rather to show all the things that happen.

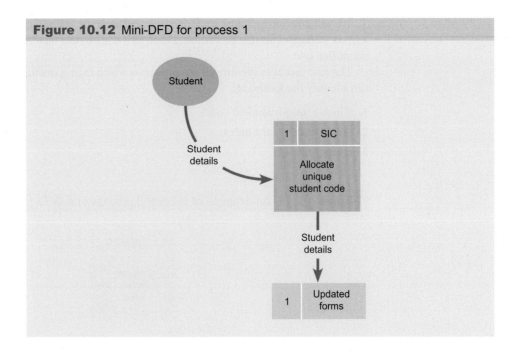

Figure 10.12 Mini-DFD for process 1

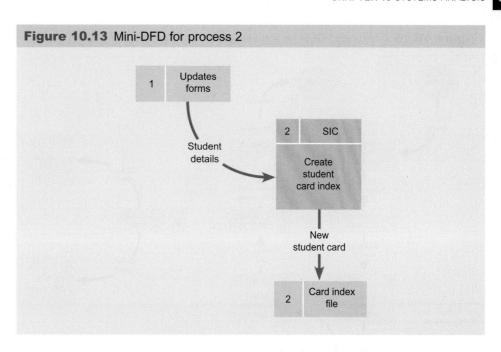

Figure 10.13 Mini-DFD for process 2

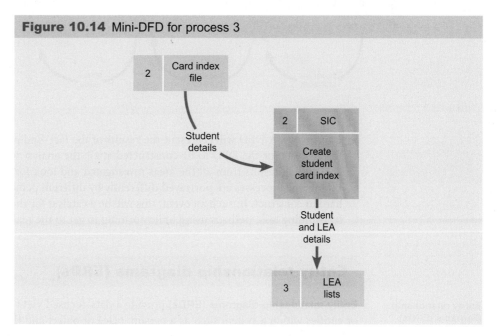

Figure 10.14 Mini-DFD for process 3

The benefits to an organisation of constructing a dataflow diagram can be summed up in the following 'three Cs':

- *Communication.* A picture paints a thousand words and DFDs are no exception. A diagram can be used by an analyst to communicate to end-users the analyst's understanding of the area under consideration. This is likely to be more successful than what Ed Yourdon describes as the 'Victorian novel' approach to writing specification reports.

- *Completeness.* A DFD can be scrutinised by functional area personnel to check that the analyst has gained a complete picture of the business area being investigated. If anything is missing or the analyst has misinterpreted anything, this will be clearer to the user if there is a diagram than if purely textual tools are used.

Figure 10.15 Completed DFD for the student record system

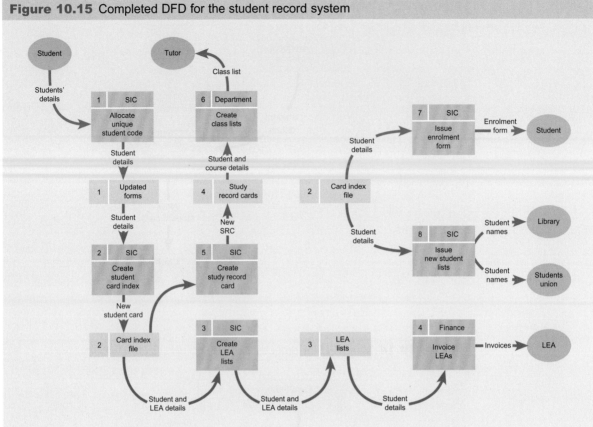

- *Consistency.* A DFD will represent the results of the fact-finding exercise conducted by the analyst. For the DFD to be constructed at all, the analyst will need to compare the fact-finding results from all the areas investigated and look for linkages between them. If the same processes are portrayed differently by different people, then the DFD will be hard to construct. In such an event, this will be a catalyst for the analyst to return to the fact-finding task, perhaps using brainstorming to get to the real facts.

Entity relationship diagrams (ERDs)

Entity relationship diagrams (ERDs)

Provide a data-focused view of the main data objects or entities within a system such as a person, place or object and the relationships between them. It is a high-level view and does not consider the detailed attributes or characteristics of an object such as a person's name or address.

Entity relationship diagrams (ERDs) provide a data-focused view of the main data objects or entities within a system such as a person, place or object and the relationships between them. It is a high-level view and does not consider the detailed attributes or characteristics of an object such as a person's name or address.

In dealing with entity relationship diagrams, we must bear in mind that we are beginning to move away from the analysis stage of the systems development lifecycle towards the design stage. This is because we are beginning to think about how data are represented and how different sets of data relate to each other. For this chapter, we will concentrate on the fundamentals of entity relationships as they exist within a particular business situation, rather than on the detail of database design which follows directly from using this tool. Database design will be covered in much more detail later (in Chapter 11) where a technique called *data normalisation* will also be covered.

In any business situation, data (whether paper-based or computerised) are processed to produce information to assist in the decision-making processes within that business area. Processes may change over time and new ones be created to provide new or different information, but very often the types of data that underpin this remain relatively unchanged.

Sometimes, data requirements change to allow new processes to be created. For example, a supermarket that moves to an electronic system from a manual one will generate new data in the form of sales of specific products at specific times and in specific quantities. The data can then be linked to automated stock ordering systems and the like.

In order to produce good-quality information, two things are needed above all others. These are:

- accurate data;
- correct processing.

If data are inaccurate, correct processing will only result in the production of incorrect information. If data are accurate, but faults exist in the processing, the information will still be incorrect. However, in the second case, the capability exists for producing correct information if the processing is adjusted. With faulty data, it may not be so easy to rectify the situation.

In the analysis context, we need to engage in fact-finding activities that reveal the data that underlie all the relevant business processes, so that they can be captured and stored correctly and then processed to produce the required information. This process will reveal details of certain *entities* which exist within the business. One of the most useful methods that can be used here is the review of records and documentation (for example, order forms, stock control cards, customer files and so on).

Entity

An object such as a person, place, thing or event about which we need to capture and store data. An entity forms a data set about a particular object.

An **entity** can be defined as *facts about a person, place, thing or event about which we need to capture and store data*. To take the example of a sales department, it would need to know facts about customers, orders, products and stock availability.

The essential symbols used in ERDs are very straightforward (Figure 10.16). Note that additional symbols are used in some notations, but they are not necessary for the detail of analysis conducted in this chapter.

There are a number of possible relationships between entities.

One-to-one relationships

For each occurrence of entity A there is one and only one occurrence of entity B.

For example, let us assume that a lecturer may teach on only one module, and that module may be taught by only one lecturer (an unlikely situation) (Figure 10.17).

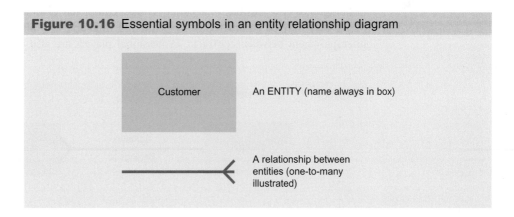

Figure 10.16 Essential symbols in an entity relationship diagram

Customer

An ENTITY (name always in box)

A relationship between entities (one-to-many illustrated)

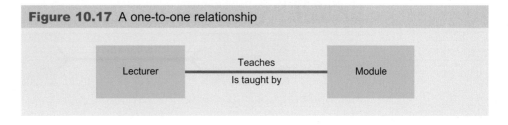

Figure 10.17 A one-to-one relationship

Lecturer

Teaches

Is taught by

Module

In Figure 10.17, we have added some additional information. This shows the nature of the relationship between the two entities. This information on the relation-ship is added to the line between the two entities. The relationship can be described in two ways according to which entity we refer to first. The relationships are:

- lecturer *teaches* module;
- module is *taught by* lecturer.

The practice of describing the relationship on the line is recommended since it helps others interpret the ERD more readily. However, the nature of the relationship is omitted on some subsequent diagrams for the sake of clarity.

One-to-many relationships

For each occurrence of entity A, there may be zero, one or many occurrences of entity B. For example, a lecturer belongs to a single division, but that division *may* contain many lecturers (it may, of course, have no staff at all if it has only just been created or if all the staff decided to leave) (Figure 10.18).

Many-to-many relationships

For each occurrence of entity A, there may be zero, one or many occurrences of entity B, *and* for each occurrence of entity B there may be zero, one or many occurrences of entity A.

For example, a course *module* may be taken by zero, one or many *students* and a student may take zero, one or many course modules (Figure 10.19).

Unfortunately, especially in database design, many-to-many relationships can cause certain difficulties. Therefore, they are usually 'resolved' into *two* one-to-many relationships through the creation of a 'linking' entity. The decomposition is shown in Figure 10.20. The linking entity will contain an item of data from each of the other entities which allows the link to be made.

The following example shows a simple ERD which illustrates each of the above possibilities in more detail.

Suppose that a nation has a professional hockey league, comprising 16 clubs. Each club may only play in this one league. Each club may employ a number of professional players (although it is also possible for a team to consist completely of amateurs). Each professional player may only be contracted to one club at a time and may also experience periods of unemployment between contracts. Professional players are also eligible to play for their

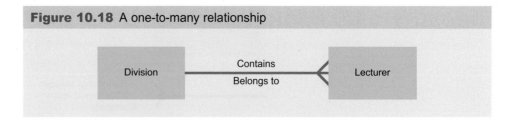

Figure 10.18 A one-to-many relationship

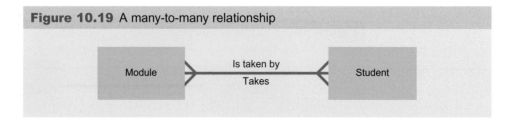

Figure 10.19 A many-to-many relationship

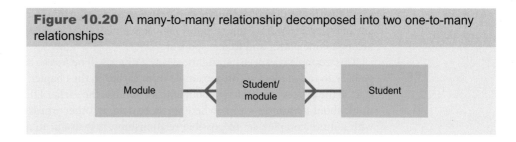

Figure 10.20 A many-to-many relationship decomposed into two one-to-many relationships

national team, but any one player may only ever play for one national team. Finally, suppose that professionals may have a number of sponsors and that each sponsor may sponsor a number of players.

If we inspect the previous paragraph, we can identify the following entities:

league;

club;

professional;

national team;

sponsor.

Our first-cut ERD is shown in Figure 10.21.

The only obvious difficulty here is the many-to-many relationship between *professional player* and *sponsor*. We can resolve this by introducing a linking entity which contains something common to both an individual player and their sponsor. This can be seen in the next ERD of Figure 10.22.

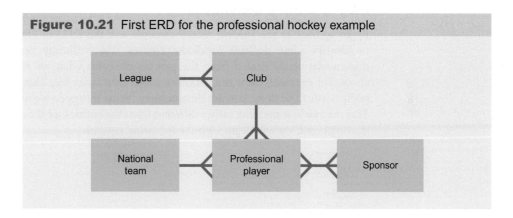

Figure 10.21 First ERD for the professional hockey example

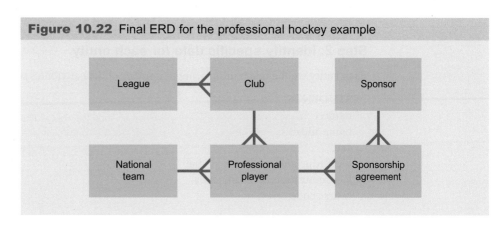

Figure 10.22 Final ERD for the professional hockey example

We have introduced the linking entity I to resolve the many-to-many relationship. Thus, any one player may have many sponsorship agreements, but any one sponsor agreement will belong to one player and to one sponsor.

This example was pretty straightforward. Others will be less so and it is therefore time to go back to our student records example from earlier in the chapter. In fact, we have already started the process of thinking about entities because the earlier DFD section required us to think about *datastores* – somewhere we store data, in other words a possible entity! Faced with a more complex set of possible relationships, it is useful to adopt a more structured approach to constructing ERDs.

There are six steps that can be helpful in producing an ERD, especially when one lacks experience in drawing them:

1. Identify all those things about which it is necessary to store data, such as customers and orders.

2. For each entity, identify specific data that need to be stored. In the case of a customer, for example, name, address and telephone number are all necessary.

3. Construct a cross-reference matrix of all possible relationships between pairs of entities and identify where a relationship actually exists. To do this, it is very helpful to identify some item of data which is common to the pair of entities under consideration.

4. Draw a basic ERD showing all the possible relationships, but not yet the *degree* of the relationship.

5. On the basic ERD, inspect each relationship and amend it to show whether it is a one-to-one, one-to-many or many-to-many relationship.

6. Resolve any many-to-many relationships by introducing an appropriate linking entity.

Step 1: Identify the entities

By going back to the student record example and the DFD in Figure 10.15, it is possible to identify some possible candidate entities. The difficulty here is that the kind of documentation generated from the process obscures what we really need to hold data about. For example, there is a datastore called *card index file*. This is hardly helpful! What really needs to be done is to ask the question: 'What things do we need to store data about?' This may yield something rather different from the entities we thought we had before. As a starting point, we will begin with the following entities:

students;

courses;

LEAs;

departments;

modules.

Step 2: Identify specific data for each entity

Each entity will be taken in turn, and a number of data attributes suggested.

STUDENTS
name;
home address;
sex;
local education authority name;
local education authority code;
course code;

term-time address;
date of birth;
next of kin;
modules taken.

COURSES
course code;
course description;
department;
course leader.

LEAs
name.

LEA CODE
address;
contact name;
telephone number;
fax number.

DEPARTMENT
department name;
department location;
office number;
head of department.

MODULES
module code;
module leader;
department;
semester run;
owning department.

Step 3: Construct cross-reference matrix

This part of the process helps novice analysts identify where relationships exist between entities. It is necessary to identify where there is a common data attribute between pairs of entities, so indicating that a probable relationship exists between them. This is the hardest part of the whole exercise. The essence is to ask the question: 'For any occurrence of entity A, are there (now or likely to be in the future) any occurrences of B that relate to it?' For example, is it likely that for a customer some orders exist that relate to it?

The cross-reference matrix in Figure 10.23 allows each pair of possible relationships to be examined for a link. In the cross-reference diagram, it is only necessary to identify each possible pair of relationships once. Also, there is no need to examine a relationship that an entity might have to itself. As a result, we are only interested in examining ten possible pairs of relationship for this small, five-entity example.

Steps 4 and 5: Construct first-cut ERD and add degree of relationship

Steps 4 and 5 will be combined, since there is nothing to be gained here from making separate diagrams. However, when drawing the diagram for Case Study 10.2, it would be wise to split the tasks as suggested.

The diagram in Figure 10.24 is almost correct, but there is still the question of the many-to-many relationship to resolve, so we must move to the final step.

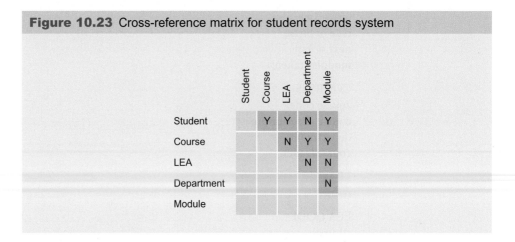

Figure 10.23 Cross-reference matrix for student records system

	Student	Course	LEA	Department	Module
Student		Y	Y	N	Y
Course			N	Y	Y
LEA				N	N
Department					N
Module					

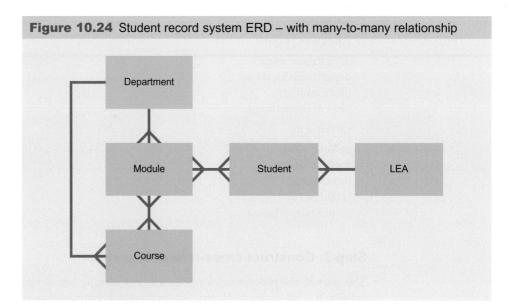

Figure 10.24 Student record system ERD – with many-to-many relationship

Step 6: Resolve any many-to-many relationships

The many-to-many relationship about which we should be concerned is the one between students and modules. A student may enrol for many modules and any modules may be taken by many students. However, what we need to represent is the ability of students to enrol for as many or as few modules as required without causing complications in either the *student* entity or the *module* entity. The many-to-many relationship is therefore resolved by introducing a linking entity which will have one occurrence for each module that one student takes and for the whole student population. So if there were 100 students each studying 8 modules, the new linking entity would contain 800 records. The final diagram is in Figure 10.25.

By working through the student record system example, we have moved from the process of identifying what the data requirements are for the system under consideration (the *analysis* part) and have made substantial progress on how a database might be constructed to hold the required data (which is a *design* task). This exercise is far from complete, however, as database design involves more than just looking at entity relationships. The detailed database design aspects will therefore be covered later (in Chapter 11) where all aspects of system design are considered.

Figure 10.25 Final student record system ERD – with many-to-many relationships decomposed

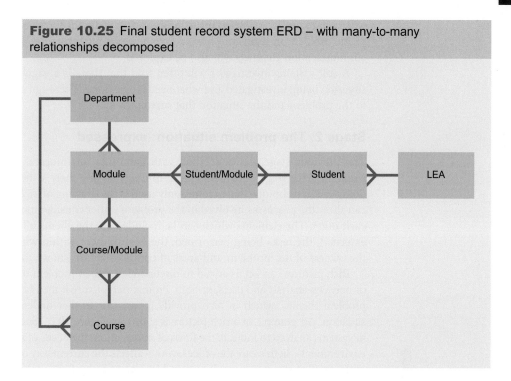

FOCUS ON... SOFT SYSTEMS METHODOLOGY

Soft systems methodology

A methodology that emphasises the human involvement in systems and models their behaviour as part of systems analysis in a way that is understandable by non-technical experts.

Soft systems methodology is a methodology that emphasises the human involvement in systems and models their behaviour as part of systems analysis in a way that is understandable by non-technical experts.

This methodology has its origins in Peter Checkland's attempt to adapt systems theory into a methodology which can be applied to any particular problem situation (Checkland, 1999). From an information systems development perspective, it is argued that systems analysts often apply their tools and techniques to problems that are not well defined. In addition, it is also argued that since human beings form an integral part of the world of systems development, a systems development methodology must embrace all the people who have a part to play in the development process (users, IS/IT professionals, managers, etc.). Since these people may have conflicting objectives, perceptions and attitudes, we are essentially dealing with the problems caused by the unpredictability of human activity systems.

Human activity system

Human activity system are non-tangible systems where human beings are undertaking some activities that achieve some purpose'.

Human activity systems are non-tangible systems where human beings are undertaking some activities that achieve some purpose.

Proponents of soft systems methodology (SSM) claim, therefore, that true understanding of complex problem situations (and in our case this means information systems development) is more likely if 'soft systems' methods are used rather than formal 'hard systems' techniques. This is not to say that 'hard' methods do not have a place. Rather, it is to suggest that the more traditional tools and techniques will have a greater chance of being used effectively if they are placed within a soft systems perspective.

Soft systems methodology has seven stages. They should be regarded as a framework rather than a prescription of a series of steps that should be followed slavishly.

Stage 1: The problem situation: unstructured

This stage is concerned with finding out as much as possible about the problem situation from as many different affected people as possible. Many different views about the problem will surface and it is important to bring out as many of them as possible. The structure of the problem in terms of physical layout, reporting structure, and formal and informal communication channels will also be explored.

A soft systems investigator will often find that there is a vagueness about the problem situation being investigated and what needs to be done. There can also be a lack of structure to the problem and the situation that surrounds it.

Stage 2: The problem situation: expressed

The previous stage was concerned with gathering an informal picture of the problem situation. This stage documents these findings. While there is no prescribed method for doing this, a technique that is commonly used is the drawing of 'rich pictures'. A rich picture can show the processes involved in the problem under consideration and how they relate to each other. The elements which can be included are the clients of the system (internal and external), the tasks being performed, the environment within which the system operates, the owners of the 'problem' and areas of conflict that are known to exist.

Rich pictures can act as an aid to discussion, between problem owner and problem solver or between analysts and users, or both. From a rich picture it then becomes possible to extract problem themes, which in turn provide a basis for further understanding of the problem situation. An example of a rich picture is shown in Figure 10.26. Such a diagram can be used in systems analysis to indicate the flows of information, the needs of staff and how the physical environment – in this case the office layout – affects the current way of working. This summary of the existing situation provides a valuable context for systems analysis and design.

Stage 3: Root definitions of relevant systems

Checkland (1999) describes a root definition as a 'concise, tightly constructed description of a human activity system which states what the system is'.

A root definition is created using the CATWOE checklist technique. CATWOE is an acronym that contains the following elements:

- *Clients or customers* – the person(s) who benefit, or are affected by or suffer from the outputs of the system and its activities that are under consideration.
- *Actors* – those who carry out the activities within the system.
- *Transformation* – the changes that take place either within or because of the system (this lies at the heart of the root definition).
- *Weltanschauung or Worldview* – this refers to how the system is viewed from an explicit viewpoint; sometimes this term is described as assumptions made about the system.
- *Owner* – the person(s) to whom the system is answerable: the sponsor, controller or someone who could cause the system to cease.
- *Environment* – that which surrounds and influences the operation of the system but which has no control over it.

The main use of the root definition is to clarify the situation so that it can be summed up in a clear, concise statement. An example of a root definition for a university might be:

> To provide students with the maximum opportunity for self-development, while at the same time safeguarding academic standards and allowing the university to operate within its budgetary constraints.

An alternative root definition might be:

> A system to maximise revenue and the prestige of academic staff!

If there are many different viewpoints to be represented, it is possible that a number of different root definitions may be constructed. These in turn will provide a basis for further discussion, so that a single agreed root definition can be produced. A single root definition that is hard to produce is indicative of sharp divisions between the CATWOE elements. From

Figure 10.26 An example of a rich picture for an estate agency showing the needs and responsibilities of different staff

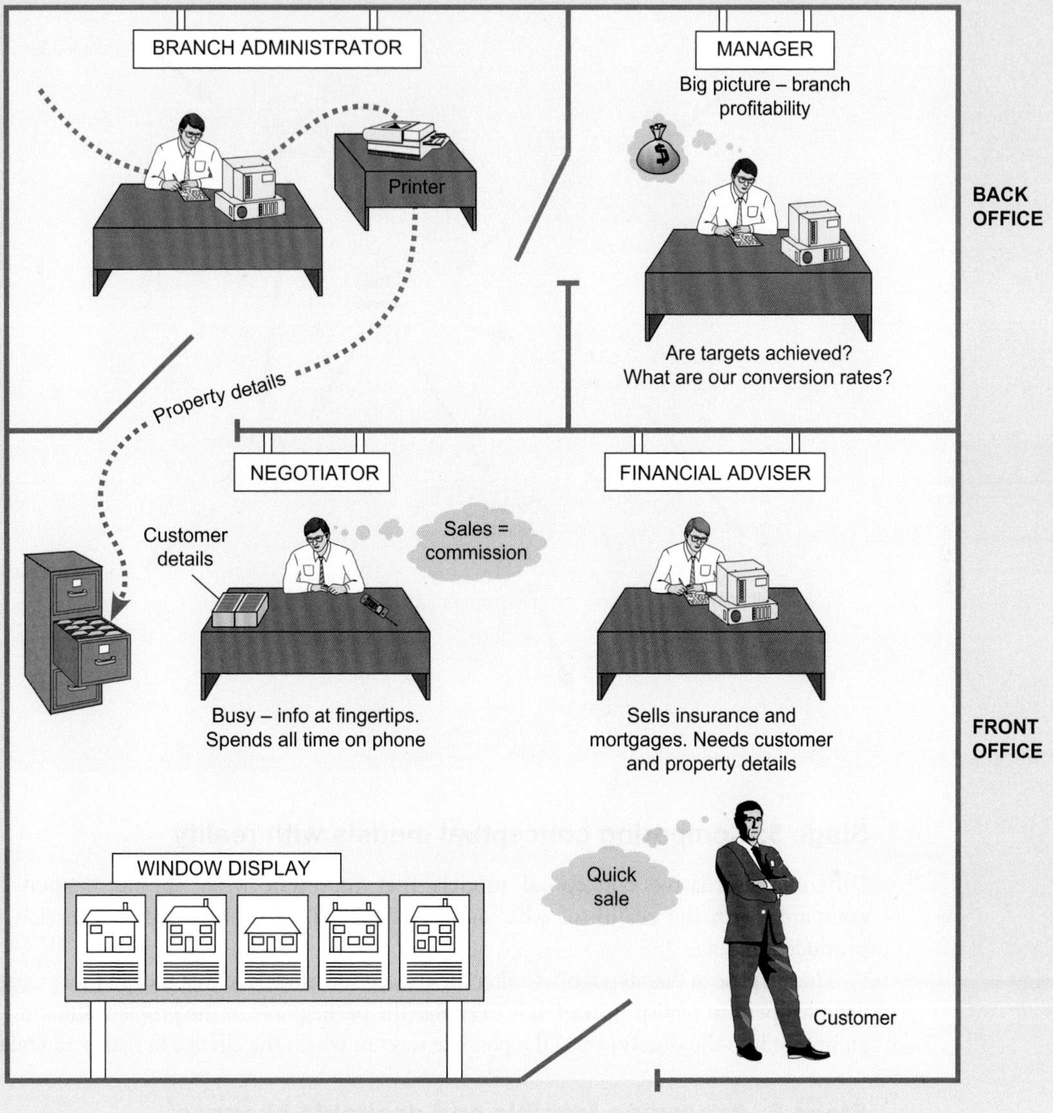

an information systems development perspective, if it is not possible to agree on a single root definition, then the systems development process is likely to be fraught with difficulties.

Stage 4: Building conceptual models

A conceptual model is a logical model of the key activities and processes that must be carried out in order to satisfy the root definition produced in Stage 3. It is, therefore, a representation of what must be done rather than what is currently done.

Conceptual models can be shown on a simple diagram where activities and the links between them can be shown. Figure 10.27 shows a simple conceptual model of a student records system.

Where several alternative root definitions have been produced, it is usual to draw a conceptual model for each one. Successive iterations through the alternative models can then lead to an agreed root definition and conceptual model. When this has happened, it is possible to move on to the next stage.

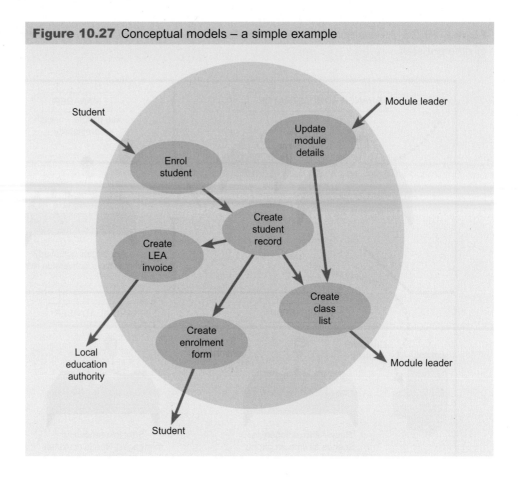

Figure 10.27 Conceptual models – a simple example

Stage 5: Comparing conceptual models with reality

Different alternative conceptual models that represent what should happen can be compared with the reality of what actually happens, as represented by the rich picture produced in Stage 2.

The purpose of this step is not to alter the conceptual models so that they fit more closely with what happens in reality. Instead, it is to enable the participants in the problem situation to gain an insight into the situation and the possible ways in which the change to reality can take place.

Stage 6: Assessing feasible and desirable changes

From the output of Stage 5, an analysis of the proposed changes can be made and proposals for change drawn up for those that are considered feasible and desirable. Such changes may relate to information systems, but there is no restriction on the type or scope of the change.

Stage 7: Action to improve the problem situation

It is perhaps here that the application of the model is most evident. SSM does *not* describe methods for implementing solutions – that lies outside the scope of the methodology. What it *does* do is to provide a framework through which problem situations can be understood. In fact, there is no reason that SSM should not be used as a tool for assisting the implementation of the required solution – the steps can be repeated, but this time the problem situation under consideration is the implementation of the required solution. This in turn may throw up alternative methods such as SSADM or rapid applications development (in Chapter 7) as the best approach to information systems development. Indeed, SSM has often been used as a 'front end' to more traditional structured development methodologies.

SYSTEMS ANALYSIS – AN EVALUATION

Any systems development project will be confronted by issues such as system size, complexity and acquisition method. These factors affect the choice of fact-finding and documentation tools. It is appropriate, therefore, to consider three alternative acquisition methods and review fact-finding and documentation needs for each.

Bespoke development

Bespoke software, which can be developed either internally or by a third party, presents the greatest scope for using the full range of analysis tools. Complex systems will require that the analyst gain a very clear and precise understanding of the business processes that take place, and all the tools at the analyst's disposal may need to be used. A combination of interviewing, documentation review and observation will yield much of the information that is needed, but if the system is a large one with many users, questionnaires may also need to be used. Brainstorming will be valuable, especially when linkages between different processes and subsystems are being investigated.

Complex projects will also require the use of all of the documentation tools we have discussed. Needless to say, the resulting diagrams will be more detailed and extensive than the ones given as examples in this chapter.

Purchasing packages off-the-shelf

Even though there is no requirement to produce something from which the system designer can produce a blueprint for the build stage, it is still necessary to gain a clear understanding of user requirements before a package is considered. Therefore, the fact-finding process will still be undertaken, but will be geared towards gaining an understanding of the features a package must support and those that are only desirable.

One benefit of deciding to purchase a package is that a number of candidate packages can be initially selected and used by the analyst as a means of identifying real user needs. It is possible, for example, for a selected group of users to review the features of a small number of packages with a view to compiling an appropriate requirements catalogue. Also, when users actually have an opportunity to experiment with a package, the analyst can gain a much greater insight into what the users' *real* requirements are.

For the analyst, it may still be useful to construct information flow and dataflow diagrams to help ensure that the package that is finally selected will support the required linkages, both between processes in the business area under consideration and to other business areas (from sales to accounts, for example). It will also be useful for the analyst to construct an entity relationship diagram to be sure that the packaged software will support the data requirements of the organisation.

User applications development

The situation here is somewhat different from the previous two acquisition methods. The end-user will have a clear idea of what the system is required to do. Also, it is less likely that the system will need to have linkages to other applications. The emphasis for the user, therefore, should be on identifying the data and processing requirements clearly so that they can be reviewed by others in the organisation, and an application can be produced which delivers good-quality information. Of the techniques discussed, the most relevant is the entity relationship diagram. By concentrating on data and how they are to be captured and represented, the user increases the probability that the data will be correct, while the use of fourth-generation language tools will help maximise the probability that the processing will also be correct.

Many user-developed applications suffer from poor database design and, as a consequence, the processing requirements are much more complex and prone to error. By taking care to consider carefully the relationships between the relevant data items, the probability of obtaining successful user-developed applications is increased.

SOFTWARE TOOLS FOR SYSTEMS ANALYSIS

Software tools are available to assist in the analysis phase. These usually focus on the diagramming rather than the enquiry stage, so much of the skill remains with the analyst in interpreting the users' requirements before producing meaningful diagrams showing the information flows and processes.

An important issue in using software tools to help the analyst is the degree to which the diagrams used to summarise processes can be converted easily into the system design and then into the final system. Traditionally, there have been separate tools for the analyst, designer and programmer. Since there is a strong overlap with the design phase, we will defer the examination of these tools until later (see Chapter 11, which has a section on computer-aided software engineering or CASE tools). Integrated CASE tools are intended to bridge the gap between analysis, design and programming.

CASE STUDY 10.2

ABC case study

Background

The following scenario is typical of many companies in the retail/wholesale business. A number of information flows exist both internally within the organisation and also with people outside. This case study is used for exercises on in-formation flow diagrams (IFDs), dataflow diagrams (DFDs) and entity relationship diagrams (ERDs).

The exercise continues in Chapter 11 when the reader is asked to produce a detailed database design based on the entity relationship diagram produced and the paper form examples.

ABC case study information

Andy's Bonsai Company (ABC) specialises in selling bonsai kits by mail order. The kits are made up of a number of ele-ments, including soil, plant pots and seeds. Other products such as mini-garden tools are also sold.

Customers place orders by telephone or by mailing an order slip which is printed as part of an ABC advert. Customers pay by cheque, credit card or debit card.

When an order is received by ABC, it is directed to a sales clerk. Each sales clerk has responsibility for a particular geographic region. The sales clerk will enter the details of the order onto a preprinted three-part order form. One part is retained by the sales clerk, one copy together with the payment is sent to the accounts department and the other is sent to the warehouse (on confirmation of the customer's creditworthiness).

On receipt of the customer orders and payment details, the accounts department ensures that the customer's payment is valid. If the payment is satisfactory, the department will inform the sales department and the order may proceed. An unsatisfactory payment situation is also communicated to the sales department, which then informs the customer of the problem.

CUSTOMER ORDER FORM

CUSTOMER NO.:
C234792
CUSTOMER ADDRESS:
26 Vicarage Drive
Thorndyke
West Yorkshire
WF24 7PL

ORDER NO.:
4214
DATE ORDERED:
29 March 1999

TELEPHONE NO.:
01482 7374

CODE	DESCRIPTION:	PRICE:	QTY:	VALUE:
1983	MINI-OAK	19.95	2	39.90
0184	MINI-MAPLE	24.50	2	49.00
2984	MINI GARDEN TOOLS (STAINLESS)	29.95	1	29.95
3775	MINI WATERING CAN (COPPER)	17.50	1	17.50
PAYMENT TYPE		Cheque	ORDER VALUE	136.35

WAREHOUSE CARD INDEX

LOCATION J82 CARD NO.: 19
PRODUCT CODE 4151
PRODUCT DESCRIPTION MINI-ASH

START QTY	TRANSACTION QTY:	DATE	SIGNATURE
37	−5	2/6/99	RON
28	−3	4/6/99	JEFF
25	−15	9/6/99	LUCY
10	+50	17/6/99	ERIC
60			

MANUFACTURING ORDER FORM

MANUFACTURING ORDER NO.	7210
PRODUCT CODE	4151
PRODUCT DESCRIPTION	MINI-ASH
QUANTITY ORDERED	50
DATE ORDERED	3/6/99
DATE REQUIRED	13/6/99
DATE DELIVERED	17/6/99
SIGNATURE	BERYL

PURCHASE ORDER FORM

SUPPLIER NO.: S165
SUPPLIER ADDRESS:
14 Wyke Trading Estate
Heckwhistle
West Yorkshire
WF9 5JJ

PURCHASE ORDER NO. 214
DATE ORDERED
29 March 1999

TELEPHONE NO.
01637 7346

CODE	DESCRIPTION	QTY	VALUE	PRICE
23	OAK CHIPPINGS	30.00	25	750.00
69	2' POTS	0.03	1000	300.00
84	SILVER SAND	1.77	10	17.70
75	MINI WATERING CAN (STAINLESS)	4.56	20	91.20
		ORDER VALUE		1158.90

The warehouse keeps a manual card-index system of stock and raw materials held together with copies of the customer orders. When an order is dispatched to the customer, the relevant order form is marked as having been dispatched. The warehouse also needs to keep track of the amount of product in stock and, when stock levels are low, it sends a manufacturing order to the manufacturing department.

The manufacturing department is responsible for ordering materials from various suppliers and then packaging them into products for sale to the customer. A three-part purchase order is made out: one part is sent to the supplier, one part is retained by the manufacturing department and the third part is sent to the accounts department. The accounts department holds copies of purchase orders for future matching with delivery notes and invoices. When the supplier delivers the ordered items, together with a delivery note, a check is made to ensure that the delivery matches the order. The supplier will send an invoice to the accounts department on confirmation that the delivery is correct so that payment can be made.

QUESTIONS

1. Using the ABC case study, produce an information flow diagram for the company by following the steps given earlier in the chapter. Does the diagram tell you anything about ABC's operations which may need some attention (such as missing or superfluous information flows)?

2. Using the ABC case study and the information flow diagram that you drew in answer to Question 1, produce a simple Level 1 dataflow diagram for the company by following the steps given earlier in the chapter. Compare your answer with that by one of your colleagues. Are the diagrams the same? If not, is it possible to say which is correct? If not, why not?

3. Using the ABC case study, including the sample forms included below the main text, construct an entity relationship diagram for the company. Make sure that you do a cross-reference matrix before attempting to draw the diagram. When you have drawn your first-cut diagram, check for many-to-many relationships and eliminate any that you find by using the appropriate technique described earlier in the chapter.

SUMMARY

Stage summary: systems analysis

Purpose:	Define the features and other requirements of the information system
Key activities:	Requirements capture (interviews, questionnaires, etc.) diagramming
Inputs:	User's opinions, system documentation, observation
Outputs:	Requirements specification

1. The analysis phase of systems development is aimed at identifying *what* the new system will do.

2. Analysis will identify the business processes which will be assisted by the software, the functions of the software and the data requirements.

3. The results of the analysis phase are summarised as a requirements specification which forms the input to the design phase, which will define *how* the system will operate.

4. Fact-finding techniques used at the analysis stage include:

   - questionnaires;
   - interviews;
   - observation;
   - documentation review;
   - brainstorming.

5. The results from the fact-finding exercise are summarised in a requirements specification and using different diagrams such as:

   - information flow diagrams which provide a simple view of the way information is moved around an organisation;
   - dataflow diagrams which show the processes performed by a system and their data inputs and outputs;
   - entity relationship diagrams which summarise the main objects about which data need to be stored and the relationship between them.

6. The depth of analysis will be dependent on the existing knowledge of requirements. A user development may have limited analysis since the user will have a good understanding of their needs. A software house will need to conduct a detailed analysis which will form the basis for a contract with the company for which it is developing software.

EXERCISES

Self-assessment exercises

1. What is the difference between the 'funnel' and 'pyramid' approaches to structuring an interview?

2. Why can closed questions still be useful in an interview?

3. Assess the relative effectiveness of interviews versus questionnaires when attempting to establish user requirements.

4. In an information flow diagram, why should we not record information flows that lie completely outside the system boundary?

5. What are the main differences between an information flow diagram and a dataflow diagram?

6. What is meant by the term 'levelling' in dataflow diagrams?

7. In a sales order processing system, which of the following are not entities? Customer, colour, size, product, telephone number, sales order, salesperson, order date.

8. Why might the construction of an ERD still be useful even if an off-the-shelf package was going to be purchased?

Discussion questions

1. Use a simple example with no more than five processes or ten information flows to examine the differences between the information flow diagram and the dataflow diagram. Which would be more effective for explaining deficiencies with an existing system to:

   (a) a business manager;
   (b) a systems designer?

Justify your reasoning.

2. Compare the effectiveness of 'soft' methods of acquiring information such as interviews and questionnaires and 'hard' methods of gathering information such as document analysis and observation of staff. In which order do you think these analysis activities should be conducted and on which do you think most time should be spent?

3. 'For producing a database, the only type of diagram from the analysis phase that needs to be produced is the entity relationship diagram. Dataflow diagrams are not relevant.' Discuss.

Essay questions

1. Compare and contrast alternative fact-finding methods and analysis documentation tools as they might relate to bespoke software development and the purchase of off-the-shelf packages.

2. Errors in the analysis stage of a systems development project are far more costly to fix than those that occur later in the systems development lifecycle. Why do some organisations seem to devalue the analysis process by seeking to get to the system build as quickly as possible?

3. Compare and contrast the relative effectiveness of the use of information flow diagrams, dataflow diagrams and entity relationship diagrams by a business analyst to demonstrate inefficiency in a company's existing information management processes. Use examples to illustrate your answer.

Examination questions

1. Briefly review the arguments for and against using interviewing as a means of determining system requirements.

2. Explain the relationship between the initiation and analysis phases of the systems development lifecycle.

3. Briefly explain (in one or two sentences) the purpose of each of the following diagramming methods:

   (a) information flow diagram;
   (b) context diagram;
   (c) dataflow diagram;
   (d) entity relationship diagram.

4. Draw a diagram showing each of the following relationships on an ERD:

   (a) The customer places many orders. Each order is received from one customer.
   (b) The customer order may contain many requests for products. Each product will feature on many customer orders.
   (c) Each customer has a single customer representative who is responsible for them. Each customer representative is responsible for many customers.

5. The final examination question is based on a detailed case study for Megatoys and is to be found on the companion web site.

References

Browne, G.J. and Rogich, M.B. (2001) 'An empirical investigation of user requirements elicitation: comparing the effectiveness of prompting techniques', *Journal of Management Information Systems*, 17, 4, 223–49

Buzan, T. and Buzan, B. (2010) *The Mind Map Book*, BBC Active, London

Checkland, P.B. (1999) *Systems Thinking, Systems Practice*, John Wiley, Chichester

Lindstrom, L. and Jeffries, R. (2004) 'Extreme programming and agile software development methodologies', *Information Systems Management*, 21, 3, 41–52

Shi, Y., Specht, P. and Stolen, J. (1996) 'A consensus ranking of information systems requirements', *Information Management and Computer Security*, 4, 1, 10–18

Taylor, D. (1995) *Business Engineering with Object Technology*, John Wiley, New York

Yeates, T. and Wakefield, T. (2004) *Systems Analysis and Design*, 2nd edition, Financial Times Prentice Hall, Harlow

Further reading

Ambler, S. and Lines, M. (2012) *Disciplined Agile Delivery: A Practitioner's Guide to Agile Software Delivery in the Enterprise*, IBM Press.

Avison, D.E. and Fitzgerald, G. (2006) *Information Systems Development: Methodologies, Techniques and Tools*, 4th edition, Blackwell, Oxford.

Kendall, K.E. and Kendall, J.E. (2013) *Systems Analysis and Design*, 9th edition, Prentice-Hall, Englewood Cliffs, NJ.

Lejk, M. and Deeks, D. (2004) *An Introduction to Systems Analysis Techniques and UML Distilled: A Brief Guide to the Standard Object Modelling Language*, 2nd edition, Prentice Hall, Hemel Hempstead.

Web links

www.cio.com CIO.com for chief information officers and IS staff has many articles related to analysis and design topics.

www.computerweekly.com *Computer Weekly* is an IS professional trade paper with UK/Europe focus which has many case studies on practical problems of analysis, design and implementation.

www.research.ibm.com/journal *IBM Systems Journal* and the *Journal of Research and Development* have many cases and articles on analysis and design related to e-business concepts such as knowledge management and security.

LINKS TO OTHER CHAPTERS

This chapter is closely linked to Chapters 10 and 12, since the design phase receives input from the requirements specification of the analysis phase and the design specification acts as input to the implementation phase.

Systems design

LEARNING OUTCOMES

After reading this chapter, you will be able to:

- define the difference between analysis and design and the overlap between them;
- synthesise the relationship between good design and good-quality information systems;
- define the way relational databases are designed;
- evaluate the importance of the different elements of design for different applications.

MANAGEMENT ISSUES

Design is also a critical phase of BIS development since errors at this stage can lead to a system that is unsatisfactory for the user. From a managerial perspective, this chapter addresses the following questions:

- What different types of design need to be conducted for a quality BIS to be developed?
- What are the key aspects of design for an e-business system?
- How do we create an effective information architecture for our organisation?

INTRODUCTION

The design phase of information systems development involves producing a specification or 'blueprint' of how the system will work. This forms the input specification for the final stage of building the system by programmers and database administrators. The design phase is also closely linked to the previous analysis phase, since the users' requirements directly determine the characteristics of the system to be designed.

The **systems design** is given in a design specification defining the best structure for the application and the best methods of data input, output and user interaction via the user interface. The design specification is based on the requirements collected at the analysis stage.

Design is important, since it will govern how well the information system works for the end-users in the key areas of performance, usability and security. It also determines whether the system will meet business requirements – whether it will deliver the return on investment. The design specification will include the architecture of the system, how security will be implemented, and methods for entry, storage, retrieval and display of data.

Before the widespread adoption of Internet technologies from the mid-1990s onwards, system design for BIS tended to focus on the design of applications for the different functional areas of the business (as described in Chapter 6). In the era of e-business, design of such applications for purposes such as electronic procurement, supply chain management and customer relationship is still required. However, the adoption of standard solutions applications such as SAP and Oracle for enterprise applications has meant that system design has changed in its nature. Many of the challenges of design now involve tailoring the user interfaces and data storage and transfer for these standard applications. It is now less common for systems to be designed without the use of pre-existing software applications or components.

A further change in the emphasis of design has been caused by the increasing volume of unstructured information that it is made available to businesses and consumers via the Internet and the World Wide Web. A design challenge faced by all organisations, large and small, is managing this content in order to deliver relevant, timely information to their stakeholders whether they be employees, customers, suppliers, partners or government agencies. So designing an effective information architecture for an organisation to enable it to deliver content via the intranets, extranet and Internet networks introduced earlier (in Chapters 5 and 6) has become a major challenge.

In this chapter, we explore the elements both of traditional application design and of delivery of web-based content. We start by introducing the concepts of effective design which apply to all types of information system. We then look at how input design, output design and interfacing with other systems occurs for traditional applications and for those delivered via web browsers. Finally, we look at approaches to building information architecture. Throughout the chapter, we will refer to the example of information systems required by a bank to illustrate today's challenges of system design.

Systems design

The design phase of the lifecycle defines how the finished information system will operate. This is defined in a design specification of the best structure for the application and the best methods of data input, output and user interaction via the user interface. The design specification is based on the requirements collected at the analysis stage.

AIMS OF SYSTEM DESIGN

In systems design we are concerned with producing an appropriate design that results in a good-quality information system that:

- is easy to use;
- provides the correct functions for end-users;

- is rapid in retrieving data and moving between different screen views of the data;
- is reliable;
- is secure;
- is well integrated with other systems.

These factors are clearly all important to delivering a satisfactory experience to end-users and a satisfactory return on investment to the business. Consider an online banking service for customers which may also be accessed by staff – all these factors are vital to the success of the system and so the design is vital to the success of the system also.

CASE STUDY 11.1

Beaverbrooks the Jewellers

Beaverbrooks the Jewellers created a system that collates data from all stores and places it in one location

Beaverbrooks the Jewellers is a family business established a century ago and with staff dispersed between branches and head office locations, increased paperwork, administration and information demands had become a significant issue. Much of Beaverbrooks' business concerns providing special order items wedding and engagement rings, necklaces, engraved silverware and watches. While each shop stocks the full range of wedding and engagement rings, it is rare that they will have all sizes in stock at every store.

Patrick Walker, head of management information systems, says that most couples choose the design of the ring together and then the ring will be ordered either from a central warehouse, another local branch or directly from a supplier. 'The result is that much of Beaverbrooks' staff time is taken up following the progression of the order', he says. 'We needed a system that would manage this for us. In addition, we discovered that there was a mass of email going round and round the organisation and not always reaching the appropriate person.' Collaboration between head office and the branches, a central repository for documentation and a framework to enable company information and knowledge to be exchanged were the desired outcomes that arose from a cross-company focus group.

All company data, regardless of its format or origin, is now held in one place on a central server where it can be easily shared, searched, retrieved, backed up and managed. KnowledgeWorker collaboration, search and workflow tools sit over the top of the data, which is accessed locally or remotely through a web browser interface. Branch staff now use the central data system extensively for stock en-quires, placing special orders, sharing company information and making sure the merchandising in each branch conforms to the current company branding and directives.

For Beaverbrooks, integrating its information and processes into a central collaborative system has led to improved productivity throughout the organisation. 'Improving our methods of storing information and then sharing it between employees has halved our administration time', says Walker.

'We keep finding more activities the system can help us with, so we are spending that extra time doing new things with our information to make us even more effective as a business.'

Source: Linda More, *Computing*, 25 October 2007, http://www.computing.co.uk/ctg/analysis/1821325/case-study-beaverbrooks-jewellers

QUESTIONS

1. Read the case study and identify the main design elements that needed to be considered.

2. Identify any design features that can be directly linked to specific business benefits.

It is also important to think forward to future releases of the software. When the software is updated in the maintenance phase, it is important to have a system that can be easily modified. Good documentation is important to this, but equally import-ant is that the design be flexible enough to accommodate changes to its structure. To achieve flexibility, simplicity in design is a requirement. Many designers and developers adopt the maxim 'KISS' or 'Keep It Simple, Stupid!'.

Whitten and Bentley (2006) point out that design does not simply involve producing an architectural and detailed design, but is also an evaluation of different implementation methods. For example, an end-user designing an application will consider whether to implement a system within an application such as Microsoft Access or develop a separate Visual Basic application. However, it is usually possible to take the 'make-or-buy' decision earlier in the software lifecycle, even when the detailed design constraints are unknown. The acquisition method is described in more detail earlier (in Chapters 7 and 8) on the start-up phases of a project.

CONSTRAINTS ON SYSTEM DESIGN

The system design is directly constrained by the user requirements specification, which has been produced as a result of systems analysis (as described in Chapter 10). This will describe the functions that are required by the user and must be implemented as part of the design. As well as the requirements mentioned in the previous section, there are environmental constraints on design which are a result of the hardware and software environment of implementation. These include:

- hardware platform (PC, Apple or Unix workstation);
- operating system (Windows XP, Apple or Unix/Linux);
- web browsers to be supported (different versions of Microsoft Internet Explorer and open-source rivals such as Opera, Mozilla, Firefox, etc.);
- data links required between the application and other programs or a particular relational database such as Oracle or Microsoft SQL Server;
- design tools such as CASE tools;
- methodologies or standards adopted by the organisation, such as SSADM;
- industry standards such as data exchange using XML;
- system development tools or development environments for programming, such as open-source technology or proprietary tools such as Microsoft Visual Studio;
- number of users to be supported concurrently and the performance required.

Design strategy

A high-level statement about the approach to developing an information system. It includes statements on the system's functionality, hardware and system software platform, and the method of acquisition.

Hoffer et al. (2010) refer to a **design strategy** as the high-level statement defining how the development of an information system should proceed which addresses all the issues described above. They identify three different aspects of design:

1. Dividing requirements (from the analysis phase discussed in the previous chapter) into sets of essential requirements and optional requirements which may be built into future versions.

2. Enumerating different potential implementation environments (hardware, system software and network platforms: discussed in Chapters 3, 4 and 5).

3. Proposing different ways to source or acquire the various sets of capabilities, for example outsourcing, purchase of pre-existing applications software or development of new capabilities (as discussed in Chapters 7 and 8 of this text).

While this is a useful way of breaking down decisions that need to be taken about design of an information system, the reality is that by the time a systems development project enters the main design phase, all three of these areas will have been agreed. They are part of the feasibility analysis described earlier (in Chapter 8). So, in this chapter we focus on the approaches to detailed design needed to implement the system requirements. These include design of the user interface, database and security of a system within the technical environment and the acquisition method that has already been selected.

THE RELATIONSHIP BETWEEN ANALYSIS AND DESIGN

As Yeates and Wakefield (2003) point out, there is considerable overlap between analysis and design. To help ensure completion of the project on time, preliminary design of the architecture of the system will start while the analysis phase is progressing. Furthermore, the design phase may raise issues on requirements that may require further analysis with the end-users, particularly with the prototyping approach.

The distinction is often made between the *logical* representation of data or processes during the analysis stage and the *physical* representation at the design stage. Consider, for example, data analysis: here the entity relationship diagram of the analysis phase described earlier (in Chapter 10) will be transformed into a physical database table definition at the design stage as described later in this chapter. A logical entity 'customer' will be specified as a physical database table 'Customer' in which customer records are stored. Similarly, the dataflow diagram will be transformed into a structure chart indicating how the different submodules of the software will interact at the design stage.

ELEMENTS OF DESIGN

The different activities that occur during the design phase of an information systems project can be broken down in a variety of ways. In this section we consider different ways of approaching system design. These alternatives are often used in a complementary fashion rather than exclusively.

A common approach to design is to consider different levels of detail. In the next main section we start by considering an overall design for the architecture of the system. This is referred to as 'system design'. Once this is established, we then design the individual modules and the interactions between them. This is known as 'module design'. Through using this approach we are tackling design by using a functional decomposition or top-down approach, similar to that referred to earlier (in Chapter 9) on project management as the 'work breakdown structure'. Major modules for an online banking system will be those for capturing and displaying data and interacting with the user, data access modules which interface to the bank's legacy customer database, and security or user access modules.

Top-down design

The top-down approach to design involves specifying the overall control architecture of the application before designing the individual modules.

Top-down or bottom-up?

Since many systems are made from existing modules or pre-built components that need to be constructed, the design approach that is most commonly employed is a **top-down** strategy. In this approach, it is best to consider the overall architecture first and then perform the detailed design on the individual functional modules of the system. The 'divide and conquer' approach can then be used to assign the design and implementation tasks for each module to different development team members. The description in this chapter will follow this approach by looking at the overall design first and then at the detailed module design.

The **bottom-up** approach to design starts with the design of individual modules such as the security module, establishing their inputs and outputs, and then builds an overall design from these modules.

Bottom-up design

The bottom-up approach to design starts with the design of individual modules, establishing their inputs and outputs, and then builds an over-all design from these modules.

Validation and verification

An aspect of the design which is quite easy to overlook is testing that the design we produce is the right one. Checking the design involves validation and verification.

In **validation** we will check against the requirements specification and ask '*Are we building the right product?*' In other words, we test whether the system meets the needs of the end-users identified during analysis such as functions required and speed of response. Validation will occur during testing of the system by the end-users; it highlights the value of prototyping in giving immediate feedback of whether a design is appropriate.

When undertaking **verification** we will 'walk through' the design and ask '*Are we building the product right?*' Since there are a number of design alternatives, designers need to consult to ensure they are choosing the optimal solution. Verification is a test of the design to ensure that the one chosen is the best available and that it is error-free.

The two questions should be considered throughout the design process and also form the basis for producing a test specification to be used at the implementation stage.

Validation

This is a test of the design where we check that the design fulfils the requirements of the business users which are defined in the requirements specification.

Verification

This is a test of the design to ensure that the design chosen is the best available and that it is error-free.

Scalability

Scalability is the potential of an information system or piece of software or hardware to move from supporting a small number of users to supporting a large number of users without a marked decrease in reliability or performance.

When designing information systems, the design target must always be for the maximum anticipated number of users. Many implementations have failed, or have had to be redesigned at considerable cost, because the system used in the development and test environment with a small number of users does not *scale* to the live system with many more users.

If the system does not scale, there may be major problems with performance which makes the system unusable. Volume or capacity planning (Chapter 12), in which the anticipated workload of the live environment is simulated, can help us foresee problems of scalability.

Scalability

The potential of an information system or piece of software or hardware to move from supporting a small number of users to a large number of users without a marked decrease in reliability or performance.

Data modelling and process modelling

Another common approach to design is to consider data modelling and process modelling separately. The design of the data structures required to support the system, such as input and output files or database tables, are considered in relation to information collected at the analysis stage as the entity relationship diagram (ERD) and data requirements. In SSADM a separate stage is identified for data design which is followed by process design although the two are often combined.

Process modelling is the design of the different modules of the system, each of which is a process with clearly defined inputs and outputs and a transformation process. (Note that this term is also used as an approach to design in business process re-engineering.) Dataflow diagrams are often used to define system processes.

Process modelling

Involves the design of the different modules of the system, each of which is a process with clearly defined inputs and outputs and a transformation process. Dataflow diagrams are often used to define processes in the system.

Data modelling

Data modelling involves considering how to represent data objects within a system, both logically and physically. The entity relationship diagram is used to model the data.

Data modelling considers how to represent data objects within a system, both logically and physically. The entity relationship diagram is used to model the data and a data dictionary is used to store details about the characteristics of the data, which is sometimes referred to as 'metadata'.

The processes or program modules which will manipulate these data are designed based on information gathered at the analysis stage in the form of functional requirements and dataflow diagrams. This approach is used, for example, by Curtis (2008). While this is a natural division, there is a growing realisation that for a more efficient design these two aspects cannot be considered in isolation. Object-oriented techniques, which are increasing in popularity, consider the design of process and associated data as unified software objects. These are considered in more detail at the end of this chapter.

Other elements of design are required by the constraints on the system. To ensure that the system is easy to use we must design the user interface carefully.

To ensure that the system is reliable and secure, these capabilities must be designed into the system. User interface and security design are elements of design that will be considered at both the overall or system design phase and the detailed design phase.

What needs to be designed?

In this chapter we will review the following major elements of systems design:

1. *Overall design or system design.* What are the best architecture and client/server infrastructure? The overall design defines how the system will be broken down into different modules and how the user will navigate between different functions and different views of the data.

2. *Detailed design of modules and user interface components.* This defines the details of how the system will operate. It will be reviewed by looking at user interface and input/output design.

3. *Database design.* How to design the most efficient structure using normalisation.

4. *User interface design.* How to design the interface to make it easy to learn and use. For web-based systems this includes the information architecture.

5. *Security design.* Measures for restricting access data and safeguarding data against deletion.

SYSTEM OR OUTLINE DESIGN

System or outline design

A high-level definition of the different components that make up the architecture of a system and how they interact.

Systems architecture

The design relationship between software applications, hardware, process and data for an information system.

System or outline design involves specifying an overall structure or **systems architecture** for all the different components that will make up the system. It is a high-level overview of the different components that make up the architecture of a system and how they interact. The components include software modules that have a particular function such as a print module, the data they access, and the hardware components that may be part of the system. Hardware will include specifying the characteristics of the client PC and servers, plus any additional hardware such as an image scanner or specialised printer.

Designing the overall architecture involves specification of how the different hardware and software components of the system fit together. To produce this design, a good starting point is to consider the business process definition that will indicate which high-level tasks will be performed using the different components of the system. Flow process charts or process maps such as Figure 11.1 can be used to inform the architectural design directly since they help to identify the different components needed and how they link. Figure 11.2 concentrates on hardware, but also describes location of data and applications.

Figure 11.1 Flow process chart for a workflow processing system

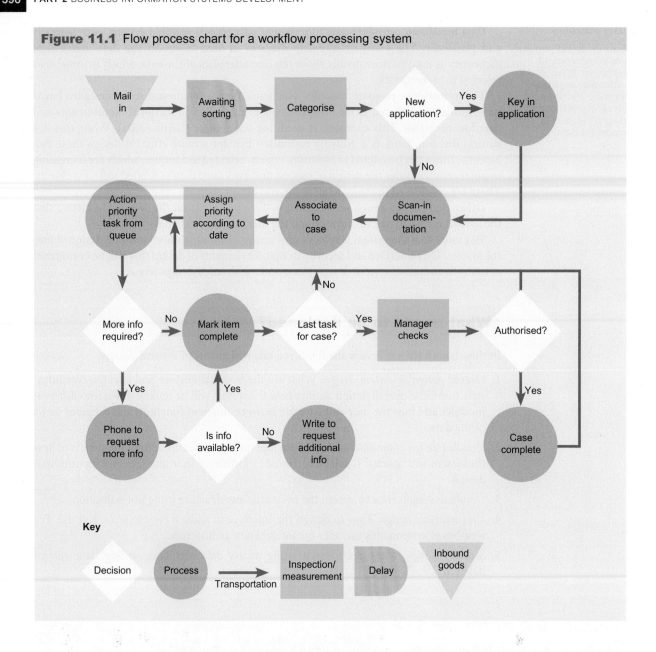

Process modelling

Process modelling is used to identify the different activities required from a system, as explained in Chapter 10. These functions can be summarised using a flow process chart as shown in Figure 11.1.

The overall architecture description will also include details of the navigation between the main screens or views of data in the application which can be based on this type of diagram.

Screen functions needed in this software are to categorise the type of mail received, associate it with a particular 'case' or customer and review items of work in the workflow queue, marking them as complete where appropriate. Table 11.1 summarises what is achieved during the different types of design.

Figure 11.2 System architecture for a workflow processing system

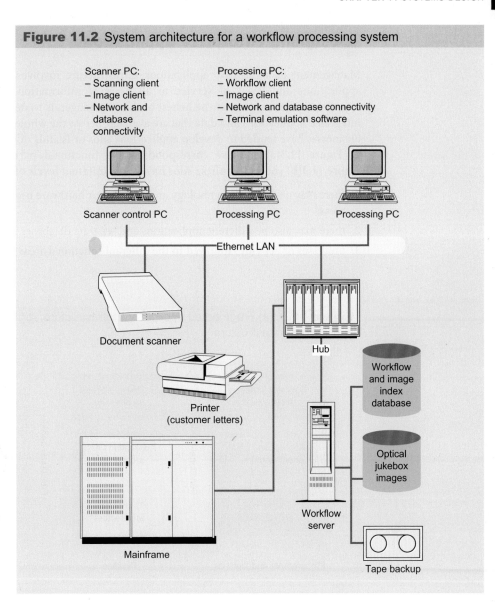

Scanner PC:
– Scanning client
– Image client
– Network and database connectivity

Processing PC:
– Workflow client
– Image client
– Network and database connectivity
– Terminal emulation software

Scanner control PC   Processing PC   Processing PC

Ethernet LAN

Document scanner

Printer (customer letters)

Hub

Workflow and image index database

Optical jukebox images

Workflow server

Mainframe

Tape backup

Table 11.1 Comparison between the coverage of system and detailed design

Design function	System design	Detailed design
Architecture	Specification of different modules and communication between them; specification of hardware components and software tools	Internal design of modules
User interface	Flow of control between different views of data	Detailed specification of input forms and dialogues
Database	Data modelling of tables	Normalisation
File structure	Main file types and contents	Detailed 'record and field structure'
Security	Define constraints	Design security method

Designing enterprise applications

Management of a business applications infrastructure involves delivering appropriate applications and levels of service to all users of information systems services. The objective of the designer, at the behest of the IS manager, is to deliver access to effective, integrated applications and data that are available across the whole company. Traditionally businesses have tended to develop applications silos or islands of information as depicted in Figure 11.3(a) – these correspond to the functional parts of the organisation. Figure 11.3(b) shows that these silos have three different levels of applications:

1. there may be different technology architectures or hardware used in different functional areas;

2. there may also be different applications and separate databases in different areas;

3. processes or activities followed in the different functional areas may also be different.

Figure 11.3 (a) Fragmented applications infrastructure, (b) integrated applications infrastructure

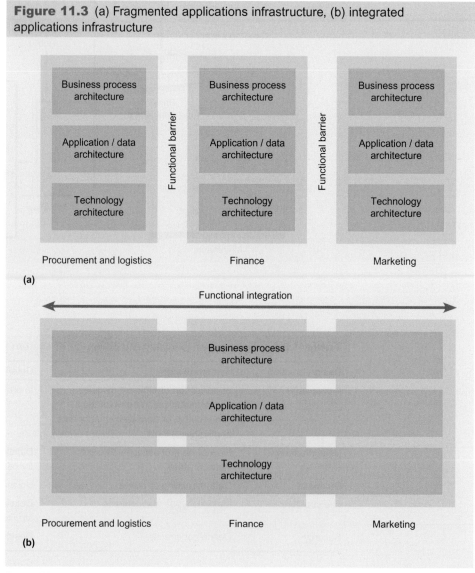

Source: Adapted from Hasselbring (2000)

These applications silos are often a result of decentralisation or poorly controlled investment in information systems, with different departmental managers selecting different systems from different vendors. An operational example of the problems this may cause is if a customer phones a B2B company for the status of a bespoke item they have ordered, the person in customer support may have access to their personal details, but not the status of their job which is stored on a separate information system in the manufacturing unit.

To avoid the problems of a fragmented applications infrastructure, companies have been attempting, since the early 1990s, to achieve the more integrated position shown in 11.3(b). Here the technology architecture, applications and data architecture and process architecture are uniform and integrated across the organisation. To achieve this many companies turned to enterprise systems vendors such as SAP and Oracle. Here, they are effectively using a pre-existing design from the off-the-shelf package, and the design involves selecting appropriate modules and tailoring them for the revised business process. Enterprise systems software is discussed in more detail earlier (in Chapter 6).

CASE STUDY 11.2

Systems management: driving innovation should be the main objective

By Jane Bird

A typical IT department is like an old house that has been mended and extended so that the original design and infrastructure have almost disappeared, says Peter Chadha, chief executive of DrPete, an IT strategy consultancy.

Nobody remembers the location of gas pipes and electricity cables or how the plumbing works, making the building difficult to adapt to a new purpose.

'The 'house' is so difficult to update and ill-suited to modern living, it is now easier to put a Portakabin in the garden than continue using it,' says Mr Chadha.

Similarly, meeting a business's technology needs can often now be better accomplished using additional products and services – such as smartphones, tablet computers, software as a service (SaaS) and outsourcing – rather than upgrading legacy IT systems.

For example, Mr Chadha helped to implement an iPad-based electronic reception logbook for The Office Group, the meetings and events organiser, using Google Apps with Google Scripting. 'It gave reception a modern feel and meant anyone in the building could instantly know who was in,' he says.

Business executives have seen how quickly apps can be implemented on their personal mobile devices, and they expect IT departments to be equally responsive to their business needs.

But most applications need to be integrated with existing systems – a difficult, expensive, time-consuming process, as IT departments point out.

Executives often think of the IT department as blocking innovation, says Roop Singh, managing partner at Bangalore-based Wipro Consulting Services.

'This is a bit unfair, because IT departments have to worry about complexity, security, risk and support,' says Mr Singh.

'Moreover, since 2009 they have been forced to focus on minimising costs, keeping the lights on rather than making a difference to the business.'

This showed in a recent UK survey of 1,000 senior IT decision makers, commissioned by KCom, a services communications provider.

Some 72.5 per cent of respondents said they had no plans to invest in IT systems during the coming year, and 26 per cent cited an inability to demonstrate that IT will help meet strategic objectives and provide a return on investment as the reason for holding back.

This lack of focus on business objectives is crucial, says Stephen Pratt, managing partner of worldwide consulting at Infosys in California. 'It is very common for the business to say it wants something done in two years and for the IT department to say it will take four,' says Mr Pratt.

'Most executives say technology infrastructure is limiting their ability to achieve business goals,' he adds. 'It ought to be doing the opposite: driving the innovation that pushes the business faster than it's comfortable with.'

Mr Pratt says IT should be split into two parts, infrastructure and innovation. Infrastructure should

➡

provide a basic service, as do the office's air conditioning and coffee machines.

Innovation should focus on ways to help the business achieve its strategic goals. You need two distinct personalities to lead these functions, Mr Pratt says.

'People focused on innovation are more likely to look for progressive ways to deploy technology – they are more likely to embrace change than resist it.'

Outsourcing applications, such as enterprise resource planning, finance and supply chain, is a good way to focus on innovation, says Brendan O'Rourke, chief information officer of TelefÓnica Digital, the telecommunications company, which outsources many applications to IT services consultancy Cognizant.

'An outsourcer can get on with the management, operation and maintenance of IT, and is best placed to optimise costs,' says Mr O'Rourke. He involves Cognizant closely in developing applications. 'This means we can hand over application maintenance to Cognizant at an early stage, and eventually send it offshore.'

Mr Chadha cites applications that make it possible to implement customer relationship systems in 'days or weeks rather than the months or years it might if organisations implemented it themselves'.

Cloud-based SaaS systems are also easier to try out, says Mr Chadha. This frees time to concentrate on improving processes and training people.

Wipro's Mr Singh says: 'IT needs to engage with the business and explain how difficult it is simply keeping the lights on.'

But he notes that IT departments are recruiting more people who understand the business side. Banks, for example, are hiring regulatory experts who can take proactive steps to ensure compliance.

In retail, communications experts are joining IT teams. This helps them not only respond better to business needs but also lets them articulate the benefits and problems with technological developments more clearly. Such approaches will help teams communicate more effectively and so drive the business forward rather than hold it back.

QUESTION

Evaluate the approach to systems management discussed in the case study.

The client/server model of computing

Client/server model

This describes a system architecture in which end-user computers access data from more powerful server computers. Processing can be split in various ways between the server and client.

The majority of modern information systems are designed with a client/server architecture. In the **client/server model**, the clients are typically desktop PCs which give the 'front-end' access point to business applications. The clients are connected to a 'back-end' server computer via a local- or wide-area network. As explained earlier (in Chapter 5), applications accessed through a web browser across the Internet are also client/server applications. These include e-commerce applications for online purchase and application service provider solutions such as remote e-mail management.

When it was introduced, the client/server model represented a radically new architecture compared with the traditional centralised processing method of a main-frame with character-based 'dumb terminals'.

Client/server is popular since it provides the opportunity for processing tasks to be shared between one or more servers and the desktop clients. This gives the potential for faster execution, as processing is shared between many clients and the server(s), rather than all occurring on a single server or mainframe. Client/server also makes it easier for end-users to customise their applications. Centralised control of the user administration and data security and archiving can still be retained. With these advantages, there are also system management problems which have led to an evolution in client/server architecture from two- to three-tier as described below. The advantages and disadvantages of client/server are discussed earlier (in Chapter 5).

When designing an information system for the client/server architecture, the designer has to decide how to divide tasks between the server and the client. These tasks include:

- data storage;
- query processing;

- display;
- application logic including the business rules.

Client/server design generally follows just two main approaches: two-tier and three-tier client/server. Two-tier client/server is sometimes referred to as fat client, the application running on the PC being a large program containing all the application logic and display code. It retrieves data from a separate database server. Three-tier client/server is an arrangement in which the client is mainly used for display, with application logic and the business rules partitioned on a server as a second tier and the database server the third tier. Here the client is sometimes referred to as a thin client, because the size of the application's executable program is smaller. It is important to understand the distinctions between these, since they involve two quite different design approaches that can have significant implications for application performance and scalability. These are the 'thin client' approach where the client only handles display and the 'fat client' approach where a larger program runs on the client and handles both display and application logic. In the 'fat client' model the client handles the display and local processing, with the server holding the data (typically in a database) and responsible for handling processing of queries on the back end. This model, which is known as two-tier client/server, is still widely used, but more recently the three-tier client/server has become widespread due to problems with unreliability and lack of scalability with two-tier systems.

Figure 11.4 shows a simple two-tier client/server arrangement. In this, a client application directly accesses the server to retrieve information requested by the user, such as a report of 'aged debtors' in an accounting system. In this two-tier model, the client handles all application logic such as control flow, the display of dialogues and formatting of views.

In a three-tier client/server model (Figure 11.4(b)), the GUI or 'thin client' forms the first tier, with the application and function logic separated out as a second tier and the data source forming the third tier. In this model there may be a separate application and database server, although these could reside on the same machine. Two-tier client/server may be the more rapid to develop in a RAD project, but it will not be the more efficient at run time or the easier to update. Through separating out the display coding and the business application into three tiers, it is much easier to update the application as business rules change (which will happen frequently). It also offers better security through fine-tuning according to the service required.

Figure 11.4 (a) Two-tier and (b) three-tier client/server architecture compared

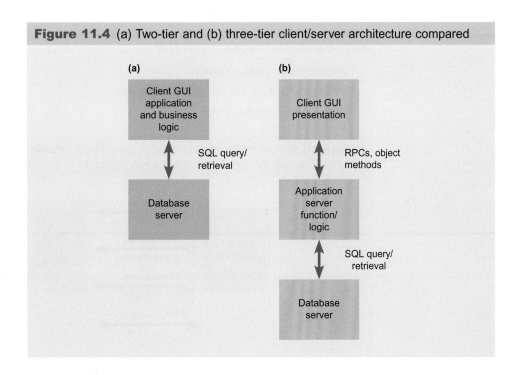

Figure 11.5 Example of a program structure chart

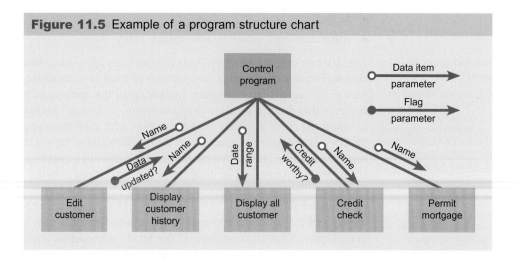

Program and module structure

The module and program structure will also be outlined at the system design stage. There are various notations used by programmers to indicate the structure that will be used. An example is the structure chart which is used in the design methodology JSD (Jackson system development – Jackson, 1983). An example of a structure chart is illustrated in Figure 11.5. A structure chart shows how the software will be broken down into different modules and gives an indication of how they will interact. Here the main control module is calling a variety of other modules with different functions. The interaction or exchange of data items between procedures is also shown. For example, the 'edit customer' module is passed the name (or customer code) of the customer to edit and if the user changes the data a 'flag' (True or False) parameter is passed back to the control module, indicating that the data were updated. Similarly, the credit check module is passed the name of the customer and a flag indicates whether the customer is creditworthy or not.

The interactions between modules will normally be defined at this stage rather than at the detailed design stage. For example, there may be a function to produce a customer report of credit history. Here, the function will need to know the customer and the time period for which a report is required. Thus the system design will specify the function with three parameters as shown in Figure 11.6:

Function: Print_Credit_history

Parameters: Cust_id, Period_start, Period_end

Return value: Print Successful

Figure 11.6 Part of a structure chart showing how parameters are passed from a control module to a module to print a credit history

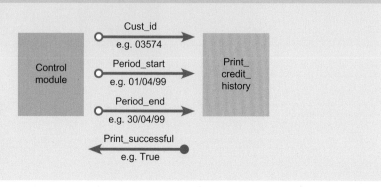

DETAILED DESIGN (MODULE DESIGN)

Detailed or module design

Detailed design involves the specification of how an individual component of a system will function in terms of its data input and output, user interface and security.

Detailed design involves considering how individual modules will function and how information will be transferred between them. For this reason, it is sometimes referred to as *module design*. A modular design offers the benefit of breaking the system down into different units which will be easier to work on by the team developing the system. It will also be easier to modify modules when changes are required in the future.

Module design includes:

- how the user interface will function at the level of individual user dialogues;
- how data will be input and output from the system;
- how information will be stored by the system using files or a database.

Detailed design is sometimes divided further into external and internal design. The external design refers to how the system will interact with users, while the internal design describes the detailed workings of the modules.

FOCUS ON... RELATIONAL DATABASE DESIGN AND NORMALISATION

Business users are often involved in the design of relational databases, either in an advisory capacity (specifying what data they should contain) or when building a small personal database, perhaps of customer contacts. For this reason, the terminology used when working with databases and the process of producing a well-designed database are described in some detail.

Relational database terminology was introduced earlier (in Chapter 4), but it is restated here since understanding the terms is important to understanding the design process. In the previous chapter we saw how entity-relationship modelling is used to analyse the conceptual design of a database. In this section we look at the next stage, which is the creation of a logical data model and then a physical database where tables and fields are created and then populated with data in records. The example used is a sales order processing database for a clothing manufacturer, 'Clothez', and we illustrate the creation of tables within a database using Microsoft Access.

Databases – fundamental terms

Databases are used for the management of information and data within organisations. The functions of a database, whether it is an address book on a phone or a corporate database supporting an entire organisation, are to enter, modify, retrieve and report information.

The terms defining the structure of a relational **database** can be considered as a hierarchy or tree structure. A single database is typically made up of several **tables**. Each table contains many **records**. Each record contains several **fields**. These terms can be related to the Clothez example as follows:

Database

All information for one business application (normally made up of many tables).

Table

Collection of records for a similar entity.

Record

Information relating to a single entity (comprising many fields).

Field

An attribute of the entity.

1. *Database* – all information for one business application (normally made up of many tables). Example: *sales order* database.

2. *Table* – a collection of records for a similar entity. Example: all customers of the company within the sales order database. Other tables in the database are *product* and *order*.

3. *Record* – information relating to a single instance of an entity (comprising many fields). Example: single customer such as Poole.

4. *Field* – an attribute of the entity. Example: *customer name* or *address* for a particular customer such as Poole.

Figure 11.7 Diagram illustrating the tree-like structure used to structure data within a relational database. This example refers to the Clothez database. The fields are only shown for the first record in each table

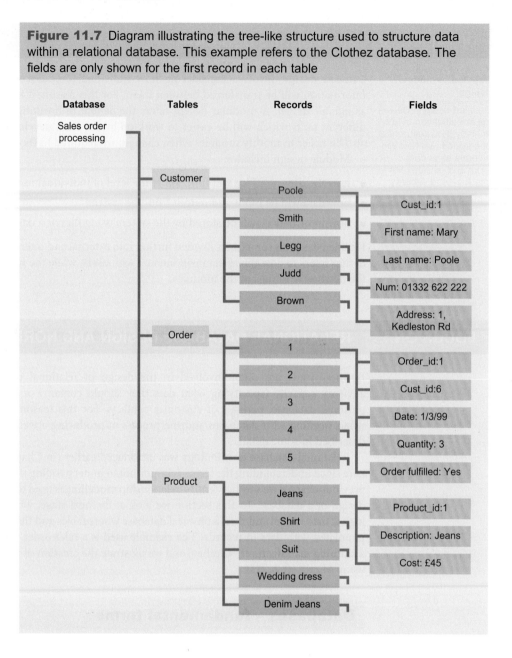

This structure is represented as a diagram in Figure 11.7 for the Clothez database. It can be seen that the sales order processing database for Clothez could be designed and implemented as three tables: customer, order and product. Each table such as customer is made up of several records for different customers and then each record is divided down further into fields or attributes which describe the characteristics of the customers such as name and address. Note that this example database is simplified and this structure only permits one product to be ordered when each order is placed. The reason for this restriction is that the database has not been fully normalised by breaking down the order table into separate order-header and order-line tables which then allow more than one product to be placed per order. The normalisation process is described in a later section.

If the data were entered into a database such as Microsoft Access, the tables and their records and fields would appear as in Figure 11.8. All three tables are shown. Fields and records for the product table are shown in Figure 11.9.

Figure 11.8 Clothez database in Microsoft Access

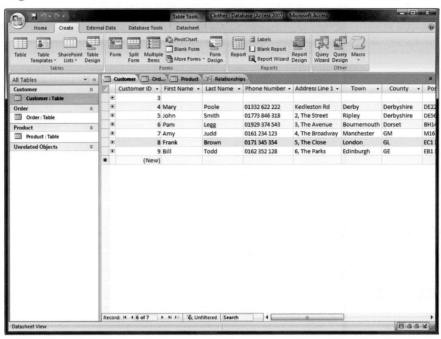

Figure 11.9 Product table showing records and fields

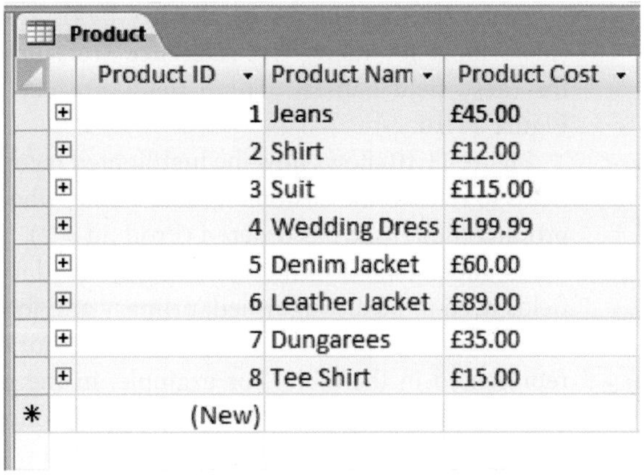

Product		
Product ID	Product Nam	Product Cost
1	Jeans	£45.00
2	Shirt	£12.00
3	Suit	£115.00
4	Wedding Dress	£199.99
5	Denim Jacket	£60.00
6	Leather Jacket	£89.00
7	Dungarees	£35.00
8	Tee Shirt	£15.00
(New)		

Key field

This is a field with a unique code for each record. It is used to refer to each record and link different tables.

A further term that needs to be introduced is **key field**. This is the field by which each record is referred, such as customer number. The key field provides a *unique* code such as '001' or '993AXR', comprising numbers or letters or both. It is required to refer to each record to help distinguish between different customers (perhaps three different customers called Smith). Key fields are also used to link different tables, as explained in the next section.

What makes an Access database relational?

The term *relational* is used to describe the way the different *tables* in a database are linked to one another. Key fields are vital to this. In recognition of the importance of key fields, Microsoft uses the key as the logo or brand icon for the Access database.

Figure 11.10 Clothez database in Microsoft Access, showing how the Order table is related to Customer and Product

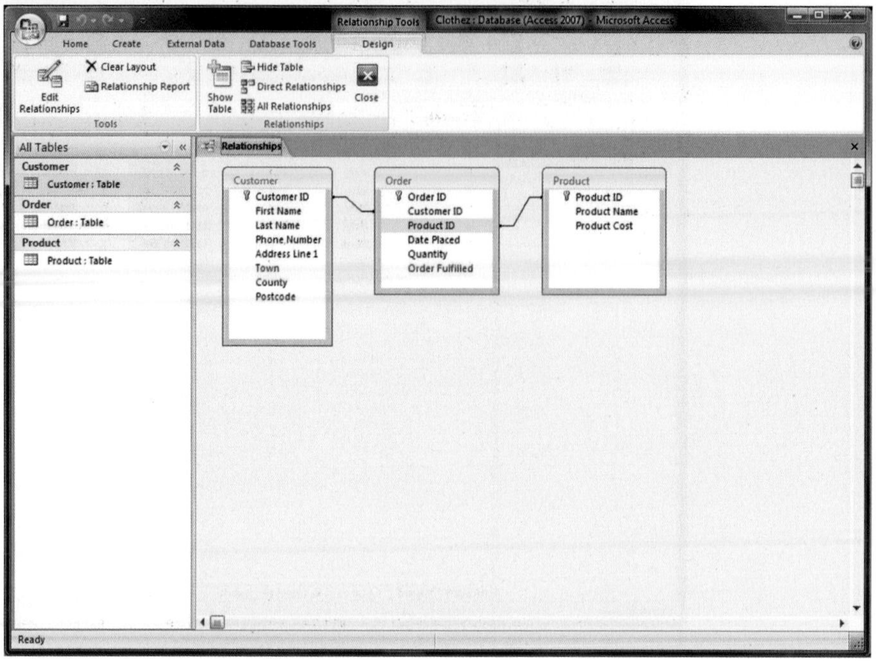

Source: Screenshot frame reprinted by permission from Microsoft Corporation

In the Clothez databases, the key fields are: Customer_id, Product_id and Order_id (id is short for identifier; reference (ref) or code number (num) could also be used for these field names). These fields are used to relate the three tables, as shown in Figure 11.10.

Figure 11.10 shows how the highlighted record in the order table (Order_id = 4) uses key fields to refer to the customer, Mary Poole, who has placed the order (Cust_id = 1) and the product (Shirt) she has ordered (Prod_id = 2).

To understand how the key fields are used to link different tables, two different types of fields need to be distinguished: primary and foreign keys.

Primary keys provide a unique identifier for each table which refers directly to the entity represented in the table. For example, in the product table, the primary key is Prod_id. There is only one primary key per table, as follows:

Customer table:	Customer_id
Order table:	Order_id
Product table:	Prod_id

Foreign keys are used to link tables by referring to the primary key of another table. For example, in the order table, the foreign key Cust_id is used to indicate which customer has placed the order. The order table also contains Prod_id as a foreign key, but neither of the other tables has foreign keys. There may be zero, one or more foreign key fields per table.

Figure 11.11 shows how the primary key fields in the customer and product tables are used to link to their corresponding foreign keys (Cust_id and Prod_id) in the order table when constructing a query in Microsoft Access. This is a summary query which summarises the details of orders by taking data from each table. The result of the query is shown in Figure 11.12. The highlighted record in Figure 11.12 is the example relationship which was used to illustrate the links between tables in Figure 11.10.

Primary key fields

These fields are used to uniquely identify each record in a table and link to similar foreign key fields (usually of the same name) in other tables.

Figure 11.11 Query design screen for the summary query in the Clothez database

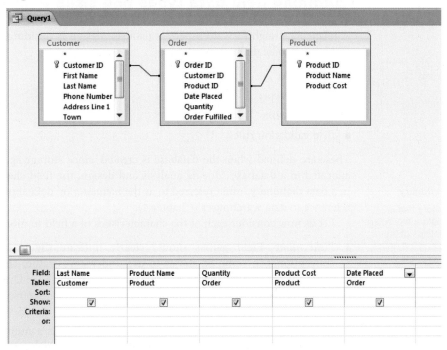

Source: Screenshot frame reprinted by permission from Microsoft Corporation

Figure 11.12 Summary query for orders placed from Clothez database

Last name	Product name	Quantity	Product cost	Date placed
Todd	Jeans	1	£45.00	01/03/2010
Legg	Wedding dress	2	£199.99	02/03/2010
Judd	Dungarees	1	£35.00	04/03/2010
Poole	Shirt	1	£12.00	05/03/2010
Poole	Suit	1	£115.00	03/03/2010

Record: |◄ ◄   4   ► ►| ►* of 5

Source: Screenshot frame reprinted by permission from Microsoft Corporation

Rules for identifying primary and foreign keys

1. Primary keys

- The primary key provides a unique identifier for each record.
- There is usually one primary key per table (unless a compound key of several fields is used).
- The name of the field is usually the name of the entity or table followed by code, reference, identifier or id.

2. Foreign key

- The foreign key always links to a primary key in another table(s).
- There may be 0, 1 or several foreign keys in each table.

Defining field data types and sizes

A relatively straightforward aspect of database design is deciding on the field definitions. Fields need to be defined in terms of:

- field name;
- field data type;
- field data size;
- field validation rules.

These are defined when the database is created, since storage space for each field is pre-allocated in a database. During analysis and design, the field characteristics are managed in a **data dictionary**, often referred to as the *metadata* or 'data about data', particularly with reference to data warehouses (Chapter 4).

Let us now consider each of the characteristics of a field in more detail:

Data dictionary

A repository that is used to store the details of the entities of the database. It will define tables, relations and field details which are sometimes referred to as metadata or 'data about data'.

1. *Field name.* Field names should clearly indicate the content of the field. It is conventional in some databases to use underscores rather than spaces to define the name, since some databases may not recognise spaces (e.g. Order_fulfilled rather than Order fulfilled). In some databases the number of characters is restricted to eight, but this is now rare.

2. *Field data type.* Data types define whether the field is a number, a word, a date or a specialised data type. The main data types used in a database such as Microsoft Access are:

   - Number. Whole number or decimal. (Most databases recognise a range of numeric data types such as integer, real, double, byte, etc.)

   - Currency. This data type is not supported for all databases.

   - Text. Often referred to as character, string or alphanumeric. Phone numbers are of this data type, since they may need to include spaces or brackets for the area code.

   - Date. Should include four digits for the year! Can also include time.

   - Yes/No. Referred to as Boolean or true/false in other databases.

   Key fields can be defined as either number or text.

3. *Field data size.* Field data sizes need to be pre-allocated in many databases. This is to help minimise the space requirements. Field size is defined in terms of the number of digits or characters which the designer thinks is required. For example, a user may define 20 characters for a first name and 40 characters for an address. It is better to overestimate than to risk having to modify the field later.

4. *Field validation rule.* Validation rules are necessary to check whether the user has entered valid data. Basic types of validation are:

   - Is field essential? For example, postcodes are usually mandatory to help identify a customer's address.

   - Is field format correct? For example, postcodes or ZIP codes usually follow a set format.

   - Is value within range? For example, an applicant for a mortgage would have to be more than 18 years of age.

   - Does field match a restricted list? An entry for marital status might need to be 'married', 'divorced' or 'single'. Restricted list choices can be defined in separate 'lookup tables'.

Table 11.2 Definition of field details for the order table in the Clothez database (with fields added to show range)

Field name	Field type	Field size	Validation rule	Key field
Order_id	Number	6	Mandatory	Primary
Cust_id	Number	6	Mandatory	Foreign
Prod_id	Number	6	Mandatory	Foreign
Date_placed	Date	10	Mandatory, must be valid date	
Order_fulfilled	Yes/No	3	Restricted, must be Yes/No	
Special_instructions	Text	120	Not mandatory	
Total_order_value	Currency	10	Not mandatory	

To maintain data quality validation is an important, but sometimes neglected, aspect of detailed design which is covered in more detail in the section on input design below.

Table 11.2 shows how the field definitions for a table can be summarised. Note that setting the key fields to a field size of six allows a maximum number of customers of 999,999.

What is normalisation?

Normalisation

This design activity is a procedure that is used to optimise the physical storage of data within a database. It involves simplification of entities and minimisation of duplication of data.

Normalisation is a design activity that is used to optimise the logical storage of data within a database. It involves simplification of entities and removal of duplication of data.

It is one of the most important activities that occurs during database design. The main purpose of data normalisation is to group data items together into database structures of tables and records which are simple to understand, accommodate change, contain a minimum of redundant data and are free of insertion, deletion and update anomalies. These anomalies can occur when a database is modified, resulting in erroneous and/or duplicate data. These anomalies are explained in the next section. Since this activity should be conducted when all databases are designed, and since databases are so widely used in business applications, we consider the process of normalisation in some detail.

Normalisation is essentially a simplifying process that takes complex 'user views' of data (such as end-user, customer and supplier) and converts them into a well-structured logical representation of the data.

Normalisation has its origins in the relational data model developed by Dr E.F. Codd from 1970 onwards and is based on the mathematics of set theory. In this section we present a brief, straightforward explanation of the steps involved in normalising data, which can be applied to simple and complex data structures alike. The description of normalisation involves a series of stages which convert unnormalised data to normalised data. There are a series of intermediate stages which are referred to as first, second, third and fourth normal forms.

Some definitions

Before commencing the steps of normalisation, it is worth providing some key definitions in order to simplify the flow of the following sections. These definitions are summarised in Table 11.3.

Table 11.3 Summary of terms used to describe databases and normalisation

Term	Definition
Normalisation	The process of grouping attributes into well-structured relations between records linked with those in other tables
Table	Used to store multiple records of different instances of the same type of entity such as customer or employee
Relation	A named, two-dimensional table of data. An equivalent term for 'table' used in normalisation
Attribute	The smallest named unit in a database; other names include 'data item' and 'field'
Update anomaly	The inability to change a single occurrence of a data item in a relation without having to change others in order to maintain data
Insertion anomaly	The inability to insert a new occurrence (record) into a relation without having to insert one into another relation first
Deletion anomaly	The inability to delete some information from a relation without also losing some other information that might be required
Functional dependency	A functional dependency is a relationship between two attributes and concerns determining which attributes are dependent on which other attributes: 'attribute B is fully functionally dependent on attribute A if, at any given point in time, the value of A determines the value of B' – this can be diagrammed as $A \rightarrow B$
Determinant	An attribute whose value determines the value of another attribute
Primary key	An attribute or group of attributes that *uniquely* identifies other non-key attributes in a single occurrence of a relation
Foreign key	An attribute or group of attributes that can be used to link different tables; the foreign key will link to the primary key in another table
Composite key	A key made up of more than one key within a relation
Candidate key	A candidate key is a determinant that can be used for a relation; a relation may have one or more determinants; determinants can be either single attributes or a composite key

Unnormalised data

Unnormalised data are characterised by having one or more repeating groups of attributes. Many user views of data contain repeating groups. Consider a customer order form for the Clothez company (Figure 11.13): there might be such information as customer name, customer address and order date recorded at the top of the form; there might also be a section in the main body of the form that allows multiple items to be ordered.

It is possible to represent the user view described above in diagrammatic form which is equivalent to a physical database table. Note that the example in Figure 11.14 uses a subset of the information shown in the order form example.

The possibility of entering multiple lines into a single order form is clearly a repeat-ing group, i.e. order no. is being used to identify multiple order lines within the view and so, therefore, is not a unique determinant of each order line and its details.

It might also be argued that address also represents a repeating group, because there are two address lines. However, in practice a set number of address lines would be given a unique data name for each line and could be identified by a customer number. (Address is

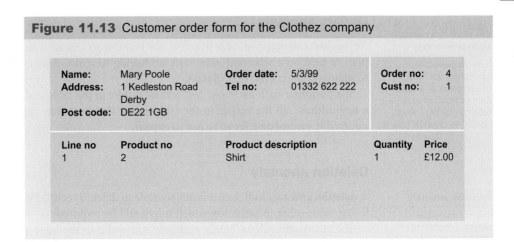

Figure 11.13 Customer order form for the Clothez company

Name:	Mary Poole	Order date:	5/3/99	Order no:	4
Address:	1 Kedleston Road	Tel no:	01332 622 222	Cust no:	1
	Derby				
Post code:	DE22 1GB				

| Line no | Product no | Product description | Quantity | Price |
| 1 | 2 | Shirt | 1 | £12.00 |

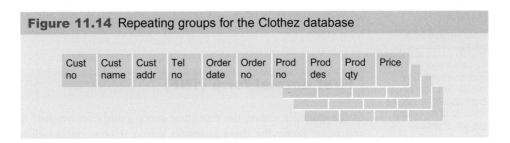

Figure 11.14 Repeating groups for the Clothez database

| Cust no | Cust name | Cust addr | Tel no | Order date | Order no | Prod no | Prod des | Prod qty | Price |

an example of a non-repeating 'data aggregate', whereas the line details are an example of a repeating data aggregate.)

By constructing such a diagram, it becomes much easier to identify repeating groups of data and thus pave the way to progressing to first normal form (1NF).

Insertion/update/deletion anomalies

At this stage it is not obvious why repeating groups of data are a bad thing! If Figure 11.14 is transformed into a table, however, updating it could result in errors or inconsistencies. Each of the three different types of anomalies is now explained in turn with reference to Table 11.4.

Insertion anomaly

If it was desired to enter a new customer into the table, it would not be possible without having an order to enter at the same time.

Insertion anomaly

It is not possible to insert a new occurrence record into a relation (table) without having to also insert one into another relation first.

Table 11.4 Table with example data for the structure shown in Figure 11.14

Customer no.	Customer name	Customer address	Tel no.	Order date	Order no.	Product no.	Product des	Product qty	Price
1	Poole	1, Ked	01332	5/03/99	4	2	Shirt	1	12
2	Smith	2, The	01773	2/03/99	6	5	Denim	3	60
3	Legg	3, The	01929	2/03/99	2	4	Wedding	2	199
3	Poole	1, Ked	01332	3/03/99	5	3	Suit	1	115

Update anomaly

An update anomaly indicates that it is not possible to change a single occurrence of a data item (a field) in a relation (table) without having to make changes in other tables in order to maintain the correctness of data.

If a customer such as 'Poole' had several orders in the table and that customer moved to a new address, all the entries in the table where that customer appeared would have to be updated if inconsistencies were not to appear.

Deletion anomaly

A deletion anomaly indicates it is not possible to delete a record from a relation without also losing some other information which might still be required.

If a customer such as 'Smith' had only one order in the table and that table entry were deleted, information about the customer would also be deleted.

The way to get round some of these problems is by normalising the data. Stage one of this process is the removal of repeating groups of data, i.e. proceeding to first normal form (1NF).

First normal form (1NF)

In the example above, the repeating group comprises *product number*, *product quantity* and *price*. Removing these attributes into a separate table will not suffice, however. For example, how could each entry in the newly created table be related to the order to which it is attached? The answer lies in including a linking attribute (also known as a 'foreign key', as described earlier in the chapter) which is present in both the modified table and the new table. In this case, a sensible attribute to use would be *order number*. The first step in normalisation has thus resulted in the transformation of one table into two new ones. The two new tables are shown in Figure 11.15. The example shows the relationship between fields at the top and example records below.

Removing insertion/update/deletion anomalies

Even though repeating groups have been removed by splitting the unnormalised data into two tables (relations), anomalies of all three types still exist.

Insert anomaly

- In the customer/order relation, an order cannot be entered without also entering the customer's name and address details, even though they may already exist on another order; a customer cannot be added if there is no order to be placed.
- In the order/product relation, an item cannot be added without also adding an order for that item.

Update anomaly

- In the customer/order relation, a customer's name and address details cannot be amended without needing to amend all occurrences (where the customer has more than one order).
- In the order/product relation, an item description could appear on many order lines for many different customers – if the description of the item were to change, all occurrences

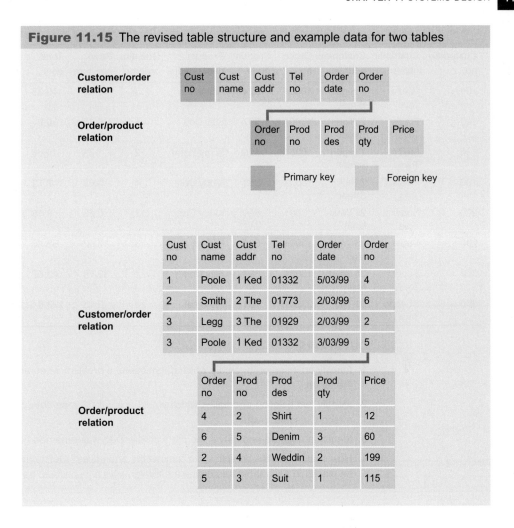

Figure 11.15 The revised table structure and example data for two tables

where that item appeared would have to be changed if database inconsistencies were not to appear.

Deletion anomaly

- In the customer/order relation, an order cannot be deleted without also deleting the customer's details.
- In the order/product relation, an order line cannot be deleted without also deleting the item number and description.

Activity 11.1 Identification and removal of insertion, deletion and update anomalies

This activity shows a prototype database that has been produced by an employee of a toy manufacturer relating to its customers and sales activities. The designer, a business user, is not aware of the need for normalisation and has stored all the data in a single table. This has resulted in some fields like customer number and customer address repeating unnecessarily.

Customer no.	Customer name	Customer address	Order no.	Product code	Product description	Quantity ordered	Price per item	Total cost	Order date	Salesperson no.
100	Fred's Toys	7 High Street	10001	324	Action Ma	3	13.46	40.38	7/10/99	007
100	Fred's Toys	7 High Street	10001	567	Silly Dog	6	5.15	30.9	7/10/99	007
100	Fred's Toys	7 High Street	10001	425	Slimy Hand	12	1.39	16.68	7/10/99	007
100	Fred's Toys	7 High Street	10001	869	Kiddy Doh	4	0.68	2.72	7/10/99	007
200	Super Toys	25 West Mall	13001	869	Kiddy Doh	12	0.68	8.16	7/17/99	021
200	Super Toys	25 West Mall	13001	637	Risky	3	17.42	52.26	7/17/99	021
200	Super Toys	25 West Mall	13001	567	Silly Dog	2	32.76	43.52	7/17/99	021
300	Cheapo Toys	61 The Arcade	23201	751	Diplomat	24	5.15	123.6	6/21/99	007

QUESTIONS

1. Identify an insertion anomaly which might cause a problem when adding a new product to the range.

2. Identify two deletion anomalies which would occur if Cheapo Toys cancelled its order and a record was removed.

3. Identify an update anomaly if the product Silly Dog was renamed Fancy Dog.

4. How could the table be split up to remove the anomalies? Define the fields which would be placed in each table and define the foreign keys which would be used to link the tables.

It is anomalies of this kind which indicate that the normalisation process needs to be taken a step further – that is, we must now proceed to second normal form (2NF).

Second normal form (2NF)

Second normal form (2NF) states that 'each attribute in a record (relation) must be functionally dependent on the whole key of that record'. To continue the normalisation process to second normal form, it is necessary to explore further some of the terms defined in the introductory section.

Functional dependencies

Within each of the relations produced above, a set of functional dependencies exists. These dependencies will be governed by the relationships that exist between different data items, which in turn will depend on the 'business rules', i.e. the purposes for which data are held and how they are used.

Once the functional dependencies have been established, it is then possible to select a candidate key for the relation.

Candidate keys

The process of analysing the functional dependencies within a relation will reveal one or more possible candidate keys – a candidate key is the minimum number of determinants (key fields) which uniquely determines all the non-key attributes. Consider the following record:

Part	Supplier	Supplier	Supplier	Price
No	No	Name	details	

An example

Consider the following record. Note that this example is different from that given in first normal form, since it illustrates the principles better.

The functional dependencies are as follows:

Part no and supplier no → Price

Supplier no → Supplier name

Supplier no → Supplier details

A possible candidate key might be thought to be supplier number. However, supplier number alone cannot be a determinant of price, since a supplier may supply many items.

Similarly, part number alone cannot be a determinant of price, because a part may be supplied by many different suppliers at different prices.

The candidate key is, therefore, a composite key comprising part number and supplier number.

We can express this more clearly by employing a dependency diagram (Figure 11.16). Two additional properties relating to candidate keys can now be introduced:

1. For every record occurrence, the key must uniquely identify the relation.

2. No data item in the key can be discarded without destroying the property of unique identification.

The dependency diagram in Figure 11.16 indicates a number of problems:

■ If supplier number is discarded, it will no longer be possible to identify the remaining attributes uniquely, even though part number remains.

■ Details of a supplier cannot be added until there is a part to supply; if a supplier does not supply a part, there is no key.

■ If supplier details are to be updated, all records which contain that supplier as part of the key must be accessed – i.e. there are redundant data.

This situation is known as a *partial key dependency* and is resolved by splitting the record into two or more smaller records (Figure 11.17).

Figure 11.16 Example of a dependency diagram for supplier example

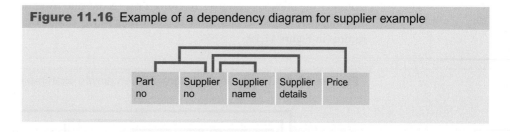

Figure 11.17 Revised dependency diagram for supplier example

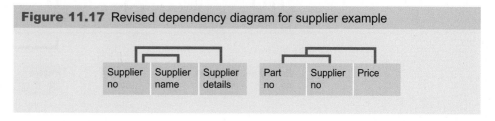

Figure 11.18 Example of a structure diagram – employee details

Employee no	Employee name	Salary	Project no	Completion date

A record is, therefore, in *at least* second normal form when any partial key dependencies have been removed.

Removing insertion/update/deletion anomalies

Consider the record structure shown in Figure 11.18. If it is assumed that an employee only works on one project at a time; then employee number is a suitable candidate key, in that all other attributes can reasonably be said to be fully functionally dependent on it.

Note: the record is already in second normal form because there is only one key attribute (therefore partial key dependencies *cannot* exist). However, some problems still exist:

- *Insertion anomaly*: before any employees are recruited for a project, the completion date for the project cannot be recorded because there is no employee record.
- *Update anomaly*: if a project completion date is changed, it will be necessary to search all employee records and change those where an employee works on that project.
- *Deletion anomaly*: if all employees are deleted for a project, all records containing a project completion date would be deleted also.

To resolve these anomalies, a record in second normal form must be converted into a number of third normal form records.

Third normal form (3NF)

Transitive dependency

A data item that is not a key (or part of a key) but which itself identifies other data items is a *transitive dependency*.

Third normal form (3NF): a record is in third normal form if each non-key attribute 'depends on the key, the whole key and nothing but the key'.

Third normal form (3NF)

A record is in third normal form if each non-key attribute 'depends on the key, the whole key and nothing but the key'.

An example

Consider the previous example. To convert the record into two third normal form records, any transitive dependencies must be removed. When this is done the result is the two records in Figure 11.19.

Figure 11.19 Dependency diagram for employee example and revised structure

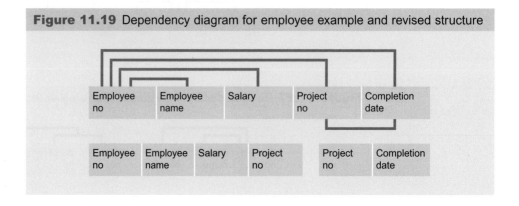

Removing insertion/update/deletion anomalies

If a record has only one candidate key and both partial key and transitive dependencies have been removed, then no insertion, update or deletion anomalies should result.

However, if a record has more than one candidate key problems can still arise. In this situation we can take the normalisation process still further.

Fourth normal form (4NF) and fifth normal form (5NF)

Further normalisation may be necessary for some applications. In these normalisation can proceed to the fourth and fifth normal forms. These are described in Hoffer et al. (2013): 'In 4NF multi-valued dependencies are removed. A multi-valued dependency exists when there are at least three attributes in a relation and for each value of A there is a well-defined set of values of B and a well-defined set of values of C. However, the set of values of B is independent of set C and vice versa.'

In 5NF it is necessary to account for the potential of decomposing some relations from an earlier stage of normalisation into more than two relations. In most practical applications, decomposition to 3NF gives acceptable database performance and is often easier to design and maintain.

Other significant database design issues

As well as the logical design of the database there are aspects of physical database design that should be taken into account. These are specialised functions performed by a database administrator or DBA. A company which does not employ a specialist risks a poor performance system or, worse still, a loss or corruption of data. These design and database implementation tasks include:

1. *Design of optimal database performance.* Use of specialist techniques such as indexes or stored procedures will accelerate the display of common user views such as a list of all customer orders. Queries can also be optimised, but this is mainly performed automatically by the database engines such as Oracle, Microsoft SQL Server or Informix. To verify the design is good, volume testing is essential to ensure that the system can cope with the number of transactions that will occur.

2. *Designing for multi-user access.* When defining a new system, it is important to consider what happens when two users want to access the same data, such as the same customer record. If access to records is unlimited, then there will be anomalous data in the database if users save data about the customer at a similar time. Since multi-user access will not be frequent, the best method for dealing with it will be to implement record locking. Here, the first user to access a record will cause the database to restrict subsequent users to read-only access to the record rather than read–write. Subsequent users should be informed that a lock is in place and access is read-only.

Activity 11.2	Database design exercise using the ABC case study

This activity builds on the ABC case study from Chapter 10. It is not necessary to have completed the Chapter 10 exercise to be able to undertake this one. You should use the extract in Chapter 10 describing ABC and in particular the paper forms of the existing system to identify which fields are required in the database.

QUESTIONS

1. Either:

   (a) Use normalisation to third normal form to identify tables and fields for an ABC database; or

   (b) Assume the following entities for the ABC database:

      - customer details;
      - salesperson details;
      - sales order header details;
      - sales order line details;
      - item details.

2. For each table in the database, define details of:

   - table names;
   - primary and foreign key fields for each table;
   - name of each field;
   - data type of each field;
   - size of each field;
   - any validation rules which may apply to each field (e.g. a limit on maximum price or quantity etc.).

   You may find it most efficient to summarise the database definition using a table (in your word processor).

3. *Planning for failed transactions*. Recovery methods can be specified in the design for how to deal with failed transactions which may occur when there is a software bug or power interruption. Databases contain the facility to 'roll back' to the situation before a failure occurred.

4. *Referential integrity*. The database must be designed so that when records in one table are deleted, this does not adversely affect other tables. Impact should be minimal if normalisation has occurred. Sometimes it is necessary to perform a 'cascading delete', which means deleting related records in linked tables.

5. *Design to safeguard against media, hardware or power failure*. A backup strategy should be designed to ensure that minimal disruption occurs if the database server fails. The main design decision is whether a point-in-time backup is required or whether restoring to the previous day's data will be sufficient. Frequently, a point-in-time backup will be required. Of course, a backup strategy is not much use if it cannot be used to restore the data, so backup and recovery must be well tested. To reduce the likelihood of having to fall back on a backup, using a fault-tolerant server is important. Specifying a server with an uninterruptible power supply, disk mirroring or RAID level 2 is essential for any corporate system. The frequency of archiving also will be specified.

6. *Replication*. Duplication and distribution of data to servers at different company locations and for mobile users is supported to different degrees by different database vendors.

7. *Database sizing*. The database administrator will size the database and perform capacity planning to ensure that sufficient space is available on the server for the system to remain functional.

8. *Data migration*. Data migration will occur at the system build phase, but it must be planned for at the design stage. This will involve an assessment of the different data sources which will be used to populate the database.

DESIGN OF INPUT AND OUTPUT

Most modern information systems use relational database management systems (RDBMS) for the storage of data. RDBMS provide management facilities which means that programmers or users do not have to become directly involved with file management. Because of this, most business users will not hear these terms unless eavesdropping on systems designers and this section is therefore kept brief. How-ever, some older systems and large-scale transaction processing systems requiring superior performance do not use RDBMS for data storage.

File access methods

File-based systems are alternatives to database systems which are traditionally used for accessing data from a file directly from program code rather than a database query. Note though that when databases are designed, these are themselves made up of many files from which data are accessed directly. Database users and database programmers are shielded from this complexity. Designers will specify systems that access data that are stored in a file using two main methods:

1. *Sequential access.* The program reading or writing a file will start processing the file record by record (usually from the beginning). Sequential access is often used when batch processing a file which involves processing each record. Sequential file access involves reading or writing each record in a file in a set order.

2. *Direct (random) access.* Access can occur to any point (record) in the file without the need to start at the beginning. Direct access is preferable when finding a subset of records such as in a query, since it is much faster. Random or direct file access allows any record to be read or written.

Sequential and random or direct file access methods

Sequential file access involves reading or writing each record in a file in a set order. Random or direct file access allows any record to be read or written.

Indexing

To enable rapid retrieval of data in a random access file (and also a database table), it is conventional to use an index which will find the location of the record more rapidly. These files are sometimes referred to as 'indexed sequential files'. A file index is an additional file that is used to 'point' to records in a direct access file for more rapid access. An index file for a customer file would contain two fields only for each record – the indexed item such as a customer number and the number of the record in the parent file (also known as the 'offset' or 'pointer') which contains details on this customer.

Index

A file index is an additional file which is used to 'point' to records in a direct access file for more rapid access.

File descriptions

In transaction processing systems which use standard native files accepted directly by programs for processing rather than through the operating system rather like RDBMS, there are additional terms that are used to describe the types of files. These types include:

1. *The master file.* This is used to store relatively static information that does not change frequently. An example would be a file containing product details.

2. *The transaction file.* This contain records of particular exchanges, usually related to a transaction such as a customer placing an order or an invoice being produced. This file has records added more frequently.

Table 11.5 Methods of file organisation

Organisation method	Access method	Application	Brief description
Sequential	Sequential	Batch process of a customer master file	An ordered sequential access file, e.g. ordered by customer number
Serial	Sequential		A sequential access file, but without any ordering
Random	Random + index	Querying data for decision support; unsuitable for frequent updates due to overhead of updating index	Organisation is provided by index
Indexed sequential	Sequential + index	Querying data for decision support and sequential batch processing	Best compromise between methods above

3. *Archive file.* To reduce storage requirements and improve performance, transactions that occurred some time ago to which businesses are unlikely to wish to refer are removed from the online system as an archive which is usually stored on a tape or optical disk. It will be still available for reference, but access will be slower.

4. *Temporary files.* These provide temporary storage space for the system which might be used during batch processing, when comparing data sets for example. The information would not be of value to a business user.

5. *Log file.* The log file is a system file used to store information on updates to other files. Its information would not be of value to a business user.

File organisation

Information can be organised in file-based systems in a variety of ways, which are not of general relevance to the business user, so the terms are only summarised in tabular form (Table 11.5). Note that the indexed-sequential technique offers the best balance between speed of access to individual records and for achieving updates.

Batch and real-time processing

Batch system

A batch system involves processing of many transactions in sequence. This will typically occur over some time after the transactions have occurred.

Real-time system

In a real-time system processing occurs immediately data are collected. Processing follows each transaction.

When designing information processing systems, designers have to decide which is the more appropriate method for handling transactions:

■ Batch – data are 'post-processed' after collection, usually at times of low system workload.

■ Real-time or online processing – data are processed instantaneously on collection.

Table 11.6 compares the merits of batch and real-time systems according to several criteria.

There is a general trend from batch systems to real-time processing, but it can be seen from the table that batch processing is superior in some areas, not least cost. For a system such as a national lottery, a real-time system must be used, but it is expensive to set up the necessary infrastructure.

Table 11.6 A comparison of batch and real-time data processing

Factor	Batch	Real-time
Speed of delivery to information user	Slower – depends on how frequently batch process is run – daily, weekly or monthly	Faster – effectively delivered immediately
Ability to deal with failure	Better – if a batch process fails overnight there is usually sufficient time to solve the problem and rerun the batch	Worse – when a real-time system is offline there is major customer disruption and orders may be lost
Data validation	Worse – validation can occur, but it is time-consuming to correct errors	Better – validation errors are notified and corrected immediately
Cost	Better – performance is less critical, so cheaper hardware communications can be purchased	Worse – high-specification databases and infrastructure are necessary to achieve the required number of transactions per second
Disruption to users when data processing needs to be performed	Better – can occur in slack periods such as at weekends or overnight	Worse – can disrupt customers if time-consuming calculations occur as each record is processed

Form

An on-screen equivalent of a paper form which is used for entering data and will have validation routines to help improve the accuracy of the entered data.

Data views

Different screens of an application which review information in a different form such as table, graph, report or map.

Batch systems are still widely used, since they are appropriate for data processing before analysis. For example, batch processing is used in data warehousing when transferring data from the operational system to the warehouse (Chapter 6). A batch process can be run overnight to transfer the data from one location to another and to perform aggregation such as summing sales figures across different market or product segments.

USER INTERFACE DESIGN

Dialog

An on-screen window (box) which is used by a user to input data or select options.

Menu

Provides user selection of options for different application functions.

Human–computer interaction (HCI) design

HCI involves the study of methods for designing the input and output of information systems to ensure they are 'user-friendly'.

The design of the user interface is key to ensuring that information systems are easy to use and that users are productive. User interface design involves three main parts: first, defining the different views of the data such as input forms and output tables; second, defining how the user moves or navigates from one view to another; and, third, providing options for the user.

Each module can be broken down into interface elements such as forms which are used to enter and update information such as a customer's details, views which tabulate results as a report or graphically display related information such as a 'to-do' list and dialogs which are used for users to select options such as a print options dialog box. Menus provide selection of different options. Figure 11.20 gives an example of these different interface components.

User interface design is a specialist field which is the preserve of graphic designers and psychologists. This field is often known as human–computer interaction (HCI) design. HCI involves the study of methods for designing the input and output of information systems to ensure they are 'user-friendly'. It is covered well in Rogers et al. (2011) and Yeates and Wakefield (2003). Many of the design parameters can be assisted by a knowledge of HCI.

Figure 11.20 Microsoft Access showing key elements of interface design

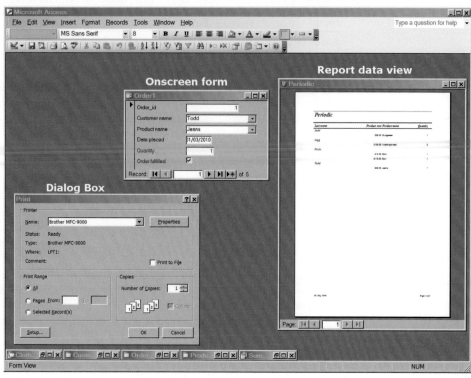

Source: Screenshot frame reprinted by permission from Microsoft Corporation

---

FOCUS ON...   WEB SITE DESIGN FOR B2C E-COMMERCE

This 'Focus on' looks at a number of issues relating to web site design. The intention is not to give an in-depth explanation of web site design specifics, but rather to look at those elements that go to make up a well-designed web site.

Cox and Dale (2002) identify a number of key quality factors that help to create web sites that meet customer needs and expectations. These include:

- *Clarity of purpose* – it must be clear to the customer whether the site is providing just information or whether it enables the customer to make transactions online; the information should be clearly and logically organised and clear instructions should be provided directly from the home page to avoid confusion and frustration.

- *Design* – a key objective here is to ensure that the image that the company is appropriately projected and that the customer will remember and return to site. Specific design factors include: *links* – valid links are needed to enable a customer to navigate around the web site and should readily enable easy navigation between the pages that the customer is most likely to want to view; *consistency, menus and site maps* – since web sites vary considerably from site to site, it is important for any one site to be internally consistent so that the same procedures occur for similar or related things wherever the user may be within the site; the use of such features as site maps, menus and a 'home page' button on every page can help guide the user around the site; pages, *text and clicks* – it is suggested the pages on a web site should ideally be short, or where this is not feasible, headings and paragraphs and other navigation aids (e.g. a button to scroll to the top of the page; for web sites that enable customer transactions, customers should be able to make purchases quickly with minimum pages in the checkout process; *communication and feedback* – in essence, the user needs to be advised what is happening inside the system in response to their interaction (e.g. confirming order details, or informing the user of a mistake by writing the information in red next to the relevant box or area); in addition, the use of graphics should be such that web page loads are not slowed down (not all users have broadband!) and that animations should not distract users from the content of the page and the information they are looking for; *search* – search mechanisms to navigate a web site are one of the first strategies used by customers to a web site, often before they use links and menus; therefore search tools should cover the whole site and return the search findings in order of relevance; *fill-in forms* – the layout of forms for personal detail entry (e.g. for site registration and ordering) should be self-explanatory and relevant to the nationality of the customers using the web site.

- *Accessibility and speed* – this refers to the ability for customers to access and navigate an organisation's web site; factors here include the speed of the home-page download, the accessibility of the web site 24 hours a day, 7 days a week, 365 days of the year and the availability of sufficient bandwidth to cope with customer demand at peak periods.

- *Content* – this refers to the information that an organisation is actually offering through its web site; important factors here include *selection* (the range of products and services on offer and the ease with which they can be found by the customer; *product/ service information and availability* including a clear picture with all the necessary information on brand, size, colour, capabilities and price so that the customer is not misled together with a clear statement of stock availability so that the customer knows before ordering whether an item is in stock; *delivery information* – this should be made accessible from the home page or with the product information so that customers are aware of the prices; in addition, customers should also be made aware of probable delivery times and any delays that may occur (e.g. during peak periods); *policies, charges, terms and conditions* – customers should be aware of all the company terms and conditions before committing to a purchase; *security and reliability* – lack of security is one of the main barriers to customers shopping online and so it is crucial that a B2C e-commerce web site offers a secure payment method online (either directly or through a third party).

- *Customer service* – customer service plays an important part in delivering service quality to the customer and since face-to-face interaction is non-existent in e-commerce transactions, services such as 'call-u-back' during office hours and e-mailing queries are needed (contact details should be on every page of the web site and not just on the home page and during the transaction process); frequently asked questions (FAQ) arranged by topic can also help to guide the customer.

- *Customer relationships* – the key to success for B2C e-commerce is to attract and retain customers that use the site and keep returning to make purchases: *recognition* – by asking customers to fill in a user ID (research suggests that it is simpler for customers if they are asked to use their e-mail address as their ID) an organisation can tailor the web sites to a particular customer; it also means that customer information such as the billing and shipping addresses do not have to be filled in again; *customer feedback platforms* – features such as product reviews (ebuyer.com is a good illustration of this) helps to create a community for customers and is more likely to lead to enhanced customer loyalty; *frequent buyer incentives* – these can include discounts, free delivery or benefits of promotions; *extra services* – examples here include a currency conversion rate mechanism on those sites engaging in international B2C e-commerce, extra or related information on the products being sold, links to other partner sites, and those that aid the customer in buying or finding the right product.

Huang et al. (2006) in an analysis of web features and functions identify a number of factors that can impact positively on the customer experience. These clearly overlap with a number of those given above and include:

- speeding up online tasks
- establishing multiple communication channels
- providing suitable access to contacts
- making the web site personal
- provision of company information and advertising online
- facilitation of customer feedback
- the ability of customers to control information detail.

Cao et al. (2005) also point out that the features that go to make for a good customer experience also have implications for web interface design. For example, in addition to the software considerations, the capabilities of the hardware (both the organisation's and the customer's) need to be taken account of (e.g. page loading times).

INPUT DESIGN

Input design

Input design includes the design of user input through on-screen forms, but also other methods of data entry such as import by file, transfer from another system or specialised data capture methods such as bar-code scanning and optical or voice recognition techniques.

User interface design can also be subdivided into input design and output design, but these terms are used more generally to refer to all methods of data entry and display, so they warrant a separate section.

Input design includes the design of user input through on-screen forms, but also other methods of data entry such as import by file, transfer from another system or specialised data capture methods such as bar-code scanning and optical or voice recognition techniques.

Data input design involves capturing data that have been identified in the user requirements analysis via a variety of mechanisms. These have been described earlier (in Chapter 3) and include:

- keyboard – the most commonly used method;
- optical character recognition and scanning;
- voice input;
- directly from a monitoring system such as a manufacturing process, or from a phone system when a caller line ID is used to identify the customer phoning and automatically bring their details on screen;
- input from a data file that is used to store data;
- import of data from another system via a batch process (for example a data warehouse will require import of data from an operational system).

Data validation

Data validation

Data validation is a process that ensures the quality of data by checking they have been entered correctly.

One of the key elements in input by all these methods is ensuring the quality of data. This is achieved through data validation. This is a process to ensure the quality of data by checking they have been entered correctly; it prompts the user to inform them of incorrect data entry.

Validation is important in database systems and databases usually supply built-in input validation as follows:

- *Data type checking*. When tables have been designed, field types will be defined such as text (alphanumeric), number, currency or date. Text characters will not be permitted in a number field and when a user enters a date, for example, the software will prompt the user if it is not a valid date.

- *Data range checking*. Since storage needs to be pre-allocated in databases, designers will specify the number of digits required for each field. For example, a field for holding the quantity of an item ordered would typically only need the range 1–999. So three digits are required. If the user made an error and entered four digits, then they would be warned that this was not possible.

- *Restricted value checking*. This usually occurs for text values that are used to describe particular attributes of an entity. For example, in a database for estate agents, the type of house would have to be stored. This would be a restricted choice of flat, bungalow, semi-detached, etc. Once the restricted choices have been specified, the software will ensure that only one of these choices is permitted, usually by prompting the user with a list of the available alternatives.

Some additional validation checks may need to be specified at the design phase which will later be programmed into the system. These include:

- *Input limits*. This is another form of range checking when the input range cannot be specified through the number of digits alone. For example, if the maximum number of an item that could be ordered is 5, perhaps because of a special offer, this would be specified as a limit of 1–5. Note that the user would not be permitted to enter 0.

- *Multiple field validation*. If there are business rules that mean that allowable input is governed by more than one field, then these rules must be programmed in. For example, in the estate agent database, there could be a separate field for commission shown as a percentage of house price, such as 1.5 per cent, and a separate field showing the amount, such as £500. In this situation the programmer would have to write code that would automatically calculate the commission amount depending on the percentage entered.

- *Checksum digits*. A **checksum** involves the use of an extra digit for ensuring the validity of long code numbers. The checksum digit is calculated from an algorithm involving the numbers in the code and their modulus (by convention modulus 11). These can be used to ensure that errors are not made in entering long codes such as a customer account number (although these would normally be generated automatically by the computer). They are often used in bar codes.

Checksum digits

A checksum involves the use of an extra digit for ensuring the validity of long code numbers. The checksum digit is calculated from an algorithm involving the numbers in the code and their modulus (by convention modulus 11).

Activity 11.3   Checksum digits example

The checksum digit is calculated using the modulus of the weighted products of the number, as follows:

1. Code number without check digit = 293643.

2. Calculate the sum of weighted products by multiplying the least significant digit by 2, the next by 3 and so on. For this example:

   (7 × 2) + (6 × 9) + (5 × 3) + (4 × 6) + (3 × 4) + (2 × 3) = 14 + 54 + 15 + 24 + 12 + 6 = 125

3. Remainder when sum divided by 11 (modulus 11) = 125/11 = 11 remainder 4.

4. Subtract remainder from 11 to find check digit (11−4) = 7. (If the remainder is 0, check digit is 0; if 1, check digit is X.)

5. New code number with check digit = 2936437.

OUTPUT DESIGN

Output design

Output design involves specifying how production of on-screen reports and paper-based reports will occur. Output may occur to database or file for storing information entered or also for use by other systems.

Output design specifies how production of on-screen reports and paper-based reports will occur. Output may occur to database or file for storing information entered or also for use by other systems.

Output data are displayed by three methods:

1. They may be directly displayed from input data.
2. They may be displayed from previously stored data.
3. They may be *derived* data that are produced by calculation.

Design involves specifying the source of data (which database tables and fields map to a point on the report), what processing needs to occur to display data such as aggregation, sorting or calculations, and the form in which the information will be displayed – graph, table or summary form.

Output design is important for decision support software to ensure that relevant information can be chosen, retrieved and interpreted as easily as possible. Given that output design involves these three factors, it will also relate to input design (to select the report needed) and database design (to retrieve the information quickly).

DESIGNING INTERFACES BETWEEN SYSTEMS

Enterprise application integration (EAI)

The process of designing software to facilitate communications between business applications including data transfer and control.

Middleware

Software used to facilitate communications between business applications including data transfer and control.

XML (eXtensible Markup Language)

A standard for transferring structured data, unlike HTML which is purely presentational.

A major challenge for the designer of today's systems is systems integration. Systems integration includes both linking the different modules of a new system together and linking the new system with existing systems often known as 'legacy systems'. For applications that span a whole organisation this challenge is referred to as enterprise application integration (EAI). Designing how the systems interoperate involves consideration of how data are exchanged between applications and how one application controls another. A special class of software, middleware or messaging software, is used to achieve this control and data transfer. In a banking system, middleware is used to transfer data between an online banking service and a legacy account system. For example, if a user wishes to transfer money from one account to another using a web-based interface this web application must instruct the legacy system to make the transfer. The web-based interface will also need to access data from the legacy system on the amount of money available in the accounts. This illustrates the role of middleware in control messaging and data transfer messaging.

XML (eXtensible Markup Language) is a standard that has been widely adopted for the transfer of information between e-business systems. XML is increasingly used to share data between partners. For example, Chem eStandards, is an XML standard for the chemical industry, which covers 700 data elements and 47 transactions and is sponsored by the Chemical Industry Data Exchange (CIDX, www.cidx.org). A more widely applicable application of XML is ebXML (www.ebxml.org). One application developed using ebXML is to enable different accounting packages to communicate with online order processing systems. For designers to ensure future flexibility of their systems it is important to ensure that interfaces with external systems can support different XML data exchange standards.

DEFINING THE STRUCTURE OF PROGRAM MODULES

The detailed design may include a definition for programmers, indicating how to structure the code of the module. The extent to which this is necessary will depend on the complexity of the module, how experienced the programmer is and how important it is to document the method of programming. A safety-critical system (Chapter 4) will always be designed in this detail before coding commences. Structured English is one of the most commonly used methods of defining pro-gram structure. Standard flow charts can be used, but these tend to take longer to produce.

Structured English

Structured English is a technique for producing a design specification for programmers which indicates the way individual modules or groups of modules should be implemented. It is more specific than a flow chart. It uses keywords to describe the structure of the program, as shown in the example box. Structured English is sometimes known as 'pseudocode' or 'program design language'. Data action diagrams use a similar notation.

Structured English has the disadvantage that it is very time-consuming to produce a detailed design. But it has the advantage that to move from here to coding is very straightforward and the likelihood of errors is reduced.

Example: Structured English

This example moves through each record of a database table totalling all employees' salaries. (Note that this could be accomplished more quickly using an SQL statement.)

```
DO WHILE NOT end of table
IF hoursrworked> basicrhours
SET pay = (hours*basicrrate) + (overtimerhours*overtimerrate)
ELSE
SET pay = (hours*basicrrate)
END if
SET totalrpay = totalrpay + pay
move to next record
ENDDO
```

SECURITY DESIGN

Data security is, of course, a key design issue, particularly for information systems that contain confidential company information which is accessed across a wide-area network or the Internet. The four main attributes of security which must be achieved through design are:

1. *Authentication* ensures that the sender of the message, or the person trying to access the system, is who they claim to be. Passwords are one way of providing authentication, but are open to abuse – users often tend to swap them. Digital certificates and digital signatures offer a higher level of security. These are available in some groupware products such as Lotus Notes.

2. *Authorisation* checks that the user has the right permissions to access the information that they are seeking. This ensures that only senior personnel managers can access salary figures, for example.

CASE (computer-aided software engineering) tools

Software that helps the systems analyst and designer in the analysis, design and build phases of a software project. They provide tools for drawing diagrams such as ERDs and storing information about processes, entities and attributes.

3. *Privacy* – in a security context, privacy equates to scrambling or encryption of messages so that they cannot easily be decrypted if they are intercepted during transmission. Credit card numbers sent over the Internet are encrypted in this way.

4. *Data integrity* – security is also necessary to ensure that the message sent is the same as the one received and that corruption has not occurred. A security system can use a checksum digit to ensure that this is the case and the data packet has not been modified.

Data must also be secure in the sense of not being subject to deletion, or available to people who don't have the 'need to know'. Methods of safeguarding data are covered in more detail in later (in Chapter 15).

DESIGN TOOLS: CASE (COMPUTER-AIDED SOFTWARE ENGINEERING) TOOLS

CASE (computer-aided software engineering) tools are software that helps the systems analyst and designer in the analysis, design and build phases of a software project. They provide tools for drawing diagrams such as entity relationship diagrams (ERDs) and storing information about processes, entities and attributes.

CASE tools are primarily used by professional IS developers and are intended to assist in managing the process of capturing requirements, and converting these into design and program code. They also act as a repository for storing information about the design of the program and help make the software easy to maintain.

ERROR HANDLING AND EXCEPTIONS

The design will include a strategy for dealing with bugs in the system or problems resulting from changes to the operating environment, such as a network failure. When an error is encountered the design will specify that:

- users should be prompted with a clear but not alarming message explaining the problem;
- the message should contain sufficient diagnostics that developers will be able to identify and solve the problem.

HELP AND DOCUMENTATION

It is straightforward using tools to construct a Windows help file based on a word-processed document. The method of generating help messages for users will also be specified in the design. Help is usually available as:

- an online help application similar to reading a manual, but with links between pages and a built-in index;
- context-sensitive help, where pressing the help button of a dialogue will take the user straight to the relevant page of the online user guide;
- ToolTip help, where the user places the mouse over a menu option or icon and further guidance is displayed in the status area;
- help associated with error messages; this is also context-sensitive.

FOCUS ON... OBJECT-ORIENTED DESIGN (OOD)

Object-oriented design

This is a design technique which involves basing the design of software on real-world objects which consist of both data and the procedures that process them rather than traditional design where procedures operate on separate data.

Object-oriented design is a popular design technique which involves basing the design of software on real-world objects that consist of both data and the procedures that process them, rather than traditional design where procedures operate on separate data. Many software products are labelled 'object-oriented' in a bid to boost sales, but relatively few are actually designed using object-oriented techniques. What makes the object approach completely different?

- Traditional development methods are *procedural*, dealing with separate data that are transformed by abstract, hierarchical programming code.
- OOD is a relatively new technique involving *objects* (which mirror real-world objects consisting of integrated data *and* code).

Examples of objects that are commonly used in business information systems include customer, supplier, employee and product. You may notice that these are similar to the entities referred to earlier (in Chapter 10), but a key difference is that an object will not only consist of different attributes such as name and address, but will also comprise procedures that process them. For example, a customer object may have a procedure (known as a 'method') to print these personal details.

The main benefits of using object orientation are said to be more rapid development and lower costs which can be achieved through greater reuse of code. Reuse in object-oriented systems is a consequence of the ease with which generic objects can be incorporated into code. This is a consequence of inheritance, where a new object can be derived from an existing object and its behaviour modified (polymorphism).

Some further advantages of the object-oriented approach are:

- easier to explain object concepts to end-users since they are based on real-world objects;
- more reuse of code – standard, tested business objects;
- faster, cheaper development of more robust code.

Object-oriented design is closely linked to the growth in use of software components for producing systems. Developers writing programs for Microsoft Windows on a PC will now commonly buy pre-built objects with functionality such as displaying a diary, a project schedule or different types of graph. Such object components are referred to as Visual Basic controls and object controls (OCX). Through using these, developers can implement features without having to reinvent the wheel of writing graphical routines.

An example of a class hierarchy is shown in Figure 11.21. The base class is a person who attends the college. All other classes are derived from this person.

Figure 11.21 A class hierarchy for different types of people at a university

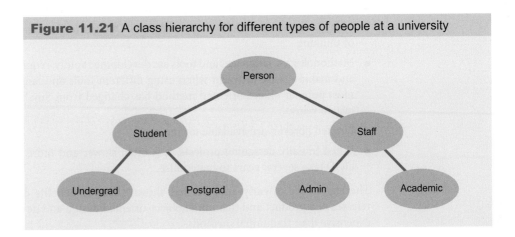

How widely is the object-oriented approach used?

There was a rapid growth in the use of object-oriented techniques in the 1990s, although original research using the Simula language dates back to the late 1960s. This growth in interest is reflected by the increase in the number of jobs advertised by companies looking to develop software using object-oriented methods, such as Smalltalk, C++ and Java which is now one of the main methods for developing interactive web sites. Specialised methodologies exist for designing object-oriented systems. One of the most commonly used is the object modelling technique (OMT) (see Blaha and Rumbaugh, 2005). This shares some elements with DFD and ERD, but differs in that a hierarchical class breakdown is an additional perspective on designing the system.

What are the main characteristics of an object-oriented system?

1. An object consists of *data* and *methods* that act on them. A customer object would contain data such as their personal details and methods that act on them such as 'print customer details'.

2. Objects communicate using *messages* which request a particular service from another object, such as a 'print current balance' service. These services are known as 'methods' and are equivalent to functions in traditional programming.

3. Objects are created and destroyed as the program is running. For example, if a new customer opens an account, we would create a new instance of the object. If a customer closes an account, the object is destroyed.

4. Objects provide *encapsulation* – an object can have private elements that are not evident to other objects. This hides complex details and gives a simple public object interface for external use by other objects. A real-world analogy is that it is possible to use a limited number of functions on a television without knowing its inner workings. In object-oriented parlance the television controls are providing different public methods which can be used by other objects. 'Abstraction' refers to the simplified public interface of the object.

5. Objects can be grouped into classes which share characteristics. For example, an organisation might contain an employee class. The classes can be subdivided using a hierarchy to create subclasses such as 'manager' or 'administrator'. Classes can share characteristics with other classes in the hierarchy, which is known as *inheritance*. This refers to the situation when an object inherits the behaviour of other objects. A specialised part-time staff class could inherit personal details data items from the employee class. If the method for calculating salary were different, then the part-time staff could override its inherited behaviour to define its own method 'calculate salary'. This is known as *polymorphism*, where an object can modify its inherited behaviour.

Despite the growth of OOD, non-object or procedural systems vastly outnumber object systems. So if OOD is nirvana, why doesn't everyone use it? The following are all practical barriers to growth:

- Millions of lines of procedural legacy computer code exist in languages such as COBOL.
- Many programmers' skills are procedural – OOD requires retraining to a different way of thinking.
- Methodologies, languages and tools are developing rapidly, requiring constant retraining and making reuse different when using different tools and languages, for example the most popular object-oriented method has changed from Small-talk to C++ to Java in just 10 years.
- Limited libraries are available for reuse.
- When initially designing projects, it is often slower and more costly – the benefits of OOD take several years to materialise.

The experience of early adopters has shown that the benefits do not come until later releases of a product and that initial object-oriented design and development may be more expensive than traditional methods.

SUMMARY

Stage summary: systems design

Purpose:	Defines *how* the system will work
Key activities:	Systems design, detailed design, database design, user interface design
Input:	Requirements specification
Output:	System design specification, detailed design specification, test specification

1. The design phase of the systems development lifecycle involves the specification of how the system should work.

2. The input to the design phase is the requirements specification from the analysis phase. The output from the design phase is a design specification that is used by programmers in the build phase.

3. Systems design is usually conducted using a top-down approach in which the overall architecture of the system is designed first. This is referred to as the systems or outline design. The individual modules are then designed in the de-tailed design phase.

4. Many modern information systems are designed using the client/server architecture. Processing is shared between the end-user's clients and the server, which is used to store data and process queries.

5. Systems design and detailed design will specify how the following aspects of the system will work:

   - its user interface;
   - method of data input and output (input and output design);
   - design of security to ensure the integrity of confidential data;
   - error handling;
   - help system.

6. For systems based on a relational database and a file-based system, the design stage will involve determining the best method of physically storing the data. For a database system, the technique for optimising the storage is known as 'normalisation'.

7. Object-oriented design is a relatively new approach to design. It has been adopted by some companies attracted by the possibility of cheaper development costs and fewer errors, which are made possible through reuse of code and a different design model that involves data and process integration.

EXERCISES

Self-assessment exercises

1. Define systems design.

2. What distinguishes systems design from systems analysis?

3. Describe the purpose of validation and verification.

4. What are process modelling and data modelling? Which diagrams used to summarise requirements at the analysis phase are useful in each of these types of modelling?

5. Explain the client/server model of computing.

6. What parts of the system need to be designed at the detailed design stage?

7. Describe the purpose of normalisation.

8. Explain insertion, update and deletion anomalies.

9. What are the differences between the sequential and direct (random) file access methods? In which business applications might they be used? What is the purpose of a file index?

10. Explain the difference between a batch and a real-time system. Which would be the more appropriate design for each of the following situations:

- periodic updating of a data warehouse from an operational database;
- capturing information on customer sales transactions?

11. What are the different types of input validation that must be considered in the design of a user input form?

12. Describe the main differences between the analysis and design phases within the systems development lifecycle.

Discussion questions

1. 'The client/server model of computing has many disadvantages, but these do not outweigh the advantages.' Discuss.

2. 'The distinction between system design and detailed design is an artificial one since a bottom-up approach to design is inevitable.' Discuss.

Essay questions

1. Explain, using an example from a human resources management database, the normalisation process from unnormalised data to third normal form (3NF).

2. Table 11.7, from a relational database, contains a number of rows and columns. When data are entered into the table, all columns must have data entered. Information about product descriptions, prices, product groups and rack locations is not held elsewhere. Explain how, because of its design, the table contains data duplicated in fields and contains the potential for insertion, update and deletion anomalies. What is meant by these anomalies and what could be done to prevent them?

3. A business-to-consumer company (B2C), a kitchenware retailer, wants to set up an e-commerce site, but first wants to produce a prototype in Microsoft Access. The data analysis has been performed and is shown in the expanded entity relationship diagram in Figure 11.22. Produce this database in Access based on the ERD. Include 4 or 5 sample records for each table.

Table 11.7 Table from a relational database

Product code	Product description	Product group	Group description	Cost	Retail price	Rack location	Quantity
0942	Small Green	KD	Kiddy Doh	0.19	1.29	A201	16
0439	Large Red	KD	Kiddy Doh	0.31	1.89	W106	35
0942	Small Green	KD	Kiddy Doh	0.19	1.29	E102	0
0902	Small Green	KD	Kiddy Doh	0.19	1.29	J320	56
1193	Spinning Top	PS	Pre-School	1.23	12.49	X215	3
2199	Burger Kit	KD	Kiddy Doh	3.25	17.75	D111	0

Figure 11.22 The expanded ERD for a kitchenware retailer

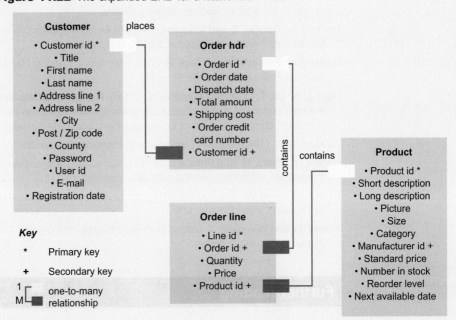

Customer
• Customer id *
• Title
• First name
• Last name
• Address line 1
• Address line 2
• City
• Post / Zip code
• County
• Password
• User id
• E-mail
• Registration date

places

Order hdr
• Order id *
• Order date
• Dispatch date
• Total amount
• Shipping cost
• Order credit card number
• Customer id +

contains   contains

Product
• Product id *
• Short description
• Long description
• Picture
• Size
• Category
• Manufacturer id +
• Standard price
• Number in stock
• Reorder level
• Next available date

Order line
• Line id *
• Order id +
• Quantity
• Price
• Product id +

Key
*   Primary key
+   Secondary key
1
M   one-to-many relationship

Examination questions

1. Explain the difference between validation and verification. Why are they important elements of systems design?

2. What benefits does three-tier client/server offer over two-tier client/server?

3. What are the main elements of system design?

4. Explain normalisation and how it can help remove different types of anomaly when modifying a database.

5. Which criteria are important in deciding whether to use a batch or real-time system?

6. What are the important aspects of user interface design?

7. Which different types of validation need to occur on data input to a system to ensure information quality?

8. What are the four main attributes of information security which need to be attained in an information system?

9. What is meant by the terms 'input design', 'output design' and 'database design'? Illustrate each of them with an example.

References

Blaha, M.R. and Rumbaugh, J. (2005) *Object Oriented Modeling and Design with UML*, 2nd edition, Prentice-Hall, Englewood Cliffs, NJ

Cao, M., Zhang, Q. and Seydel, J. (2005) 'B2C e-commerce web site quality: an empirical examination', *Industrial Management and Data Systems*, 105, 5, 645–61

Cox, J. and Dale, B.G. (2002) 'key quality factors in Web site design and use: an examination', *International Journal of Quality and Reliability Management*, 19, 7, 862–88

Curtis, G. and Cobham, D. (2008) *Business Information Systems: Analysis, Design and Practice*, 6th edition, Addison-Wesley, Harlow

Hoffer, J.A., George, J. and Valacich, J. (2010) *Modern Systems Analysis and Design*, 6th edition, Prentice-Hall, Upper Saddle River, NJ

Hoffer, J.A., Ramesh, V. and Topi, H. (2013) *Modern Database Management*, 11th edition, Prentice-Hall, Upper Saddle River, NJ

Huang, W., Le, T., Li, X. and Gandha, S. (2006) 'Categorizing web features and functions to evaluate commercial web sites: an assessment framework and an empirical investigation of Australian companies', *Industrial Management and Data Systems*, 106, 4, 523–39

Jackson, M.A. (1983) *System Development*, Prentice Hall, London

Rogers, Y., Sharp, H. and Preece, J. (2011) *Interaction Design: Beyond Human-Computer Interaction*, 3rd edition, Addison-Wesley, Wokingham

Whitten, J.L. and Bentley, L.D. (2006) *Systems Analysis and Design Methods*, 7th edition, McGraw-Hill Irwin, Boston, MA

Yeates, D. and Wakefield, T. (2003) *Systems Analysis and Design*, 2nd edition, Financial Times Pitman Publishing, London

Further reading

Booch, G. (2011) *Object Oriented Analysis and Design with Applications*, 2nd edition, Addison-Wesley, Upper Saddle River, NJ

Hasselbring, W. (2000) 'Information system integration', *Communications of the ACM*, June, 43, 6, 33–8

Hoffer, J.A., Ramesh, V. and Topi, H. (2013) *Modern Database Management*, 11th edition, Prentice-Hall, Upper Saddle River, NJ. A comprehensive text on the process of database design and normalisation together with applications such as data warehousing.

Hoffer, J.A., George, J. and Valacich, J. (2010) *Modern Systems Analysis and Design*, 6th edition, Prentice-Hall, Upper Saddle River, NJ. A complementary text to *Modern Database Management*, this has specific chapters on issues involved with designing user interfaces and Internet systems.

Kendall, K. and Kendall, J. (2013) *Systems Analysis and Design*, 9th edition, Prentice-Hall, Upper Saddle River, NJ. A longer text than the other two partly due to the extensive case on designing a student record system that runs through the book.

Rosenfeld, L. and Morville, P. (2007) *Information Architecture for the World Wide Web*, 3rd edition, O'Reilly & Associates, Sebastopol, CA. An excellent guide to analysis and design approaches to defining structured storage and access to information using web-based information systems.

Web links

www.cio.com CIO.com for chief information officers and IS staff has many articles related to analysis and design topics.

http://database.ittoolbox.com Channel of IT Toolbox giving topical news and whitepapers on database design, for example data quality, security design, data warehousing. Also has a series of useful introductory articles.

Usability and accessibility

www.uie.com/articles This site focuses on usability, but offers a counterpoint with different views based on research of user behaviour.

www.rnib.org.uk/accessibility Royal National Institute for the Blind web accessibility guidelines.

www.w3.org/WAI World Wide Web Consortium web accessibility guidelines.

LINKS TO OTHER CHAPTERS

This chapter focuses on the build and implementation stage of a systems project before a system goes 'live' within a business. It is related to previous Chapters 7–11 which describe preceding phases of systems development.

System build, implementation and maintenance: change management

CHAPTER AT A GLANCE

MAIN TOPICS

CASE STUDIES

LEARNING OUTCOMES

After reading this chapter, you will be able to:

- state the purpose of the build phase, and its difference from changeover and implementation;
- specify the different types of testing required for a system;
- select the best alternatives for changing from an old system to a new system;
- recognise the importance of managing software, IS and organisational change associated with the introduction of a new BIS.

MANAGEMENT ISSUES

Effective systems implementation is required for a quality system to be installed with minimal disruption to the business. From a managerial perspective, this chapter addresses the following questions:

- How should the system be tested?
- How should data be migrated from the old system to the new system?
- How should the changeover between old and new systems be managed?
- How can the change to a process-oriented system be managed?

INTRODUCTION

System build

The creation of software by programmers involving programming, building release versions of the software and testing by programmers and end-users. Writing of documentation and training may also occur at this stage.

System implementation

Involves the transition or changeover from the old system to the new and the preparation for this, such as making sure the hardware and network infrastructure for a new system are in place, testing of the system and also human issues of how best to educate and train staff who will be using or affected by the new system.

System build occurs after the system has been designed. It refers to the creation of software using programming or incorporation of building blocks such as existing software components or libraries. The main concern of managers in the system build phase is that the system be adequately tested to ensure it meets the requirements and design specifications developed as part of the analysis and design phases. They will also want to closely monitor errors generated or identified in the build phase in order to control on-time delivery of the system. **System implementation** follows the build stage. It involves setting up the right environment in which the test and finished system can be used. Once a test version of the software has been produced, this will be tested by the users and corrections made to the software followed by further testing and fixing until the software is suitable for use throughout the company.

Maintenance deals with reviewing the IS project and recording and acting on problems with the system.

Change management in this chapter is considered at the level of software, information systems and the organisation. Software change management deals with meeting change requests or variations to requirements that arise during the systems development project from business managers, users, designers and programmers. IS change management deals with the migration from an old to a new IS system. Organisational change management deals with managing changes to organisational processes, structures and their impact on organisational staff and culture. Business process management (BPM) provides an approach to this challenge.

SYSTEM BUILD AND IMPLEMENTATION

Maintenance

This deals with reviewing the IS project and recording and acting on problems with the system.

Change management

The management of change which can be considered at the software, information system and organisational levels.

System development

System development, which includes programming and testing, is the main activity that occurs at the system build phase.

The coverage of programming in this book will necessarily be brief, since the technical details of programming are not relevant to business people. A brief coverage of the techniques used by programmers is given since a knowledge of these techniques can be helpful in managing technical staff. Business users also often become involved in end-user development, which requires an appreciation of programming principles.

Software consists of program code written by programmers that is compiled or built into files known as 'executables' from different modules, each with a particular function. Executables are run by users as interactive programs. You may have noticed *application or executable files* in directories on your hard disk with a file type of '.exe', such as winword. exe for Microsoft Word, or '.dll' library files.

There are a number of system development tools available to programmers and business users to help in writing software. Software development tools include:

- Third-generation languages (3GLs) include Basic, Pascal, C, COBOL and Fortran. These involve writing programming code. Traditionally this was achieved in a text editor with limited support from other tools, since these languages date back to the 1960s. These languages are normally used to produce text-based programs rather than interactive graphical user interface programs that run under Microsoft Windows. They are, however, still used extensively in *legacy systems*, in which there exist millions of lines of COBOL code that must be maintained.

- Fourth-generation languages (4GLs) were developed in response to the difficulty of using 3GLs, particularly for business users. They are intended to avoid the need for programming. Since they often lack the flexibility for building a complex system, they are often ignored.

- Visual development tools such as Microsoft Visual Studio, Visual Basic and Visual C++ use an 'interactive development environment' that makes it easy to define the user interface of a product and write code to process the events generated when a user selects an option from a menu or button. They are widely used for prototyping and some tools such as Visual Basic for Applications are used by end-users for extending spreadsheet models. These tools share some similarities with 4GLs, but are not true application generators since programming is needed to make the applications function. Since they are relatively easy to use, they are frequently used by business users.

- **CASE or computer-aided software engineering tools** (see Chapter 11 for coverage of CASE tools) are primarily used by professional IS developers and are intended to assist in managing the process of capturing requirements, and converting these into design and program code.

Computer-aided software engineering (CASE) tools

Primarily used by professional IS developers to assist in managing the process of capturing requirements, and converting these into design and program code.

Software or systems quality

Measures software quality according to its suitability for the job intended. This is governed by whether it can do the job required (Does it meet the business requirements?) and the number of bugs it contains (Does it work reliably?).

Assessing software quality

Software metrics are used by businesses developing information systems to establish the quality of programs in an attempt to improve customer satisfaction through reducing errors by better programming and testing practices. **Software or systems quality** is measured according to its suitability for the job intended. This is governed by whether it can do the job required (Does it meet the business requirements?) and the number of bugs it contains (Does it work reliably?). The quality of software is dependent on two key factors:

1. the number of errors or bugs in the software;
2. the suitability of the software to its intended purpose, i.e. does it have the features identified by users which are in the requirements specification?

It follows that good-quality software must meet the needs of the business users and contain few errors. We are trying to answer questions such as:

- Does the product work?
- Does it crash?
- Does the product function according to specifications?
- Does the user interface meet product specifications and is it easy to use?
- Are there any unexplained or undesirable side-effects to using the product which may stop other software working?

The number of errors is quite easily measured, although errors may not be apparent until they are encountered by end-users. Suitability to purpose is much more difficult to quantify, since it is dependent on a number of factors. These factors were referred to in detail earlier (in Chapters 8 and 11) which described the criteria that are relevant to deciding on a suitable information system. These quality criteria include correct functions, speed and ease of use.

Software bug

Software bugs are defects in a program which are caused by human error during programming or earlier in the lifecycle. They may result in major faults or may remain unidentified.

What is a bug?

Problems, errors or defects in software are collectively known as 'bugs', since they are often small and annoying! **Software bugs** are defects in a program which are caused by human error during programming or earlier in the lifecycle. They may result in major faults or may remain unidentified. A major problem in a software system can be caused by one wrong character in a program of tens of thousands of lines. So it is often the source of the problem that is small, not its consequences.

Computing history recalls that the first bug was a moth which crawled inside a valve in one of the first computers, causing it to crash! This bug was identified by Grace Hopper, the inventor of COBOL, the first commercial programming language.

Software quality also involves an additional factor which is not concerned with the functionality or number of bugs in the software. Instead, it considers how well the software operates in its environment. For example, in a multitasking environment such as Microsoft Windows, it assesses how well a piece of software coexists with other programs. Are resources shared evenly? Will a crash of the software cause other software to fail also? This type of interaction testing is known as 'behaviour testing'.

Software metrics

Software metrics

Measures which indicate the quality of software.

Software metrics have much in common with measures involved with assessing the quality of a product in other industries. For example, in engineering or construction, designers want to know how long it will take a component to fail or the number of errors in a batch of products. Most measures are defect-based, measuring the number and type of errors. The source of the error and when it was introduced into the system are also important. Some errors are the result of faulty analysis or design and many are the result of a programming error. By identifying and analysing the source of the error, improvements can be made to the relevant part of the software lifecycle. An example of a comparison of three projects in terms of errors is shown in Table 12.1. It can be seen that in Project 3, the majority of errors are introduced during the coding (programming) stage, so corrective action is necessary here.

While the approach of many companies to testing has been that bugs are inevitable and must be tested for to remove them, more enlightened companies look at the reasons for the errors and attempt to stop them being introduced by the software developers. This implies that longer should be spent on the analysis and design phases of a project. Johnston (2003) suggests that the balance between the phases of a project should be divided as shown in Table 12.2, with a large proportion of the time being spent on analysis and design.

Errors per KLOC

Errors per KLOC (thousand lines of code) is the basic defect measure used in systems development.

In software code the number of errors or 'defect density' is measured in terms of **errors per 1000 lines of code** (or KLOC for short). The long-term aim of a business is to reduce the defect rate towards the elusive goal of 'zero defects'.

Errors per KLOC is the basic defect measure used in systems development. Care must be taken when calculating defect density or productivity of programmers using KLOC, since this will vary from one programming language to another and according to the style of the programmer and the number of comment statements used. KLOC must be used consistently between programs, and this is usually achieved by only counting executable statements, not comments, or by counting function points (function point analysis is covered in Chapter 9).

Table 12.1 Table comparing the source of errors in three different software projects

	Project 1	Project 2	Project 3
Analysis	20%	30%	15%
Design	25%	40%	20%
Coding	35%	20%	45%
Testing	20%	10%	20%

Table 12.2 Ideal proportions of time to be spent on different phases of a systems development project, focusing on details of build phase

Project activities	Suggested proportion
Definition, design and planning	20%
Coding	15%
Component test and early system test	15%
Full system test, user testing and operational trials	20%
Documentation, training and implementation support	20%
Overall project management	10%

The technical quality of software can also be assessed by measures other than the number of errors. Its complexity, which is often a function of the number of branches it contains, is commonly used.

Another metric, more commonly used for engineered products, is the mean time between failures. This is less appropriate to software since outright failure is rare, but small errors or bugs in the software are quite common. It is, however, used as part of outsourcing contracts or as part of the service-level agreement for network performance.

A more useful measure for software is to look at the customer satisfaction rating of the software, since its quality is dependent on many other factors such as usability and speed as well as the number of errors.

Data migration

Data migration

Data migration is the transfer of data from the old system to the new system. When data are added to a database, this is known as populating the database.

A significant activity of the build phase is to transfer the data from the old system to the new system. **Data migration** is the transfer of data from the old system to the new system. When data are added to a database, this is known as 'populating the database'. One method of transferring data is to rekey manually into the new system. This is impractical for most systems since the volume of data is too large. Instead, special data conversion programs are written to convert the data from the data file format of the old system into the data file format of the new system. Con-version may involve changing data formats, for example a date may be converted from two digits for the year into four digits. It may also involve combining or aggregating fields or records. The conversion programs also have to be well tested because of the danger of corrupting existing data. Data migration is an extra task which needs to be remembered as part of the project manager's project plan. During data migration data can be 'exported' from an old system and then 'imported' into a new system.

Import and export

Data can be 'exported' from an old system and then 'imported' into a new system.

When using databases or off-the-shelf software, there are usually tools provided to make it easier to import data from other systems.

Testing information systems

Testing is a vital aspect of implementation, since this will identify errors that can be fixed before the system is live. The type of tests that occur in implementation tend to be more structured than the ad hoc testing that occurs with prototyping earlier in systems development.

Note that often testing is not seen as an essential part of the lifecycle, but as a chore that must be done. If its importance is not recognised, insufficient testing will occur. Johnston (2003) refers to the 'testing trap', when companies spend too long writing the software without changing the overall project deadline. This results in the amount of time for testing being 'squeezed' until it is no longer sufficient.

During prototyping, the purpose of testing is to identify missing features or define different ways of performing functions. Testing is more structured during the implementation phase in order to identify as many bugs as possible. It has two main purposes: the first is to check that the requirements agreed earlier in the project have been implemented, the second is to identify errors or bugs. To achieve both of these objectives, testing must be conducted in a structured way by using a **test specification** which details tests in different areas. This avoids users' performing a general usability test of the system where they only use common functions at random. While this is valid, and is necessary since it mirrors real use of the software, it does not give a good coverage of all the areas of the system. Systematic tests should be performed using a test script which covers, in detail, the functions to be tested.

Test specification

A detailed description of the tests that will be performed to check the software works correctly.

Mini case study

Jim Goodnight: crunching the numbers

By Michael Dempsey

Addressing a recent business intelligence conference in London, Jim Goodnight's considered responses and soft Southern drawl left the impression of a thoughtful figure who just happens to be chief executive of a $1.34bn business.

His taciturn aspect changed when the absolute quality of his company's software was raised. 'SAS is still quicker and better', he states.

Despite the waves of re-labelling that have allowed his business to surf through management information systems and data warehousing to reach today's focus on business intelligence and performance management, Mr Goodnight defines SAS in the light of a very old-fashioned customer grouse. 'When we ship software, it's almost bug-free. We learnt about doing that the hard way, many years ago.'

During the 1980s, SAS released some software before it was fully tested and provoked a vocal reaction from the users. 'They let us know what was wrong with it.' He jokes about the number of bugs that are still found in other large commercial systems and then generously redeems his competitors with the remark 'but then we do so much more testing'.

 Source: Dempsey, M. (2005) Jim Goodnight: crunching the numbers. *Financial Times.* 23 March.
© The Financial Times Limited 2005. All Rights Reserved.

Test plan

Plan describing the type and sequence of testing and who will conduct it.

Given the variety of tests that need to be performed, large implementations will also use a **test plan**, a specialised project plan describing what testing will be performed when, and by whom. Testing is always a compromise between the number of tests that can be performed and the time available.

The different types of testing that occur throughout the software lifecycle should be related to the earlier stages in the lifecycle against which we are testing. This approach to development (Figure 12.1) is sometimes referred to as the 'V-model of systems development', for obvious reasons. The diagram shows that different types of testing are used to test different aspects of the analysis and design of the system: to test the requirements specification a user acceptance test is performed, and to test the detailed design unit testing occurs.

We will now consider in more detail the different types of testing that need to be conducted during implementation. This review is structured according to who performs the tests.

Figure 12.1 The V-model of systems development relating analysis and design activities to testing activities

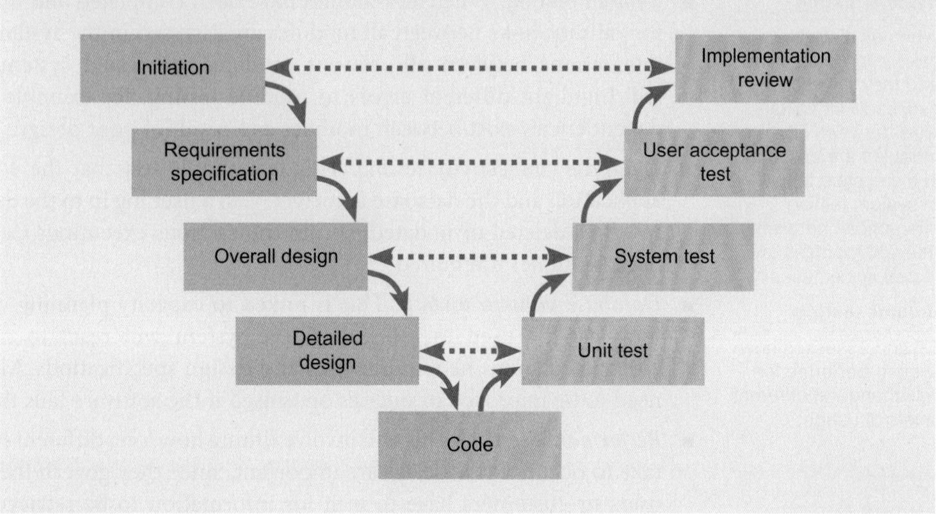

Developer tests

There are a variety of techniques that can be used for testing systems. Jones (2008) identifies 18 types of testing, of which the most commonly used are subroutine, unit, new function, regression, integration and systems testing. Many of the techniques available are not used due to lack of time, money or commitment. Some of the more common techniques are summarised here.

Module or unit testing

Individual modules are tested to ensure they function correctly for given inputs.

■ **Module or unit tests**. These are performed on individual modules of the system. The module is treated as a 'black box' (ignoring its internal method of working) as developers check that expected outputs are generated for given inputs. When you drive a car this can be thought of as black box testing – you are aware of the inputs to the car and their effect as outputs, but you will probably not have a detailed knowledge of the mechanical aspects of the car and whether they are functioning correctly. Module testing involves considering a range of inputs or test cases, as follows:

   (a) Random test data can be automatically generated by a spreadsheet for module testing.

   (b) Structured or logical test data will cover a range of values expected in normal use of the module and also values beyond designed limits to check that appropriate error messages are given. This is also known as 'boundary value testing' and is important, since many bugs occur because designed boundaries are crossed. This type of data is used for regression testing, explained below.

   (c) Scenario or typical test data use realistic example data, possibly from a previous system, to simulate day-to-day use of the system.

These different types of test data can also be applied to system testing.

■ Integration or module interaction testing (black box testing). Expected interactions such as messaging and data exchange between a limited number of modules are assessed. This can be performed in a structured way, using a top-down method where a module calls other module functions as stubs (partially completed functions which should return expected values) or using a bottom-up approach where a driver module is used to call complete functions.

■ New function testing. This commonly used type of testing refers to testing the operation of a new function when it is implemented, perhaps during prototyping. If testing is limited to this, problems may be missed since the introduction of the new function may cause bugs elsewhere in the system.

- **System testing.** When all modules have been completed and their interactions assessed for validity, links between all modules are assessed in the system test. In system testing, interactions between all relevant modules are tested systematically. System testing will highlight different errors to module testing, for example when unexpected data dependencies exist between modules as a result of poor design.

- *Database connectivity testing.* This is a simple test that the connectivity between the application and the database is correct. Can a user log in to the database? Can a record be inserted, deleted or updated, i.e. are transactions executing? Can transactions be rolled back (undone) if required?

- *Database volume testing.* This is linked to capacity planning of databases. Simulation tools can be used to assess how the system will react to different levels of usage anticipated from the requirements and design specifications. Methods of indexing may need to be improved or queries optimised if the software fails this test.

- *Performance testing.* This will involve timing how long different functions or transactions take to occur. These delays are important, since they govern the amount of wasted time users or customers have to wait for information to be retrieved or screens refreshed. Maximum waiting times may be specified in a contract, for example.

- *Confidence test script.* This is a short script which may take a few hours to run through and which tests all the main functions of the software. It should be run before all releases to users to ensure that their time is not wasted on a prototype that has major failings which mean the test will have to be aborted and a new release made.

- *Automated tests.* Automated tools simulate user inputs through the mouse or keyboard and can be used to check for the correct action when a certain combination of buttons is pressed or data entered. Scripts can be set up to allow these tests to be repeated. This is particularly useful for performing regression tests.

- *Regression testing.* This testing should be performed before a release to ensure that the software performance is consistent with previous test results, i.e. that the outputs produced are consistent with previous releases of the software. This is necessary, as in fixing a problem a programmer may introduce a new error that can be identified through the regression test. Regression testing is usually performed with automated tools.

End-user tests

The purpose of these is twofold: first, to check that the software does what is required; and second, to identify bugs, particularly those that may only be caused by novice users.

For ease of assessing the results, the users should be asked to write down for each bug or omission found:

1. module affected;
2. description of problem (any error messages to be written in full);
3. relevant data – for example, which particular customer or order record in the database caused the problem;
4. severity of problem on a three-point scale.

Different types of end-user tests that can be adopted include:

- *Scenario testing.* In an order processing system this would involve processing example orders of different types, such as new customers, existing customers without credit and customers with a credit agreement.

- **Functional testing.** Users are told to concentrate on testing particular functions or modules such as the order entry module in detail, either following a test script or working through the module systematically.

- *General testing.* Here, users are given free rein to depart from the test specification and test according to their random preferences. Sometimes this is the only type of testing used, which results in poor coverage of the functions in the software!

- **Multi-user testing.** The effect of different users accessing the same customer or stock record. Software should not permit two users to modify the same data at the same time. Tests should also be made to ensure that users with different permissions and rules are treated as they should be, e.g. that junior staff are locked out of company financial information.

- *Inexperienced user testing.* Staff who are inexperienced in the use of software often make good 'guinea pigs' for testing software, since they may choose an illogical combination of options that the developers have not tested. This is surprisingly effective and is a recommended method of software testing. The staff involved often also like the power of being able to 'break' the software.

- **User acceptance testing.** This is the final stage of testing which occurs before the software is signed off as fit for purpose and the system can go live. Since the customer will want to be sure the software works correctly, this may take a week or more.

- *Alpha and beta testing.* These terms apply to user tests which occur before a packaged software product is released. They are described in the section on configuration management later in this chapter.

Multi-user testing

The effect of different users accessing the same customer or stock record is tested. Software should not permit two users to modify the same data at the same time.

User acceptance testing

This is the final stage of testing which occurs before the software is signed off as fit for purpose and the system can go live.

Benefits-based testing

An alternative approach to testing is not to focus only on the errors when reviewing a system, but rather to test against the business benefits that the system confers. A system could be error-free, but if it is not delivering benefits then its features may not have been implemented correctly. This approach can be used with prototyping, so that if a system is not delivering the correct features it can be modified. When undertaking structured testing, the software will be tested against the requirements specification to check that the desired features are present.

Testing environments

Testing occurs in different environments during the project. At an early stage prototypes may be tested on a single standalone machine or laptop. In the build phase, testing will be conducted in a *development environment*, which involves programmers' testing data across a network on a shared server. This is mainly used for module testing. In the implementation phase, a special **test environment** will be set up which simulates the final operating environment for the system. This could be a room with three or more networked machines accessing data from a central server. This test environment will be used for early user training and testing and for system testing. Finally, the **production or live environment** is that in which the system will be used operationally. This will be used for user acceptance testing and when the system becomes live. When a system goes live, it is worth noting that there may still be major problems despite extensive testing.

Test environment

A specially configured environment (hardware, software and office environment) used to test the software before its release.

Live (production) environment

The term used to describe the setup of the system (hardware, software and office environment) where the software will be used in the business.

Documentation

Software documentation refers to end-user guidance such as the user guide and technical maintenance documentation such as design and test specifications.

Documentation

Producing **documentation** occurs throughout the software lifecycle, such as when requirements are specified at the analysis stage, but it becomes particularly import-ant at the implementation and maintenance stages of a project. At this stage user guides will be used as part of user acceptance testing and system developers will refer to design documents when updating the system. The main types of documentation required through the project are referred to in Figure 12.1. The important documentation used at the testing stage includes:

- the requirements specification produced at the analysis stage; this is used in the user acceptance test, to check that the correct features have been implemented;

- the user manual, which will be used during testing and operational use of the system by business users;
- the design specification, which will be used during system testing and during maintenance by developers;
- the detailed design, which will be used in module testing and during maintenance;
- the data dictionary or database design, which will be used in testing and maintenance by database administrators and developers;
- detailed test plans and test specifications, which will be used as part of developer and user testing;
- quality assurance documents such as software change request forms, which will be used to manage the change during the build and implementation phases.

The writing of documentation is often neglected, since it tends to be less interesting than developing the software. To ensure that it is produced, strong project management is necessary and the presence of a software quality plan will make sure that time is spent on documentation, since a company's quality standard is assessed on whether the correct documentation is produced.

Example of a user guide structure

User guides are normally structured to give a gradual introduction to the system, and there may be several guides for a single system. A common structure is:

1. *A brief introductory/overview guide*, often known as 'Getting started'. The aim of this is to help users operate the software productively with the minimum of reading. The introductory section will also explain the purpose of the system for the business.

2. *Tutorial guide*. This will provide lessons, often with example data to guide the user through using the package. These are now often combined with online 'guided tours'.

3. *Detailed documentation* is often structured according to the different screens in an application. However, it is usually better to structure such guides according to the different functions or applications a business user will need. Chapter titles in such an approach might include 'How to enter a new sales order' or 'How to print a report'. This guide should also incorporate information on trouble-shooting when problems are encountered.

4. *Quick reference guide, glossary and appendix*. These will contain explanations of error messages and a summary of all functions and how to access them.

User guides

The user guide has become a less important aspect of systems documentation with the advent of online help such as the help facility available with Windows applications and web-site-based help. Online help can give general guidance on the software, or it can give more specific advice on a particular screen or function – when it is known as 'context-sensitive'. It is often a good idea to ask business users to develop the user guide, since if programmers write the guide it will tend to be too technical and not relevant to the needs of users. Since business users are sometimes charged with producing a user guide, approaches to structuring these is covered in a little more detail.

MAINTENANCE

The maintenance phase of a project starts when the users sign off the system during testing and it becomes a live production system. After a system is live, there are liable to be some errors that were not identified during testing and need to be remedied. When

Maintenance

Maintenance occurs after the system has been signed off as suitable for users. It involves reviewing the project and recording and acting on problems with the system.

problems are encountered, this presents a dilemma to the system manager, since they will have to balance the need for a new release of the system against the severity of an error. It is not practical or cost-effective to introduce a new release of the software for every bug found, since each release needs to be tested and installed and fresh problems may exist in the new system. Most systems managers would aim not to make frequent, immediate releases to correct problems because of the cost and disruption this causes. Instead, faults will be recorded and then fixed in a release that solves several major problems. This is known as a *maintenance* release and it might occur at monthly, six-monthly or yearly intervals according to the stability of the system. This is usually a function of the age of the system – new systems will have more errors and will need more frequent maintenance releases.

With the advent of customer-facing e-commerce systems that need to be available 24 hours a day, 7 days a week for 365 days a year, periodic maintenance releases are not appropriate. Significant problems must be rectified immediately with the minimum of disruption. In 2001 Barclays Bank was censured by the UK advertising standard authority for suggesting in their television adverts that their systems were continuously available 24 hours per day. In fact, some users of their system complained that it was not available for a short period after midnight each night due to maintenance. Consequently Barclays had to change the advert, and may eventually change their approach to maintenance.

Maintenance releases will not only fix problems, but may also include enhancements or new features requested by users.

Major and minor releases are denoted by the release or version number. If a system changes from version 1.1 to 2.0, this will be a major release. When moving from version 2.0 to 2.1, some new features might be involved. From version 2.1 to 2.1.1 might represent a patch or interim release to correct problems.

To help make the decision of installing a new release to correct the problem, a scale of severity of the fault is used by companies to govern what action is required. Such a scale may form part of the contract if a company has outsourced its systems development to a third party. An example of such a scale is shown in Table 12.3.

Most systems now have a modular design such that it is not necessary to reinstall the complete system if an error is encountered – rather the module where the error lies can be replaced. This is described in a rather primitive way as applying a **patch** to the system. Patches to off-the-shelf systems are now available for download over the Internet. Because

Software patch

This is an interim release of part of an information system that is intended to address deficiencies in a previous release.

Table 12.3 Fault taxonomy described in Jorgenson (1995)

Category	Example	Action
Mild	Misspelt word	Ignore or defer to next major release
Moderate	Misleading or redundant information	Ignore or defer to next major release
Annoying	Truncated text	Defer to next major release
Disturbing	Some transactions not processed correctly, intermittent crashes in one module	Defer to next maintenance release
Serious	Lost transactions	Defer to next maintenance release may need immediate fix and release
Very serious	Crash occurs regularly in one module	Immediate solution needed
Extreme	Frequent, very serious errors	Immediate solution needed
Intolerable	Database corruption	Immediate solution needed
Catastrophic	System crashes, cannot be restarted – system unusable	Immediate solution needed
Infectious	Catastrophic problem also causes failure of other systems	Immediate solution needed

of the competitive pressures of releasing software as soon as possible, a large number of off-the-shelf packages require some sort of patch. For example, web browser software such as Netscape Navigator and Microsoft Internet Explorer has required frequent patches to correct errors in the security of the browser which permit unauthorised access to the computer on which the browser is running.

Post-implementation review

Post-implementation review

A meeting that occurs after a system is operational to review the success of the project.

A **post-implementation review** or project closedown review occurs several months after the system has gone live. Its purpose is to assess the success of the new system and decide on any necessary corrective action. The review could include the following:

- faults and suggested enhancements with agreement on which need to be implemented in a future release;
- success of system in meeting its budget and timescale targets;
- success of system in meeting its business requirements – has it delivered the anticipated benefits described in the feasibility study?
- development practices that worked well and poorly during the project.

An additional reason for performing a post-implementation review is so that lessons can be learnt from the project. Good practices can be applied to future projects and attempts made to avoid techniques which failed.

CHANGE MANAGEMENT

The main activities undertaken by a manager of systems development projects are essentially concerned with managing change. Managing change takes different forms. First, we will look at managing technical changes to the software requirements as the system is developed through prototyping and testing. We will then look at how organisations can manage the transition or changeover to a new information system from an old system. Another important aspect of change we will review is how the introduction of a new system can affect the business users and action that can be taken to manage this organisational change. The role of organisational culture in influencing this will also be considered.

Software change management

Change (modification) requests

A modification to the software thought to be necessary by the business users or developers.

At each stage of a systems development project, **change (modification) requests** or variations to requirements will arise from business managers, users, designers and programmers. These requests include reports of bugs and of features that are missing from the system as well as ideas for future versions of the software.

These requests will occur as soon as users start evaluating prototypes of a system and will continue through to the maintenance phase of the project when the system has gone live. As the users start testing the system in earnest in the implementation phase, these requests will become more frequent and tens or possibly hundreds will be generated each week. This process of change needs to be carefully managed, since otherwise it can develop into *requirements creep*, a problem on many information systems projects. As the number of requirements grows, more developer time will be required to fix the problems and the project can soon spiral out of control. What is needed is a mechanism to ensure, first, that all the changes are recorded and dealt with, and second, that they are reviewed in such a way that the number of changes does not become unmanageable.

The main steps in managing changed requirements are:

1. Record the change requests, indicating level of importance and module affected.
2. Prioritise them with the internal or external customer as 'must have', 'nice to have' or 'later release' (Priority 1, 2 or 3). This will be done with reference to the project constraints of system quality, cost and timescale.
3. Identify responsibility for fixing the problem, since it may lie with a software house, internal IS staff, systems integrator or hardware vendor.
4. Implement changes that are recorded as high-priority.
5. Maintain a check of which high-priority errors have been fixed.

When a system is being implemented, it is useful to have a three-way classification of errors to be fixed, since this highlights the errors or missing features that must be implemented and avoids long discussions of the merits of each solution.

When the system is live, a more complex classification is often used to help in deciding how to 'escalate' problems up the hierarchy according to their severity. This could be structured as follows:

1. Critical problem, system not operational. This may occur due to power or server failure. Level 1 problems need to be resolved immediately, since business users cannot access the system at all. With customer-facing applications such as e-commerce systems, this type of problem needs to be corrected as soon as possible since every minute the system is not working transaction revenue is lost.
2. Critical problem, making part of the system unusable or causing data corruption. These would normally need to be resolved within 12 to 24 hours, depending on the nature of the problem.
3. Problem causing intermittent system failure or data corruption. Resolve within 48 hours.
4. Non-severe problem not requiring modification to software until next release.
5. Trivial problem or suggestion which can be considered for future releases.

If the system has been tailored by a systems integrator, these will be their responsibility to fix and this will be specified in the contract or service-level agreement (SLA), together with the time that will be taken for the change to be made. If the system has been developed or tailored internally by the IS department or even within a department, an SLA is still a good idea. If the problem occurs from a problem with packaged software, you will have to hope that an update release that solves the problem is available; if not, you will have to lobby the supplier for one.

Software quality assurance

As we have seen, procedures should be followed throughout the software lifecycle to try to produce good-quality systems. These quality assurance (QA) procedures have been formalised in the British Standard BS 5750 Part 1 and its international equivalent ISO 9001 (TickIT). These procedures do not guarantee a quality information system, but their purpose is to ensure that all relevant parts of the software lifecycle, such as requirements capture, design and testing, are carried out consistently. Business users can ask whether suppliers have quality accreditation as a means of distinguishing between them. QA procedures would not specify a particular method for design or testing, but they would specify how the change was managed by ensuring that all changes to requirements are noted and that review mechanisms are in place to check that changes are agreed and acted on accordingly.

If a business buys software services from a company that has achieved the quality standards, then there is less risk of the services' being inadequate. For a company to achieve a quality standard it has to be assessed by independent auditors and if successful it will be audited regularly.

Configuration management: builds and release versions

Configuration management is control of the different versions of software and program source code used during the build, implementation and maintenance phases of a project.

Throughout the implementation phase, updated versions of the software are released to users for testing. Before software can be used by users it needs to be released as an executable, built up from compiled versions of all the program code modules that make up the system. The process of joining all the modules is technically known as the *linking or build process*. The sequence can be summarised as:

1. programmers *write* different code modules;
2. completed code modules are *compiled* to form object modules;
3. object modules are *linked* to form executables;
4. executables are installed on machines;
5. executables are loaded and run by end-users testing the software.

Each updated release of the software is therefore usually known as a new 'build'. With large software systems there will be hundreds of program files written by different developers that need to be compiled and then linked. If these files are not carefully tracked, then the wrong versions of files may be used, with earlier versions causing bugs. This process of version control is part of an overall process known as configuration management, which ensures that programming and new releases occur in a systematic way. One of the problems with solving the millennium bug was that in some companies configuration management was so poor that the original program code had been lost!

During the build phase, updated software versions will become more suitable for release as new functions are incorporated and the number of bugs is reduced. Some companies, such as Microsoft, call these different versions 'release candidates', others use the terminology alpha, beta and gold to distinguish between versions. These terms are often applied to packaged software, but can also be applied to bespoke business applications.

- *Alpha releases and alpha testing.* Alpha releases are preliminary versions of the software released early in the build phase. They usually have the majority of the functionality of the complete system in place, but may suffer from extensive bugs. The purpose of alpha testing is to identify these bugs and any major problems with the functionality and usability of the software. Alpha testing is usually conducted by staff inside the organisation developing the software or by favoured customers.

- *Beta releases and beta testing.* Beta releases occur after alpha testing and have almost complete functionality and relatively few bugs. Beta testing will be conducted by a range of customers who are interested in evaluating the new software. The aim of beta testing is to identify bugs in the software before it is shipped to all customers.

- *Gold release.* This is a term for the final release of the software which will be shipped to all customers.

IS change management

Choosing the method to be used for migrating or changing from the old system to the new system is one of the most important decisions that the project management team must make during the implementation phase. Changeover can be defined as moving from the old information system to the new information system. Note that this changeover is required whether the previous information system is computer- or paper-based. Before considering the alternatives, we will briefly discuss the main factors that a manager will consider when evaluating them. The factors are:

- *Cost.* This is, of course, an important consideration, but the quality of the new system is often more important.

Configuration management

Procedures that define the process of building a version of the software from its constituent program files and data files.

Alpha release

Alpha releases are preliminary versions of the software released early in the build process. They usually have the majority of the functionality of the system in place, but may suffer from extensive bugs.

Alpha testing

The purpose of 'alpha testing' is to identify bugs and any major problems with the functionality and usability of the software. Alpha testing is usually conducted by staff inside the organisation developing the software or by favoured customers.

Beta release

Beta releases occur after alpha testing and have almost complete functionality and relatively few bugs.

Beta testing

Will be conducted by a range of customers who are interested in evaluating the new software. The aim of beta testing is to identify bugs in the software before it is shipped to a range of customers.

Changeover

The term used to describe moving from the old information system to the new information system.

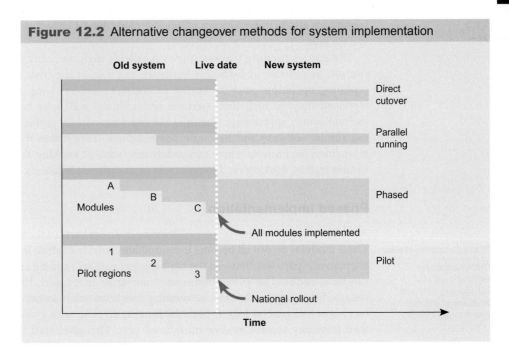

Figure 12.2 Alternative changeover methods for system implementation

- *Time.* There will be a balance between the time available and the desired quality of the system which will need to be evaluated.
- *Quality of new system after changeover.* This will be dependent on number of bugs and suitability for purpose.
- *Impact on customers.* What will be the effect on customer service if the change-over overruns or if the new system has bugs?
- *Impact on employees.* How much extra work will be required by employees during the changeover? Will they be remunerated for this?
- *Technical issues.* Some of the options listed below may not be possible if the system does not have a modular design.

There are four main alternatives for moving from a previous system to a new system. The options are shown in Figure 12.2 and described in more detail below.

Immediate cutover or big-bang method

Immediate cutover (big-bang changeover)

Immediate cutover is when a new system becomes operational and operations transfer immediately from the previous system.

The **immediate cutover** method involves moving directly from the original system to the new system at a particular point in time. On a designated date, the old system is switched off and all staff move to using the new system. Clearly, this is a high-risk strategy since there is no fallback position if serious bugs are encountered. However, this approach is adopted by many large companies since it may be impractical and costly to run different systems in parallel. Before cutover occurs, the company will design the system carefully and conduct extensive testing to make sure that it is reliable and so reduce the risk of failure. The case study shows a relatively successful example of the cutover method and indicates why this is necessary for the implementation of large systems. The success factors of this project are described.

Parallel running

Parallel running

This changeover method involves the old and new systems operating together at the same time until the company is certain the new system works.

With **parallel running** the old and new systems are operated together for a period until the company is convinced that the new system performs adequately. This presents a lower risk than the immediate cutover method, since if the new system fails, the company can revert to the old system and customers will not be greatly affected. Parallel running sometimes also involves using a manual or paper-based system as backup in case the new system fails.

The cost of running two systems in parallel is high, not only in terms of maintaining two sets of software and possibly hardware, but also in the costs of the human operators repeating operations such as keying in customer orders twice. Indeed, the increase in workload may be such that overtime or additional staff may be required. The parallel method is only appropriate when the old and new systems perform similar functions and use similar software and hardware combinations. This makes it unsuitable for business re-engineering projects where completely new ways of working are being introduced that involve staff in working on different tasks or in different locations.

Phased implementation

Phased implementation

This changeover method involves introducing different modules of the new system sequentially.

A phased implementation involves delivering different parts of the system at different times. These modules do not all become live simultaneously, but rather in sequence. As such, this alternative is part-way between the big-bang and parallel running approaches. Each module can be introduced as either immediate cutover or in parallel. In a modular accounting system, for example, the core accounting functions, such as accounts payable, accounts receivable and general ledger, could be introduced first, with a sales order processing and then inventory control module introduced later. This gives staff the opportunity to learn about the new system more gradually and problems encountered on each module can be fixed as they are introduced.

Although this may appear to be an attractive approach, since if a new module fails the other modules will still be available, it is difficult to implement in practice. To achieve a phased implementation requires that the architecture of the new system and old system be designed in a modular way, and that the modules can operate independently without a high degree of coupling. For all systems, however, data exchange will be required between the different modules and this implies that common data exchange formats exist between the old and the new systems. This is often not the case, particularly if the software is sourced from different suppliers. Designers of systems are using techniques such as object-oriented design to produce modules with fewer and clearer dependencies between them. This should help in making phased implementations more practical. In the example given for the modular accounting system, modules in the old and new systems would have to have facilities to transfer data.

Pilot system

Pilot implementation

The system is trialled in a limited area before it is deployed more extensively across the business.

In a pilot implementation, the system will be trialled in a limited area before it is deployed more extensively. This could include deploying the system in one operating region of the company, possibly a single country, or in a limited number of offices. This approach is common in multinational or national companies with several offices. Such a pilot system usually acts as a trial before more extensive deployment in a big-bang implementation.

Using combinations of changeover methods

The different changeover methods are often used in conjunction for different stages of an implementation. For example, in a national or international implementation it is customary to trial the project in a single region or country using a pilot of the system. If a pilot system is considered successful there is then a choice of one of the following:

- immediately implementing the system elsewhere using the big-bang approach;
- running the new and old systems in parallel until it is certain that the new system is stable enough;

Table 12.4 Advantages and disadvantages of the different methods of implementation

Method	Main advantages	Main disadvantages
Immediate cutover	Rapid, lowest cost	High risk if serious errors in system
Parallel running	Lower risk than immediate cutover	Slower and higher-cost than immediate cutover
Phased implementation	Good compromise between immediate cutover and parallel running	Difficult to achieve technically due to interdependencies between modules
Pilot system	Essential for multinational or national rollouts	Has to be used in combination with the other methods

- if the new system is modular in construction, it is possible for the implementation to be phased, with new modules gradually being introduced as they are completed and the users become familiar with the new system;

- parallel running will probably also occur in this instance, in case there is a need to revert to the old system in the event of failure of the new system.

Once the system is proved in the first area, then further rollout will probably occur through the big-bang approach.

The advantages and disadvantages of each of these changeover methods are summarised in Table 12.4.

Deployment planning

Deployment plan

A deployment plan is a schedule that defines all the tasks that need to occur in order for changeover to occur successfully. This includes putting in place all the infrastructure such as cabling and hardware.

A **deployment plan** is necessary to get all 'kit' or hardware in place in time for user acceptance testing. A deployment plan is a schedule that defines all the tasks that need to occur in order for changeover to occur successfully. This includes putting in place all the infrastructure such as cabling and hardware. This is not a trivial task, because often a range of equipment will be required from a variety of manufacturers. A deployment plan should list every software deliverable and hardware item required, when it needs to arrive and when it needs to be connected. The deployment plan will be part of the overall project plan or Gantt chart. A deployment plan is particularly important for large implementations involving many offices, such as the Barclays system referred to earlier in the chapter. Several people may be responsible for this task on large projects.

When planning deployment, advanced planning is required due to possible delays in purchasing and delivery. The burden of purchasing will often be taken by a systems integrator, but it may be shared by the purchasing department of the company buying the new system. This needs careful liaison between the two groups.

With installation of new hardware, a particular problem is where changes to infrastructure are required – for example upgrading cabling to a higher bandwidth or installing a new router. This can take a considerable time and cause a great deal of disruption to users of existing systems.

Organisational change management

Business process re-engineering (BPR)

Identifying radical, new ways of carrying out business operations, often enabled by new IT capabilities.

This section deals with managing changes to organisational processes, structures and their impact on organisational staff and culture.

In the early-to-mid 1990s organisation-wide transformational change was advocated under the label of **business process re-engineering (BPR)**. It was popularised through the pronouncements of Hammer and Champy (1993) and Davenport (1993). The essence of BPR is the assertion that business processes, organisational structures, team structures and employee responsibilities can be fundamentally altered to improve business performance. Hammer and Champy (1993) defined BPR as:

> the fundamental rethinking and radical redesign of business processes to achieve dramatic improvements in critical, contemporary measures of performance, such as cost, quality, service, and speed.

The key words from this definition that encapsulate the BPR concept are:

- *fundamental rethinking* – re-engineering usually refers to changing of significant business processes such as customer service, sales order processing or manufacturing;
- *radical redesign* – re-engineering is not involved with minor, incremental change or automation of existing ways of working. It involves a complete rethinking about the way business processes operate;
- *dramatic improvements* – the aim of BPR is to achieve improvements measured in tens or hundreds of per cent. With automation of existing processes only single-figure improvements may be possible;
- *critical contemporary measures of performance* – this point refers to the importance of measuring how well the processes operate in terms of the four important measures of cost, quality, service and speed.

Willcocks and Smith (1995) characterise the typical changes that arise in an organisation with process innovation as:

- work units changing from functional departments to process teams;
- jobs change from simple tasks to multidimensional work;
- people's roles change from controlled to empowered;
- focus of performance changes from activities to results;
- values change from protective to productive.

In *Re-engineering the Corporation* Hammer and Champy have a chapter giving examples of how IS can act as a catalyst for change (disruptive technologies). These technologies are familiar from those described earlier (in Chapter 6) and include tracking technology, decision support tools, telecommunications networks, teleconferencing and shared databases. Hammer and Champy label these as 'disruptive technologies' which can force companies to reconsider their processes and find new ways of operating.

Many re-engineering projects were launched in the 1990s and failed due to their ambitious scale and the problems of managing large information systems projects. Furthermore, BPR was also often linked to downsizing in many organisations, leading to an outflow of staff and knowledge from businesses. As a result BPR as a concept has fallen out of favour and more caution in achieving change is advocated.

Business process improvement (BPI)

Optimising existing processes typically coupled with enhancements in information technology.

Less radical approaches to organisational transformation are referred to as **business process improvement (BPI)** or by Davenport (1993) as 'business process innovation'. Taking the example of a major e-business initiative for supply chain management, an organisation would have to decide on the scope of change. For instance, do all supply chain activities need to be revised simultaneously or can certain activities such as procurement or outbound logistics be targeted initially? Modern thinking would suggest that the latter approach is preferable.

Business process automation (BPA)

Automating existing ways of working manually through information technology.

If a less radical approach is adopted, care should be taken not to fall into the trap of simply using technology to automate existing processes which are sub-optimal – in plain words, using information technology 'to do bad things faster'. This approach of using technology to support existing procedures and practices is known as **business process automation (BPA)**. Although benefits can be achieved through this approach, the improvements may not be sufficient to generate a return on investment. These alternative terms for business process change are summarised in Table 12.5.

Table 12.5 Alternative terms for using IS to enhance company performance

Term	Involves	Intention	Risk of failure
Business process re-engineering	Fundamental redesign of all main company processes through organisation-wide initiatives	Large gains in performance (>100%?)	Highest
Business process improvement	Targets key processes in sequence for redesign	(<50%)	Medium
Business process automation	Automating existing process Often uses workflow software	(<20%)	Lowest

A staged approach to the introduction of BPR has been suggested by Davenport (1993). This can also be applied to e-business change. He suggests the following stages that can be applied to e-business as follows:

- *Identify the process for innovation* – these are the major business processes from the organisation's value chain which add most to the value for the customer or achieve the largest efficiency benefits for the company. Examples include customer relationship management, logistics and procurement.

- *Identify the change levers* – these can encourage and help achieve change. The main change levers are innovative technology and, as we have seen, the organisation's culture and structure.

- *Develop the process vision* – this involves communication of the reasons for changes and what can be achieved in order to help achieve buy-in throughout the organisation.

- *Understand the existing processes* – current business processes are documented. This allows the performance of existing business processes to be benchmarked and so provide a means for measuring the extent to which a re-engineered process has improved business performance.

- *Design and prototype the new process* – the vision is translated into practical new processes which the organisation is able to operate. Peppard and Rowland (1995) provide a number of areas for the potential design of processes under the headings of Eliminate, Simplify, Integrate and Automate (ESIA) (see Table 12.6). Prototyping the new process operates on two levels. First, simulation and modelling tools can be used to check the logical operation of the process. Second, assuming that the simulation model shows no significant problems, the new process can be given a full operational trial. Needless to say, the implementation must be handled sensitively if it is to be accepted by all parties.

Table 12.6 ESIA areas for potential redesign

Eliminate	Simplify	Integrate	Automate
Over-production	Forms	Jobs	Dirty
Waiting time	Procedures	Teams	Difficult
Transport	Communication	Customers	Dangerous
Processing	Technology	Suppliers	Boring
Inventory	Problem areas		Data capture
Defects/failures	Flows		Data transfer
Duplication	Processes		Data analysis
Reformatting			
Inspection			
Reconciling			

Source: Peppard and Rowland, 1995.

Business process management (BPM)

Business process management (BPM)

Both a philosophy towards process change and a collection of supporting technologies for process change.

Business process management (BPM) is an important approach to process management that can be considered both in terms of a philosophy towards process change and as a supporting technology to process change in the form of tools for process design.

The philosophy of BPM recognises that business processes, and the way they are managed, are the key mechanisms that allow the organisation to deliver value to its customers. The approach thus entails an analysis of the structure of the organisation, the way people work together and the way technology is utilised. The focus of business process change will be provided by performance objectives for business processes that are derived from an analysis of how the company achieves its competitive advantage. Due to the far-reaching nature of the BPM approach it is likely that in most organisations a significant degree of organisational change, including a change of culture will be required. These aspects are covered in the later organisational culture section in this chapter.

Underpinning the philosophy of BPM are a number of process design tools that allow the approach to be put into operation. These tools include process maps, business process simulation, business activity monitoring and service-oriented architecture.

CASE STUDY 12.1

Business-process management (BPM)

When image document circulation first appeared in the 1990s, the idea of applying computer technology to this kind of labour-intensive business process was considered cutting edge. Everyone in IT understood the potential of centralised computing for numerical computation and transaction processing, but few envisioned that this type of application would fit a broader set of distributed business processes.

Since the 1990s, leading companies have found more innovative ways to automate their business processes. E-forms, process modelling, simulation, EAI, integration services, rules engines, event services, real-time monitoring and process analytics are among the systems being applied to processes that include order management, billing, financial reporting, credit-card issuance, product returns and dispute resolution.

IT and operations executives have now understood that their current technology has done little to link the processes that run their companies to the transactions that result from those processes – transactions at the heart of corporate growth and profitability. This disconnect is rooted in a basic misunderstanding of the purpose of enterprise resource planning (ERP) and the role of business-process management – relationships that are now examined more carefully.

It is no secret that work gets done by people through business processes and that technology only supports those processes, whether distributing goods to customers, collaborating with suppliers, or co-ordinating employee efforts, business processes add value to products and brands.

Yet most ERP systems have a functional focus and lack process models that explain business operations. As a result, when managers tried to innovate or solve business problems – customer satisfaction was one of the most widespread – the 'fix' is often myopic and transaction-centric. What is missing is good business-process management.

Business-process management provides methods to automate and/or improve activities and tasks for particular business purposes. Its goal is not only efficiency and productivity, but also control, responsiveness and improvement. Control assures that company resources are aligned to execute strategies. Responsiveness and improvement support the competitive differentiation that enables a company to excel.

IT executives can assert control by basing the direction and flow of transactions on a predefined set of rules and work flows – for example, determining how a purchase order is acknowledged or merchandise is returned. Responsiveness enables individuals to react quickly to business events and maximise interactions, as when expediting a critical customer order across the customer-service and warehouse teams. As for improvement, you want to systematically measure and monitor processes; doing so will lead to innovation and optimal performance.

An integral part of business-process management is performance management, which is intended to steer the organisation and its partners toward corporate goals. Performance management focuses on the collaboration and empowerment of all individuals in the business network or value chain. It enables them to work across strategic, tactical and operational levels to align actions that produce rapid and effective responses to business challenges.

In the same way you define and document processes, you need to detail performance-management objectives. These objectives are the analytics used to measure all process-improvement projects. The metrics will provide the basis for an ongoing cycle of measurement, evaluation and improvement. It is also critical that your company tie these process-improvement metrics to high-level performance-improvement goals, not to low-level or transaction-oriented metrics.

Done right, performance management should shed light on why some processes do not function well and how to go about improving them. During analysis, the tools will provide the project teams with data to assess the productivity impact of proposed solutions. That data should also help business and IT departments arrive at a common understanding of particular business needs and their solutions. Collaboration between these groups is particularly important in good business process management.

Once you have addressed the overall issue of performance management and built the framework for a sustainable business-process management practice, you can begin to assess requirements for the IT systems that will support it. For this part of the project, five components are necessary: assessing current systems, building a business case, developing and communicating the plan, evaluating software and architecture options and, lastly, deploying the initiative. Here is further detail on each of the steps.

First, conduct an independent assessment of the process you want to innovate and the systems that currently support it. Establish a benchmark for the current levels of efficiency and effectiveness, and then identify areas for improvement. Of course, you will need to evaluate financial and operational requirements in this approach, including ROI and total-cost-of-ownership calculations.

Next, build a business case to demonstrate the value and results that the project will deliver, citing clear definitions of the value and cost of your programme, as well as compelling productivity and financial reasons for going ahead. Address the cultural, business and technology barriers to ensure you have support for your initiative.

Third, create a well-defined plan and communicate it to the process owners and participants. This will have to be articulated at different levels of the organisation, so make clear to all stakeholders what is in it for them. It should also show how the effectiveness of operations will improve through this process innovation.

After that, architecture and software needs should be identified in several ways. First, evaluate solutions with appropriate criteria to ensure that the programme is timely and responsive to the organisation. Consolidation in the business software market has changed the landscape of business-process management systems significantly. It has been recommended that you evaluate all viable options including service-oriented architectures. Also, be wary of promises from vendors of single solutions that do only BAM or only process modelling – these products may not be functionally rich enough.

It was also recommended to keep performance management capabilities in mind when making vendor evaluations as good business-process management requires both simulation and BAM tools. Simulation aids process design and modelling by letting designers preview how a process flows and look at how the logic, events and rules work together – before the process is rolled out into a production environment. Using such a tool should discover and remove bottlenecks and accurately predict process performance. The best process models allow multiple simulation scenarios to be performed across sub-processes. The engine should be able to track resource usage, including cost and time analysis, and monitor usage that exceeds preset thresholds.

Other things to consider: a robust simulation tool will allow you to deploy new versions of processes without interrupting those already in use and the best solutions allow controlled migration from old processes to new ones. This capability is critical not only for safety reasons but also for benchmarking and measuring results.

Business-activity monitoring aggregates, analyses and presents relevant and timely internal information as well as data involving your customers and partners. BAM solutions can alert individuals to changes in the business that may require action from them. Once again, the purpose is to produce rapid insight into process innovations by identifying issues in real time, improving process performance and reducing operating costs.

Most BAM solutions provide post-process metrics, such as when and how many times the process was executed and which user performed which tasks. Some go further to provide visual representations of business activity with maps, technical drawings, charts, blueprints or graphs.

However, keep in mind that real-time process monitoring requires considerable development and integration work. Consider tying these activities to a company's performance management objectives, measuring and tracking them in an active, balanced scorecard. It is well worth the effort. After all, how will you know if you are aligning current process activities to your performance objectives if you don't properly score the results?

Once you have evaluated all software and architecture options, the fifth and final step is to roll out your solution and ensure widespread adoption of your business-process management initiative. To succeed, you must understand how to minimise interruptions to your current business processes, culture and technology usage.

➡

Make sure you do not skip any of these steps – especially the second, where you benchmark your current process performance and build a business case. Doing so will enable you to showcase the value of your innovation after adoption. Following these steps will increase efficiency and effectiveness and improve the alignment of your operational processes. Through a simple organisation-wide approach, you can transform your staff, processes and systems in an efficient manner that ultimately will be reflected on the company's bottom line.

Source: Based on *Optimize,* September 2005, Issue 47

Tools for business process management

Tools and techniques that are used to assist in the implementation of the business process management approach include:

- diagramming techniques such as process mapping;
- modelling techniques such as business process simulation (BPS);
- improvement approaches such as business process reengineering (BPR);
- implementation of information technologies such as workflow systems;
- use of performance management technologies such as business activity monitoring (BAM);
- use of the service-oriented architecture (SOA) and web services.

BPR is considered earlier is this section. (Workflow systems are covered in Chapter 6 and BAM is covered in Chapter 4.) This section now considers process mapping, business process simulation, service-oriented architecture and web services.

Process mapping

Process mapping

The use of a flowchart to document the process incorporating process activities and decision points.

Documenting the process can be undertaken by the construction of a **process map**, also called a flowchart. This is a useful way of understanding any business process and showing the interrelationships between activities in a process. For larger projects it may be necessary to represent a given process at several levels of detail. Thus a single activity may be shown as a series of sub-activities on a separate diagram. Table 12.7 shows the representations used in a simple process mapping diagram.

Figure 12.3 shows a process map of activities undertaken by traffic police in response to a road traffic accident (RTA) incident in the UK. The process map shows that following the notification of a road traffic incident to the police by the public, a decision is made to attend

Table 12.7 Symbols used for a process map

Meaning	Symbol
Process/activity	▭
Decision point	◇
Start/end point	◯
Direction of flow	→

Figure 12.3 A road traffic accident reporting process map

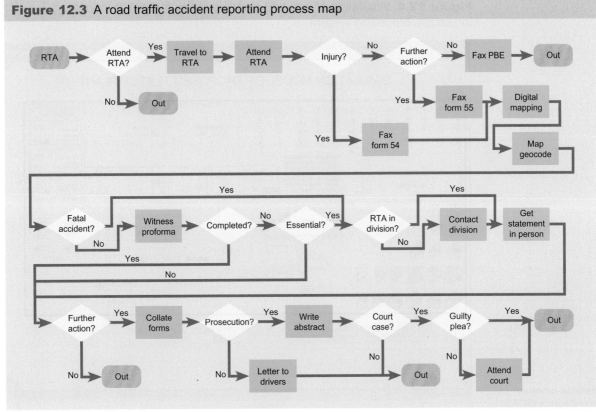

the scene of the incident. If it is necessary to attend the RTA scene the officer travels to the location of the incident. After an assessment is made of the incident the officer returns to the station to complete and submit the appropriate paperwork. If a court case is scheduled and a not guilty plea has been entered then the officer will be required to attend the court proceedings in person. Otherwise this is the end of the involvement of the officer.

Process maps are useful in a number of ways. For example, the actual procedure of building a process map helps people define roles and see who else does what. This can be particularly relevant to public-sector organisations in which modelling existing processes can be used to build consensus on what currently happens. The process map can also serve as a first step in using business process simulation as it identifies the processes and decision points required to build the model.

Business process simulation

The use of a simulation model on a computer to mimic the operation of a business means that the performance of the business over an extended time period can be observed quickly and under a number of different scenarios. **Business process simulation (BPS)** is usually implemented using discrete-event simulation systems which move through time in (discrete) steps. BPS software is implemented using graphical user interfaces employing objects or icons that are placed on the screen to produce a model (see Figure 12.4).

Although BPS requires a significant investment in time and skills it is able to provide a more realistic assessment of the behaviour of organisational processes than most other process design tools. This is due to its ability to incorporate the dynamic (i.e. time-dependent) behaviour of organisational systems. The two aspects of dynamic systems which need to be addressed are variability and interdependence. Most business systems contain variability in both the demand on the system (e.g. customer arrivals) and the durations (e.g. customer service times) of activities within the system. The use of fixed

Business process simulation

The use of computer software, in the context of a process-based change, that allows operation of a business to be simulated.

Figure 12.4 Simulation of a textile plant using the ARENA™ Visual Interactive Modelling system

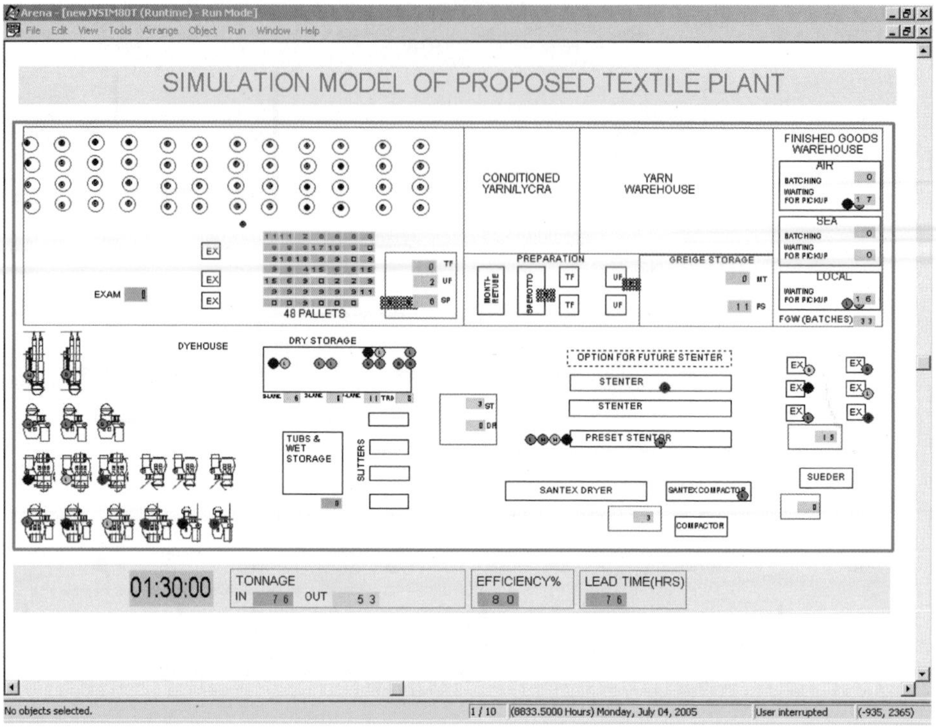

Source: Courtesy of Oracle Corporation

Service-oriented architecture (SOA)

An approach that incorporates reusable business-aligned IT services that can be utilised in a manner that is independent of the underlying application and technology platforms.

Service inventory/ service catalogue

A collection of standardised services that are designed to be used in a number of business processes.

Service composition

A selection of services from the service inventory that are allocated to a particular business process.

Interoperability

The ability to allow computer systems from different manufacturers to work together.

Loose coupling

The capability of services to be joined together on demand to create composite services.

(e.g. average) values will provide some indication of performance, but simulation permits the incorporation of statistical distributions and thus provides an indication of both the range and variability of the performance of the system. Most organisational systems also contain a number of decision points that affect the overall performance of the system. The simulation technique can also incorporate the 'knock-on' effect of these many interdependent decisions over time.

Service-oriented architecture (SOA)

The concept of **SOA** is to develop a number of reusable business-aligned IT services that span multiple applications across the organisation. SOA defines the services in such a way as to be utilised in a manner that is independent of the underlying application and technology platforms. A collection of standardised services forms the basis of a **service inventory** or **service catalogue**. Individual services from the service inventory can be deployed in multiple business processes. Each collection of services used in a particular business process is termed a **service composition**. The advantage of this approach for business process management is that a business process can link with the business services which are activated by the business processes without the need to know about the underlying application and technology platforms. The relationship between the business process, services, application and technology layers is shown in Figure 12.5. The use of SOA provides **interoperability**, the ability to allow computer systems from different manufacturers to work together and **loose coupling**, the capability of services to be joined together on demand to create composite services. These capabilities are particularly useful in increasing the flexibility of enterprise systems covered earlier (in Chapter 6). Read Case Study 12.2 'Service-oriented architecture' for more details of SOA.

Figure 12.5 Relationship between the business process, services, application and technology layers in the organisation

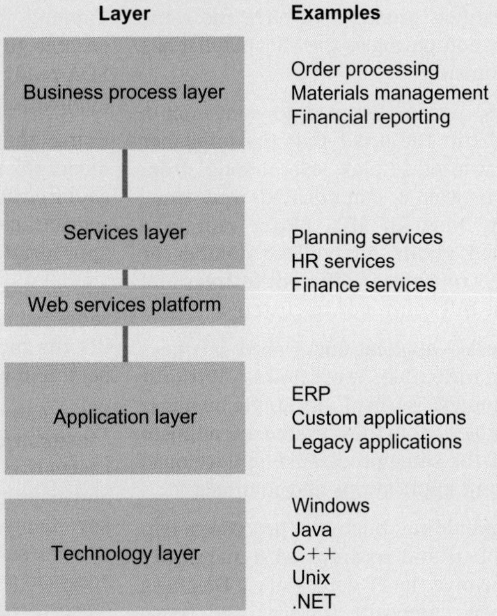

Web services

A collection of industry standards which represents the most likely technology connecting services together to form a service-oriented architecture.

WSDL (web services description language)

Provides a means to define the functionality of a web service in terms of the XML schema definition language

SOAP (simple object access protocol)

Consists of a framework for XML format messages sent between distributed information systems.

Web services

SOA will most often be implemented on the web platform and the term web services is used for the technology which is derived from the convergence of service-oriented architecture and internet technologies. The web services platform is defined through a number of industry standards including WSDL (web services description language) which provides a means to define the functionality of a web service in terms of the XML schema definition language (Chapter 11). Another standard SOAP (simple object access protocol) consists of a framework for XML format messages sent between distributed information systems.

In practical terms a web service is really just reusable software code that can be combined with other web services to develop new applications. In order to use a web service a consumer searches for existing services in a web services registry either inside the organisation (private registry) or outside the organisation (public registry). Once the service is found it is retrieved and a fee is paid if appropriate. The service provider is then able to provide the web service to the service consumer.

CASE STUDY 12.2

Play pick-and-mix to innovate with SOA

By George Ravich, Executive Vice-President and Chief Marketing Officer of Fundtech

Business opportunities abound for financial institutions with the flexibility and agility to respond to rapidly changing market conditions and regulatory pressures. But when it requires a lengthy IT project to create new products or services, those business opportunities remain tantalisingly out of reach.

Services-Oriented Architecture offers the ability for non-technical business users to build new products and

➡

services by picking and choosing from existing processes contained within an "SOA services catalogue".

An SOA services catalog promises to have the same impact on enterprise computing as the MP3 playlist has had on listening to music.

Before MP3 players, people listened to songs on a vinyl record or a CD in the order that the publisher determined. If you wanted to play several songs from different albums, it was a complicated and time-consuming activity. Now an MP3 player can take individual songs and create an endless number of playlists. Each song is reusable in different settings and situations, under the full control of the listener.

Before SOA, enterprise applications placed business processes within inflexible workflows. Without extensive IT development, reuse of any single business process was not feasible within these systems, leading to multiple versions of the same process being developed separately for different applications and channels.

Now, with SOA, individual business processes can be discovered, modified and recombined dynamically without having to involve the IT department. Business users can create new composite services and reuse services outside of their original context.

In the current environment, it is virtually impossible to define in advance the workflow that best fits the needs of the business. With services-oriented payments architecture (Sopa), managers can respond to the evolving needs of the business by tapping into a complete set of reusable, SOA-enabled business assets.

An example would be a fee calculation for a foreign exchange transaction. Given any currency pair, an amount, a transaction date and a customer type, the fee calculation service would determine the applicable fee to the customer. Usually, a function such as this would be part of a point solution for foreign exchange

capabilities, and you would only be able to use it in a prescribed set of circumstances.

Tapping into the SOA services catalog, you would be able to embed the same fee calculator into other SOA-ready systems, including web applications, mobile applications, branch applications and ATM systems.

Using the fee calculator, product specialists could model the revenue impact of a price change, marketers could craft special offers for preferred customers, and service agents could help customers to choose the most appropriate service plan.

All of these business users would be able to use the same fee calculation service, with the knowledge that it's the most up-to-date version available, meeting all pertinent regulatory standards and company policies.

Sopa can transform an enterprise from a reactive consumer of pre-built systems into an active creator of innovative new services. Whether it's modifying terms and conditions, updating service-level agreements for key clients or creating new products based on parts of existing services, business users will have unprecedented access to powerful capabilities without having to embark on costly and time-consuming IT projects.

Instead, they will have a nimble response to external regulatory pressures, and be able to build products faster, and deploy new capabilities at a cost advantage to competitors.

The role of IT doesn't go away with the adoption of SOA. When it's time to improve the underlying services by making them faster or more efficient, or when expanded capabilities are called for, IT developers can create new versions of existing services or build entirely new ones.

Once completed, these new and improved services are immediately available through the SOA services catalog for enterprise use.

QUESTIONS

Explain the advantages and disadvantages of the SOA approach

Achieving organisational change

Approaches such as business process management are concerned with the implementation of change involving both IS systems and employees. Implementation of processes that are performed by employees requires consideration of organisational change management including factors such as managing a change in culture.

An essential part of managing change associated with IS introduction is education to communicate the purpose of the system to the staff – in other words, to sell the system to them. It is not sufficient to simply provide training in the use of the software. This education should target all employees in the organisation who will be affected by the change. It involves:

- explaining why the system is being implemented;
- explaining how staff will be affected;
- treating users as customers by involving them in specification, testing and review;
- training users in use of the software;
- above all, listening to users and acting on what they say.

Kurt Lewin and Edgar Schein suggested a model for achieving organisational change that involves three stages:

1. Unfreeze the present position by creating a climate of change through education, training and motivation of future participants.
2. Quickly move from the present position by developing and implementing the new system.
3. Refreeze by making the system an accepted part of the way the organisation works.

Note that Lewin and Schein did not collaborate on developing this model of personal and organisational change. Lewin developed the model in unpublished work and this was then extended by Edgar Schein who undertook research into psychology based on Lewin's ideas (Schein, 1956). Later, Kurt Lewin summarised some of his ideas (Lewin, 1972). More recently, Schein (1992) concluded that three variables are critical to the success of any organisational change:

1. the degree to which the leaders can break from previous ways of working;
2. the significance and comprehensiveness of the change;
3. the extent to which the head of the organisation is actively involved in the change process.

'Change' was defined by Kurt Lewin as a transition from an existing quasi-equilibrium to a new quasi-equilibrium. This model was updated and put into an organisational context by Kolb and Frohman (1970). Although this is now an old model, it remains relevant to the implementation of information systems today.

Organisational culture

Culture

This concept includes shared values, unwritten rules and assumptions within the organisation as well as the practices that all groups share. Corporate cultures are created when a group of employees interact over time and are relatively successful in what they undertake.

Understanding social relationships within an organisation, which are part of its culture, is also an important aspect of change management. The efficiency of any organisation is dependent on the complex formal and informal relationships that exist within it. Formal relationships include the hierarchical work relationships within and between functional business areas. Informal relationships are created through people working and socialising with each other on a regular basis and will cut across functional boundaries. Major change, such as the move to e-business, has the capacity to alter both types of relationships as it brings about change within and between functional business areas.

Schein (1992) also claims that the notion of organisational culture provides useful guidance on what must be changed within a corporate culture, if organisational change is to be successfully accomplished. He provides a threefold classification of culture that helps to identify what needs to be done:

- Assumptions are the invisible core elements of an organisation's culture such as a shared collective vision within the organisation. One of the challenges in change management is to question core assumptions where appropriate, especially if they are seen to be obstructing organisational change.
- Values are preferences that guide behaviour such as attitudes towards dress codes and punctuality within an organisation or ethics within a society. Often such values

are transmitted by word of mouth rather than being enshrined in written documents or policy statements. As with organisational assumptions, values are hard to change, especially when the views that embody them are firmly held.

- Artefacts are tangible material elements of cultural elements. These will be identifiable from the language used in the policies, procedures and acronyms of the organisation, and the spoken word and dialects of the society. In some ways they are also the easiest to change. Policies can be created or rewritten, but it is the organisation's values and assumptions that will determine how they are perceived and acted upon.

The implications of organisational culture for information systems implementation are important. While the 'artefacts' associated with information systems developments may be clear, it is the 'assumptions' and 'values' that will ultimately determine the success of the implementation and it is to these that the change management process must be largely directed.

Boddy et al. (2005) summarise four different types of cultural orientation that may be identified in different companies. These vary according to the extent to which the company is inward-looking or outward-looking, in other words to what extent it is affected by its environment. They also reflect whether the company is structured and formal or has a more flexible, dynamic, informal character. The four cultural types of cultural orientation are:

1. *Survival (outward-looking, flexible)* – the external environment plays a significant role (an open system) in governing company strategy. The company is likely to be driven by customer demands and will be an innovator. It may have a relatively flat structure.

2. *Productivity (outward-looking, ordered)* – interfaces with the external environment are well structured and the company is typically sales-driven and is likely to have a hierarchical structure.

3. *Human relations (inward-looking, flexible)* – this is the organisation as family, with interpersonal relations more important than reporting channels, a flatter structure and staff development, and empowerment is thought of important by managers.

4. *Stability (inward-looking, ordered)* – the environment is essentially ignored with managers concentrating on internal efficiency and again managed through a hierarchical structure.

Different approaches to change management that may be required according to the type of culture are explored in the activity.

Activity 12.1	Changing the culture for e-business

The purpose of this activity is to identify appropriate cultural changes that may be necessary for e-business success.

Review the four general categories of organisational cultural orientation summarised by Boddy et al. (2005) and take each as characterising four different companies and then suggest which will most readily respond to the change required for a move to an e-business. State whether you think the cultures are most likely to occur in a small organisation or a larger organisation.

Achieving user involvement

Efforts should be made to involve as many staff as possible in the development. The following types of involvement (summarised by Regan and O'Connor, 2001) can occur in a systems development project:

1. *Non-involvement* – here, users are unwilling to participate or are not invited to.

2. *Involvement by advice* – user advice is solicited through interviews or questionnaires during analysis.

3. *Involvement by sign-off* – users approve the results produced by the project team, such as requirements specifications.

4. *Involvement by design team membership* – active participation occurs in analysis and design activities (including interviews of other users, creation of functional specifications and prototyping).

5. *Involvement by project team membership* – user participation occurs throughout the project since the user manages and owns the project.

While it will not be practical to involve everyone, representatives of all job functions should be polled for their requirements for the system at the analysis stage. As many user and manager representatives as possible should be involved in the active analysis and design involved in prototyping.

Promotion of the system can also be achieved by appointing particular managers to champion the new system:

- Senior managers or board members are used as system sponsors. Sponsors are keen that the system should work and will fire up staff with their enthusiasm and stress why introducing the system is important to the business and its workers.

- System owners are managers in the organisation who will use the system to create the business benefits envisaged.

- Stakeholders should be identified at every location in which the system will be used. These people should be respected by their co-workers and will again act as a source of enthusiasm for the system. The user representatives used in specification and testing can also fill this role.

- Legitimisers protect the norms and values of the system; they are experienced in their job and regarded as the experts by fellow workers; they may initially be resistant to change and therefore need to be involved early.

- Opinion leaders are people whom others watch to see whether they accept new ideas and changes. They usually have little formal power, but are regarded as good 'ideas' people who are receptive to change, and again need to be involved early in the project.

System sponsors

System sponsors are senior managers or board members who are responsible for a system at a senior level in a company.

System owners

These are managers who are directly responsible for the operational use of a system.

Stakeholders

All staff who have a direct interest in the system.

Resistance to change

Some resistance to change is inevitable, but this is particularly true with the introduction of systems associated with business process re-engineering, because of the way that work is performed and people's job functions will be changed. If the rationale behind the change is not explained, then all the classic symptoms of resistance to change will be apparent. Resistance to change usually follows a set pattern. For example, Hopson and Scully (1997) have used the transition curve in Figure 12.6 to describe the change from when staff first hear about a system to when the change becomes accepted.

While outright hostility manifesting itself as sabotage of the system is not unheard of, what is more common is that users will try to project blame on to the system and will identify major faults where only minor bugs exists. This will obviously damage the reputation of the system and senior managers will want to know what went wrong with the project. Another problem that can occur if the system has not been introduced well is avoidance of the system, with users working around the system to continue their previous ways of working. Careful management is necessary to ensure that this does not happen. To summarise the way in which resistance to change may manifest itself, the following may be evident:

- *aggression* – in which there may be physical sabotage of the system, deliberate entry of erroneous data or abuse of systems staff;

- *projection* – where the system is wrongly blamed for difficulties encountered while using it;

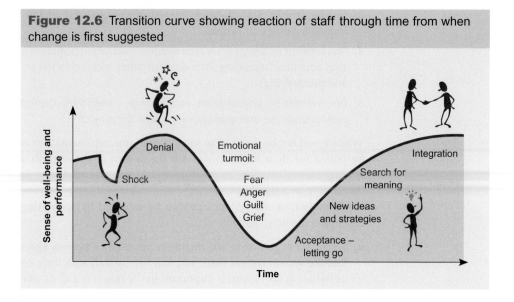

Figure 12.6 Transition curve showing reaction of staff through time from when change is first suggested

- *avoidance* – withdrawal from or avoidance of interaction with the system, non-input of data, reports and enquiries ignored, or use of manual substitutes for the system.

There are many understandable reasons for people to resist the technological change that comes from the development of new information systems. These include:

- social uncertainty;
- limited perspectives and lack of understanding;
- threats to power and influence of managers (loss of control);
- perception that costs of the new system outweigh the benefits;
- fear of failure, inadequacy or redundancy.

It is evident that training and education can be used to counter many of these issues. Additionally, other steps can be taken to reduce resistance to change, namely:

- ensure early participation and involvement of users;
- set realistic goals and raise realistic expectations of benefits;
- build in user-friendliness to the new system;
- don't promise too much and deliver what was promised;
- develop a reliable system that is easy to maintain;
- ensure support of the various stakeholders;
- bring about agreement through negotiation.

Training

Appropriate education and training are important in implementation. Many companies make the mistake of not training staff sufficiently for a new system. This is often because of the cost of training or of taking staff away from their daily work for several days. If companies do provide training, it is often the wrong sort. Practical, operational training in how to use the software, such as which menu options are available and which buttons to press, is common. What is sometimes missing is ideological training: an explanation of why the system is being brought in – why are the staff's existing ways of working being overturned? This educational part of training is very important. Previous projects or examples of how systems have improved the business of competitors may be used here.

SUMMARY

Stage summary: systems build

Purpose:	To produce a working system
Key activities:	Programming (coding), system and user documentation, testing
Input:	Design specification and requirements specification
Output:	Preliminary working system which can be tested by end-users

Stage summary: systems implementation

Purpose:	To install the system in the live environment
Key activities:	Install computers and software, user acceptance test, change-over, sign off
Input:	Preliminary versions of software
Output:	Tested, release version of software

Stage summary: systems maintenance

Purpose:	To ensure system remains available to end-users
Key activities:	Monitoring errors, reviewing and fixing problems, releasing patches
Input:	Tested, release version of software
Output:	Revised version of software

1. The build stage of systems development involves programming, testing and transferring data from the old system to the new system.

2. The main types of testing are unit testing of individual modules, system testing of the whole system by developers and user acceptance testing by the business. Sufficient time for testing must be built in using a quality assurance system to ensure that the delivered system is of the right quality.

3. The implementation stage involves managing the changeover from the old sys-tem to the new system. There are several alternative changeover approaches that can be used together if required:

   ■ run the old and new systems in parallel;
   ■ a phased approach where different modules are gradually introduced;
   ■ cutover immediately to the new system;
   ■ pilot the system in one area or office before 'rolling out' on a larger scale.

4. Some of the main reasons that information systems projects may fail at the build or implementation stage include:

   ■ *Forgetting the human issues.* New systems are usually accompanied by a new way of working, so managers need to explain through training why the change is occurring and then train people adequately in the use of the system.
   ■ *Cutting corners through using RAD.* Some corners cannot be cut, especially in design, optimising system performance and testing. If insufficient time is spent on these activities, the system may fail. Documentation may also be omitted, which is serious during maintenance.
   ■ *Computer resources are inadequate.* The project managers need staff to check, for example, that the server can handle the load at critical times of the day, such as when scanning is occurring or at peak times in a call centre. Checks will also be made to ensure that the system performance does not degrade as the number of users of the systems or customers' records held increase.
   ■ *Poor management of change process.* Staff who are involved with the new system should be trained so that they can use the software easily and understand the reasons for its introduction.
   ■ *Lack of support from the top or from stakeholders.* Top management and appropriate stakeholders must support the cultural changes necessary to introduce the new system.
   ■ *Using a big-bang method of changeover.* Using this approach is high-risk unless there has been extensive testing and methodical design.

5. The maintenance phase is concerned with managing the system once it is live. This will involve responding to errors as they are found. If serious, the problems will have to be solved immediately through issuing a 'patch' release to the system; otherwise they will be recorded for a later release.

6. A post-implementation review will occur to assess the success of the systems development project so that lessons are recorded for future projects.

7. Change management can be considered at the software, IS and organisational levels.

8. Software change management involves managing the process of modification to software thought to be necessary be business users or developers.

9. IS change management involves managing the change from the old to the new information system. The four main alternative methods of changeover are immediate cutover, parallel running, phased implementation and pilot system.

10. Organisational change management deals with managing changes to organisational processes, structures and their impact on organisational staff and culture. Business process management (BPM) provides a methodology for change management in the organisation.

EXERCISES

Self-assessment exercises

1. What are the main activities that occur in the build and implementation phases of a systems development project?

2. What is the difference between unit and system testing?

3. How can resistance to change among staff affect a new information system?

4. What are the most important factors in reducing resistance to change?

5. Why is it important to manage software change requests carefully?

6. What is the difference between the direct changeover method and the parallel changeover method?

7. What is the best option for an end-user to program a system?

8. What is the purpose of a post-implementation review?

9. What is the purpose of the concept of SOA?

Discussion questions

1. 'All the different project changeover methods are likely to be used on any large project.' Discuss.

2. 'The most important aspect of software quality assurance is to make sure that bugs are identified during the testing phase.' Discuss.

3. 'Companies should aim to minimise the number of patch releases, provided that no serious system errors occur.' Discuss.

4. 'The combination of BPM and SOA is more powerful than either is alone.' Discuss.

Essay questions

1. You are a business manager responsible for the successful implementation of a new information system. What problems would you anticipate from staff when the new system is introduced? What measures could you take to minimise these?

2. Discuss the advantages and disadvantages of the different methods of changeover from an old system to a new one. Which is the optimal method?

3. Discuss the philosophy and describe the tools of BPM.

Examination questions

1. Describe the direct changeover method. How does this differ from phased implementation?

2. What different classes of fault will a user be aiming to identify in a user acceptance test?

3. What are the three classical signs of resistance to change by end-users?

4. Distinguish between system testing and unit testing.

5. What different types of documentation will be used during the implementation phase of a project?

6. What elements of staff training should a new system receive?

7. What is the purpose of volume testing?

8. Which criteria should be used to measure the successful outcome of a systems development project?

9. In the maintenance phase of the systems development lifecycle, why might an information system need to be maintained?

10. Briefly outline the considerations that a company needs to take into account in deciding between the two main methods of changeover to a new information system: direct and parallel running.

11. Evaluate the concept of BPM.

12. How could BPS and BAM work together?

References

Boddy, D., Boonstra, A. and Kennedy, G. (2009) *Managing Information Systems: Strategy and Organisation*, 3rd edition, Financial Times Prentice Hall, Harlow

Davenport, T.H. (1993) *Process Innovation: Re-engineering Work through Information Technology*, Harvard Business School Press, Boston

Hammer, M. and Champy, J. (1993) *Re-engineering the Corporation: A Manifesto for Business Revolution*, HarperCollins, New York

Hopson, B. and Scully, M. (1997) *Transitions: Positive Change in Your Life and Work*, Prentice Hall, Harlow

Johnston, A.K. (2003) *A Hacker's Guide to Project Management*, 2nd edition, Butterworth-Heinemann, Oxford

Jones, C. (2008) *Applied Software Measurement: Global Analysis of Productivity and Quality*, 3rd Edition, McGraw-Hill, New York

Jorgenson, P. (1995) *Software Testing: A Craftsman's Approach*, CRC Press, Boca Raton, FL

Kolb, D.A. and Frohman, A.L. (1970) 'An organizational development approach to consulting', *Sloan Management Review*, 12, 51–65

Lewin, K. (1972) 'Quasi-stationary social equilibria and the problems of permanent change', in N. Margulies and A. Raia (eds), *Organizational Development: Values, Process and Technology*, McGraw-Hill, New York, pp. 65–72

Peppard, J. and Rowland, P. (1995) *The Essence of Business Process Re-engineering*, Prentice Hall, Hemel Hempstead

Regan, E.A. and O'Connor, B.N. (2001) *End-user Information Systems: Implementing Individual and Work Group Technologies*, 2nd edition, Prentice-Hall, Upper Saddle River, NJ

Schein, E. (1956) 'The Chinese indoctrination program for prisoners of war', *Psychiatry*, 19, 149–72

Schein, E. (1992) *Organizational Culture and Leadership*, Jossey Bass, San Francisco

Willcocks, L. and Smith, G. (1995) 'IT enabled business process reengineering: organisational and human resource dimension', *Strategic Information Systems*, 4, 3, 279–301

Further reading

Erl, T. (2007) *Service Oriented Architecture: Principles of Service Design*, Prentice-Hall, Upper Saddle River, NJ.

Greasley, A. (2008) *Enabling a Simulation Capability in the Organisation*, Springer Verlag.

Hallows, J. (2005) *Information Systems Project Management: How to Deliver Function and Value in Information Technology Projects*, 2nd edition, Amacom, New York.

Kerzner, H. (2013) *Project Management: A Systems Approach to Planning Scheduling and Controlling*, 11th edition, John Wiley, New York.

Newcomer, E. and Lomow, G. (2005) *Understanding SOA with Web Services*, Addison Wesley, Upper Saddle River, NJ.

Smith, H. and Fingar, P. (2006) *Business Process Management: The Third Wave*, Meghan Kiffer, Tampa, FL.

Weske, M. (2012) *Business Process Management: Concepts, Languages, Architectures*, 2nd edition, Springer, Berlin, New York.

Web links

www.bitpipe.com A repository for white papers on many IT topics including systems testing, change management and business process management. Many of these are sponsored by vendors so research is not independent.

www.bpm.com Provides news and in-depth articles about both the business and technology perspectives of business process management.

www.bptrends.com Provides a source of news and information relating to all aspects of business process change, focused on trends, directions and best practices.

www.bpmi.org Business Process Management Institute. An introduction to the concept and specifications for modelling business processes.

www.computerweekly.com This online trade paper for the IT industry has many case studies of the problems that can occur if the build process is not managed adequately.

www.cio.com CIO.com for chief information officers and IS staff has many articles related to analysis and design topics in different research centres such as security.

www.service-architecture.com Consultancy website containing information on SOA.

www.scs.org The Society for Modeling and Simulation International. Conference details and links to journal and publications.

www.scs-europe.net The Society for Modeling and Simulation: European Council. European Conference details and links to journal and publications.

www.stickyminds.com Portal with articles on software test, measurement and defect removal techniques.

Business information systems management

Introduction to Part 3

Managing BIS within an organisation involves two main elements: strategic planning; and operational management of systems, to give reliable access to IS for end-users and third parties such as customers, suppliers and distributors. In Part 3, we start by reviewing approaches to IS strategy and then go on to describe key operational aspects of IS that need to be managed. These include:

- managing the portfolio of IS/IT investments (Chapter 14);
- protecting IS from security breaches (Chapter 15);
- providing end-user services (Chapter 16);
- adhering to moral, legal and ethical constraints (Chapter 17).

The IS strategy will define the future applications portfolio of business information systems required to support the business objectives of the organisation. The IS strategy will also seek to improve the quality of information used by the company. Since information is an increasingly important asset of the company, it must be managed to ensure it is well protected and of suitable quality for decision making. IS management should also ensure that audits and appropriate follow-up actions occur to be certain that the company is complying with legal and ethical codes relating to the use of information systems. This will involve asking questions such as:

- Has the company's applications software been purchased legally?
- Is personal information accurate and well protected?

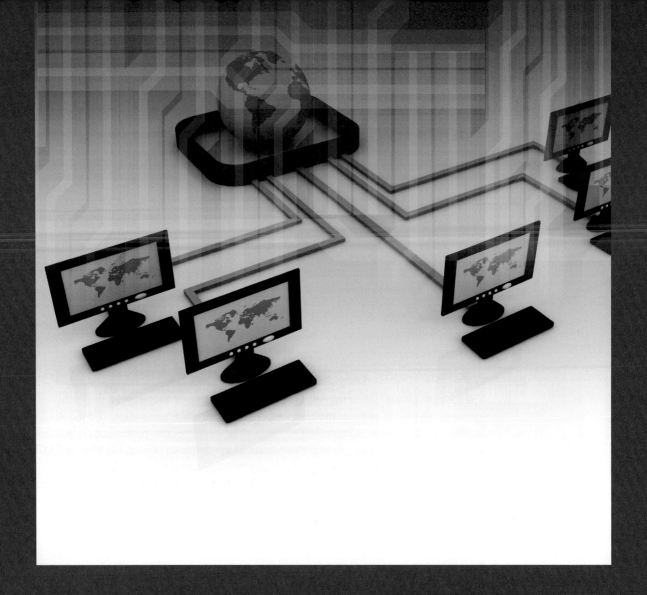

LINKS TO OTHER CHAPTERS

This chapter introduces some elements of IS strategy. It does not link directly to subsequent chapters in Part 3, since these describe specific aspects of managing information systems which are separate elements of strategy implementation. The aspects of business information systems management covered in Part 3 are managing IS/IT infrastructure (Chapter 14), protecting information quality (Chapter 15), managing end-user services in a business (Chapter 16), and professional issues such as data privacy and protection (Chapter 17). Chapter 8 in Part 2 covers cost–benefit analysis and investment appraisal for a single information system in more detail than the coverage in this chapter.

Information systems strategy

CHAPTER AT A GLANCE

MAIN TOPICS

FOCUS ON . . .

CASE STUDY

LEARNING OUTCOMES

After reading this chapter, you will be able to:

- define approaches for integrating IS strategy with business strategy;
- apply simple strategic analysis tools to determine IS strategy.

MANAGEMENT ISSUES

Annual investment in BIS is significant for many companies. But what return do organisations receive for this investment? To achieve more effective investment, a well-planned BIS strategy is required that supports the corporate goals. In this chapter we aim to answer the questions a newly installed manager seeking to develop an IS strategy would ask:

- Which process can we follow to develop an IS strategy?
- How can we ensure the IS strategy supports the business strategy?
- What analysis tools are available to assess current use of IS within the organisation and its environment and formulate IS strategy?
- Where should we locate the IS function and to what extent should some services be outsourced?

INTRODUCTION

Organisations that make the most effective use of business information systems (BIS) are those that make BIS strategy an integral part of their overall business strategy. The development of the e-business concept is intended to further support the integration of BIS with business strategy. This chapter looks at the approaches an organisation can use to develop a strategy for putting information systems in place which will support and enhance its overall business strategy.

THE STRATEGIC CONTEXT

In its original sense, 'strategy' referred to the development of plans for deceiving or outwitting an enemy. Today, corporate strategy is developed not to conquer a single competitor, but rather to compete within a chosen market. Johnson et al. (2011) use a definition that places strategy in the context of the marketplace environment and stresses its role in utilising internal resources to be best able to compete in this environment. The elements of this environment are summarised in Figure 1.2. These authors define strategy as:

> the direction and scope of an organization over the long-term: which achieves advantage for the organization through its configuration of resources within a changing environment to meet the needs of markets and to fulfil stakeholder expectations.

Strategy

Definition of the future direction and actions of a company defined as approaches to achieving specific objectives.

BIS is one of the resources deployed to help meet the needs of the market by developing and promoting new, innovative products and services that increase customer value. Most companies use a **hierarchy of strategies** to support the business strategy. For example, a marketing strategy is developed to assist in implementing the business strategy and this in turn will inform a marketing communications strategy. Similarly an information strategy will support the business strategy and this will be achieved by implementing separate IS and IT strategies as explained in the next section.

Hierarchy of strategies

A collection of sub-strategies developed to help achieve corporate objectives.

Effective use of BIS can also result in increased efficiency of internal processes and outward-facing processes which are part of supply chain management. This can help reduce costs and lead to increased profitability.

Any organisation's strategy can be rooted in four areas:

- *vision* – an image of a future direction that everyone can remember and follow;
- *mission* – a statement of what a business intends to achieve and what differentiates it from other businesses;
- *strategies* – a conditional sequence of consistent resource allocations that defines an organisation's relationships with its environment over time;
- *policies* – guidelines and procedures used in carrying out a strategy.

These areas in turn can be applied at a number of levels within an organisation:

- *corporate strategy* – view of the lines of business in which the company will participate and the allocation of resources to each line;
- *strategic business units (SBU)* – subsidiaries, divisions, product lines;

■ *functional strategy* – each functional area within a business unit must develop a course of action to support the SBU strategy. Examples include marketing strategy and logistics strategy.

This straightforward definition masks an underlying complexity of strategy. Indeed, the way in which an organisation can formulate its strategy is the subject of some debate. Claudio Ciborra (Ciborra and Jelassi, 1994) contrasts the mechanistic or prescriptive approach to business strategy with more flexible and eclectic approaches. The former is characterised by such elements as:

■ *Conscious and analytical thought*, where strategies emerge from a structured process of human thought and rigorous analysis; it is suggested that implementation can only follow when the strategy has been analytically formulated.

■ *Top-down and control orientation*, where strategy is formulated at the peak of the managerial pyramid and responsibility for strategy lies with the organisation's chief executive officer.

■ *Simple and structured models of strategy formulation*, where data analysis and internal and external scanning are undertaken so that the resulting model is clear and simple.

■ *Separation* between the formulation of strategy and its implementation; diagnosis is followed by prescription and then by action; an organisation structure must therefore follow the formulation of the strategy rather than the other way around.

Flexible, eclectic or emergent approaches, on the other hand, are characterised by responsiveness to gradual changes through evolutionary decision-making processes that often prevail in organisations that profess to adhere to formal and mechanistic approaches to strategy formulation. Mintzberg (1990), as cited by Ciborra and Jelassi (1994), questions the mechanistic, prescriptive school of thought on three counts:

1. During strategy implementation, surprises occur that question previously developed plans. To be successful, the strategic plan needs to be modified to reflect the new situation and this contradicts the previously stated rationality and rigidity that characterise the mechanistic approach. Organisational learning is also hampered by an unduly inflexible approach.

2. While the mechanistic approach to strategy features the strategist as an impartial and independent observer and participant in the strategy development process, the reality in organisations is that organisational structure, culture, inertia and politics themselves influence the strategy development process. Strategy formulation is therefore profoundly influenced by the environment it is seeking to affect.

3. The mechanistic approach to strategy formulation is an intentional process of design. However, the reality is that organisations acquire knowledge on a continual basis and this knowledge can have a profound influence on the contents of strategy and, therefore, its formulation process.

Since both corporate and IS strategy formulation will always involve the need to react to unforeseen circumstances, resulting in sudden changes to overall corporate objectives, an effective strategy formulation process must embrace adaptation, organisational learning and incremental development that reflect a constantly changing business environment.

INTRODUCTION TO BIS STRATEGY

We have seen that all business strategies must be responsive to the external environment, but what are the elements of a strategy for managing BIS and how do they relate? Ward and Peppard (2002) identify three different elements of IS strategy:

1. *Business information strategy*. This defines how information, knowledge and the applications portfolio will be used to support business objectives. Increasingly, a chief information officer (CIO) or chief knowledge officer (CKO) who is part of, or reports to the senior management team is appointed to be responsible for defining and implementing this strategy.

2. *IS functionality strategy*. This defines, in more detail, the requirements for e-business services delivered by the range of business applications (the **applications portfolio**).

3. *IT strategy (IS/IT strategy)*. This defines the software and hardware standards and suppliers which make up the e-business infrastructure.

Applications portfolio

The range of different types of business information systems deployed within an organisation.

IT strategy

Determination of the most appropriate technological infrastructure comprising hardware, networks and software applications.

IS strategy

Determination of the most appropriate processes and resources to ensure that information provision supports business strategy.

These strategies are part of the organisation's hierarchy of strategies discussed in the previous section.

IT strategy determines the technological infrastructure of the organisation. It ensures the most appropriate technologies and best standards are used in terms of cost, efficiency and supporting the needs of the business users and integration with customers and other partners. A recent strategic decision taken by many companies is to use the Internet protocol (IP) to support deployment of business applications via an intranet. The hardware and software elements of the IT infrastructure were described earlier (in Chapters 3 to 6). Approaches for controlling the total cost of ownership (TCO) of the IT infrastructure are described earlier (in Chapter 16).

IS strategy determines how IT is applied within an organisation. It should ensure that the IT deployed supports business strategies and that the appropriate resources and processes are in place for the deployment to be effective.

Note that, in reality, there is some overlap between elements of IS and IT strategy. For example, it can be argued that the selection of the optimal portfolio of software applications is an aspect of both IS and IT strategy. For this reason a convention preferred by many authors such as Ward and Peppard (2002) refers to both elements together (IS/IT strategy). This convention is used in this chapter.

The relationship between these elements is indicated in Figure 13.1. It is evident that these three elements can be considered to be hierarchical. Here, business information strategy should be driven by the objectives of the business strategy – by its information needs. IS functionality, delivered by BIS applications, should in turn be driven by the

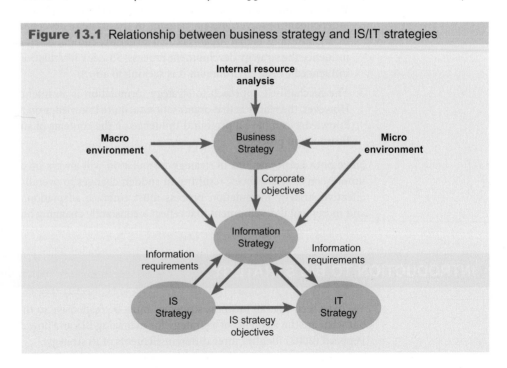

Figure 13.1 Relationship between business strategy and IS/IT strategies

information requirements of the organisation, and finally IT strategy is the implementation of IS strategy through the delivery of IT infrastructure. Such a model is useful for debate. For example, does this model represent reality in most organisations? Do organisations have separate information, IS and IT strategies? What are the benefits and disadvantages of this approach? Although the top-down approach implies strong control of IS and alignment with business strategy, it may have limited responsiveness in taking advantage of opportunities provided by IS. If IS strategy development identifies a business opportunity it is difficult to feed this back up the hierarchy to be incorporated into the business strategy. We return to this issue in a later section where we review the merits of business-impacting and business-aligning techniques.

The importance of a coherent strategy to manage information is highlighted by Willcocks and Plant (2000) who found in a study of 58 major corporations in the USA, Europe and Australasia that the leading companies were astute at *distinguishing the contributions of information and technology, and considering them separately*. They make the point that competitive advantage *comes not from technology, but how information is collected stored, analysed and applied*.

IS/IT strategy and an organisation's environment

All organisations operate within an environment that influences the way in which they conduct business. Strategy development is strongly influenced by considering the environment the business operates in. Environmental influences can be broken down into:

Micro-environment

Immediate environment includes customers, competitors, suppliers and distributors.

- the immediate competitive environment (micro-environment) which includes customer demand and behaviour, competitor activity, marketplace structure and relationships with suppliers and partners;

Macro-environment

Wider environment of social, legal, economic, political and technological influences.

- the wider environment (macro-environment) in which a company operates includes economic development and regulation by governments in the forms of law and taxes together with social and ethical constraints such as the demand for privacy.

For IS/IT strategy, the most significant environmental influences are those of the immediate marketplace which is shaped by the needs of customers and how services are provided to them through competitors and intermediaries and via upstream suppliers. We concentrate on managing these influences here (and in Chapter 14). Wider influences are provided by local and international economic conditions and legislation together with what business practices are acceptable to society. Finally, technological innovations are vital in providing opportunities to provide superior services to competitors or through changing the shape of the marketplace. Later (in Chapters 15 to 17) we look at issues involved in managing some of the external factors related to information systems.

Activity 13.1   Why are environment influences important?

Purpose

To emphasise the importance of monitoring and responding to a range of environment influences.

Activity

For each of the environment influences shown in Figure 1.3, give examples of why it is import-ant as part of IS/IT strategy to monitor and respond in an information systems strategy context. Environmental influences are clearest for a company operating an e-commerce service.

The environment and the modern management imperatives

Paul Licker refers to seven 'modern management imperatives' (Licker, 1997) summarised as the 'seven Rs of strategy'. These highlight how an organisation must compete by using information systems strategy to respond to its external environment. Each of the seven Rs is described below together with how IS can be used to respond to the influence.

- *Reach* – this recognises that businesses increasingly compete globally rather than locally or within national boundaries. As a result organisations need the ability to compete with everyone else, regardless of geographic constraints.

  IS/IT both allows global competition and is required to compete; organisations need information and the tools to process it to allow quick, accurate response, any time and anywhere; global competition implies information networks and inter-organisational systems.

- *Reaction* – customers are becoming ever more demanding and customers will make their views known and wish to have them respected. This means that organisations need quick customer feedback on products and services in order to offer what customers are demanding.

  IS/IT is needed to access and interpret customer feedback. It can be used to keep track of customers, products and projects – it is particularly important to bring order to the data to facilitate fast and accurate response so that managers will be able to anticipate customer needs because they understand the customer. A consequence of this is that software needs to be flexible and quickly developed.

- *Responsiveness* – the process of turning an idea into a product or service that can be marketed is shortening – global reach means that there will be a greater probability that a competitor will be able to offer a good or service that more closely meets customers' requirements. The response to this situation is to shorten the concept-to-customer cycle time so that the organisation can tailor goods and services to meet customers' specific needs.

  There needs to be a rapid movement of product ideas to the market. Organisations need IS/IT to help manage this process: efficiency and speed as well as accuracy and reliability are required and information needs to be relevant and well formatted.

- *Refinement* – greater customer sophistication and specificity means that customers are more able than ever to distinguish fine differences between products and compare them with their needs and desires.

  More customer sophistication means increased turbulence in the market, so more information and the tools to manage and manipulate it are needed. Customers are better at communicating precise requirements which means that niche markets appear, grow and disappear rapidly. As a result increased breadth of information is required to create and market products. Also, customers respond well to systems that respond well to them.

- *Reconfiguration* – as a consequence of changing customer needs and preferences, it may be necessary to re-engineer work patterns and organisational structures to change the structure of work and workflow from idea to product or service.

  As business processes need to evolve and adapt to market needs, there is a big impact on information resource requirements needed for organisational learning (crossing functional boundaries). Complex work structures generate complex data, and management support systems are needed to help manage continually evolving work patterns and structures. Also, new architectures (e.g. client/server) allow decentralisation of IS/IT and greater customer responsiveness.

■ *Redeployment* – changing an organisation's configuration may require the reorganisation and redesign of the financial, physical, human and information resources that are required to create and market a product or service.

Rapid redeployment of resources is required to meet customer needs. An organisation needs to be able to visualise complex arrangements for resources and models to manage them. Therefore, it is necessary to maintain detailed, relevant information on resources at all times and be able to redeploy them. Information itself has become a competitive resource, as well as allowing more control over other resources.

■ *Reputation* – an organisation's reputation will be determined, at least in part, by the satisfaction that a customer experiences. This will be enhanced when the product or service meets or exceeds expectations and requirements. Therefore, an organisation needs to pay attention to the quality and reliability of its products or services and processes by which they are produced.

IS/IT can be used to support product development, testing, marketing and customer post-sales service. It can also help to reduce the gap between expectation and performance. Organisations need to enhance the quality and reliability of the product, and information systems can help in such areas as quality benchmarks, measurement and group-based control techniques.

Figure 13.2 illustrates how an organisation's IS/IT strategy increasingly forms the bridge between the external business environment and internal business processes and activities. Consider an airline: the quality of all customer interactions, often referred to as 'moments of truth' by marketers, whether by phone, Internet or in person, require the support of IS. Similarly most supplier services will also be arranged and delivered through IS support.

An organisation's IS/IT capability will determine, at least in part, how well it can respond to demands placed on it by the external business environment and how it can manage and revise its internal business processes to meet those external demands.

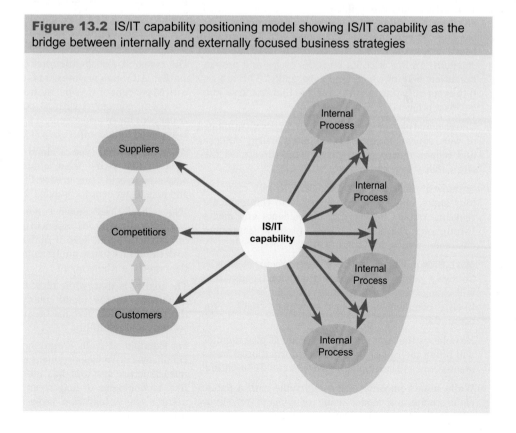

Figure 13.2 IS/IT capability positioning model showing IS/IT capability as the bridge between internally and externally focused business strategies

CASE STUDY 13.1

Which cloud model will prevail?

By Paul Taylor

Enthusiasm for the cloud continues to grow. Companies from banking groups with thousands of branches to five-person start-ups are embracing it to obtain the benefits of its pay-as-you-go pricing and on-demand flexibility.

'Cloud computing is one of the biggest game-changers in computing since e-business emerged 15 years ago,' says Steve Caniano, who is in charge of AT&T's hosting, cloud and application services businesses.

'It helps companies directly align business needs to IT consumption, tie revenues to expenses, and control costs,' he adds. 'Using the cloud, businesses can scale their infrastructure at will and create opportunities to [take advantage] of services previously unavailable or unthinkable.

'Based on our work with thousands of businesses, we estimate that approximately 70 per cent of corporate information technology infrastructure runs on customer premises with less than 20 per cent utilisation. The cloud helps companies avoid wasted investment on idle resources.'

Two AT&T customers illustrate the point. One an engineering group, the other a regional energy company. The engineering group uses AT&T's network-based cloud to increase or decrease its computing capability in line with its business cycles and project execution, both of which tend to be 'spiky'. This allows it to avoid investing in infrastructure that would sit idle between projects.

The regional energy company had to cope with millions of web requests for information about energy outages and repairs during a big storm. This threatened the site's ability to work.

'It moved the site's infrastructure to our cloud in four hours, enabling it continuously to communicate real-time outage information to residents and media throughout the service area, greatly improving customer service,' Mr Caniano says.

Mark Brown, IT risk and assurance director at Ernst& Young, a consultancy, agrees that cloud computing will change the operating landscape, but believes it is likely to complement, rather than replace, client server computing.

He believes that traditional large-scale IT programmes will retain their place in the chief information officer's arsenal, but will be supplemented with cloud computing.

While some companies are comfortable with a public cloud computing model using on-demand resources such as Amazon's Web Services, others are building private clouds using their own virtualised servers, or adopting hybrid public-private models.

But the basic drivers are often the same and, perhaps surprisingly, cost savings are not at the top of the list.

As a recent report by Gartner, the IT research company, noted: 'The cloud promises to deliver a range of benefits, including a shift from capital-intensive to operational cost models, lower overall cost, greater agility and reduced complexity. It can also be used to shift the focus of IT resources to higher-value-added activities for the business, or to support innovation and, potentially, lower risks.'

When asked about the main customer benefits of cloud computing, 67 per cent of Europe-based respondents to a survey published this month by CA Technologies, a software company, pinpointed scalability. Businesses using the cloud have more flexibility to expand or contract IT services as required.

A further 54 per cent highlighted the significance of 'agility', again emphasising the importance of being able to deliver services in a shorter time.

The survey investigated the cost benefits from cloud services and found users making savings of about 11.5 per cent on their annual IT budgets, up from 9.7 per cent reported in last year's study.

The research also highlighted the maturation of the market. Although private clouds dominate the industry, with 55 per cent of CA's partners saying their customers use them, compared with 33 per cent for public and 22 per cent for hybrid clouds, it is the hybrid model that is expected to take off.

When asked what type of cloud will be predominantly used in five years' time, almost half (47 per cent) answered hybrid, compared with 37 per cent for private and just 16 per cent for public.

'The hybrid cloud model combines the best of both worlds by allowing customers to maximise their existing infrastructure and keep it under internal control, but with the ability to use public cloud resources as needed,' the report's authors noted.

The reality is that, while most companies are looking at moving to the cloud, many are cautious about the public model, perhaps because of concerns about security and reliability.

For example, at Wells Fargo, the banking group, Scott Dillon, executive vice-president and head of technology infrastructure services, has used what he calls 'cloud like' technologies to help steer the company through a three-year integration project following the $15bn acquisition of Wachovia.

'We think the cloud is here to stay, but not a public cloud The attributes of the cloud or what we refer to as 'cloudlike computing' are something we have been embracing for about three years. We have been working on a road map to move towards that and evolve,' he says.

'We started by commoditising the hardware itself, moving into virtualisation and standardising software,' he explains.

In the process, Wells Fargo reduced its number of top 'tier 4' data centres from seven to three, cut its regional data centres from 13 to 10, reduced the number of applications by 25 per cent to 3,000 and accelerated server provisioning (starting up a new application server) from months to 10 days.

By the end of last year, almost two-thirds of the bank's servers were virtualised and 80 per cent were standardised. As a result, Wells Fargo achieved $1bn in savings with a significant portion attributed to its infrastructure efficiency efforts.

But like other IT professionals, Mr Dillon notes that making this type of change is not just about the technology. 'You really have to start [focusing on] your operational readiness and capabilities,' he says.

'Moving to the cloud is not just another IT project, it represents a transformation of the business,' says Mr Brown.

Daryl Plummer, a Gartner fellow and expert on web services and the cloud, strongly agrees. 'There is a stronger recognition today that this is more than just a shift of technology,' he says.

Unlike the move from mainframe to client-server, which was a switch from one technology architecture to another, 'this shift moves out of the realm of technology architecture change and into the realm of behavioural relationship and business change, so it's more akin to the change from on-premises systems with client-server mainframe to the web and e-business.'

Mr Plummer adds: 'I use Amazon as a great example of the shift that happened then, the kind of dynamic change that can happen to markets, and now we're seeing the same thing happening because of the cloud phenomenon.'

But he cautions that, although most companies recognise they need a cloud strategy, 'the problem is that a lot of them are deluding themselves. Some of them are being fooled by marketing strategy, and others are just not educated enough about what cloud computing is to be able to come up with a credible strategy'.

He adds: 'The gulf between knowing you need a strategy, and having a credible one, is a big one. We have to point out that, because companies are still just educating themselves about what it means to be doing cloud computing'

QUESTION

Discuss the cloud model in terms of IS strategy.

TOOLS FOR STRATEGIC ANALYSIS AND DEFINITION

In this section we present six tools commonly used in BIS strategic analysis and definition. We start by considering tools that are mainly used to assess the external environmental constraints and options for strategy and then move on to tools that assess the existing internal situation and are used to generate options about future strategy. The tools selected form only a small proportion of those available, but those covered provide a firm foundation for further analysis. In addition, each tool will be examined in the context of the way in which it can be used to help derive an IS strategy that is an integral part of an organisation's business strategy. We will review the application of these six tools:

1. *Porter and Millar's five forces model* – analyses the different *external* competitive forces that affect an organisation and how information can be used to counter them.

2. *Porter's competitive strategies* – assesses how *external* competitive forces can be harnessed.

3. *Nolan's stage model* – an evolutionary maturity model for assessing the current development of information systems *within* an organisation.

4. *McFarlan's strategic grid* – a model for assessing the current and future applications portfolio *within* an organisation.

5. *Value chain analysis* – a tool for analysing the value-adding of information *within* an organisation. Note that value chain or value stream analysis can also be used to assess value-adding activities *outside* an organisation.

6. *Critical success factors (CSFs) analysis* – a model for assessing those factors *within* an organisation that are required to achieve strategic objectives.

1. Porter and Millar's five forces model

Porter and Millar's five forces model

Porter and Millar's five forces model analyses the following competitive forces which impact on an organisation: rivalry between existing competitors, threat of new entrants, threat of substitutes, the power of buyers and the power of suppliers.

Porter and Millar's five forces model is a model for analysing the different external competitive forces that affect an organisation and how information can be used to counter them. The five forces are rivalry between existing competitors, threat of new entrants, threat of substitutes, the power of buyers and the power of suppliers.

This model originated in 1985 and has remained one of the classic tools by which an organisation can assess its current competitive position in relation to a number of external factors:

■ *Rivalry between existing competitors.* This will determine the immediate competitive position of the business and will depend principally on the number of firms already in the industry and the maturity of the industry itself. For example, a mature or declining industry will probably experience a high degree of rivalry, since survival is the key issue at stake.

■ *Threat of new entrants.* A new entrant to an industry will cause the existing competitive situation to be disrupted. This has been evident in many countries over the last few years, where many of the formerly nationalised industries which were then privatised are now facing competition that they have never faced before.

■ *Threat of substitutes.* The substitutes in question already exist within the industry, but because of differentiation they are not quite perfect substitutes for each other. The danger here, therefore, is that a company may lose market share if a rival can supply a substitute that more closely matches the needs of certain customers.

■ *Power of buyers.* The phrase 'the customer is king' is never more true than here where buyers, especially in a business area where there are relatively few of them, can exert power by threatening to switch their purchasing to an alternative supplier. This is also true for businesses where the items being purchased are particularly high-value items (e.g. aero engines).

■ *Power of suppliers.* This may appear a little odd given the previous point, since a business is going to be the customer to its suppliers. However, there are still competitive pressures to be addressed. For example, in a situation where a material is in short supply, a business is going to be at risk from its competitors bidding up material prices and suppliers selling to the highest bidder. An illustration of this is the worldwide shortage of PC memory chips in the early 1990s, where computer manufacturers effectively had to endure a large hike in prices if they were still to manufacture and sell personal computers.

Figure 13.3 illustrates how the five forces outlined above provide the main external pressure on the successful operation of a typical business.

These five forces can exert a profound influence on how business is conducted. If the model is to be used successfully, it will require a thorough analysis of the industry under consideration. Of itself, the resulting information will not automatic-ally generate a business strategy for the organisation. However, it will create a vivid picture of the market environments within which the organisation is operating and provide some pointers towards avenues of further investigation.

From an information systems strategy perspective, the tool provides further pointers towards how IS can be used to affect one or more of the five forces. Each one of the five forces will be taken and an illustration of how IS can be used to benefit the business will be given:

Figure 13.3 Porter and Millar's five forces model

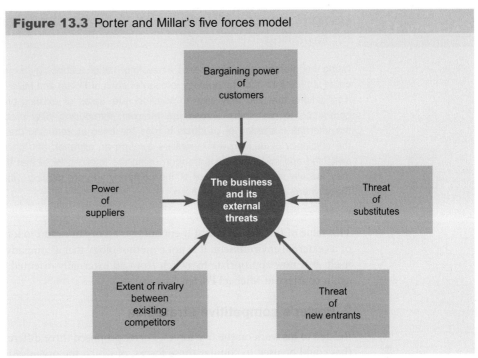

- *Rivalry between existing competitors.* The greater the extent of rivalry within the industry, the higher the costs that will be incurred by a business as it seeks to compete with its rivals. In addition, industry rivalry will be profoundly influenced by the positioning of its products in both the industry and product lifecycles. In a declining industry, for example, collaborative efforts between industry rivals may help reduce costs or raise the profile of the industry.

- *Threat of new entrants.* Businesses such as the financial services industry are competing increasingly on the basis of quality and service, and information systems are one enabler in this process. Investment in systems that support these two aspects of competition can deter potential entrants if they themselves have to make a significant investment in such systems before they can hope to compete successfully.

- *Threat of substitutes.* The threat here is greater if the substitute products are a close alternative. In the shape of CAD/CAM and computer-integrated manufacturing, IS can be used to speed up development of new products and therefore reduce the ability of competitors to provide products that are acceptable substitutes.

- *Power of buyers.* IS can be used to lock customers into a company's products and so reduce the risk of the customer switching to a rival. For example, a business specialising in organising corporate travel may locate terminals at its main corporate customers so that they will be more likely to book flights, hotels and car hire with that company rather than a competitor.

- *Power of suppliers.* If a supplier believes that its customers will always buy from it because there are few perceived alternatives, it is in a position to exert upward pressure on prices and to dictate trading terms to the customer rather than the other way around. Through external databases and now the Internet, IS can help businesses identify equipment and raw material suppliers much more efficiently than before and so reduce the bargaining power of suppliers.

Activity 13.2	Using Porter and Millar's model to devise strategies for exploiting the Internet

Using the Internet as an example of a new information technology, examine how a business could apply information technology to counter each of Porter and Millar's competitive forces. Applications that you may wish to consider are: sales of existing products by electronic commerce to customers across the Internet; introducing new products available over the Internet; marketing of products across the Internet; reducing the cost and increasing the efficiency of dealing with suppliers through an extranet; and changes in the ease of switching and switching costs through using the Internet. Note that the new technologies may actually improve the power of the company you are dealing with in some instances. State where you feel this is the case.

The value of this model is that it encourages an organisation to look at itself in the context of its external environment. It is not a methodology that a company can follow to transform itself. It is now appropriate to switch from an externally oriented view to an internal one, again courtesy of Michael Porter.

2. Porter's competitive strategies

Related to his work on the five forces, Porter proposed three different competitive strategies that could be used to counter these forces, of which the organisation may be able to adopt one (Porter, 2004). Once a competitive strategy has been identified, all marketing efforts can be applied to achieving this and IS can help support the aim. The three competitive strategies, which are covered in more detail in Chapter 1, are:

- *Overall cost leadership* – the firm aims to become the lowest-cost producer in the industry. The strategy here is that, by reducing costs, one is more likely to retain customers and reduce the threat posed by substitute products. An example of how this might be achieved is to invest in systems that support accurate sales forecasting and therefore projected materials requirements so that good, long-term deals can be struck with suppliers, thus reducing materials costs.

- *Differentiation* creates a product perceived industry-wide as being unique. By being able to tailor products to specific customers' requirements or by offering an exceptional quality of service, the risk of customers' switching is reduced.

- *Focus or niche* involves identifying and serving a target segment very well (e.g. buyer group, product range, geographic market). The firm seeks to achieve either or both of 'cost leadership' and 'differentiation'.

There is also a possible undesirable outcome:

- *'Stuck in the middle'* – the firm is unable to adopt any of the above approaches and, therefore, is ultimately at the mercy of competitors that are able to offer these approaches.

3. Nolan's stage model

Nolan's stage model

This model is a six-stage evolutionary model of how IS can be applied within a business.

Nolan's stage model is a six-stage maturity model for the application of information systems to a business.

It must be stressed at the outset that this model dates back to the mainframe era and, therefore, provides a way of looking at an organisation's response to ongoing IS investment and management that is fundamentally influenced by this. However, the model does have value since it is simple to understand, provides an evolutionary view of business use of IS and demonstrates that an organisation's approach to the management of IS will change over time. The model demonstrates that, over time and with experience, an organisation's approach to computer applications, specialist IS personnel and methods of management will evolve to a level of maturity where the planning and development of information systems are embedded into the strategic planning process for the business as a whole.

The six-stage 1979 version of the model is the one on which we will focus here:

1. *Initiation.* The first cautious use of a strange technology, characterised by:
   - low expenditures for data processing;
   - small user involvement;
   - lax management control;
   - emphasis on functional applications to reduce costs.

2. *Contagion.* The enthusiastic adoption of computers in a range of areas:
   - proliferation of applications;
   - users superficially enthusiastic about using data processing systems;
   - management control even more lax;
   - rapid growth of budgets;
   - treatment of the computer by management as just a machine;
   - rapid growth of computer use throughout the organisation's functional areas;
   - computer use is plagued by crisis after crisis.

3. *Control.* A reaction against excessive and uncontrolled expenditures of time and money on computer systems:
   - IS raised higher in the organisation;
   - centralised controls placed on the systems;
   - applications often incompatible or inadequate;
   - use of database and communications, often with negative general management reaction;
   - end-user frustration.

4. *Integration.* Using new technology to bring about the integration of previously unintegrated systems:
   - rise of control by the users;
   - large DP (data processing) budget growth;
   - demand for database and online facilities;
   - DP department operates like a computer utility;
   - formal planning and control within DP;
   - users more accountable for their applications;
   - use of steering committees, applications financial planning;
   - DP has better management controls, standards, project management.

5. *Data administration.* There is a new emphasis on managing corporate data rather than information technology:
   - identification of data similarities, their usage and meanings within the whole organisation;
   - the applications portfolio is integrated into the organisation;
   - DP (MIS – management information systems) department serves more as an administrator of data resources than of machines;
   - the emphasis changes to IS rather than DP.

6. *Maturity.* Information systems are put in place that reflect the real information needs of the organisation:
   - use of data resources to develop competitive and opportunistic applications;
   - MIS organisation viewed solely as a data resource function;
   - MIS emphasis on data resource strategic planning;
   - ultimately users and MIS department *jointly* responsible for the use of data resources within the organisation.

Data processing (DP) department

Commonly used in the 1970s and 1980s to describe the functional area responsible for management and implementation of information systems.

Data processing (DP) department is a term commonly used in the 1970s and 1980s to describe the functional area responsible for management of what is now referred to as information systems and applications development. It is interesting to note that the term focuses on the processing of data rather than the application of information. The head of this department was referred to as DP manager rather than chief information officer or IS manager.

There are a number of implications of Nolan's model which, if taken into account, may help provide a clearer path towards the maturity stage. Both general and IS management must:

- verify the state of IS development in order to plan for the future;
- recognise the fundamental organisational transition from computer management to information resource management;
- recognise the importance of and the future trends in information technology;
- introduce and maintain the appropriate planning and control devices for the IS function (steering committees etc.).

While it is clear that the model has value, there are clearly a number of shortcomings, particularly in respect of the lack of a human dimension. Galliers and Sutherland (1991) extended the model so that it is a socio-technical one rather than merely a technical one. They did this by including reference to the organisation's goals, culture, skills and structure. Nevertheless, we should not dismiss Nolan's model, despite its age, since it can still provide a useful framework for information systems planning. Indeed, the maturity stage implies what all organisations should aspire to: true integration between IS and business planning!

4. McFarlan's strategic grid

McFarlan's strategic grid

This model is used to indicate the strategic importance of information systems to a company now and in the future.

Applications portfolio

The range of different types of business information systems deployed within an organisation.

McFarlan's strategic grid model is used to indicate the strategic importance of information systems to a company now and in the future. It is sometimes referred to as an **applications portfolio** model since it assesses the current mix of business information systems within an organisation.

This matrix model was developed by Cash et al. (1992) to consider the contribution made currently by information systems and the possible impact of future IS investments. It is suggested in the original model that any business will occupy one of the segments in the matrix (Figure 13.4):

- The *strategic* segment indicates that the business depends on both its existing IS and its continued investment in new IS to sustain continued competitive advantage.

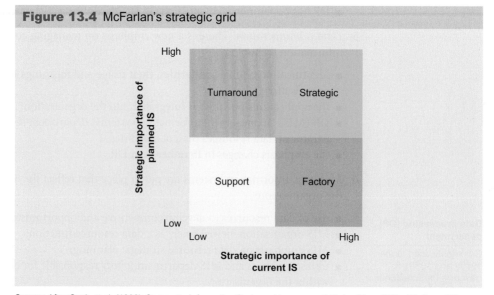

Figure 13.4 McFarlan's strategic grid

Source: After Cash et al. (1992) *Corporate Information Systems Management*, 3rd edition. © The McGraw-Hill Companies, Inc.

- The *turnaround* segment suggests that, while a business in this position does not currently derive significant competitive benefits from its current IS, future investment in this area has the potential to positively affect the business's competitive position.

- On the other hand, a business operating in the *factory* segment, while depending on its current IS to operate competitively, does not envisage further IS investment having a positive impact on its competitive position.

- Finally, a business in the *support* segment does not, and believes it will not, derive significant competitive advantage from information systems.

Note that it is not likely to be the aim for every company to move to a high strategic importance for IS. In some industries such as manufacturing, it is unlikely that IS will ever attain high importance. In others, such as retailing, it may become more important. Given the varying significance of IS in different industries, there are a number of ways in which this model can be applied:

- across industries for analysing the strategic importance that particular industries attach to IS;

- within an industry, different competitors can be plotted according to the relative significance they attach to IS;

- within a company, different departments within an organisation can be classified and goals set in relation to the future planned importance of IS.

Ward and Peppard's (2002) modified matrix provides a useful variation on this model by categorising information systems and their business contribution in terms of an applications portfolio. This model recognises that the information systems used by a single company will not fit into a single quadrant on such a matrix, but rather there will be a portfolio of IS, some of which may lie in different quadrants.

The four sectors, which are shown in Figure 13.5, are:

- *Support.* These applications are valuable to the organisation but not critical to its success.

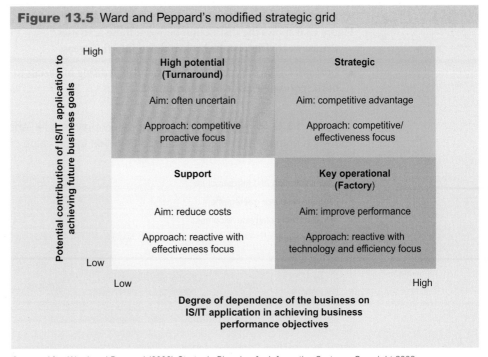

Figure 13.5 Ward and Peppard's modified strategic grid

Source: After Ward and Peppard (2002) *Strategic Planning for Information Systems.* Copyright 2002.
© John Wiley & Sons Ltd.

- *Key operational.* The organisation currently depends on these applications for success (mission-critical).

- *High potential.* These applications may be important to the future success of the organisation.

- *Strategic.* Applications that are critical to sustaining future business strategy.

Each of an organisation's applications will fall into one of these categories. It is quite feasible that applications will move from one sector to another over time (e.g. today's strategic application may become tomorrow's key operational one). It is quite possible, for example, that a current key operational system needs to be developed to replace an old legacy system that no longer meets all the organisation's requirements (e.g. in respect of year 2000 compliance).

The McFarlan matrix and its variant do not of themselves provide a methodology to assist an organisation with its information systems planning. However, especially in its Ward and Peppard guise, the matrix can be effective in providing a framework through which an organisation can explore current and planned IS, both from an IS perspective and from that of functional business managers.

5. Value chain analysis

Value chain

Michael Porter's value chain is a framework for considering key activities within an organisation and how well they add value as products and services move from conception to delivery to the customer.

This is an analytical framework for decomposing an organisation into its individual activities and determining the value added at each stage. In this way, the organisation can assess how effectively resources are being used at the various points on the **value chain**. Michael Porter's value chain is a framework for considering key activities within an organisation and how well they add value as products and services move from conception to delivery to the customer. The relevance for information systems is that for each element in the value chain, it may be possible to use IS to increase the efficiency of resource usage in that area. In addition, IS may be used between value chain activities to increase organisational efficiency.

Value chain analysis makes a distinction between *primary activities*, which contribute directly to getting goods and services closer to the customer (physical creation of a product, marketing and delivery to buyers, support and servicing after sale), and *support activities*, which provide the inputs and infrastructure that allow the primary activities to take place. Figure 13.6 shows the distinction between these activities.

Primary activities can be broken down into five areas:

- *Inbound logistics.* Receiving, storing and expediting materials to the point of manufacture of the good or service being produced.

Figure 13.6 Michael Porter's internal value chain model, showing the relationship between primary activities and support activities to the value chain within a company

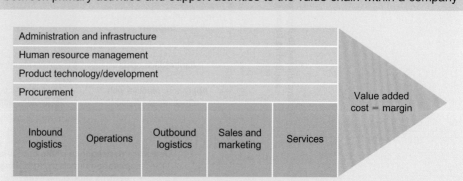

- *Operations*. Transforming the inputs into finished products or services.

- *Outbound logistics*. Storing finished products and distributing goods and services to the customer.

- *Marketing and sales*. Promotion and sales activities that allow the potential customer to buy the product or service.

- *Service*. After-sales service to maintain or enhance product value for the customer.

Secondary activities fall into four categories:

- *Corporate administration and infrastructure*. This supports the entire value chain and includes general management, legal services, finance, quality management and public relations.

- *Human resource management*. Activities here include staff recruitment, training, development, appraisal, promotion and rewarding employees.

- *Technology development*. This includes development of the technology of the pro-duct or service, the processes that produce it and the processes that ensure the successful management of the organisation. It also includes traditional research and development activities.

- *Procurement*. This supports the process of purchasing inputs for all the activities of the value chain. Such inputs might include raw materials, office equipment, production equipment and information systems.

It is probably easier to see how IS can be applied within this model than in the five forces model that we looked at earlier. For example, sales order processing and warehousing and distribution systems can be seen to be very relevant to the inbound and outbound logistics activities. Similarly, accounting systems have an obvious relevance to administration and infrastructure tasks. What is perhaps less clear is how IS can be used between value chain elements. The case study on 'Applying the value chain to a manufacturing organisation' helps illustrate the use of IS to provide linkages between some of the value chain elements.

How can an organisation have a positive impact on its value chain by investing in new or upgraded information systems? Porter and Millar (1985) propose the following five-step process:

1. *Step 1*. Assess the information intensity of the value chain (i.e. the level and usage of information *within* each value chain activity and *between* the levels of activity). The higher the level of intensity and/or the higher the degree of reliance on good-quality information, the greater the potential impact of new information systems.

2. *Step 2*. Determine the role of IS in the industry structure (for example, banking will be very different from mining). It is also important to understand the information linkages between buyers and suppliers within the industry and how they and competitors might be affected by and react to new information technology.

3. *Step 3*. Identify and rank the ways in which IS might create competitive advantage (by affecting one of the value chain activities or improving linkages between them). High-cost or critical activity areas present good targets for cost reduction and performance improvement.

4. *Step 4*. Investigate how IS might spawn new businesses (for example, the Sabre computerised reservation system spawned a multi-billion-dollar software company which now has higher earnings than the original core airline business).

5. *Step 5*. Develop a plan for taking advantage of IS. A plan must be developed that is business-driven rather than technology-driven. The plan should assign priorities to the IS investments (which, of course, should be subjected to an appropriate cost–benefit analysis).

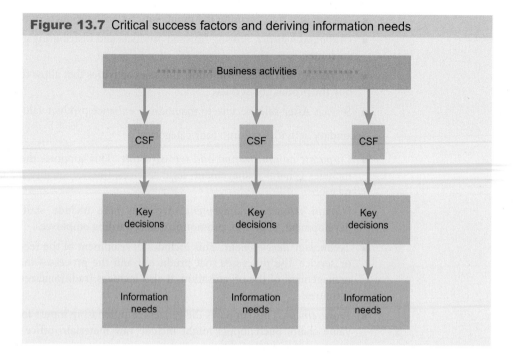

Figure 13.7 Critical success factors and deriving information needs

6. Critical success factors (CSFs) analysis

Critical success factors (CSFs)

Measures that indicate the performance or efficiency of different parts of an organisation and its processes.

Critical success factors (CSFs) are measures that indicate the performance or efficiency of different parts of an organisation. Good performance of processes measured by these factors is vital to the business unit or organisation.

This technique is one of the most useful for an organisation in pinpointing what are its precise information needs. The essence of CSF analysis is summarised in Figure 13.7.

Critical success factors will exist in every functional area of the business and they indicate those things which must be done right if that functional area in particular and the organisation as a whole are to flourish. CSFs will also relate to the level within each functional area. For example, in the sales function, a CSF for an account handler may be the accurate and speedy recording and retrieval of sales data. On the other hand, for a senior manager, a CSF may involve achieving the right mix of products.

Once CSFs have been determined across process and hierarchical levels, it is possible to consider the key decisions that have to be made if those CSFs are to be achieved.

An example of the application of CSFS in sales order processing

When a customer places an order, a number of decisions need to be made, the results of which will determine the processing actions for the order and the effectiveness of the process. The critical success factor for this process will be to achieve a high conversion rate of orders received to orders fulfilled while minimising the risk of bad debts.

One of the first decisions will be whether to accept the customer order at all. Such a decision will hinge on the creditworthiness of the customer. Second, a decision will have to be made about when the customer can receive his or her order. This may be a complex process, depending on the size and importance of the customer, the size and complexity of the order and finally existing stock levels for the ordered items and planned manufacturing or purchasing lead times. If the order is delayed, the customer may seek an alternative supplier.

Having identified the range of key decisions that need to be supported, consideration must turn to the information needed to support the decision-making processes for each relevant functional business area or operational level. To pursue the sales example to its logical conclusion, one of the first information needs is, therefore, the creditworthiness of the customer as expressed by his or her credit line or limit and the current outstanding amount. Both of these items of information would normally be drawn from a mixture of existing sales and accounts receivable data. The sales account handler needs this information before a decision can be made to continue with the customer order. Second, information relating to order item availability needs to be known before a delivery date commitment can be made to the customer. This information will probably be drawn from:

1. Customer data (for example, is the customer an important one who needs to be looked after?).

2. Stock control data (is there sufficient stock in the warehouse to fulfil this customer's requirements?).

3. Production planning data (if there is currently insufficient stock on hand, will there be sufficient stock in time to meet the customer's requirements?).

Through improving the quality of information available to support decision making, it should be possible to improve the efficiency of sales order processing and achieve the CSF.

IS AND BUSINESS STRATEGY INTEGRATION

This section examines how strategic models can be applied to ensure that there is good congruence between business and IS strategies. The aim is to apply tools that enable us either to *align* the IS strategies with the business needs or use IT/IS to have a favourable impact on the business. Aligning techniques are top-down in nature, beginning with the organisation's generic business strategy and from this deriving information systems strategies that support business activities. Before these tools can be applied, it is necessary to consider the organisational strategy and the environment in which the business operates.

It is useful to consider tools for strategy definition in the context of whether they are intended to support an existing business strategy directly (business alignment), or whether they are intended to indicate new opportunities which may have a positive impact on a business strategy (business-impacting).

In a business-alignment IS strategy the IS strategy will be generated from the business strategy through techniques such as CSF analysis. In a business-impacting IS strategy the IS strategy will have a favourable impact on the business strategy through the use of innovative techniques and technologies, often as part of business process re-engineering. CSF analysis is fundamentally a business-aligning technique rather than an impacting one.

Business impacting could be achieved through the use of value chain analysis where an organisation, through an analysis of the potential for the use of IS within and between value chain elements, may seek to identify strategic IS opportunities. Perhaps the ultimate expression of using IS to impact business performance is through business process re-engineering.

Business-aligning IS strategy

The IS strategy is derived directly from the business strategy in order to support it.

Business-impacting IS strategy

The IS strategy is used to favourably impact the business strategy, perhaps by introducing new technologies.

The importance of strategic alignment

Figure 13.8 attempts to illustrate one of the key problems in strategic information systems planning. T1 represents the point in time when it is recognised that the current IS/IT capability (C1) is insufficient to meet the needs of the organisation (represented by the IS/IT capability gap G1). Plans are therefore developed to acquire the applications and/or infrastructure which will meet the needs of the business. At time T1 it is anticipated that a level of IS/IT capability represented by C2 will be sufficient when implemented at

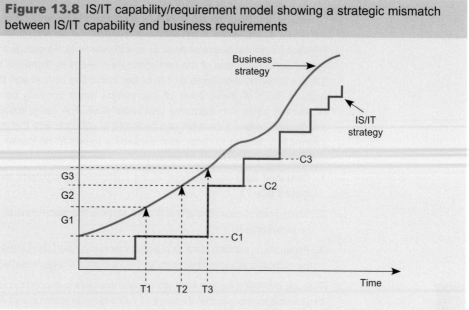

Figure 13.8 IS/IT capability/requirement model showing a strategic mismatch between IS/IT capability and business requirements

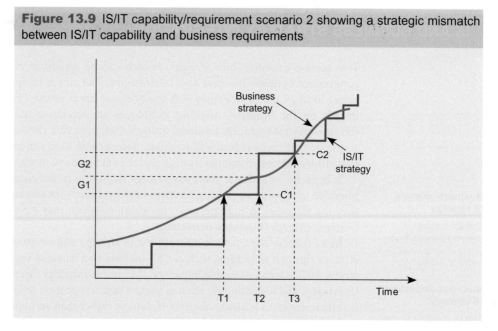

Figure 13.9 IS/IT capability/requirement scenario 2 showing a strategic mismatch between IS/IT capability and business requirements

time T3 (thus making up the anticipated IS/IT capability gap G2). However, developments in an organisation's business strategy may mean that, by T3, IS/IT requirements are greater than those envisaged earlier on, thus resulting in a new IS/IT capability gap, G3. The response to this can be a shortening of the cycle time between new software releases so that the cap-ability gap is smaller and for a shorter period. However, the implication of this is that IS/IT and business strategies run the risk of never being fully and consistently aligned.

It is possible to take the misalignment argument further (Figure 13.9). At time T1, an organisation may anticipate significant demands for additional IS/IT development and construct an IS plan that will deliver capability C2 by time T2. However, it is possible that the organisation may only need part of that capability by T2 and will only be capable of using the IS/IT resource C2 by time T3. Therefore, the time from T2 to T3 may represent wasted resources. Furthermore, it may also represent a period of organisational change and upheaval while there is a misalignment of this type. In an extreme case, the resulting mismatch could result in business failure since the organisation's business strategy has been neglected at the expense of an over-emphasis on the perceived benefits of IS/IT investments alone.

These misalignment problems lie at the heart of IS planning and mean that there is a risk of ever-moving goalposts when attempting to specify, acquire and implement new computer-based information systems.

Strategic alignment barriers

Weill and Broadbent (1998) summarise the alignment of business strategy and in-formation technology in Figure 13.10. The elements to be aligned include:

- *Environment* – the external business environment provides opportunities through the availability of technology, threats from competitors and constraints from external regulations.

- *Information technology portfolio* – this comprises the IT infrastructure and the informational, transactional and strategic information systems part of the portfolio.

- *IT strategy* – here, three aspects need to be balanced: the role of information techno-logy in the firm (for example whether it is perceived to be a core or support function); the way information services are delivered (e.g. the degree or centralisation or decentralisation and the extent to which services are insourced or outsourced); technology policies and standards as they relate to the acquisition and operation of hardware and software solutions.

- *Strategic context* – the two aspects here include the strategic intent of the organisation as it drives long-term investments in the IT (infrastructure) portfolio and the current strategy which drives the acquisition of strategic, informational and transactional information systems in response to changing internal and external needs.

Figure 13.10 Barriers to business and IS/IT alignment

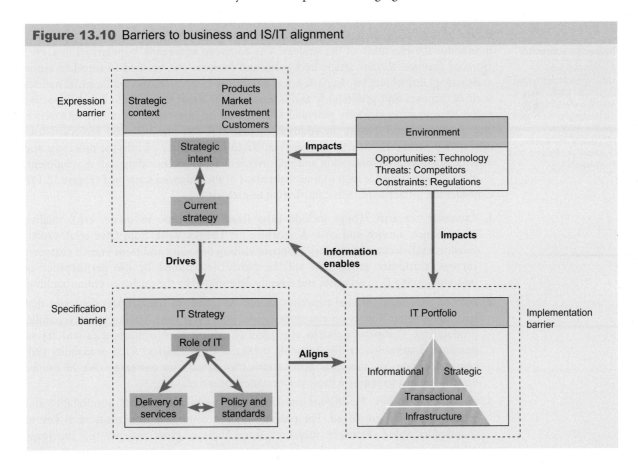

The barriers identified by Weill and Broadbent in aligning business strategy, technology strategy and the information technology portfolio fall into three categories: expression barriers, specification barriers and implementation barriers.

Expression barriers include lack of direction in the business strategy which can result in an information technology strategy being set in isolation from the business strategy, changing strategic intents where the long-term goals of the firm are unstable and lead to difficulties in articulating a technology infrastructure, and insufficient awareness of information technology whereby the vision for how technology will be used can restrict business opportunities.

Specification barriers can include lack of information technology involvement where the impact of IT industry developments is not seriously considered in an organisation's strategy-setting process, the communications gap that can exist between IT professionals and business managers which can lead to misunderstandings and inappropriate decisions, and uncoordinated information technology where investment in IT takes place without an overview of the organisation's total IT portfolio and its relationship to strategic objectives.

Implementation barriers occur when one or more parts of the organisation perceive themselves as being somehow different from the other functional areas or business units and, therefore, they opt out of the shared infrastructure because they believe that it will not meet their needs.

Balanced scorecards and strategic alignment

A consequence of the barriers discussed above is that organisations can make significant investments in their IT portfolio which do not necessarily lead to any real business benefits, thus leading to the notion of the 'productivity paradox' (discussed in Chapter 14).

Integrated metrics such as the balanced scorecard have become widely used as a means of translating organisational strategies into objectives and then providing metrics to monitor the execution of the strategy. The balanced scorecard, popularised in a 1993 *Harvard Business Review* article by Kaplan and Norton, can be used to translate vision and strategy into objectives. In part, it was a response to over-reliance on financial metrics such as turnover and profitability and a tendency for these measures to be retrospective rather than looking at future potential as indicated by innovation, customer satisfaction and employee development. In addition to financial data the balanced scorecard uses operational measures such as customer satisfaction, efficiency of internal processes and also the organisation's innovation and improvement activities including staff development.

Balanced scorecard

A framework for setting and monitoring business performance. Metrics are structured according to customer issues, internal efficiency measures, financial measures and innovation.

We will now consider each of four main areas of the balanced scorecard (Figure 13.11). Consider the influence of IS in contributing to each area:

1. *Customer concerns.* These include time (lead time, time to quote, etc.), quality, performance, service and cost. A measure for Halifax Bank from Olve et al. (2000) considers satisfaction of mystery shoppers visiting branches and from branch customer surveys. Customer satisfaction will be partly determined by the performance of customer-facing IS in branches and directly determined by the quality of online banking.

2. *Internal measures.* Internal measures should be based on the business processes that have the greatest impact on customer satisfaction: cycle time, quality, employee skills, productivity. Companies should also identify critical core competencies and try to guarantee market leadership. Example measures from Halifax: ATM availability (%), conversion rates on mortgage applications (%), arrears on mortgage (%). IS can be directly applied to improve these performance measures.

3. *Financial measures.* Traditional measures such as turnover, costs, profitability and return on capital employed. For publicly quoted companies this measure is key to shareholder value. Example measures from Halifax: gross receipts (£), mortgage offers (£), loans (£).

Figure 13.11 The balanced scorecard process

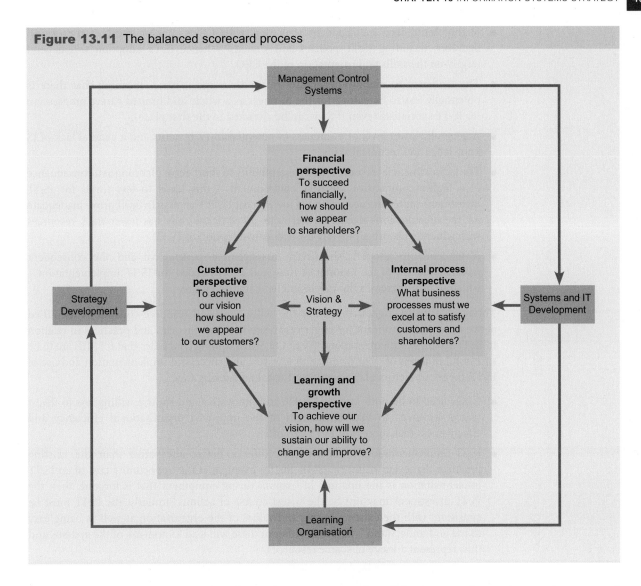

4. *Learning and growth: innovation and staff development.* Innovation can be measured by change in value through time (employee value, shareholder value, percentage and value of sales from new products). Examples: management performance, training performance, new product development. Some companies such as Skandia Life use measures such as staff IT skills or access to the IT to assess performance in this area.

For each of these four areas management teams will define objectives, specific measures, targets and initiatives to achieve these targets. For some companies, such as Skandia Life, the balanced scorecard becomes much more than a performance measurement system but provides a framework for the entire business strategy process. Olve et al. (2000) make the point that a further benefit of the scorecard is that it does not solely focus on outcomes, but also considers measures that are performance drivers that should positively affect the outcomes. Examples of performance drivers are investment in technology and employee training.

FOCUS ON... IS/IT AND SMEs

James Thong (1999) whilst lamenting the lack of empirical research on the determinants of IS/IT adoption in small businesses nevertheless identifies a number of factors that can apply in SMEs. These include:

- Highly centralised management structures with CEOs making most of the critical decisions including IS/IT policies and strategy – hence IS/IT adoption will depend largely on the skills and orientation of the CEO.

- The tendency to employ generalists rather than specialists – meaning that there is potentially less to be gained for the business as a whole and limited career progression for IS/IT specialists (even if they can be attracted in the first place).

- A generally lower level of awareness of potential IS/IT benefits and a general lack of IS knowledge and technical skills.

- The lack of financial resources and susceptibility to short-term planning as a consequence of a highly competitive business environment – this leads to less funds for IS/IT investment and/or the acquisition of lowest-cost IS/IT that may in itself prove inadequate for the organisation's needs; furthermore, an SME typically has fewer slack resources with which to absorb a possibly unsuccessful adoption of IS/IT.

- A tendency to adopt a short-term management perspective and the consequent underestimation of the amount of time and effort needed for IS/IT implementation – which in turn increases the risk of implementation failure.

Thong goes on to suggest that since the skills, time and resource constraints identified above are not as significant for larger organisations, then theories and practices in relation to IS/IT strategy implementation may not fit SMEs. Thong concludes that if SMEs are to be successful in terms of their orientation towards, and successful implementation and use of IS/IT, then four factors play a significant role in achieving this:

- CEOs need to be both knowledgeable and innovative and show a willingness to invest scarce resources to take advantages of the improved organisational efficiency and effectiveness that successful IS/IT can offer.

- IS/IT implementation in SMEs must offer a better alternative than the existing practices that exist within the SME. So, for example, if the opportunity cost of an IS/IT implementation is the upgrade in manufacturing equipment that is forgone, then the IS/IT investment may not be the wisest course of action. Similarly, the IS/IT must be consistent with the existing norms and values of the organisation as well as being easy to use and understand – failure in either of these will lead to non-use of the systems and thus represent a waste of scarce resources.

- Despite the acknowledged lack of financial resources and IS/IT-knowledgeable employees in many SMEs, sufficient financial and human resources still need to be devoted to an IS/IT implementation if it is to be successful.

- Where there is a greater need for information processing within an SME (one dealing with financial services, rather than a small builder for example), there is likely to be a greater adoption of IS/IT. This still means, however, that sufficient financial and IS/IT-knowledgeable human resources will be needed, and that these are more likely, the larger the organisation.

Thoburn et al. (1999) point out that traditionally, SMEs have concentrated on the '4 Ms' – money, materials, machine and manpower, whilst neglecting the effective management of information, resulting in fragmented information systems that do not meet the operational or strategic needs of the organisation. Indeed, they suggest that appropriate management of information lies at the heart of an agile organisation. However, in their 15-month analysis of three manufacturing companies in the SME sector, they found such factors as:

- poor strategic awareness with a lack of internal and external intelligence;

- limited, uncoordinated and unplanned technology where computers were seen as an answer by simply being present;

- lack of direct integration of IT systems and connectedness of IT and people-centred systems;

■ people that were highly trained, valued and rewarded but where there was a failure in communications in people-centred systems.

In response to some of the difficulties encountered by SMEs as they seek to make better use of IS/IT, Pavic et al. (2007) propose a four-stage model whereby it may be possible for some SMEs to integrate new IS technology into an overall strategy and that this new technology could lead to a competitive advantage:

■ *Implementation of appropriate IT infrastructure.* IT infrastructure integration is seen as a starting element of an e-business implementation strategy and investment is needed in the hardware and software required for the business to work. Their study shows that companies that are highly IT-capable and employ more skilled staff outperformed others in terms of profit.

■ *Changed organisational structure and business strategies.* Structural change within organisations is seen as essential and a company must accept that the Internet technology will become an integral part. They see structural change as an import-ant element of sustaining value creation by firms in the future, and point out that organisations need an integrated and coordinated approach towards knowledge, technology and relationship management.

■ *Integration within an organisation.* This refers to complete internal integration where all aspects of organisational operations must be synchronised and co-aligned with the business goal of focusing on cost reduction and internal efficiency. It is suggested that SMEs that are able to integrate internally are more successful and employ skilled and knowledgeable staff.

■ *Full integration with free information flow between suppliers, the organisation and customers.* Final and full integration with free information flows enables the business goal of creating market value and competitive advantage by using the Internet technology to be achieved. It also enables supply chain integration and more effective insourcing and outsourcing. It is suggested that this stage is seen as an essential part of implementing an e-business strategy for an SME.

Pavic et al. summarise by saying that if SMEs are to create competitive advantage and e-customers, it is absolutely essential for them to have a sound and well-resourced integration plan of new technologies. However, as they also point out, the literature in this field consistently argues that effective adoption and implementation of IS may rely quite a lot on individual factors such as organisational size and structure, and the mix of available human and financial resources and capabilities. They also suggest that although SMEs are more flexible and more adaptable to change, they lack the human and financial resources and capabilities of large firms and, therefore, they face limitations in purchasing and implementing new systems. The challenge then for SMEs is to embed IS/IT technologies (including web-based systems) as soon as possible into their business model.

CASE STUDY 13.2

Next generation of clients forces pace of IT change

By Jennifer Thompson

Any retail high street bank chief will tell you that IT investment and development is critical in maintaining loyalty in a fast-changing market. For example, it allows customers to check balances on mobile phones before making a purchase.

The picture in private banking, whose members compete on the strength of their brand and the personal services they provide, is more fragmented.

'A big chunk of their offering is in the 'white glove' service,' says Matthew Thomas, partner in investment management at KPMG, referring to the face-to-face advice offered by wealth managers that private banking customers know and trust, and typically work with for many years. 'However, that's not necessarily tracking what customers want.'

Doing nothing about this latest technological revolution is not an option. Where they once primarily catered to long-established 'old money' clients, many private banks have started to note the number of Generation Y clients in their 20s and 30s among the customers they have attracted over the past couple of years. These are young and digitally savvy individuals, some of them technology entrepreneurs.

'The new generation of private banking customers has grown in a different way,' says Nicolas Debaig, head of strategy and business development at ABN Amro private banking. 'They have different expectations.'

The sector has mainly regarded technology as a cost and a support function, not as a means of competing. Such attitudes are changing.

'People are the mainstay but IT is now playing a more and more important role,' adds Mr Thomas.

Technology investment offers an opportunity for individual banks to shine in customer service as well as risk management.

'For a while, technology has been a big deal for private bankers and potentially a key differentiator,' says Ralf Dreischmeier, global leader of the information technology practice at Boston Consulting Group.

Better technology can assist wealth managers with risk and compliance by recording how they interact with clients and documenting agreements or discussions about risk appetite or investment exposure. Investing in platforms and software could help smaller banks scale up quickly if they add a significant number of clients.

The costs of investment are typically in the range of at least tens of millions of pounds or dollars, unproblematic sums for big private banks. Barclays, for instance, has dedicated about two-thirds of Project Gamma, a £350m investment programme in its wealth and investment management business, to IT. One innovation was

the launch last year of voice recognition technology in its telephone banking services, a move aimed at personalising the service and reducing call times that have been lengthened by standard security checks.

'We're trying to use technology to get some of the awkward modern realities out of the way,' says Matt Smallman, vice-president in charge of the client experience at Barclays.

Meanwhile, ABN Amro has concentrated on developing technology around its core systems relating to customer relationship and portfolio management, developing an online tool that allows clients to see the exposure of their portfolio.

Can smaller banks compete? Some insiders wryly note that at least they are not burdened by legacy IT systems that can wreak havoc in the event of glitches.

Many analysts regard outsourcing, or small groups sharing an IT platform with other businesses or alongside a bigger bank, as the only economically feasible route for such organisations.

'When it comes to efficiency in the back office, that is almost the only way they can compete,' argues Mr Dreischmeier.

Others suggest they could make their online offering stand out with distinctive apps, which cost thousands of pounds to develop rather than millions, and can be used to tailor the customers' experience to their individual needs.

One small business that has developed its own system is Weatherbys Bank, which grew out of a seventh-generation family-owned firm dedicated to horseracing services. It was granted a bank licence in 1994 and has had no trouble developing its own IT platform, thanks to its unusual heritage. This meant it had a pre-existing IT business to manage a database of the pedigree of foals born in the UK and Ireland.

Even for those who currently find themselves ahead in the technology stakes, continuing innovation and investment are essential. 'You need to update,' says Roger Weatherby, chief executive of the bank that bears his name. 'There's always something to add to.'

QUESTION

What does the case study show about the strategic role of IT?

SUMMARY

1. Business strategy will embrace business decisions, the broad objectives and direction of the organisation and how it might cope with change – in other words, where the business is going and why. IS has an impact on this and provides potential for competitive advantage.

2. A company needs an information systems strategy that is rooted in business needs, meets the demand for information to support business processes and provides applications for key functional areas of the business.

3. If an organisation does not have a clear picture of what its strategy is, it is difficult to see how the right information systems can be put in place. In turn, if the information needs are unclear, it is difficult to see how the right techno-logy can be put in place to satisfy those needs.

4. Since business strategies have the potential to be subjected to sudden and unpredictable change (or even evolutionary change), the IS and IT strategies that are needed to support changing business strategies must themselves be capable of adaptation and change if they are to continue to reflect the existing business strategy at any time. In reality, IS strategy must be embedded in an organisation's business strategy and be a fundamental part of it. Separation between the two is likely to result in a suboptimal solution, with organisations failing to gain the full benefits that information systems and the technology associated with them can bring.

EXERCISES

Self-assessment exercises

1. How do strategic systems differ from high-potential projects?

2. Why do information systems projects fail?

3. Explain the difference between project size and project complexity when evaluating information systems risk.

4. Why might the mechanistic approach to strategy formulation be considered inadequate?

5. How might Porter's five forces model be helpful in determining information systems requirements?

6. Explain how a fast-food restaurant may use Porter's value chain analysis to help determine its information system needs.

7. How might Nolan's stage model be useful to an organisation that is struggling with spiralling IS costs?

8. Identify three critical success factors for the maternity department of a busy hospital. How do those CSFs translate into key decisions and then information requirements?

Discussion questions

1. 'The millennium bug has demonstrated that organisations, more often than not, take a short-term view in their approach to information systems rather than a strategic one.' Discuss.

2. 'The barriers relating to the relationship between business and IS/IT strategies mean that successful alignment is likely to be the exception rather than the rule.' Discuss.

Essay questions

1. Top-down and bottom-up approaches to formulating information systems strategy are fine as far as they go. However, is there a case for a more eclectic or selective approach to the strategy formulation process?

2. Evaluate the importance of information systems knowledge amongst senior business managers in achieving successful alignment of business and IS/IT strategies.

Examination questions

1. Explain the concept of Porter's value chain and how it can be used to identify a company's information needs.

2. How can McFarlan's strategic grid be used to define an information systems strategy for a company?

3. Explain the difference between a business-impacting and a business-aligning approach to a company's IS strategy. Give examples of strategy tools that can help support each method.

4. Using the potential business applications of the Internet, show how Porter's five forces model can help identify opportunities for deploying information systems.

References

Cash, J., McKenney, J. and McFarlan, F.W. (1992) *Corporate Information Systems Management*, 3rd edition, Irwin, Homewood, IL

Ciborra, C. and Jelassi, T. (1994) *Strategic Information Systems: A European Perspective*, John Wiley, Chichester

Galliers, R.D. and Sutherland, A.R. (1991) 'Information systems management and strategy management and formulation: the stages of growth model revisited', *Journal of Information Systems*, 1, 2, 89–114

Johnson, G., Scholes, K. and Whittington, R. (2011) *Exploring Strategy*, 9th edition, Prentice Hall Europe, Hemel Hempstead

Kaplan, R.S. and Norton, D.P. (1993) 'Putting the balanced scorecard to work', *Harvard Business Review*, Sep–Oct, 134–42

Licker, P.S. (1997) *Management Information Systems: A Strategic Leadership Approach*, Dryden Press, London

Mintzberg, H. (1990) 'The design school: reconsidering the basic premises of strategic management', *Strategic Management Journal*, 11, 171–95

Nolan, R. (1979) 'Managing the crisis in data processing', *Harvard Business Review*, Mar–Apr, 115–26

Olve, N., Roy, J. and Wetter, M. (2000) *Performance Drivers. A Practical Guide to Using the Balanced Scorecard*, John Wiley, Chichester

Pavic, S., Koh, S.C.L., Simpson M. and Padmore, J. (2007) 'Could e-business create a competitive advantage in UK SMEs?' *Benchmarking: An International Journal*, 14, 3, 320–51

Porter, M.E. (2004) *Competitive Strategy*, Free Press, New York

Porter, M.E. and Millar, V.E. (1985) 'How information gives you competitive advantage', *Harvard Business Review*, July/August, 149–60

Thong, J.Y.L. (1999) 'An integrated model of information systems adoption in small businesses', *Journal of Management Information Systems*, Spring, 15, 4, 187

Thoburn, J.G., Arunachalam, S. and Gunasekaran A. (1999) 'Difficulties arising from dysfunctional information systems in manufacturing SMEs – case studies', *International Journal of Agile Management Systems* 1, 2, 116–26

Ward, J. and Peppard, J. (2002) *Strategic Planning for Information Systems*, 3rd edition, John Wiley, Chichester

Weill, P. and Broadbent, M. (1998) *Leveraging the New Infrastructure: How Market Leaders Capitalize on Information*, Harvard Business School Press, Boston

Willcocks, L. and Plant, R. (2000) 'Business Internet strategy – moving to the Net', in L. Willcocks and C. Sauer (eds) *Moving to E-Business*, Random House, London, pp. 19–46

Further reading

Curtis, G. and Cobham, D. (2008) *Business Information Systems: Analysis, Design and Practice*, 6th edition, Addison-Wesley, Harlow.

Johnson, G., Scholes, K. and Whittington, R. (2011) *Exploring Corporate Strategy*, 9th edition, Prentice Hall Europe, Hemel Hempstead.

Kearns, G.S. and Sabherwal, R. (2007) 'Strategic alignment between business and information technology: a knowledge-based view of behaviors, outcome, and consequences', *Journal of Management Information Systems*, Winter 2006–7, 23, 3, 129–62.

Kendall, K.E. and Kendall, J.E. (2013) *Systems Analysis and Design*, 9th edition, Prentice-Hall, Englewood Cliffs, NJ.

Lynch, R. (2006) *Corporate Strategy*, 4th edition, Financial Times Prentice Hall, Harlow.

Smith, P. R. and Zook, Z. (2011) *Marketing Communications: Integrating Offline and Online with Social Media*, 5th edition, Kogan Page, London.

Ward, J. and Peppard, J. (2012) *Strategic Planning for Information Systems*, 4th edition, John Wiley, Chichester. This book provides an excellent review of current thinking on IS strategy.

Web links

www.outsourcing.com Outsourcing Institute web site.

LINKS TO OTHER CHAPTERS

This chapter follows on logically from Chapter 13 by concentrating primarily on the financial and locational aspects of IS/IT management. It does not link directly to subsequent chapters in Part 3, since these describe specific aspects of managing information systems which are separate elements of strategy implementation. The remaining aspects of business information systems management covered in Part 3 are protecting information quality (Chapter 15), managing end-user services in a business (Chapter 16), and professional issues such as data privacy and protection (Chapter 17). Chapter 8 in Part 2 also covers cost–benefit analysis and investment appraisal for a single information system in more detail than that provided in this chapter.

Information systems management

CHAPTER AT A GLANCE

MAIN TOPICS

FOCUS ON . . .

CASE STUDIES

LEARNING OUTCOMES

After reading this chapter, you will be able to:

- evaluate the relationship between IS spending and business benefits;
- evaluate location alternatives for an organisation's IS function;
- assess the arguments for and against outsourcing;
- apply IS governance concepts to the management of an organisation's IS function.

MANAGEMENT ISSUES

Annual investment in BIS is significant for many companies. But what return do organisations receive for this investment? To achieve more effective investment, a well-planned BIS strategy is required that supports the corporate goals. In this chapter we aim to answer the questions a newly installed manager seeking to develop an IS strategy would ask:

- How can we ensure that our proposed IS/IT solutions will deliver value for money?
- What are the main considerations when deciding where to locate the management of the IS/IT function within the organisation?
- How can we determine the extent to which IS/IT services should be outsourced?
- What management tools and techniques exist to help us manage the IS/IT portfolio effectively?

INTRODUCTION

Earlier (in Chapter 13), we explored a number of tools and issues relating to the development if IS/IT strategies and their integration with an overall business strategy. This chapter explores a range of issues relating to the management of information systems within an organisation including investment appraisal, outsourcing and the organisation and implementation of the IS/IT management function within an organisation. By combining effective IS/IT strategies with effective implementation and management, it will then become more likely that an organisation will have IS/IT solutions that provide significant business benefits rather than ones which act as a drain on the organisation.

INFORMATION SYSTEMS INVESTMENT APPRAISAL

There has been considerable discussion in academic journals regarding both 'information systems value' and 'evaluating IS/IT investments'. While the former relates more closely to the 'productivity paradox' mentioned above, the latter deals more with the analysis of how organisations can identify and evaluate IS/IT investments and their associated benefits. Lubbe and Remenyi (1999) in their analysis of the management of IS/IT evaluation identified seven benefit objectives that provide a stimulus to organisational IS/IT investment. In descending order of significance these are:

- productivity;
- new opportunities;
- change;
- competitive advantage;
- contribution to organization;
- increased turnover;
- reduced risk.

Coupled with these factors, Lubbe and Remenyi also identified seven IS/IT investment drivers that will help determine the organisation's response to the IS/IT investment opportunity. In descending order of importance, these are:

- organisational strategy;
- management decisions;
- interfacing (of systems);
- quality of service;
- evaluation of IS/IT (tangible and intangible benefits);
- business modelling (improving business processes);
- budgets.

Given that there is a range of drivers that affect the IS/IT investment process and that both tangible and intangible benefits will be generated as a result of the IS/IT investment, a range of techniques can be employed to assess tangible benefits (typically through financial measures) and intangible benefits (using qualitative methods). Indeed, the existence of both financial and non-financial approaches to IS/IT investment appraisal could give us some clue as to why the so-called productivity paradox may appear to exist. In other words, there may not be a financial payback in the short or even medium term, but the very fact that business benefits (such as improved customer service) are perceived to come from particular investments that have been assessed from a qualitative perspective, would lend some credence to the 'time lag' explanation of the paradox.

Financial approaches to information systems investment appraisal have already been covered earlier (in Chapter 8).

DETERMINING INVESTMENT LEVELS FOR INFORMATION SYSTEMS IN AN ORGANISATION

Earlier (in Chapter 8) we described the assessment of costs at the initiation phase of a single information systems project. In this chapter, we consider at an organisational level the amount of investment that should occur in information systems.

Managers in many organisations are concerned with the level of investment in information systems and whether they are getting value for money from that investment. One of the difficulties with measuring this is that while costs tend to be tangible in nature, benefits are often more difficult to quantify.

Investment levels

How much an organisation will spend on IS will depend both on the size of the organisation and on the nature of its business operations. Spending as a proportion of turnover will also vary over time, depending on the maturity of an organisation's systems and on the organisation itself. There is a tendency for the proportion of spending on IS to increase as organisations mature and have to maintain legacy systems. Regardless of any of these considerations, the task facing senior managers remains the same: can we be sure that investment in IS will deliver more benefit than the costs incurred?

Information systems costs

As described earlier (in Chapter 8), costs can be both tangible and intangible. As you would expect, tangible costs are more easily identified than intangible ones. Hochstrasser and Griffiths (1990) produced a checklist which can help organisations identify, quantify and evaluate information system costs. The main cost elements include:

- hardware costs;
- software costs;
- installation costs;
- environmental costs;
- running costs;
- maintenance costs;
- security costs;
- networking costs;
- training costs;
- wider organisational costs.

Since every information system that is acquired incurs operational and maintenance costs, IS expenditure will always be split between *development* costs and *operational and maintenance* costs.

Information system benefits

While information systems costs are relatively easy to identify, the benefits that accrue from IS investment are harder to quantify. This is because benefits are often intangible in nature and, therefore, harder to ascribe a financial value to. Broadly speaking, benefits from IS investment result from the capability of the organisation to do things that it could not do or did not do very well before. This must be supported by information of good quality, as defined in Chapter 2. This will include:

- Information relevance – is the information being provided relevant to the business decisions being made?
- Is accurate information available on which business decisions can be made?
- Speed of information delivery – does information reach the decision makers when they need it?
- The functionality of the IS to support decision making – will the system do what we want it to do?
- The reliability of the IS – can we rely on the system to give us the information we want when we want it?

If the above questions can be answered positively, then the investment in IS is providing benefits to the organisation and, therefore, allows it to do things that it could not do before.

In making an IS investment decision, the value that accrues from the above elements must be measured in some way. However, as noted above, value from IS investment can often be intangible in nature and, therefore, harder to measure. Such items of intangible benefit include:

- improved customer service;
- gaining competitive advantage and avoiding competitive disadvantage;
- support for core business functions;
- improved management information;
- improved product quality;
- improved internal and external communication
- impact on the business through innovation;
- job enhancement for employees.

Each of these elements has a level of difficulty attached when we attempt to determine the value of the benefit. For example, impact on the business through innovation is very hard to measure quantitatively, while the benefit of improved product quality may be easier to measure.

IS investment – balancing costs and benefits

We can deduce from the above discussion that the more accurately we can identify the contribution of IS towards the value of business gain, the more accurately we can identify the value accruing from IS investments. It follows from this that in order to assess the value of future investments in IS, we must come up with a framework that allows us to weigh up the relative costs and benefits and so enables us to make properly considered IS investment decisions.

There are a number of approaches that attempt to evaluate IS investment decisions. In essence, a proposed or ongoing investment should proceed if the benefits from the investment outweigh the costs incurred. However, as Robson (1997) indicates, one of the main difficulties is the intangible benefits, which can amount to at least 30 per cent of all benefits obtained. In addition, even if a benefit can be quantified (e.g. a new system speeds up customer response to queries from an average of 10 minutes to 10 seconds), it is not always easy to put a monetary value on it. This leads to a division in approaches between those that concentrate purely on financial measures and those that attempt a non-monetary evaluation.

Earlier (in Chapter 8) we considered the basis of investment decisions taken at the feasibility assessment stage of the initiation of an individual project. It is the role of the IS manager to ensure that individual IS project decisions are consistent with the company's overall IS strategy.

Financial justification methods look at the relationship between the monetary costs of IS investment and the monetary benefits that might be obtained from it. There are a number of techniques that can be used, including:

- return on investment (ROI);
- discounted cashflow (DCF), such as net present value (NPV) and internal rate of return (IRR);
- payback period.

These are described in more detail elsewhere (in Chapter 8), which also reviews how they are applied to a proposal for an individual system.

Risk assessment methods, on the other hand, look at a number of factors other than those related to pure financial return. Such considerations include:

- the benefits that are designed to accrue from investment in different categories of IS;
- the reasons that systems fail;
- categories of risk and their likely impact on systems success.

Information systems fail when they do not deliver the benefits they were intended to achieve. Clearly, the greater the investment in IS, the greater the impact of a failed project, especially as that investment could have been made in another part of the business (e.g. investment in additional plant, people or equipment) with much greater effect.

We will now look at an alternative approach for prioritising investment in IS.

Investment categories of the IS applications portfolio

Sullivan (1985) identified four investment categories for information systems that provide a framework within which the strategic value of the investment to the company can be placed. It is useful to identify in which category a new system lies within the IS portfolio, in order to assess its importance and allocate resources to it accordingly. The investment categories are:

1. *Strategic systems.* These are designed to bring about innovation and change in the conduct of business and so bring about a competitive edge. Business processes may need to be designed and relationships with customers and suppliers changed. Risk occurs because of the level of uncertainty associated with these kinds of systems (we are dealing with unstructured decision making, the results of which are often hard to quantify).

2. *Key operational systems.* Existing processes are rationalised, integrated or reorganised in order to carry out the activities of business more effectively. The risk occurs in the complexity of the systems in this category and the need to integrate them with other systems (externally as well as internally).

3. *Support systems.* Such systems support well-structured, stable and well-understood business processes (i.e. decisions are usually made in a climate of relatively high business certainty). Benefits derive either from eliminating unnecessary processes or from automating regular and routine procedures. In either case, the aim is to reduce cost and raise efficiency. The risks occur in selecting the right kind of software (often packaged) and implementing it effectively to gain the benefits.

4. *High-potential projects.* These are of research and development orientation and may have the capacity to deliver significant business benefits in the future. They are usually high-risk projects (in the sense that they may not deliver anything at all) and the main business risk lies in committing too much money to the project (i.e. the attitude that if we invest more, we must realise some benefits!).

The challenge for the organisation is to channel investment into the areas that are likely to yield the highest level of potential benefit at the lowest level of acceptable risk.

Risk factors

These have been summarised by Ward and Peppard (2002). They should be considered at the start of a project to attempt to reduce the risk of project failure. Risk management is described in more detail elsewhere (in Chapter 8).

LOCATING THE INFORMATION SYSTEMS MANAGEMENT FUNCTION

There are two basic approaches to locating the information system function in an organisation that operates at more than one location. These are the centralisation of all IS services at one office (usually the head office) and decentralisation. It is unusual for a company to choose one extreme or the other; typically, the approach will vary for the different types of services. The approach chosen is significant, since it will have a direct correspondence to the quality of service available to the end-user departments and the cost of providing this service.

What needs to be managed?

It is useful to make a distinction between information systems and information technology. As has been stated before, we can view IT as the infrastructure and an enabler, while information systems give a business the applications that produce the information for decision-making purposes. IS cannot exist without the IT to support them, but IT on its own does not of itself confer any business benefits.

For information technology the following must be managed:

- *Hardware platforms.* These need to be selected and supported (for example, it may be decided only to operate a client/server environment using Unix workstations).

- *Network architectures.* An organisation currently operating a mixture of AS/400 computers and PCs may wish to focus on a particular network architecture for the PCs in order to facilitate easier integration with the AS/400 systems.

- *Development tools.* It may be desirable to adopt tools that permit more rapid development of new information systems. Such tools will need to be able to run on the selected hardware platform and also be compatible with chosen database management systems.

- *Legacy systems.* These systems may run on old hardware platforms and be difficult to integrate with planned systems development. While strictly an IS issue rather than an IT one, it may still be necessary in the short-to-medium term to provide the necessary IT support to allow these systems to continue to operate.

- *Operations management.* This covers a number of areas, including hardware management, capacity planning, security (backups, access control, error detection, archiving), technical support (for hardware and systems software), telecommunications and network management.

The areas that relate to information systems management are:

- *Business systems development.* Applications development falls into two broad categories: those applications that deal with corporate data and those that are departmental or personal in nature.

- *Migration and conversion strategy.* While strictly being part of the systems development process, migration from one system to another involves specialists from both IS/IT and functional business areas. For corporate information systems, many functional areas may be involved.

- *Database administration.* Today's information systems depend very much on database management systems (such as DB2, Oracle, Informix and Access).

- *User support and training.* All applications software users require support at some point. The objective is to get the right support to the right people at the right time.

- *End-user application development.* This is becoming increasingly popular, especially in medium-to-large organisations. Such development will not only require support (e.g. advice on appropriate development tools) but will require explicit management to ensure that wheels are not being re-invented and bug-ridden software not being produced.

- *Shared services.* Recent innovations such as e-mail and collaborative work systems have both local and corporate application. The objective should be to maximise local flexibility while at the same time ensuring that organisation-wide standards are adhered to (the same could be said of end-user development).

- *IS/IT staffing.* While this is more of a human resources issue than an IT one, it is, nevertheless, important to stress that for an IT strategy to be implemented, there need to be staff with expertise in hardware, communications, systems software and development software. Naturally, for a small business this expertise will be limited.

This analysis indicates that there are some aspects of IS/IT that need central control and management, but at the same time there are local needs that have to be addressed within individual functional areas of the business. Therefore, we should now move from *what* needs to be managed to *where* IS/IT needs to be managed and the factors that influence this.

Structuring information systems management

In a large company with several sites, IS/IT management must be organised and located in such a way as to ensure full integration of business and IS/IT strategies, as well as full support for the IS/IT needs of each functional area of the business.

Questions that should be asked when ascertaining the best approach include:

- *Is information systems management (ISM) in tune with corporate strategy?* Structures need to exist in such a way that an organisation's information systems strategy is fully embedded within its business strategy. This means that mechanisms must exist that embrace all functional areas of the business as well as the most senior management.

- *Is ISM in tune with organisational shape?* A heavily centralised approach to managing all aspects of IS/IT may conflict with a geographically dispersed organisation, or with one where individual functional areas enjoy a high degree of local autonomy.

- *Is the focus of ISM inward-looking on managing technology?* If this is the case, it suggests that IS/IT is operating mainly in a support capacity rather than a strategic one. An alternative, less palatable explanation is that the IS/IT department is rooted in the past and does not see IS/IT as being an integral part of business strategy.

- *Is the focus of ISM outward-looking on helping the business plan the best use of technology?* A positive answer to this question indicates a modern approach to IS/IT management. One can look at all aspects of IS/IT, from getting the best management information from existing transaction processing systems to implementing a company-wide communications strategy to enable business processes to be re-engineered and facilitate better links to customers and suppliers.

There are a number of additional factors that will influence the structuring of information systems management. An organisation that operates in a single geographic location will have different needs from one that is spread over many sites (perhaps over many countries). Similarly, a business that has a diverse range of products and business operations may need an ISM different from that of a single-product company. If a large organisation has a number of discrete strategic business units, it may be appropriate to treat each distinct SBU as a separate entity in its own right for ISM purposes.

One must also not ignore the impact of organisational culture and management style on ISM structure. An organisation that has a decentralised management philosophy may find it easier to decentralise certain ISM functions than one that is highly centralised.

There are two approaches to IS/IT management. The centralised approach will concentrate all aspects of IS/IT management at a single point within the organisation, such as the data processing or management information systems (MIS) department. An MIS department may either report into a single functional business area (traditionally, the accounting department has been a popular choice) or it may report directly at board level. The modern trend is for MIS managers or chief information officers (CIOs) to report directly at board level in the same way as heads of functional areas such as HRM, sales and finance.

The decentralised approach recognises that some aspects of IS/IT management are best located close to the point of use. If any degree of decentralisation exists, the inference is that there will be staff located within the parts of the organisation that enjoy a degree of local autonomy. In some cases, the staff will be IS/IT professionals who might otherwise be located in a more centralised structure.

Alternatively, there may be 'hybrid' personnel who have both functional area expertise and good IS/IT skills. Aspects of IS/IT that lend themselves well to a degree of decentralisation are the development of end-user applications, use of report generators with corporate data as the main input, and information systems in functional areas that carry out discrete activities not connected with primary business functions (such as plant maintenance or HRM systems).

For centralised and decentralised approaches there are advantages. With the centralised approach, it is suggested that it is possible to:

- achieve and control consistent IS/IT strategy without having to worry about what individual functional business areas are doing;
- coordinate IS/IT activities more easily;
- implement simpler control systems, since it will not be necessary to monitor the quality of the distributed IS/IT activities;
- allocate resources more efficiently, using the benefit of economies of scale and eliminating the risk of similar applications being developed in different parts of the organisation;
- achieve speedier strategic decision making because of fewer parties being involved.

Supporters of the decentralised approach also claim a number of advantages:

- The presence of IS/IT expertise at a functional level allows for a rapid response to local problems without the competition for resources that exists with the centralised approach.
- Where local decisions can be made about IS/IT that directly affects that area, improved motivation and commitment among staff to their information systems is likely.
- The cumbersome overhead associated with purely centralised systems is reduced.

Decentralised IS management

Management of some IS services in individual operating companies or at regional offices, but with some centralised control.

Centralised IS management

The control of all IS services from a central location, typically in a company head office or data centre.

The decentralised approach also has a number of problems associated with it:

- Where responsibilities are split (e.g. between operational and strategic matters), they need to be very carefully defined if matters are not to be forgotten.
- Central management may become frustrated by what it perceives as an idiosyncratic approach being adopted within the functional business areas (and vice versa).
- Split responsibilities may result in complicated control procedures which make decision making more difficult and time-consuming. No one location will be correct for all organisations. Indeed, as an organisation moves towards the maturity stage, it will evolve different locations for different areas of information systems management.

For those who get the balance right between centralised and decentralised services, they can expect to enjoy:

- rapid information systems development;
- harmonious IS and business relationships;
- an IS service that is tailored for the user community;
- a cost-effective IS/IT function;
- development of technology infrastructures that support the required information systems;
- business success through successfully implemented IS/IT strategies;
- adoption of appropriate IS strategies;
- effective change management processes;
- encouragement of end-user computing where appropriate;
- accurate assessment of IS/IT costs and benefits, thus ensuring value for money from IS/IT investments.

On the other hand, those organisations that fail can expect:

- continual conflict between functional business areas and the IS/IT function;
- continual complaints about information systems management as a whole;
- business decline or inefficient service provision;
- lack of interest in information systems by non-IS/IT personnel;
- skills problems – either shortages in certain areas or wasteful duplication;
- high staff turnover;
- gaps and overlaps in the provision of IS/IT services.

Information systems outsourcing

All or part of the information systems services of a company are subcontracted to a third party.

Activity 14.1	Location of the IS function at Security Services Limited (SSL)

This is an additional case study on the companion web site. You should suggest an appropriate strategy for SSL which is distributed over several sites in the UK.

OUTSOURCING

Outsourcing occurs when a function of a company that was traditionally conducted internally by company staff is instead completed by a third party. The main reasons for doing this are usually cost reduction and to enable focus on the core business. Functions that are commonly outsourced include catering, cleaning, public relations and information systems.

Outsourcing is a major trend in the development and management of information systems. Major public and private organisations in the UK such as the Inland Revenue and Rolls-Royce have outsourced its IS management to Electronic Data Systems (EDS).

Types of outsourcing

There are different degrees of outsourcing, varying from total outsourcing to partial management of services. It is best to consider the types of outsourcing services offered rather than specifics such as facilities management and time sharing, which are open to different interpretations. The main categories of services that can be managed include:

1. *Hardware outsourcing.* This may involve renting time on a high-capacity mainframe computer. Effectively, the company is sharing the expense of purchasing and maintaining the network with other companies that are also signed up to an outsourcing contract. This arrangement is sometimes known as a **time-sharing** contract.

2. *Network management.* Network management may also be involved when managing hardware: here a third party is responsible for maintaining the network. This is often referred to as **facilities management (FM)**, and may also include management of PC and server hardware.

3. *Outsourcing systems development.* When specialised programs are required by a business, it is necessary either to develop bespoke software or to modify existing systems. This is also a significant outsourcing activity. When EDS undertook its contract with the Inland Revenue in the UK, one of its main tasks was to write the software to deal with changes to the way in which tax forms were submitted.

4. *IS support.* A company help desk can be outsourced to a third party. This could cover answering queries about operating systems, office applications or specific company applications. It could also include fixing problems, in which case an on-site presence would be required. Microsoft outsources much of its support for Windows 95 and 98 to third parties such as Digital.

5. *Management of IS strategy.* Determining and executing the information systems strategy is less common than the other types of outsourcing outlined above, because many companies want to retain this control. A great deal of trust will be placed in the outsourcing partner in this arrangement and it is most common in a total outsourcing contract.

6. *Total outsourcing.* An example of total outsourcing is the 1996 agreement between Thorn Europe and IBM Global Services. This five-year contract involves IBM taking over all IT operations on hardware from five different vendors, managing 90 staff and defining and implementing the IT strategy as well.

Time sharing

The processing and storage capacity of a mainframe computer is rented to several companies using a leasing arrangement.

facilities management (FM)

The management of a range of IT services by an outsourcing provider. These commonly include network management and associated software and hardware.

Mini case study | **Customers admit blame for outsourcing failures**

Many businesses accept that poor management on their part and unrealistic expectations are largely to blame for failed IT outsourcing deals, according to a new report released today by sourcing advisory firm TPI.

Meanwhile, a separate study has concluded that the potential for significant savings through outsourcing is expected to fuel growth in the offshoring market for the next 20 years at least.

The TPI report, which is based on responses from 40 large firms undertaking outsourcing projects, found that almost a third admitted to placing more emphasis on setting up an outsourcing contract than they did on managing it. Over half also said that their own 'unrealistic' expectations were a major barrier to the success of the project.

'Contrary to popular belief, many companies blame themselves at least as much as the service providers for their own dissatisfaction with outsourcing relationships', said Stuart Harris, partner at TPI. 'Moreover, problems encountered with outsourcing contracts prior to renegotiations often stem from a lack of clarity between the client and the service provider about the scope of the services to be provided – not the quality of the services themselves.'

Harris said the fact that only 18 percent of respondents had looked to replace their incumbent supplier during contract renegotiations suggested that most customers understood that relationships with outsourcers could change over time.

'Most clients conclude that the industry's service providers are generally adept at delivering on contractual commitments, and that courses of remedy must necessarily involve changes to service management and governance processes in the first instance', explained Harris.

The report will prove reassuring to outsourcing providers, many of whom have been roundly blamed for the high proportion of IT outsourcing projects that are deemed to have failed. However, it also suggests that some outsourcers may be exploiting customers' weak outsourcing management skills, with almost a third of respondents claiming their bargaining position had weakened during the renegotiation process compared with when the original deal was signed.

Worryingly for the outsourcing sector, the report also found that best practice outsourcing management techniques are still not widespread. Almost half of respondents said they had no formal governance structure, while over a third fail to hold regular meetings for monitoring outsourcing deals.

The findings are particularly concerning in the wake of a recent study from management consultancy AT Kearney that predicts offshore outsourcing sites such as India and China will retain their cost advantage for another 20 years, despite wage inflation.

Paul Laudicina, managing office of AT Kearney, said that the report also revealed that while salaries in offshore locations are climbing, the quality and stability of their services are also improving. 'These findings reinforce the message that corporations making global location decisions should focus less on short-term cost considerations, and more on long-term projections of talent supply and operating conditions', he said.

The report also identified Indonesia, Malaysia, the Philippines, Singapore, Thailand and Vietnam, as the strongest challengers to India and China in the offshore outsourcing market.

Source: IT Week, 20 March 2007, www.computing.co.uk/itweek/news/2185966/customers-admit-blame

Why do companies outsource?

The main reasons for IS outsourcing are to achieve the following:

- *Cost reduction.* An outsourcing vendor can share its assets, such as mainframes and staff, between different companies and achieve economies of scale. It is also argued by outsourcing vendors that lower costs are achieved since they are in a contractual relationship, unlike most internal providers of IT services.

- *Quality improvements and customer satisfaction.* Through outsourcing IS functions to a company that is expert in this field, it should be possible to deliver better-quality services to internal and external customers. Better quality could be in the form of systems that are more reliable and have appropriate features, a more reliable company network and better phone support.

- *Enables focus on core business.* A company can concentrate its expertise on what it is familiar with, i.e. its market and customers, rather than being distracted by information systems development. This particular argument is weak in some industries such as the financial services sector where information systems are critical to operating in a particular market.

- *Reduce risk of project failure.* Owing to the contract, there is more pressure on the supplier compared with internal developers to deliver a quality product on time, hence it is more likely to succeed.

- *Implementation of a strategic objective.* To implement a strategic objective may involve considerable risk if it is undertaken internally or resources are not available. For example, in the mid-1990s many companies undertook outsourcing to ensure that the 'millennium bug' could be fixed by using a third party with the expertise to solve the problem. Similarly, in the mid-1990s many companies were undertaking business process re-engineering initiatives that often involved major changes to information systems.

Reasons for outsourcing

The top 10 reasons companies outsource (in alphabetical order), according to The Outsourcing Institute:

1. Accelerate re-engineering benefits

2. Access to world-class capabilities

3. Cash infusion

4. Free resources for other purposes

5. Function difficult to manage or out of control

6. Improve company focus

7. Make capital funds available

8. Reduce operating costs

9. Reduce risk

10. Resources not available internally

Source: The Outsourcing Institute, © 1998 The Outsourcing Institute, Jericho, NY.

Whether these benefits are achievable is currently the subject of a great deal of debate, with the detractors of outsourcing arguing that although costs may be reduced, the quality of the service will also decline. Since outsourcing is a relatively new phenomenon, it is not clear whether the promises are achieved, but the number of companies signing up to outsourcing contracts indicates that it is a major industry trend. Other problems that may occur are that IT staff are likely to be unhappy, as they are transferred to a third-party company with new contracts. To summarise this section, reasons given by companies as to why they use outsourcing are given in Table 14.1.

Table 14.1 Main reasons for outsourcing

Reason	Percentage mentioning
Cost savings	57%
Improved quality of service	40%
Access to specialist expertise	37%
Increased flexibility	27%
Strategic business decision	21%
Free management time	19%
Lack of resources	11%
Improved financial control	8%

Activity 14.2 — Reasons for outsourcing

Examine Table 14.1 and assess which of the reasons for outsourcing would be important to the following:

1. Financial manager (chief finance officer).

2. Information systems manager.

3. Managing director.

4. Departmental manager in human resources, marketing or production.

Problems of outsourcing

Strassmann (2002) checked on some of the largest recent multi-year contracts for firms that outsourced more than half their computing resources. An analysis of detailed financial information from 1996 to 2000 that was available for eight firms revealed that each of them had delivered declining returns on (shareholder) equity (ROE), with the average ROE for the entire group declining from 18.2 per cent in 1996 to 2.5 per cent in 2000.

This observation raises an interesting question: is it the outsourcing of computing resources that is the cause of the decline, or is it a symptom of outsourcing being used by a business in trouble as an attempt to reduce costs?

Collins and Millen (1995) cite the following concerns over outsourcing:

- loss of control of IS
- loss or degradation of internal IS services
- corporate security issues
- qualifications of outside personnel
- negative impact on employee morale.

In addition to these problems, case studies seem to suggest that the principal objective of undertaking outsourcing, cost reduction, may not be achieved in many cases. Cost reduction is usually thought to occur because of a reduction in the number of staff employed and savings on the cost of acquisition of hardware and software through discounts available through economies of scale.

Lacity and Hirscheim (1995), in their classic study of outsourcing, identify the following reasons for escalating costs:

- not identifying present and future requirements fully, and leaving loopholes in the contract;
- failing to identify the full costs and service levels of existing in-house operations, with the result that contracts turn out to cost more than originally anticipated because in-house calculations were too low;
- change-of-character clauses prompting excess fees for any changes in service or functions;
- software licence transfer clauses making customers responsible for fees;
- fixed prices that soon exceed market prices because the cost of IT is decreasing;
- fluctuations in data processing volumes not covered by fixed limits under the contract, and incurring significantly higher fees.
- paying extra for services that the customer assumed were included in the fixed price, because of poor analysis beforehand of services provided by the in-house group leading to a limited fixed-price contract;

- subsidising the vendor's learning curve;
- changes in technology: vendors offer services on existing platforms and subsequent moves into new technology often cost more than anticipated.

To avoid some of the problems outlined above, the design of the contract is critical to ensure that the supplier provides a full service. For network management this can be achieved through service-level agreements (SLAs) that specify minimum acceptable values for availability of the network, such as 99.8 per cent access, or give the maximum number of failures per month. It is more difficult to specify in a contract services to be provided for developing software. As a result of this, the costs of outsourced software development can spiral. Further details on defining contracts for information systems development are given later in this chapter.

Human factors and outsourcing

Outsourcing IS developments will have a direct impact on information systems staff and this needs to be managed. In the worst case staff may be made redundant, but in the majority of cases the outsourcing company will agree to employ existing IS staff while a core of IS staff remain with the company to manage the contract or functions that have not been outsourced. Redundancies tend not to occur, because this is part of the agreement between the company and the outsourcer to avoid resistance to change. Additionally, due to shortages of IS staff it is usually possible for the outsourcing company to redeploy staff if necessary.

Even if staff are not made redundant, transfer of staff will cause major disruption and often resentment. One main cause of this is that staff will be forced to sign a new contract when they transfer. While remuneration may be better, terms and conditions will change. For example, there may be no paid overtime, or staff may be asked to work elsewhere in the country on other outsourcing contracts. Positive aspects of outsourcing for staff may include:

- improved rates of pay;
- better training;
- greater career opportunities for improving knowledge and promotion through working in a range of companies.

Making outsourcing work

The critical role of the contract in ensuring that an outsourcing initiative will work has already been mentioned. In addition to this, other factors must be incorporated. These include:

- Outsourcing strategy must be consistent with the business and information management strategy.
- Level of outsourcing should be appropriate to the business: selective outsourcing for most businesses or total outsourcing where information systems play a mainly supporting role.
- A method of retaining control and leverage over the suppliers is necessary. This could include a shorter-term contract, a risk and reward contract, and not including strategic planning in the services to be outsourced.
- Human factors involved in outsourcing must be considered in conjunction with the human resources department, particularly where staff may be displaced or made redundant.

Table 14.2 Decision matrix for deciding which IS services stay in-house

Business characteristics	Outsource	Don't outsource
Business positioning impact	Low	High
Links to business strategy	Low	High
Future business uncertainty	Low	High
Technological maturity	High	Low
Level of IT integration	Low	High
In-house v. market expertise	Low	High

- If a company does not have previous experience of outsourcing, it may be valuable to get an independent specialist to assist in drawing up the outsourcing agreement.
- Allocating time and using measurement systems to manage the outsourcing contract.

Feeny et al. (1995) have identified alternative scenarios to help an organisation decide whether to stay in-house or to outsource. These are summarised in Table 14.2.

The same authors cite the following statistics from the organisations they surveyed:

- 80 per cent had considered outsourcing;
- 47 per cent outsourced some or all of their information systems;
- 70 per cent did not have formal outsourcing policy in place;
- only 43 per cent of organisations that had outsourced actually have an outsourcing policy;
- few organisations approach outsourcing in a strategic manner.

These rather alarming statistics clearly show that more than half of those organisations that outsource some of their information systems provision do not have a formal outsourcing policy in place. Perhaps it is not surprising then, that Paul Strassmann (2002) has described outsourcing as a 'game for losers'.

In a review of outsourcing success factors, Gonzalez et al. (2005) summarise a number of success factors in the literature. The key success factors include:

- *Provider's understanding of clients' objectives* – the client–provider relationship management should focus on the achievement of the clients' aims; suppliers that have a good understanding and an interest in the outsourcing firm's business will be better positioned to help define those goals essential for the middle- and long-term continuity of the outsourcing relationship.
- *Choosing the right provider* – this can be key to the success or failure of the outsourcing agreement; therefore, prior to contract signature, a detailed evaluation and selection of potential vendors must be carried out and the provider must be chosen from a wide range of IT vendors in order to locate a potential outsourcing provider; an organisation should also investigate current outsourcing partnerships in the same sector as well as in related industries; factors such as the stab-ility, quality and reputation of the provider should also be considered.
- *A clear idea of what is sought through outsourcing* – an accurate definition of the project's scope and specifications is a clear prerequisite for outsourcing success; if firms resort to outsourcing with only a vague idea of what they want to obtain from the vendor, unavoidable uncertainty relating both to technological aspects of the IS service and to the volume of needs that must be met will result; the solution, therefore, is to outsource only those activities that are clearly understood and for which a solid contract can be drawn up. It is also recommended to sign the contract for a length of time that allows the firm to monitor its business requirements whilst the client firm must also make an effort to clarify the business objectives that will be reached through outsourcing.

- *Provider's attention to clients' specific problems* – since each organisation is different, firms are advised against standard contracts and clients want to feel that the provider will take into account their special technological and business characteristics.

- *Frequent client–provider contacts* – the literature suggests that these contacts will make it possible to build working relationships, confidence, comfort and trust; ensure the provider's extensive acclimatisation to understand their customer's style, standards and culture; good communication between client and vendor in order to make the outsourcing deal successful for everybody; enable continuity by designing relationships that anticipate change as business conditions and technology evolve, thus requiring relationship structures and management mechanisms that ensure successful work with the outsourcing vendor over time

- *A good-value-for-money relationship* – since financial justification is seen as one of the top ten outsourcing success factors, outsourcing is likely to be successful when financial expectations such as the achievement of a cash infusion, cost reduction, production and transaction cost economies, financial slack or even tax advantages are covered.

- *Top management's support and involvement* – given that the involvement of the top management in IT-related decisions is largely the key determining factor for the good or bad performance of IS departments within organisations, senior management support is also crucial in the IT outsourcing process where both senior management and IT management involvement is required to conduct a rational outsourcing evaluation; by involving both in the outsourcing decision, financial, business and technical objectives can be defined, thus establishing the scope of the outsourcing evaluation, developing bid analysis criteria, and verification of the bid analysis, whilst the IT management 'assumes the critical role of creating the detailed request for proposal, evaluating the legitimacy of vendor economies of scale, estimating the effects of price/performance improvements, and providing insights on emerging technologies that might affect the business'.

- *Proper contract structuring* – if an organisation outsources its information systems, a written outsourcing contract is the only certain way to ensure that expectations will be realised – it is therefore essential to outsourcing success. Good outsourcing contracts must be as comprehensive as possible, defining all pertinent issues; they must discuss the obligations of each party, cost, duration, terms and conditions and must include clauses that refer to its evolution, reversibility, termination and penalisation. The contract can, therefore, 'be viewed as a set of master terms and conditions, with details about the specific work required and the compensation for that work treated as additional components'.

CASE STUDY 14.1

Outsourcing: beware false economies

By Jane Bird

Letting a contractor deal with 'your mess for less' is the conventional attraction of outsourcing – customers save money by handing over their hardware, software, networking and even information technology staff to a third party.

Clients often say they want to outsource to focus on their core business, to improve flexibility or to access

skilled staff, says Neville Howard, a partner in the technology integration team at Deloitte, the business advisers. 'But I haven't seen one yet that doesn't want to save money on operating costs.'

Traditional IT outsourcing contracts last five, seven or even 10 years, and offer annual savings of about 20 per cent. Suppliers tend to lose money in the first year or two because of the investment required in taking over legacy systems.

Over the long term, they save by shedding staff, streamlining systems and achieving economies of scale. In recent years, this pricing model has become harder to achieve because of a shortage of capital to borrow.

Clients' discomfort with the idea of their IT being handled at long distances has also made it more difficult for suppliers to cut costs by offshoring. The advent of cloud computing and software as a service, with their pay-as-you-go pricing, has also increased the financial pressure on outsourcing suppliers.

Many have made unrealistic promises to win contracts and then underinvested. 'Service levels dip and customers become frustrated. We hear that again and again,' says Mr Howard. Customers should be careful about driving a hard bargain, he says, because what looks like a lower price might end up costing more.

Martin Burvill, group vice-president of global solutions at Verizon Business, the US IT services provider, says that customers who just want to save money by outsourcing and ruthlessly drive down suppliers on price are making a big mistake. 'Suppliers try to recover their losses by charging for all the extras or cutting back resources, so there is a huge gulf between expectation and execution.'

Customers can't expect to get a cheaper service unless they are prepared to let suppliers change the operating model and methodology, Mr Burvill says. 'Without transformation, the supplier won't make money. This is pure logic, but it gets forgotten,' he says.

Customers have to be prepared to adapt, he adds, and the more they can move to the outsourcing provider's systems, the greater the potential savings.

Customers can often get better value for money by focusing on how the outsourcing provider can make them more competitive or help to bring out products faster, says Jonathan Cooper-Bagnall, head of outsourcing at PA Consulting.

'That might mean switching some services off or scaling them back, or shifting the speed of transition from legacy infrastructure to new customer-focused applications.' They could also request fewer estimates for new applications, which are expensive, he says.

For outsourcing providers, moving away from guaranteed returns and minimum commitments is a big step, says Mr Cooper-Bagnall. 'It fundamentally changes the way they can sell, because it's not about

length of contract. They have to change the incentive structure for sales staff, and think about whether it cannibalises a service they already provide.'

Nick Grossman, group business development director of 2e2, an IT services provider, suggests that customers should set challenges for outsourcing suppliers, such as reducing the time and cost of processing documents. 'With measurable targets, suppliers can be offered a share in the risks and rewards of improving business efficiency,' he says.

Keeping outsourcing providers to a minimum also helps to reduce costs, says Don Herring, the New Jersey-based senior vice-president of network sourcing at AT&T, the communications company. AT&T encourages clients to engage a maximum of three suppliers to handle computing, applications and networking respectively, and to expect them to collaborate. This can result in savings of up to 35 per cent, says Mr Herring.

Having multiple suppliers can also help to keep prices low by introducing competition. It is smart to have a couple of providers for activities such as maintenance and application development, says Deloitte's Mr Howard. Then you can have a mini contest between the two.

'Otherwise,' he says, 'it's very hard to know how long they need; you might get a low hourly rate that ends up costing more than another provider that charges more but does the job quicker.

Minimising the use of consultants also saves money, says Mr Burvill at Verizon. 'Being paid by the day motivates consultants to prolong their contracts by continuously changing the specification.'

There is a lot of emotion in outsourcing, especially as it often involves transferring staff, which is upsetting and causes upheaval. This disruption is one reason why about 40 per cent of clients for which Deloitte looks at outsourcing end up keeping the service in-house. They decide there are not enough cost savings, or the risks outweigh the benefits, particularly for small and medium-sized businesses.

A number of Deloitte's clients that have tried outsourcing are bringing it back in house, Mr Howard says. 'It is a bit like marriage – there can be lots of suffering and violence, and occasionally a messy divorce.'

To avoid breakdown, customers should be prepared to share the financial rewards of improved efficiency. A level of mild dissatisfaction is not unusual in customers, Mr Howard says. 'But responsibility for making it work rests as much with them as with suppliers.'

 Source: Bird, J. (2011) Outsourcing: beware false economies. *Financial Times*. 6 December.
© The Financial Times Limited 2011. All Rights Reserved.

QUESTION

Discuss the economics of outsourcing.

BEYOND STRATEGIC INFORMATION SYSTEMS – THE IMPORTANCE OF IS CAPABILITY

Until relatively recently, the management of information systems within organisations can largely be described as belonging to the 'strategic information systems (SIS) era: that is, management typically seeks out opportunities for competitive advantage through investment in IS/IT where those investments are aligned with corporate strategy and also where those investments can be used to shape business strategy. Peppard and Ward (2004), however, propose an alternative perspective whereby management of IS/IT in organisations can 'continuously derive and leverage value through IT'. In a summary of antecedent literature, they point out that only IS management skills are likely to be a source of sustained competitive advantage and that 'these skills are the ability of IS managers to understand and appreciate business needs; their ability to work with functional managers; the ability to co-ordinate IS activities in ways that support other functional managers; and the ability to anticipate future needs'.

In promoting a resource-based view of competitive advantage, Peppard and Ward identify three main elements of resource-based theory (RBT) to help establish a context for developing a model of IS/IT capability. These elements are:

- *Resources* – resources in this context are available factors of production that are owned or controlled by the firm, including the information, systems and techno-logy owned or available to the firm are and 'in the context of IS management the critical resources are the knowledge and skills residing in employees or the employees of third-party vendors'.

- *Competencies* – the RBT perspective indicates that resources of themselves do not create value, but that value is created by an organisation's ability to utilise and mobilise those resources. From an IS management perspective, competencies can be portrayed as the ability to deploy combinations of firm-specific resources to accomplish a given task and that they represent the collective knowledge of the firm in initiating or responding to change.

- *Capability* – this refers to the strategic application of competencies and their use and deployment to accomplish given organisational goals; an organisation's current capability is based on its existing competencies, will be either an enabler or inhibitor in terms of the goals it can actually achieve.

Peppard and Ward go on to suggest that one way to apply RBT to the management of IS is to focus on competencies within the IS function and that research has identified six domains of IS competence: strategy, defining the IS contribution, defining the IT capability, exploitation, delivering solutions and supply. They are defined as follows:

Strategy – ability to identify and evaluate the implications of IT based opportunities as an integral part of business strategy formulation and define the role of IS/IT in the organization

Define the IS contribution – the ability to translate the business strategy into processes, information and systems investments and change plans that match the business priorities (i.e. the IS strategy)

Define the IT capability – the ability to translate the business strategy into long term information architectures, technology infrastructure and resourcing plans that enable the implementation of the strategy (i.e. the IT strategy)

Exploitation – the ability to maximize the benefits realized from the implementation of IS/IT investments through effective use of information, applications and IT services

Deliver solutions – the ability to deploy resources to develop, implement and operate IS/IT business solutions, which exploit the capabilities of the technology

Supply – the ability to create and maintain an appropriate and adaptable information, technology and application supply chain and resource capacity.

Figure 14.1 A model of the IS capability

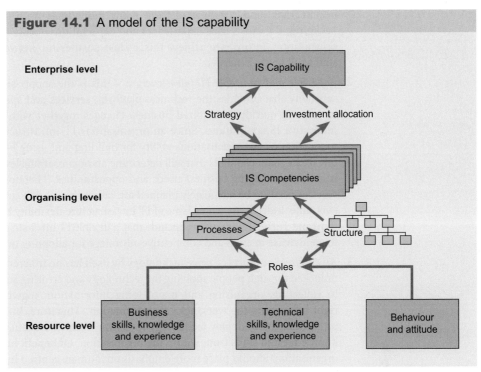

Source: Peppard and Ward (2004)

Peppard and Ward propose that a model that can be constructed to represent the components of the IS capability as illustrated in Figure 14.1.

In order to arrive at an understanding of IS capability, they suggest that first one needs to understand the relationship between resources and IS competencies and then between IS competencies and IS capability. Competencies, it is suggested, are embedded in organisational processes which in turn are bounded by the structure of the organisation. By performing roles in organisational structures, people apply and integrate their knowledge by interacting with others and coordinating their actions. A competency is, therefore, an emergent property of organisational processes. From an information systems perspective, *processes* include 'formulating strategies, management decision making processes for investments in IS/IT, managing the organisational and business changes required to deliver value, and the responsibilities and accountabilities for realizing specific benefits'. The *roles* that need to be performed to deliver these processes require individuals to have certain abilities including their *skills* (e.g. the ability to draw data flow diagrams), *know-ledge* (e.g. what might be involved in constructing a workable outsourcing contract) and *behaviours and attitudes* that make knowledge useful and enable skills to be acquired (e.g. having IS staff who empathise with the user in delivering IS services). Finally, structures need to be put in place that enable processes to be performed effectively and which allow skills to be harnessed (e.g. structures that easily facilitate cross-functional communication and delivery).

When examining the relationship between IS competency and IS capability, it is suggested that an organisation's *strategy* and its *investment decisions* are the two key contributing factors. These two factors can determine whether an organisation's IS capability is a source of competitive advantage, competitive parity or competitive disadvantage. IS capability, according to Peppard and Ward, has three interrelated attributes.

1. *Fusing IS knowledge and business knowledge* – this is essential to ensure that strategies involving technological innovation can be formulated, and appropriate IS choices made and implemented quickly and effectively. In addition, knowledge will need to

be integrated and coordinated from many individuals from different disciplines and backgrounds, with varied experiences and expectations, located in different parts of the organisation. In order to achieve this, a close partnership between IS staff and business staff at all levels is needed.

2. *A flexible and re-usable IT infrastructure* – this is the supply-side component of the IS capability that provides the technical platform, services and specialist resources needed to respond quickly to required business changes together with the capacity to develop innovative IS applications. Since an organisation's IT infrastructure provides the shared foundation of the organisation's ability for building and using business applications, it is one of the main elements that will determine an organisation's level of agility as it seeks to respond to changing business needs and opportunities. Therefore, IT infrastructure and services needs to be adequately planned for, rather than simply grow in an ad-hoc manner over time. Indeed, the whole issue of IT infrastructure flexibility has been well explored by Byrd and Turner (2000) who conclude that 'a flexible IT infra-structure is positively related to an increase in costs and competitive advantage for adopting organisations'.

3. *An effective use process* – since technology by itself has no inherent value, its value must be unlocked through people applying the technology and creating an environment conducive to collecting, organising and maintaining information, together with embracing the right behaviours for working with information. Therefore, business and management processes need to deploy technology to deliver business benefits, which in turn requires knowledge and skills from within the organisation. Of benefit here is the suggestion that organisations should place more emphasis on 'human-centred information management' in order to improve the ways in which people use and share information.

This section has emphasised the importance of management processes in providing organisations with an IS capability that is a source of competitive advantage through the harnessing of human and technical resources. Peppard and Ward rather wistfully conclude in their 2004 paper that 'the recent re-labelling of IS/IT as "e" seemed to re-ignite that inherently flawed notion (that merely possessing a technology will deliver untold benefits). The stock market boom in technology stocks and unsubstantiated claims for the "new economy" increased that misplaced confidence for a short time – but long enough for vast sums to be wasted on failed IT investments! This suggests a significant level of incompetence exists.'

FOCUS ON... IT INFRASTRUCTURE FLEXIBILITY

Byrd and Turner (2000) have noted that, on average, IT infrastructure expenditures account for over 58 per cent of an organisation's IT budget and this is growing annually at a rate of 11 per cent. Given that an organisation's IT infrastructure is a key factor in its ability to respond to changing information system needs, it is useful to consider what is meant by infrastructure flexibility.

Byrd and Turner also highlight a Society for Information Management (SIM) Delphi study where IT managers indicated that the building and development of a flexible and responsive IT infrastructure was the most important issue of IT management. In a review of relevant literature they also note that there are two main components of IT infrastructure: a *technical IT infrastructure* relating to applications, data and technology configurations and a *human IT infrastructure* relating to the knowledge and capabilities required to manage effectively the IT resources within the organisation. They also point to relevant management literature where flexibility is defined as 'the degree to which an organisation possesses a variety of actual and potential procedures, and the rapidity with which it can implement these procedures to increase the control capability of the management and improve the controllability of the organisation over its environment'.

They go on to suggest that 'IT infrastructure is the shared IT resources consisting of a technical physical base of hardware, software, communications technologies, data, and core applications and a human component of skills, expertise, competencies, commitments, values, norms, and knowledge that combine to create IT services that are typically unique to an organisation. These IT services provide a foundation for communications interchange across the entire organisation and for the development and implementation of present and future business applications.' And when combining the above definition with the concept of flexibility, IT infrastructure flexibility can be defined as 'the ability to easily and readily diffuse or support a wide variety of hardware, software, communications technologies, data, core applications, skills and competencies, commitments, and values within the technical physical base and the human component of the existing IT infrastructure.'

As Duncan (1995) points out, infrastructure flexibility is perceived as critical to information-intensive firms because of the amount of unplanned systems requirements faced by IT departments. Inflexibility exists when developers have difficulties with users' demands that require systems to do things they were not designed to do. In this situation, the historic solution has been either to update the systems to do those things, or to build a new system to reflect the new requirements. The alternative approach is to develop an infrastructure that allows flexible manufacturing of systems so that the systems developers' ability to design and build systems is improved.

The links here with agile approaches to software development, reusable code, open hardware and communications technologies are clear. From a systems management perspective, it suggests that if an organisation is to be agile in its response to a changing internal and external business environment, then it needs a flexible IS/IT infrastructure, embracing both technical and human infrastructures.

PULLING IT TOGETHER: IT GOVERNANCE AND COBIT

Very few models and texts embrace an overall methodology for determining the relationship between IS/IT processes, IS/IT resources and information to organisational strategies and objectives. The Control Objectives for Information and related Technology (COBIT) approach aims to address these relationships and, according to the IT Governance Institute, 'integrates and institutionalises good (or best) practices of planning and organising, acquiring and implementing, delivering and supporting, and monitoring IT performance to ensure that the enterprise's information and related technology support its business objectives' (COBIT, 3rd edition, Executive Summary, July 2000).

Business objectives and the organisational activities that stem from them both provide an input to the COBIT IT processes and are themselves informed by the capabilities afforded by IS/IT. Effective governance of an organisation requires that individual and group expertise be applied where it can be most productive. IT governance provides the structure that enables IT resources and information to be incorporated as an integral part of organisational strategies and objectives. COBIT in its Control Objectives document summarises the relationship thus:

> Enterprise activities require information from IT activities in order to meet business objectives. Successful organisations ensure interdependence between their strategic planning and their IT activities. IT must be aligned with and enable the enterprise to take full advantage of its information, thereby maximising benefits, capitalising on opportunities and gaining a competitive advantage.

The COBIT framework adopts seven requirements to which an organisation's systems should comply, together with five principal categories of IT resource that are used to deliver business information. The business inputs to the COBIT framework stem from business events including business objectives, business opportunities, external requirements, regulations and risks, and it is through the application of the five categories of IT resource that the seven information requirements can be controlled. These requirements are:

- *Effectiveness*: delivery of relevant information that is pertinent to the business process in a timely, correct and consistent manner.
- *Efficiency*: the provision of information through the optimal use of resources.
- *Confidentiality*: the protection of sensitive information from unauthorised disclosure.
- *Integrity*: the accuracy, validity and completeness of information.
- *Availability*: information being available as and when required by the business process; it also refers to the safeguarding of necessary resources and associated capabilities.
- *Compliance*: the externally imposed business criteria that apply, such as laws, regulations and contractual arrangements.
- *Reliability of information*: the provision of appropriate information such that the organisation can continue to operate and for the management to exercise its fiscal and compliance reporting responsibilities.

The resources used to achieve these information objectives are:

- *Data*: both internal and internal, structured and non-structured that need to be captured and stored.
- *Application systems*: the sum of all manual and programmed procedures (i.e. paper-based as well as computer-based applications).
- *Technology*: the hardware, operating systems, DBMS, networks etc. within the organisation.
- *Facilities*: the resources needed to house and support information systems.
- *People*: this includes staff skills needed to plan, organise, acquire, deliver, support and monitor information systems and services.

The complete COBIT framework identifies four domains with a total of 34 high-level control objectives. These high-level control objectives are broken down into 318 detailed control objectives. In addition to the framework is a set of Management Guidelines which

provides management direction for getting the enterprise's information and related processes under control, for monitoring achievement of organisational goals, for monitoring performance within each IT process and for benchmarking organisational achievement.

Management guidelines

These comprise four elements and we will deal with each in turn.

Maturity models

The thinking here is not unlike Nolan's stage model discussed earlier (in Chapter 13). An organisation can analyse its own position with respect to the model and in so doing can identify the steps needed to improve its IT governance. The six stages are as follows:

0. *Non-existent*: There is a complete lack of any recognisable IT governance process and the organisation may not even realise that there is an issue to be addressed.
1. *Initial/ad hoc*: IT governance is recognised as an issue, but management's approach is chaotic; no standardised processes exist, but one-off approaches may be taken on a case-by-case basis.
2. *Repeatable but intuitive*: There is awareness of IT governance issues and IT governance activities are under development; basic measurement and assessment

methods and techniques are in use, but they have not been adopted across the organisation.

3. *Defined process*: The need to act with respect to IT governance is understood and accepted; procedures have been standardised, documented and implemented; balanced business scorecard ideas are being adopted by the organisation; individuals are left to get training, follow standards and apply them; root cause analysis is rarely applied.

4. *Managed and measurable*: There is full understanding of IT governance issues at all levels, supported by formal training; responsibilities are clear and process ownership is established; all process stakeholders are aware of risks, the importance of IT and the opportunities it can offer; continuous improvement is beginning to be addressed; IT governance activities are becoming integrated with the enterprise governance process.

5. *Optimised*: There is advanced and forward-looking understanding of IT governance issues and solutions; processes have been refined to a level of external best practice; the organisation, people and processes are quick to adapt and fully support IT governance requirements; all problems and deviations are root-cause-analysed and efficient action taken; risks and returns of IT processes are defined, balanced and communicated across the organisation; enterprise and IT governance are strategically linked so that technology, human and financial resources can be leveraged to increase the competitive advantage of the enterprise.

The maturity model would suggest that the adoption of a framework such as COBIT will result in a seamless interface and integration between business and IS/IT strategies. The following three tools can be used to help with the alignment process.

Critical success factors

These are discussed in more detail in earlier (Chapter 13). Within the context of the COBIT model, CSFs define the most important management-oriented implementation guidelines to achieve control over and within an organisation's IT processes. Example CSFs include:

- integration and smooth interoperability of the more complex IS/IT processes such as problem, change and configuration management;
- the implementation of management practices that increase the efficient and optimal use of resources and increase the effectiveness of IS/IT processes;
- the integration of IS/IT governance activities into the enterprise governance process and leadership behaviours;
- focusing IS/IT governance on the organisational goals, strategic initiatives, the use of technology to enhance the business and on the availability of sufficient resources and capabilities to keep up with the business demands.

Key goal indicators

These define the measures that tell management whether an IT process has achieved its business requirement. An example might be an organisation that is seeking to be the most profitable company in the industry, and that to help achieve this, investment in procurement software to help reduce materials costs has been undertaken. Therefore, the measures used might include a 'before and after' analysis of materials purchase costs. Needless to say, this is an 'after the fact' approach! Further indicators might include the following:

- improved time-to-market;
- reaching new and satisfying existing customers;
- creation of new service delivery channels;

- appropriately integrated and standardised business processes;
- improved return on major IS/IT investments.

Key performance indicators (KPIs)

KPIs are the lead indicators that define measures of how well the IT process is performing in enabling a key goal to be reached. For example, suppose that a hospital has a required systems availability of 99.99 per cent up-time in order to ensure that patient care is fully supported. A KPI would be the reported systems up-time when compared with the target value. Further examples include:

- improved performance as measured by balanced scorecards;
- improved staff productivity and morale;
- increased satisfaction of stakeholders;
- increased availability of knowledge and information for managing the enterprise;
- increased linkage between IS/IT and enterprise governance.

COBIT IT processes – the four domains

It is easiest to consider these if COBIT is considered as a 'lifecycle' model. Figure 14.2 illustrates the approach and also shows how information and IS/IT resources are embedded in the process. The diagram illustrates that the information both drives and enables business objectives and that business objectives generate the need for information as enabled through the utilisation and application of IS/IT resources. We will now consider each of the four domains.

Figure 14.2 COBIT's four domains

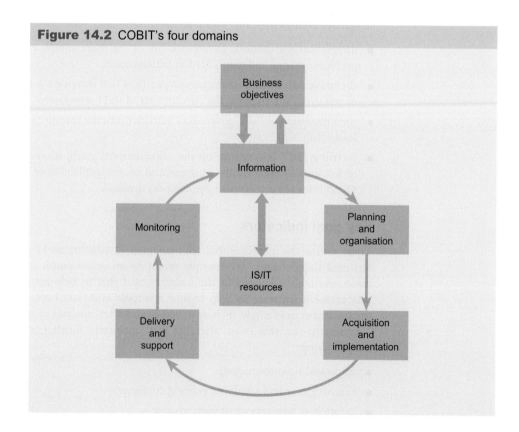

Planning and organisation

This domain is principally concerned with the way IS/IT can best contribute to the achievement of the business objectives. This means that an IS/IT strategy needs to be clearly articulated, particularly with respect to linkages with the overarching business strategy. The strategic vision needs to be planned, communicated and managed for different perspectives within the organisation (for example, those perspectives identified as part of the balanced scorecard method). Finally, a proper organisation as well as technological infrastructure must be put in place. This will include hardware, operating environment and communications technologies (in other words the delivery platforms that enable the right information to be delivered to decision makers). As with each of the following domains, there are a number of specific processes involved with implementing the control objectives:

- define a strategic IT plan;
- define the information architecture;
- determine technological direction;
- define the IT organisation and relationships;
- manage the IT investment;
- communicate management aims and direction;
- manage human resources;
- ensure compliance with external requirements;
- assess risks;
- manage projects;
- manage quality.

Acquisition and implementation

Earlier chapters have dealt with issues relating to information systems acquisition and implementation. Therefore, in order to bring about the IS/IT strategy, solutions need to be identified, developed or acquired, as well as implemented and integrated into business processes. In addition, ongoing systems evolution and maintenance are included in this domain to make sure that the lifecycle is continued for these systems (which naturally become legacy systems once implemented). The processes involved in this domain include:

- identify automated solutions;
- acquire and maintain application software;
- acquire and maintain technology infrastructure;
- develop and maintain procedures;
- install and accredit systems;
- manage changes.

Delivery and support

This domain is concerned with the actual delivery of required services, which range from traditional operations over security and continuity aspects to training. In order to deliver services, the necessary support processes must be set up. One thing that perhaps sets this apart from more traditional strategy models is the fact that the actual processing of data by application systems is included, even though this would typically be regarded as more the operational domain of the functional business area concerned. The specific processes involved within this domain are:

- define and manage service levels;
- manage third-party services;

- manage performance and capacity;
- ensure continuous service;
- ensure systems security;
- identify and allocate costs;
- educate and train users;
- assist and advise customers;
- manage the configuration;
- manage problems and incidents;
- manage data;
- manage facilities;
- manage operations.

Monitoring

It is necessary to assess regularly all IS/IT processes to ensure that they meet the required quality standards and that they comply with control requirements. This domain, therefore, helps to address management's oversight of the organisation's control process through internal and external auditing and/or benchmarking against best practice. Specific activities include the following processes:

- monitor the processes;
- assess internal control adequacy;
- obtain independent assurance;
- provide for independent audit.

In conclusion, COBIT would appear to provide a control framework whereby IS/IT strategy can be more readily aligned with an organisation's business strategy. In particular, it articulates a number of processes that organisations need to perform in order to deliver appropriate and cost-effective IS/IT strategies.

CASE STUDY 14.2

IT trends shape future corporate strategies

By Paul Taylor

As the impact of technology change on business grows, McKinsey, has identified 10 IT-enabled business trends that it says will help shape corporate strategies over the next decade.

In the article, published in the McKinsey's Quarterly, authors Jacques Bughin, Michael Chui and James Manyika argue that since they last reviewed the IT landscape in 2010, 'the implications of those trends for companies' strategies, business models, organisational approaches and relationships with customers and employees have only grown.'

Since then, they say the pace of technology change, innovation and business adoption since then has been

stunning. 'Consider that the world's stock of data are now doubling every 20 months; the number of Internet-connected devices has reached 12bn; and payments by mobile phone are hurtling toward the $1,000bn mark.'

In particular, the authors argue that the dramatic pace at which two trends in particular have been advancing is transforming them into 21st-century business 'antes': competitive necessities for most if not all companies.

'Big data and advanced analytics have swiftly moved from the frontier of our trends to a set of capabilities that need to be deeply embedded across functions and operations, enabling managers to have a better basis for understanding markets and making business decisions,' they write. 'Meanwhile, social technologies are becoming a powerful social matrix – a key piece of organisational infrastructure that links and engages employees, customers and suppliers as never before.'

They note that the 'Internet of All Things,' the linking of physical objects with embedded sensors, is being exploited at breakneck pace, simultaneously creating massive network effects and opportunities.

Meanwhile 'the cloud,' with its ability to deliver digital power at low cost and in small increments, is not only changing the profile of corporate IT departments but also helping to spawn a range of new business models by shifting the economics of 'rent versus buy' trade-offs for companies and consumers.

'The result is an acceleration of a trend we identified in 2010: the delivery of anything as a service,' they say. 'The creeping automation of knowledge work, which affects the fastest-growing employee segment worldwide, promises a new phase of corporate productivity.

'Finally, up to 3bn new consumers, mostly in emerging markets, could soon become fully digital players, thanks chiefly to mobile technologies. Our research suggests that the collective economic impact (in the applications that we examined) of information technologies underlying these four trends could range from $10,000bn to $20,000bn annually in 2025.'

The next three trends identified in the article, 'will be most familiar to digital marketers, but their relevance is expanding across the enterprise, starting with customer-experience, product and channel management,' say the authors.

'The integration of digital and physical experiences is creating new ways for businesses to interact with customers, by using digital information to augment individual experiences with products and services. Consumer demand is rising for products that are free, intuitive and radically user oriented. And the rapid evolution of IT-enabled commerce is reducing entry barriers and opening new revenue streams to a range of individuals and companies.'

Finally, McKinsey highlights the extent to which government, education and healthcare – which often seem outside the purview of business leaders – could benefit from adopting digital technologies at the same level as many industries have.

'Productivity gains could help address the imperative (created by ageing populations) to do more with less, while technological innovation could improve the quality and reach of many services. The embrace of digital technologies by these sectors is thus a trend of immense importance to business, which indirectly finances many services and would benefit greatly from the rising skills and improved health of citizens everywhere.'

The trends identified in the report are:

1. Joining the social matrix – Social technologies are much more than a consumer phenomenon: they connect many organisations internally and increasingly reach outside their borders. Now it has become the environment in which more and more business is conducted.

2. Competing with 'big data' and advanced analytics – Three years ago, McKinsey described new opportunities to experiment with and segment consumer markets using big data. As with the social matrix, the firm now sees data and analytics as part of a new foundation for competitiveness.

3. Deploying the Internet of All Things – Tiny sensors and actuators, proliferating at astounding rates, are expected to explode in number over the next decade, potentially linking over 50bn physical entities as costs plummet and networks become more pervasive. What McKinsey described as nascent three years ago is fast becoming ubiquitous, which gives managers unimagined possibilities to fine-tune processes and manage operations.

4. Offering anything as a service – The buying and selling of services derived from physical products is a business-model shift that's gaining steam. An attraction for buyers is the opportunity to replace big blocks of capital investment with more flexible and granular operating expenditures. A prominent example of this shift is the embrace of cloud-based IT services.

5. Automating knowledge work – Physical labour and transactional tasks have been widely automated over the last three decades. Now advances in data analytics, low-cost computer power, machine learning and interfaces that 'understand' humans are moving the automation frontier rapidly toward the world's more than 200m knowledge workers.

6. Engaging the next 3bn digital citizens – As incomes rise in developing nations, their citizens are becoming wired, connected by mobile computing devices, particularly smartphones that will only increase in power and versatility. Although several emerging markets have experienced double-digit growth in internet adoption, enormous growth potential remains. Rising levels of connectivity will stimulate financial inclusion, local entrepreneurship and enormous opportunities for business.

7. Charting experiences where digital meets physical – The borders of the digital and physical world have been blurring for many years as consumers learnt to shop in virtual stores and to meet in virtual spaces. In those cases, the online world mirrors experiences of the physical world. Increasingly, we're seeing an inversion as real-life activities, from shopping to factory work, become rich with digital information and as the mobile internet and advances in natural user interfaces give the physical world digital characteristics.

8. 'Freeing' your business model through Internet-inspired personalisation and simplification – After nearly two decades of shopping, reading, watching, seeking information and interacting on the internet, customers expect services to be free, personalised and easy to use without instructions. This ethos presents a challenge for business, since customers expect instant results, as well as superb and transparent customer service, for all interactions – from web sites to brick-and-mortar stores. Fail to deliver, and competitors' offerings are only an app download away.

9. Buying and selling as digital commerce leaps ahead – The rise of the mobile Internet and the evolution of core technologies that cut costs and vastly simplify the process of completing transactions online are reducing barriers to entry across a wide swath of economic activity. Amped-up technology platforms are enabling peer-to-peer commerce to replace activities traditionally carried out by companies and giving birth to new kinds of payment systems and monetisation models.

10. Transforming government, healthcare, and education – The private sector has a big stake in the successful transformation of government, healthcare, and education, which together account for a third of global GDP. They have lagged behind in productivity growth at least in part because they have been slow to adopt Web-based platforms, big-data analytics, and other IT innovations. Technology-enabled productivity growth could help reduce the cost burden while improving the quality of services and outcomes, as well as boosting long-term global-growth prospects.

What does all this mean for busy senior executives? The McKinsey authors suggest that the era of pervasive connectedness underlying these trends also implies a need for more focused attention on issues such as transparent and innovative business models, talent, organisation, privacy and security.

'In short, as these trends take hold, leaders must prepare for the disruption of longstanding commercial and social relationships, as well as the emergence of unforeseen business priorities, the authors say. 'The difficulty of embracing those realities while addressing related risks and concerns may give some leaders pause. But it's worth keeping in mind that if the future traces past experience, these technology-enabled business trends will not only be a boon for consumers but also stimulate growth, innovation and a new wave of pacesetting companies.'

 Source: Taylor, P. (2013) IT trends shape future corporate strategies. *Financial Times*. 23 May.
© The Financial Times Limited 2013. All Rights Reserved.

QUESTION

Write a short essay on any of the 10 IT trends described in the case study.

SUMMARY

1. The relationship between IS/IT investments and productivity can be problematic. The intangible nature of many benefits means that it can be difficult to put a money value on them.

2. Appropriately targeted IS/IT investments need to be rooted in a coherent IS/IT strategy so that the IS/IT applications portfolio is distributed as needed between support, key operational, high potential and strategic information systems.

3. The alternatives for structuring or locating IS within an organisation range from centralised to decentralised. A hybrid approach is often used with some aspects of IS management, such as IS strategy and security centralised and others such as user support decentralised.

4. Outsourcing is a significant trend in IS management. It involves a third party undertaking some or all of the following IS activities:

   ■ hardware outsourcing;
   ■ network management or facilities management (FM);
   ■ systems development;
   ■ IS support;
   ■ management of IS strategy.

   When all activities are performed by the external company, this is known as 'total outsourcing'. When some activities are performed by the external company, this is known as 'selective outsourcing'. Outsourcing is driven by a desire to reduce costs while improving the quality of IS and user services. The debate on whether this is frequently achieved is still raging!

EXERCISES

Self-assessment exercises

1. When information systems costs are being considered, what kinds of costs would be considered *development* costs and what would be considered *operations/maintenance* costs?

2. How do strategic systems differ from high-potential projects?

3. Why do information systems projects fail?

4. Explain the difference between *project size* and *project complexity* when evaluating information systems risk.

5. What are the main different types of outsourcing?

Discussion questions

1. 'The millennium bug has demonstrated that organisations, more often than not, take a short-term view in their approach to information systems rather than a strategic one.' Discuss.

2. 'Public-sector organisations such as the police and health service are incapable of delivering good-quality information systems because they are dominated by the need to demonstrate tangible benefits before any investment decisions are made.' Discuss.

3. Would you outsource the HRM or accounting functions of a company? If not, what is so different about IS/IT?

Essay questions

1. Why do many new information systems seem to deliver poor value for money?

2. It has been said that when making IS investment decisions, organisations are dominated by organisational politics. Is this really true or are there other, more important issues at stake?

3. What do you see as the main problems with outsourcing, and how can they be overcome?

4. 'The IS capability model proposed by Peppard and Ward reaffirms the old adage that "technology is easy, people are difficult".' Discuss.

Examination questions

1. What are the two main alternatives for a company's location of its information systems? Summarise the benefits and disadvantages in terms of cost and control.

2. What information systems management activities would occur with a total outsourcing contract?

References

Byrd, T. and Turner, D.E. (2000) 'Measuring the flexibility of information technology infrastructure: exploratory analysis of a construct', *Journal of Management Information Systems*, 17, 1, 167–208

Collins, J.S. and Millen, R.A. (1995) 'Information systems outsourcing by large American firms: choices and impacts', *Information Resources Management Journal*, 8, 1, 9–14

Duncan, N.B. (1995) 'Capturing flexibility of information technology infrastructure: a study of resource characteristics and their measure', *Journal of Management Information Systems*, 12, 2, 37–57

Feeny, D., Fitzgerald, G. and Willcocks, L. (1995) 'Outsourcing IT: the strategic implications', *Long Range Planning*, 28, 5, 59–71

Gonzalez, R., Gasco, J. and Llopis, J. (2005) 'Information systems outsourcing success factors: a review and some results', *Information Management and Computer Security*, 13, 5, 399–418

Hochstrasser, B. and Griffiths, C. (1990) *Regaining Control of IS Investments: A Handbook for Senior UK Managenment*, Kobler Unit, Berlin

Lacity, M.C. and Hirscheim, R. (1995) *Beyond the Information Systems Outsourcing Bandwagon – the Insourcing Response*, John Wiley, Chichester

Lubbe, S. and Remenyi, D. (1999) 'Management of information technology evaluation – the development of a managerial thesis', *Logistics Information Management*, 12, 1/2, 145–56

Peppard, J. and Ward, J. (2004) 'Beyond strategic information systems: towards an IS capability', *Journal of Strategic Information Systems*, 13, 167–94

Robson, W. (1997) *Strategic Management and Information Systems: An Integrated Approach*, Financial Times Pitman Publishing, London

Strassmann, P. (2002) 'Still a loser's game', *Computerworld*, 4 February.

Sullivan, C.H. (1985) 'Systems planning in the information age', *Sloan Management Review*, Winter, 3–12

Ward, J. and Peppard, J. (2002) *Strategic Planning for Information Systems*, 3rd edition, John Wiley, Chichester

Further reading

Curtis, G. and Cobham, D. (2008) *Business Information Systems: Analysis, Design and Practice*, 6th edition, Addison-Wesley, Harlow.

Johnson, G., Whittington, R., Scholes, K., Angwin, D. and Regnér, P. (2014) *Exploring Strategy*, 10th edition, Prentice Hall Europe, Hemel Hempstead.

Kendall, K.E. and Kendall, J.E. (2013) *Systems Analysis and Design*, 9th edition, Prentice-Hall, Englewood Cliffs, NJ.

Ward, J. and Peppard, J. (2012) *Strategic Planning for Information Systems*, 4th edition, John Wiley, Chichester.

Web links

www.outsourcing.com Outsourcing Institute web site.

www.strassmann.com The web site of Paul Strassmann includes many of his articles on the value of information and issues such as outsourcing and IS investment.

www.isaca.org/cobit.htm This website provides further information about the COBIT methodology for IT security and governance. COBIT is issued by the IT Governance Institute.

LINKS TO OTHER CHAPTERS

Chapter 17   deals with ethical issues of relevance to the developers and managers of computer-based information systems.

Managing information security

CHAPTER AT A GLANCE

MAIN TOPICS

FOCUS ON . . .

CASE STUDIES

LEARNING OUTCOMES

After reading this chapter, you will be able to:

- understand and assess potential threats to a computer-based information system;
- propose an overall strategy for ensuring the security of a computer-based information system;
- identify specific techniques that might be used to protect a computer-based information system against damage or unauthorised access.

MANAGEMENT ISSUES

The concept that information is an important and valuable business asset has been stressed throughout this text. The responsibility for ensuring the security of organisational information systems is one that cannot be taken too lightly. In addition to ensuring that the organisation has uninterrupted access to its information resources, managers must also deal with the threat of outsiders attempting to gain access to those same resources. From a managerial perspective, this chapter addresses the following areas:

- An understanding of approaches towards information systems security will help managers to develop and implement an overall strategy for security.
- An understanding of the threats to information systems will help in predicting and anticipating acts such as denial-of-service attacks.
- Knowledge of specific techniques for protecting information systems will help in the development of effective counter measures.
- As organisations turn to the Internet for business purposes, it becomes important to understand some of the new threats that must be faced.

INTRODUCTION

The first section of this chapter discusses the need for controls on information systems, paying particular attention to unauthorised access. Having established some of the threats facing modern computer-based systems, several strategies are introduced for ensuring the integrity of an information system. A brief description of some of the controls that can be placed on information systems is followed by a more detailed examination of two areas of contemporary interest: malicious software and threats to Internet services.

THE NEED FOR CONTROLS

Controls upon information systems are based upon two underlying principles:

- the need to ensure the accuracy of the data held by the organisation;
- the need to protect against loss or damage.

Although this chapter is largely concerned with unauthorised access and the physical security of information systems, it should be noted that many of the issues raised are also relevant to the discussion of accuracy and privacy that is provided later (in Chapter 17).

The most common threats faced by organisational information systems can be placed into the following categories:

- accidents
- natural disasters
- sabotage (industrial and individual)
- vandalism
- theft
- unauthorised use (hacking)
- computer viruses and malware.

The following box charts a number of major incidents that made national or international headlines between 2007 and 2011. As can be seen, there has been a marked increase in threats related to the Internet and organisational intranets.

Accidents

A number of estimates suggest that 40–65 per cent of all damage caused to information systems or corporate data arises as a result of human error. The DTI's Information Security Breaches Survey 2006, for example, states that: 'Human error rather than flawed technology is the root cause of most security breaches.' Some examples of the ways in which human errors can occur include:

Why do we need controls? Some computer-related security incidents reported in the media 2007–12

February 2007

Two Dutch hackers received prison sentences and fines for creating a botnet of up to 1.5 million computers. As well as using the network of hijacked computers to steal confidential information from computer users, they also blackmailed companies by threatening to launch denial-of-service attacks.

September 2007

The New Zealand secret service suggested the Chinese government had launched cyberattacks against the country's networks and information systems. Other reports alleged that additional cyberattacks had been launched by China against the UK, France, Germany and the United States.

September 2007

Estimates of the size of the botnet created by the Storm Worm launched in January 2007 range from 10 to 50 million computers.

January 2008

A French bank, Société Générale, lost £3.6 billion as a result of the unauthorised activity of a rogue trader. Jerome Kerviel used his knowledge of anti-fraud procedures to circumvent the banks security systems.

August 2008

A senior financial analyst at Countrywide Financial Corp. was arrested for stealing and selling confidential information. The man was said to have downloaded 20,000 customer profiles each week which he sold for around $500. The information was sold to people in the mortgage industry so that they could make approaches to potential customers. Up to 17 million records were compromised.

October 2008

The FBI and other agencies around the world concluded an undercover operation that resulted in 56 arrests worldwide and saved up to $70 million in potential losses. The case involved an electronic forum called 'Dark Market' where criminals bought and sold stolen financial information, such as credit card details. At its peak, Dark Market had more than 2,500 members.

April 2009

The Conficker worm infected up to 15 million computers and resulted in estimated losses of $9.1 billion worldwide. The worm continues to infect computers today (see June 2011). Some specific incidents involving Conficker include:

- In February 2009, an infection at Manchester City Council resulted in losses of approximately £1.5 million. Removing the worm cost an estimated £1.2 million. Other costs involved £169,000 for hiring extra staff to handle backlogs of work and compensation payments because of delays in issuing benefit payments.
- In May 2009 computer systems at Ealing Council became infected by the worm from a memory stick used by an employee. The incident cost the Council more than £500,000 in repairs and lost revenues.

December 2009

A hacker gained access to 32 million records owned by social game developer, RockYou. The information compromised included log-in information from social networking sites such as Facebook and MySpace.

March 2010

Albert Gonzalez was sentenced to 20 years in prison for stealing more than 90 million credit and debit card numbers from TJX and other retailers.

September 2010

A mobile phone virus, Zombie, begins to infect phones in China. By November 2011, the virus is reported to have infected more than 1 million phones and was costing phone owners $300,000 a day. The problem is made more difficult by the fact that antivirus software is unable to detect Zombie.

September 2010

HSBC received fines of £3 million from the Financial Services Authority related to incidents involving confidential customer records, such as losing unencrypted data in the post.

November 2010

Five British teenagers, including two girls, went on trial for selling stolen identities and credit card details from a site called Gh0stMarket.net. Losses were estimated at between £12 million and £16 million from the credit card details found on the site. Four members of the group eventually received prison sentences of between 18 months to five years.

May 2011

Lulz Security (LulzSec), a group of hackers, began a '50 day cruise' of incidents, attacking web sites or releasing confidential information taken from a variety of organisations. Victims reportedly included Sony, Nintendo, The *Sun* newspaper, the US version of the X Factor, the Arizona police department, the Serious Organised Crime Agency (SOCA), AT&T, Fox.com, US broadcaster PBS, the CIA and the United States Senate.

June 2011

A joint operation between the FBI and the Security Service of Ukraine (SBU) closed down a 'scareware' ring operating across a number of countries including the US, the Ukraine, the Netherlands, Latvia, Germany, France, Lithuania, Sweden and the United Kingdom. The ring used the Conficker worm to infect computers then frighten the owners into paying for worthless security software. The worm was also used to collect confidential information from infected machines. Estimates suggest that the ring managed to collect at least $72 million before being closed down.

September 2011

Kweku Adoboli, a 31-year-old trader at UBS, was arrested by London police in relation to rogue trading that was estimated to have cost the Swiss bank £1.3 billion.

June 2012

The *New York Times* publishes an in-depth article stating that Stuxnet, a computer virus aimed at hindering the Iranian nuclear research programme, was created as a **cyberweapon** by the United States and Israel. It is later alleged that other cyberweapons were created and used by both countries, including programs called Flame and Gauss.

Cyberweapon

Computer code intended to cause harm to structures, systems or people.

Update query

Used to change records, tables and reports held in a database management system.

- *Inaccurate data entry.* As an example, consider a typical relational database management system, where **update queries** are used to change records, tables and reports. If the contents of the query are incorrect, errors might be produced within all of the data manipulated by the query. Although extreme, significant problems might be caused by adding or removing even a single character to a query.

- *Attempts to carry out tasks beyond the ability of the employee.* In smaller computer-based information systems, a common cause of accidental damage involves users attempting to install new hardware items or software applications. In the case of software applications, existing data may be lost when the program is installed or the program may fail to operate as expected.

- *Failure to comply with procedures for the use of organisational information systems.* Where organisational procedures are unclear or fail to anticipate potential problems, users may often ignore established methods, act on their own initiative or perform tasks incorrectly.

- *Failure to carry out backup procedures or verify data backups.* In addition to carrying out regular backups of important business data, it is also necessary to verify that any backup copies made are accurate and free from errors.

A survey from the Computing Technology Industry Association found that in more than 63 per cent of IT security breaches human error played a role. Technological failures accounted for only 8 per cent of security problems (source: Jupitermedia Corporation).

Mini case study

Complacent staff weak link in combating cyber criminals

By Kate Burgess

If your password is 'password' or '123456', change it this minute. For even as the civil liberties brigade rails against state snooping and mythologises cyber leakers such as Edward Snowden, cyber crime is bringing down small companies and destroying livelihoods.

At the business end, the victims of cyber crime are piling up. About 90 per cent of all British companies suffered some kind of attack last year, according to the government's department of business.

It comes in all forms – staff siphoning off cash, competitors filching customer data, contract details or product designs, or gangs (some possibly sponsored by foreign states) infecting software with viruses and worms for financial gain. Web-based crime has cost the UK as much as £27bn this year, according to the National Audit Office. The government reckons that the costs to business have tripled in a year.

The average price paid for the worst breaches by companies with fewer than 250 staff is £35,000- £65,000.

For bigger companies, the average cost is £850,000. But the grief caused to the UK's smallest and most vulnerable enterprises is more than just financial. The combination of clean-up costs, the threat of fines for failing to protect customer data, the damage to reputation and client losses can prove fatal.

Worryingly, the unscrupulous are now targeting these small enterprises. For the first time, almost as many small companies say they were attacked last year as bigger ones.

It will only get worse, too, given the reach of the internet and the fact that almost everything we do is recorded and stored somewhere on the web. The full extent of the damage may never be known.

Many companies – like the world's superpowers – are loathe to admit explicitly just how much data they have collected and would be embarrassed to own up to a cyber attack. Governments are working to encourage more disclosure to help to form a united defence. Police forces are wising up, too, setting up specific cyber crime units such as the Europol Cybercrime (yes, really) centre.

Prevention, though, must be the best cure. Nearly all breaches are because hackers have been able to exploit the vulnerability of staff and systems through weak passwords, out-of-date security software and the misuse of social networking sites.

The problem is that few of us, executives of small companies included, think we have much worth stealing. But even corporate minnows should not underestimate their usefulness as a route into the databases of bigger companies with which they are linked, or the importance of innovative small caps as repositories of big, groundbreaking ideas.

> The lesson is that the top brass of big and small companies have to spend more on web security. We must also stop moaning about the number of times we are asked to change our passwords and guard against how we pass on corporate tittle tattle. Careless talk may not cost lives, but it certainly costs.

Source: Burgess, K. (2013) Complacent staff weak link in combating cyber criminals. *Financial Times*. 30 June.
© The Financial Times Limited 2012. All Rights Reserved.

Natural disasters

Safety-critical system

Where human lives rely on the correct operation of a computer-based information system.

Where human lives rely on the proper operation of an information system, this is usually known as a **safety-critical system**. Perhaps a better way of describing a critical system is to suggest that it is an information system that must not fail. A good example of a critical system is an air traffic control system.

All information systems are susceptible to damage caused by natural phenomena, such as storms, lightning strikes, floods and earthquakes. In Japan and the United States, for example, great care is taken to protect critical information systems from the effects of earthquakes. Although such hazards are of less concern in much of Europe, properly designed systems will make allowances for unexpected natural disasters.

Sabotage

With regard to information systems, sabotage may be deliberate or unintentional and carried out on an individual basis or as an act of industrial sabotage.

Individual sabotage

Logic bomb

Sometimes also known as a time bomb, a logic bomb is a destructive computer program that activates at a certain time or in reaction to a specific event.

Back door

A section of program code that allows a user to circumvent security procedures in order to gain full access to an information system.

Individual sabotage is typically carried out by a disgruntled employee who wishes to exact some form of revenge upon their employer. The **logic bomb** (sometimes known as a 'time bomb') is a well-known example of how an employee may cause deliberate damage to the organisation's information systems. A logic bomb is a destructive program that activates at a certain time or in reaction to a specific event. In most cases, the logic bomb is activated some months after the employee has left the organisation. This tends to have the effect of drawing suspicion away from the employee. Another well-known example is known as a **back door**. The back door is a section of program code that allows a user to circumvent security procedures in order to gain full access to an information system. Although back doors have legitimate uses, such as for program testing, they can also be used as an instrument of sabotage. It should be noted, however, that individual sabotage is becoming more infrequent due to legislation such as the Computer Misuse Act.

Industrial sabotage

Industrial sabotage is considered rare, although there have been a number of well-publicised cases over the past few years. Industrial sabotage tends to be carried out for some kind of competitive or financial gain. The actions of those involved tend to be highly organised, targeted at specific areas of a rival organisation's activities, and supported by access to a substantial resource base. Industrial sabotage is considered more serious than individual sabotage since, although occurrences are relatively few, the losses suffered tend to be extremely high. A well-known example concerns the legal battle between British Airways and Richard Branson's Virgin during the 1990s, where it was alleged that BA gained access to Virgin's customer databases and used this information to 'poach' Virgin's customers. More recently, it has been claimed that governments have used their resources to give some companies an advantage in the marketplace. At the turn of the century, for example, it was alleged that both the United States and the United Kingdom were passing commercially sensitive information gathered via the Echelon surveillance network to certain companies.

Unintentional sabotage

An intent to cause loss or damage need not be present for sabotage to occur. Imagine the case of an organisation introducing a new information system at short notice and without proper consultation with staff. Employees may feel threatened by the new system and may wish to avoid making use of it. A typical reaction might be to enter data incorrectly in an attempt to discredit the new system. Alternatively, the employee might continue to carry out tasks manually (or with the older system), claiming that this is a more efficient way of working. In such cases, the employee's primary motivation is to safeguard their position – the damage or loss caused to the organisation's information systems is incidental to this goal.

Vandalism

Deliberate damage caused to hardware, software and data is considered a serious threat to information systems security. The threat from vandalism lies in the fact that the organisation is temporarily denied access to some of its resources. Even relatively minor damage to parts of a system can have a significant effect on the organisation as a whole. In a small network system, for example, damage to a server or shared storage device might effectively halt the work of all those connected to the network. In larger systems, a reduced flow of work through one part of the organisation can create bottlenecks, reducing the overall productivity of the entire organisation. Damage or loss of data can have more severe effects since the organisation cannot make use of the data until they have been replaced. The expense involved in replacing damaged or lost data can far exceed any losses arising from damage to hardware or software. As an example, the delays caused by the need to replace hardware or data might result in an organisation's being unable to compete for new business, harming the overall profitability of the company.

In recent years, vandalism has been extended to the Internet. A number of incidents have occurred where company web sites have been defaced.

Theft

As with vandalism, the loss of important hardware, software or data can have significant effects on an organisation's effectiveness. Theft can be divided into two basic categories: physical theft and data theft.

Independent insurance broker Bland Bankart plc estimates that the cost of computer and electronic office equipment theft exceeds £50 million each year (Bland Bankart plc). Even the theft of a single piece of hardware can result in significant loss. A survey by Kensington, producers of notebook security equipment, found that the theft of a single notebook computer cost £11,500 when factors such as lost productivity were taken into account.

Physical theft, as the term implies, involves the theft of hardware and software. The DTI's 2012 'Information Security Breaches Survey' reported that 7 per cent of the worst security incidents suffered by large organisations and 5 per cent of the worst incidents suffered by small organisations involved the physical theft of equipment. It is worth noting that physical theft is not restricted to computer systems alone; components are often targeted by criminals because of their small size and relatively high value.

Data theft

This can involve stealing sensitive information or making unauthorised changes to computer records.

Data theft normally involves making copies of important files without causing any harm to the originals. However, if the original files are destroyed or damaged, then the value of the copied data is automatically increased. The Ponemon Institute (www.ponemon.org) estimates that the average cost of a "compromised" record is $214.

Service organisations are particularly vulnerable to data theft since their activities tend to rely heavily upon access to corporate databases. Imagine a competitor gaining access to a customer list belonging to a sales organisation. The immediate effect of such an event would be to place both organisations on an essentially even footing. However, in the long term, the first organisation would no longer enjoy a competitive edge and might, ultimately, cease to exist. In the United States alone, lost sales due to the theft of technology and business ideas are valued at $100 billion to $250 billion a year.

Both data theft and physical theft can take a number of different forms. As an example, there has been growing concern over the theft of customer information, such as credit card details, from company web sites.

Unauthorised use

One of the most common security risks in relation to computerised information systems is the danger of unauthorised access to confidential data. Contrary to the popular belief encouraged by the media, the risk of hackers gaining access to a corporate information system is relatively small. Most security breaches involving confidential data can be attributed to the employees of the organisation. In many cases, breaches are accidental in that employees are unaware that particular sets of information are restricted. Deliberate breaches are typically the result of an employee wanting to gain some personal benefit from using the information obtained. A good example concerns the common myth of the police officer using the Police National Computer to check up on a car they wish to buy. In reality, strict guidelines cover the use of the Police National Computer and a log is kept of every enquiry made.

However, we must consider that the threat posed by hackers is starting to increase as more organisations make use of the Internet for business purposes. In addition, it should be noted that even a relatively small number of hacking incidents can account for significant losses to industry. As an example, a survey commissioned by the UK National High Tech Crime Unit (now part of SOCA – Serious Organised Crime Agency) found that 167 companies had lost £195 million to high-tech crime, such as hacking, over a period of twelve months. Furthermore, even a small number of hackers can cause a significant amount of damage. For instance, a single hacker arrested in 2006 was accused of compromising over 150 US government systems, resulting in $1.36 million in losses to NASA and nearly $100,000 in losses for the Energy Department and the Navy.

Hacker

Hackers are often described as individuals who seek to break into systems as a test of their abilities. Few hackers attempt to cause damage to systems they access and few are interested in gaining any sort of financial profit.

Cracker

A person who gains access to an information system for malicious reasons is often termed a cracker rather than a hacker. This is because some people draw a distinction between 'ethical' hackers and malicious hackers.

The term **hacker** is used for a person who attempts to gain unauthorised access to a computer-based information system, usually via a telecommunications link. However, this is the *popular* use of this term and is considered incorrect by many IT professionals. Traditionally, 'hacking' referred to the process of writing program code, so hackers were nothing more than skilled computer programmers. Even today, many people consider themselves to be 'hackers' of the traditional kind and dislike being associated with the stereotype of a computer criminal. Furthermore, many people draw distinctions between those who attempt to gain unauthorised access to computer-based information systems for malicious reasons and those with other motivations. A person who gains access to an information system for malicious reasons is often termed a **cracker** rather than a hacker. Similarly, many people claim to use hacking for ethical purposes, such as helping companies to identify security flaws or assisting law enforcement agencies in apprehending criminals. These people tend to be referred to as 'white-hat hackers' and their counterparts are termed 'black-hat hackers'. However, for the purposes of this chapter, we will continue to use the term 'hacker' in its popular sense.

In general, most people consider hackers to fall into one of four categories:

■ those who wish to demonstrate their computer skills by outwitting the designers of a particular system;

■ those who wish to gain some form of benefit (usually financial) by stealing, altering or deleting confidential information;

- those who wish to cause malicious damage to an information system, perhaps as an act of revenge against a former employer;

- those who wish to make a political statement of some kind.

Understandably, the most common crime committed by hackers involves telecommunications fraud. Clearly, the first task carried out by most hackers is to obtain free access to telecommunications, so that the time-consuming task of breaking into a given system can be carried out without incurring a great deal of expense. However, the growth of digital communications technology means that it is possible to implement countermeasures against hacking.

An excellent example concerns a well-known 1989 case, where a hacker managed to access information systems in more than 35 military bases across the United States. The hacker's intention was to steal information on the Strategic Defense Initiative (SDI) – the so-called Star Wars project. The hacker was traced on the basis of an anomaly found by Clifford Stoll in telephone records. The unauthorised use of 75 cents of telephone time led to an investigation that lasted more than 18 months. Finally, following a number of failed attempts to trace the hacker via the telecommunications system, he was caught and sentenced to imprisonment.

Hacktivist

Describes a person who uses hacking as a means of making a political statement, usually as a form of protest.

A fairly recent development in relation to hacking concerns the emergence of **hacktivists**. Hacktivists are those who deface web sites, carry out denial of service attacks or publish confidential information in order to make a political statement. Although hacktivism has existed for several decades, several recent high profile cases have brought it to the attention of the public. The wars in Iraq and Afghanistan, for instance, saw various groups attempting to promote their views by attacking web sites belonging to the government or other organisations connected to the conflicts in some way. More recently, a great deal of public controversy began when Wikileaks (http://wikileaks.org) began to publish a body of confidential documents considered embarrassing to the United States and other countries.

CASE STUDY 15.1

Online cybercrime rings forced to home in on smaller prey

By Vanessa Kortekaas

Wall Street's banks and brokerages came under a sustained cyber attack last Thursday as hackers attempted to bring down online banking and trading operations at 50 top institutions.

Websites were subjected to distributed denial of service (DDoS) attacks to put them out of action, and a 'malware' infection was aimed at trading platforms, in a digital offensive dubbed 'Quantum Dawn 2'.

If this sounds more like a film than reality, that may be because the cyber warfare was part of a simulated exercise to test financial institutions' ability to withstand global threats.

It came two months after eight members of an international cybercrime ring were indicted for allegedly hacking into the systems of global banks, stealing customer data, and inflicting $45m of losses on the global banking system.

But, as the multinational banks have increased their efforts to thwart such security breaches, the cyber criminals have been forced to target smaller prey – and these include London's wealth managers and stockbrokers.

'We are seeing a trend [for cyber criminals] to target smaller institutions who have higher value customers,' explains Stephen Bonner, a partner within KPMG's information protection and businesses resilience team in the UK.

'Very effective work by large retail banks to protect online retail banking is moving the attacker away to easier targets,' he warns. 'We're seeing them attack smaller institutions that historically didn't have enough customers to make it worthwhile.'

Mr Bonner says that this 'displacement' phenomenon in the cyber security landscape has also pushed the online security to the top of the agenda for UK wealth managers and stockbrokers.

Rathbone Brothers, a wealth manager with about £20bn of funds under management, says it is aware of attempts to hack in to its client data.

'We've got 40,000 clients, and the fraudsters are just becoming more sophisticated,' says Andy Pomfret, chief executive of Rathbones. 'You constantly have a few people trying to [hack] in.'

Rathbones has emulated the big banks in putting its systems to the test, by having so-called 'ethical hackers' attempt to access its data.

Mr Pomfret says he also encourages his investment managers to talk to their clients as much as possible, to reduce the risk of identity theft. 'It's much harder for someone to impersonate a client when you're actually talking to them,' he says.

Rathbones is not alone. According to the Association of Private Client Investment Managers and Stockbrokers (Apcims), cyber criminals are targeting the clients of UK brokerages.

In recent months, one Apcims member firm found that online fraudsters had set up a website identical to its own, and urged clients to buy certain shares – in an online version of a 'boiler-room' scam.

'It turned out [the firm's clients] were buying into a Ponzi type fund, which means you don't get your money back,' explains John Barrass, Apcims' deputy chief executive.

Although the scam was caught quickly, Mr Barrass says the attack has served as a 'very big warning sign' to financial companies about the need to protect themselves against cyber crime.

Many UK companies have increased their spending on methods to combat cyber attacks.

KPMG says the number of wealth managers and brokers that have approached the firm for advice on online security has roughly doubled in the past 18 months.

Charles Stanley, the stockbroker and wealth manager, sends its IT staff for cyber security training at the Chartered Institute of Securities and Investment (CISI). It is one of many seeking to make its staff more aware of the risk.

'Over the past year or so, I've seen much greater attendance from middle ranking firms, from the wealth management side and from the wealth management [business] of the big global banks,' says George Little john, a senior adviser at the CISI.

KMPG says that wealth managers have one advantage over the large banks in tackling cybercrime: they are 'closer to their clients' behaviour', and therefore more able to detect unusual activity in their accounts.

However, they also bring one disadvantage. 'With the very high-net-worth individuals, they expect a much more personal touch,' says Mr Bonner. '[They] are less willing to accept some of the inconveniences of higher security.'

 Source: Kortekaas, V. (2013) Online cybercrime rings forced to home in on smaller prey. *Financial Times*. 19 July.
© The Financial Times Limited 2012. All Rights Reserved.

QUESTION

What is the key approach to combating cybercrime discussed in the case study?

Computer viruses

Whilst some methods, such as logic bombs, are beginning to decline, others are becoming more common. The release of the 'virus construction kits' and 'virus mutation engines' places the construction of a new computer virus within the hands of most users. Additionally, whilst methods such as virus scanning provide a degree of protection against virus infection, no completely secure prevention technique has yet been found.

Computer viruses are considered in more detail later on.

CONTROL STRATEGIES

In the previous section it was shown that there is a need to:

- control access to information systems;
- maintain the integrity of the information held within a computer-based information system;

- implement procedures to ensure the physical security of equipment;
- safeguard the overall security of an information system.

In this section, strategies for reducing threats to information systems are discussed. In general, there are four major approaches that can be taken to ensure the integrity of an information system. These are containment, deterrence, obfuscation and recovery. Although each strategy is discussed separately, it is important to note that an effective security policy will draw upon a variety of concepts and techniques.

Containment

The strategy of containment attempts to control access to an information system.

One approach involves making potential targets as unattractive as possible. This can be achieved in several ways but a common method involves creating the impression that the target information system contains data of little or no value. It would be pointless, for example, attempting to steal data that had been encrypted – the data would effectively be useless to anyone except the owner.

A second technique involves creating an effective series of defences against potential threats. If the expense, time and effort required to gain access to the information system is greater than any benefits derived from gaining access, then intrusion becomes less likely. However, defences must be continually improved and upgraded in order to keep up with advances in technology and the increasing sophistication of hackers. Thus, such an approach tends to be expensive in terms of organisational resources.

A third approach involves removing the target information system from potential threats. Typical ways in which this might be achieved include distributing assets across a large geographical area, distributing important data across the entire organisation or isolating important systems.

Deterrence

A strategy based upon deterrence uses the threat of punishment to discourage potential intruders. The overall approach is one of anticipating and countering the motives of those most likely to threaten the security of the system.

A common method involves constantly advertising and reinforcing the penalties for unauthorised access. It is not uncommon, for example, to dismiss an employee for gaining access to confidential data. Similarly, it is not uncommon for organisations to bring private prosecutions against those who have caused damage or loss to important information systems. Attempts to breach the security of the information system are discouraged by publicising successful actions against employees or other parties.

A second approach involves attempting to detect potential threats as early as possible, for example by monitoring patterns of information system usage and investigating all anomalies. However, although such a technique can prevent some attacks and reduce the damage caused by others, it can be expensive in terms of organisational resources.

The third technique used commonly involves predicting likely areas of attack and then implementing appropriate defences or countermeasures. If an organisation feels, for example, that it is particularly vulnerable to computer viruses, it might install virus-scanning software across the entire organisation.

Obfuscation

Obfuscation concerns itself with hiding or distributing assets so that any damage caused can be limited.

One means by which such a strategy can be implemented is by monitoring *all* of the organisation's activities, not just those related to the use of its information systems. This provides a more comprehensive approach to security than *containment* or *deterrence* since it also provides a measure of protection against theft and other threats.

A second method involves carrying out regular audits of data, hardware, software and security measures. In this way, the organisation has a more complete overview of its information systems and can assess threats more accurately. A regular software audit, for example, might result in a reduction in the use of illegal software. In turn, this might reduce the number of virus infections suffered by the organisation, avoid potential litigation with software companies and detect illegal or unauthorised use of programs and data.

The dispersal of assets across several locations can be used to discourage potential intruders and can also limit the damage caused by a successful attack. The use of other techniques, such as backup procedures, can be used to reduce any threats further.

Recovery

A strategy based upon recovery recognises that, no matter how well defended, a breach in the security of an information system will eventually occur. Such a strategy is largely concerned with ensuring that the normal operation of the information system is restored as quickly as possible, with as little disruption to the organisation as possible.

The most important aspect of a strategy based upon recovery involves careful organisational planning. The development of emergency procedures that deal with a number of contingencies is essential if a successful recovery is to take place. The process of developing and maintaining these procedures is often called business continuity planning (sometimes also called *disaster recovery*).

In anticipating damage or loss, a great deal of emphasis is placed upon backup procedures and recovery measures. In large organisations, a backup site might be created, so that data processing can be switched to a secondary site immediately in the event of an emergency. Smaller organisations might make use of other measures, such as RAID facilities or data warehousing services (Chapter 4).

As cloud computing becomes more popular, many individuals and organisations have seen this as an ideal way of ensuring business continuity. Several copies of important data may be distributed across the cloud and even software applications can be accessed anywhere there is an Internet connection. However, it can be argued that cloud computing simply replaces one set of problems with another. As an example, how could a company maintain normal operations if Internet access was lost or if a service provider suffered a major breakdown? In April 2011, Amazon's EC2 cloud computer network crashed, taking thousands of company websites offline. Some sites took two days to restore and Amazon later announced that some customer data had been permanently lost. In October 2011, Blackberry phone users in Europe, India, South America and other regions suffered disruptions to e-mail, Internet and instant messaging services for a number of days. Services were disrupted again in September 2012.

Planning for emergencies involves more than merely restoring hardware, software and data. Since the 11 September 2001 terrorist attacks in the United States and the 7 July 2005 attack in the UK, a great deal of emphasis has been placed on protecting employees from danger and making sure that competent staff are available in an emergency. This is sometimes known as 'skills continuity'.

Audit

The process of monitoring an organisation's hardware and software resources. In general, audits are used as a deterrent against theft and the use of illegal software.

Recovery

The process which is used to restore backup data.

Business continuity planning

The process of developing procedures aimed at restoring the normal operation of an information system in the event of an emergency or disaster.

Backup site

This houses a copy of the organisation's main data processing facilities, including hardware, software and up-to-date data files. In the event of an emergency, processing can be switched to the backup site almost immediately so that the organisation's work can continue.

RAID

This stands for 'redundant array of inexpensive disks'. Essentially, identical copies of important data files are kept upon a number of different storage devices. If one or more of the storage devices fails, additional devices are activated automatically, allowing uninterrupted access to the data and reducing the possibility of losing transactions or updates.

TYPES OF CONTROLS

There are five major categories of controls that can be applied to information systems. These are:

- physical protection;
- biometric controls;
- telecommunications controls;
- failure controls;
- auditing.

Physical protection

Physical protection involves the use of physical barriers intended to protect against theft and unauthorised access. The reasoning behind such an approach is extremely simple: if access to rooms and equipment is restricted, risks of theft and vandalism are reduced. Furthermore, by preventing access to equipment, it is less likely that an unauthorised user can gain access to confidential information. Locks, barriers and security chains are examples of this form of control.

Biometric controls

These controls make use of the unique characteristics of individuals in order to restrict access to sensitive information or equipment. Scanners that check fingerprints, voice prints or even retinal patterns are examples of biometric controls.

Until relatively recently, the expense associated with biometric control systems placed them out of reach of all but the largest organisations. In addition, many organisations held reservations concerning the accuracy of the recognition methods used to identify specific individuals. However, with the introduction of more sophisticated hardware and software, both of these problems have been largely resolved. As a result, laptop computers, PDAs and USB flash drives are all now available with built-in fingerprint scanners.

Many organisations have now begun to look at ways in which biometric control systems can be used to reduce instances of fraud. Within five years, for example, banks are expected to introduce automated teller machines (ATMs) that use fingerprints and retinal patterns to identify customers.

Activity 15.1   Biometric security

Devices employing biometric security measures are now within the reach of a typical computer user. Using the Internet, magazines, product catalogues and other sources, locate at least two examples of low-cost products that employ biometrics.

Telecommunications controls

These controls help to verify the identity of a particular user. Common types of communications controls include passwords and user validation routines.

As an example, when a new network account is created for a given user, they may be asked to supply several pieces of personal information, such as the name of their spouse or their date of birth. When the user attempts to connect to the network system from outside of the organisation, they are asked to confirm their identity by providing some of the information given when the account was created.

Failure controls

Failure controls attempt to limit or avoid damage caused by the failure of an information system. Typical examples include recovery procedures and regular backups of data. Backups are explained in more detail later on.

Auditing

Auditing involves taking stock of procedures, hardware, software and data at regular intervals.

With regard to software and data, audits can be carried out automatically with an appropriate program. Auditing software works by scanning the hard disk drives of any computers, terminals and servers attached to a network system. As each hard disk drive is scanned, the names of any programs found are added to a log. This log can then be compared to a list of the programs that are legitimately owned by the organisation. Since the log contains information concerning the whereabouts of each program found, it is relatively simple to determine the location of any unauthorised programs. In many organisations, auditing programs are also used to keep track of software licences and allow companies to ensure that they are operating within the terms of their licence agreements.

A **software licence** enables a company to make several copies of a program, allowing it to acquire important programs at reduced cost. Typically, a company will purchase a single copy of the program and install this on as many computers as required. Since only one copy of the program and any accompanying documentation is required, costs are reduced for both the company and the supplier. The terms of the software licence will determine how many copies of the program can be made. A ten-user licence, for example, allows a company to make up to ten copies of a program for use by its employees.

Software licence

This sets out the terms under which a piece of software can be used. In general, licences are required for every piece of software owned and used by a company. A company using ten copies of a word processor, for instance, must own ten individual licences or a single licence giving the right to use ten copies of the program.

SOME TECHNIQUES FOR CONTROLLING INFORMATION SYSTEMS

Some of the most common techniques used to control computer-based information systems are:

- formal security policies;
- passwords;
- file encryption;
- organisational procedures governing the use of computer-based information systems;
- user validation techniques;
- backup procedures.

The following describes each of these techniques in more detail.

Formal security policy

Perhaps the simplest and most effective control is the formulation of a comprehensive policy on security. Amongst a wide variety of items, such a policy will outline:

> In 2010, only 67 per cent of small UK organisations had a formal information management security policy in place compared to 90 per cent of large organisations.
>
> *Source*: DTI, 2010

- what is considered to be acceptable use of the information system;
- what is considered unacceptable use of the information system;
- the sanctions available in the event that an employee does not comply with the security policy;
- details of the controls in place, including their form and function and plans for developing these further.

Once a policy has been formulated, it must be publicised in order for it to become effective. In addition, the support of management is essential in order to ensure that employees adhere to the guidelines contained within the policy.

It is worth noting that many European countries have national standards that can be used to develop and assess organisational security policies. In the UK, for example, compliance with BS 7799 demonstrates that a company has established an effective information security management infrastructure. Standards such as ISO/IEC 27001, ISO 17799 and BS 7799 are extremely useful in that they provide a framework that can be used to develop a series of policies and procedures in order to maintain the security of computer-based information systems.

Passwords

The password represents one of the most common forms of protection for computer-based information systems. In addition to providing a simple, inexpensive means of restricting access to equipment and sensitive data, passwords also provide a number of other benefits. Amongst these are the following:

- Access to the system can be divided into levels by issuing different passwords to employees based on their positions and the work they carry out.
- The actions of an employee can be regulated and supervised by monitoring the use of their password.
- If a password is discovered or stolen by an external party, it should be possible to limit any damage arising as a result.
- The use of passwords can encourage employees to take some of the responsibility for the overall security of the system.

> The InfoSecurity Europe 2007 survey found that 64 per cent of workers questioned were prepared to reveal their computer password in exchange for a small gift, such as a chocolate bar. Although this fell to 21 per cent in 2008, 60 per cent of workers were still willing to reveal personal information, such as contact details, many without needing any reward at all.
>
> *Source*: *PC Pro*, 16 April 2008

Encryption

An additional layer of protection for sensitive data can be provided by making use of encryption techniques. Modern encryption methods rely upon the use of one or more keys. Without the correct key, any encrypted data are meaningless – and therefore of no value – to a potential thief.

Activity 15.2	Pretty Good Privacy (PGP)

Using the Internet as a resource, locate information related to a well-known product called GNU Privacy Guard (GPGP, sometimes also called GnuPG). Describe how GPGP works and explain why you think the system is so popular.

Procedures

Under normal circumstances, a set of procedures for the use of an information system will arise from the creation of a formal security policy. Such procedures should describe in detail the correct operation of the system and the responsibilities of users. Additionally, the procedures should highlight issues related to security, should explain some of the reasoning behind them and should also describe the penalties for failing to comply with instructions.

User validation

User validation

Checks made to ensure the user is permitted access to a system. Also known as access control systems, they often involve user names and passwords, but can also include biometric techniques.

Of relevance to telecommunications is the use of **user validation** techniques. It is necessary to verify the identity of users attempting to access the system from outside of the organisation. A password is insufficient to identify the user since it might have been stolen or accidentally revealed to others. However, by asking for a date of birth, National Insurance number or other personal information, the identity of the user can be confirmed. Alternatively, if the location of the user is known, the system can attempt to call the user back at their current location. If the user is genuine, the call will be connected correctly and the user can then access the system. Although such methods do not offer total security, the risk of unauthorised access can be reduced dramatically.

Backup procedures

The effects of a sudden loss of data can affect a company's activities in a variety of ways. The disruption caused to a company's normal activities can result in significant financial losses due to factors such as lost opportunities, additional trading expenses and customer dissatisfaction.

The cumulative effects of data loss can prove detrimental to areas as diverse as corporate image and staff morale. Perhaps the single most compelling reason for introducing effective backup procedures is simply the expense involved in reconstructing lost data. A 2008 study of UK data breaches by the Ponemon Institute in collaboration with Symantec and PGP Corporation found that the cost of a lost record ranges from £47 to £59.

Grandfather, father, son

A common procedure used for creating backup copies of important data files.

One of the most common methods of protecting valuable data is to use the '**grandfather, father, son**' technique. Here, a rotating set of backup disks or tapes are used so that three different versions of the same data are held at any one time.

To illustrate this method, imagine a single user working with a personal computer and using three flash drives to store their data on. Each day, all of the data being worked on are copied onto the flash drive containing the oldest version ('grandfather') of that data. This creates a continuous cycle that ensures that the oldest backup copy is never more than three days old.

Table 15.1 illustrates the operation of the 'grandfather, father, son' method. As can be seen, each flash drive or other storage device moves through three generations. Since three copies of the data are maintained, the risk of data loss is reduced considerably. In the event of the original data becoming corrupted or damaged in some way, only the changes made

Table 15.1 The 'grandfather, father, son' backup method

Day 1	Day 2	Day 3
Device 1	Device 2	Device 3
Grandfather	Grandfather	Grandfather
Device 2	Device 3	Device 1
Father	Father	Father
Device 3	Device 1	Device 2
Son	Son	Son

since the last backup copy was made would be lost. In most cases, this would amount to new or altered data produced during the previous day. In addition, since only three sets of reusable media are required in order to make backups, the costs involved can be considered low.

It is worth noting several general points concerning backups of data:

- The time, effort and expense involved in producing backup copies will be wasted unless they are made at regular intervals. How often backups are made depends largely upon the amount of work processed over a given period of time. In general, backups will be made more frequently as the number of transactions carried out each day increases.

- Backup copies of data should be checked each time they are produced. Faulty storage devices and media may sometimes result in incomplete or garbled copies of data. In addition, precautions should be taken against computer viruses, in order to prevent damage to the data stored.

- The security of backup copies should be ensured by storing them in a safe location. Typically, an organisation will produce two sets of backup copies: one to be stored at the company premises, the other to be taken off the premises and stored at a separate location. In this way, a major accident, such as a fire at the company premises, will not result in the total destruction of the organisation's data. Many companies take additional precautions, such as storing important data online, using cloud storage as an extra safeguard.

- Not all data need be backed up at regular intervals. Software applications, for example, can normally be restored quickly and easily from the original media. In a similar way, if a backup has already been made of a given item of data, the production of additional copies may not be necessary.

Incremental backup

Includes only those files that have changed in some way since the last backup was made.

Full backup

A method of producing copies of important data files by including all data files considered to be important.

In order to reduce the time taken to create backup copies, many organisations make use of software that allows the production of **incremental backups**. Initially, a backup copy of all data files is made and care is taken to ensure the accuracy of the copy. This initial, complete backup is normally referred to as a **full backup** (sometimes also known as an 'archival backup'). From this point on, specialised backup software is used to detect and copy only those files that have changed in some way since the last backup was made. In the event of data loss, damaged files can be replaced by restoring the full backup first, followed by the incremental backups. One of the chief advantages of creating incremental backups is that it is possible to trace the changes made to data files over time. In this way, any version of a given file can be located and restored. However, incremental backups can also have a significant disadvantage: should the full backup made initially become lost or corrupted, it may not be possible to restore any data at all. For this reason, it is essential that all backups be checked carefully as soon as they are made.

Many companies have started to adopt disk-imaging software as a way of producing backups of important programs and data. The latest and most sophisticated packages allow users to create incremental backups of an entire hard disk drive. This helps to avoid redundancy and makes the overall process faster and easier to manage. Disk images are discussed in more detail a little later on.

FOCUS ON... MALWARE

What is malware?

The term 'malware' (malicious software) is a generic term for software intended to gather confidential information from a computer system, or cause harm to valuable data. In general, malware can be broken down into a number of categories, each of which is discussed in more detail in the following sections:

- computer viruses;
- Trojans and key loggers;
- spyware.

The computer virus

Computer virus

This is a computer program that is capable of self-replication, allowing it to spread from one 'infected' machine to another.

The origin of the term computer virus is credited to Fred Cohen, author of the 1987 paper 'Computer viruses – theories and experiments'. However, 'natural' computer viruses were reported as early as 1974 and papers describing mathematical models of the theory of epidemics were published in the early 1950s.

There are several different types of computer virus, for example *parasitic viruses* (sometimes known as 'file infectors') insert copies of themselves into legitimate programs, such as operating system files, often making little effort to disguise their presence. In this way, each time the program file is run, so too is the virus.

In recent years, a great deal of attention has been paid to the emergence of *macro viruses* (sometimes called 'script viruses'). These programs are created using the high-level programming languages found in e-mail packages, web browsers and applications software, such as word processors. Technically, such viruses are extremely crude but are capable of causing a great deal of damage. Table 15.2 provides some examples of estimated losses caused by computer viruses over the years 1999–2008. As the table shows, some of the largest losses experienced were the result of relatively unsophisticated viruses distributed via e-mail.

All viruses should be considered to be harmful. Even if a virus program does nothing more than reproduce itself, it may still cause system crashes and data loss. In many cases, the damage caused by a computer virus might be accidental, arising merely as the result of poor programming.

Until quite recently, it was thought that computer viruses could not be attached to data files, such as word processing documents or e-mail messages. However, the built-in programming languages featured within many modern applications mean that data files may now be used to transmit viruses. A typical example is the Word for Windows macro viruses, which attach themselves to a document template and duplicate each time a new document is created. Using an infected document on another machine automatically infects the user's copy of Word for Windows. However, it remains true that viruses cannot be transmitted by a conventional e-mail message. A virus can only be transmitted as an attachment to a message, or if the e-mail package being used allows active content.

Table 15.2 Examples of estimated losses due to computer viruses from 1999 to 2008

Year	Virus	Estimated loss ($ billions)
1999	Melissa	1.10
2000	LoveLetter	8.80
2001	Code Red	2.60
2001	SirCam	1.15
2002	Klez	9.00
2003	Slammer	1.20
2004	MyDoom	4.75
2004	Sasser	3.50
2004	NetSky	2.70
2004	Bagle	1.50
2007	Conficker	9.80
2008	Storm Worm	8.50

Sources: Bocij, 2006; www.howstuffworks.com

The transmission of computer viruses and malware

A number of reports suggest that consultants, maintenance engineers and employees are responsible for approximately 40 to 60 per cent of all virus infections. Often, a virus infection occurs as a result of employees' transferring files to and from their machines at home. Other ways in which viruses and other malware may be transmitted include through the use of illegal software, software downloaded via the Internet and, occasionally, through commercial software and magazine cover-mounted discs.

It can be argued that computer users themselves are often responsible for damage arising as a result of malware, such as viruses and worms. Few users take adequate security measures, such as backing up data. It is estimated that fewer than 5 per cent of computer users are capable of carrying out backup procedures. Furthermore, inadequate training and incorrect responses to security breaches often exaggerate the problem, since anxious users may cause more damage than the malware itself.

There are few accurate estimates of the financial loss caused by computer viruses, Trojans and other forms of malware each year. This is undoubtedly due to the reluctance of major companies to disclose the fact that their systems have been compromised. Despite this, surveys have suggested that over 60 per cent of major corporates come into contact with computer viruses each year. However, the real rate of infection may be substantially higher since companies are unlikely to admit any major losses arising as a result of computer virus infections. In the UK, the Department for Trade and Industry's *Information Security Breaches Survey 2012* found that 40 per cent of large organisations had experienced virus infections, as had 43 per cent of smaller organisations. Worldwide, *Fox News* reported that total losses from malware infections amounted to $86 billion in 2009.

Detecting and preventing virus infection

The risk of virus infection can be reduced to a minimum by implementing a relatively simple set of security measures:

- unauthorised access to machines and software should be restricted as far as possible;
- machines and software should be checked regularly with a virus detection program;
- all new disks and any software originating from an outside source should be checked with a virus detection program before use;

Virus scanner

Intended to detect and safely remove virus programs from a computer system.

Signature

Unique features of a virus such as the unique series of values in its program file or message displayed on screen or hidden text.

Polymorphic virus

Capable of altering its form, so that the 'standard' signature of the virus is not present. This means that a virus scanner may not always identify the virus correctly.

Stealth virus

Specifically designed to avoid detection. Such programs are normally written with the intention of defeating common or well-known virus-scanning programs.

Heuristics

Involves monitoring a system to detect common behaviours associated with computer viruses, such as attempts to access certain areas of the hard disk drive.

Erasing

Erasing a file removes its details from the disk's directory structure. This leaves the file essentially intact and can allow it to be recovered.

Deleting

Deleting a file removes its details from the disk's directory structure and overwrites it with new data. This makes it virtually impossible to recover the file.

Payload

This refers to the action that will be carried out once a computer virus becomes active. This can range from displaying a message on the screen, to deleting valuable data.

- the use of flash drives on company systems should be monitored and controlled, especially if employees take data files to/from their homes;
- regular backups of data and program files must be made in order to minimise the damage caused if a virus infects the system.

Virus scanners are intended to detect and then safely remove virus programs from a computer system. The most common method of detection used by these programs involves scanning for the signatures of particular viruses. It is often possible to locate a virus by simply searching every file on an infected disk for these identifying characteristics. However, since new viruses are discovered quite frequently, the list of signatures contained within a detection program quickly becomes dated. For this reason, most software developers insist that regular program updates are essential. In fact, some programs are updated every few *hours*, rather than once a day or less frequently.

The introduction of new kinds of viruses, such as polymorphic and stealth viruses, means that signature checking alone can no longer be regarded as a completely secure method of detection. For this reason, most virus scanners use a combination of techniques to enhance their efficiency. Amongst the methods used are checksums, virus shields, anti-viruses, heuristics and inoculation. The use of heuristics, for example, involves monitoring the computer system to detect common behaviours associated with computer viruses, such as attempts to access certain areas of the hard disk drive.

Once a virus has been detected there are three methods of removing it. The first, *disinfection*, attempts to restore damaged files and directory structures to their original condition. However, disinfection is not possible in all cases. The second technique involves *overwriting* the virus program so that it is permanently and irrevocably deleted from the disk. The third and final method of removing a virus is by restoring a backup of the infected disk to the system. The process of writing files to the disk effectively overwrites the virus and restores the system to its original state.

A distinction is made between erasing and deleting a file. Erasing a file merely removes its entry in the disk's directory structure: the file remains intact until another file overwrites it. For this reason, virus killers delete the virus completely by overwriting it with new data.

Despite the sophistication of scanning programs, none is capable of offering complete protection against infection. Many tests have been carried out to determine the efficiency of specific virus-scanning programs. In some cases, the detection rate of some programs was found to be as low as 50 per cent.

The action that a virus carries out when activated is normally referred to as the payload. An example of a payload might be issuing the command to delete all of the files from the user's hard disk drive when a certain condition is met, such as when a particular date or time is reached.

In recent years many companies have come to recognise that virus scanners and other software, such as firewalls, are no longer enough to provide high levels of protection in the face of sophisticated viruses and malware. For instance, computer viruses and Trojans now exist that can disable or delete security software whilst maintaining the appearance that they are working properly. Many companies have started to adopt other methods of protecting their systems, for example by investing in disk-imaging software.

Using appropriate software, it is possible to take a 'snapshot' of a hard disk drive at a given date and time. The entire contents of the drive can be copied into a special disk image file while the user carries on working. In the event of a disaster, the image file can be written back to the hard disk, restoring the system to the same state as when the image was created. Disk images can even be copied onto other hard disk drives, allowing users to transfer programs and data onto a new system. One of the reasons companies have started to use disk images is because the disk drive is completely erased when the image is restored. At present, no known malware can survive this process, so restoring an image to a hard disk can be taken to guarantee the destruction of a virus or Trojan. Of course,

Disk image

A perfect copy of the entire contents of a hard disk drive. Disk images are used to back up whole systems since they provide a snapshot of the system at a specific date and time.

this process can only be successful if no virus or other malware was present when the disk image was created.

The use of disk images has become so popular that many companies use them as the basis for their backup routines. Although disk images can be somewhat wasteful in terms of storage, they have the advantage of being very quick and easy to make. A good example of disk-imaging software is Acronis TrueImage (www.acronis.com), which can be used on individual systems or across a network. This package also allows users to restore individual files if they wish, removing the need to overwrite the entire hard disk.

Trends

There are many different estimates concerning the growth in numbers of viruses, Trojans and worms. In 1989, it was believed that there were fewer than 50 viruses in circulation. However, by the end of 2004 it was estimated that the number of viruses had grown to more than 100,000 (Bocij, 2006) and to more than one million by 2008 (*Sunday Times*, 10 April 2008). There has been a similar growth in the number of new viruses and similar malware that is being discovered each month. As an example, at the end of 2002, Sophos – a leading developer of anti-virus products – reported that it had detected more than 7000 new viruses, worms and Trojans during the whole of the year. By 2004, some antivirus companies were reporting the discovery of up to 1700 new viruses every month and by 2008 a leading antivirus company, Symantec, reported that it had discovered 711,000 new viruses in a single year. In 2012, McAfee reported that it was receiving 100,000 malware samples each day and attributed much of the growth to a surge in malware aimed at mobile applications and devices.

Improved access to technology, an increase in the use of networks and new communications technology have all increased the vulnerability of many users to virus infections. At most risk are universities and other large sites, such as public services.

Activity 15.3	Computer viruses

Using the Internet as a resource, find details of at least three major virus incidents over the past three years. For each incident, describe:

1. where the virus originated and how it spread;
2. how many machines were infected around the world;
3. estimated losses resulting from the infection.

Trojans and key loggers

Worm

A small program that moves through a computer system randomly changing or overwriting pieces of data as it moves.

Trojan

A Trojan presents itself as a legitimate program in order to gain access to a computer system. Trojans are often used as delivery systems for computer viruses.

Two other kinds of programs are related to computer viruses: worms and Trojans. A **worm** is a small program that moves through a computer system randomly changing or overwriting pieces of data as it moves.

A **Trojan** appears as a legitimate program in order to gain access to a computer system. In the past few years, the use of Trojans to disrupt company activities or gain access to confidential information has grown sharply. Most of the Trojans en-countered by business organisations are designed to gather information and transmit regular reports back to the owner. Typically, a Trojan will incorporate a *key logging* facility (sometimes called a 'keystroke recorder') to capture all keyboard input from a given computer. Capturing keyboard data allows the owner of the Trojan to gather a great deal of information, such as passwords and the contents of all outgoing e-mail messages.

Although Trojans are often used as delivery systems for spyware and other forms of malware, some are designed to give owners control over the target computer system.

Bot

A computer that has been infected by a zombie program is sometimes referred to as a bot. See botnet and zombie.

Zombie

A type of Trojan capable of taking full or partial control of a computer when activated by the author. Zombie computers are usually organised into large networks (called botnets) so that their combined resources can be used to send spam or launch distributed denial-of-service attacks.

Botnet

A group of zombie computers capable of being directed towards various tasks, such as launching denial of service attacks. See zombie.

Spyware

Describes a category of software intended to collect and transmit confidential information without the knowledge or consent of a computer user.

Adware

Describes a type of software that contains spyware intended to monitor a user's online activities, usually so that advertising can be targeted more accurately.

Effectively, the Trojan acts as a remote control application, allowing the owner to carry out actions on the target computer as if they were sitting in front of it. Sometimes, the owner of the Trojan will make no effort to conceal their activities: the victim sees actions being carried out but is unable to intervene, short of switching off the computer. More often, however, the Trojan operates silently and the victim is unaware that their computer is running programs, deleting files, sending e-mail, and so on. Back Orifice is an example of a Trojan that can be used in both of these ways. This program was designed to target Microsoft's operating systems and is arguably the most famous program of its kind.

Some programs are designed to disrupt company activities by initiating denial-of-service attacks or by attacking company servers. In recent years, hackers have started to use specialised programs to create networks of zombie computers that can be used to send commercial spam or launch distributed denial-of-service attacks. Some Trojans are designed to take full or partial control of a computer when they receive instructions from the author. The Trojan remains inactive most of the time, only connecting to the Internet every now and then to check for new instructions. When activated by the author, the Trojan begins to generate e-mail or fake web traffic directed towards one or more specific targets. A computer infected by this type of Trojan is often called a **bot** or a **zombie**. Hackers use these networks – called **botnets** – to generate an income by renting them out to spammers, extortionists and other criminals, or by extorting money from companies themselves.

Spyware

Spyware represents a new type of threat for business and home users. In general, spyware describes a category of software designed to capture and record confidential information without a user's knowledge or consent. As an example, an earlier section described how key loggers record every key pressed by a user. Such programs are often used to collect passwords and other information – such as the contents of documents and e-mail messages – over a period of time. At regular intervals, the program will attempt to connect to the Internet and transmit a report to its owner by e-mail. Often, key loggers will attempt to avoid detection by waiting until the computer user is working on the Internet before attempting to transmit any data.

Applications for spyware range from monitoring the actions of a spouse to industrial espionage. Although early spyware programs were relatively crude, modern applications have a number of sophisticated features that make them difficult to detect and remove. As an example, some programs can be installed at a distance, without needing direct access to the target computer.

Spyware is also produced and disseminated as **adware** (advertising-supported software). Many companies produce useful software tools that are distributed free of charge or at low cost. In order to generate revenues, the software displays advertisements on behalf of other companies. However, some companies attempt to target their advertising more effectively by monitoring how people use their computers and the Internet. The software collects information, such as details of any web sites visited, and reports back to a central server. Although most companies claim that they do not collect any data that can identify a specific individual, many people frown upon the idea that their activities are being constantly monitored and reported on.

Detecting Trojans and spyware

Many modern virus scanners are also capable of detecting Trojans and spyware, however, it is also possible to detect this software in two other ways. First, it is possible to purchase specialised software that functions in much the same way as a virus scanner. *The Cleaner,* for instance, is a specialised Trojan scanner capable of detecting thousands of common Trojans, as well as continuously monitoring a computer for behaviour indicative of a Trojan infection. Similar applications exist to deal with spyware, such as *Ad-Aware*, a package claimed to be capable of removing all known adware products.

Second, since many spyware programs need to communicate via the Internet, it is often possible to detect them by looking for unusual activity, such as attempts to send e-mail by unfamiliar programs or components. A firewall often provides a good defence against Trojans since it will detect and prevent any unauthorised Internet access.

CASE STUDY 15.2

Cybercrime costs US $100bn a year, report says

By Paul Taylor in New York

Cybercrime and cyberspying are costing the US economy $100bn a year and the global economy perhaps $300bn annually, according to a first-of-its-kind report published on Tuesday.

The report, 'Estimating the Cost of Cybercrime and Cyber Espionage', prepared by the Washington-based Center for Strategic and International Studies (CSIS) and sponsored by McAfee, the security firm now owned by Intel, also estimates that malicious cyber activity costs as many as 508,000 jobs in the US alone.

'It begs several important questions about the full benefit to the acquirers and the damage to the victims from the cumulative effect of continuous losses in cyberspace,' the report said.

'We believe the CSIS report is the first to use actual economic modelling to build out the figures for the losses attributable to malicious cyber activity,' said Mike Fey, chief technology officer at McAfee.

'Other estimates have been bandied about for years, but no one has put any rigour behind the effort. As policy makers, business leaders and others struggle to get their arms around why cyber security matters, they need solid information on which to base their actions.'

The figures confirm that malicious cyberactivites do indeed represent what some have termed 'the greatest transfer of wealth in human history'.

'Losses to the US [the country where data are most accessible] may reach $100bn annually,' the report says. 'The cost of cybercrime and cyberespionage to the global economy is some multiple of this likely measured in hundreds of billions of dollars.'

To put this in perspective, the World Bank suggests that global GDP was about $70,000bn in 2011. 'A $300bn loss – and losses are probably in this range – would be four tenths of 1 per cent of global income.'

'This seemingly trivial amount begs several important questions about the full benefit to the acquirers and the damage to the victims from the cumulative effect of continuous losses in cyberspace,' the report authors say.

The report's authors note that the cost of malicious cyberactivity involves more than the loss of financial assets or intellectual property. There are opportunity costs, damage to brand and reputation, consumer losses from fraud, the opportunity costs of service disruptions 'cleaning up' after cyber incidents and the cost of increased spending on cybersecurity.

To help measure the real loss from cyberattacks, CSIS enlisted economists, intellectual property experts and security researchers to develop the report. The general accepted range for cybercrime launch was between $100bn and $500bn to the global economy. Researchers used real-world analogies like figures for car crashes, piracy, pilferage and drugs to build the model.

They noted the difficulty of relying on methods such as surveys because companies that reveal their cyber losses often cannot estimate what has been taken, intellectual property losses are difficult to quantify and the self-selection process of surveys can distort the results.

'This report is also the first to connect malicious cyberactivity with job loss,' said James Lewis, director and senior fellow of the Technology and Public Policy Program at CSIS and a co-author of the report. 'Using figures from the Commerce Department on the ratio of exports to US jobs, we arrived at a high-end estimate of 508,000 US jobs potentially lost from cyberespionage. As with other estimates in the report, however, the raw numbers might tell just part of the story. If a good portion of these jobs were high-end manufacturing jobs that moved overseas because of intellectual property losses, the effects could be more wide ranging.'

A second report from the CSIS, which is under way, will look at the ramifications of cybersecurity losses on the pace of innovation, the flow of trade and the social costs associated with crime and job loss.

Mr Lewis and co-author Stewart Baker of Steptoe & Johnson, point out that as thoroughly as they plan to develop their estimates, the dollar amount might not fully reflect all the damaging effects that cyber espionage and cybercrime have on the global economy.

Both activities slow the pace of innovation, distort trade and bring the spate of social costs associated with crime and job loss, according to the report.

The authors say the larger effect may be more important than any actual number, and it will be the focus of the next report.

 Source: Taylor, P. (2013) Cybercrime costs US $100bn a year, report says. *Financial Times*. 23 July.

QUESTION

What are the indirect costs of cybercrime described in the report?

THREATS RELATED TO INTERNET SERVICES

Since 1999, a number of significant new threats to organisational information systems have emerged. Many of these threats reflect an increasing reliance on intranets and the Internet as basic tools for conducting transactions with partners, suppliers and customers. Although the following material focuses on the Internet, much of it is also relevant to company intranets.

Denial of service (DoS)

Denial of service (DoS)

This is a form of attack on company information systems that involves flooding the company's Internet servers with huge amounts of traffic. Such attacks effectively halt all of the company's Internet activities.

As companies begin to rely on network technology to reduce costs, they become more vulnerable to certain risks. For example, more harm can be caused if an individual gains access to a network server than if they merely gain access to a single PC. Similarly, companies relying on the Internet for business communications may find themselves subject to **denial-of-service (DoS)** attacks. Typically, these attacks involve blocking the communications channels used by a company. For example, an e-mail system might be attacked by sending millions of lengthy messages to the company. Other techniques involve altering company web pages or attacking the systems used to process online transactions. In these cases, companies are usually forced to shut down services themselves until the problem can be dealt with. Such attacks were almost unheard of before 1999 but have recently started to become more common. The DTI's 'Information Security Breaches Survey 2012' found that 30 per cent of companies had experienced DoS attacks in the previous year, a figure that has grown significant from 2004 when only 5 per cent of companies reported such incidents.

The impact of a denial-of-service attack can be extremely severe, especially for organisations that rely heavily on the Internet for e-commerce. As an example, an attack on Yahoo in 2000 involved servers being flooded with 1 billion hits per minute. The attack was estimated as costing £300,000 in lost advertising revenue alone (*Financial Times*, 17 November 2000).

In the past few years, denial-of-service attacks have started to be used to extort money from companies that rely heavily on the Internet. Often, an initial DoS attack is accompanied by a demand for money and the threat of a more serious and prolonged attack. A well-known case took place in 2004, when Russian extortionists launched a number of DoS attacks against UK bookmakers before demanding between £10,000 and £30,000 to stop the attacks. Bookmakers who refused to pay suffered losses of approximately £40 million through lost business caused by repeated attacks. Recent studies by the FBI, Ponemon Institute and others have suggested that DoS and other attacks on a single organisation can result in losses of up to $36.5 million.

Activity 15.4   Denial-of-service attacks

Using the Internet as a resource, locate three examples of recent denial-of-service attacks. For each example, describe how the attack occurred and the losses suffered by the victim.

Identity theft and brand abuse

Identity theft involves using another person's identity to carry out acts that range from sending libellous e-mail to making fraudulent purchases. It is considered relatively easy to impersonate another person in this way, but far harder to prove that communications did not originate from the victim.

For business organisations, there is a threat that employees may be impersonated in order to place fraudulent orders. Alternatively, a company may be embarrassed if rumours or bogus press releases are transmitted via the Internet.

The term brand abuse is used to cover a wide range of activities, ranging from the sale of counterfeit goods, for example software applications, to exploiting a well-known brand name for commercial gain. As an example, the name of a well-known company might be embedded into a special web page so that the page receives a high ranking in a search engine. Users searching for the name of the company are then likely to be diverted to the special web page where they are offered a competitor's goods instead. Some estimates suggest that the total cost of brand abuse, including counterfeiting, costs UK companies between £4 billion and £6.6 billion per year. This figure rises to between £28 and £40 billion across the EU and between $200 to $400 billion per year worldwide.

With regard to identity theft, CIFAS (www.cifas.org), a UK-based fraud prevention service, reports that there were 80,000 cases of identity theft in the UK in 2006. According to figures published on the organisation's web site, identity fraud cost the UK economy £1.5 billion in 2005 and generates an income of £10 million per day for criminals. More recent figures suggest that identity theft costs the UK around £2.7 billion per year, affecting 1.8 million people (SkyNews, 18 October 2010).

Brand abuse

This describes a wide range of activities, ranging from the sale of counterfeit goods (e.g. software applications) to exploiting a well-known brand name for commercial gain.

Extortion

Various approaches can be used to extort money from companies. Two examples include 'cybersquatting' and the threat of divulging customer information.

Cybersquatting involves registering an Internet domain that a company or celebrity is likely to want to own. Although merely registering a domain is not illegal in itself, some individuals attempt to extort money from companies or celebrities in various ways. Typically, the owner of the domain will ask for a large sum in order to transfer the domain to the interested party. Sometimes, however, demands for money may be accompanied by threats, such as the threat the domain will be used in a way that will harm the victim's reputation unless payment is forthcoming. Although there is an established mechanism for dealing with disputes over domain names, many victims of cybersquatting choose not to use these procedures since they do not wish to attract negative publicity.

A more common form of extortion usually occurs after a security breach in which sensitive company information has been obtained. Often, the threat involves making the information available to competitors or the public unless payment is made. One of the best-known cases involved an incident when an online music retailer's e-commerce systems were compromised and the details of some 300,000 credit cards were obtained. When a demand for a payment of $100,000 was not met, 25,000 credit card numbers were published on the Internet (*Financial Times*, 17 November 2000). A 2011 report from Detica and the Cabinet Office suggested that annual losses to UK business resulting from extortion linked to cybercrime are between £0.56 billion and £2.7 billion annually.

Cybersquatting

The act of registering an Internet domain with the intention of selling it for profit to an interested party. As an example, the name of a celebrity might be registered and then offered for sale at an extremely high price.

Abuse of resources

Organisations have always needed to ensure that employees do not take advantage of company resources for personal reasons. Whilst certain acts, such as sending the occasional personal e-mail, are tolerated by most companies, the increased availability of Internet access and e-mail facilities increases the risk that such facilities may be abused. Two examples of the risks associated with increased access to the Internet involve libel and cyberstalking.

Cyberstalking is a relatively new form of crime that involves the harassment of individuals via e-mail and the Internet. Of interest to business organisations is the fact that many cyberstalkers make use of company facilities in order to carry out their activities. There have also been cases of 'corporate stalking' where an organisation has used its resources to harass individuals or business competitors. Individuals can also harass companies and government departments. Although this kind of behaviour often has a financial motive, it can also result from a desire for revenge against the organisation, or even from political beliefs. For an organisation, the consequences of cyberstalking can include a loss of reputation and the threat of criminal and civil legal action.

A number of cases where employees have abused company e-mail facilities have received a great deal of publicity. Well-known cases include an incident where Norwich Union was forced to pay £450,000 in damages after staff libelled a competitor in internal e-mails and a case where Royal & Sun Alliance dismissed ten members of staff after an internal investigation uncovered a series of lewd e-mails circulating. These cases demonstrate that allowing Internet resources to be used inappropriately can have serious repercussions for organisations. In addition to the legal and financial consequences of libel and harassment, a great deal of harm can be caused to a company's public image and its relationships with customers and suppliers.

Other risks

A thorough discussion of the risks to organisations that arise from increased reliance on the Internet is beyond the scope of this chapter. However, in closing this section we provide two additional examples of emerging threats: cyberterrorism and stock fraud.

Cyberterrorism describes attacks made on information systems that are motivated by political or religious beliefs. Organisations involved in the defence industries are often the victims of such attacks. As an example, it is estimated that 20,000 UK and US web sites were attacked during the first week of the Iraq conflict in 2003. However, many other companies are also at risk from politically motivated attacks. For example, companies trading in countries that are in political turmoil or companies with business partners in these countries also face the risk of such attacks.

A number of recent cases have highlighted the danger of allowing inaccurate or misleading information to propagate across the Internet. Online stock fraud involves artificially increasing or decreasing the values of stocks by spreading carefully designed rumours across bulletin boards and chat-rooms. Whilst such activities may seem relatively harmless, companies can suffer significant losses. One of the best-known examples was reported on by the *Financial Times* some years ago (7 February 2001): 'In separate incidents, Lucent Technologies, the telecoms network equipment giant, and Emulex, a computer network hardware vendor, saw $7.1bn and $2.6bn wiped off their respective stock market values within hours of bogus press releases appearing on the web.'

Incidences of online stock fraud highlight an extremely important issue: organisations are at risk from the distribution of false information across the Internet. It is important to note that the effects of online stock fraud are not limited to influencing stock prices. Imagine, for example, what might happen if bogus press releases began to appear when a company was in the process of negotiating a merger or strategic alliance. Preventing inaccurate or misleading information from appearing on the Internet is fraught with difficulty. The sheer size of the Internet means that monitoring web sites, chat-rooms and news services places an unacceptable burden on the resources of even the largest organisations. However, the use of intelligent agents, offline readers and meta-search tools, as described in Chapter 4, can go some way towards helping an organisation monitor how it is being portrayed on the Internet.

Cyberstalking

This refers to the use of the Internet as a means of harassing another individual. A related activity is known as corporate stalking, where an organisation uses its resources to harass individuals or business competitors.

Cyberterrorism

This describes attacks made on information systems that are motivated by political or religious beliefs.

Online stock fraud

Most online stock fraud involves posting false information to the Internet in order to increase or decrease the values of stocks.

Although social engineering has existed for several decades, it has become of more concern in recent years because of developments such as phishing. Social engineering involves tricking people into providing confidential information that will allow access to a computer system. As an example, someone might pose as a technician during a telephone call and ask for information, such as passwords or user names.

A relatively new development related to social engineering concerns phishing which involves attempting to obtain information through bogus e-mails and web sites. As an example, computer users might receive an official-looking e-mail message from a bank asking them to confirm the details of a transaction via a web site. When users access the web site, they are asked for security information, such as an account number and password. Using this method, criminals are able to gather access to thou-sands of bank accounts and credit card accounts. As well as leading to financial losses, phishing also causes secondary damage by harming a company's reputation and damaging public confidence in services such as online shopping and online banking.

In the United States, a Consumer Reports 2007 survey found that American consumers lost $7 billion over the last two years to viruses, spyware and phishing schemes (*Information Week*, 6 August 2007). Approximately 8 per cent of respondents had been taken in by phishing schemes at a median cost of $200 per incident. Similar figures have been reported for the UK and the rest of Europe, though the UK remains the most popular target for such attacks. In the UK, ZDNet (11 March 2011) found that while phishing attacks rose significantly, actual losses fell to £46.7 million in 2009–10.

In terms of companies, the DTI's 2012 'Information Security Breaches Survey' looked at how often UK companies were impersonated or subjected to phishing attacks: 36 per cent of respondents said they experienced 'a few' attacks over the period of a year and a further 4 per cent said they experienced hundreds of attacks a day.

Social engineering

This involves tricking people into providing information that can be used to gain access to a computer system.

Phishing

A relatively new development, phishing involves attempting to gather confidential information through fake e-mail messages and web sites.

Infosecurity (1 June 2011) reports:

Online fraud continues to grow. The UK Fraud Barometer, for example, suggests that the average loss from online fraud currently stands at £697/$1120 per person, against £352/$566 in March 2010. One in 10 people report that they have been victims of online fraud or theft.

Managing threats to Internet services

In general terms, threats to information systems that originate from the Internet can be managed using the basic approaches and techniques outlined in this chapter.

Of the four basic strategies outlined earlier, an emphasis is likely to be placed on containment, obfuscation and recovery. Whilst an approach based on deterrence is likely to reduce problems associated with staff abuse of facilities, it is unlikely to discourage threats originating from outside the organisation. For example, it would be extremely difficult to take legal action against an attacker based in another country.

In terms of the specific techniques used to control access to information systems, whilst a great deal of emphasis will usually be placed on telecommunications controls, other methods are also of value. Encryption, for example, is used in a variety of circumstances to ensure that any information transmitted via the Internet is only of value to its intended recipient.

It is also important to remember that a formal security policy will play a key role in ensuring that an organisation is prepared to deal with Internet-based threats. Unfortunately, as evidenced by the DTI's 'Information Security Breaches Survey 2010', around 10 per cent of large organisations have no formal security policy in place.

Recently, a range of specialised software applications have appeared that help individuals and companies maintain the security of their systems. Examples include:

Firewalls

A specialised software application mounted on a server at the point the company is connected to the Internet to prevent unauthorised access into the company from outsiders.

- **Firewalls**. Firewalls act as a barrier between an information system and the Inter-net. The software attempts to monitor and control all incoming and outgoing traffic in an attempt to prevent outsiders gaining access to the information system.

- *Intrusion detection software*. This type of software monitors activity on a network in order to identify intruders. Typically, the software will look for characteristic patterns of behaviour that might identify the fact that someone has gained access to the network.

- *AI software*. Many organisations have begun to develop applications that use artificial intelligence in order to detect intrusion attempts or unusual activity that might indicate a breach in security. As an example, Searchspace has developed a system that detects unusual activity on the London Stock Exchange in order to detect attempts at insider trading.

SUMMARY

1. Controls upon computer-based information systems are needed to ensure the accuracy of data held by an organisation and to prevent loss or damage.

2. The most common threats to computer-based information systems include accidents, natural disasters, sabotage, vandalism, theft, unauthorised use and computer viruses.

3. Accidental damage to computer-based information systems can arise from a number of sources including: inaccurate data entry, attempts to carry out tasks beyond the ability of the employee, failure to comply with procedures for the use of organisational information systems and failure to carry out backup procedures or verify data backups.

4. In some cases, a computer-based information system may be vulnerable to damage caused by natural disasters, such as flooding.

5. Computer-based information systems should be protected against deliberate or unintentional sabotage. The damage or loss caused by unintentional sabot-age is often incidental to the actions taken by an employee in pursuit of a different goal.

6. Vandalism can result in an organisation's being deprived of critical hardware, software and data resources.

7. Theft can involve the physical theft of equipment or data theft. Whilst problems caused by physical theft can normally be overcome quickly and easily, data theft can result in significant long-term losses to an organisation.

8. The threat of unauthorised access to confidential data can arise from internal or external sources. Most security breaches involving confidential data can be attributed to the employees of the organisation.

9. There are four basic control strategies that can be applied to the security of computer-based information systems: containment, deterrence, obfuscation and recovery. Containment attempts to control access to an information system and often involves making potential targets as unattractive as possible. A strategy based upon deterrence uses the threat of punishment to discourage potential intruders. Obfuscation concerns itself with hiding or distributing assets so that any damage caused can be limited. A strategy based upon recovery recognises that, no matter how well defended, a breach in the security of an information system will eventually occur. Such a strategy is largely concerned with ensuring that the normal operation of the information system is restored as quickly as possible.

10. Types of control for computer-based information systems include: physical protection, biometric controls, telecommunications controls, failure controls and auditing. Physical protection involves the use of physical barriers intended to protect against theft and unauthorised access. Biometric controls make use of the unique characteristics of individuals, such as fingerprints, in order to restrict access to sensitive information or equipment. Telecommunications controls, such as user validation routines, help to verify the identity of a particular user. Failure controls attempt to limit

or avoid damage caused by the failure of an information system. Auditing involves taking stock of procedures, hardware, software and data at regular intervals.

11. Techniques used to control computer-based information systems include: formal security policies, passwords, file encryption, organisational procedures governing the use of computer-based information systems and user validation techniques.

12. A formal security policy should be supported by management and widely publicised. The policy will outline what is considered to be acceptable use of the information system and the sanctions available in the event that an employee does not comply with the policy.

13. Encryption involves encoding data so that they are meaningless to anyone except the rightful owner.

14. Backup procedures enable an organisation to protect sensitive files by making copies that can be stored at a safe location. The 'grandfather, father, son' technique is one of the most popular methods of making backups. An incremental backup provides a means of copying only those files that have changed in some way since the last backup was made. This provides a number of benefits, such as the ability to trace the changes that a given file has undergone over time.

15. Computer viruses, worms, Trojans and logic bombs represent a growing threat to information systems security. A computer virus is a computer program that is capable of self-replication, allowing it to spread from one 'infected' machine to another. All computer viruses are considered harmful and steps should be taken to protect valuable data from infection.

16. As organisations begin to rely on the Internet as a means of conducting business transactions, new threats to the security of information systems have begun to emerge. Some of these threats include denial-of-service attacks, brand abuse, identity theft, extortion and online stock fraud.

EXERCISES

Self-assessment exercises

1. What are the two basic reasons for the need to control computer-based information systems?

2. List some of the advantages and disadvantages of using passwords to protect equipment and sensitive data from unauthorised users.

3. What types of controls can be used to protect a computer-based information system against vandalism, theft and unauthorised access?

4. What are the advantages and disadvantages of an approach to controlling computer-based information systems that is based on containment?

5. Describe some of the ways in which accidental damage can occur to a computer-based information system.

6. Explain why virus-scanning software and anti-virus programs are often of only limited value in detecting and removing computer viruses.

7. What is malware?

8. What is the difference between spyware and adware?

9. Why do some security specialists recommend the use of disk imaging software?

10. What is phishing?

Discussion questions

1. What motivates an individual or organisation to create a computer virus?

2. 'No computer-based information system can be considered completely secure – all organisations should base their control strategies on recovery.' Make a case in favour of or against this argument.

3. 'An increased reliance on the Internet exposes organisations to increased risk in terms of threats to information systems security.' Make a case in favour of or against this argument.

4. How can companies reduce their vulnerability to social engineering attacks?

Essay questions

1. Conduct any research necessary and produce a formal security policy governing student access to the computer systems at the institution that you attend. In addition to providing details of any controls already in place, your work must also address the areas listed below. For each of these areas, you should also justify any decisions or choices made:

   (a) what activities are considered acceptable;
   (b) what activities are considered unacceptable;
   (c) the sanctions that may be used against those failing to comply with the policy.

2. Select an organisation that you are familiar with, such as a university or bank. Conduct any research necessary to address the following tasks:

   (a) Describe the potential impact of infection by computer viruses and other malware on the organisation's computer-based information systems.
   (b) Consider the effectiveness of tools, methods and procedures designed to protect computer-based information systems from computer viruses and other malware.
   (c) Evaluate the level of risk posed to the organisation by computer viruses and other malware. Produce a set of recommendations that may assist the organisation in reducing this risk.

3. Outline some of the threats to information systems that arise as a result of doing business via the Internet. Illustrate your response with appropriate examples and indicate how the risks you identify can be mitigated.

Examination questions

1. Computer viruses represent a significant threat to the security of organisational computer-based information systems. Some sources have estimated that as many as 1700 new computer viruses may appear each month. You are required to:

   (a) Provide a definition of the term 'computer virus'.
   (b) Using relevant examples, describe the ways in which computer viruses can be transmitted.
   (c) Discuss some of the ways in which organisations can protect against computer viruses. Highlight some of the advantages and disadvantages of each method described.

2. With regard to the control of computer-based information systems, answer the following:

   (a) Describe some of the common security threats facing organisational computer-based information systems.

(b) Explain the four basic approaches to controlling computer-based information systems. Highlight the advantages and disadvantages of each approach.

(c) 'More effective protection for a computer-based information system can be achieved by employing a combination of the four basic approaches to control.' Using relevant examples, discuss this statement.

3. A formal security policy can provide an effective means of protecting an organisation's computer-based information systems against theft, damage and other hazards.

(a) Provide an overview of the areas that will be outlined by a typical formal security policy document.

(b) Describe the ways in which a formal security policy can help to protect an organisation's computer-based information systems.

(c) A number of factors will determine whether or not a security policy works effectively. Using relevant examples, provide a brief discussion of some of these factors.

References

Bocij, P. (2006) *The Dark Side of the Internet and How to Protect Your Family*, Praeger Press, Westport, CT

Cohen, F. (1987) 'Computer viruses – theory and experiments', *Computers and Security*, 6, 1, 22–35

Department of Trade and Industry (2010) 'Information Security Breaches Survey 2010', Department of Trade and Industry. Available online at: http://www.infosec.co.uk/files/isbs_2010_technical_report_single_pages.pdf

Further reading

Andress, J. (2011) *The Basics of Information Security: Understanding the Fundamentals of InfoSec in Theory and Practice, Syngress*, Waltham, MA

Bocij, P. (2004) *Cyberstalking: Harassment in the Internet Age and How to Protect Your Family*, Praeger Press, Westport, CT.

Bocij, P. (2006) *The Dark Side of the Internet*, Praeger Press, Westport, CT.

Laudon, K. and Laudon, J. (2013) *Management Information Systems: Managing the Digital Firm*, 13th edition, Prentice-Hall, Upper Saddle River, NJ. Although some might find this book a little dense and difficult to read, it is detailed and comprehensive in its coverage. Chapter 8 looks at security.

O'Brien, J. and Marakas, G. (2011) *Management Information Systems*, 10th edition, McGraw-Hill, Boston. Chapter 13 deals with issues such as security and ethics.

Web links

http://csrc.nist.gov The NIST (National Institute of Standards and Technology) site hosts a Computer Security Resource Centre containing numerous articles, bulletins and other information.

http://www.sans.org/security-resources/ The SANS Institute publishes a huge number of articles dealing with computer security. This site is considered one of the most authoritative sources of information on computer security by IS professionals worldwide.

www.security-resources.com Security-resources.com offers a selection of introductory articles dealing with topics like how firewalls work.

www.lockdown.co.uk LockDown is a site aimed at home computer users. It provides information on security threats rated by severity. This site gives an excellent overview of the very large and diverse range of security problems that computer users face. Note that many of the problems listed in the site's database also apply to business computer users.

www.cert.org The Computer Emergency Response Team provides up-to-date information on security issues related to the Internet. The site publishes some interesting statistics concerning the number of incidents investigated.

www.infosyssec.org Information Systems Security Alert. This is a highly respected site that contains links to literally hundreds of resources. Of particular interest is a sophisticated search facility that allows information to be located on all aspects of security.

www.boran.com/security The IT Security Cookbook. A set of documents that provide detailed information on security management. There is a particularly good section on firewalls.

www.mcafee.com McAfee publishes Virus Scan, widely regarded as the best virus detection package available. The site contains a great deal of information on individual computer viruses.

www.vmyths.com This site sheds light on common myths related to viruses and computer security.

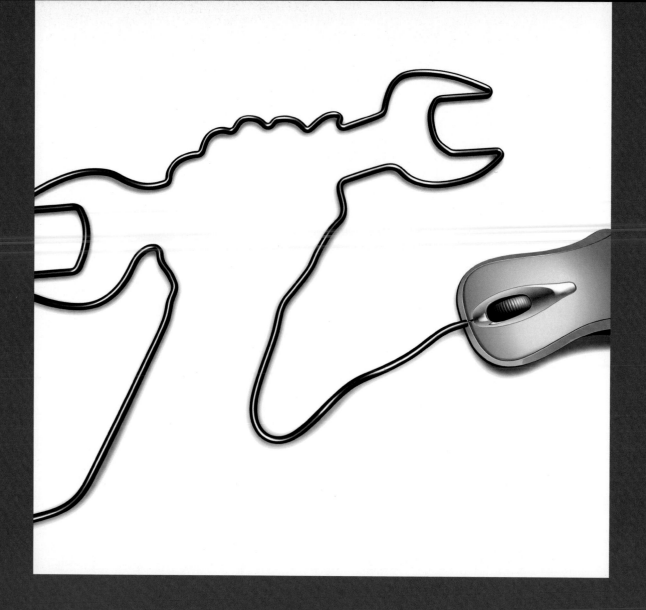

LINKS TO OTHER CHAPTERS

Protecting information, another key role of the IS manager, is covered in Chapter 15. Attributes of good-quality data were covered in Chapter 1.

End-user computing and the location of support services are elements of overall IS strategy which is described in Chapter 13.

Issues involved with employee monitoring are described in Chapter 17.

End-user computing – providing end-user services

CHAPTER AT A GLANCE

LEARNING OUTCOMES

After reading this chapter, you will be able to:

- define the range of services that must be delivered to support end-users effectively;
- distinguish between the general term 'end-user computing' and the more specific 'end-user development';
- analyse the risks associated with pursuing end-user development of information systems as part of a company's IS strategy;
- recommend policies for the effective management of end-user computing within an organisation;
- recommend new information systems applications that could reasonably be developed by end-user staff within an organisation.

MANAGEMENT ISSUES

End-user computing plays a significant role in the majority of organisations since, as we have seen throughout the book, many business users regularly use BIS as an essential part of their role. Managerial issues involved with controlling the use of information systems by end-users include:

- assessing the emphasis to be placed on end-user software development activities;
- providing a suitable support function to assist end-users in their use of computers;
- ensuring the appropriate skill levels for end-users through staff development and training;
- controlling the cost of end-user activities and support.

INTRODUCTION

This chapter considers some of the many tasks to support end-users that need to be performed by an information systems manager in the modern organisation. At the top of the list of priorities is the management of user information within the organisation – ensuring that it is secure, that backups are made and that its quality is maintained. A further important aspect of managing the information quality is ensuring that it is delivered to the user in a reliable and timely way. The management of the network is key to achieving this, but ensuring reliable access to the applications needed to work with the data is also important. This is particularly true with mission-critical applications – the operational systems used to deal with customers for taking orders and reservations. When a new version of the EuropCar car reservation system failed, for example, it is estimated to have cost the company $300,000 in lost orders over three days. In 2011, research from CA Technologies (**www.ca.com**) estimated that the total cost of downtime each year across the EU is in the region of €17 billion. The average annual cost of downtime per company is in excess of €263,000.

The protection of information is one type of end-user service that was covered earlier (in Chapter 15). As well as managing information, the network and applications, the IS manager has to manage other services provided to end-users to help them work with this application. These 'soft' services include advice, trouble-shooting various problems and assisting users in developing their own applications.

End-user computing (EUC)

All uses of computers by business people who are not information systems professionals.

End-user development (EUD)

Systems development and programming undertaken by non-IS staff.

End-user application development is also an increasingly important activity with the move to PCs from a central mainframe and dumb terminal arrangement, giving more opportunities for tailoring of applications. This chapter will focus on the management of these 'soft' services and examine how they should be integrated into a company's overall IS strategy.

End-user service provision is often considered under the heading 'end-user computing'. This covers a wide range of activities. In this chapter, the distinction is made between the use of applications created by others for the end-user (**end-user computing**) and the *creation* of applications by the end-user (**end-user development**). The chapter considers how to provide services to support both classes of activity. Supporting both activities is certainly important – even the most conservative estimates suggest that end user computing accounts for more than 50 per cent of IS budgets (McGill et al., 1998), while others (e.g. Robson, 1997) argue that it accounts for up to 75–90 per cent.

END-USER IS SERVICES

End-user IS services

All services required to support end-users in running their computers and developing and using applications.

The main **end-user services** that the information systems manager has to provide are as follows:

1. *Provide a help-desk service.* This will solve problems that users are having in using their software. It will involve trouble-shooting to work out the source of the problem, which could be caused by:

   - the way the user is using the software;
   - a problem with the way the software has been installed;
   - a bug in the software;
   - an underlying hardware or networking problem.

2. This service must be delivered as rapidly as possible, but this is often difficult to achieve since a help desk will have to juggle many requests, some of which may be quite time-consuming to solve.

3. *Achieve standardisation of software.* Applications used across departments should be standardised to reduce the cost of purchase through volume discounts and to ensure easy transfer of information through the organisation (Chapter 4).

4. *Ensure network efficiency.* Users should not experience 'downtime' when the network is unavailable (Chapter 5).

5. *Provide training.* Users require training in the use of standard and company applications and where necessary in how to develop applications or manage information when end-user development is undertaken.

6. *Delivering services to end-users cost-effectively.* This is referred to as 'minimising the total cost of ownership', which includes both the initial cost of purchase of hardware and software and the ongoing cost of maintenance.

At a more strategic level, the IS manager will be responsible for:

■ setting the organisation's IS strategy covering issues such as integration with business strategy, investment levels and whether services are centralised or decentralised (Chapter 14);

■ establishing IS infrastructure (networks, hardware and software services);

■ implementation of corporate strategy through developing line-of-business systems;

■ ensuring that the company follows ethical or legal codes for health and safety and data protection (Chapter 17).

MANAGING NETWORK SERVICES

Network management services

Network management services are part of the goal of integrated information management. This will include the following end-user services that are normally managed centrally:

■ maintaining servers, including file (document) servers, database servers and web servers for intranets (Chapter 5 describes types of servers);

■ ensuring availability of end-user applications;

■ backup and restoration of information;

■ network maintenance.

In many companies, the magnitude of the cost of managing user services is not recognised. To start with, the number of PCs and the different applications they run must be audited. The number of PCs that have been purchased and applications being used may be a surprise. For example, on completing its first audit, Nottinghamshire County Council discovered 6500 PCs across 830 sites. A survey in the UK of 500 IT and finance directors by market research company Banner discovered that 47 per cent had no tools to help in auditing the software applications used or for trouble-shooting. This shows that network management and end-user services can be neglected in some organisations.

Cost-effective delivery of IS services

A growing realisation among many IS and financial managers is that the total cost of ownership of each PC in a company is significant when summed across all PCs in the organisation. Traditionally, companies have costed PCs on the initial purchase price or the cost of leasing, without explicitly costing the other services required to support a PC and its users. These other costs are all the end-user services referred to above, such as running a help desk to solve end-user problems and managing user information. The costs involved with running a help desk are indicated by the Help Desk Institute Practices and

Salary Survey 2010 (**www.thinkhdi.com**) which shows that the median cost of an incident reported via phone is $20. Handling incidents via e-mail and chat is lower at $15 each, but these are still significant costs when multiplied across a large organisation.

The significance of IT costs additional to purchase cost is highlighted by the Gartner Group with their **total cost of ownership (TCO)** measure (Gartner Group, 1996).

TCO also includes other costs such as:

- the loss of productive work time when users are unable to use their computer;
- the loss of productive work time when someone is trying to fix a colleague's problem (this type of unofficial support can be very costly);
- the cost of consumables such as paper and toner for printing.

Total cost of ownership (TCO)

TCO refers to the total cost for a company operating a computer. This includes not only the purchase or leasing cost, but also the cost of all the services needed to support the end-user.

Gartner (Troni and Silver, 2006) suggests that the 'most effective way for an enterprise to reduce the total cost of ownership of its PCs is through the implementation of management best practices across all phases of the PC life cycle'. The company argues that adopting up-to-date best practices can realise significant savings throughout the useful life of a PC or other piece of equipment.

Hardware manufacturers, such as Hewlett Packard, tend to support this view, suggesting that organisations can reduce TCO effectively when they make three complementary investments: (1) training people, (2) streamlining processes and (3) acquiring technologies that are easy to manage, service and support. This approach can be summarised like this:

- People – training end-users and IT staff to make optimal use of cost-controlling processes and technologies.
- Processes – automating some tasks and streamlining others, ranging from asset tracking to software updating.
- Technologies – deploying information technologies that minimise and in some cases eliminate the widest range of labour-intensive tasks.

The TCO can also be reduced by using simpler, less expensive hardware, which is the idea behind 'network computers' (sometimes called 'thin clients'), the use of virtualization and cloud computing.

Various companies, such as Gartner, have published formulae that can be used to calculate TCO for a given organisation. There are also a number of sophisticated software tools available that can be used to forecast costs related to areas such as training, support and maintenance. A combination of careful planning and product research before purchase can help to reduce TCO significantly. As an example, Bloor Research (**www.bloorresearch.com**) suggests that replacing networked PCs with thin clients can reduce TCO by up to 70 per cent each year. In a similar vein, a 2006 study by Gartner found that moving towards thin clients can result in annual savings like this:

- 79 per cent less downtime cost per user;
- 16 per cent capital cost savings;
- 34 per cent less in maintenance;
- 19 per cent less to operate;
- 48 per cent overall lower total cost.

Managing employee access to the Internet

A further network management issue is the level of staff access to the Internet to send and receive e-mail and access web sites. Governments incite employers to empower employees by widening access in order to increase competitiveness. However, is it practical to give all employees access or should it be limited? An example of the type of problem that can arise is highlighted by the case of Neath Port Talbot Council. In July 2007, three council workers lost their jobs because of excessive Internet use while at work. One employee was dismissed and two resigned after it was found that they were spending up to two hours a day on eBay. As with many similar cases, matters were not clearcut – the union representing the workers claimed that managers were partly to blame for allowing Internet access to employees in the first place.

Many recent cases have seen hundreds of employees sacked for access to and distribution of material interpreted as 'lewd' by their employers. In 2006, for instance, the DVLA dismissed 14 members of staff for distributing pornographic e-mail attachments to people outside the centre. In 2008, Virgin Atlantic dismissed 13 cabin crew after posts made on Facebook called passengers 'chavs' and suggested that the planes were full of cockroaches. In 2011, Argos dismissed an employee for alleged gross misconduct after he posted a complaint about his work following his return from annual leave. His comments read: 'Had a great day back at work after my hols who am I kidding!!' and 'Back to the shambles that is work.' The case can be considered significant as the post did not identify the store at which he worked (**www.clarkslegal.com**). More recently, The *Guardian* (30 December 2011) reported on a number of incidents involving inappropriate posts made on Facebook: 'At least two police officers have been sacked, seven have resigned and 150 faced disciplinary action after posting inappropriate photos or comments on Facebook in the past four years.'

| Activity 16.1 | Controlling employee access to the Internet |

In this scenario, you are a senior manager at a company that currently limits employee access to the Internet. You are considering relaxing company restrictions on the personal use of company e-mail and Internet resources but are concerned about issues such as staff time-wasting and the need to monitor how staff use these facilities.

1. Prepare a list of advantages and disadvantages of enabling widespread employee access.
2. Make another list of actions you will need to take when you proceed with granting wider access.

Mini case study

Cyberslacking: employees surf non-work-related web sites

Employees who have access to the internet at work spend almost a quarter of their time online visiting news, weather and other websites that have nothing to do with their jobs, according to a new study of web surfing habits. The three-part US study, the third section of which will be published on Wednesday, found that 61 per cent of people who use the internet at work admitted to visiting non-work-related sites. Workers spent an average of 12.8 hours online each week, with 24 per cent of that time devoted to non-work sites. The study was sponsored by Websense, an internet security group that specialises in web filtering software.

Half of more than 850 people surveyed said they would rather give up their morning coffee than their ability to access the internet for personal use, suggesting that companies that block employee access to personal sites such as web-based e-mail risk draining workforce morale. Still, many employees said they feared that some of their personal web surfing habits could put their jobs at risk. Sixteen per cent of men and 8 per cent of women admitted to having viewed online pornography at work, even though most respondents said they feared they could be fired if caught. A majority of both genders said they had accessed those sites by accident.

Spyware was also a source of concern. Six per cent of employees said they had visited sites known to contain spyware programmes, but only 42 per cent of those whose computers became infected with spyware called their IT help desk. The number of people who were aware of 'phishing' e-mail scams rose to 49 per cent in 2006, up from just 33 per cent last year. Map, news and weather sites were the most popular non-work sites visited in the survey. Last month, a US court ruled that a New York City government employee could not be fired from his job solely for surfing the internet at work. The judge hearing the case ruled that such activity was akin to taking personal telephone calls or reading the newspaper – activities commonly allowed at work, so long as they do not interfere with an employee's overall job performance.

Source: Allison, K. (2006) Cyberslacking: employees surf non-work-related web sites. *Financial Times*. 17 May.
© The Financial Times Limited 2006. All Rights Reserved.

Cyberslacking

Making use of the Internet for personal reasons while at work.

In recent years, unproductive use of the Internet and e-mail has become known as **cyberslacking** (or sometimes *cyber-skiving*). A survey of 2000 office workers carried out by Thomas Cook in 2006 found:

- one in 20 members of staff spend two hours per day chatting to friends via the Internet;
- one in 20 members of staff spend an hour a day looking for another job;
- some staff spend two-and-a-half hours a day using the Internet for personal business, such as researching holidays or buying goods;
- most time is wasted on e-mail and instant messaging.

The results of this survey – and many others – suggest that personal use of the Internet during work time is costly and unproductive. Figures from SpamTitan (**www.spamtitan .com**) claim that cyberslacking costs an average business £40,000 per year. According to CEO, Ronan Kavanagh, a company employing 52 people, who each spend 20 minutes a day on sites such as Facebook and Twitter, loses 5 per cent of its annual wage bill to non-productive time.

However, the problem of cyberslacking may not be quite as serious as suggested by some people. In 2007, the TUC advised British companies not to implement an outright ban on employees using the Internet during working hours. This was because it was suggested that some companies might benefit from employees making use of social networking sites, such as Facebook and MySpace, It was also feared that a ban might result in a backlash from employees. Instead of a ban, companies were advised to set up formal policies for acceptable use of the Internet while at work.

Over the past few years some commentators have suggested that cyberslacking may actually improve productivity. Writing in Psychology Today (25 March 2011), for instance, Tomas Chamorro-Premuzic reported: 'some studies suggest that cyber-slacking can also be beneficial even in terms of contributing to higher employee productivity levels (Oravec, 2002). Indeed, it has been reported that cyberslacking does not always lead to work inefficiency (Mahatanankoon et al., 2004) as previously thought'.

Complete Activity 16.1 for a discussion of actions a company can take to deal with these problems of employee access.

Monitoring of electronic communications

Employee communications monitoring

Companies monitor staff e-mails and web sites they access.

Electronic communications are regularly monitored by both government and private organisations. Employee communications monitoring or surveillance is used by organisations to reduce productivity losses through time-wasting. Time can be wasted when a member of staff spends work time when they are paid to work checking personal e-mail messages or accessing the Internet for personal interests.

Communications monitoring of employees may be warranted if it is felt they are sending or receiving e-mails or accessing web sites which contain material the organisation deems unacceptable. Typical examples of such content are pornography and racist material. However, some organisations even block access to news, sports or web-based e-mail sites because of the amount of time staff spend in accessing them. To define permissible content, many organisations now have acceptable use policies. For example, many universities, at log-in, or in computer labs and libraries have notices about 'acceptable use policy'. This will describe the types of material it is not acceptable to access and is also a means of explaining monitoring procedures.

Acceptable use policy

Statement of employee activities involving use of networked computers that are not considered acceptable by management.

Scanning software

Identifies e-mail or web page access that breaches company guidelines or acceptable use policies.

Filtering software

Software that blocks specified content or activities.

Scanning software and filtering software are the two most common forms of monitoring. Scanning software identifies the content of e-mails sent or received and web pages accessed. Tools such as WebSense or NetIQ Mail Marshal or WebMarshal will look for the occurrence of particular words or images – pornography is indicated by skin colour tones for example. Rules will also be set up, for example to ban e-mail attachments over a particular size or containing swearing.

Such software usually also has blocking or filtering capabilities. Filtering software such as WebSense (**www.websense.com**) can detect and block other activities such as:

- peer-to-peer (P2P) file sharing, for example of MP3 audio files;

- instant messaging using Yahoo! Messenger or Microsoft Instant Messenger;

- manage the use of streaming media (e.g. audio and video) and other high-bandwidth applications;

- access to specified sites, e.g. some companies block all news sites such as **www.bbc.co.uk** or **www.msn.co.uk** since analysis has shown that staff spend so much time using them. Access to personal e-mail programs such as GMail or Hotmail may also be blocked.

- spyware which seeks to send out confidential information collected from Internet users;

- adware programs which display adverts or pop-ups;

This topic is covered further later (in Chapter 17) since there are legal constraints on employee monitoring.

END-USER COMPUTING

What is end-user computing?

The term *end-user computing* (EUC) has different meanings according to the context in which it is used. The following statements could all refer to end-user computing:

- all tools by which non-data-processing staff handle their own problems without professional programmers;

- creative use of data processing by non-data-processing experts;

- complex computing by non-data-processing professionals to answer organisational information needs;

- non-technical end-users using user-friendly, fourth-generation languages (4GLs) and PCs to generate reports or build decision support systems;

- the use of computer hardware and software by people in organisations whose jobs are usually classified as users of information systems rather than developers of information systems.

The common theme is that staff whose main job function is not building information systems are doing some system development. The definitions vary in what is meant by 'system development'. For some staff this may mean just that: developing a complete information system. More frequently, it will mean users' building their own spreadsheet model or using a report generator. The three main types of end-user computing can be defined as:

1. end-user-developed computer-based information systems for personal, departmental or organisation-wide use, where the end-user is a non-IT professional;
2. end-user control of which hardware and package applications are purchased for use in their department;
3. end-user use of existing information systems.

Clearly, each type of end-user computing represents a different challenge for the information systems manager. In the following sections we will consider end-user computing and end-user development separately.

What are the drivers for end-user computing?

The primary business driver for EUC from the *organisational perspective* is greater control in end-user departments over choosing which applications are developed. Where there is a backlog of applications that need to be developed, this also leads to a reduced time for a system to be implemented if it is developed by end-users. EUC can also lead to the empowerment of staff in functional areas of an organisation to follow through creative ideas for using information systems to improve the efficiency of their work. Innovative ideas may be fostered in this way when they would otherwise be stifled if there were no outlet or mechanism for their being implemented.

The reasons given above for the development of end-user computing have been supported by *technology* becoming more readily available to support end-user development. Such technical support has become possible through increased availability of:

- personal computers or workstations on users' desktops with graphical user interfaces that (unlike simple terminals) are appropriate for end-user development;
- visual development tools such as the Visual Studio range of products or Real Basic, which make it easier to prototype application screen layouts and navigation between data views – these tools also enable screen elements such as tables to be readily integrated with information from a database;
- support for extending productivity applications. For example, Microsoft Word or Excel can be extended to an end-user application using the Visual Basic for Applications tools.

Finally, EUC has also been enabled by IS skills among the workforce increasing as the overall standard of IT familiarity grows through staff using IT throughout their education and into the workplace.

Which company staff are involved in end-user computing?

A common method of describing end-user computing is according to the skills of the end-user. This method was described in a paper from the early 1980s by Rockart and Flannery, summarised in Table 16.1. Some of the terms used have been superseded (updated equivalents are shown in brackets), but the basic definition remains valid. The classification does not

Table 16.1 Different types of end-user personnel. Updated descriptions based on original classes of Rockart and Flannery (1983)

Class	Term	Description
1	Non-programming end-users	These are users of software developed by others
2	Command-level end-users (power users)	These are users who use more sophisticated functions of a package, such as formulas and macros in a spreadsheet such as Excel
3	Programming-level end-users	Here users write their own functions using add-on application languages such as Visual Basic for Applications
4	Functional support personnel (business analysts and developers)	These are support staff who work in one area of the business to provide end-user development and support
5	End-user computing support personnel (help-desk staff)	These are the support staff who exist to trouble-shoot hardware and software problems that are encountered by users in Classes 1 to 3
6	Data-processing programmers (application developers)	This type of programming staff has traditionally worked on company operational or reporting systems

represent a continuum from Class 1 to 6, but rather two different groupings: first, business users of different skills levels in Classes 1 to 3, and then support personnel in Classes 4 to 6. Blili et al. (1996) present a more recent review of how end-user computing can be defined, grouping work into types of user, types of application and end-user behaviour.

A further important method of describing end-user computing is according to the way in which it is controlled. This will typically vary in line with the maturity of end-user computing in an organisation. Initially there will be no control and an organic growth of EUC. As EUC becomes more prevalent, problems caused by the lack of control will occur and a need will be identified by business and IS managers to take measures to control it. Control measures are referred to below.

THE IT HELP DESK

Help desk

A central facility in an organisation which provides end-user help-desk services such as phone support for trouble-shooting end-user software and hardware problems, training, guidance on end-user development and management of user information.

The **IT help desk** is a central facility in an organisation which provides end-user help-desk services such as phone support for trouble-shooting end-user software and hardware problems, training, guidance on end-user development and management of user information. In the past, an American term 'information center' based on a concept developed by IBM in the 1980s was used. Typical information centres developed at this time are described by White and Christy (1987). In the UK and Europe, the equivalent is usually referred to by the less grand terms 'IT support' or 'help desk'. However, the modern IT help desk offers much more than phone support to users – it provides all the services required for end-users to use and develop applications.

The range of services offered by a typical IT help desk are:

1. *Help-desk support for user problems.* Support can be offered via a number of routes, including telephone, e-mail, instant messaging and in person.

2. *Advice on software purchase.* This ensures that the software is suitable for its purpose and is compatible with hardware, other software and company purchasing schemes.

3. *Advice on hardware purchase.* This will usually be a centralised standard, again to take advantage of discounts and limiting support contracts.

4. *Advice on how end-user development should be approached.* The support person will suggest the best approaches for developing software, such as following the main parts of the lifecycle. These can be defined through more detailed training.

5. *Application development.* For larger systems, the help-desk staff may be involved in performing the systems analysis and design or more difficult aspects of the programming.

6. *Training.* In particular, on packages or development techniques.

7. *Data management.* Management and supply of data to end-users or explanations of formats used.

The main difficulty with managing a help desk is getting the balance right between providing a flexible service and exerting controls that are too restrictive. The information centre can be valuable in providing controls to prevent the type of problems that are described in the following section.

As part of the trend to outsourcing of IS described earlier (in Chapter 14), many help desks are now outsourced to other companies. For example, support for cloud computing within Royal Mail is provided by Capgemini. Microsoft outsources its help desk for its applications and operating systems to companies such as HP.

Help-desk technologies

In this section we briefly review the way in which information systems are used to support the use of other information systems within a company!

1. *Asset management software.* Help-desk staff need to know the technical details of the systems being used in the company and the software loaded on them. This is achieved by asset management software such as Microsoft Systems Management server. This can also distribute new software automatically.

2. *Computer telephony integration (CTI).* CTI gives automatic phone number identification and the system will then load up the details of the computer, its current user and configuration. This allows first-tier calls to be answered much faster.

3. *Case-based reasoning.* These systems use artificial intelligence techniques (Chapter 6) to guide the user or help-desk staff through the process of solving the problem.

4. *Web-based intranet access.* Users can access frequently asked questions, send an e-mail or type in keywords describing their problems. Problems solved this way will save help-desk staff the time spent dealing with straightforward queries.

5. *Workflow.* Workflow systems can be used to prioritise user queries and assign them to the staff best placed to deal with them. An example of a workflow queue used in a help desk is shown in Figure 16.1.

Further details on the type of facilities available in help-desk software are provided by Utopia, one of the most frequently used products worldwide (see **www.utosoft.com**).

Some IT help desk facts

- Every help desk analyst handles 471 user requests every month, and many help desks still process these manually.

- In the UK and the USA, the average PC user raises a help desk ticket 1.2 times every month, amounting to approximately 150 million requests, calls and emails made to help desks every month.

- End-user contacts with the help desk service desk cost every organisation between $18 and $75, depending on the nature of the call and the seniority of the analyst involved.

Source: Vanson Bourne, Help Desk Efficiency Report 2010 (**www.vansonbourne.com**)

Figure 16.1 Workflow system from TIBCO Software being used to prioritise support calls

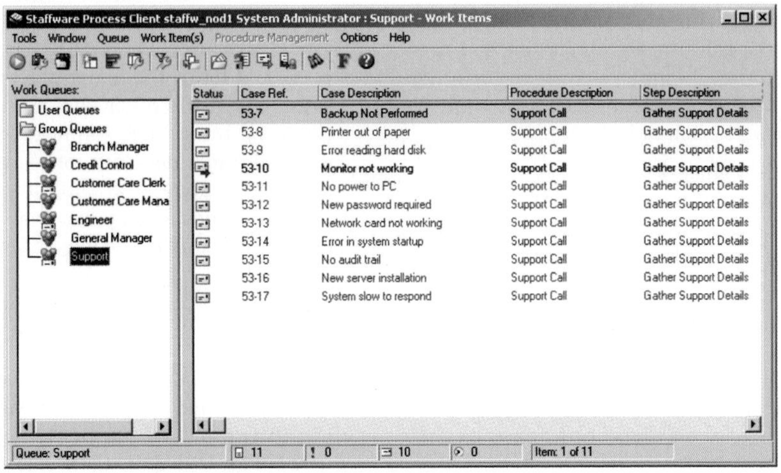

Source: TIBCO Software screenshot.

CASE STUDY 16.1

The 21st-century help desk

There is something about the IT help-desk that seems to bring out the worst in people. For employees of the average enterprise, it is often among the least appreciated, most maligned departments they come into contact with.

On both sides of the fence – among helpdesk agents and their 'customers' – arrogance, impatience, even outright hostility have soured what ought to be a straightforward relationship where every-one is singing from the same hymn sheet. Now the IT helpdesk, the agents who work on it and the people who use it are having to move with the times.

In the 21st century, every department has to make a contribution to the development of the business. The IT department may not directly generate revenues from external customers, but the beginning of the end has arrived for the 'log, follow-up and close' culture that has bedevilled helpdesks in the past.

The new mantras are 'business value' and 'customer satisfaction'. The modern helpdesk is viewed as a core business function and not just simply the face – or the voice – of the IT department. It is a key element of an overall service management strategy that is meant to deliver a better-functioning IT infrastructure from which the enterprise can benefit.

There is a lot of money at stake. IT service management can typically account for 7–10 per cent of an enterprise's IT budget, says Michele Hudnall, senior research analyst at Meta Group. 'Most of the activity at the moment is centred around operating efficiency', she says. 'Over the past three years technology has come along to automate mature processes.' Rather than simply logging problems, she says, the emphasis has switched to proactive management of problems, and even managing them away.

The most important tool for achieving this is knowledge management, which is getting good enough to allow companies to find and collect the information they need, says Esteban Kolsky, research director at Gartner, another IT research company. 'There is a need to capture as much knowledge as possible from people solving the issues, so that agents and users can access it [if the problem occurs again]', he says.

Some 40 per cent of enterprises, Mr Kolsky estimates, have been using some form of advanced, automated knowledge management in their external, customer-facing service desks – which in most companies have tended to be a higher priority for investment. 'People have been getting good success externally, so now they are moving it internally', he says, estimating adoption rates at 25 per cent for internal service desks.

Efficient, intelligent use of updated data on IT problems and issues lies at the heart of the push towards reducing costs and increasing customer satisfaction from IT helpdesks over the past two years. The success of emerging self-help solutions on corporate intranets will largely depend on giving employees easy access to the information they need for, say, resetting a password, along with a quick way to log and track faults or requests.

It is much the same with one of the great holy grails of IT service departments recently – improving the first-time or first-call fix rate. According to Gartner it costs $1.50–$2 a time if employees can be encouraged to fix their own problems, and as much as 10 times that if they have to call the helpdesk.

It is when the helpdesk cannot fix the problem in the first instance, however, that the cost can rise exponentially – to as much as $100 if a highly-paid engineer or developer has to be called in, distracting them from their other work.

But with knowledge-based systems at their disposal, and fewer footling queries about expired passwords or printers that won't print, helpdesk staff should be better placed to fix the more complex problems themselves.

That is the theory, at least. On self-help, companies such as British Airways are enthusiastic, but many people still prefer to talk to someone if they have an IT problem, lacking the confidence to do anything about it themselves.

There is also the question of finding the right balance between relieving the pressure of calls on the helpdesk and increasing the workload and stress of employees.

On first-call fix rates, there seems to be room for improvement, too. 'There is plenty of technology available to the helpdesk to fix problems on the first call', says Paul Clayton, a senior IT consultant at PA Consulting, 'but many of our clients are struggling with making this work'. PA suggests that some of the technology has become too complex for helpdesks to exploit properly.

There are similar pitfalls for the unwary in another of the big trends of the past two years – the consolidated helpdesk. More and more functions are becoming part of these larger, automated helpdesks, says Mr Kolsky, and increasing numbers of enterprises plan to introduce them. Compared with smaller, undermanned helpdesks, they can offer better support for longer hours – never closing, if necessary. Nor do they need to exist physically – they can be virtual helpdesks, manned by agents using mobile devices or even sitting at home.

Ms Hudnall says organisations which have introduced consolidated service desks correctly – with investment and resources, with a common repository of data and a centralised view of their support systems – have reaped benefits and exploited the technology to eliminate some of their IT problems. 'But if you just do it for cost-control reasons, creating a centralised place to call into, you are simply managing larger volumes of calls with less cost.'

Howard Kendall, founder director of the Help Desk Institute, says implementation of the consolidated, knowledge management-based helpdesk has been patchy. 'A lot of the major players have gone for it', he says, 'but at the other end, there are still people with the very basic "log, follow-up and close" mentality, and there is a hell of a lot of room for improvement. [Internal] helpdesks are still low profile, they don't get the budget despite the fact that there will be a return for the company in the longer term.'

Meanwhile, vendors of IT service desk tools are fighting for a share of a market estimated by Meta at $3bn a year worldwide.

The market is growing at about 5 per cent a year, says Meta, and is a fairly typical IT subsector with big, integrated vendors – Hewlett-Packard, Computer Associates, and BMC Software, which owns Remedy – and specialised companies which concentrate on the helpdesk, service management and IT asset management market. These include Peregrine Systems, FrontRange Solutions, Hornbill Systems, RightNow Technologies, Touchpaper and Axios Systems. These systems are used by enterprises and by outsourcers.

Ms Hudnall says companies need to think about integration issues upfront to get the most from their investments, but will probably end up with a mixture of broad-based and niche solutions.

The long-term future, experts suggest, will see more self-help solutions, more 'self-healing' systems and pro-active, preventative technologies. 'The ultimate will be when you receive a message to say "Your PC's about to fail", says Lindsay Miller, group director of management information systems at LogicaCMG. 'That is a Utopia, and on the way to that environment, you have to take advantage of what is available.'

So will helpdesks wither away as all these trends bear fruit? 'There will be fewer people, answering more intelligent questions, but there will always be people', says Mr Miller.

Mr Kendall at the Help Desk Institute agrees: 'They won't disappear entirely for the more complex questions or transactions', he says. 'Reports on the self-help software will have to go somewhere, and the responsibility of helpdesks will move up a level to track all this. But that's a good 20 years away.'

What the experts say

John Sansbury, senior consultant of Compass Management Consulting

'Although it is an IT function, the service desk is largely a product of its people and the support they receive from the tools and their colleagues and managers.

However, issues such as impatience and arrogance are people attributes and you do not fix these with a toolset. Achieving high performance is about understanding customers' requirements and responding to them appropriately. Implicitly, that is not the function of the toolset.'

Lionel Lamy, research manager at IDC

'When CIOs are considering a helpdesk or services management vendor, they should be looking at the likely impact on the business rather than wearing a technical hat. Both niche players and providers of end-to-end solutions can do the job, but I would choose vendors that can do more than the simple task – you will then be a bigger fish to them. When outsourcing,

look at how confident the provider is that service levels can be met – if it goes wrong, the CIO still gets the blame.'

Richard Harrison, global IT consulting group practice, PA Consulting Group

'Many companies have spent millions on sophisticated software for their helpdesks but I genuinely believe people don't get true value out of the more sophisticated tools. If you have all the basics, and you do things in a consistent way to deliver what the business expects, it is remarkable how effective a helpdesk can be. I would advocate a back-to-basics approach – often it is only when taking the complexity out that companies obtain real value.'

Source: Baxter, A. (2004) It's not just an IT issue any more. *Financial Times.* 21 July.
© The Financial Times Limited 2004. All Rights Reserved.

QUESTIONS

You are a placement student who has joined the help-desk team as assistant manager in an organisation with 5,000 PCs and their users who require support. To familiarise you with the business requirements of the help-desk team, your manager has asked you to prepare a report based on the article which summarises:

1. How the success of the IT Help desk can be measured.

2. Emerging trends in technology and practice in managing the IT help desk more effectively.

Use the article to identify alternatives under both of the headings above.

END-USER DEVELOPMENT

End-user development of applications represents a major trend in the use of information technology in organisations. McGill et al. (2003) explain that:

> User-developed applications (UDAs) are computer-based applications for which non-information systems professionals assume primary development responsibility. They support decision-making and organizational processes in the majority of organizations.

An increasing number of users are writing their own software or spreadsheet models to help in decision making. This was not possible before there was a PC on every desktop. The widespread use of office software like Microsoft Excel, Microsoft Word and Microsoft Access has accelerated this trend since they contain macro languages and a complete language and applications development environment through Visual Basic for Applications (VBA). It is worth noting that many other major office applications also contain fully featured programming tools. Developing and using spreadsheet models and reporting systems is the predominant example of end-user development today. There is also use of end-user tailoring of specialist software. For example, business intelligence tools such as Business Objects (**www.businessobjects.com**) and Cognos (**www.cognos.com**) have special query languages based on SQL for users to define ad hoc database queries and create standard reports.

Previously, before the advent of such software and hardware, the user was totally reliant on the IS department or third-party suppliers to write applications. Because the IS department focused on strategic applications, the users' requests for small-scale applications would often be ignored.

Applications and tools for end-user development

There is a wide range of possible applications for end-user-developed software listed below. Typically it is the smaller-scale, departmental applications that are most appropriate for end-user development. The development tools reflect these. These tools are usually high-level reporting and programming tools. It is rare for the end-user to program using a lower-level language such as C++ or Java, which would require extensive training. Possible types of applications include:

- reports from a corporate database using standard enquiries defined by the IS/IT function;

- simple ad hoc queries to databases defined by the user. For someone in an airline, for example, these might include access to a frequent flyer database, customer reservation system or crew rostering system to monitor performance of each;

- what-if? analysis using tools such as spreadsheet models or more specialised tools such as risk or financial management packages or business intelligence software, used for monitoring sales and marketing performance of information stored in a data warehouse;

- writing company information for a company intranet;

- development of applications such as a job costing tool or production scheduling system, using easy-to-use, high-level tools such as application generators, PC database management systems such as Microsoft Access or Filemaker, or visual programming environments such as Microsoft Visual Studio or Embarcadero Delphi.

An example of a visual programming environment is shown in Figure 16.2. The user has easy-to-use tools to draw graphs and tables and to populate these with information from a database. Program code (shown in the window) may be required to achieve this.

Figure 16.2 Visual Studio development environment showing onscreen forms and development code

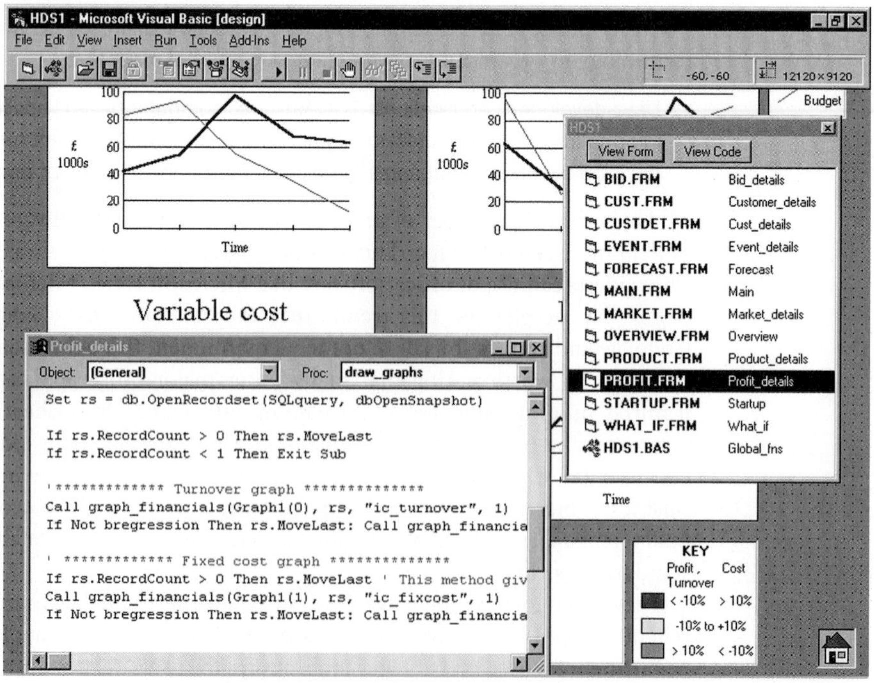

Source: Screenshot frame reprinted by permission from Microsoft Corporation.

Reasons for the growth of end-user development

The reason for the increase in end-user-developed applications is a combination of two main factors. The first is that it only became practical for end-users to develop software with the introduction of the PC and graphical systems development tools. With earlier mainframe and minicomputer systems, it was not practical for people who were not in the IS department to develop software; neither the tools nor the access were available. In addition, end-users seldom had the necessary knowledge and skills needed to build their own applications. As computer literacy has increased, more people have become capable of customizing the software packages they use or creating new programs.

The second reason is that users were not receiving the required response from the IS department in terms of building systems for them. This is often known as the applications backlog. Galliers and Leidner (2003) have suggested that there is a *visible backlog* made up of genuine requests for maintenance and the development of new systems as well as an *invisible backlog* that is made up of genuine requests that are no longer being pursued by disillusioned users. The invisible backlog is several times larger than the visible one. This is important when it is considered that various estimates suggest the visible backlog alone is between two to five years.

The IS department has rightly to focus on corporate, mission-critical applications such as production, financial and customer services applications. It follows that they will not have the resources available to develop smaller-scale systems required in departments. As an example of this, one UK travel industry organisation has a backlog of nearly 100 systems required by users to add to over 120 existing systems. Any new system requested will almost certainly not be authorised by the IS department. For example, if the marketing department requires a new system to analyse sales performance and it requests this from the central IS department, it will almost certainly be of a lower priority than items that were requested a year ago. As a result, the *only* option may be for it to be developed in the marketing department or to ask an outside consultant to develop it. Viewed in this way, end-user development could be considered as a failure of the IS department and IS strategy.

Less significant reasons for the growth of end-user development are:

- the desire by users to query and analyse data and generate reports from information stored on databases available across the corporate network;

- a trend to decentralisation of computing to user departments for systems to support departmental activities;

- reduced expense of application development when conducted by end-users (from departmental rather than information systems budget);

- better fit between end-user-developed software and their requirements (since no requirements translation is needed between the users and third-party developers). End-users are also less likely to 'over-engineer' a solution to a basic problem than an IS professional who will want to treat every problem with rigour.

Applications backlog

The demand for new applications by users exceeds the capacity of the IS department or IS outsourcing company to develop them.

Benefits of end-user development

There are many benefits claimed for end-user development. Some are those experienced by the end-users, such as more varied work and being able to use applications sooner. Additionally, IS personnel can concentrate on key, mission-critical applications. Improvements in both these areas also accrue benefits to the organisation as a whole. The full range of benefits includes:

- reduction in the number of professional analysts and programmers and IS staff employed by a company (and reduced cost of employing outside consultants);

- reduction in communications overheads of users explaining requirements to IS professionals and also reduced risk of mistranslation of requirements;

- help in reducing the applications development backlog associated with centralising applications development in an IS department;

- IS staff can focus on tasks requiring their expertise, such as the maintenance of corporate systems;

- it allows applications in departments to be developed more quickly, so the business can benefit from new facilities more quickly and gain competitive advantage;

- it can encourage innovation and creativity in the use of IS/IT, since bureaucratic barriers can be removed.

McGill et al. (2003) emphasise the most important benefits when they say:

> Perhaps the most important benefit claimed for user development of applications is improvement in employee productivity and performance, resulting from a closer match between applications and user needs since the end user is both the developer and the person who best understands the information requirements.

A useful way to assess the benefits of end-user-developed applications suggested by McGill et al. (2003) is the model of DeLone and McLean (1992). These authors reviewed the IS literature concerning factors for development of information systems and created a model that showed that success was dependent on the quality characteristics of the IS itself (system quality); the quality of the output of the IS (information quality); consumption of the output of the IS (use); the IS user's response to the IS (user satisfaction); the effect of the IS on the behaviour of the user (individual impact); and the effect of the IS on organisational performance (organisational impact). This straightforward model, which can usefully be applied to all types of information systems is shown in Figure 16.3.

McGill et al. (2003) used this model to assess end-user perception of these different quality factors (within spreadsheets created for a business simulation) and found that there was often a variance between perception and reality. They found that there was no relationship between user developers' perceptions of system quality and independent experts' evaluations, and user ratings of individual impact were not associated with organisational impact measured as company performance.

Figure 16.3 A model of IS success that can be applied to end-user-developed applications

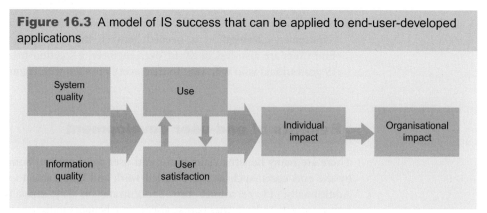

Source: Reprinted by permission, DeLone, W. and McLean, E. 'Information success: The quest for the dependent variable', *Information Systems Research*, 3, 1, 1992. Copyright 1992, the Institute for Operations Research and the Management Sciences (INFORMS), 7240 Parkway Drive, Suite 310, Hanover, MD 21076 USA.

This study suggests some of the potential problems of end-user development arising out of the inexperience of end-user developers. These include lack of standardisation, which leads to different software tools being selected by different users, giving rise to incompatible software and data sources. Users may also take short cuts during development, such as missing out application design or testing, which will give rise to poor-quality software with bugs in it.

McGill et al. (2003) recognise the problems associated with end-user development when they say:

> However, the realization of these benefits may be put at risk because of problems with information produced by UDAs that may be incorrect in design, inadequately tested, and poorly maintained.

These problems, and how to counter them, are described in more detail below.

The development of EUD in an organisation

The stage model of Huff et al. (1988) indicates how the use of end-user computing might develop in a typical organisation. This is loosely based on Nolan's stage model of computing use in organisations (Chapter 13). The stages of development are:

1. *Isolation*. A few scattered pioneers of EUD develop small-scale business tools within their area. Initially, little support from central IS.

2. *Standalone*. Larger-scale applications are developed that may be of importance to a department. Examples might include a staff rostering system or an application for anticipating demand for raw materials. At this stage, an information centre may be developed to support an increase in demand for user computing services.

3. *Manual integration*. Here, different end-user applications need to exchange data. This happens through manual intervention, with files being transferred by floppy disk or across the network or even with rekeying of information. Information centre development has continued to support the needs of these larger-scale applications by providing training and skills and specifying standards for hardware, software and the development process.

4. *Automated integration*. Users start to link into corporate applications to gain seamless access to information. For example, end-users may download information from a central data warehouse, which is then used to profile customers for a new product launch or marketing campaign.

5. *Distributed integration*. At this stage of development, there is a good level of integration between different end-user applications and corporate systems. Good standards of metadata (or data describing data in a data dictionary) are required to help achieve this.

Since this model was proposed, experience indicates that although a natural progression can be seen in many organisations, the development beyond Stage 3 may not be practical or desirable. Once end-user-developed applications become important or 'mission-critical' to a department or an organisation, the question that must be asked is: 'Are end-users the right people to maintain an application of this importance?' The answer will usually be 'no', since end-users will not have the skills to develop such an application, and if they are trained to levels necessary to do this, they will no longer be end-users fulfilling their original function, but specialist application developers!

Problems of end-user development

The problems of end-user development are usually the result of a lack of sufficient training in software development or the inability of management to ensure that this training occurs. This can manifest itself in different ways. Perhaps the best way to consider these problems is to review where they may occur over the course of end-user development using the software lifecycle model as a framework (Table 16.2).

The problems referred to in Table 16.2 could have serious consequences if they occurred during the development of a large, new information system. However, for small-scale end-user-developed software that will only be used by a limited number of staff and is not vital to the business, such errors are less important.

Note that Table 16.2 is based on assuming that end-user development follows a similar pattern to a large-scale systems development. However, some authors, such as Lally (1995), note that additional stages of promotion or dissemination of information about the product are required. The product may then need to evolve for it to be adopted more widely in a company.

Among the general risks or misuse of information associated with end-user-developed information systems are:

- using information that is out of date;
- information requires export from other information systems before it can be analysed by the end-user application;
- corruption of centrally held data by uploading erroneous data;
- development of insecure systems without password control that are vulnerable to accidental and deliberate damage.

Table 16.2 Review of problems associated with EUD and where they occur in the systems development lifecycle (SDLC)

Stage of SDLC	Typical problem
Initiation	Absent or limited feasibility study. If omitted, the user may be developing a system that is not required or solving a problem that has been solved before. Insufficient review of cost–benefit and acquisition alternatives. Other end-user software with the same function may be available elsewhere in the organisation. Off-the-shelf software may also be available.
Analysis	Limited analysis. Since the end-user may know their own requirements, they may not consult others in the company who may have a different perspective. This may alienate potential users and mean that the software is unsuitable for its application.
Design	Omitted completely! This stage is often omitted and programming will occur straightaway. This may occur since users may not have the design skills or understand the importance of design. This will adversely affect the usability, speed and security of the software.
Build	Programming will occur as normal; the problem is that ancillary activities may be omitted. Documenting the work and testing are areas that should not be omitted.
Implementation	Implementation becomes more difficult for large systems. For a standalone piece of end-user-developed software, there should not be too many problems.
Maintenance	Problems at this stage are minor compared to those that may have happened before. Users may not keep an adequate list of problems that need to be fixed. There is also a tendency to release updates to the software without good version control.

A final problem to be mentioned is the hazard of personal or private systems that are unreadable, undocumented and not transferable to any other users. This is a particular problem if the developer of the software leaves. This can be a common scenario with end-user-developed software. The only solution to this problem is often to rewrite the software, since the source code and documentation may be impossible to follow or non-existent.

MANAGING EUC AS PART OF IS STRATEGY

It could be argued that the IS manager has two basic choices when considering the relationship between IS strategy and end-user computing. These could be paraphrased as 'ignore it or embrace it'. The 'ignore it' option may be appealing to the IS manager who sees EUC as a threat that is eroding their control. In reality, they will not ignore it completely, rather they will not take any steps to encourage it. Those IS managers who wish to embrace it will probably have realised that EUC is inevitable, given the reasons mentioned earlier in the chapter such as insufficient availability of staff to develop applications, increasing skills among staff and availability of tools to produce the applications. EUC should be encouraged to reduce the applications backlog and will help in ensuring that the requirements of end-users are well understood and are met by the software developed.

We have seen that quite serious problems can develop with EUC due to inexperience in systems development and management among the end-users and their managers. Given this, it is vital that there be a strategy to support *and* control EUC, whether the IS manager is ignoring it or embracing it. Many of these risks and problems arise through a lack of experience of system development, coupled with a lack of training for end-users. End-user development should be recognised as part of the IS strategy and guidelines should be developed that cover the techniques below. Techniques that could be used to improve control of end-user development include:

1. *Training.* Provision of relevant training courses both in how to program and in how to approach systems development in a structured way (the second of these is often omitted). This happened at the Open University, where many of the end-users wanted to omit the analysis course.

2. *Suitability review.* Authorisation of major end-user new developments by business and IS managers to check that they are necessary (this should not be necessary for smaller-scale developments since otherwise creativity may be stifled).

3. *Standards for development.* Such standards will recommend that documentation and structured testing of all user-developed software occurs. Detailed standards might include clear data definitions, validation rules, backup and recovery routines and security measures.

4. *Guidance from end-user support personnel.* Help-desk staff can provide training in techniques used to develop software.

5. *Software and data audits.* Regular audits should occur of software produced by end-users for data and application quality. The European Spreadsheet Risks Interest Group (see www.eusprig.org) provides links to a number of stories showing what can happen when spreadsheet users make mistakes as they enter data, formulas or program code. In many of the cases described millions of dollars have been lost as a result of a single error!

6. *Ensuring corporate data security.* Ensure that users are not permitted to enter data directly into central databases except via applications especially written for the purpose by the IS department which have the necessary validation rules to ensure data quality. For analysis of corporate data, data should regularly be downloaded from the central database to the PC for analysis, where they can be analysed without causing performance problems to the corporate system.

It will be apparent from the list of potential measures that a careful balance has to be struck between being over-restrictive, which may cause a stifling of innovation, or too open, which will result in the type of problems referred to above.

CASE STUDY 16.2

Time to call the help desk?

Among medical personnel working in war zones, disaster scenes and casualty departments, the process of sorting and prioritising patients for treatment is commonly known as 'triage'. The approach was developed in response to situations where the needs of the injured far outstrip the medical skills available – a situation that will sound all-too familiar to those who work on the frontline of corporate computing, otherwise known as the IT helpdesk. Helpdesk analysts may not be dealing with life-or-death situations, but they do face overwhelming demand for a limited pool of skills. Increasingly, they are using tactics that look very much like triage when responding to end-users scuppered by technology snags. They perform preliminary assessments; provide basic 'first aid'; and only refer the most critical cases to more qualified colleagues. Furthermore, they do all this against a stressful backdrop of rising call volumes, sky-high end-user expectations and increasingly complex interdependencies between different pieces of IT kit, says Howard Kendall, founding director of the Help Desk Institute (HDI), an international membership organisation for the IT service and support industry.

A former IT support manager at Citibank and the Prudential, Mr Kendall reckons the job of helpdesk analyst has never been tougher, for two reasons. 'First, end-users are more dependent on technology than ever before in order to get on with their work. When IT systems fail, productivity suffers immediately, so the pressure is on for the helpdesk to get it fixed quickly', he says. 'Second, employees are using a much broader range of more complex technologies – multiple applications, remote working and mobile devices are now the norm, and the helpdesk is expected to be able to deal with it all.'

But despite those pressures, as the 'public face' of the IT department, helpdesk agents are still expected to deliver a high level of customer service – and that means resolving issues 'quickly, efficiently and sympathetically', says Elizabeth Hackenson, chief information officer of telecommunications giant Alcatel-Lucent. 'The helpdesk is here to support our customers, who are internal IT users, so that they in turn can support the company's customers out in the wider marketplace', explains Ms Hackenson, who runs a team of more than 400 helpdesk agents worldwide, supporting 80,000 staff.

'When end-users call the helpdesk, they're not productive, and that's a big issue for the company as a whole. Our goal is to solve the majority of problems at the first level of the helpdesk, so that issues are resolved within minutes of a call being made and callers are not bounced from agent to agent along the way.' There are also sound cost reasons behind empowering frontline, or first-level, helpdesk staff to tackle as many problems as possible, says Gianluca Tramacere, a research director at Gartner. The bulk of IT service and support cost is related to personnel, he points out: 'Therefore, it makes sense that less-qualified, lower paid employees – typically first-level support agents – handle the majority of calls, so that higher paid IT personnel handle only those issues that require complex technical troubleshooting.' Or, as Arlen Beylerian, director of product management for service management solutions at Computer Associates, puts it: 'You don't want your top network analyst or database administrator attending to printer problems and resetting passwords'. As a general rule, says Mr Tramacere, helpdesk best practice states that between 54 and 75 per cent of all IT service requests should be managed by the first-level helpdesk analyst at the first point of contact – this is known as the first-call resolution rate. There is, he says, a clear correlation between first-call resolution and customer satisfaction.

This kind of thinking has transformed IT helpdesk software in recent years. Early systems merely enabled first-level helpdesk analysts to log the basic details of a call to the helpdesk: the date and time it was received, the unique identifier number assigned to the problem, the IT support staff member assigned to deal with it, the time it was resolved. Incidents were typically dealt with on a first come, first served basis. Now, most helpdesk software enables agents to prioritise calls according to complex business rules, says Peter Armstrong, corporate strategist at BMC Software. 'A number of factors will dictate how quickly an issue needs to be addressed: the time of day, the number of people affected, the seniority of those affected, which business processes are impacted, how much the issue is costing the company', he says.

The software uses those rules in order to guide the helpdesk analyst through the process of prioritising calls by automatically prompting them to ask pertinent questions of the caller and gather relevant information about the problem at hand. In addition, most helpdesk software now comes with integrated knowledge management tools that enable companies to build an electronic reference library of common IT problems and their solutions. 'The collective knowledge that resides among the helpdesk team can be really powerful in terms of improving service quality – but only if it can be captured and shared by the whole team', explains Mr Armstrong. When helpdesk agents have access to an effective knowledge base, he explains, they are not 'starting from scratch' on every call. They can search the knowledge base for information on similar incidents, their underlying causes and how they've been fixed in the past. In this way, knowledge can be transferred from more experienced IT staff to frontline help-desk agents, enabling them to take the most appropriate action and reducing training time for new hires, explains Tony Adams, global product manager for workplace services at EDS, the IT services giant. 'Knowledge management tools also help counteract the problem of staff leaving the company and taking their knowledge with them.' In addition, they can be used as the basis for a self-help portal that end-users can visit in order to find solutions to simple problems such as password resets that they can apply themselves', he adds. According to Mr Beylerian of CA, a good knowledge base will also provide frontline staff with details of second and third-level colleagues with the skills to fix specific problems, enabling them to route jobs to the right person.

Collaboration tools are also enabling helpdesk analysts to meet exacting customer service levels, according to Simon Presswell, EMEA managing director of Citrix Online, which provides helpdesk software as a hosted service. The latest version of the company's GoToAssist product enables agents to work with their helpdesk colleagues on solving problems, he explains. 'While speaking with a customer, a support representative can, via the keyboard, silently invite more experienced experts into the session to view the customer's screen and evaluate the problem. Experts can participate invisibly, so callers can experience uninterrupted, end-to-end contact with just one represent-ative', he says. But achieving better levels of customer satisfaction with helpdesk operations is not just a question of technology – it requires a whole change in approach and attitude, he says. 'In my experience, many companies tend to view the frontline helpdesk agent in rather crude productivity terms. Traditional helpdesk metrics, for example, concentrate on volume of calls handled and call handling times – customer satisfaction doesn't even enter into it.' That has to change if corporate IT is to remain fighting fit.

QUESTIONS

1. Why is it essential that calls to the help desk be dealt with as quickly and efficiently as possible?

2. Why is it important to make sure that help desk staff are able to deal with the widest possible range of problems?

3. What are the benefits of establishing a comprehensive knowledge base?

SUMMARY

1. End-user computing (EUC) describes the use of information systems by non-IT staff.

2. Providing end-user services is an important function of the IS department, since many company staff rely on analysing data for decision making.

3. End-user development (EUD) is one type of EUC that is significant in many organisations, since it provides a low-cost method of reducing the applications backlog.

4. The key benefits of end-user development are:
   - shorter wait for system before it can be used in the organisation;
   - users understand their requirements better than IS specialists;
   - lower cost than paying a third party.

5. The principal problem with end-user development is that users may omit some essential activities in software development, such as assessing the best solution, documenting their work, design or thorough testing.

6. An information centre or help desk is provided by many medium and large organisations to provide guidance, support and trouble-shooting for end-users.

7. Given the potential problems of end-user-developed applications, they are most appropriate for small-scale applications within departments.

8. The cost of providing end-user services can be high, which is partly responsible for the high total cost of ownership (TCO) of PCs in many organisations and a trend to using thin clients to reduce this.

9. EUC and EUD have great potential, but enthusiasm can be misdirected due to inexperience. EUC must be an element of overall IS strategy to ensure that it is effectively controlled and supported.

EXERCISES

Self-assessment exercises

1. What are the principal end-user services that must be provided by the information systems manager?

2. What is the significance of the total cost of ownership?

3. What is the role of the network computer and other thin clients in reducing the total cost of ownership?

4. What is the difference between end-user computing and end-user development?

5. What are the different types of end-user development?

6. What are the main reasons for the growth in end-user development?

7. Which activities in the software development lifecycle are often omitted by end-users?

8. What facilities can be provided to support end-user development?

Discussion questions

1. It has been argued that end-user computing has been driven by a failure of central information systems departments to develop applications quickly enough (the applications backlog). Is this statement true or is there an alternative explanation?

2. Examine the reasons for the growth of end-user computing in companies of all sizes. You should consider the balance between practical necessity and strategic planning.

3. What do you see as the future for end-user computing? Will the growth continue, or will there be a backlash against the problems experienced by some companies using this approach?

Essay questions

1. End-user applications development poses a new set of management problems in companies that adopt this approach. Identify the nature of these problems and suggest measures to overcome them.

2. Intranets are now widely used by many companies. Examine the suitability of end-users for the control, development and maintenance of intranets.

3. End-user computing can only be successful if users have a knowledge of the software lifecycle and the activities required to produce good-quality information systems. Which activities do you consider essential to achieving this, and which are likely to be omitted?

4. Imagine that you are the IS manager of a medium-to-large company with 500 staff. Explain the strategy you would develop to encourage end-user computing, while seeking to control any problems that may arise.

Examination questions

1. What are the main benefits provided by end-user computing?

2. Why are end-user-developed applications unsuitable for cross-enterprise applications?

3. What factors contribute to the total cost of ownership? Why is it significantly higher than the purchase cost?

4. How does the network computer differ from the personal computer? Why might this appeal to:

    (a) the IS manager;
    (b) the finance manager;
    (c) the end-user.

5. Name and explain three services that can be provided by an information centre.

6. What is the applications backlog and how is end-user development significant in relation to this?

7. Give three reasons why it is important for end-user computing to be part of a company's overall IS strategy. Briefly justify each.

References

Blili, S., Raymond, L. and Rivard, S. (1996) 'Definition and measurement of end user computing sophistication', *Journal of End User Computing*, 8, 2, 13–23

DeLone, W. and McLean, E. (1992) 'Information systems success: the quest for the dependent variable', *Information Systems Research*, 3, 1, 60–95

Galliers, R. and Leidner, D. (2009) *Strategic Information Management: Challenges and Strategies in Managing Information Systems*, 4th edition, Butterworth-Heinemann, Oxford

Gartner Group (1996) *Total Cost of Ownership: Reducing PC/LAN Costs in the Enterprise*, 9 February, The Gartner Group, Boston

HDI, U.S. (2010) *2010 HDI Practices and Salary Survey*. Summary of main findings within Press Release. Available online from: www.thinkhdi.com

Huff, S., Munro, M. and Martin, B. (1988) 'Growth stages of end-user computing', *Communications of the ACM*, 31, 5, 542–50

Lally, L. (1995) 'Supporting appropriate user-developed applications: guidelines for managers', *Journal of End User Computing*, 7, 3, 3–11

McGill, T., Hobbs, V. and Klobas, J. (2003) 'User-developed applications and information systems success: a test of DeLone and McLean's model', *Information Resources Management Journal*, 16, 1, 24–45

McGill, T., Hobbs, V., Chan, R. and Khoo, D. (1998) 'User satisfaction as a measure of success in end user application development: an empirical investigation', in M. Khosrowpour (ed.), *Effective Utilization and Management of Emerging Information Technologies*, Idea Group Inc., New York, pp. 352–7

Robson, W. (1997) *Strategic Management and Information Systems: An Integrated Approach*, Financial Times Pitman Publishing, London

Rockart, J. and Flannery, L. (1983) 'The management of end-user computing', *Communications of the ACM*, 26, 10, 776–84

Troni, F. and Silver, M. (2006) *Use Processes and Tools to Reduce TCO for PCs, 2005–2006 Update*, Gartner, Stamford, CT. Available online at www.gartner.com/DisplayDocument? doc_cd=136769

White, C.E. and Christy, D.P. (1987) 'The Information Centre concept: a normative model and a study of six installations', *MIS Quarterly*, December, 450–8

Further reading

Clarke, S. (2007) *End User Computing Challenges and Technologies: Emerging Tools and Applications*, Information Science Reference, Hershey, PA.

Mahmood, M. (ed.) (2007) *Contemporary Issues in End User Computing (Advances in End User Computing)*, Idea Group, Hershey, PA.

Regan, E.A. and O'Connor, B.N. (2002) *End-user Information Systems: Perspectives for Managers and Information Systems Professionals*, 2nd edition, Macmillan, New York. Second edition contains updates on knowledge management and help-desk management, although most review of strategy and planning is generic to end-user systems.

Web link

www.epolicyinstitute.com E-policy Institute: commercial site with examples of e-mail problems faced by companies and sample guidelines.

LINKS TO OTHER CHAPTERS

Chapter 13 deals with a number of issues relevant to this material, such as managing organisational change.

Chapter 15 considers common threats to the security of computer-based information systems, such as unauthorised access.

Ethical, legal and moral constraints on information systems

CHAPTER AT A GLANCE

MAIN TOPICS

FOCUS ON . . .

CASE STUDIES

LEARNING OUTCOMES

After reading this chapter, you will be able to:

- analyse decisions and courses of action from professional, ethical and moral perspectives;
- select appropriate and legal courses of action in keeping with professional codes of conduct;
- understand and respond to issues of concern, such as personal privacy.

MANAGEMENT ISSUES

This chapter illustrates the huge number of demands that must be balanced in order to ensure that an organisation functions efficiently, responsibly and legally. From a managerial perspective, this chapter addresses the following areas:

- Managers must deal with moral, ethical, professional and legal issues that often conflict with one another.
- Responsible organisations must show an awareness of issues that cause concern for employees and the public such as monitoring of employees.
- An understanding of legislation is required to ensure that the organisation operates within the law.

INTRODUCTION

This chapter considers the moral, legal and ethical responsibilities of those involved in designing, developing and managing computer-based information systems.

After studying this chapter, readers should have obtained an understanding of:

legislation relevant to the management and use of computer-based information systems;

the social and professional responsibilities of those involved in the management, development and use of computer-based information systems;

major and contemporary social issues related to computer-based information systems, such as the impact of technology on employment and personal privacy.

PROFESSIONALISM, ETHICS AND MORALITY

We expect the developers, managers and users of computer-based information systems to behave in a professional manner at all times. They are expected to balance the needs of their employer and the requirements of their profession with other demands such as a responsibility to society. The terms ethics, morality and professionalism are often used to describe our expectations of managers and employees:

Professionalism

Acting to meet the standards set by a profession in terms of individual conduct, competence and integrity.

Ethics

In general terms, describes beliefs concerning right and wrong that can be used by individuals to guide their behaviour.

Morality

Individual character or personality and beliefs governing right and wrong.

- **Professionalism** can be described as acting to meet the standards set by a profession in terms of individual conduct, competence and integrity.

- **Ethics** describes beliefs concerning right and wrong that can be used by individuals to guide their behaviour.

- **Morality** is concerned with an individual's personal beliefs of what is right and wrong.

The IS professional is in a difficult position when undertaking their work since there are a number of constraints affecting their behaviour. These constraints are indicated in Figure 17.1. These constraints may not necessarily conflict, but the employer may place demands on the manager which go against any of the constraints in Figure 17.1.

What should a project manager do, for instance, if the company asks them to reduce the time taken for testing on a project (in order to meet a deadline) which may affect public safety? The sections that follow examine some of the responsibilities and values on the IS manager in each of these areas.

Figure 17.1 Constraints and potential areas of conflict related to the duties and responsibilities of the IS professional

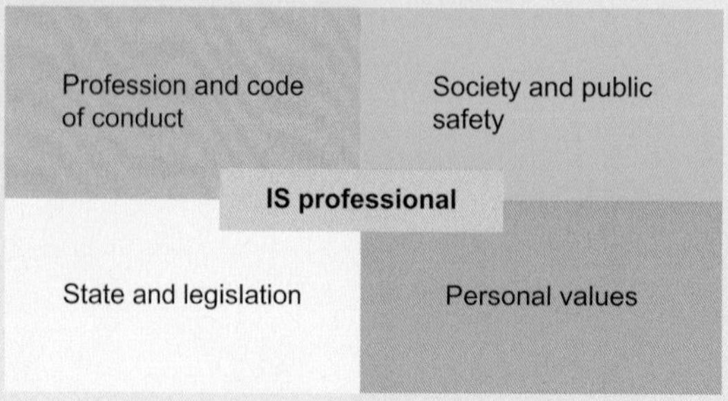

Profession and code of conduct	Society and public safety
IS professional	
State and legislation	Personal values

CODES OF CONDUCT

Code of conduct

Members of professional associations are expected to abide by a set of principles that set out minimum standards of competence, conduct and behaviour.

British Computer Society (BCS)

Widely regarded as the UK's leading professional association for those involved in the management and development of computer-based information systems.

In addition to personal beliefs concerning right and wrong, professionals must also ensure that they obey the law and meet the standards set by their professional association.

A professional association is entitled to set entrance requirements that govern minimum levels of experience and qualifications for new members. Gaining membership affords status to the member and implies that they have achieved a high level of competence in their field. Membership also provides a variety of other benefits, such as training and official representation. However, in return for membership, the individual accepts a duty to meet certain standards of conduct and behaviour. All professional associations expect members to adhere to a code of conduct that sets out a number of the association's principles.

In the UK, the British Computer Society (BCS) is regarded as the leading professional association for those involved in the design, use and management of computer-based information systems. The BCS code of conduct provides clear and firm guidance concerning a member's duties and responsibilities.

The British Computer Society Trustee Board Regulations – Schedule 3 Code of Conduct for BCS Members

Introduction

This Code sets out the professional standards required by the Society as a condition of membership. It applies to members of all grades, including Students, and Affiliates, and also non-members who offer their expertise as part of the Society's Professional Advice Service.

Within this document, the term 'relevant authority' is used to identify the person or organisation which has authority over your activity as an individual. If you are a practising professional, this is normally an employer or client. If you are a student, this is normally an academic institution.

The Code governs your personal conduct as an individual member of the BCS and not the nature of business or ethics of the relevant authority. It will, therefore, be a matter of your exercising your personal judgement in meeting the Code's requirements.

Any breach of the Code of Conduct brought to the attention of the Society will be considered under the Society's Disciplinary procedures. You should also ensure that you notify the Society of any significant violation of this Code by another BCS member.

The public interest

1. In your professional role you shall have regard for the public health, safety and environment. This is a general responsibility, which may be governed by legislation, convention or protocol. If in doubt over the appropriate course of action to take in particular circumstances, you should seek the counsel of a peer or colleague.

2. You shall have regard to the legitimate rights of third parties. The term 'Third Party' includes professional colleagues, or possibly competitors, or members of 'the public' who might be affected by an IT System without their being directly aware of its existence.

3. You shall ensure that within your professional field/s you have knowledge and understanding of relevant legislation, regulations and standards, and that you comply with such requirements. As examples, relevant legislation could, in the UK, include the Public Interest Disclosure Act, Disability Discrimination Act, Data Protection or Privacy legislation, Computer Misuse law, legislation concerned with the export or import of technology, possibly for national security reasons, or law relating to intellectual property. This list is not exhaustive, and you should ensure that you are aware of any legislation relevant to your professional responsibilities. In the international context, you should be aware of, and understand, the requirements of law specific to the jurisdiction within which you are working, and, where relevant, to supranational legislation such as EU law and regulation. You should seek specialist advice when necessary.

4. You shall conduct your professional activities without discrimination against clients or colleagues. Grounds of discrimination include, but are not limited to race, colour, ethnic origin, gender, sexual orientation, age and disability. All colleagues have a right to be treated with dignity and respect. You should adhere to the relevant law within the jurisdiction where you are working and, if appropriate, the European Convention on Human Rights. You are encouraged to promote equal access to the benefits of IT by all groups in society, and to avoid and reduce 'social exclusion' from IT wherever opportunities arise.

5. You shall reject and shall not make any offer of bribery or inducement.

Duty to relevant authority

6. You shall carry out work or study with due care and diligence in accordance with the relevant authority's requirements, and the interests of system users. If your professional judgement is overruled, you shall indicate the likely risks and consequences. The crux of the issue here, familiar to all professionals in whatever field, is the potential conflict between full and committed compliance with the 'relevant authority's wishes, and the independent and considered exercise of your judgement.' If your judgement is overruled, you are encouraged to seek advice and guidance from a peer or colleague on how best to respond.

7. You shall avoid any situation that may give rise to a conflict of interest between you and your relevant authority. You shall make full and immediate disclosure to them if any conflict is likely to occur or be seen by a third party as likely to occur. You shall endeavour to complete work undertaken on time to budget and shall advise the relevant authority as soon as practicable if any overrun is foreseen.

8. You shall not disclose or authorise to be disclosed, or use for personal gain or to benefit a third party, confidential information except with the permission of your relevant authority, or at the direction of a court of law.

9. You shall not misrepresent or withhold information on the performance of products, systems or services, or take advantage of the lack of relevant knowledge or inexperience of others.

Duty to the profession

10. You shall uphold the reputation and good standing of the BCS in particular, and the profession in general, and shall seek to improve professional standards through participation in their development, use and enforcement. As a Member of the BCS you also have a wider responsibility to promote public understanding of IT – its benefits and pitfalls – and, whenever practical, to counter misinformation that brings or could bring the profession into disrepute. You should encourage and support fellow members in their professional development and, where possible, provide opportunities for the professional development of new members, particularly student members. Enlightened mutual assistance between IT professionals furthers the reputation of the profession, and assists individual members.

11. You shall act with integrity in your relationships with all members of the BCS and with members of other professions with whom you work in a professional capacity.

12. You shall have due regard for the possible consequences of your statements on others. You shall not make any public statement in your professional capacity unless you are properly qualified and, where appropriate, authorised to do so. You shall not purport to represent the BCS unless authorised to do so. The offering of an opinion in public, holding oneself out to be an expert in the subject in question, is a major personal responsibility and should not be undertaken lightly. To give an opinion that subsequently proves ill founded is a disservice to the profession, and to the BCS.

13. You shall notify the Society if convicted of a criminal offence or upon becoming bankrupt or disqualified as Company Director. This does not apply, in the UK, to convictions spent under the Rehabilitation of Offenders Act 1974, to discharged bankruptcy, or to expired disqualification under the Company Directors Disqualification Act 1986. Not all convictions are seen as relevant to membership in the Society and each case will be considered individually.

Professional competence and integrity

14. You shall seek to upgrade your professional knowledge and skill, and shall maintain awareness of technological developments, procedures and standards which are relevant to your field, and encourage your subordinates to do likewise.

15. You shall not claim any level of competence that you do not possess. You shall only offer to do work or provide a service that is within your professional competence. You can self-assess your professional competence for undertaking a particular job or role by asking, for example,

    (a) am I familiar with the technology involved, or have I worked with similar technology before?

    (b) have I successfully completed similar assignments or roles in the past?

    (c) can I demonstrate adequate knowledge of the specific business application and requirements successfully to undertake the work?

16. In addition to this Code of Conduct, you shall observe whatever clauses you regard as relevant from the BCS Code of Good Practice and any other relevant standards, and you shall encourage your colleagues to do likewise. You shall accept professional responsibility for your work and for the work of colleagues who are defined in a given context as working under your supervision.

Activity 17.1   Professional associations

Using the Internet as a resource, locate some of the other professional associations that help to regulate the activities of those employed in the IT industry. You should attempt to locate both national and international associations. In addition, you should try to compare what you locate in terms of entrance requirements, codes of conduct and the benefits offered to members.

Professional responsibilities

Another way in which the responsibilities of managers, developers and users can be described is by considering some of their obligations to their employers, the public and the state. In this way, we can illustrate some of the areas in which conflicts of interest might occur.

Employers and employees

Both managers and employees are expected to balance a number of duties and responsibilities in the course of their activities. These can be divided into two broad areas: the responsibilities of all staff to the employer and the responsibilities of managers to the staff they supervise.

Some of the responsibilities employers expect their staff to assume include:

- All employees should look for ways in which they can help the company to achieve its aims. In many cases, this will involve finding new or more efficient ways to complete their work.

- All staff should take responsibility for their actions and the quality of their work.

- Managers should assess projects carefully, considering areas such as cost and risk in relation to the aims of their employer.

- Staff should work to ensure the security of equipment, software and data.

- All employees should attempt to protect and maintain the accuracy of the data held by the company.

- All employees should only attempt work they feel competent to perform. In the event that they feel unable to manage a task correctly, they should seek appropriate help and advice.

■ All employees should maintain an up-to-date knowledge of their area of expertise and seek training when required. This is often described in terms of *continuing professional development* (CPD).

In addition to their responsibilities to their employer, managers must also assume additional responsibilities for the staff under their supervision. Some of these responsibilities include:

■ Managers should assign tasks to employees based on skills and experience. Staff should not feel that their skills are being under-employed, nor should they feel pressured into attempting work they are not capable of carrying out competently.

■ Managers should ensure that their staff are adequately trained and should assign responsibilities carefully and fairly.

■ Resources should be applied in the most efficient ways possible. Managers should be accountable for how the resources they control are used.

These points should help to illustrate some of the difficulties that can arise in the workplace. As an example, consider a manager charged with completing a complex technical project with only a limited budget. Some of the possible approaches to the task might be as follows:

1. The manager might approach a superior and ask for additional resources or could continue with the work knowing that the assigned budget will be exceeded.

2. The manager could attempt to distribute the work amongst staff members, potentially placing them under extreme stress by asking them to complete work that might be beyond their capabilities.

3. The manager could use part of the budget to provide additional training for staff. This would enable the work to be completed but might affect the timescale allowed for the project and cause difficulties for the company later on.

In each of these cases, there is a clear conflict between the manager's responsibilities to the employer and their responsibilities towards staff. In attempting to seek a solution to such a problem, the manager must deal with a number of professional and ethical issues, often relying upon personal judgement and experience.

The public

The responsibilities of managers, developers and users to the public can also raise a number of ethical and professional issues. Two of the most important obligations placed upon professionals concern the duty to protect confidential information and a duty towards public safety.

The duty to protect sensitive or confidential information is normally described in terms of developing security measures to prevent hackers and other unauthorised users from gaining access to company data. However, in terms of a duty to the public, this responsibility can be extended to encompass areas relevant to civil liberties, such as censorship, the right of individuals to view personal data held on them and the privacy of e-mail messages and other communications.

Safety-critical system

Where human lives rely on the correct operation of a computer-based information system, this is normally referred to as a critical system.

In a similar way, the duty to maintain public safety is not to be restricted to simply ensuring that **safety-critical systems** function correctly. Managers and developers must also take responsibility for the quality of the systems they work with.

Many computer-based information systems can have an indirect impact on public safety by producing inaccurate or incomplete information that is relied upon by users. As an example, many companies publish medical software programs designed to help home users find information related to illnesses and their treatment. Despite the prominent warnings displayed by these programs, there is clearly a danger that users may accept a suggested diagnosis or treatment and act upon the information.

If some people can place too much reliance upon computer-based information systems, then the opposite is also true. An unreliable or ineffective system can also have consequences for public safety. A well-known example concerns a case in 1990 where the pilot of a British Airways aircraft, Captain Tim Lancaster, was nearly sucked out of his cockpit window after the bolts securing the windscreen gave way. It was later found that an engineer had used the wrong bolts when fitting the windscreen. Although the engineer had access to a computer-based information system that could have been used to identify and select the correct bolts, he had chosen not to use it since it was considered unreliable and inaccurate (*Independent on Sunday*, 15 November 1992).

In some cases, an information system can be perfectly functional but problems can result from poor user interface design or inadequate checks on data entered by people. Such incidents are often avoidable through various means, such as thorough testing. As an example, in 2011 a judge found that a woman's death from breast cancer resulted from a simple data entry error (*Daily Mail*, 14 March 2011). The patient missed important hospital appointments because they were sent to the wrong address after part of her address was recorded as '16' instead of '1b'. In such a case, one might ask how much responsibility lies with the creator of the information system, who might easily have introduced mechanisms for verifying a patient's address?

A controversial aspect of public safety involves issues related to child pornography and information that could be used to support criminal and terrorist activities. Whilst some argue that all information should be freely available, others are concerned that steps should be taken to control potentially dangerous information and protect the vulnerable, such as children. However, this raises questions of censorship and how we determine what information is 'safe' for the public to receive. In 2011, for instance, Home Secretary, Teresa May, stated: 'Terrorists are increasingly using online technology, including Google Earth and Street View for attack planning' (ComputerActive, 14 July 2011).

The state

The state attempts to maintain standards and behaviour by enacting legislation to regulate the behaviour of companies and employees. Although specific pieces of legislation, such as the Computer Misuse Act 1990, are aimed directly at those working in the field of computer-based information systems, companies and employees must also observe more general laws. As an example, the Health and Safety at Work Act 1974 means that all employees are responsible for safety in the workplace. Staff are required to take immediate action in response to any hazard or danger to health. Furthermore, employers are expected to ensure that the workplace is safe through actions such as providing safety equipment.

Other aspects of legislation relevant to those working in the field of computer-based information systems are described in more detail later on.

CASE STUDY 17.1

Small mistakes attract the biggest trouble

By Lucy Kellaway

Scott Thompson, one assumes, is a clever man. And yet the new CEO of Yahoo has done something incredibly stupid. Claiming to have a degree in computer sciences and accountancy when you've only got a degree in accountancy is an idiotic thing to do.

Quite possibly the people at Diageo are also clever enough. But preventing a little brewer from winning a prize last week was a fabulously boneheaded piece of work.

Most definitely the bankers at JPMorgan are clever. Too clever by half, one might say. But that didn't stop them

➡

losing $2bn through what its CEO Jamie Dimon called 'error, sloppiness and poor judgment'.

Nearly always, it's the bad little things we do that get us into the biggest trouble. It's the things that we know are stupid even at the time we are doing them, but do anyway.

There is a new word for the idea of smart people making moronic errors: 'disrationalia'. It has been coined by Keith Stanovich, a psychologist at the University of Toronto, who argues that we are preprogrammed to make daft mistakes. Partly it's because we think we are better than we are. We also look for evidence that supports what we believe. And we get easily distracted.

To understand how deep this human stupidity goes, I need look no further than myself. Only last week I managed to say something disparaging in an open-plan office about a colleague – only to find the man in question standing behind me. My gaffe was relatively unserious because it was delightfully low-tech. I wasn't linked to a microphone or connected in any way, so only three people were involved.

Thanks to mass-connectivity, most small gaffes are no longer small – they are ginormous. The internet made it much easier to detect the Yahoo CV cock-up and then for the world to make a great stink about it.

Email – as well as texting – is still the fastest way to get into huge trouble over not very much. Never mind the fact that we all know perfectly well that we must never write anything in a work email that we would not be happy for the world to see, the penny still isn't dropping.

The people at Goldman Sachs are as clever as they come, and the corporate bellowing of ethical messaging couldn't be louder. But that didn't stop former trader Fabrice Tourre from boasting in an email about the 'pure intellectual masturbation' of a product he had created and how the market was too stupid to price it. More recently, the bank was on the defensive again, hunting through its emails to find the culprits who had apparently been calling clients muppets.

It's not just that we take no care over what we say in emails. We can't even address them to the right person. Ten years after the invention of electronic messages we still haven't learnt to get the correct name in the address field.

Last week, Eastern Michigan University managed by mistake to sack the entire student body, sending everyone a message that was aimed at just a few. It told them that their academic performance was not up to scratch and they were being kicked out. The same day I read about this I got a text from my usually technically competent son that he had intended to send to a friend, in which he reported that his mother had turned into a madwoman.

Is there any chance that we will ever learn anything? For me, it's not looking good. Last week I took a solemn vow that I would never say anything about a third party unless I was locked in a soundproof cell. But I've made a similar vow a hundred times in the past, and broken it equally often.

I've been sifting through expert papers on this and there seems to be a consensus that the only way to stop making small mistakes is to understand why we make them.

I understand why I say bad things about people: to amuse the person I'm talking to, because I like saying what I think.

I can also see why people falsify CVs: to make themselves look better. I suppose people fiddle prizes for the same reason. And above all I can understand why we are sloppy and careless – because it's a lot less effort than being careful. The easiest thing of all is to understand why we always think we'll get away with it – because we did last time, because we know others have and because it's what we want to believe.

I've understood all this for a long time. But I also understand that understanding it isn't going to make a shred of difference. Any company that thinks it can reprogramme our 'disrationalia' with a few rules and ethics courses is not making a small mistake. It is making a huge one.

 Source: Kellaway, L. (2012) Small mistakes attract the biggest trouble. *Financial Times.* 13 May. © The Financial Times Limited 2012. All Rights Reserved.

QUESTION

How can a company reduce 'disrationalia' amongst its workforce?

SOCIAL ISSUES

The **information society** is a term that has been coined to describe a modern population that is conversant with – and reliant upon – information and communications technology. In this section, we consider a selected range of social issues that concern both individuals and organisations.

Information society

Describes a modern population that is conversant with – and reliant upon – information and communications technology.

Employment

There can be no doubt that technology has made a significant impact on patterns of employment. In the office environment, the positions and tasks of many employees have been taken over by computer-based information systems. Where a number of clerks may have been needed to maintain records or handle everyday transactions, many tasks are now carried out automatically through web-based technologies. In manufacturing organisations, industrial robots and automated manufacturing processes have replaced many thousands of skilled workers.

However, whilst it is certainly true that technology has been responsible for the loss of many jobs within manufacturing and service industries, it is also apparent that a wealth of new employment opportunities has been created in their place:

- As the demand for highly skilled IS professionals continues to grow, new positions have opened up in areas such as computer training and higher education.

- As more companies adopt IT on a larger scale, demand increases for people to develop, maintain and manage the software and equipment used.

- The Internet has created a huge demand for people skilled in areas such as web page design, e-commerce and networking.

Skills shortage

Describes the significant shortage of educated and highly skilled IT practitioners entering the industry.

At present, the demand for skilled IS professionals far outstrips supply, leading to what has been termed a **skills shortage**. According to recruitment specialist Hays (www.hays.co.uk) 110,000 new IT professionals were needed in 2011 alone to meet immediate employer demand. It was also predicted that over the next decade IT employment will increase at a rate that is five times faster than other job markets. Furthermore, approximately 17 per cent of employees will be sourced from higher education, though demand may exceed supply as fewer young people take an interest in ICT subjects at school. Worldwide, staff shortages have become so severe that 'headhunting' agencies can command fees of hundreds of thousands of pounds when recruiting an experienced manager for a large IS department. In some cases, the situation has become so severe that some companies have begun to monitor staff e-mail in order to learn when an employee is approached by another company or a recruitment agency. A secondary effect of staff shortages has been to increase salaries across the entire industry.

In recent years, many companies have turned to 'offshoring': moving business processes abroad, where it is possible to recruit staff more easily and reduce costs by up to 40 per cent. The expansion of the European Union to include new member states has also encouraged some companies to relocate projects to countries such as Poland.

Skilling versus deskilling

A subject of great debate over the past two decades has been whether or not technology leads to the deskilling of employees. In general, the debate concerns a single central question: are employees being given the opportunity to develop new skills in depth, or are they developing a broader range of skills, but failing to develop any real expertise in one or more specific areas?

Some people have expressed concerns about the development of a labour force made up of a large proportion of relatively unskilled employees and just a small number of 'elite' (highly skilled) employees. The belief is that we will eventually rely and depend on a very small number of highly competent people to manage companies, develop new products, and so on.

It is certainly true that there are relatively few employees in the IT industry who could be described as highly skilled. For example, the British Computer Society has approximately 70,000 members, of which more than a quarter have Chartered status (BCS, 2011) but the total number of people involved in the UK IT industry is estimated at more than 2 million. However, we should recognise that there may be many highly skilled people in the labour force who go unrecognised because they have not joined a professional association or come to our attention in other ways. In addition, society always has the opportunity to produce more skilled employees by investing in training and education.

The digital divide

Concern is growing that society may eventually become divided into two distinct groups. One group will be made up of those who have access to technology and are able to obtain information via the Internet. The other will be made up of those who are unable to gain access to technology and information.

The concept of a digital divide can be viewed from national and international perspectives. From an international point of view, consider the availability of Internet access across different countries. In Africa, for example, Ethiopia had just 960000 Internet users in 2012, representing around 1.1 per cent of the total population of approximately 87 million. However, Nigeria had more than 48 million Internet users during the same period, representing around 28 per cent of the population, and almost 29 per cent of all Inter-net users on the continent (see Internet World Stats, **www.internetworldstats.com**).

The existence of a digital divide can be illustrated further by looking at Internet access across continents. As a whole, some estimates suggest that as little as 15.6 per cent of the population of Africa have Internet access. In contrast, the total number of Internet users in Europe is estimated at almost 519 million, representing approximately 63 per cent of the population (Internet World Stats). In the UK alone, around 53 million people have access to the Internet, amounting to approximately 84 per cent of the population.

There is also evidence that a digital divide exists within individual countries. However, in countries such as the UK, where most people have access to the Internet through schools, Internet cafés, public libraries and other organisations, the concept of a digital divide has changed somewhat since the turn of the century. Many governments and organisations now talk about access to high-speed services, such as broadband Internet and video-on-demand, as well as the information-seeking skills needed to use those services effectively. In the UK, for example, some rural areas have only limited access to high-speed Internet connections. In addition, many adults lack basic literacy skills, preventing them from making the best use of the Internet. Overall, the European Commission estimates that 40 per cent of European citizens suffer from 'digital illiteracy' (Silicon.com, 28 September 2007).

For business, the implications of a digital divide provide cause for concern. For example, attempts to open new premises in certain parts of the country could be hindered by an inability to recruit suitably qualified and experienced staff from the local area.

Access to high speed Internet services is now considered so important that it has become a human right in some countries. In 2012, the United Nations Human Rights Council passed a resolution titled 'The promotion, protection and enjoyment of human rights on the Internet' which has been interpreted by the media as meaning 'that broadband access is a basic human right, right up there with the right to healthcare, shelter and food' (Lane, 2011). Countries reported to have made Internet access a basic human right include Costa Rica, Estonia, Finland, France, Greece and Spain. In the EU as a whole the situation is less clear but an internet freedom provision adopted in 2010 stated that any measures taken by member states that may affect citizen's access to or use of the internet 'must respect the fundamental rights and freedoms of citizens' (BBC News, 8 March 2010). In the UK, a 2012 case involving a voyeur who spied on a 14-year-old girl resulted in a legal ruling that it was 'entirely unreasonable' for anyone to be denied

Internet access in modern Britain. The *Telegraph* (13 November 2012) argued that the ruling 'effectively renders access to the internet as a human right, [when] Appeal Court judges ruled it is "unreasonable nowadays to ban anyone from accessing the internet in their home"'. A similar ruling in 2013 was made in Germany, where Federal Justice Minister Sabine Leutheusser-Schnarrenberger was quoted as saying: 'The ruling shows how fundamental the Internet has become for an informed life. Internet use is becoming recognized as a civil right.'

Source: Deutsche Welle, 27 January 2013.

Personal privacy

Surveillance society

This describes a society where the actions of individuals are closely monitored by government departments and major companies, and where these organisations routinely gather and process large amounts of personal information.

Dataveillance

The use of technology to automate the monitoring of individuals.

It has long been recognised that technology enables companies, government departments and other organisations to collect large amounts of personal information. Although the use of such information is controlled by various mechanisms, such as legislation, many people are concerned by the potential threat to personal privacy. The surveillance society is a term used to describe a society where the actions of individuals are closely monitored by government departments and major companies, and where these organisations routinely gather and process large amounts of personal information.

The threat to personal privacy is perceived to arise from the basic functions of computer-based information systems, namely their ability to store, process and retrieve data quickly and efficiently. Advances in technology now make it possible to monitor people via automated systems, often using data pooled from a wide variety of different sources. This kind of monitoring has been termed dataveillance by Australian academic Roger Clarke (Clarke, 1988). The Surveillance Studies Network describes dataveillance like this: 'Dataveillance monitors or checks people's activities or communications in automated ways, using information technologies. It is far cheaper than direct or specific electronic surveillance and thus offers benefits that may sometimes act as incentives to extend the system even though the data are not strictly required for the original purpose' (Wood, 2006).

While tools capable of profiling Internet users automatically are in their infancy, they are starting to become of concern to privacy campaigners and researchers. A 2010 study by Balduzzi et al. (2010) reported that it was possible to collate information about users across numerous social networks. This allowed the researchers to discover information that individuals might not want known, for example identifying people using different names or ages on dating web sites. Kosinskia, Stillwella and Graepelb (2013) also discuss how Internet users can be automatically profiled using information taken from Facebook. In their work, they found that they were able to predict the IQ, personality, ethnicity, sexuality and political beliefs of individuals by examining their 'Likes'. Of significance was the accuracy of such predictions; a person's sexuality could be determined with 95 per cent accuracy, for instance.

Two examples can be used to illustrate common concerns related to privacy:

■ The use of computer-based information systems enables an organisation to combine or analyse data in ways not previously possible with manual systems. As an example, a bank might build up profiles of its customers by analysing their spending, borrowing and saving habits. This information could then be supplied to other organisations involved in marketing relevant goods or services. In 2005, Tesco faced controversy over a decision to begin tagging items with RFID (radio-frequency identification) chips. Campaigners claimed that the supermarket was using 'spy chips' to track the behaviour of customers and called for a global boycott of the company (BBC News, 26 January 2005). Another example of a controversy relating to privacy involves Google Street View. This project involves a fleet of cars taking street-level photographs of all public streets and roads in a number of different countries. The data collected can be integrated with other data owned by Google to offer a range of sophisticated services. As an example, you might use a web search to find a restaurant in your local area, plot a route to it using Google Maps, then look at a photograph of the restaurant using Street View. As can be imagined, many privacy concerns have been raised over Street View and it has faced restrictions or outright bans in a number of countries, such as Greece and the Czech Republic. Outraged citizens have even held protests or grouped together to prevent Street View vehicles from photographing their streets. In a 2013 settlement with 38 US states, Google agreed to pay a $7 million (£4.6 million) fine for collecting people's personal data without authorisation as part of its Street View service.

- Communications technology allows organisations to share data, allowing them to develop a comprehensive pool of information regarding individuals. An insurance company, for example, might gather medical information before deciding whether or not to offer a policy to an individual.

A further issue related to privacy concerns the quantity and accuracy of the personal data held on individuals. In the late 1990s it was estimated that an average adult might be listed on as many as 200 computer files and that there might be a 2 per cent error rate in the information held (*Guardian*, 12 May 1997). It is difficult to find up-to-date information on how many files an average person is listed on today but the total is likely to be much higher, thanks to changes in the way we use technology. As an example, many organisations routinely collect information whenever someone buys a product from them or requests support.

Holding inaccurate personal data on an individual can result in a number of problems, affecting areas such as health, employment and education. A good example involves the Criminal Records Bureau (CRB), the agency responsible for vetting job applicants wishing to work with children or vulnerable people. In a 2006 report from the Surveillance Studies Network, an international non-profit research organisation, it was stated that the CRB had incorrectly identified 2,700 people as having criminal records with the result that a number were refused jobs. The report also noted that 22 per cent of records entered into the Police National Computer contained errors, even after being checked by a supervisor. More recently, the Inland Revenue acknowledged that almost one in five records it held contained errors (*Telegraph*, 7 September 2010), while a review of electronic patient records in Birmingham found that one in ten records contained errors or out-of-date information (*Telegraph*, 17 July 2010). Such cases are significant since agencies like these often share data with other government departments and organisations.

Another area of concern is the use of computer monitoring to gather information concerning the behaviour of people in the workplace. Although such monitoring has legitimate uses, for example measuring workflow and productivity, it can also be used to violate an employee's privacy.

Computer monitoring

The use of computer and communications technology to monitor the activities of individuals.

Computer monitoring is also used in a number of other areas, for example a security firm may use a combination of computers, video cameras, sensors and other devices to maintain the security of a large building.

The monitoring of communications, such as telephone calls and e-mail messages is also a major area of concern for many users. Although there seems little evidence to suggest that *all* communications are monitored at *all* times, many companies and individuals have turned towards methods such as encryption in order to protect sensitive business or personal information.

There are 4.2 million CCTV cameras in the UK, roughly one camera for every 14 people. Although the UK accounts for less than 1 per cent of the world's population, it has 20 per cent of the world's cameras. The average Londoner may be monitored up to 300 times every day.

Source: This Is London, 26 March 2007 (www.thisislondon.co.uk)

In the UK, the introduction of legal measures that allow government agencies to monitor e-mail messages has sparked a huge controversy that still continues today. Businesses have expressed concern that such measures will harm competitiveness and damage business relations. Other people are concerned that the ability to gather this kind of information could be abused, causing untold harm to industry and individuals. In 2000, for example, it was alleged that American intelligence agencies were sharing information – such as the contents of e-mail messages – with certain companies, giving them an unfair advantage in international markets.

Echelon

Many people are concerned at what appears to be the indiscriminate monitoring of communications, the majority of which are almost certain to be both innocent and legitimate.

Echelon is a global surveillance system that monitors communications around the world. The project is operated by the USA, the UK, Canada, Australia and New Zealand. Each day, millions of telephone calls, faxes and e-mail messages are intercepted and scanned for key words and phrases. Messages matching the search criteria used are collected and sent to the United States for further analysis.

In May 2000, allegations were made that US intelligence services were found to be passing sensitive information to American companies, effectively giving them an unfair advantage over British and European competitors. Similar concerns were raised in a 2001 report to the European Parliament which reported that the CIA and other agencies were involved in monitoring 'on a targeted basis communications by individual firms in connection with contract-award procedures in order to prevent corruption-related distortions of competition to the detriment of US firms'.

It should be noted that some of the fears surrounding Echelon may not be valid. For instance, it is unlikely that Echelon is capable of monitoring the sheer volume of messages sent around the world each day. For instance, a 2010 estimate from the Radicati Group claims that 294 billion messages are sent every day. Similarly, given the sophistication of modern encryption techniques, it is highly unlikely that Echelon would be capable of decrypting even a tiny fraction of the messages transmitted every day. However, concern over Echelon is such that in 2004 the EU announced plans to invest a 11 million in developing new encryption techniques that would prevent anyone – including Echelon – from intercepting and decoding e-mail messages.

Sources: Security.ITWorld.com, 17 May 2004; Federation of American Scientists; Inside Echelon (www.cyberdelix.net); Radicati Group (www.radicati.com)

Activity 17.2   Personal privacy

As mentioned in this section, it is estimated that a typical adult may be listed in as many as 200 computer files.

1. How many organisations hold data on you? List as many organisations as possible and describe the data held.

2. Imagine that you have access to all of this data and wish to build a profile of the characteristics of a person. Describe what such a profile would contain and what other assumptions could be made.

3. If a government department or commercial organisation were given access to all of this information, what uses could they put it to?

Crime

As the use of technology has become more widespread, so too have the incidences of computer crime. Acts such as theft, fraud, unauthorised access and vandalism have become almost commonplace and the losses or damage caused by such acts have increased dramatically.

The Information Security Breaches Survey 2010 (**http://www.infosec.co.uk/files/ isbs_2010_technical_report_single_pages.pdf**) found that 80 per cent of large UK businesses had been affected by theft or fraud. The most common breaches were malware infections (35 per cent), systems failure or data corruption (14 per cent), fraud or theft involving computers (13 per cent) and staff misuse of Internet or email (12 per cent). Taking a more global view, the Computer Security Institute (**www.gocsi .com**) publishes an annual Computer Crime and Security Survey. The 2010–11 survey gathered responses from around 350 organisations. The survey found that the most common breaches experienced by respondents were malware infections (67.1 per cent), laptop or mobile device theft (33.5 per cent), phishing (38.9 per cent), bots on network (28.9 per cent), misuse of Internet or email (24.8 per cent) and denial of service attacks(16.8 per cent).

Computer criminals

Those who commit computer-related crimes can be divided into three basic categories:

Computer criminals

Make use of technology to perform a variety of criminal acts, ranging from vandalism and sabotage to hacking and fraud.

Information warrior

Seeks to obtain data by any means necessary. Such people may resort to illegal methods, such as hacking, in order to obtain the information they require.

Hacker

Individuals who seek to break into systems as a test of their abilities. Few hackers attempt to cause damage to the systems they access and few are interested in gaining any sort of financial profit.

1. **Computer criminals** are typically well-educated, white-collar workers who feel undervalued or bear some resentment to an employer or former employer (Parker, 1976). Such individuals resort to sabotage, vandalism or theft as a means of revenge against the employer. Other computer criminals may stumble upon ways of compromising system security and take advantage of these in order to steal money, goods or services.

2. Schwartau (1994) describes as **information warriors** those who seek to obtain data by any means necessary. Such people may resort to illegal methods, such as hacking, in order to obtain the information they require. It is worth noting that the information obtained may not necessarily be used in pursuit of criminal activities, for example a police officer might feel the need to resort to such methods in order to gather evidence against a suspect.

3. **Hackers** are often described as individuals who seek to break into systems as a test of their abilities. As the points below demonstrate, we can make distinctions between different kinds of hackers and the terms used to describe them. This area was considered briefly in Chapter 15. Comparatively few hackers attempt to cause damage to the systems they access and few are interested in gaining any sort of financial profit. It can be argued that there are four basic motives behind the actions of hackers (Johnson, 1994):

   (a) Some hackers hold the belief that all information should be free. Such individuals feel a duty to ensure free access to information held by government departments and private companies.

   (b) Many hackers believe that they provide an important service to companies by exposing flaws in security.

   (c) Some people believe that hacking serves an educational purpose by helping them to improve their knowledge and skills. Since no harm is caused to any systems accessed, their actions are acceptable and should not be considered threatening.

   (d) A final motive for hacking is simply for enjoyment or excitement. Many hackers find stimulation in the challenge of defeating the designers of the security measures used by a given system.

Types of computer crime

Computer crime can be divided into a number of different categories:

Theft

In terms of computing, theft normally, but not always, involves altering computer records to disguise the theft of money. The theft of services can include a variety of acts, such as the unauthorised use of a company's information systems.

- **Theft** normally, but not always, involves altering computer records to disguise the theft of money. An employee of an insurance company, for example, might create a number of fictitious clients and then make claims on their behalf.

- The *theft of services* can include a variety of acts, such as the unauthorised use of a company's information systems. Although many of these acts may appear innocuous, it should be noted that their effect can lead to significant losses. Making intensive use of a company's computer systems, for example, can temporarily deprive the organisation of its resources, leading to financial losses through decreased productivity. Botnets involve the theft of services on a very large scale. They are normally created by planting malware on a large number of computers. The malware allows the controller of the botnet to issue commands to all of the infected machines. Botnets are often used to mount distributed denial of service attacks (DDoS), where large numbers of compromised computers flood a web site with traffic in order to prevent it from functioning. They can also be used for large scale harvesting of confidential information, such as passwords or credit card details, or even for tasks that require large amounts of computing power, such as decrypting data.

Software theft

Software theft, also known as software piracy, involves making unauthorised copies of software applications.

- **Software theft** involves making unauthorised copies of software applications. This topic is described in more detail later on.

Data theft

Data theft can involve stealing sensitive information or making unauthorised changes to computer records.

- **Data theft** can involve stealing sensitive information or making unauthorised changes to computer records.

- The *destruction of data and software*, for example by creating and disseminating computer viruses, can lead to significant losses.

A report from Symantec (**www.symantec.com**) stated that the company recorded 3 billion malware attacks in 2010 and that there were 286 million unique variants of malware in existence. In the UK alone, a report to the Houses of Parliament in September 2011 said that 'common types of attack, such as cyber fraud and intellectual property theft that are estimated to cost the UK £27 billion a year'.

Some of the emerging trends in computer crime with a particular emphasis on activities related to the Internet were described earlier (see Chapter 15).

LEGAL ISSUES

In this section, we consider some of the legislation relevant to managers, users and developers of computer-based information systems.

It is worth noting that whilst this section is primarily concerned with UK legislation, many other countries have similar laws and guidelines that deal with the same issues. In general, the majority of the material in this section will be relevant to all European Union members, the United States and other nations, such as South Africa, Australia and New Zealand.

Data Protection Act 1984, 1998

The full title of the Data Protection Act 1998 is:

An Act to make new provision for the regulation of the processing of information relating to individuals, including the obtaining, holding, use or disclosure of such information.

As can be seen, the Act tries to ensure that organisations use personal information in a responsible way. The Act gives individuals limited rights concerning how information on them is gathered, stored and used. Any company that makes use of personal information must register under the Act.

The **Data Protection Act** is based upon a number of general principles. These include:

Data Protection Act 1984

Legislation setting out the rights of organisations and individuals in terms of how personal information is gathered, stored, processed and disclosed.

- Information shall be obtained and processed 'fairly and lawfully'.

- Information shall be held only for one or more specific and lawful purposes.

- Companies should not hold information that is excessive or not relevant to the purposes the company has registered under the Act.

- Information held on individuals should be accurate and up to date.

- Information should not be held for longer than needed.

- Individuals have the right to see the data held on them and have corrections made where necessary.

- Companies must take measures to protect information from unauthorised access.

As of April 2010, the penalties for failing to comply with the Act include fines of up to £500,000 and custodial sentences. However, to date, there have been relatively few prosecutions brought under the Act and many of these have been for relatively minor offences, such as the failure to register as a data user.

There are three major criticisms levelled at the Data Protection Act:

1. It is considered fairly easy for companies to obtain exemption from the conditions set out in the Act.

2. It is sometimes very difficult for individuals to gain access to the information held on them.

3. It is sometimes difficult for users to ensure that corrections are made to the information held on them.

The adoption of EU regulations dealing with the processing of personal data has brought the UK's legislation in line with the rest of the Union. However, the changeover has not been without difficulty and UK companies have now started to share some of the problems of their European counterparts. Examples of the difficulties now faced by UK and other European organisations include:

- *Conflicts with other legislation.* For example, the adoption of the Human Rights Act 1998 has provided UK citizens with a set of fundamental rights, including a right to privacy. Already there have been a number of cases where the requirements of the Human Rights Act have come into conflict with the activities permissible under the Data Protection Act. Note that such a situation is not unique to the UK: the basic principles set out in UK legislation apply to all EU members.

- *Difficulty in trading across international boundaries.* EU regulations place strict controls on the transfer of personal data to organisations based outside of the EU. Since many organisations have close relationships with companies in the United States and Asia, this has served to constrain some business activities. Of particular importance is the impact of restrictions on areas such as e-commerce. Again, this issue impacts upon all EU members.

- *Lack of clear guidance.* Many organisations have found it difficult to incorporate new data protection legislation into existing company policies and procedures. Although the amended Data Protection Act came into force in 2000, there have also been a number of new developments, such as the introduction of the Human Rights Act in 2000. Unfortunately, clarification of some of the issues raised by these changes has been slow to arrive.

Safe Harbor

The European Union Directive on the Protection of Personal Data took effect in October 1998. The Directive prohibits the transfer of personal data outside of the European Economic Area to any nation that does not have sufficiently rigorous data protection practices. In order to allow US companies to work effectively with their EU counterparts, the United States Department of Commerce has developed a set of Safe Harbor Principles to underpin a formal EU-US Safe Harbor agreement:

- *Notice* – people must be told that their data is being collected and how it will be used.
- *Choice* – people must be able to opt out of the collection and transfer of the data to third parties.
- *Onward transfer* – data may only be transferred to a third party if they follow adequate data protection principles.
- *Security* – reasonable security precautions must be taken to protect information from loss, unauthorised access, and so on.
- *Data integrity* – data must be relevant, accurate, current and appropriate to the purpose it has been collected for.
- *Access* – people must be able to access information about them and correct, amend, or delete information that is inaccurate.
- *Enforcement* – there must be effective mechanisms for enforcing these principles.

As can be seen, these principles are similar to those of UK and EU legislation. However, it is worth noting that significant criticism has been levelled at the EU-US Safe Harbor agreement in relation to enforcement and ensuring compliance.

One of the issues often associated with the Data Protection Act involves monitoring staff e-mail and Internet use at work. This is a complex area and the available guidance is not always clear. As an example, current guidance suggests that if an employee is away from work, the employer has the right to read any business-related e-mail but is *not* entitled to any personal e-mail. If the subject line of a message is missing or unclear, how is the employer supposed to tell whether the message is personal or business-related without reading it?

Many companies allow staff to make personal use of company e-mail and Internet resources, providing these privileges are not abused. *Cyberslacking* (see Chapter 16) is a term used to describe employees making personal use of the Internet while at work. Cyberslacking can lead to a number of problems, including significant losses in productivity. A survey from the Cranfield School of Management, for instance, found that 30 per cent of the companies questioned were losing more than a day's work per week through cyberslacking. The survey also found that company profits might be increased by 15 per cent if the problem were dealt with effectively (BBC News, 1 November 2002). The cost of cyberslacking was also investigated in a 2010 survey of 1000 workers by MyJobGroup.co.uk. The survey found that 6 per cent of workers spent more than one hour a day using social media sites. The company estimated that £14 billion a year is lost due to employees spending time on social networking sites. Around 14 per cent of respondents admitted they were less productive as a result of using social media though 10 per cent claimed social media actually made them more productive.

In addition to reduced profits, companies also expose themselves to risks such as legal action if employees libel a competitor within e-mail messages. However, monitoring e-mail messages and Internet use can also lead to significant problems. In addition to the threat of legal action, for example, companies must consider the expense involved in monitoring employees.

Although the government has issued guidance on monitoring employees, the guidelines are not legally binding and following them may not provide protection against legal action brought under the Data Protection Act or other legislation. However, the guidance does promote good practice and attempts to find a balance between meeting the needs of employers and respecting the privacy of employees.

CASE STUDY 17.2

Sony fined after lapses at games network

By Bede McCarthy, Technology Correspondent

Sony's European subsidiary has been hit with a £250,000 fine by the UK Information Commissioner's Office over the attack on its PlayStation Network in 2011.

Names, addresses, email addresses, dates of birth and passwords for millions of customers were accessed by hackers in the attack on the Japanese electronics maker's network and the commissioner's office said payment card details were also at risk.

PlayStation Network is the online element of Sony's PlayStation gaming console and mobile gaming products, where customers can buy games and rent films with credit cards as well as chat and play against each other online.

The fine against Sony Computer Entertainment Europe is the third-largest imposed by the ICO, which is charged with enforcing the Data Protection Act in the UK but cannot issue penalties of more than £500,000. The two larger fines were both handed to local authorities.

The commissioner's office said the 2011 attack could have been prevented if the network's software had been up-to-date and that technical developments had made passwords unsecure. According to the fine document, it said Sony 'did not ensure a level of security appropriate to the harm that might result from unauthorised or unlawful processing and the nature of the data'.

David Smith, deputy commissioner and director of data protection, said Sony was a company that traded on its technical expertise and therefore should have had the knowhow to keep customer data safe.

'When the database was targeted, albeit in a determined criminal attack, the security measures in place were simply not good enough,' he said.

Sony said on Thursday that it planned to appeal against the fine.

The company pointed to passages in the penalty notice that said there was no evidence that encrypted card payment details were accessed and that personal data were unlikely to have been used for fraudulent purposes after the attack.

'Criminal attacks on electronic networks are a real and growing aspect of 21st century life and Sony continually works to strengthen our systems... The reliability of our network services and the security of our consumers' information are of the utmost importance to us.'

The breach forced Sony to take the platform offline for a month and rebuild it to be more secure. At the time, it said 10m users had used their credit cards on the PlayStation Network online gaming platform, but tried to reassure its mainly US members that the chances of card data having been accessed were low.

Even so, the breach, part of a series of attacks, continued to haunt the company for much of 2011, contributing to a management reshuffle, a tumbling share price and the company's fourth straight loss that year.

QUESTION

Discuss the consequences for companies that are attacked by hackers.

Computer Misuse Act 1990

Computer Misuse Act 1990

Legislation intended to protect sensitive equipment and data from unauthorised access, alteration and damage.

The full title of the Computer Misuse Act 1990 can be used to clarify its intent:

> An Act to make provision for securing computer material against unauthorised access or modification; and for connected purposes.

A number of offences are covered by the Act. Amongst these are the following:

- unauthorised access to computer material;
- unauthorised access with the intention of carrying out or assisting others with the commission of further offences;
- unauthorised modification of computer material;
- impairing the operation of a program or the reliability of data;
- preventing or hindering access to any program or data.

It is interesting to note that the Act deliberately made no attempt to define what was meant by a computer. It was recognised very early on that it would be impossible to create a definition that could encompass the technological changes likely to occur over the next few decades. Instead, it was decided that the courts should use the common, everyday meaning of the term. It was felt that this would enable the Act to remain relevant for longer by allowing it to keep pace with technology. Despite this, the Act quickly became outdated because it did not take into account developments such as the growth of the Internet. As an example, the Act did not cover certain acts, such as denial-of-service attacks. In order to address these problems, a number of amendments were proposed as part of the Police and Justice Bill 2006. The Bill gained royal assent in November 2007, enabling the scope of the Computer Misuse Act to be broadened significantly.

It is worth noting several general points in relation to the Act and the amendments made as part of the Police and Justice Bill 2006. The original Act made the unauthorised modification of computer material a criminal offence. The amendments now mean that anyone who 'commits an unauthorised act in relation to a computer' is guilty of an offence if the person has the knowledge and intent:

- to impair the operation of any computer;
- to prevent or hinder access to any program or data held in any computer; or
- to impair the operation of any such program or the reliability of any such data.

This wording encompasses a broader range of acts, including making denial-of-service attacks, distributing malware and publishing passwords on the Internet. The new wording is also broad enough to deal with situations where someone is paid to commit an offence, such as when a hacker is hired to launch a denial-of-service attack. It is also now an offence to make, supply or obtain tools or software intended to be used to assist or commit a computer misuse offence. This effectively makes it illegal to create hacker tools or malware of any kind; previously it was illegal to distribute malware but not to create it.

The wording of the Act makes it clear that offences need not be directed at any particular program, data or computer system. This provides the legislation with far-reaching authority, allowing action to be taken in a wide variety of circumstances.

The Act also states that an individual is guilty of an offence if they have the 'requisite intent and the requisite knowledge', meaning that individuals must have the intention to cause some form of damage or harm and must be aware that their actions are unauthorised. This offers a measure of protection to those users who unintentionally gain unauthorised access to a computer system or cause accidental damage.

There is also no distinction between acts that cause permanent or temporary changes to programs or data. In this way, even a practical joke, such as changing a user's password without their permission, could be considered a criminal act.

It is interesting to note that the Act does not appear to extend to damage caused to data held on offline storage media, such as compact discs and magnetic tapes. However, other legislation can be used to provide additional protection. It is an offence under the Criminal Damage Act 1971, for example, to destroy or damage any property. This legislation has been extended to cover storage media by suggesting that certain actions, such as deleting data from a floppy disk, can be said to cause damage by reducing the value or usefulness of the media.

Other notable omissions from the Act include electronic eavesdropping and software piracy. Although relatively uncommon at the time the Act was passed, incidences of electronic eavesdropping have grown rapidly. Much of this growth can be attributed to increased sales of mobile telephones and the rapid development of e-commerce. Software piracy is considered to be covered adequately by existing counterfeiting and copyright legislation.

The penalties for offences covered by the Act can include an unlimited fine and up to a maximum of five years' imprisonment.

Electronic eavesdropping describes the act of gaining access to confidential information by intercepting or monitoring communications traffic. Some examples include:

■ Calls made using cellular telephones can be monitored using relatively inexpensive radio receivers.

■ Police, emergency services and air traffic control radio transmissions can be monitored using a domestic radio receiver.

■ Material sent via the Internet, such as e-mail messages, can be intercepted at a number of different points. This allows individuals to gain access to any sensitive information transmitted in this way, such as credit card numbers.

■ Comparatively inexpensive receivers can be used to view the display shown on a computer monitor being used in another location. Although monitors can be shielded to prevent this, relatively few organisations seem aware of the risk.

The Privacy and Electronic Communications (EC Directive) Regulations 2003

This legislation came into force in December 2003 and brought the UK into compliance with the rest of the European Union regarding issues such as e-mail marketing and telesales. For industry, this legislation regulates the use of publicly available electronic communications services for direct marketing purposes. The legislation also covers unsolicited direct marketing activity by telephone, fax, e-mail and automated calling systems and even text messages.

For consumers, this legislation introduces several important rights. Of these, perhaps the most important are:

■ The right to register with the Telephone Preference Service, which helps to make sure that their telephone number is not made available to telemarketing companies and others. Although it has been possible to register with the Telephone Preference Service for a number of years, the legislation makes it an offence to make unsolicited direct marketing calls to individuals who have indicated that they do not want to receive such calls.

■ The right to make a complaint to the Information Commissioner if it is felt that any regulations have been breached. This allows the Information Commissioner to take enforcement action against a marketing company, if they feel it necessary.

The legislation also brings in controls for dealing with unsolicited e-mail (spam) and the processing of cookies. In terms of marketing messages sent by e-mail, for instance, companies may not conceal their identities and must provide a valid means for opting-out.

Although this legislation should be welcomed for attempting to deal with problems such as spam, critics have argued that it is unlikely to be effective. This is because most spam originates from countries outside of the EU; any company wishing to sidestep the legislation needs only to set up a subsidiary in a country outside of the EU. However, it will take several years before it is possible to assess whether or not this legislation has been successful.

What are cookies?

Cookies are small files that contain information about an Internet user. Cookies are often used to record a user's preferences when they visit a web site, allowing the site to 'remember' how to display information. However, some companies use cookies to record other information secretly, such as the addresses of any web sites visited. This information can then be processed for various purposes, such as targeting advertising.

Copyright, Designs and Patents Act 1988

The **Copyright, Designs and Patents Act** provides organisations and software developers with protection against unauthorised copying of designs, software, printed materials and other works. In general, most countries have legislation that mirrors the principles of the Copyright, Designs and Patents Act.

Copyright legislation allows a company to safeguard its *intellectual property rights (IPR)* against competitors and others who might wish to profit from the company's research and investment.

Intellectual property is a generic term used to describe designs, ideas and inventions. In general, intellectual property covers the following areas: patents, trade marks, designs and copyright.

Copyright

Copyright exists automatically as soon as a given work is completed and no action is necessary to gain copyright. The copyright to a given work can exist for up to 50 years following the author's death. Authors of copyrighted works can transfer their rights to others, selling or leasing them if they wish.

For managers involved with computer-based information systems, copyright legislation raises a number of important issues. We will now describe the two most significant.

Ownership of bespoke software developed for the company by a consultant

The possibility of disputes means that organisations should introduce procedures that can be used to establish ownership of copyright. Quite a common problem is when a bespoke system is developed for a company by a consultant. Unless specified in the contract, the copyright or IPR will reside with the consultant. The consultant can then sell the same software (which was of course paid for) to a competitor of the first company. This is obviously undesirable and needs to be included in the contract for development of the system.

Consider a dispute concerning two writers claiming ownership over the contents of a book or article. Unless one of the authors can prove that they were the original creator of the material, it may not be possible to resolve the argument. For a company, such copyright disputes might result in lengthy and expensive legal battles, leading to lost revenues and adverse publicity. A common solution to this problem is to register all copyright materials with an agency, government department or legal firm. However, this requires organisations to set procedures in place in order to ensure that all important materials are protected in this way.

In the UK it is worthwhile including a **source escrow** clause in a contract for bespoke software. Under this arrangement software (both media and source code instructions) is stored at the National Computing Centre in Manchester and if the company developing the software becomes insolvent the company that originally contracted them can still attempt to use the source code to fix maintenance problems.

Many countries allow companies to lodge materials with a government department in order to register copyright. In the United States, for example, materials can be lodged with the US Copyright Office for a small fee.

Employee 'takes' software to another company

Another problem concerning ownership of copyright involves materials produced by the employees of an organisation. Although many organisations assume automatic ownership to the copyright of any materials produced by their employees, this may not necessarily be the case. Unless specifically stated by the employee's contract, or implied on the basis of the employee's usual work for the organisation, the company may have no rights to any materials created.

Activity 17.3   Copyright

You are employed as a clerk in a large sales organisation. In your spare time, for example during lunch breaks, you develop a computer program that could be of significant value to your employer. Your employer claims ownership of the program on two grounds: that the program is related to your normal activities as an employee and that you used their equipment when creating the program. You dispute this on the grounds that the work was carried out during your own time and that the majority of the work was completed at home, using your own personal computer.

1. What legal, moral and ethical issues are involved in this case?

2. Who owns the program?

An example may help to make this point clearer. A computer programmer moves to another company, taking with them a program that was under development. The programmer argues that they are entitled to take the program since the contract they worked under made no reference to ownership of copyright. However, since the programmer was formerly employed to produce computer programs, the original employer has implied rights concerning the uncompleted program. In such a case, it is likely that the original employer would be successful if they took legal action against the employee.

This example should help to illustrate the importance of ensuring that employees' contracts take account of copyright issues. Many organisations routinely issue employment contracts containing clauses that concern copyright to all employees, regardless of their position or function.

Note that copyright protection applies only to materials that have been recorded in some way and it cannot be used to protect ideas or concepts. The operation of a computer program, for example, is not normally protected by copyright legislation; although the actual source code may be subject to copyright, there may be little to stop a competitor creating a similar program to fulfil the same purpose.

In general, breach of copyright involves making a direct copy of part or the whole of a given work, such as an article. However, copyright can sometimes be extended to include the expression of a work and derivative works. As an example consider what might happen if a programmer developed a program that produced precisely the same screen displays, in terms of content and presentation, as an existing commercial product. Copyright infringement could be argued on the basis that the new program was merely an expression of the original commercial product. However, if the displays produced by the program were sufficiently different from the original, it might not be possible to prove infringement.

For business organisations, these aspects of copyright legislation can present a major dilemma. Although copyright legislation can be used to gain a measure of protection for certain works, for example computer programs, such protection is often limited and may not be sufficient in the case of particularly valuable or important works. As a result, large amounts of expense and time can be involved in pursuing copyright infringement via legal action.

Software piracy

Copyright is also infringed when software is copied by employees in the organisation so that it can be installed on more machines than licences have been paid for. This is an important topic and the 'Focus on software piracy' section later in this chapter describes some of the consequences of copyright theft in the form of software piracy.

Patents

Patent

Provides its owner with a monopoly allowing them to exploit their invention without competition. The protection offered by a patent lasts for a number of years but does not begin until the patent has been granted.

A **patent** provides its owner with a monopoly allowing them to exploit their invention without competition. The protection offered by a patent lasts for a number of years but does not begin until the patent has been granted. The application process for a patent can take as long as five years. During this time, the applicant must not disclose the details of the invention or the application will be rejected.

A patent can only be granted for original inventions that are considered to be 'non-obvious'. A simple modification to an existing item, for example, would be considered obvious and unoriginal.

Since the patent application will describe the method used to create the item and the way in which it functions, the owner's work is protected in its entirety. Once the patent has been granted, competitors are prohibited from duplicating the item.

Unlike copyright, where international agreements provide automatic protection for an author's work in other countries, separate applications may need to be made to patent offices in other countries. It is common, for example, for companies to register patents in the UK, other countries in Europe and the United States in order to protect these potential markets from competitors.

Cross-licensing agreement

Agreements allow companies to share patents so that each can produce and market a wider range of products.

The rights assigned by a patent can be sold or licensed to others. This enables smaller companies to form partnerships with others in order to exploit foreign markets. **Cross-licensing agreements** allow companies to share patents so that each can produce and market a wider range of products.

In many countries, patents can be used to protect computer programs by registering the methods and techniques used in their creation. As an example, PKZIP is a leading data compression utility that uses a number of specialised techniques to compress data quickly and efficiently. It is these techniques that distinguish the program from others, allowing it to provide an original and non-obvious approach to data compression. In the UK, patents are not granted for computer programs, although this may change in the near future. In the rest of the EU, the European Patent Convention prohibits the patenting of software programs, although it is possible to patent the function of the software.

Reverse engineering

Attempts to recreate the design of software or hardware by analysing the final product.

Reverse engineering represents one of the ways in which companies attempt to circumvent the restrictions imposed by copyright and patent legislation. Reverse engineering attempts to recreate the design of an item by analysing the final product. This can be compared to the 'black box' approach to systems analysis, where the outputs from the system are analysed in order to determine the inputs and processes involved.

Microprocessors compatible with Intel's range of Pentium processors are often created using reverse engineering methods. Typically, a team of developers is assembled and made to work in a 'clean room', that is, an environment where there is no access to information concerning the item to be reproduced. The development team is then given information concerning the functions performed by the processor to be duplicated and works to reproduce all of these functions. Since the developers have no access to the original processor and information concerning its operation, the new processor design cannot be claimed to be an identical copy. However, this does not necessarily mean that reverse engineering is considered an acceptable activity; this area continues to be a subject of legal controversy.

Registered designs

The aesthetic aspects of items such as clothing, furniture, electrical goods and jewellery can be protected by registering their designs. Registered designs can be thought of as similar to patents except that they deal only with the appearance of a given item.

Trade marks

A trade mark distinguishes a company's goods or services from those of its competitors. Intel's advertising campaigns featuring their Pentium processors are an excellent example of how a trade mark can help to establish a strong product or brand identity. As with patents and designs, trade marks can be protected by form-ally registering them.

Regulation of Investigatory Powers Act 2000

Although many people felt that the Regulation of Investigatory Powers Act 2000 – known as the RIP Act – would have a profound effect on business organisations, its impact has not been as serious as predicted. The Act introduced measures that allow electronic communications to be monitored by government agencies. In some circumstances, companies can be obliged to comply with requests to supply information considered confidential. Companies may also be required to provide agencies with the encryption keys they use, so that information can be decoded.

WEEE Directive

E-waste

Short for 'electronic waste' and refers to any electronic equipment disposed of by individuals and organisations.

The EU Waste Electrical and Electronic Equipment Directive deals with the safe and environmentally responsible disposal of electrical equipment, including computers and other common office technology. The Directive sets out targets for the collection, recycling and recovery of electrical equipment. While much of the responsibility for dealing with electronic waste, or e-waste, lies with manufacturers, all organisations have legal and moral responsibilities for the safe disposal of equipment that might cause harm to people or the environment.

Other legislation

We conclude this section by describing some of the other legislation that may have an impact on organisations and individuals working in the technology industry.

- The Human Rights Act 1998 provides UK citizens with a set of fundamental rights, including a right to privacy. The provisions made in the Human Rights Act are important since the principles described by the Act apply to the whole of the European Union.

- The Freedom of Information Act 2000 gives people the right to request any information held by a public authority, subject to a number of exemptions. The Act also requires public bodies to publish information on a routine basis. One of the benefits of the Act is that it sets out the rights of UK citizens in terms of personal privacy by distinguishing between personal and public life and by strengthening parts of the Data Protection Act. Although other legislation, such as the Human Rights Act 1998, deals with areas such as personal privacy, many people feel that the Freedom of Information Act will help to make government agencies and other organisations more accountable to the public since there is a statutory duty to meet requests for information.

- The Police Act 1997 was set up the National Criminal Intelligence Centre, a specialised police organisation charged with preventing and detecting computer-related crime. As with the RIP Act, this Act gives the police and other agencies the power to monitor communications. However, unlike the RIP Act, this Act has received a better welcome since it has been seen as less intrusive in terms of personal privacy.

- The Official Secrets Act 1911–1989 prevents individuals from disclosing any information related to national security. In addition, both individuals and organisations are required to take appropriate measures in order to prevent such information from being disclosed. This legislation is of particular importance to companies and individuals that work in areas related to defence.

- The Obscene Publications Act 1959 and the Protection of Children Act 1978 prohibit the publication of material considered pornographic or excessively violent. This legislation would deal with issues such as copying pornographic materials from the Internet.

- The Malicious Communications Act 1988 makes it an offence to send any message that might be considered obscene or threatening.

- The Defamation Act 1996 is concerned with slander and libel. This legislation extends to comments made in e-mail messages and material displayed on web sites.

- The Electronic Communications Act 2000 is intended to support the growth of e-commerce in the UK. Amongst other things, the Act serves to make electronic signatures legally binding and outlaws spam.

- In the wake of the 11 September terrorist attack on the United States, the Anti-terrorism, Crime and Security Act 2001 was introduced in the UK as a means of strengthening existing anti-terrorism legislation. Of particular importance to the IS industry is a requirement to make sure that certain companies retain data on consumers' Internet and telephone activities, and to make sure the data are searchable. As an example, guidelines from the Home Office suggest that ISPs should keep telephone subscriber and call information for twelve months, e-mail and ISP subscriber data for six months, and web activity information for four days.

Activity 17.4   Major points of the 2002 Regulations

Referring to a web site such as Out-Law (www.out-law.com) outline the major points of the Electronic Commerce (EC Directive) Regulations 2002.

FOCUS ON...   **SOFTWARE PIRACY**

Copyright theft, in the form of software piracy, continues to be one of the most common crimes associated with computer systems. This section considers software piracy from several perspectives with a view to improving understanding of this complex area.

Background

The recognition of software theft as a major problem to software companies and distributors can be traced back to the early 1980s. During this period, the personal computer 'boom' began with the launch of the original IBM personal computer in the United States and the launch of a series of inexpensive home computers by Sir Clive Sinclair in the UK. The sudden popularity of personal computers created a huge demand for software applications and resulted in the creation of thousands of small software companies around the world. However, as the number of applications increased, so too did incidences of illegal copying.

Prior to the widespread adoption of the CD-ROM, most software applications were distributed via floppy disk and magnetic tape. Programs distributed via magnetic media, such as the floppy disk, were relatively simple to copy since few software companies made use of copy protection methods. However, even the use of copy protection techniques did little to deter users. A number of companies existed that supplied various hardware and software items that could be used to circumvent common copy protection techniques. Such items were often sold as legitimate pro-ducts, for example special utility programs designed to help users to duplicate copy-protected software were often sold as legitimate backup utilities.

Copy protection

Methods that can be used to prevent unauthorised copies being made of a software package.

Dongle

A hardware device used to prevent unauthorised copies of a program being made. The hardware 'key' must be connected to the computer in order for the software to function.

Copy protection describes a number of methods that can be used to prevent unauthorised copies being made of a software package. The most common form of copy protection is the use of passwords and registration codes; unless the user possesses the correct registration information, the software will not function. It is worth noting that some software companies make use of hardware copy-protection devices. Specialised programs are sometimes supplied with a hardware key, often called a **dongle**. The hardware key must be connected to the computer in order for the software to function. This provides a highly effective, if inconvenient, means of preventing illegal copies of the program from being made.

As more sophisticated personal computers became available, the cost of software began to increase and the problem of software theft grew even greater. Many individuals saw an opportunity to profit by distributing counterfeit versions of popular programs. Organised groups began to sell counterfeit software through a number of different channels, for example via mail order. New programs were obtained through a variety of different methods. As an example, *cracking groups* were made up of users who gained satisfaction by defeating the copy protection methods used by software companies. Collections of programs where all copy protection had been disabled were created and sold on to others. In some cases, individuals imported software from countries without effective copyright legislation or where software theft was regarded as unimportant.

The advent of CD-ROM as a distribution medium in the early 1990s briefly obstructed the making of illegal copies. The sheer quantity of data held on a CD made it impractical for individuals to transfer data onto magnetic tape or floppy disk. In addition, the costs involved in duplicating large numbers of disks or tapes also served to hinder the activities of the organised groups. However, the introduction of inexpensive CD-recordable (CD-R) units reversed the situation by making it possible to store and distribute numerous applications on a single CD.

As DVD (digital versatile disc) units became widespread, the problem of software theft was expected to decline. This was because the DVD format offers a number of features designed to prevent illegal copying of software and data. However, as recordable DVD units have become more affordable, software piracy has started to grow once more.

The growth of software piracy

Business Software Alliance (BSA)

An organisation formed to act against software piracy.

Produced on behalf of the **Business Software Alliance (BSA)** and IDC Global Software, the annual 'Global Software Piracy Report' charts changes and trends in software piracy across the world.

The 2010 report (published in May 2011) provides a number of statistics that illustrate the severity of the problem of software piracy:

- Worldwide losses from software piracy were estimated at $58.8 billion in 2010 (up from $40 billion in 2006, $30 billion in 2003 and $12 billion in 1999).
- The highest losses due to software piracy in 2006 were attributed to the Asia Pacific region ($18.7 billion).
- In the UK, the piracy rate for 2010 was estimated at 27 per cent or $1.85 billion.

Table 17.1 illustrates selected software piracy rates by region.

Music piracy has become an important issue since the turn of the century with more than 1 billion counterfeit CDs being sold in 2002 and up to 1.7 billion discs in 2003 (IFPI, **www.ifpi.org**). However, the Internet has also become a distribution medium for music through P2P services such as BitTorrent and Gnutella. Some of the largest P2P services have more than 100 million active members and can allow thousands of transfers to take place

Table 17.1 Software piracy rates by region 2010

Region	Piracy rate (%)	Losses ($m)
North America	22	8,104
Western Europe	34	10,630
Asia Pacific	55	11,596
Middle East/Africa	60	1,997
Central/Eastern Europe	68	4,124
Latin America	66	3,125
European Union	36	11,003

Source: Based on data from Fourth Annual BSA and ISC Global Software Piracy Study, www.bsa.org.

simultaneously. Although a number of services have been shut down, others have quickly emerged to take their place.

A report from the IFPI (International Federation of the Phonographic Industry) found that 76 per cent of all music obtained online in the UK in 2010 was unlicensed. The report also cited research from April 2010 claiming that 89 per cent of all torrent files linked to illegal content. The report concluded that 'virtually all P2P content is illegal'.

In an attempt to tackle piracy, a number of companies have introduced services that allow people to download music legally in exchange for a small fee. Such services have become remarkably successful within a very short time. For instance, more than 2 million tracks were downloaded from the Apple iTunes service within the first 16 days of operation (BBC News, 16 May 2003). In February 2006, iTunes reported that it had sold one billion tracks since launch and that three million downloads were being recorded each day (PC Pro, March 2006). By 2010 the service reached 10 billion downloads and 3.75 million downloads a day (*Guardian*, 25 February 2010).

While sales of CDs are declining, figures from the IFPI show that the digital music market has grown by 1000 per cent between 2004 and 2010, reaching $4.6 billion in 2010. However, the IFPI's figures also show that overall the global music industry has declined by 31 per cent over the same period.

Over the past few years, concern has started to grow regarding movie piracy. As an example, the Motion Picture Association of America estimates that the annual losses due to movie piracy were $58 billion in 2010. The sheer scale of movie piracy can be illustrated with the example of *Avatar*, the highest grossing movie ever with worldwide box office sales of £1.8 billion. The most popular film of 2010 also became the most pirated film of 2010, with 16.5 million downloads recorded from just one file sharing site (BBC News, 22 December 2010).

Mini case study

Pirate Bay hacker jailed for two years

By Richard Milne, Nordic Correspondent

A founder of the infamous file-sharing website Pirate Bay has been sentenced to two years in jail for his part in one of the biggest hacking attacks to take place in Sweden.

Gottfrid Svartholm Warg was convicted of hacking into the computer system of Nordea, the Nordic region's biggest bank, and seeking to transfer several million Swedish krona electronically. He was also found guilty of gaining unauthorised access to the personal data for thousands of people from Sweden's population registry.

The 28-year-old was extradited last year from Cambodia back to Sweden to serve a prison sentence for copyright infringement.

A Swedish court this week also ruled he could be extradited to Denmark to face hacking charges there over attacks on various government databases, but it is now unclear when that might take place.

Pirate Bay shot to notoriety after being set up in 2003 by Svartholm Warg and three others.

It facilitated the download of popular films and music for free, and quickly surpassed Kazaa and Napster to become one of the biggest file-sharing sites.

But authorities around the world have renewed efforts to block such websites with US authorities last year closing Megaupload, another file-sharing service, and UK courts ordering internet providers to block Pirate Bay.

Sweden itself has repeatedly tried to shut down Pirate Bay, which has been forced to move from country to country and is now using a domain name registered in Sint Maarten, an island in the north-eastern Caribbean. It is still possible to download material from the site including, for instance, the current number one US album: Black Sabbath's 13.

In retaliation for the Swedish crackdown on internet piracy, hackers launched last October a concerted attack against Swedish government websites, forcing those for institutions such as the central bank, security services and prosecutors' office to be taken offline.

Sentencing the Pirate Bay founder yesterday, the Nacka district court, near Stockholm, said the hacking attacks have 'been very extensive and technically advanced. The attacker has affected very sensitive systems.'

Svartholm Warg, who denied the charges saying his own computer had been hacked, is likely to appeal, according to his lawyer. The court dismissed his argument that somebody else had performed the hacking from his computer.

The details of about 10,000 Swedes, held on the systems of IT company Logica, were published on the web after the attack.

Perspectives on software piracy

In this section, we consider software piracy from three perspectives: a typical end-user, software development companies and business organisations.

End-users

Although we refer to software packages in the following section, much of the material applies equally to music, movies and other digital products, such as ring tones.

On an individual basis, making illegal copies of computer programs, music and movies holds a number of attractions:

- Software packages can be acquired at a very low cost. After an initial outlay for any specialised software or hardware needed, users face only the ongoing costs of blank media.

- Many users collect software applications in order to trade with others or create a library of applications that can be used to support their activities. It is not unusual, for example, for a person interested in programming to acquire a collection of editors, compilers and interpreters.

- Many users consider software piracy a trivial offence; some even believe that making copies of software is perfectly legal. In truth, since software piracy is extremely widespread, individual users who make copies of programs for their own use are unlikely to be pursued by agencies such as FAST (the Federation against Software Theft). In the event that a user is caught in possession of illegal software, prosecution is unlikely because of the time and expense involved in taking legal action. However, in recent years FAST has pursued a number of high-profile prosecutions against individuals as a way of publicising the problem of software piracy and warning users of the risks they face.

- A significant minority of users produce and distribute illegal copies of software in order to generate an income that can be used to support their hobby. In many cases, the distribution of software is seen as a business venture and used as a source of revenue.

Federation against Software Theft (FAST)

An organisation formed to act against software piracy.

There are several common arguments put forward by individuals who advocate the copying of software and associated materials, such as manuals.

One argument suggests that software houses provide too little information concerning their products. Software houses and retailers are also seen as being reluctant to provide demonstrations or allow users to purchase products on a trial basis. These factors can sometimes mean that the software chosen for a particular task proves to be unsuitable. In some cases, the user may not be able to reclaim the cost of the software since retailers and manufacturers are sometimes reluctant to offer refunds. In view of these factors, many users feel that it is unfair to ask them to bear the full cost of a decision made on the incomplete or inaccurate information provided by the retailer or software house. Copying a given package, some argue, allows a full and careful evaluation to be made of the software. If it is felt that the package is appropriate to their needs, users are likely to purchase a genuine copy of the program in order to receive manuals, technical support and other benefits. On the other hand, if the software is considered unsuitable, the user will delete any copies made since they are of little or no value.

A second argument in favour of copying software involves the sometimes restrictive licence conditions adopted by software houses. When a user purchases a software package, they are merely buying the right to make use of the package for an unspecified period of time. In general, the software house retains ownership of the software, all accompanying documentation and the distribution medium itself. A licence agreement may also forbid users from making a backup copy of a package and the software may incorporate *copy protection* in order to prevent users from making copies. In addition, licence agreements often include statements that disclaim responsibility if the software does not function correctly or if the distribution media become damaged or corrupt. If the terms set out in the software licence agreement are broken, the user may be required to return all of the materials supplied at their own expense. Many users believe that they should have the right to safeguard their investment in a software package by making one or more backup copies. Such users will see the terms of the licence agreement as being unreasonable and will often disregard any clauses regarding backup copies.

A third argument concerns the pricing policies adopted by software companies. Some users argue that software companies have deliberately inflated their prices, placing some packages out of the reach of individuals and small companies. Copying software, it is argued, causes no harm to the software companies involved since the software would never have been purchased in the first place.

Software developers

Software companies make a number of powerful arguments against the copying of software.

Perhaps the simplest and most compelling argument made by software companies is that software is protected under international copyright laws. In most countries, the copying of software is regarded as theft and exposes the individual to both criminal and civil liability.

A second argument involves a defence of the pricing policies adopted by many software companies. The costs involved in the development of a sophisticated, comprehensive application program can be extremely high. The effort involved in developing an application is normally measured in terms of *labour hours*. A word processing program, for example, may take several years to develop and can involve the efforts of hundreds of staff. Such a program might require many millions of labour hours before it is released to the public. Since the cost of development must be recovered, it is reflected within the price of the application. In addition, the cost of the software also includes sums that support the continued development of the application and research into new products. Copying software, it is argued, reduces the revenues generated from the sale of the software and jeopardises new developments.

This leads to a related argument concerning the pricing of software. As incidences of illegal copying increase, software companies face a need to safeguard profit margins and recover development costs as quickly as possible. In order to do this, prices must be increased so that the losses made due to illegal copying can be recovered. In this way, it is argued, those that make illegal copies of software are directly responsible for the higher prices faced by legitimate customers.

Business organisations

The preceding sections should make clear some of the problems that face modern business organisations.

Smaller organisations, with limited budgets, are sometimes tempted to make additional copies of a given software package. As mentioned earlier, although the risk of detection is relatively low, the use of illegal software can lead to a number of repercussions. Some examples include:

- Organisations found in breach of copyright can suffer severe financial penalties. It is not uncommon for an organisation to be required to purchase licences for all illegal programs found on the company's premises. In addition, the company may face criminal or civil proceedings that result in significant fines.

- By encouraging employees to make use of illegal software, the company exposes itself to action from unions, employees and other parties. As an example, an employee accused of using illegal software in the course of their duties might take legal action against the employer. In addition, staff morale might be reduced, leading to productivity losses and labour disputes.

- Action taken by organisations such as the Business Software Alliance (BSA) often result in negative publicity for an organisation. This could have a major impact on relationships with customers and suppliers.

- The organisation's profitability can be damaged if it is deprived of the applications software needed to support day-to-day activities. In some companies, even a temporary disruption might lead to long-term effects. As an example, relationships with clients could be harmed if a sales organisation were unable to offer high levels of customer service.

It is worth noting that, as the size of the organisation increases, so too does the risk of detection and the severity of the possible consequences. Organisations such FAST and BSA, for example, encourage employees to report software piracy by their employers, sometimes offering a substantial reward for information leading to a successful prosecution.

Large organisations must also recognise a number of issues and responsibilities that influence the way in which they operate. A key issue facing many organisations is the need to reduce or eliminate the use of illegal software within their computer-based information systems. Only by taking an active stand against software piracy can a company gain a measure of protection against prosecution and the other losses outlined in this section. In addition, only such a stance can protect the company's reputation and industry status.

At the simplest level, an organisation seen to be making an effort to control how software is used in its computer systems is likely to be dealt with less severely than one that takes no action at all. However, such an approach can also lead to a number of other, somewhat more tangible benefits. Consider some of the benefits to be gained by using methods such as regular software audits in order to control which software applications are used by a company's computer-based information systems:

- In the UK and many other countries, an employer, ultimately the managing director, is held responsible for the actions taken by employees during the course of their work. In this way, the employer could be held jointly responsible if an employee uses illegal software with the company's computer-based information systems. The use of methods such as software audits can help to reduce instances where employees install or use illegal programs on the company's systems. In turn, this acts to reduce the risk of the company facing prosecution due to the employee's actions.

- By reducing the number of illegal or unauthorised programs used with the company's systems, employees can be encouraged to focus on their work more closely. Games and Internet browsers, for example, are well-known distractions that cost organisations many millions of labour hours each year.

- With a reduction in the use of unauthorised or illegal software also comes a reduction in the risk of infection by computer viruses and other malware. In turn, this decreases the costs and damage associated with removing infections.

- By preventing the use of unauthorised or illegal software, employees can be encouraged to adhere to organisational standards for the use of the company's computer-based information systems. This can provide a number of benefits related to the way in which the organisation produces, manages and makes use of its data. As an example, if only programs that have been approved by the organisation are used, then the accuracy of data can be maintained or improved.

Activity 17.5   **The ASP software model**

A new approach to the distribution of software may help to reduce levels of software piracy whilst ensuring that legitimate users gain benefits such as improved support and access to the very latest applications. Using the Internet as a resource, locate information related to application service providers (ASP) and answer the following questions.

1. How does this model of software distribution work?

2. What are the benefits of ASP to business organisations?

3. What are the benefits of ASP to software companies?

SUMMARY

1. Managers, developers and users of computer-based information systems are required to balance the needs of their employer and the requirements of their profession with other demands such as a responsibility to society.

2. Membership of a professional association brings with it the requirement to abide by a professional code of conduct. The code of conduct provides guidance related to the individual's legal, social and professional responsibilities.

3. An alternative view of the responsibilities of managers, developers and users involves considering some of their obligations to their employers, the public and the state. Conflicts of interest can arise from the need to serve the duties and responsibilities imposed upon the individual.

4. The impact of technology on personal privacy has manifested itself in many different ways. A contemporary issue related to personal privacy is the increase in the use of computer monitoring techniques. Computer monitoring can involve a wide variety of activities, from observing the behaviour of employees in the workplace to intercepting private e-mail messages.

5. Acts of computer crime can include theft of goods or services, software theft, data theft, damage to data or software, and hacking.

6. Some of the legislation relevant to those involved in managing or developing computer-based information systems include:

   ■ The Copyright, Designs and Patents Act 1988 provides limited protection for an organisation's intellectual properties. Such legislation also places a responsibility upon companies to ensure that they do not infringe the copyright of others, for example by making or using unauthorised copies of computer programs.
   ■ The Computer Misuse Act 1990 attempts to prevent unauthorised access to computer-based information systems. In addition, such legislation also makes it an offence to cause damage to hardware, software or data.
   ■ The Data Protection Act 1998 defines the way in which companies may gather, store, process and disclose personal data. In addition, the Act provides individuals with a number of rights allowing them to view or modify the personal data held on them.
   ■ The Human Rights Act 1998 has implications for personal privacy, including the privacy of employees.
   ■ The Regulation of Investigatory Powers Act 2000 has caused concern for many business organisations since, under certain circumstances, it allows confidential e-mail traffic and business data to be monitored by security forces.

7. Software developers see software piracy as a major threat to their business activities and the continued growth of the software industry. Business organisations face severe penalties unless they take an active stand against software piracy.

EXERCISES

Self-assessment exercises

1. Describe the offences are covered by the Computer Misuse Act 1990.

2. What is meant by computer monitoring?

3. What are eight guiding principles of the Data Protection Act?

4. What are the most common types of computer crime?

5. Identify the legislation that covers the following actions:

   (a) distributing a computer virus;
   (b) making an unauthorised copy of a computer program;
   (c) gaining unauthorised access to a computer-based information system;
   (d) vandalising computer hardware;
   (e) creating a computer virus;
   (f) placing an unauthorised computer program on a network system;
   (g) stealing a backup copy of a data file;
   (h) photocopying a software manual.

6. For each of the following acts, state whether or not they are permissible under the Computer Misuse Act 1990 or Data Protection Act 1998:

    (a) storing inaccurate or misleading personal data;
    (b) damaging data held on offline storage media;
    (c) electronic eavesdropping;
    (d) preventing access to personal data held in manual files, such as microfilm;
    (e) software piracy;
    (f) accidental damage to hardware, software or data;
    (g) disclosing personal data without the permission of the individual;
    (h) preventing access to personal data.

7. What is reverse engineering?

8. What is a professional code of conduct?

Discussion questions

1. You are given the responsibility of managing a technical project that may result in hundreds of job losses. Decide whether or not you should continue with the project and justify your decision on professional, moral and ethical grounds.

2. Do the security services and government departments have the right to monitor personal communications, such as e-mail messages? Justify your answer.

3. 'The cost of software applications leaves some users no choice but to make illegal copies.' Make a case in favour or against this argument.

4. Are file sharing services harming the music and entertainment industries? Consider services that allow people to download music legally, as well as services associated with music, video and software piracy.

5. Is there a digital divide?

Essay questions

1. Discuss changes in employment patterns brought about by increased levels of automation and the introduction of computer-based information systems.

2. What are some of the moral, ethical and professional issues faced by the managers of information systems? Illustrate your answer with relevant examples.

3. Using relevant examples, critically review the major pieces of legislation relevant to the ways in which organisations use computer-based information systems. Your discussion should refer to areas such as copyright, unauthorised access, the use of personal data and any other relevant issues.

Examination questions

1. The Data Protection Act 1988 regulates the ways in which organisations may gather, store, process and disclose personal information. You are required to:

    (a) describe the principles upon which the Act is based;
    (b) discuss some of the responsibilities placed on organisations by the Act;
    (c) critically evaluate the strengths and weaknesses of the Act in terms of the right given to individuals to view and amend any personal data held on them.

2. The ability of computer-based information systems to store, process and retrieve data quickly and efficiently raises concerns related to the privacy of individuals. You are required to:

   (a) explain the meaning of 'personal privacy';
   (b) describe some of the ways in which technology can allow an individual's personal privacy to be invaded
   (c) using relevant examples, discuss the moral and ethical issues involved in gathering, storing and making use of personal data.

3. Members of associations, such as the British Computer Society, are required to abide by a professional code of conduct.

   (a) describe the areas that a professional code of conduct is likely to include;
   (b) using relevant examples, discuss some of the ways in which a manager's ethical and professional responsibilities can conflict;
   (c) adopt a position in favour or against this argument: 'An individual's professional and legal obligations always take precedence over moral and ethical concerns' and justify your response.

References

Balduzzi, M., Platzer, C., Holz, T., Kirda, E. et al. (2010) 'Abusing social networks for automated user profiling', RAID'10 Proceedings of the 13th international conference on Recent advances in intrusion detection, 422–41, Springer-Verlag Berlin, Heidelberg

Clarke, R. (1988) 'Information technology and dataveillance', *Communications of the ACM*, 31, 5, 498–512

Johnson, D.G. (2003) *Computer Ethics*, 4th edition, Prentice-Hall, Englewood Cliffs, NJ

Kosinskia, M., Stillwella, D. and Graepelb, T. (2013) 'Private traits and attributes are predictable from digital records of human behavior', Proceedings of the National Academy of Sciences of the United States of America [online], 11 March. National Academy of Sciences. Available at: http://www.pnas.org/content/early/2013/03/06/1218772110?cited-by=yes&legid=pnas;1218772110v1#cited-by

Lane, R. (2011) 'The United Nations Says Broadband Is Basic Human Right', *Forbes* [online], 15 November. Available at: www.forbes.com/sites/randalllane/2011/11/15/the-united-nations-says-broadband-is-basic-human-right/

Parker, D.B. (1976) *Crime by Computer*, Charles Scribner's Sons, New York

Parliamentary Office of Science & Technology (2011) 'Cyber Security in the UK', POSTNOTE, 389, September

Schwartau, W. (1996) *Information Warfare*, 2nd edition, Thunder's Mouth Press, New York

Wood, D. (ed.) (2006) *A Report on the Surveillance Society*, Milton Keynes: Surveillance Studies Network. Available online at: www.ico.gov.uk/upload/documents/library/data_protection/practical_application/surveillance_society_full_report_2006.pdf

Further reading

Bocij, P. (2006) *The Dark Side of the Internet and How to Protect Your Family*, Praeger Press, Westport, CT

Capron, H. and Johnson, J. (2004) *Computers: Tools for an Information Age*, 8th edition, Prentice-Hall, Upper Saddle River, NJ. This book is very easy to read and the material is highly accessible. However, the material is a little lacking in depth, making it unsuitable for students working at a high level. Despite this, the book provides a useful reference for anyone having difficulty in grasping technical concepts and explanations related to hardware, software and other topics.

Furnell, S. (2002) *Cybercrime: Vandalizing the Information Society*, Addison-Wesley, Harlow. Although this book focuses on hackers, it covers a broad range of issues relavent to security, ethics and professional standards of behaviour.

Mitnick, K. and Simon, W. (2002) *The Art of Deception*, John Wiley, Indianapolis, IN. Mitnick's text focuses on 'social engineering' and offers detailed guidance on developing procedures to deal with this threat.

O'Brien, J. (2009) Management Information Systems, 9th edition, McGraw-Hill, Boston. Chapter 9 deals with security and ethics.

Power, R. (2000) *Tangled Web*, QUE, Indianapolis, IN. Although dated, this book is highly regarded by computer professionals and covers computer crime in great detail.

Room, S. (2007) *Data Protection and Compliance in Context*. Swindon: British Computer Society

Schwartau, W. (2000) *Cybershock: Surviving Hackers, Phreakers, Identity Thieves, Internet Terrorists and Weapons of Mass Disruption*, Thunder's Mouth Press, New York. Winn Schwartau's book covers a broad range of interesting ideas.

Spinello, R. and Tavani, H. (eds) (2001) *Readings in Cyberethics*, Jones & Bartlett, Sudbury, MA. This book is made up of a large collection of papers organised into a number of different sections. Although each paper tackles a slightly different topic, the collection as a whole provides comprehensive coverage of the legal, professional and ethical issues faced by modern managers. Chapter 3 covers intellectual property. Chapter 4 covers privacy and the Internet, including issues such as how data mining impacts on privacy. Chapter 5 focuses on security and the Internet. Chapter 6 covers ethical issues connected with the work of IS professionals.

Whitman, M. and Mattord, H. (2011) *Principles of Information Security*, 4th edition, Thomson Course Technology, Boston. Chapter 3 discusses legal, ethical and professional issues in depth.

Web links

www.bsa.org Business Software Alliance. Provides reports and information on international software piracy.

http://cyberethics.cbi.msstate.edu Good selection of resources on computer ethics, including case studies.

www.wired.com HotWired is the electronic sister of *Wired* magazine. It carries a range of popular articles and covers areas such as anonymity, freedom of speech and so on.

http://eserver.org/cyber/mainfram.html A body of articles and other materials covering a wide range of issues related to privacy, software theft, hacking and other issues.

http://library.thinkquest.org/26658 An interactive guide to computer ethics. A little simplistic, but offers a good introduction to this area and provides links to other resources.

www.infosyssec.org/infosyssec/compcrim1.htm Information Systems Security provides a huge array of links and resources related to computer ethics.

www.gilc.org/privacy/survey Information on privacy legislation around the world.

www.hmso.gov.uk The full text of all the Acts is provided via a simple search.

Glossary

access control See *user validation*.

access time In terms of storage devices, the access time refers to the average time taken to locate a specific item of data. Access times are normally given in milliseconds, for example a typical hard disk drive might have an access time of 11 Ms.

active content Describes a method by which a browser can restrict access to WWW pages that have been rated for their content.

Active-X A programming language standard developed by Microsoft which permits complex and graphical customer applications to be written and then accessed from a web browser. An example might be a form for calculating interest on a loan. A competitor to Java.

actors People, software or other devices that interface with a system. See *use-case*.

ad clicks An IFABC standard indicating the number of audited occasions a web banner or interstitial has been clicked on by a user to view an advert.

adaptive system In general, an adaptive system has the ability to monitor and regulate its own performance. In many cases, an adaptive system will be able to respond fully to changes in its environment by modifying its behaviour.

address book A folder that contains frequently used email addresses. Rather than identifying other users by their email addresses, individuals or groups can be given aliases or nicknames. Email addressed to an alias is automatically sent to the user(s) associated with that name.

adoption levels The proportion of the population or businesses that have access to the Internet, are influenced by it or purchase using it.

agent The term 'agent' is used to describe a specialised program that automatically searches the Internet for information meeting a user's requirements.

alias The process of sending email messages to specific individuals or groups of users can be simplified by making use of aliases. An alias – sometimes known as a 'nickname' – usually consists of a description and the email addresses of those grouped under the alias.

alpha release and alpha testing Alpha releases are preliminary versions of the software released early in the build process. They usually have the majority of the functionality of the system in place, but may suffer from extensive bugs. The purpose of 'alpha testing' is to identify these bugs and any major problems with the functionality and usability of the software. Alpha testing is usually conducted by staff inside the organisation developing the software or by favoured customers.

analogue Analogue data is continuous in that an infinite number of values between two given points can be represented. As an example, the hands of a clock are able to represent every single possible time of the day.

annotation A note or message that can be attached to a document. Voice annotations are spoken messages that can be embedded within a document.

anti-virus An anti-virus is a benevolent virus program that copies itself to the boot sectors of unprotected floppy disks. If another virus attempts to overwrite the anti-virus, it displays a message on the screen warning the user of infection. See *computer virus*.

Apple Macintosh A family of personal computers produced by Apple Computers. Although less popular than IBM-compatible personal computers, the Apple Macintosh is widely used for professional desktop publishing applications, graphics and animation.

applets Small programs with limited functions typically running from within a web browser.

application service provider (ASP) A company that supplies software and services to a client organisation over a network, usually the Internet.

applications backlog An applications backlog occurs when the demand for new applications by users exceeds the capacity of the IS department or IS outsourcing company to develop them. Over a period of a year a large number of applications are in the queue of required new work.

applications generator An applications generator performs an action or creates a computer program based on a set of requirements given by the user. Many applications generators allow users to define a series of actions or requirements by arranging icons on a special design screen. The resulting design is then converted into a series of instructions or an executable program.

applications portfolio The range of different types of business information systems deployed within an organisation.

artificial intelligence (AI) Artificial intelligence (AI) methods attempt to make a computer system behave in the same way as a human being. One application for AI is in natural language processing, where users can communicate with a computer system using English-like statements.

assembly language Assembly language represented an attempt to simplify the process of creating computer programs. Symbols and abbreviations were used to create sequences of instructions. An assembler was used to translate a completed assembly language program into the machine code required by the computer.

asymmetric digital subscriber line (ADSL) A relatively new development in telecommunications, ADSL makes use of conventional telephone lines to provide extremely high data transmission rates.

asynchronous When collaborators send messages that can be accessed at a later time these are known as asynchronous. Asynchronous exchange occurs with email or discussion groups.

attributes of information quality A group of characteristics by which the quality of information can be assessed. These attributes are normally grouped into three categories: time, content and form. Examples of attributes of information quality include accuracy, reliability and timeliness.

audits This describes the process of monitoring an organisation's hardware and software resources. In general, audits are used as a deterrent against theft and the use of illegal software.

autoresponder This describes a program that automatically responds to incoming email messages by scanning for key words or phrases and returning an appropriate reply.

B

back door The back door is a section of program code that allows a user to circumvent security procedures in order to gain full access to an information system.

backbones High-speed communications links used to enable Internet communications across a country and internationally.

backup site A backup site houses a copy of the organisation's main data processing facilities, including hardware, software and up-to-date data files. In the event of an emergency, processing can be switched to the backup site almost immediately so that the organisation's work can continue.

balanced scorecard A framework for setting and monitoring business performance. Metrics are structured according to customer issues, internal efficiency measures, financial measures and innovation.

bandwidth The term 'bandwidth' is often used to describe how many pieces of data can be transmitted or received at one time by a given device. Bandwidth is usually expressed in hertz (Hz) or in bits or bytes per second.

banner A rectangular graphic displayed on a web page for the purposes of advertising. It is normally possible to perform a click-through to access further information. Banners may be static or animated.

bar code A bar code is a means of displaying a unique identification number as a series of thick and thin lines. The sequence and width of the lines in the bar code can be translated into a sequence of digits. Bar code numbers are normally produced according to a specific method. The Universal Product Code, for example, is a standard method for creating and using bar codes.

bar-code reader A bar-code reader measures the intensity of a light beam reflected from a printed bar code to identify the digits making up a unique identification number. The digits making up the identification number are also printed at the foot of the bar code. If a label containing a bar code becomes damaged or cannot be read for some other reason, it may still be possible to enter the identification number manually.

batch processing Data is 'post-processed' following collection, often at times when the workload on the system is lower. Batch processing usually occurs without user interaction as a 'background job'.

baud A simple means of measuring the performance of a modem or other device. Early modems operated at speeds of 1200 baud, the equivalent of approximately 100 characters per second. Data transmission rates can also be expressed in bits per second (bps). In general, the higher the baud rate or bps value, the faster and more efficient the device.

benchmarks This describes the process of testing the performance of computer equipment. Having carried out a series of benchmark tests, the results can be compared against similar items in order to make the best selection.

bespoke development An IS is developed 'from scratch' by an IS professional to suit the business requirements of the application.

beta release and beta testing Beta releases occur after alpha testing and have almost complete functionality and relatively few bugs. Beta testing will be conducted by a range of customers who are interested in evaluating the new software. The aim of beta testing is to identify bugs in the software before it is shipped to a range of customers.

big-bang changeover Immediate cutover when a new system becomes operational and operations transfer immediately from the previous system.

BIOS (basic input/output system) Housed in a memory chip on the computer's motherboard, the BIOS contains software that controls all of the computer's most basic activities. It is the BIOS that allows the keyboard, display, hard disk drives, serial ports and other devices to function. The BIOS is stored in ROM so that it is always available and cannot be accidentally damaged or erased.

bit A single binary digit representing a zero (0) or a 1.

bit-map image A bit-map image is made up of small dots (pixels) arranged in a grid. The finer the grid, the higher the resolution of the image.

bluetooth A common standard for wireless communications between devices such as laptop computers, PDAs and mobile phones.

bookmarks All web browsers allow users to maintain a directory of WWW sites. The directory will enable users to add, edit, delete and organise addresses in the form of bookmarks.

bot A computer that has been infected by a zombie program is sometimes referred to as a bot. See *botnet* and *zombie*.

botnet A group of zombie computers capable of being directed towards various tasks, such as launching denial-of-service attacks. See *zombie*.

bottom-up design The bottom-up approach to design starts with the design of individual modules, establishing their inputs and outputs, and then builds an overall design from these modules.

boundary This describes the interface between a system and its environment. Everything within the boundary forms part of the system, everything outside the boundary forms part of the external environment.

brainstorming Uses the interaction between a group of staff to generate new ideas and discuss existing problems. It is the least structured of the fact-finding techniques.

brand abuse This describes a wide range of activities, ranging from the sale of counterfeit goods (e.g. software applications) to exploiting a well-known brand name for commercial gain.

British Computer Society (BCS) The British Computer Society is widely regarded as the UK's leading professional association for those involved the management and development of computer-based information systems.

broadband services Telecommunications services provided using a high-capacity transmissions network.

bubble jet printer A bubble jet printer works in similar manner to an inkjet printer, but transfers the character by melting the ink droplets onto the paper.

bug Software bugs are defects in a program which are caused by human error during programming or earlier in the lifecycle. They may result in major faults or may remain unidentified.

bulk emailer The use of mass email programs, called bulk emailers, enables an organisation to issue documents, such as questionnaires, at a fraction of the cost of traditional methods.

bus width Describes how many pieces of data can be transmitted or received at one time by the bus connecting the processor to other components of the PC.

Business Activity Monitoring (BAM) This is software designed to monitor, capture and analyse business performance data in real time and present them visually in order that rapid and effective decisions can be taken.

business-aligning IS strategy This IS strategy is used to support the business strategy.

business-impacting IS strategy This IS strategy is used to favourably impact the business strategy, perhaps by introducing new technologies.

business information systems This describes information systems used to support the functional areas of business. For example, an organisation might use specialised information systems to support sales, marketing and human resource management activities.

business intelligence (BI) software BI software is a general term used to describe analysis software which makes use of functions available in data warehouses, data marts and data mining.

business model A summary of how a company will generate revenue identifying its product offering, value-added services, revenue sources and target customers.

business process automation (BPA) Automating existing ways of working manually through information technology.

business process improvement (BPI) Optimising existing processes typically coupled with enhancements in information technology.

business process management (BPM) An approach supported by software tools intended to increase process efficiency by improving information flows between people as they perform business tasks.

business process re-engineering (BPR) Identifying and implementing radical new ways of carrying out work, often enabled by new IT capabilities.

business resource base The resources that a company has available to it are known collectively as the business resource base. The business resource base is made up of physical and conceptual resources (also known as 'tangible' and 'intangible' assets).

business rule A rule defines the actions that need to occur in a business when a particular situation arises. For example, a business rule may state that if a customer requests credit and they have a history of defaulting on payments, then credit will not be issued. A business rule is broken down into an event which triggers a rule with test conditions which result in defined actions.

Business Software Alliance (BSA) An organisation formed to act against software piracy. See *software theft*.

business-to-business (B2B) Commercial transactions that are between an organisation and other organisations.

business-to-consumer (B2C) Commercial transactions that are between an organisation and consumers.

buy-side e-commerce E-commerce transactions between a purchasing organisation and its supplier.

byte Made up of eight bits and represents the amount of space required to hold a single character.

C

cable modems These devices allow users to make use of the fibre-optic cables that have been installed in most major cities by cable television companies. Cable modems offer very high data transfer rates, up to a theoretical maximum of 30 Mbps.

cache (browser) In order to increase the speed and efficiency with which a web browser functions, a temporary storage space is used to store copies of any pages that the user has viewed. If the user returns to a given location, the web browser retrieves the required page from the temporary storage space (known as a cache), rather than transfer a fresh copy from a remote computer.

cache memory In a computer system, cache memory is used to improve performance by anticipating the data and instructions that will be needed by the processor. The required data are retrieved and held in the cache, ready to be transferred directly to the processor when required.

call centre An office which is devoted to answering telephone enquiries from customers; call centres are commonly used for financial services and retail customer support.

capacity loading graphs Capacity loading graphs show the resources required to undertake activities in a project.

CD-R (CD-recordable) This describes a variation on the traditional CD-ROM. CDR drives can not only read conventional compact discs but can also write data to special 'gold' discs. Compact discs produced in this way are known as 'write-once discs', that is, once data have been stored on the disc they cannot be altered or erased. See *CD-ROM*.

CD-ROM A computer storage device offering a relatively high capacity. The acronym CD-ROM stands for compact disc – read only memory, denoting the fact that CD-ROM discs are read-only devices; data cannot be written to a CD-ROM by a conventional player.

CDRW A more recent development in terms of compact disc storage is CD re-writable drives. In addition to providing the functionality of the CDR drive, the CDRW drive also allows the use of special compact disc media that can be written and erased many times. However, discs produced in this way are not compatible with standard CD-ROM drives and can only be used with a CDRW unit. See *CD-R* and *CD-ROM*.

central processing unit (CPU) This describes the microprocessor found in a computer system. The CPU controls all of the computer's main functions and enables users to execute programs or process data.

centralised IS management Centralised IS management will involve the control of all IS services from a central location, typically in a company head office or data-centre.

CGI (common gateway interface) CGI offers a way of providing interactivity through the web, with a form-type HTML document, a user type in information and structured information or queries sent using the web.

change (modification) requests A modification to the software thought to be necessary by the business users or developers.

changeover The term used to describe moving from the old information system to the new information system.

channels Channels (sometimes described as 'netcasting') enable users to subscribe to particular sites on the Internet, in much the same way that one might subscribe to a newspaper or magazine. The use of channels allows both the user and the information provider to select the information to be sent and schedule its transmission.

checksum digits A checksum involves the use of an extra digit for ensuring the validity of long code numbers. The checksum digit is calculated from an algorithm involving the numbers in the code and their modulus (by convention modulus 11).

chip theft Chip theft describes a relatively new phenomenon involving the removal of small but valuable components from computers, such as memory modules and processors.

Chromebook A laptop running the Chrome operating system which is primarily connected to the internet using applications residing in the cloud.

CISC A complex instruction set computer is a specific type of microprocessor which has a wide range of instructions to enable easy programming and efficient use of memory. CISC processors are best known as the Intel processors from 8086 to 80486 and the Motorola 68000 used in early Apple Macintoshes.

client/server The client/server architecture consists of client computers such as PCs sharing resources such as a database stored on a more powerful server computers. Processing can be shared between the clients and the servers.

client/server model This describes a system architecture in which end-user computers access data from more powerful server computers. Processing can be split in various ways between the server and client.

closed questions Closed questions have a restricted choice of answers such as Yes/No or a range of opinion on a scale from strongly agree to strongly disagree (Lickert scale). Approach is useful for quantitative analysis of results.

closed system No or limited interaction occurs with the environment.

code of conduct Members of professional associations, such as the British Computer Society, are expected to abide by a set of principles that set out minimum standards of competence, conduct and behaviour.

cognitive style This describes the way in which a manager absorbs information and reaches decisions. A manager's cognitive style will fall between analytical and intuitive styles.

comma-separated values (CSV) A CSV file is a simple text file made up of items enclosed within quotation marks and separated by commas. The use of commas and quotation marks enables a program reading the file to identify individual items.

command line interpreter (CLI) A CLI is used to pass instructions from a user to a computer program. The CLI accepts instructions from a user in the form of brief statements entered via the keyboard.

commercial languages This category of programming languages is intended to create applications that meet the basic information processing requirements of business organisations.

commoditisation The process whereby product selection becomes more dependent on price than differentiating features, benefits and value-added services.

compact disc (CD) This describes the media used by CD-ROM players. The data on a compact disc are encoded as a series of dips and raised areas. These two states represent binary data – the same number system used by microprocessors. The CD-ROM player shines a laser beam onto the surface of the disc and measures the light that is reflected back. The intensity of the light that is reflected back enables the player to distinguish individual binary digits. See *CD-ROM*.

competitive advantage In order to survive or expand, organisations must seek to gain dominance over their competitors in the marketplace. This can be achieved by using a variety of strategies to gain control of a market or prevent others from gaining control.

compiler The instructions that make up a computer program are often stored as a simple text file, usually called a 'source code file'. A compiler produces an executable program by converting instructions held as source code into machine language.

compound key In a relational database, it is possible to retrieve data from several tables at once by using record keys in combination, often known as a compound key. See *record key* and *primary key fields*.

computer-aided design (CAD) Provides interactive graphics that assist in the development of product and service designs. Connects to a database, allowing designs to be recalled and developed easily.

computer-aided manufacture (CAM) CAM involves the use of computers directly to control production equipment and indirectly to support manufacturing operations.

computer-aided software engineering (CASE) tools CASE tools are software which helps the systems analyst and designer in the analysis, design and build phases of a software project. They provide tools for drawing diagrams such as ERDs and storing information about processes, entities and attributes.

computer-based information system This describes an information system that makes use of information technology in order to create management information.

computer criminals In general, computer criminals are well-educated, white-collar workers who feel undervalued or bear some resentment against an employer or former employer. Computer criminals make use of technology to perform a variety of criminal acts, ranging from vandalism and sabotage to hacking and fraud.

Computer Misuse Act 1990 This legislation is intended to protect sensitive equipment and data from unauthorised access, alteration and damage.

computer monitoring The use of computer and communications technology to monitor the activities of individuals.

computer network A computer network can be defined as: 'a communications system that links two or more computers and peripheral devices and enables transfer of data between the components'.

computer output to microfilm (COM) COM, also known as computer output microfilm, is often used to archive large quantities of information for future reference. Information is processed via a personal computer and sent directly to a device that produces microfilm negatives.

computer system A computer system consists of a number of interrelated components that work together with the aim of converting data into information. In a computer system, processing is carried out electronically, usually with little or no intervention from a human user. The components of a computer system include hardware and software.

computer virus A computer virus is a computer program that is capable of self-replication, allowing it to spread from one 'infected' machine to another.

conceptual resources Conceptual resources are the non-physical resources owned by a company. Conceptual resources are also known as 'intangible assets'. Examples include knowledge, experience and judgement.

configuration management Procedures which define the process of building a version of the software from its constituent program files and data files.

constructive cost model (COCOMO) A model used to estimate the amount of effort required to complete a project on the basis of the estimated number of lines of program code.

contact manager This describes a software application that can be used to maintain lists of information relating to customers, suppliers and other important individuals or organisations.

content Content is the design, text and graphical information which forms a web page.

content dimension This describes several characteristics of information quality related to the scope and contents of the information. Amongst these characteristics are the accuracy, relevance and conciseness of information. As an example, information may be considered to be of high quality if it is accurate. Other dimensions of information characteristics include time and form. See *time dimension*, *form dimension*.

content management system (CMS) A software application intended to help users create and manage sophisticated web sites quickly, easily and without any technical knowledge.

context diagrams A simplified diagram which is useful for specifying the boundaries and scope of the system. They can be readily produced after the information flow diagram (IFD) since they are a simplified version of the IFD showing the external entities.

control mechanism If alterations are needed to the system, adjustments are made by some form of control mechanism. The function of a control mechanism is to ensure that the system is working to fulfil its objective.

Control Objectives for Information and related Technology (CobiT) This approach aims to achieve best practice in ensuring that the enterprise's information and related technology support its business objectives.

copy protection This describes a number of methods that can be used to prevent unauthorised copies being made of a software package.

Copyright, Designs and Patents Act 1988 Legislation that can be used to provide organisations and software developers with protection against unauthorised copying of designs, software, printed materials and other works.

core competencies Resources, including skills or technologies, that provide a particular benefit to customers.

cost of ownership The cost of ownership describes a range of different expenses incurred by purchasing and maintaining a computer system. Such costs include the original cost of the hardware and software, upgrades, maintenance, technical support and training.

cost per megabyte The cost per megabyte presents a simple means of gauging the costs associated with a given storage device.

cost per page The cost per page provides a simple means of determining the overall running costs of a given printer. The figures given usually refer to the costs of consumables such as ink and replacement components (toner cartridges, drums and so on).

countermediation Creation of a new intermediary by an established company.

coupling Defines how closely linked different subsystems are. 'Loose coupling' means that the modules pass only the minimum of information between them and do not share data and program code. 'Close-coupled systems' are highly dependent on each other.

CPM Cost for advertising is specified as CPM or cost per thousand page impressions.

cracker A person who gains access to an information system for malicious reasons is often termed a cracker rather than a hacker. This is because some people draw a distinction between 'ethical' hackers and malicious hackers.

critical path Activities on the critical path are termed 'critical activities'. Any delay in these activities will cause a delay in the project completion time.

critical path method (CPM) Critical path diagrams show the relationship between activities in a project.

critical success factors (CSFs) CSFs are measures which indicate the performance or efficiency of different parts of an organisation.

critical system See *safety-critical system*.

cross-licensing agreement Cross-licensing agreements allow companies to share patents so that each can produce and market a wider range of products. See *patent*.

customer relationship management (CRM) CRM involves a company in forming a long-term business relationship with its customers for mutual benefit. The essential aim of CRM is to improve customer service without harming company profitability. Typically, information technology is used to obtain and analyse information on customer behaviour. Such an analysis might result in various actions, such as improving the products and services offered to customers.

customer value Dependent on product quality, service quality, price and fulfilment time.

cybermall A single web site which gives online access to goods from a range of shops in a similar way to how physical shopping malls enable shoppers to make purchases in one location.

cyberslacking Making use of the Internet for personal reasons while at work.

cyberspace The prefix 'cyber' indicates a blurring in distinction between humans, machines and communications. Cyberspace is a synonym for Internet.

cybersquatting The act of registering an Internet domain with the intention of selling it for profit to an interested party. As an example, the name of a celebrity might be registered and then offered for sale at an extremely high price.

cyberstalking This refers to the use of the Internet as a means of harassing another individual. A related activity is known as corporate stalking, where an organisation uses its resources to harass individuals or business competitors.

cyberterrorism This describes attacks made on information systems that are motivated by political or religious beliefs.

D

daisywheel printer The daisywheel printer functions in much the same way as a conventional typewriter. Characters are mounted on hammers arranged in the shape of a wheel. The wheel is rotated until the correct character is in the correct position for printing. As one of the earliest forms of printing technology, daisywheel printers are considered slow and noisy. However, they are also considered inexpensive and reliable. It should be noted that daisywheel printers are unable to print graphics.

data Data can be described as a series of facts that have been obtained by observation or research and recorded.

data dictionary A repository which is used to store the details of the entities of the database. It will define tables, relations and field details which are sometimes referred to as 'metadata' or 'data about data'.

data entry form In an electronic database, a data entry form provides a convenient means of viewing, entering, editing and deleting records.

data marts These are small-scale data warehouses which do not hold information across an entire company, but rather focus on one department.

data migration Data migration is the transfer of data from the old system to the new system. When data are added to a database, this is known as 'populating the database'.

data mining This involves searching organisational databases in order to uncover hidden patterns or relationships in groups of data. Data mining software attempts to represent information in new ways so that previously unseen patterns or trends can be identified.

data modelling Data modelling involves considering how to represent data objects within a system, both logically and physically. The entity relationship diagram is used to model the data.

data process A process used to convert data into information. Examples include summarising, classifying and sorting.

data processing This describes the process of handling the large volumes of data that arise from an organisation's daily activities. Although data processing describes a wide range of activities, the most common are transaction processing and process control.

data processing (DP) department The data processing (DP) department was a term commonly used in the 1970s and 1980s to describe the functional area responsible for management of what is now referred to as 'information systems and applications development'. It is interesting to note that the term focuses on the processing of data rather than the application of information. The head of this department was referred to as DP manager rather than chief information officer or IS manager.

Data Protection Act 1984 This legislation sets out to define the rights of organisations and individuals in terms of how personal information is gathered, stored, processed and disclosed. One of the most important aspects of the Act is a focus on the individual's rights to view the information stored on them and ensure that it is accurate.

data theft Data theft can involve stealing sensitive information or making unauthorised changes to computer records. See also *software theft* and *theft*.

data transfer rate In terms of storage devices, the data transfer rate describes how quickly a device is able to read continuous blocks of data. This figure is normally expressed in terms of kilobytes or megabytes.

data validation Data validation is a process to ensure the quality of data by checking they have been entered correctly.

data warehouses Data warehouses are large database systems (often measured in gigabytes or terabytes) containing detailed company data on sales transactions which are analysed to assist in improving the marketing and financial performance of companies.

data views Different screens of an application which review information in a different form such as table, graph, report or map.

database A database can be defined as a collection of related information. The information held in the database is stored in an organised way so that specific items can be selected and retrieved quickly. See *database management system*.

database management system (DBMS) The information held in an electronic database is accessed via a database management system. A DBMS can be defined as one or more computer programs that allow users to enter, store, organise, manipulate and retrieve data from a database. For many users, the terms *database* and *database management system* are interchangeable. A *relational database management system (RDBMS)* is an extension of a DBMS and allows data to be combined from a variety of sources.

dataflow diagrams (DFD) Define the different processes in a system and the information which forms the input and output datastores to the processes. They may be drawn at different levels. Level 0 provides an overview of the system with levels 1 and 2 providing progressively more detail.

dataveillance The use of technology to automate the monitoring of individuals.

decentralised IS management Decentralised IS management involves management of some services in individual operating companies or at regional offices.

decision behaviour Describes the way in which people make decisions.

decision support systems Decision support systems provide managers with information needed to support semi-structured or unstructured decisions.

decision table A matrix showing all the alternative outcomes of different decisions which occur when certain input conditions occur.

decision tree A diagram showing the sequence of events, decisions and consequent actions that occur in a decision-making process.

deleting a file Deleting a file removes its details from the disk's directory structure and overwrites it with new data. This makes it virtually impossible to recover the file.

deletion anomaly It is not possible to delete a record from a relation without also losing some other information which might still be required.

denial of service (DoS) This is a form of attack on company information systems that involves flooding the company's Internet servers with huge amounts of traffic. Such attacks effectively halt all of the company's Internet activities until the problem is dealt with.

deployment plan A deployment plan is a schedule which defines all the tasks that need to occur in order for changeover to occur successfully. This includes putting in place all the infrastructure such as cabling and hardware.

desktop computer The desktop computer is intended for office use and supports the day-to-day activities of an organisation's employees. These machines tend to be placed in a fixed location and connected permanently to items such as printers, scanners and other devices. The desktop computer is the most common type of microcomputer and is found in the majority of organisations.

detailed design Detailed design involves the specification of how an individual component of a system will function in terms of its data input and output, user interface and security.

development programs Development programs allow users to develop their own software in order to carry out processing tasks.

dial-up networking (DUN) Dial-up networking software allows users to access a network at a remote location via a modem. Most home computer users, for example, access the Internet via dial-up networking.

dialogue An onscreen window (box) which is used by a user to input data or select options.

digital Digital data can only represent a finite number of discrete values. For example, at the most basic level, a computer recognises only the values 0 (zero) and 1. Any values *between* 0 and 1, for example 0.15, cannot be represented.

digital audio tape (DAT) A storage medium that combines some of the characteristics of magnetic tape and compact disc. Digital audio tape couples high storage capacities with improved speed and reliability.

digital camera A digital camera captures and stores still images in much the same way as a traditional camera. Images are held in the camera's memory or stored on disk until they can be transferred to a personal computer. The image is recorded using a charge-coupled device which recognises the different colours and intensity of light in the image.

digital certificates A method of ensuring privacy on the Internet. Certificates consist of a private key for encrypting data or documents and a corresponding public key for reading the data. An independent certification authority issues public and private keys. They are the basis for SET (Secure Electronic Transactions).

digital ID A digital ID provides a means of confirming the identity of a specific user through the use of a small data file called a 'personal certificate'. The certificate contains encrypted information relating to the user's identity.

digital versatile disc (DVD) Although superficially similar to Cd-ROM, DVD devices offer two important benefits to users. First, the discs used by a DVD player offer extremely high storage capacities, typically between 4 Gb and 7 Gb. Secondly, data held on DVD can be accessed at very high speeds. One of the most common applications for DVD is as a distribution medium for full-length feature films. See *CD-ROM*.

direct capture This describes a method of acquiring and storing data automatically with little or no human intervention. As an example, the sensors on an automated production line can be described as direct capture devices.

direct file access Random or direct file access allows any record to be read or written.

disaster recovery companies These maintain copies of important data on behalf of an organisation. They may also provide a service which can immediately supply replacement systems.

disintermediation The removal of intermediaries such as distributors or brokers that formerly linked a company to its customers.

document image processing (DIP) DIP systems are used in industry to convert printed documents into an electronic format so that they can be stored, organised and retrieved more easily.

documentation Software documentation refers to end-user guidance such as the user guide and technical maintenance documentation such as design and test specifications.

documentation review Uses information on existing systems such as user guides, or requirements specifications together with paper or on-screen forms used to collect information such as sales order forms.

domain name Refers to the name of the web server and is usually selected to be the same as the name of the company and the extension will indicate its type. The extension is also commonly known as the global top-level domain (gTLD), e.g. http://www.domain-name.extension/filename.htm.

dongle This describes a hardware device used to prevent unauthorised copies of a program being made. The hardware 'key' must be connected to the computer in order for the software to function.

dot-matrix printer The dot-matrix printer arranges a series of pins to form the shape of a required character. The character is transferred to the paper by striking the pins against an ink ribbon. The greater the number of pins used, the more detailed the character can be produced. As one of the earliest forms of printing technology, dot-matrix printers are considered slow and noisy. However, they are also considered inexpensive and reliable.

dot-pitch This describes a common method of gauging the quality of a monitor's display and involves measuring the distance – known as the dot-pitch – between the pixels on the screen. The smaller the distance between pixels, the finer the image will appear.

dots per inch (DPI) The quality of a printer's output is normally measured in dots per inch. This describes the number of individual dots that can be printed within a space of one square inch. Quality is normally compared against professional typesetting, such as the equipment used to produce a book or magazine.

duty cycle When referring to printers, this describes the typical monthly workload in terms of the number of pages printed.

dynamic systems development methodology (DSDM) A methodology which describes how RAD can be approached.

dynamic web page A page that is created in real time, often with reference to a database query, in response to a user request.

early adopter Early adopters are companies or departments that invest in new technologies when they first become available in an attempt to gain a competitive advantage despite the risk in deploying new systems.

economic feasibility An assessment of the costs and benefits of different solutions to select that which gives the best value. (Will the new system cost more than the expected benefits?)

editing The process of entering or correcting text is known as editing.

effort time Effort time is the total amount of work that needs to occur to complete a task.

EISA (Extended Industry Standard Architecture) This describes a common standard governing the way in which an expansion card interacts with a computer's motherboard and CPU. See *expansion card* and *motherboard*.

elapsed time Elapsed time indicates how long in time (such as calendar days) the task will take (duration).

electronic business (e-business) All electronically mediated information exchanges, both within an organisation and with external stakeholders, supporting the range of business processes.

electronic commerce Transactions of goods or services for which payment occurs over the Internet or other wide-area networks.

electronic data interchange (EDI) The electronic exchange of information between businesses using a wide-area network. EDI transactions transfer structured data such as an electronic payment and also documents.

electronic document management software (EDMS) Systems that convert documents into a digital format which allows storage, retrieval and manipulation of the document on computer.

electronic eavesdropping This describes the act of gaining access to confidential information by intercepting or monitoring communications traffic. See also *computer monitoring*.

electronic funds transfer Automated digital transmission of money between organisations and banks.

electronic mail (email) Email can be defined as the transmission of a message over a communications network.

electronic meeting systems This describes a category of office automation systems that seek to improve communications between individuals and groups. Examples of these systems include those that support teleconferencing, teleworking and groupwork. See *office automation systems*.

electronic publishing systems This describes a category of office automation systems that supports the production of documents, such as letters, reports and catalogues. Some of the typical programs used include word processors and desktop publishing packages. See *office automation systems*.

end-user computing (EUC) End-user computing includes all uses of computers by business people who are not information systems professionals. This may range from use of business applications through spreadsheet modelling to developing programs to solve specific problems.

end-user development (EUD) End-user development is programming undertaken by non-IS staff. It typically involves development of small applications for solving departmental problems rather than cross-departmental applications.

end-user IT services These include all services required to support end-users in running their PCs and applications.

enterprise application integration (EAI) The process of designing software to facilitate communications between business applications including data transfer and control.

environment This describes the surroundings of a system. The environment of a system can contain other systems and external agencies.

EPROM (erasable programmable read-only memory) This is a form of ROM that retains its contents until changed using a special device known as a 'burner'. See *read-only memory*.

erasing a file Erasing a file removes it from the disk's directory structure. This leaves the file essentially intact and can allow it to be recovered.

error rate In many cases, it may be acceptable if an input device generates a certain number of errors. This is often referred to as the error rate and the acceptable level will vary according to the input device being used and the business application. Optical character recognition, for example, is generally considered a comparatively unreliable means of entering data. At present, a typical OCR software package will have an error rate of between 5 and 10 per cent.

errors per KLOC Errors per KLOC (thousands of line of code) is the basic defect measure used in systems development.

estimation Estimation allows the project manager to plan for the resources required for project execution through establishing the number and size of tasks that need to be completed in the project.

e-tailing The use of the Internet by manufacturers to sell goods directly to customers.

ethics In general terms, ethics describes beliefs concerning right and wrong that can be used by individuals to guide their behaviour. See *morality* and *professionalism*.

executive information systems These systems are used by senior management to select, retrieve and manage information that can be used to support the achievement of an organisation's business objectives. They need not be directly concerned with decision-making activities, but can help senior managers to become more efficient and productive in a number of other ways, for example by helping them to manage their time more efficiently.

expansion card Expansion cards can be used to extend a computer's capabilities by adding new devices to the system. An expansion card usually takes the form of a small circuit board that can be inserted into an expansion slot on the computer's motherboard. Some examples of expansion cards include modems, graphics cards and sound cards.

expert systems Expert systems are used to represent the knowledge decision-making skills of specialists so that non-specialists can take decisions. They encapsulate the knowledge of experts by providing tools for the acqusition of knowledge and representation of rules and their enactment as decisions.

explicit knowledge Knowledge that can be readily expressed and recorded within information systems.

export The process of saving a file in a format compatible with another software package is known as exporting.

extensible markup language See *XML*.

extranet An intranet with restricted access which is extended to suppliers, collaborators or customers.

fax-modem A fax-modem combines the capabilities of a modem with the ability to send and receive fax transmissions.

fax-on-demand A service that allows users to select from a range of documents by using the keys on the telephone handset. Once a document has been selected, the system automatically telephones the user's fax machine and transmits the document.

feasibility study This is the activity that occurs at the start of the project to ensure that the project is a viable business proposition. The feasibility report analyses the need for and impact of the system and considers different alternatives for acquiring software. Input: Idea for initiation of a new information system. Output: Feasibility report and recommendation to proceed.

Federation against Software Theft (FAST) An organisation formed to act against software piracy. See *software theft*.

feedback control In feedback closed-loop control systems the control loop compares the output of the process to the desired output and if a difference is found, adjusts the input or process accordingly.

feedback mechanism This provides information on the performance of a system. An example of feedback might include quality control measurements taken on a production line.

feedforward control Feedforward incorporates a prediction element in the control feedback loop.

field The data in an electronic database is organised by fields and records. A field is a single item of information, such as a name or a quantity.

file attachment Email messages can be used to transmit data files to other users. Files can be attached to messages and transmitted in the usual way. All types of data can be sent in this way including word processor files, spreadsheet data, graphics and database files.

filter In a spreadsheet or database, a filter can be used to remove data from the screen temporarily. This allows users to work with a specific group of records. Filters do not alter or delete data but simply hide any unwanted items.

financial EDI Aspect of electronic payment mechanism involving transfer of funds from the bank of a buyer to a seller.

firewall This is a specialised software application mounted on a server at the point the company is connected to the Internet. Its purpose is to prevent unauthorised access into the company from outsiders. Firewalls are essential for all companies hosting their own web server.

firewire A common standard for wireless communications between devices that require very high data transfer speeds, such as digital video equipment and external hard disks.

first normal form (1NF) Transforming unnormalised data into its first normal form state involves the removal of repeating groups of data.

flat file database A flat file database can be described as being self-contained since it contains only one type of record – or table – and cannot access data held in other database files.

flexible manufacturing systems (FMS) A group of machines with programmable controllers linked by an automated materials handling system and integrated by an IS that enables a variety of parts with similar processing requirements to be manufactured.

floppy disk Consists of a plastic disk, coated with a magnetic covering and enclosed within a rigid plastic case.

font The typeface used in a document is referred to as the font. The size of the characters used is referred to as the 'point size'.

foreign (secondary) key fields These fields are used to link tables together by referring to the primary key in another database table.

form An on-screen equivalent of a paper form which is used for entering data and will have validation routines to help improve the accuracy of the entered data.

form dimension This describes several characteristics of information quality related to how the information is presented to the recipient. Amongst these characteristics are clarity, level of detail and the order of information. As an example, information may be considered to be of high quality if it is presented in a clear and consistent fashion (clarity). Other dimensions of information characteristics include time and content. See *time dimension* and *content dimension*.

formal communication Formal communication involves presenting information in a structured and consistent manner. Such information is normally created for a specific purpose, making it likely to be more comprehensive, accurate and relevant than information transmitted using information communication. An example of formal communication is an accounting statement. See *informal communication*.

formula In a spreadsheet, a formula is a calculation that is entered by the user and performed automatically by the spreadsheet program.

free-form database A free-form database allows users to store information in the form of brief notes or passages of text. Each item held can be placed within a category or assigned one or more key words. Information is organised and retrieved by using categories or key words.

FTP file transfer The file transfer protocol is used as a standard for moving files across the Internet. The most common use is for releasing fixes to software applications. Documents can be transferred by this means. FTP is available as a feature of web browsers for downloading files.

full backup A method of producing backup copies of important data files. A full backup includes all data files considered to be important. See also *incremental backup*.

function In a spreadsheet, a function is a built-in command that carries out a calculation or action automatically.

function point analysis A method of estimating the time it will take to build a system by counting up the number of functions and data inputs and outputs and then comparing to completed projects.

functional testing Testing of particular functions or modules either following a test script or working through the module systematically.

functionality A term used to describe whether software has the features necessary to support the business requirements.

G

Gantt charts Show the duration of parallel and sequential activities in a project as horizontal bars on a chart.

GPRS (General Packet Radio Service)

Geographical Information System (GIS) Uses maps to display information about different geographic locations such as catchment areas or branches. They are commonly used for performance analysis by marketing staff.

GIF (graphics interchange format) A graphics format and compression algorithm best used for simple graphics.

gigabyte (Gb) A measure of storage capacity. Approximately 1000 Mb, or the equivalent of one billion characters.

global business The global business is a company that operates in several countries and uses information technology to assist in the control of operation and performance in each country.

goal seeking In a spreadsheet, goal seeking describes a way of automatically changing the values in a formula until a desired result is achieved.

grandfather, father, son A common procedure used for creating backup copies of important data files.

graphical user interface (GUI) A graphical user interface allows the user to control the operation of a computer program or item of computer hardware using a pointing device, such as a mouse. In general, commands are issued by selecting items from menus, buttons and icons.

graphics accelerator card A type of graphics card containing its own memory and featuring a coprocessor. The coprocessor reduces the burden placed on the CPU by taking over the intensive calculations needed to produce complex graphical displays.

graphics tablet A graphics tablet is used in the same way as a writing pad. A stylus is used to draw images on a rigid pad located near to the computer. As the user draws with the stylus, the image is duplicated on the computer's display.

green computing Adopting policies and procedures to ensure resources are used as efficiently as possible so that environmental impact is minimised.

groupware Software which enables information and decision making to be shared by people collaborating within and between businesses.

H

hacker Hackers are often described as individuals who seek to break into systems as a test of their abilities. Few hackers attempt to cause damage to systems they access and few are interested in gaining any sort of financial profit.

hard data See *quantitative data*.

hard disk A magnetic medium that stores data upon a number of rigid platters that are rotated at very high speeds.

hardware Describes the physical components of a computer system. The hardware of a computer system can be said to comprise: input devices, memory, central processing unit, output devices and storage devices.

hierarchical systems Systems that are hierarchical in nature, being made up of subsystems that may themselves be made up of other subsystems.

hierarchy of strategies Sub-strategies developed to help achieve corporate objectives.

hits A measure of individual files delivered to the browser when requesting a URL. Hits usually overstate access to a web page. Page-impressions and ad-impressions are more accurate.

hot plugging This describes the ability to add or remove new devices whilst the computer is running and have the operating system automatically recognise any changes made.

hot spots A geographical area with a signal to allow wireless connection to the internet.

HTML (hypertext markup language) HTML is the method used to create web pages and documents. The HTML code used to construct pages has codes or tags such as to indicate to the browser what is displayed.

human activity system A human activity system can be defined as a 'notional system (i.e. not existing in any tangible form) where human beings are undertaking some activities that achieve some purpose'.

human–computer interaction (HCI) design HCI involves the study of methods for designing the input and output of information systems to ensure they are 'user-friendly'.

hybrid disk drive Storage devices that combine solid-state drive (SSD) with hard disk drive (HDD) technology.

hyperlink A link from a hypertext document to another location, activated by clicking on a highlighted word or image.

hypertext Hypertext is highlighted words or phrases that represent links to other documents activated by clicking the mouse.

hypertext database In a hypertext database information is stored as series of objects and can consist of text, graphics, numerical data and multimedia data. Any object can be linked to any other, allowing users to store disparate information in an organised manner.

IBM-compatible The modern personal computer found in most business organisations developed from a family of personal computers launched by IBM in the early 1980s. The IBM-compatible computer is considered the standard for general business use.

If Then Else statements These are common within programs since they govern the different actions taken by the program according to a condition. They are usually in the form:

    IF Condition Then.
    Action if condition is TRUE
    Else.
    Action if condition is FALSE
    End If.

image processing systems This describes a category of office automation systems that allows users to create, edit, store and retrieve documents in electronic format. Document image processing (DIP) is an example of an image processing system. See *office automation systems*.

immediate cutover (big-bang) changeover Immediate cutover is when a new system becomes operational and operations transfer immediately from the previous system.

import The process of loading a file created with another package is known as importing.

incremental backup A method of producing backup copies of important data files. An incremental backup includes only those files that have changed in some way since the last backup was made. See *full backup*.

index In an electronic database, an index stores information concerning the order of the records in he database. The index lists the locations of records but does not alter the actual order of the database.

informal communication This describes information that is transmitted by informal means, such as casual conversations between members of staff. The information transmitted in this way is often less structured and less detailed than information transmitted by formal communication. In addition, the information may be inconsistent or may contain inaccuracies. Furthermore, the information may also include a subjective element, such as personal opinions. See *formal communication*.

information Data that have been processed so that they are meaningful.

information centre (IC) An IC is a central facility in an organisation which provides end-user services such as phone support for trouble-shooting end-user software and hardware problems, training, guidance on end-user development and management of user information.

information flow diagram (IFD) A simple diagram showing how information is routed between different parts of an organisation. It has an information focus rather than a process focus.

information kiosk A multimedia system usually integrated with a touch screen to provide information for retail or community applications such as libraries or local government is known as an information kiosk.

information leadership Information leadership involves enhancing a product or service with an organisation's specialised information or expertise. In many cases, organisations achieve information leadership by selling information or expertise in the form of a separate product. A good example might be selling a mailing list created from an organisation's customer database.

information need The object of producing information is to meet a specific purpose or requirement.

information reporting systems These systems are used to generate reports containing information that can be used to support managerial decision making.

information society The information society is a term that has been coined to describe a modern population that is conversant with – and reliant upon – information and communications technology.

information system This describes a system designed to produce information that can be used to support the activities of managers and other workers.

information systems acquisition Acquisition describes the method of obtaining an information system for a business. The main choices are off-the-shelf (packaged), bespoke applications developed by an in-house IT department or a software house, and end-user-developed systems.

information systems strategy Determination of the most appropriate processes and resources to ensure that information provision supports business strategy.

information technology strategy Determination of the most appropriate technological infrastructure comprising hardware, networks and software applications.

information warrior Information warriors seek to obtain data by any means necessary. Such people may resort to illegal methods, such as hacking, in order to obtain the information they require. However, the information obtained may not necessarily be used in pursuit of criminal activities.

initiation phase The startup phase in an IS development project. Its aims are to establish whether the project is feasible and then prepare to ensure the project is successful. Input: Creative thought and/or systematic evaluation of IS needs. Output: Idea for initiation of a new information system.

inkjet printer An inkjet printer uses a print-head containing 50 or more small nozzles. Each nozzle can be controlled individually by electrostatic charges produced by the printer. Characters are formed by squirting small droplets of directly onto the paper. Inkjets are considered relatively inexpensive, near-silent in operation and capable of producing good-quality results. It should be noted that inkjet printers also represent an economical means of printing in colour.

input The input to a system can be thought of as the raw materials for a process that will produce a particular output. Examples of inputs might include data, knowledge, raw materials, machinery and premises.

input design Input design includes the design of user input through on-screen forms, but also other methods of data entry such as import by file, transfer from another system or specialised data capture methods such as bar-code scanning and optical or voice recognition techniques.

input device Input devices are used to enter data, information or instructions into a computer-based information system.

insertion anomaly It is not possible to insert a new occurrence record into a relation (table) without having to also insert one into another relation first.

intangible assets Intangible assets describe the non-physical resources owned by a company. Intangible assets are also known as 'conceptual resources'. Examples include knowledge, experience and judgement.

intangible value A value or benefit that is difficult or impossible to quantify.

intellectual property Intellectual property is a generic term used to describe designs, ideas and inventions. In general, intellectual property covers the following areas: patents, trade marks, designs and copyright.

intelligent agent An intelligent agent is a semi-autonomous computer program capable of carrying out one or more tasks specified by the user. You can think of an intelligent agent as a software 'robot' capable of being programmed to carry out a wide variety of tasks.

interactive kiosk A typical application for touch screen systems, an interactive kiosk allows a user to purchase items or browse through a list of products by pressing buttons or other controls shown on the screen. Such kiosks are often found in banks, music stores and large catalogue stores. Many bookings systems, such as those used by airlines, theatres and travel agents, also make use of touch screens. See *touch screen*.

interdependence Interdependence means that a change to one part of a system leads to or results from changes to one or more other parts.

interface In terms of systems, the interface describes the exchanges between a system and its environment or between the system and other systems. In the field of information technology, the interface describes ways in which information is exchanged between users and computer software or hardware.

interlaced An interlaced display is one where each complete image shown on a monitor's display is drawn in two steps. A non-interlaced monitor refreshes the display in a single pass. A good-quality monitor is normally capable of supporting a non-interlaced display at a refresh rate of 70 Hz or more.

internal rate of return (IRR) A discounted cashflow technique used to assess the return of a project by considering the interest rate which would produce an NPV of zero.

Internet The Internet refers to the physical network that links computers across the globe. It consists of the infrastructure of servers and communication links between them which is used to hold and transport the vast amount of information on the Internet.

Internet economy This encompasses all of the activities involved in using the Internet for commerce.

Internet EDI Use of EDI data standards delivered across non-proprietary Internet protocol networks.

Internet pure-play A company trading online that has limited or no physical presence such as retail units.

Internet relay chat (IRC) This is a synchronous communications tool which allows a text-based 'chat' between different users who are logged on at the same time. It is not used for many business applications since asynchronous discussions are more practical – not all team members need to be present at the same time.

Internet service providers (ISPs) Companies which provide access to the Internet and web page hosting for home and business users. Online service providers give access to the Internet plus their own content.

interoperability A general term used to describe how easily different components of a system can be integrated.

interpreted An interpreted computer program can be run directly, without the need for compilation. As the program runs, each instruction is taken in turn and converted into machine language by a command interpreter.

interstitial A small, rectangular area within a web page used for advertising. May be animated or static.

interviewing Recommended practice: a range of staff are interviewed using structured techniques to identify features and problems of the current system and required features of the future system.

intranet An intranet uses web servers, browsers and email within a company to share company information and software applications. The intranet is only accessible to company employees.

IP address The unique numerical address of a computer.

ISA (Industry Standard Architecture) This describes a common standard governing the way in which an expansion card interacts with a computer's motherboard and CPU. See *expansion card* and *motherboard*.

ISDN (integrated services digital network) ISDN represents a standard for communications that allows data transfer rates that are up to five times faster than a 56,600 bps modem. An ISDN telephone line provides two separate 'channels' allowing simultaneous voice and data transmissions. Since ISDN lines transmit digital data, a modem is not required to make use of the service. Instead, a special terminal adapter (often called an 'ISDN modem') is used to pass data between the computer and the ISDN line. See *modem* and *baud*.

J

Java An object-orientated programming language standard supported by Sun Microsystems which permits complex and graphical customer applications to be written and then accessed from a web browser. An example might be a form for calculating interest on a loan. A competitor to Active-X.

Javascript A simple scripting programming language, which offers a subset of the features of the Java programming language.

JPEG (joint photographics experts group) A graphics format and compression algorithm best used for photographs.

justification In a word processor, the alignment of text with the left and right margins can be controlled by specifying the justification. Text can be left-justified, right-justified or fully justified.

K

kilobyte (kb) A measure of storage capacity. Approximately 1000 bytes, or the equivalent of 1000 characters.

knowledge Knowledge can be thought of as the combined result of a person's experiences and the information they possess. See *explicit knowledge* and *tacit knowledge*.

knowledge management Techniques and tools for collecting, managing and disseminating knowledge within an organisation.

L

label printers These are small units specifically designed to print on rolls of self-adhesive labels. Although various kinds of label printer exist, one of the most common types is used for printing bar codes.

laser printer The laser printer is commonly used for business applications requiring a combination of speed with high print quality.

legacy system When a new computer-based information system is developed, it may be necessary to retain hardware – but more often software – from the earlier system. In these cases, the software that has been retained is referred to as a legacy system.

leverage A way of increasing returns without increasing investment, usually by maximising the use of existing resources.

lightpen A lightpen is a pointing device that can be used to control applications by pointing to items on the screen. Lightpens are also used for applications involving graphics, such as drawing packages, since images can be drawn directly onto the screen. See *pointing device*.

line printer A line printer processes a document one line at a time. In contrast, a page printer processes a document one entire page at a time.

live (production) environment The term used to described the setup of the system (hardware, software and office environment) where the software will be used in the business.

local-area network (LAN) This is a computer network that spans a limited geographic area, typically a single office or building. It consists of a single network segment or several connected segments which are limited in extent.

logic bomb Sometimes also known as a 'time bomb', a logic bomb is a destructive computer program that activates at a certain time or in reaction to a specific event.

low-level language A low-level programming language requires the programmer to work directly with the hardware of the computer system. Instructions are normally entered in machine code or assembly language.

M

machine language This describes the natural language of a computer. Machine language instructions are made up of binary digits and use only the values of 0 (zero) and 1.

machine-orientated A machine-orientated programming language focuses on the requirements of the computer hardware being used, where programs are produced in a form that suits the way in which the microprocessor functions.

macro A macro is a sequence of instructions that can be used to automate complex or repetitive tasks. Macros can be used to emulate a sequence of keys pressed on the keyboard or can be programmed so that they can carry out more complicated processes.

macro-environment Wider environment of social, legal, economic, political and technological influences.

magnetic ink character recognition (MICR) This involves capturing data that have been printed using a special magnetic ink. This technology is normally associated with the banking industry, especially cheque processing. Some of the details on a cheque, such as the cheque number, are printed in a special typeface using magnetic ink. The shape of each character means that it can be recognised by its magnetic field.

mainframe A traditional view of computing saw three main categories of computers: mainframes, minicomputers and microcomputers. Mainframes were considered the most powerful computers and were used for large-scale data processing.

management information systems These systems provide feedback on organisational activities and help to support managerial decision making.

materials requirements planning (MRP) software MRP software is used to plan the production of goods in a manufacturing organisation by obtaining components, scheduling operations and controlling production. MRP II integrates the information system with other functional areas in the business such as finance and marketing.

McFarlan's strategic grid This model is used to indicate the strategic importance of information systems to a company now and in the future.

M-commerce Describes selling goods or services via wireless technology, especially mobile phones and PDAs.

media centre A computer designed specifically for entertainment. Media centres usually have a remote control and are constructed using a special case that features a digital display.

megabyte (Mb) A measure of storage capacity. Approximately 1000 kb, or the equivalent of one million characters.

megapixel A measurement that is often used to describe the quality of the image captured by a digital camera. A megapixel represents one million individual picture elements – the dots that make up an image. Early digital cameras produced images at a quality of 0.5 megapixel. modern devices can produce images at a quality of 3.5 megapixels or higher.

memory Computer memory is used as a temporary means of storing data and instructions. Memory is used to store data awaiting processing, instructions used to process data or control the computer system, and data or information that has been processed.

metadata Reference data describing the structure and content of data in a data warehouse are known as metadata.

metropolitan area network (MAN) A network covering a city or university campus.

metropolitan ethernet A network covering a metropolitan area based on the ethernet standard.

microcomputer A traditional view of computing saw three main categories of computers: mainframes, minicomputers and microcomputers. Microcomputers were considered less powerful than other types of computer but were more flexible and relatively inexpensive to purchase.

micro-environment Immediate environment including customers, competitors, suppliers and distributors.

middleware A type of software that acts as a layer between other software to facilitate communications between business applications including control and data transfer between incompatible systems.

milestone This denotes a significant event in the project such as completion of a prototype.

minicomputer A traditional view of computing saw three main categories of computers: mainframes, minicomputers and microcomputers. Minicomputers offered an intermediate stage between the power of mainframe systems and the relatively low cost of microcomputer systems.

mission statement A statement intended to encapsulate the overall goal(s) of an organisation.

modelling Modelling involves creating a numerical representation of an *existing* situation or set of circumstances, whilst simulation involves *predicting* new situations or circumstances. In both cases, a model is produced that provides a numerical representation of the situation or circumstances being studied. Modelling and simulation are common activities carried out with the use of spreadsheet software. See *spreadsheet*.

modem (modulator–demodulator) A modem is a communications device that allows users to send and receive data via an ordinary telephone line. See also *fax-modem*.

module design Detailed design involves the specification of how an individual component of a system will function in terms of its data input and output, user interface and security.

module or unit testing Individual modules are tested to ensure they function correctly for given inputs.

monitoring and control Monitoring involves ensuring the project is working to plan once it is started. Control is taking corrective action if the project deviates from the plan.

morality In general terms, morality is concerned with individual character or personality and beliefs governing right and wrong. See *ethics* and *professionalism*.

motherboard The motherboard is the main circuit board within a computer and houses the processor, memory, expansion slots and a number of connectors used for attaching additional devices, such as a hard disk drive.

mouse A pointing device found on most modern personal computers. Moving the mouse over a flat surface causes a corresponding movement to a small pointer on the screen. Selections, such as menu items, are made by clicking one of the buttons on the mouse. See *pointing device*.

multi-core processor The latest CPUs combine two or more cores (processors) within a single physical device.

multidimensional data Data broken down in analysis for a data warehouse into dimensions such as time period, product segment and the geographical location. Dimensions are broken down into categories. For time these could be months, quarters or years.

multimedia Multimedia can be defined as the combination of several media under the control of an interactive computer program. Such media can include text, graphics, sound, video and animation. In terms of computer hardware, a multimedia computer will incorporate a CD-ROM drive and sound card. In addition, current standards for multimedia computers specify minimum graphics capabilities and processor speed.

multi-user testing The effect of different users accessing the same customer or stock record is tested. Software should not permit two users to modify the same data at the same time.

natural keyboard A variation on the conventional computer keyboard, a natural keyboard has the keys arranged so that users can locate them more quickly and easily. The keyboard itself is often shaped in a way that makes prolonged use more comfortable.

navigating The act of moving from one section of the Internet to another.

net PC A hybrid between a traditional PC and a network computer, it will usually feature no floppy or hard drive and limited memory and processor since it will use the power of the server to provide applications.

net present value (NPV) A measure of the return from a system which takes into account the variation in monetary value through time.

network computer (NC) The purpose of the network computer is to provide access to a network system, such as the Internet, at minimal cost. A typical network computer will feature limited disk storage, memory and expansion potential. In addition, the computer may also feature an older, less powerful processor than its desktop counterpart. Network computers are often associated with the thin client architecture and the concept of zero administration. See *thin client* and *zero administration*.

network interface card A network interface card is an expansion card that allows a personal computer to be connected to a network. The network card deals with all communications between the network and the computer.

network operating system (NOS) This describes the software needed to operate and manage a network system.

network topology The physical layout of a local-area network is known as a network topology. Bus, star, ring and combinations are most common.

neural networks These systems use a similar process to biological intelligence to learn problem-solving skills by 'training' or exposure to a wide range of problems. The learning occurs through interactions between nodes which are similar to the neurons of the brain.

node name The name used to identify a particular computer system on the Internet.

Nolan's stage model This model is a six-stage maturity model for the application of information systems to a business.

non-interlaced An interlaced display is one where each complete image shown on a monitor's display is drawn in two steps. A non-interlaced monitor refreshes the display in a single pass. A good quality monitor is normally capable of supporting a non-interlaced display at a refresh rate of 70 Hz or more.

non-volatile memory The memory found in a personal computer is considered volatile, that is, anything held in memory is lost once the power to the computer system is switched off. However, non-volatile memory retains its contents until altered or erased.

normalisation This design activity is a procedure which is used to optimise the physical storage of data within a database. It involves simplification of entities and minimisation of duplication of data.

notebook A small portable computer, which is approximately the size of an A4 sheet of paper.

object-orientated database An object-orientated approach to database design employs the concept of reusable objects in order to develop sophisticated or complex applications. An object combines data structures with any functions needed to manipulate the object or the data it holds.

object-orientated design This is a design technique which involves basing the design of software on real-world objects which consist of both data and the procedures that process them rather than traditional design where procedures operate on separate data.

observation This analysis technique is useful for identifying inefficiencies in an existing way of working with either a computer-based or a manual information system. It involves timing how long particular operations take and observing the method used to perform them. It can be time-consuming and the staff who are observed may behave differently from normally.

office automation systems In business organisations, productivity software is often used to reduce the time needed to complete routine administrative tasks, such as producing documents or organising meetings. By attempting to automate many of the activities carried out within a typical office, organisations seek to improve efficiency, reduce costs and enhance internal communications. Computer-based information systems used in this way are generally referred to as office automation systems.

office management systems This describes a category of office automation systems that assists users in scheduling projects and tasks. Examples of office management systems include personal information managers (PIMs) and project management software. See *office automation systems*.

offline When a user is not connected to their Internet account, they are said to be offline.

offline reader Sometimes called an 'offline browser'. An offline reader allows a single page, a group of pages, or an entire web site to be copied to the user's hard disk drive so that the material can be viewed at a later date.

off-the-shelf purchase of packaged software An acquisition method which involves direct purchase of a pre-written application used by more than one company.

online When a user is connected to their Internet account, usually by a modem link, they are said to be online.

online analytical processing (OLAP) OLAP can be considered to be a synonym for a data warehouse. It refers to the ability to analyse in real time the type of multidimensional information stored in data warehouses. The term 'online' indicates that users can formulate their own queries compared to standard paper reports. The originator of OLAP, Dr E. Codd, defines OLAP as the dynamic synthesis, analysis and consolidation of large volumes of multidimensional data.

online or Internet revenue contribution An assessment of the direct or indirect contribution of the Internet to sales, usually expressed as a percentage of overall sales revenue.

online stock fraud Most online stock fraud involves posting false information to the Internet in order to increase or decrease the values of stocks.

open profiling standard A standard method of collecting personal details about customers. An initiative, begun by Netscape and Firefly, now supported by many players including Microsoft.

open questions Not restricted to a limited range of answers such as Yes/No (closed questions). Asked to elicit opinions or ideas for the new system or identify commonly held views amongst staff. Open questions are not typically used for quantitative analysis, but can be used to identify a common problem.

open source An alternative approach towards software development and acquisition. Open-source applications are made available free of charge to individuals and organisations.

open system Interaction occurs with elements beyond the system boundary.

open systems interconnection (OSI) model An international standard defining connectivity of links between computers at different levels.

open-loop control system An open-loop control system is one in which there is an attempt to reach the system objective, but no control action to modify the inputs or process is taken once the process has begun.

operating environment This describes a number of programs intended to simplify the way in which users work with the operating system. Early versions of Windows, for example, provided a graphical user interface that removed the need for users to work with the more complex aspects of MS-DOS.

operating system (OS) The operating system interacts with the hardware of the computer at a very low level in order to manage and direct the computer's resources. The basic functions of the operating system include: allocating and managing system resources, scheduling the use of resources and monitoring the activities of the computer system.

operational feasibility An assessment of how the new system will affect the daily working practices within the organisation. (Is the system workable on a day-to-day basis?)

operations information systems These systems are generally concerned with process control, transaction processing, communications (internal and external) and productivity.

optical character recognition (OCR) Optical character recognition involves using software that attempts to recognise individual characters. An optical scanner is normally used to capture an image of a document. As the image is processed, the OCR program creates a text file containing all of the characters recognised. This file can then be edited further using a word processor, text editor or other suitable program. See *optical scanner*.

optical mark recognition (OMR) A variation on optical character recognition is optical mark recognition, which involves detecting and recognising simple marks made on a document. See *optical character recognition*.

optical scanner The optical scanner can be used to capture graphics and text from printed documents. A photograph, for example, can be captured and converted into a form suitable for use with a number of different applications. Images captured in this way are normally incorporated into word processing or desktop publishing documents.

organisational culture This concept includes shared values, unwritten rules and assumptions within the organisation as well as the practices that all groups share. Corporate cultures are created when a group of employees interact over time and are relatively successful in what they undertake.

organisational feasibility Reviews how well the solution meets the needs of the business and anticipates problems such as hostility to the system if insufficient training occurs. (Considers the effect of change given a company's culture and politics.)

outline design A high-level definition of the different components that make up the architecture of a system and how they interact.

output An output is a finished product that is created by a system. Examples include information, products and services.

output design Output design involves specifying how production of on-screen reports and paper-based reports will occur. Output may occur to database or file for storing information entered or also for use by other systems.

output devices Output devices translate the results of processing – output – into a human-readable form.

outsourcing Outsourcing occurs when all or part of the information systems services of a company are subcontracted to a third party.

packaged software An acqusition method that involves direct purchase of a pre-written application used by more than one company.

packets Units of data that are exchanged between different devices over communications media. The entire message to be sent is broken down into smaller packets since if an error occurs in transmission, only the packet with the error needs to be retransmitted.

page impressions Number of occasions a single page has been delivered to a user. Several hits may be recorded during one page impression according to the number of separate graphics and text blocks that need to be downloaded.

page printer A page printer processes a document one entire page at a time. In general, page printers are capable of printing documents quickly and at high quality. In contrast, line printers process a document one line at a time.

pages per minute (ppm) This describes a simple means of measuring the speed of a printer. The speed of a page printer, such as a laser printer or modern inkjet model, is measured in terms of pages per minute.

pages per month (ppm) Manufacturers often provide ratings for their printers that describe the typical workload appropriate for a given model. This value is often described in terms of pages per month.

page requests See *page impressions*.

paint programs Paint programs serve the same purpose as a sketch pad or easel and enable users to produce drawings using a variety of different techniques.

paperless office Describes the office environment of the future where paper documents are redundant and have been replaced by their electronic counterparts.

parallel port A type of connector that allows various devices to be attached to a computer system. Examples of common parallel devices include printers and external storage devices.

parallel running This changeover method involves the old and new system operating together at the same time until the company is certain the new system works.

patent A patent provides its owner with a monopoly allowing them to exploit their invention without competition. The protection offered by a patent lasts for a number of years but does not begin until the patent has been granted.

payback period The period after the initial investment before the company achieves a net benefit.

payload This refers to the action that will be carried out once a computer virus becomes active. This can range from displaying a message on the screen, to deleting valuable data.

PCI (peripheral component interconnect) This describes a common standard governing the way in which an expansion card interacts with a computer's motherboard and CPU. PCI devices often support the plug and play installation of devices. See *expansion card*, *plug and play* and *motherboard*.

peer-to-peer network A simple type of local-area network which provides sharing of files and peripherals between PCs.

personal certificate A data file containing encrypted information relating to the user's identity.

personal digital assistant (PDA) This can be thought of as a sophisticated personal organiser. A PDA is normally a hand-held device, often no larger than a pocket calculator. The purpose of the PDA is to help users manage their time more efficiently and effectively. The typical functions of a PDA can include: address book, appointment scheduler, calculator, expenses tracking, currency conversion, alarm clock, world time display and a variety of other features that allow users to store notes, such as to-do lists.

personal information manager (PIM) A PIM can be thought as an electronic personal organiser. The program allows users to store, organise and retrieve personal information such as appointments, personal expenses, telephone numbers and addresses, reminders and to-do lists.

PERT Sometimes used to refer to a critical path network diagram (PERT charts), but more accurately PERT replaces the fixed activity duration used in the CPM method with a statistical distribution which uses optimistic, pessimistic and most-likely duration estimates.

phablet A device with a screen size which is between a smartphone and a tablet computer

phased implementation This changeover method involves introducing different modules of the new system sequentially.

photo-editing packages Photo-editing packages enable users to capture, view and edit scanned images.

physical resources Physical resources are the tangible resources owned by a company. Examples include land, buildings and plant. Physical resources are also known as 'tangible assets'.

pilot system The system is trialled in a limited area before it is deployed more extensively across the business.

plotter A plotter uses a number of different coloured pens to draw lines upon the paper as it moves through the machine. Although capable of producing characters, the quality of the text created is often very poor. Plotters are primarily used to create technical drawings, such as engineering diagrams but can also be used to record the results of the continuous monitoring of various events by creating charts. Some cardiac monitors, for example, use a simple plotter device to produce charts showing a patient's heart activity over time.

plug and play (PnP) This describes a means by which expansion cards can be added to a computer system and configured automatically without the user needing to enter settings or make other changes. See *expansion card*.

plug-in A plug-in is a small program or accessory that can be used to extend a web browser's capabilities. For example, a number of different plug-ins exist that allow a web browser to display video or animation sequences.

pointing device An input device that allows the user to control the movement of a small pointer displayed on the screen. The pointer can be used to carry out actions by selecting items from a menu or manipulating icons.

portable computer The portable computer is largely self-contained, featuring its own power supply, keyboard, pointing device and visual display unit. Variations on the portable computer include the notebook and sub-notebook.

portal Site which provides the main method of access to other web sites through providing services to locate information on the WWW are now commonly referred to as portals. Such portals are often set to the default or home page of the user's web browser. Examples of portals include Yahoo (www.yahoo.com), Microsoft's MSN (www.msn.com) and the Netscape Netcenter (http://home.netscape.com).

Porter and Millar's five forces model Porter and Millar's five forces model is for analysing the different competitive forces which impact on an organisation. The five forces are: rivalry between existing competitors, threat of new entrants, threat of substitutes, the power of buyers and the power of suppliers.

positive and negative feedback Negative feedback is used to describe the act of reversing any discrepancy between desired and actual output. Positive feedback responds to a variance between desired and actual output by increasing that variance.

post-implementation review A meeting that occurs after a system is operational to review the success of the project and learn lessons for the future.

power supply unit (PSU) All modern personal computers feature a power supply unit used to convert AC current into DC current. The PSU regulates the amount of power supplied to the motherboard and any other devices installed within the case.

presentation software Presentation software enables users to create, edit and deliver presentations via a computer system.

primary key fields These fields are used to uniquely identify each record in a table and link to similar secondary key fields (usually of the same name) in other tables.

primary storage Data and instructions are loaded into memory such as random access memory. Such storage is temporary.

PRINCE A project management methodology that has been developed to be compatible with system development methodologies such as SSADM.

PRINCE structure PRINCE defines an organisational structure and standard set of job descriptors.

print preview The print preview feature displays a document exactly as it will be printed, enabling users to check and correct the document without making unnecessary printouts.

printer sharer A printer sharer allows several computers to be attached to a single printer.

Privacy and Electronic Communications (EC Directive) Regulations 2003 This legislation regulates the use of use of publicly available electronic communications services for direct marketing purposes. The legislation also covers unsolicited direct marketing activity by telephone, fax, email and automated calling systems and even text messages.

private branch exchange (PBX) Enables switching between phones or voice and data using existing telephone lines.

problem-orientated A problem-orientated language focuses on the expression of a problem or set of information processing requirements. The language will provide a variety of features that allow programmers to express their requirements in a natural form.

process Inputs are turned into outputs by using a transformation process.

process control systems These systems deal with the large volume of data generated by production processes.

process modelling Involves the design of the different modules of the system, each of which is a process with clearly defined inputs, outputs and a transformation process. Dataflow diagrams are often used to define processes in the system.

processor Uses instructions from software to control the different components of a PC.

production (live) environment The term used to described the setup of the system (hardware, software and office environment) where the software will be used in the business.

productivity paradox Research results indicating a poor correlation between organisational investment in information systems and organisational performance measured by return on equity.

productivity software This describes a category of computer software that aims to support users in performing a variety of common tasks.

professionalism In general terms, professionalism can be described as acting to meet the standards set by a profession in terms of individual conduct, competence and integrity. See *ethics* and *morality*.

programming language Programming languages enable users to develop software applications in order to carry out specific information processing tasks.

Project(s) Projects are unique, one-time operations designed to accomplish a specific set of objectives in a limited timeframe.

project constraints Projects can be resource-constrained (limited by the type of people, monetary or hardware resources available) or time-constrained (limited by the deadline).

project costs graphs Show the financial cost of undertaking the project.

project crashing Refers to reducing the project duration by increasing spending on critical activities.

project documentation Documentation is essential to disseminate information during project execution and for reference during software maintenance.

project plan This shows the main activities within the project, providing an overall schedule and identifying resources needed for project implementation.

proprietary related to an owner or ownership

protocols The Internet functions using a series of standard protocols which allow different computers to communicate with each other. Passing of data packets around the Internet occurs via the TCP/IP protocol which stands for transfer control protocol/Internet protocol. The HTTP (hypertext transfer protocol) is used to allow computers to transfer and process HTML files.

prototyping A prototype is a preliminary version of part or a framework of all of an information system which can be reviewed by end-users. Prototyping is an iterative process where users suggest modifications before further prototypes and the final information system are built.

pull technology Information sent out as a result of receiving a specific request, for example a page is delivered to a web browser in response to a request from the user.

push technology Push is used to deliver web pages to the user's desktop PC without specifically requesting each page. It is the Internet equivalent of a TV channel, hence it is sometimes also known as NetCasting. Important players are Marimba, Pointcast, Microsoft (Internet Explorer 4.0) and Netscape (Netcaster).

Q

qualitative data Also known as *soft data*, qualitative data describes the qualities or characteristics of an object or situation. Such data are often collected in order to help achieve a better understanding of a given situation. An interview, for example, might help the interviewer to understand an individual's personal beliefs and opinions.

quantitative data Also known as *hard data*, quantitative data tend to make use of figures, such as statistics. These data are often collected in order to measure or quantify an object or situation.

query In a spreadsheet or database, a query can be used to extract data according to a set of conditions specified by the user. The results of a query can be stored in another part of the worksheet or database so that the original data remain intact.

questionnaires Used to obtain a range of opinion on requirements by targeting a range of staff. They are open to misinterpretation unless carefully designed. They should consist of both open and closed questions.

R

RAID RAID stands for 'redundant array of inexpensive disks'. Essentially, identical copies of important data files are kept upon a number of different storage devices. If one or more of the storage devices fail, additional devices are activated automatically, allowing uninterrupted access to the data and reducing the possibility of losing transactions or updates.

random access memory (RAM) RAM is used as working storage by a computer, holding instructions and data that are waiting to be processed. The contents of RAM are volatile, that is, any data held are lost when the power to the computer system is switched off. See *volatile memory*.

random file access Random or direct file access allows any record to be read or written.

rapid applications development (RAD) A method of developing information systems which uses prototyping to achieve user involvement and faster development compared to traditional methodologies such as SSADM.

ratings Many web browsers support the use of ratings in order to restrict access to inappropriate content, for example pornography. When a web browser is used to access a site belonging to a given ratings scheme, the site's ratings are checked against the list of criteria set within the browser. If a site does not meet the criteria specified within the browser, access to the site is denied.

read-only In terms of storage devices, a read-only device can only be used to access data that are already present on the medium. A CD-ROM player, for example, is unable to write data to a compact disc and can only read from it. See also *read-only memory*.

read-only memory (ROM) The contents of ROM are fixed and cannot be altered. ROM is also non-volatile, making it ideal as a means of storing the information needed for a device to function properly. In a computer system, for example, the basic information needed so that the computer can access disk drives and control peripherals is stored in ROM. See *non-volatile memory*.

real-time processing Data are processed immediately on collection.

record In an electronic database, a record is a collection of *related* fields. See *field*.

record key In order to identify a specific item of information within a database, all records must contain an identifier, normally called the record key. The record key usually takes the form of a number or code and will be different for each record in the database.

recovery The process which is used to restore backup data.

refresh rate This describes a common method of gauging the quality of a monitor's display and involves measuring the number of times the image is drawn upon the screen each second. The refresh rate is normally measured in hertz, for example a refresh rate of 60 Hz means that the image will be drawn upon the screen 60 times each second.

regression testing Testing performed before a release to ensure that the software performance is consistent with previous test results, i.e. that the outputs produced are consistent with previous releases of the software.

re-intermediation The creation of new intermediaries between customers and suppliers providing services such as supplier search and product evaluation.

relational database(s) Data are stored within a number of different tables with each dealing with different subjects that are related (linked) using key fields.

relational database management system (RDBMS) This is an extension of a DBMS and allows data to be combined from a variety of sources.

relationship In a relational database, data can be combined from several different sources by defining relationships between tables.

remote access Remote-access describes a means of accessing a network from a distant location. A modem and specialised software allow users to send and receive information from home or an office when travelling.

replication (server) A process in which information on server computers at different locations is transferred and synchronised so users in different locations can view the same data.

replication (virus) The process by which a virus copies itself.

request for proposals (RFP) A specification drawn up to assist in selecting the supplier and software.

requirements specification The main output from the systems analysis stage. Its main focus is a description of what all the functions of the software will be.

resolution The resolution of the monitor describes the fineness of the image that can be displayed. Resolution is often expressed in terms of pixels (picture elements) – the individual dots that make up an image on the screen.

resource allocation This activity involves assigning a resource to each task.

response time Many organisations make use of external companies to provide maintenance and technical support for their computer-based information systems. In such cases, the organisation may require the maintenance provider to guarantee a minimum response time for important repairs.

return on investment (ROI) An indication of the returns provided by an IS. Calculated by dividing the benefit by the amount of investment. Expressed as a percentage.

revenue models Describe methods of generating income for an organisation.

reverse engineering Reverse engineering attempts to recreate the design of an item by analysing the final product. This can be compared to the 'black box' approach to systems analysis, where the outputs from the system are analysed in order to determine the inputs and processes involved. Reverse engineering can be used to duplicate both hardware and software.

RISC (reduced instruction set computer) processor Designed so that it has to perform fewer instructions than a CISC processor and it can then operate at a higher speed. The IBM RS/6000 workstation is a well-known example of a computer that uses the PowerPC RISC processor. As new designs of Pentium processor are produced these are incorporating RISC features and are also making use of parallel processing.

risk management Risk management aims to anticipate the future risks of an information systems project and to put in place measures to counter or eliminate these risks.

RSS (Really Simple Syndication) A format used for documents that contain regularly updated information, such as news headlines and blog entries.

S

safety-critical system Where human lives rely on the correct operation of a computer-based information system, this is normally referred to as a critical system.

scalability The potential of an information system or piece of software or hardware to move from supporting a small number of users to supporting a large number of users without a marked decrease in reliability or performance.

scenario A particular path or flow of events or activities within a use case.

scientific languages Scientific programming languages are designed to serve scientific and mathematical applications.

scoring system A means of selecting hardware, software and suppliers using a point-scoring system. Each item or supplier is assigned scores against a number of selection criteria. Final selection is based upon the total score achieved by each item or supplier. The relative importance of the selection criteria can be recognised through the use of weighting factors, resulting in the creation of a weighted ranking table.

script All modern web browsers are capable of executing special commands that have been embedded within the body of a WWW page. These scripts can be used to control the appearance of the page or can provide additional facilities, such as on-screen clocks and timers.

SCSI (small computer system interface) This describes a common standard governing the way in which an expansion card interacts with a computer's motherboard and CPU. Up to seven separate devices can be attached to a single SCSI interface simultaneously. Connecting several devices in sequence is known as daisy-chaining. See *expansion card*, *plug and play* and *motherboard*.

SDLC stages Initiation, feasibility study, analysis of business requirements, systems design, system build and implementation and, finally, review and maintenance.

search engine Search engines provide an index of all words stored on the World Wide Web. Keywords typed in by the end-user are matched against the index and the user is given a list of all corresponding web pages containing the keywords. By clicking on a hyperlink the user is taken to the relevant web page.

second normal form (2NF) Second normal form states that 'each attribute in a record (relation) must be functionally dependent on the whole key of that record'.

secondary key fields These fields are used to link tables together by referring to the primary key in another database table.

secondary storage Floppy disks and hard disks are secondary storage which provide permanent storage.

Secure Electronic Transactions (SET) A method developed by Visa and Mastercard proposed for enabling credit-card-based electronic commerce based on digital certificates.

secure sockets layer (SSL) A standard used within web browsers to encrypt data such as credit-card details sent over the Internet.

security breach A security breach is a deliberate or unintentional act that leads to unauthorised access to or loss or damage to information or an information system.

sell-side e-commerce E-commerce transactions between a supplier organisation and its customers.

semantic web A movement that promotes common data formats on the world wide web in order to create a 'web of data'

sensing device Modern personal computers are capable of communicating with external devices via a number of different means. This allows them to be connected to a variety of sensing devices. Amongst these are motion detectors, light sensors, infra-red sensors (which can detect heat), microphones and many others.

sequential access method Sequential file access involves reading or writing each record in a file in a set order.

serial port A type of connector that allows various devices to be attached to a computer system. Examples of common serial devices might include mouse, modem and printer.

server A server is a powerful computer used to control the management of a network. It may have a specific function such as storing user files or a database or managing a printer.

service-level agreements A contractual specification of service standards a contractor must meet.

signature Most computer viruses contain a message to be displayed on screen or a hidden piece of text. Additionally, a virus program may also contain a unique series of values in its program file. These unique features are known as the signature of the virus.

signature file A signature file contains information such as an address and phone number that can be automatically added to the end of an email message.

site certificate A site certificate contains information regarding the identity of a particular site on the Internet. The site certificate is encrypted to protect the information it contains. When a user's web browser accesses a given site on the Internet, the corresponding certificate is checked to ensure the authenticity of the site.

skills shortage Describes the significant shortage of educated and highly skilled ICT practitioners entering the industry.

smartphone Describes a device that is primarily a mobile phone but incorporates the features of a PDA.

soft systems methodology A methodology that emphasises the human involvement in systems and models their behaviour as part of systems analysis in a way that is understandable by non-technical experts.

software A series of detailed instructions that control the operation of a computer system. Software exists as programs that are developed by computer programmers.

Software as a Service (SaaS) A software distribution model where users access software and data via a network, such as the Internet, using a web browser.

software bug Software bugs are defects in a program which are caused by human error during programming or earlier in the lifecycle. They may result in major faults or may remain unidentified.

software licence This sets out the terms under which a piece of software can be used. In general, licences are required for every piece of software owned and used by a company. A company using ten copies of a word processor, for instance, must own ten individual licences or a single licence giving the right to use ten copies of the program.

software metrics Measures which indicate the quality of software.

Software Publishers Association (SPA) An organisation formed to act against software piracy. See *software theft*.

software quality Measured according to its suitability for the job intended. This is governed by whether it can do the job required (does it meet the business requirements?) and the number of bugs it contains (does it work reliably?).

software theft Software theft, also known as 'software piracy', involves making unauthorised copies of software applications. Software theft represents a serious and growing problem for the software industry. Global losses due to software piracy were estimated at more than $11 billion in 1996.

sound card A sound card allows a personal computer to play speech, music and other sounds. A sound card can also be used to capture sound, music and speech from a variety of sources.

source escrow An arrangement where a third party stores software that can be used for maintenance purposes if the original developer of the software becomes insolvent.

spam Unwanted messages, such as advertisements, are received by most email users. The act of sending out these messages is usually called 'spamming'.

speech synthesis Speech synthesis software allows text to be converted into speech. The contents of spreadsheet files, email messages, word processing documents and other files can be converted into speech and played back via a sound card or other device.

spiral model An iterative systems development model developed by B. Boehm in which the stages of analysis, design, code and review repeat as new features for the system are identified.

spreadsheet A spreadsheet can be described as a program designed to store and manipulate values, numbers and text in an efficient and useful way. The work area in a spreadsheet program is called the 'worksheet'. A worksheet is a grid made up of cells. Each cell is uniquely identifiable by its horizontal (row) and vertical (column) coordinates. A cell can contain text, numbers or a formula that relates to information held in another cell.

stage models Used to assess the current and future application of technology in an organisation.

stakeholders All who have a direct interest in the system.

static web page A page on the web server that is invariant.

storage devices Storage devices provide a means of storing data and programs until they are required.

strategy Definition of the future direction and actions of a company defined as approaches to achieving specific objectives.

strategy process model A framework for approaching strategy development.

streaming media Sound and video that can be experienced within a web browser without the need to download a complete file.

structured decisions Structured decisions tend to involve situations where the rules and constraints governing the decision are known. They tend to involve routine or repetitive situations where the number of possible courses of action is relatively small.

structured English A technique for producing a design specification for programmers which indicates the way individual modules or groups of modules should be implemented.

structured query language (SQL) This describes a form of programming language that provides a standardised method for retrieving information from databases.

sub-notebook A small portable computer which is usually significantly smaller than a notebook due to its small screen and keyboard.

subsystem Large systems can be composed of one or more smaller systems. These smaller systems are known as subsystems.

suprasystem This describes a larger system that is made of one or more smaller systems (subsystems).

surveillance society This describes a society where the actions of individuals are closely monitored by government departments and major companies, and where these organisations routinely gather and process large amounts of personal information.

synchronous When people exchange information simultaneously, as is the case with real-time chat or a telephone conversation, this is known as synchronous.

synergy Synergy means that the whole is greater than the sum of the parts.

system A system can be defined as a collection of interrelated components that work together towards a collective goal.

system build System build is the term used to describe the creation of software by programmers. It involves writing the software code (programming), building release versions of the software, constructing and populating the database and testing by programmers and end-users. Writing of documentation and training may also occur at this stage. Inputs: Requirements and design specification. Outputs: Working software, user guides and system documentation.

system implementation Implementation covers practical issues such as making sure the hardware and network infrastructure for a new system are in place; testing of the system and also human issues of how best to educate and train staff who will be using or affected by the new system. Implementation also involves the transition or changeover from the old system to the new. Input: Working system, not tested by users. Output: Signed-off, operational information system installed in all locations.

system maintenance Maintenance occurs after the system has been signed off as suitable for users. It involves reviewing the project and recording and acting on problems with the system.

system objective All systems are created to meet a specific objective or purpose. All of the components of the system are related to one another by a common objective. When the components of a system no longer share the same objective, a condition of 'sub-optimality' is said to exist.

system or outline design A high-level definition of the different components that make up the architecture of a system and how they interact.

system owners These are managers who are directly responsible for the operational use of a system.

system sponsors System sponsors are senior managers or board members who are responsible for a system at a senior level in a company.

system testing When all modules have been completed and their interactions assessed for validity, links between all modules are assessed in the system test. In system testing interactions between all relevant modules are tested systematically.

systems analysis Systems analysis refers to the capture of the business requirements of a system from talking to or observing end-users and using other information sources such as existing system documentation. Input: Terms of reference in feasibility report describing outline requirements. Output: Detailed requirements specification summarising system functions. Supported by diagrams showing the information flow and processes that are required.

systems analysis and design method (SSADM) A methodology that defines the methods of analysis and design that should occur in a large-scale software development project. It is used extensively in the UK, particularly in government and public organisations.

systems development lifecycle (SDLC)

systems design The systems design phase defines how the system will work in key areas of user interface, program modules, security and database transactions. Input: Requirements specification. Output: Detailed design specification.

systems dynamics Based on the view that the world can be regarded as a set of interdependent systems, it usually uses simulation models to try to understand why systems behave as they do.

systems software This form of software manages and controls the operation of the computer system as it performs tasks on behalf of the user.

systems theory The study of the behaviour and interactions within and between systems.

table In an electronic database, data are organised within structures known as tables. A table defines the structure of a specific record.

tacit knowledge Mainly intangible knowledge that is typically intuitive and not recorded since it is part of the human mind.

talk-through A user verbally describes their required actions.

tangible assets Tangible assets are the physical resources owned by a company. Examples include land, buildings and plant.

tangible value A value or benefit that can be measured directly, usually in monetary terms. With regard to information, tangible value is usually calculated as: value of information minus cost of gathering information.

tape streamer A common form of storage device that uses magnetic tape as a storage medium.

TCP/IP The transmission control protocol is a transport-layer protocol that moves data between applications. The Internet protocol is a network-layer protocol that moves data between host computers.

technical feasibility Evaluates to what degree the proposed solutions will work as required and whether the right people and tools are available to implement the solution. (Will it work?)

telecommunications Telecommunications is the method by which data and information are transmitted between different locations.

telecommunications channels The media by which data are transmitted. Cables and wires are known as 'guided media' and microwave and satellite links are known as 'unguided media'.

teleworking The process where company staff work remotely from their company office. Most commonly it is applied to 'home workers' who spend at least three days a week working in this way.

Telnet This allows remote access to computer systems. For example, a system administrator on one site could log-in to a computer elsewhere to check it is running successfully. Telnet is widely used in the retail industry. For example, a retailer could check to see whether an item was in stock in a warehouse using a telnet application. Such telnet applications will not usually be run over the public Internet, but rather over secure lines.

tender document A document used as an invitation to suppliers, asking them to bid for the right to supply an organisation's hardware, software and other requirements.

terminate and stay resident (TSR) A program that is stored in the computer's memory and functions as a background task, receiving only a small share of the processor's time.

test environment A specially configured environment (hardware, software and office environment) used to test the software before its release.

test plan Plan describing the type and sequence of testing and who will conduct it.

test specification A detailed description of the tests that will be performed to check the software works correctly.

theft In terms of computing, theft normally, but not always, involves altering computer records to disguise the theft of money. The theft of services can include a variety of acts, such as the unauthorised use of a company's information systems. See also *software theft* and *data theft*.

thermal printer Thermal printers operate by using a matrix of heated pins to melt ink from a ribbon directly onto the paper.

thin client In a network system, this describes an architecture where the bulk of the processing is carried out by a central server. The results of the processing are then relayed back to a terminal or network computer. See *network computer*.

third normal form (3NF) A record is in third normal form if each non-key attribute 'depends on the key, the whole key and nothing but the key'.

three-tier client/server The client is mainly used for display with application logic and the business rules partitioned on a second-tier server and a third-tier database server. Here the client is sometimes referred to as a 'thin client', because the size of the executable program is smaller.

time dimension This describes several characteristics of information quality related to the time period that the information deals with and the frequency at which the information is received. Amongst these characteristics are the timeliness, currency and frequency of information. As an example, information may be considered to be of high quality if it is received in good time (timeliness). Other dimensions of information characteristics include content and form. See *content dimension*, *form dimension*.

top-down design The top-down approach to design involves specifying the overall control architecture of the application before designing the individual modules.

total cost of ownership (TCO) TCO refers to the total cost for a company operating a computer. This includes not only the purchase or leasing cost, but also the cost of all the services needed to support the end-user.

touch screen The touch screen is a transparent, pressure-sensitive covering that is attached to the screen of a monitor. Users make selections and control programs by pressing on the screen. Although touch screens are simple to use, they are comparatively expensive and require special software to operate.

trackball A trackball is a pointing device that is controlled by rotating a small ball with the fingertips or palm of the hand. Moving the ball causes corresponding movement to a small pointer on the screen. Buttons are used to select items in the same way as the mouse. See *pointing device*.

transaction log files A web server file that records all page requests from site visitors.

transaction processing This involves dealing with the sales and purchase transactions that an organisation carries out in the course of its normal activities. Banks, for example, handle millions of deposits and withdrawals each day.

transaction processing systems (TPS) Transaction processing systems (TPS) manage the frequent external and internal transactions such as orders for goods and services which serve the operational level of the organisation.

transformation process A transformation process is used to convert inputs into outputs. A power station, for example, converts fuel into electricity.

trojan A trojan presents itself as a legitimate program in order to gain access to a computer system. Trojans are often used as delivery systems for computer viruses.

two-tier client/server Sometimes referred to as 'fat client', the application running on the PC is a large program containing all the application logic and display code. It retrieves data from a separate database server.

ultraportable One of the smallest types of laptop computer, weighing less than 3 lb (1.4 kg) and with a screen measuring 10" (25 cm) or less.

UML A language used to specify, visualise and document the artefacts of an object-orientated system.

uniform (universal) resource locators (URL) A web address used to locate a web page on a web server.

unit testing Individual modules are tested to ensure they function correctly for given inputs.

universal product code A standard for defining bar codes used frequently in retailing.

universal serial bus (USB) This describes a relatively new standard that governs the way in which an expansion card interacts with a computer's motherboard and CPU. In addition to offering very high data transmission speeds, USB also supports Plug and Play, the connection of up to 127 devices and hot plugging. See *expansion card*, *plug and play*, *hot plugging* and *motherboard*.

unstructured decisions Unstructured decisions tend to involve complex situations, where the rules governing the decision are complicated or unknown. Such decisions tend to be made infrequently and rely heavily on the experience, judgement and knowledge of the decision maker.

update anomaly It is not possible to change a single occurrence of a data item (a field) in a relation (table) without having to change others in order to maintain the correctness of data.

update query An update query can be used to change records, tables and reports held in a database management system.

use-case The sequence of transactions between an actor and a system that support the activities of the actor.

use-case modelling A user-centred approach to modelling system requirements.

Usenet newsgroups Usenet is mainly used by special-interest groups such as people discussing their favourite pastimes. They are not used much by businesses, unless it is as a means of studying consumer behaviour.

user acceptance testing This is the final stage of testing which occurs before the software is signed off as fit for purpose and the system can go live.

user-centred design Design based on optimising the user experience according to all factors, including the user interface, which affect this.

user validation Checks made to ensure the user is permitted access to a system. Also known as 'access control systems', they often involve user names and passwords, but can also include biometric techniques.

utility programs Utility programs provide a range of tools that support the operation and management of a computer system.

validation This is a test of the design where we check that the design fulfils the requirements of the business users which are defined in the requirements specification.

value-added networks (VANs) Value-added networks (VANs) give a subscription service enabling companies to transmit data securely across a shared network.

value chain Michael Porter's value chain is a framework for considering key activities within an organisation and how well they add value as products and services move from conception to delivery to the customer.

value network The links between an organisation and its strategic and non-strategic partners that form its external value chain.

vector image Vector graphics are made up of shapes, rather than individual dots. Mathematical formulae determine the size, position and colour of the shapes that make up a given image.

verification This is a test of the design to ensure that the design chosen is the best available and that it is error-free.

VGA (video graphics array) A common standard for graphics cards. All graphics cards support the VGA standard which specifies a maximum image size of 640 by 320 pixels, displayed in 16 colours.

video capture card The video capture card records and stores video sequences (motion video). A playback device, for example a video cassette recorder, is connected to the video capture card and special software is used to capture, edit and manipulate video sequences. Once a motion video sequence has been processed, it can then be output to a television, video cassette recorder or other device.

video projector A computer system can be connected directly to a projector so that output is directed to a projection screen. Some projectors convert the computer's output into a television picture before displaying it.

virtual organisation An organisation which uses technologies to allow it to operate without clearly defined physical boundaries between different functions. It provides customised services for customers by linking different human resources and suppliers at different locations.

virtual private network (VPN) A data network that makes use of the public telecommunication infrastructure and Internet, but information remains secure by the use of a tunnelling protocol and security procedures such as firewalls.

virtual reality (VR) An interactive, artificial reality created by the computer. Users perceive the environment in three dimensions and are able to interact with objects and people. Using virtual-reality goggles, for example, a user might interact with a body of data that appears as a three-dimensional model.

virus See *computer virus*.

virus scanner Virus scanners are intended to detect and then safely remove virus programs from a computer system. The most common method of detection used by these programs involves scanning for the signatures of particular viruses. See also *signature*.

virus shield Virus shields are TSR programs that constantly monitor and control access to a system's storage devices. Any unusual attempt to modify a file or write to a disk drive will activate a message asking the user to authorise the operation. See also *terminate and stay resident*.

visual display unit (VDU) This is normally used to describe the monitor connected to a computer system, but can also refer to any other form of display device.

visualisation This describes a variety of methods used to produce graphical representations of data so that they can be examined from a number of different perspectives.

voice annotations These can be described as spoken notes or reminders that can be inserted into data files, such as word processing documents. Annotations are created and played back via a sound card. See *sound card*.

voice–data integration Sometimes known as *computer telephony*. A combination of different communications technologies that provide a range of sophisticated facilities, for example automated call-switching, telephone answering services and fax-on-demand. See *fax-on-demand*.

voice modem Voice modems offer greater flexibility than conventional modems by combining voice, fax and data facilities. At a simple level, a voice modem can be used as a speaker phone or answering machine.

voice recognition This describes the facility to control a computer program or carry out data entry through spoken commands. The user issues instructions via a microphone connected to a sound card. Specialised software then attempts to interpret and execute the instruction given.

VoIP (Voice over IP) A relatively recent technology that enables users to make and receive telephone calls via the Internet.

volatile memory The memory found in a personal computer is considered volatile, that is, anything held in memory is lost once the power to the computer system is switched off. However, non-volatile memory retains its contents until altered or erased.

volume testing Testing assesses how system performance will change at different levels of usage.

W

walk-through A user executes their actions through using a system or mock-up.

wax printers Printers which employ a ribbon with a coloured wax coating to form images by heating sections of the ribbon and pressing it against the paper (dye-sublimation).

web addresses Web addresses refer to particular pages on a web server which are hosted by a company or organisation. The technical name for these is 'uniform resource locators', so you often see them referred to as 'URLs'.

web browsers Browsers such as Netscape Navigator and Microsoft Explorer provide an easy method of accessing and viewing information stored as web documents on different servers. The web pages stored as HTML files on the servers are accessed through a particular standard supported by the web browsers (this is the hypertext transfer protocol (http), which you will always see preceding the web address of a company). For example, http://www.derby.ac.uk defines the university home page at Derby.

web directories or catalogues Web directories provide a structured listing of web sites. They are grouped according to categories such as business, entertainment or sport. Each category is then subdivided further, for example into football, rugby, swimming, etc.

web servers Web servers such as Microsoft Internet Information Server are used to store the web pages accessed by web browsers. They may also contain databases of customer or product information which can be queried and retrieved from the browser.

what if? analysis This describes the ability to see the predicted effect of a change made to a numerical model. See *modelling* and *spreadsheet*.

wide-area network (WAN) These networks cover a large area to connect businesses in different parts of the same city, different parts of a country or different countries.

WIMP (windows, icons, mouse and pull-down menus) Often used to describe a GUI (graphical user interface) environment.

wireless application protocol (WAP) WAP is a technical standard for transferring information to wireless devices, such as mobile phones.

wireless markup language (WML) Standard for displaying mobile pages such as transferred by WAP.

word processor A word processor provides the ability to enter, edit, store and print text. In addition, word processing packages allow users to alter the layout of documents and often provide a variety of formatting tools.

word wrap In a word processor, as users type text and move towards the end of a line, the program automatically moves to the beginning of a new line.

work breakdown structure (WBS) This is a breakdown of the project or a piece of work into its component parts (tasks).

workbook In a spreadsheet program, this describes a collection of worksheets.

workflow management (WFM) Systems for the automation of the movement and processing of information in a business according to a set of procedural rules.

workgroup A workgroup can be defined as a group of individuals working together on a given task. Each member of the workgroup will be attached to the organisation's network system so that tasks can be organised and information can be shared with other members.

worksheet An individual area or sheet for entering data in a spreadsheet program.

workstation This describes a powerful terminal or personal computer system, usually applied to specialised applications, such as computer-aided design (CAD) and animation.

World Wide Web The World Wide Web is a medium for publishing information on the Internet. It is accessed through web browsers which display web pages and can be used to run business applications. Company information is stored on web servers which are usually referred to as 'web sites'.

worm (virus) A worm is a small program that moves through a computer system randomly changing or overwriting pieces of data as it moves.

WORM (write once, read many) A WORM (write once, read many) storage device allows data to be written only once. Once the data have been written, they cannot be changed or erased.

XML (extensible markup language) XML describes a standard for creating documents that can store almost any kind of data. XML is extremely flexible since it offers the ability to create new language elements – or whole new languages – using standard XML elements. XML is seen as a key technology in the area of business-to-business communications since it provides a simple and effective way for organisations to share data. XML is also seen as a key technology for areas such as e-commerce and distributed databases. Finally, XML forms part of Microsoft's .Net strategy, which is intended to shape the future of operating systems, applications software, software development and the use of the Internet.

zero administration In a network system, zero administration describes a point where the centralised management and control of the computers attached to a network server makes administration costs almost negligible. Zero administration is often associated with network computers. See *network computer*.

zombie A type of Trojan capable of taking full or partial control of a computer when activated by the author. Zombie computers are usually organised into large networks (called botnets) so that their combined resources can be used to send spam or launch distributed denial-of-service attacks.

Index

Note: page numbers in **Bold** indicate Glossary entries.

C

U

V

W